London

"All you've got to do is decide to go
and the hardest part is over.

So go!"

TONY WHEELER, COFOUNDER – LONELY PLANET

THIS EDITION WRITTEN AND RESEARCHED BY
Emilie Filou, Steve Fallon, Damian Harper, Vesna Maric

Contents

Plan Your Trip 4

Explore London 78

Understand London 351

Survival Guide 399

London Maps 427

BERTRAND GARDEL / GETTY IMAGES ©

ANTIDE S.N.C. / GETTY IMAGES ©

Left: 30 St Mary Axe (Gherkin; p157), designed by Foster and Partners

Above: Oxo Tower Restaurant & Brasserie (p180)

Right: Hyde Park (p195)

JOHNNIE PAKINGTON / GETTY IMAGES ©

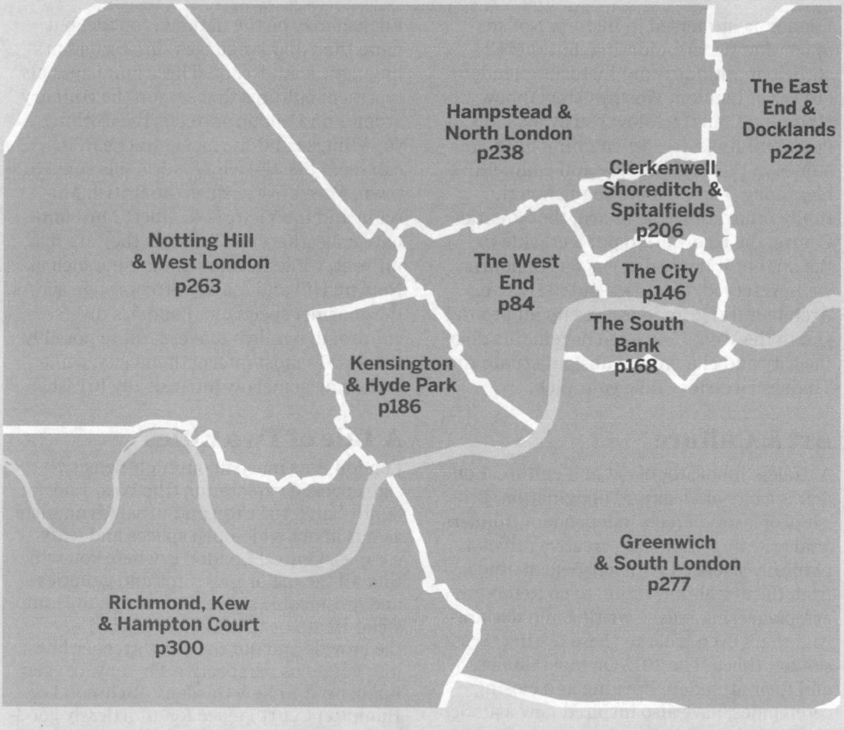

Welcome to London

One of the world's most visited cities, London has something for everyone: from history to culture, art to architecture.

Time Travel

London is immersed in history. Not so much that it's intimidating, but there's sufficient antiquity and historic splendour (Tower of London, Westminster Abbey, Hampton Court) to blow you away. London's buildings are eye-catching milestones in the city's unique and compelling biography. There's more than enough funky innovation (the Shard, the Aquatics Centre, the Gherkin) to put a crackle in the air, but it never drowns out London's well-preserved, centuries-old narrative. Architectural grandeur rises up all around you in the West End, ancient remains dot the City and charming pubs punctuate the Thames riverside. Take your pick.

Art & Culture

A tireless innovator of art and culture, London is a city of ideas and imagination. British people are fiercely independent thinkers (and critics), so London's creative milieu is naturally streaked with left-field attitude, from theatrical innovation to contemporary art, pioneering music, writing and design. And that's even truer in these testing recessionary times. The 2012 Olympic Games, and their attendant opening and closing ceremonies, have also inspired new artistic vigour and confidence.

Diversity

English may be the national tongue, but more than 300 languages shape London's linguistic soundscape. These languages also represent cultures that season the culinary aromas on London's streets, the clothing you glimpse and the music you hear. It can seem like the whole world has come to town. Museums, such as the British Museum and the Victoria & Albert Museum, have collections as diverse as they are magnificent, while flavours at markets such as Notting Hill and Maltby Street range across the gourmet spectrum. London's diverse cultural dynamism makes it quite possibly the world's most international city, while still being somehow intrinsically British.

A Tale of Two Cities

London is as much about high-density, sight-packed exploration (the West End, South Bank, the City) and urban dynamism as it is about wide-open spaces and leafy escapes. Central London is where you will find all the major museums and galleries and most iconic sights, but escape to Hampstead Heath or Greenwich Park to flee the crowds and put the city's greener hues into gorgeous perspective. Or venture even further out to Kew Gardens, Richmond or Hampton Court Palace for effortlessly good-looking panoramas of riverside London.

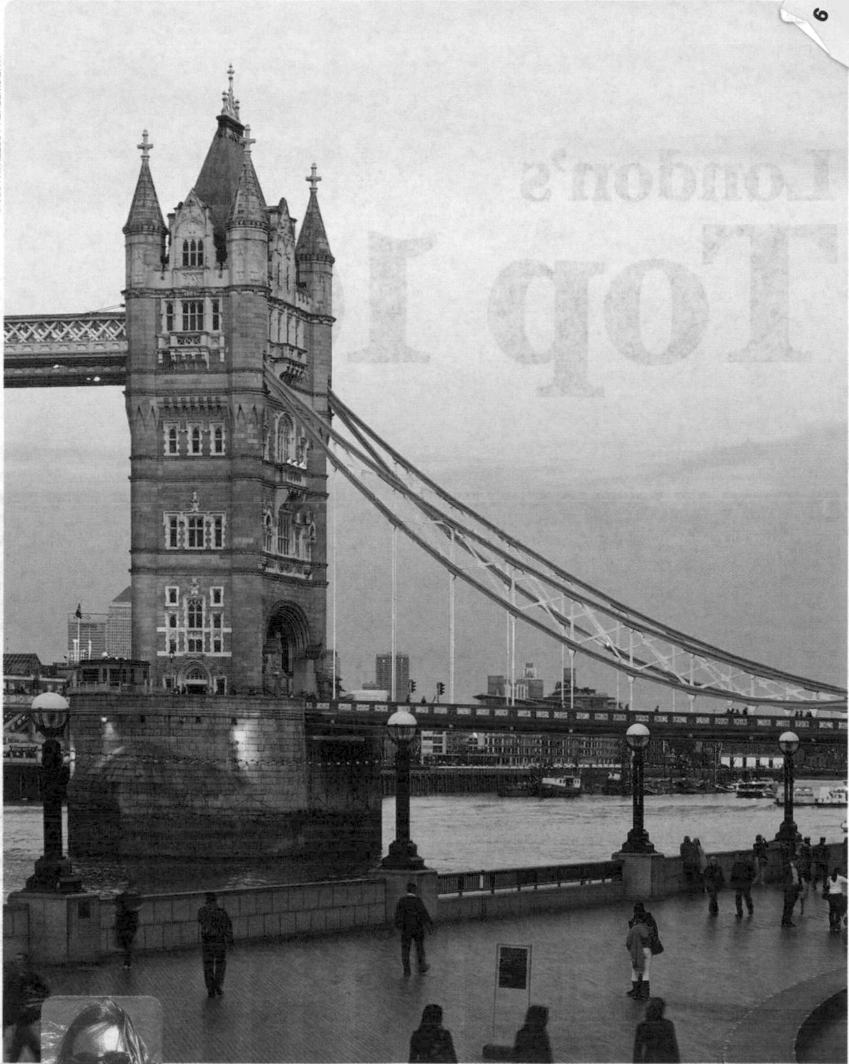

Why I Love London

By Emilie Filou

I was born in Paris, France, and while the Gallic capital never did much for me, I have fallen head over heels for London. It's been 10 years and I still revel in its energy, its amazing diversity and its unparalleled green spaces. Swimming in Hampstead Heath's ponds has to be one of my favourite things to do, followed closely by a pub quiz with friends and cocktails in Soho. And then there is the food – London is, without a doubt, the culinary capital of the world. Just come and see for yourself!

For more about our authors, see p472.

Tower Bridge (p158) on the River Thames

London's Top 16

1

National Gallery *(p97)*

1 This superlative collection of (largely pre-modern) art at the heart of London is one of the largest anywhere, and a roll-call of some of the world's most outstanding artistic compositions. With highlights including work from Leonardo da Vinci, Michelangelo, Gainsborough, Constable, Turner, Monet, Renoir and Van Gogh, it's a bravura performance and one not to be missed. The on-site restaurants and cafes are also exceptional, rounding out a terrific experience and putting the icing on an already eye-catching cake.

The West End

British Museum *(p89)*

2 With five million visitors trooping through its doors annually, the British Museum in Bloomsbury is London's most popular tourist attraction. You could spend a lifetime in this vast and hallowed collection of artefacts, art and age-old antiquity and still make daily discoveries (admission is free, soyou could just do that, if so inclined). Otherwise join everyone else on the highlights tours (or eyeOpener tours) for a précis of the museum's treasures.

The West End

CHRISTER FREDRIKSSON / GETTYIMAGES ©

ORIEN HARVEY / GETTYIMAGES ©

3

4

Tate Modern (p170)

3 The favourite of Londoners (and quite possibly the world), this contemporary art collection enjoys a triumphant position right on the River Thames. Housed in the former Bankside Power Station, the Tate Modern is a vigorous statement of modernity, architectural renewal and accessibility. The permanent collection is free, but make sure you enter by the ramp down into the Turbine Hall, where the gallery's standout temporary exhibitions push the conceptual envelope and satisfy more cerebral art-hunters. JACKSON POLLOCK'S SUMMERTIME: NUMBER 9A

The South Bank

Tower of London (p148)

4 Few parts of the UK are as steeped in history or as impregnated with legend and superstition as the titanic stonework of this fabulous fortress. Not only is the tower an architectural odyssey but there's also a diamond almost as big as the Ritz, free tours from magnificently attired 'beefeaters', a dazzling array of armour and weaponry and a palpable sense of ancient history at every turn. Because there is simply so much to see, it's well worth getting here early as you will need at least half a day of exploration.

The City

London Pubs (p57)

5 London minus its pubs would be like Paris sans cafes or Beijing shorn of its charming *hutong*. Pub culture is an indispensable element of London DNA and the pub is the place to be if you want to see local people in their hop-scented element. Longer hours for many pubs have only cemented them as the cornerstone for a good night out across the capital. Once no-go zones for discerning foodies, pubs long ago upped their game: standout gastropubs now dot London's culinary cosmos in highly tasty and appetising proportions, frequently putting top-tier restaurants to shame.

Drinking & Nightlife

Culinary London *(p47)*

6 Don't let anybody tell you that the food in England isn't good: London has long been a shining light in culinary excellence, with a kaleidoscope of cuisines unrivalled in Europe. The capital is particularly strong in Indian and other Asian food (such as Chinese, Japanese and Thai) but don't miss the opportunity of trying traditional or Modern British cuisine, either in a good gastropub or the finer restaurants. For those with a sweet tooth, an afternoon tea or a treat from the capital's many cake shops is a must. EXMOUTH MARKET

Eating

Camden Town *(p245)*

7 A foray into trendy North London, away from the central sights, is a crucial part of the London experience. Camden's market – actually four markets in one great melange – may be a hectic and tourist-oriented attraction, but snacking on the go from the international food stalls is a great way to enjoy browsing the merchandise, while Camden's terrific dining scene, throbbing nightlife and well-seasoned pub culture is well known to night owls citywide.

Hampstead & North London

6

Victoria & Albert Museum *(p188)*

8 You could spend your entire London trip in this huge museum and still be astounded at its variety and depth. Located in stylish South Kensington, the world's leading collection of decorative arts has something for everyone, from imposing 19th-century architecture to antique Chinese ceramics, Japanese armour, Islamic textiles, works by Raphael, a beautiful collection of jewellery and the revolutionary Sony Walkman (plus other modern design classics). And don't overlook the fabulous architecture of the museum, a major attraction in itself.

⊙ Kensington & Hyde Park

Kew Gardens *(p306)*

9 Where else in London can you size up an 18th-century 10-storey Chinese pagoda and a Japanese gateway while finding yourself among one of the world's most outstanding botanical collections? Kew Gardens is loved by Londoners for its 19th-century Palm House and other Victorian glasshouses, conservatories, tree canopy walkway, architectural follies and mind-boggling plant variety. You'll need a day to do it justice, but you could find yourself heading back for more. PALM HOUSE, KEW GARDENS

Richmond, Kew & Hampton Court

Hyde Park & Kensington Gardens *(p195)*

10 London's urban parkland is virtually second to none and is *the* place to see locals at ease and in their element. Hyde Park alone ranges across a mighty 142 hectares; throw in Kensington Gardens and you have even more space to roam and everything you could want: a central London setting, a royal palace, extravagant Victoriana, boating opportunities, open-air concerts, an art gallery, magnificent trees and a tasteful granite memorial to Princess Diana. HYDE PARK

Kensington & Hyde Park

West End Performances *(p135)*

11 The West End is synonymous with musicals and no trip to London would be complete without an evening of *Matilda*, *Les Misérables* or *Phantom of the Opera*. If musicals don't float your boat, there are more alternatives than you'll have evenings to fill: theatre, dance, opera, small gigs, big-ticket concerts or live jazz. London truly is the capital of the arts. The trick is to book either far in advance if you have a particular show in mind or last minute for bargains. LONDON COLISEUM

Entertainment

9

10

11

London Eye (p173)

12 You may have eyed up London from altitude as you descended into Heathrow, but your pilot won't have lingered over the supreme views of town that extend in every direction from London's great riverside Ferris wheel. The queues move as slowly as the Eye rotates (there are ways to fast-track your way on), but that makes the occasion even more rewarding once you've lifted off and London unfurls beneath you. Avoiding grey days is the top tip – but with London's notoriously overcast skies that might be a tall order. If you've only a few days in the capital, make this your first stop and you can at least say you've seen the sights. LONDON EYE DESIGNED BY DAVID MARKS AND JULIA BARFIELD

The South Bank

12

13

Notting Hill Carnival *(p265)*

13 Every August, trendy Notting Hill throws a big, long and loud party. Europe's leading street festival is a vibrantly colourful three-day celebration of Afro-Caribbean music, culture and food. Over a million people visit every year, taking part in the celebrations, thronging the streets and letting their hair down. The festival is a must if you want a spirited glimpse of multicultural London and its cross-pollination of music, food, clothing, language and culture.

Notting Hill & West London

Westminster Abbey *(p86)*

14 Adorers of medieval ecclesiastic architecture will be in seventh heaven at this sublime abbey, hallowed place of coronation for England's sovereigns. Almost every nook and adorable cranny has a story attached to it but few sights in London are as beautiful, or as well preserved, as the Henry VII chapel. Elsewhere you will find the oldest door in the UK, Poet's Corner, the Coronation Chair, 14th-century cloisters, a 900-year-old garden, royal sarcophagi and much more. Be warned that the crowds are almost as solid as the abbey's unshakeable stonework, so aim to join the queue first thing in the morning.

The West End

Sporting London *(p76)*

15 Even if you don't land tickets to the FA Cup Final at Wembley Stadium or front-row seats for the Wimbledon finals, there are plenty of ways to enjoy sport in London. You could find yourself doing anything from watching the Oxford–Cambridge boat race, cheering runners at the London Marathon, hopping on a Barclays bike to weave through the central London traffic or jogging around Battersea Park – there's lots on offer. And why not check out the impressive new facilities in Olympic Park, which hosts the Olympic Stadium, the stunning Aquatics Centre and the cutting-edge Velodrome. WIMBLEDON

Sports & Activities

15

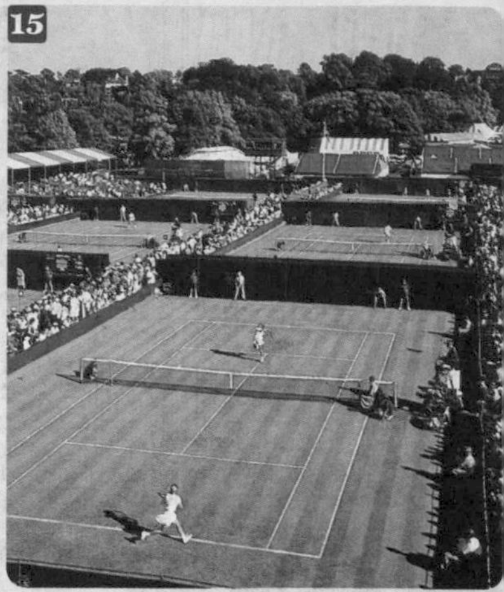

16

Natural History Museum *(p192)*

16 With its thunderous, animatronic Tyrannosaurus Rex, magical Wildlife Garden, outstanding Darwin Centre and architecture straight from a Gothic fairy tale, the Natural History Museum is quite simply a work of great curatorial imagination. Kids are the target audience but, looking around, you'll see adults equally mesmerised. Popular sleepovers in the museum have young ones snoozing alongside the towering diplodocus skeleton, while winter brings its own magic, when the glittering ice rink by the east lawn swarms with skaters.

Kensington & Hyde Park

What's New

Cutty Sark

It was six years in the making, but the refurbishment of this legendary clipper was worth it: the Cutty Sark is now one of Greenwich's top sights. (p282)

Maltby Street Market

Hailed as the new Borough Market (the famous food market on the South Bank), Maltby Street is small, quirky, delicious and a joy to laze an afternoon in. (p179)

Charles Dickens Museum

After a £3.5 million renovation, the only surviving London residence of the great novelist is bigger and better than ever. (p106)

View from the Shard

London's latest statement skyscraper, the Shard, pierces the sky from the south bank of the river. Head up top for sweeping panoramas of the city. (p177)

Theatrical Tours of Benjamin Franklin's House

Benjamin Franklin spent 17 years in London trying to broker peace with Britain in the late 18th century. Visit the modest abode where the 'First American' spent his London years. (p113)

One New Change

Designed by architect Jean Nouvel, city mall One New Change, aka the Stealth Bomber, is trying to breathe weekend life into the City with shops, restaurants and cocktail bars open weekdays as well as weekends. (p147)

Cocktail Craze

Londoners have always loved their designer cocktails, but they keep upping the ante with ever fancier bars and concoctions: it's all about rare spirits, flower infusions and homemade exotic fruit syrups. (p62)

William Morris Gallery

Fans of the Arts and Crafts movement will revel in the details of this completely overhauled gallery in northeast London, once the family home of Arts and Crafts figurehead William Morris, of wallpaper fame. (p249)

Two Temple Place

Once the home of William Waldorf Astor, of hotel fame, this opulent neo-gothic mansion is now a gallery showcasing art from outside the capital. (p116)

New Broadcasting House

The BBC moved lock, stock and barrel from its old home in Bush House on the Strand to this equally historic but recently refurbished and extended building in 2012, ready to write the next instalment in the corporation's history. (p107)

Emirates Air Line Cable Car

Forget about bridges, boats or tunnels; the newest and coolest way to cross the Thames is by cable car between the O2 on the Greenwich Peninsula and the Excel Centre in the Docklands of East London. (p407)

For more recommendations and reviews, see **lonelyplanet.com/london**

Need to Know

For more information, see Survival Guide (p399)

Currency

Pound sterling (£).
100 pence = £1.

Language

English (and over 300 others).

Visas

Not required for US, Canadian, Australian, New Zealand or South African visitors for stays of up to six months. European Union nationals can stay indefinitely.

Money

ATMs widespread. Major credit cards accepted everywhere.

Mobile Phones

Buy local SIM cards for European and Australian phones, or a pay-as-you-go phone. Set other phones to international roaming.

Time

London is on GMT; during British Summer Time (BST; late March to late October), London clocks are one hour ahead of GMT.

Tourist Information

Visit London (☎0870 156 6366; www.visitlondon.com) can fill you in on everything from attractions and events to tours and accommodation.

Daily Costs

Budget: Less than £80

➡ Dorm bed £10-30

➡ Market-stall lunch £5, supermarket sandwich £3-4

➡ Many museums free

➡ Standby theatre tickets £5-15

➡ Barclays bike daily charge £2

Midrange: £80-180

➡ Double room £100-150

➡ Two-course dinner with glass of wine £30

➡ Theatre ticket £10-50

Top End: Over £180

➡ Four-star/boutique hotel room £200

➡ Three-course dinner in top restaurant with wine £60-90

➡ Black cab trip £30

➡ Top theatre ticket £65

Advance Planning

Three months before Book weekend performances of top shows; make dinner reservations for renowned restaurants; snatch up tickets for must-see exhibitions; book accommodation at popular or boutique properties.

One month before Check listings on entertainment sites such as www.timeout.com for fringe theatre, live music and festivals, and book tickets.

A few days before Check the weather on www.tfl.gov.uk/weather.

Useful Websites

Lonely Planet (www.lonelyplanet.com/london) Bookings, traveller forum and more.

Time Out London (www.timeout.com/london) Up-to-date and comprehensive listings.

60by80 (www.60by80.com/london) Fantastic city guide for modern gay (and straight) travellers.

Londonist (www.londonist.com) A website about London and everything that happens in it.

Transport for London (www.tfl.gov.uk) Essential tool for staying mobile in the capital.

WHEN TO GO

Summer is peak season: days are long and festivals are afoot, but expect crowds; spring and autumn are cooler, but delightful. Winter is cold but quiet.

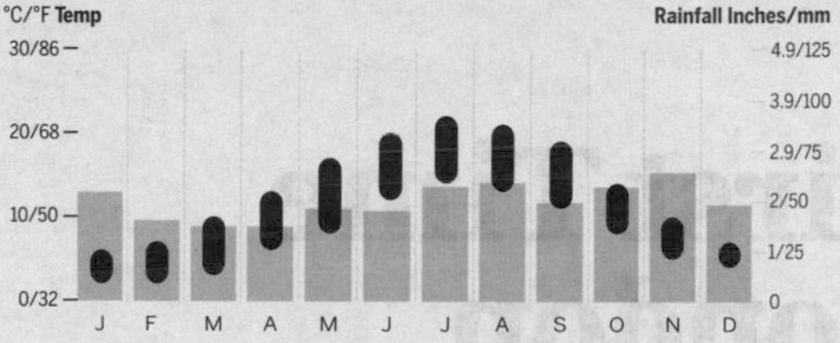

Arriving in London

Heathrow Airport Trains, London Underground (tube) and buses to central London from 5.25am to midnight (night buses run later) £5-20; taxi £45-65.

Gatwick Airport Trains to central London from 4.30am to 1.35am £8-20; hourly buses to central London from 6am to 9.45pm £7-10; taxi £90.

Stansted Airport Trains to central London from 5.30am to around midnight £23.40; round-the-clock buses to central London £8-10; taxi £90.

Luton Airport Trains to central London from 7am to 10pm £15; round-the-clock buses to central London £10-15; taxi £90.

London City Airport Trains to central London from 5.30am to 12.30am Monday to Saturday, 7am to 11.30pm Sunday £2; taxi £30.

St Pancras International Train Station In Central London (for Eurostar train arrivals from Europe) and connected by many underground lines to other parts of the city.

For much more on **arrival** see p400

Digital London

There are dozens of cool apps for travellers. Here are some of our favourites (all free), from the inspirational to the downright practical. Many museums and attractions also have their own.

➡ **StreetMuseum** Historical images (photographs, paintings, drawings etc) of modern-day locations.

➡ **Street Art Tours London** Hand-picked grafitti and other street-art locations. First tour free, then £1.99.

➡ **Soho Stories** Social history of London's most Bohemian neighbourhood told through poems and extracts from novels and newspapers.

➡ **Hailo** Summons the nearest black cab.

➡ **Kabbee** Offers you quotes and bookings from nearby licensed minicabs at the tap of a button.

➡ **Bus London** Confused by buses? Not any more thanks to this handy real-time route finder.

➡ **London Cycle** Find a 'Boris bike', a route and a place to return it.

➡ **ToiletFinder** Where to spend a penny.

For much more on **staying connected** see p409

Sleeping

Hanging your hat in London can be expensive, and as the city is busy at the best of times, you'll need to book your room well in advance. Decent, central hostels are easy enough to find and also offer reasonably priced double rooms. Bed and breakfasts are a dependable and inexpensive, if rather simple, option. Hotels range from cheap, no-frills chains through boutique choices to luxury five-star historic hotels.

Useful Websites

➡ **Lonely Planet** (www.lonelyplanet.com/london) Hundreds of properties from budget hostels to luxury apartments.

➡ **London Town** (www.londontown.com) Excellent last-minute offers on boutique hotels and B&Bs.

➡ **Alastair Sawdays** (www.sawdays.com) Hand-picked selection of abodes in the capital.

➡ **Visit London** (www.visitlondon.com) Huge range of listings from the city's official tourism portal.

For much more on **sleeping** see p332

First Time London

For more information, see Survival Guide (p399)

Checklist

- ➡ Make sure your passport is valid for at least six months past your arrival date
- ➡ Check airline baggage restrictions (liquids and fresh products in particular)
- ➡ Arrange travel insurance (or get a European Health Insurance Card if you hail from the EU)
- ➡ Inform your debit/credit card company of your travels
- ➡ Book tickets for popular plays, shows or festivals to avoid disappointment

What to Pack

- ➡ An umbrella, because the rumours about the weather are true
- ➡ Good walking shoes – the city is best explored on foot
- ➡ UK plug adaptor
- ➡ A few extra layers – even summer can be cool
- ➡ A small day pack

Top Tips for Your Trip

- ➡ London is huge – work by neighbourhood to avoid wasting time (and money) on transport.
- ➡ Get an Oyster card, the cheapest and most convenient way to use public transport in London.
- ➡ Walk – it's cheaper than transport and the best way to discover the city.
- ➡ For West End performances at bargain prices, opt for standby tickets (which you buy on the day at the venue) or last-minute ticket-booth tickets on Leicester Sq.
- ➡ To treat yourself to fine dining without breaking the bank, opt for lunch rather than dinner, or try for pre- or post-theatre dinner deals.

What to Wear

Fashion is big in London but very eclectic so you're unlikely to stand out, whatever your sartorial choice.

Dress codes are rare (although you'll need smart shoes for some restaurants and clubs), but many Londoners make an effort in the evening, whether they're kitted out in cool T-shirts or more formal gear.

The weather has a mind of its own, regardless of the season: always carry an umbrella or a jacket that can withstand a shower or two. And do wrap up warm in winter, the wind can be punishing.

Be Forewarned

- ➡ London is open for business every day of the year, except Christmas Day (25 December) when absolutely everything shuts down, including the transport network. Hotel restaurants are about the only thing you'll find open.
- ➡ London is a relatively safe city; common sense applies such as avoiding deserted streets at night and being mindful of pickpockets in crowded areas.
- ➡ Be discreet with your tablet/smartphone – snatching happens.
- ➡ Always use black cabs or licensed minicabs.

Money

ATMS are everywhere, and will generally accept Visa, MasterCard, Cirrus or Maestro cards. There is nearly always a transaction surcharge for cash withdrawals with foreign cards.

Credit and debit cards are accepted almost universally in London. American Express and Diners Club are less widely used than Visa or MasterCard.

The best place to change money is in post office branches, which do not charge a commission. You can also change money in most banks as well as in numerous bureaux de change.

For more information, see p410.

Taxes & Refunds

Value-added tax (VAT) is a 20% sales tax levied on most goods and services. Restaurants must always include VAT in their prices, but the same requirement doesn't apply to hotel room prices so double-check when booking.

It's sometimes possible for visitors to claim a refund of VAT paid on goods; see p412 for details.

Tipping

➡ **Hotels** One pound per bag is standard; gratuity for cleaning staff at your discretion.

➡ **Pubs** Not expected unless table service is provided, then £1 for a round of drinks.

➡ **Restaurants** Service charge often included in the bill. If not, 10% for decent service, up to 15% if exceptional.

➡ **Taxis** Round fare up to nearest pound.

MICHAEL COYNE / GETTY IMAGES ©

Changing of the Guard, Buckingham Palace (p93)

Etiquette

Although largely informal in their everyday dealings, Londoners do observe some (unspoken) rules of etiquette.

➡ **Greetings** Shake hands with men, women and children when meeting for the first time and when saying goodbye. Female friends are greeted with a single (air) kiss.

➡ **Queues** The English are notoriously polite, especially when it comes to queuing. Any attempt to 'jump the queue' will result in an outburst of tutting.

➡ **Bargaining** Haggling over the price of goods (but not food) is okay in markets, but rare in shops. Politeness is key.

Staying connected

Smartphone users can turn their data-roaming off: there are numerous ways to get online for free in London (aside from your hotel):

➡ Chains such as Pret a Manger, McDonalds or Starbucks all have free wi-fi.

➡ Most cafes these days have complimentary wi-fi.

➡ The City of London is one giant hotspot as is Upper St in Islington.

➡ Art centres like the Barbican, the Southbank Centre or the British Library all offer free wi-fi.

➡ Wi-fi is also available in some Overground stations (free) and some Underground stations (depending on your home network, access fees may apply).

Getting Around

For more information, see Transport (p400)

Underground (Tube)
The quickest (but most expensive) form of public transport; trains run from 5.30am to 12.30am (7am to 11.30pm Sunday).

Bus
Slow-going but cheap, with ace views from double-deckers. Large number of night buses.

Bicycle
The Barclays Bike Hire Scheme is the ideal way to get around central London on a dry day. Cheap, fast and scenic.

Walking
Free, healthy and immersive, you can't beat it for neighbourhood exploration.

Overground
Runs all the way around London across Zones 2 and 3. Similar operating hours to the Underground but less frequent trains (every 10 to 20 minutes).

Taxi
Available everywhere and round-the-clock. Hail in the street (black cabs) or book ahead (minicabs).

Train
Best to get to/from the airport, go to Hampton Court or on day trips to places further afield such as Oxford or Windsor.

Key Phrases

Black Cab London's signature clunky taxi, which can be hailed anywhere in the city. Note that despite the name, they are not all black!

Boris bike A colloquialism for the blue Barclays-branded bikes for hire all over London. Named after current mayor Boris Johnson, although the initiative was set in motion by previous mayor Ken Livingstone.

DLR Docklands Light Railway, an overground, driver-less train in East London, almost as frequent as the tube.

Minicab A taxi that cannot be hailed in the street and must be pre-booked over the phone or in person with the dispatcher (offices can generally be spotted by an orange flashing light outside).

Oyster card Smart card ticket for London's transport network.

The Tube London's underground metro system.

Key Routes

Bus: Routes 9 and 15 These 'heritage' bus routes use the classic London double-decker buses.

DLR: Bank to Greenwich Bag the seats at the front of this driverless, overground train for an amazing sightseeing trip through the Docklands and Canary Wharf.

Tube: Piccadilly Line This tube line stops at some of London's key sights and neighbourhoods – Piccadilly Circus, Covent Garden, Hyde Park and Knightsbridge.

How to Hail a Taxi

➡ To hail a black cab, look for a stationary or approaching cab with its 'For Hire' sign lit up.

➡ If the car is approaching, stand in a prominent place on the side of the road and stick out your arm.

➡ Use a smartphone app such as Hailo, which uses your phone's GPS to find the nearest available black cab.

➡ See p406 for how to hire a minicab.

TOP TIPS

- ➡ As a general rule, eschew the tube within Zone 1 unless going from one end to the other: cycling, walking or the bus will be cheaper/quicker.
- ➡ Check www.tfl.gov.uk or advance notices in tube stations for planned engineering works and line closures at weekends.
- ➡ Get an Oyster card – and return it when you leave to get the £5 deposit back along with any remaining credit.
- ➡ If you're only travelling a short distance, try using a Barclays bike – they're free for up to 30 minutes.

When to Travel

➡ Rush hour is between 7.30am and 9.30am and from 4.30pm to 7pm.

➡ Travelling at these times can be uncomfortably crowded: think stealthy seat races, face-in-armpit and toe-treading. Tube fares are also more expensive at rush hour and tempers easily fray.

➡ Weekends are notorious for engineering works, when entire tube lines or sections of lines shut down. Replacement bus services are usually in place, but they often take longer so try to plan around these restrictions.

➡ The tube stops running around 12.30am, much to the annoyance of revellers. Night buses are the universal public transport Plan B, but note that some services only run every half hour, so check times before leaving lest you fancy hanging around at a bus stop at 3am.

Travel Etiquette

➡ Have your ticket or Oyster card ready before you go through the gate. Londoners are well-practiced at moving through ticket barriers without breaking stride.

➡ On escalators, stand on the right-hand side and use the left if you want to walk down. Failure to observe this can cause consternation among other users, especially during rush hour.

➡ Take your rucksack off at rush hour to avoid sweeping off somebody's newspaper, tablet or child.

➡ Give up your seat for people less able to stand than you – people with reduced mobility actually have priority over the seats closest to the doors on the tube.

Tickets & Passes

➡ The cheapest and most convenient way to pay for public transport is to buy an Oyster card, a smart card on which you can store credit. The card works on the entire transport network and can be purchased from all tube and train stations and some shops.

➡ Oyster cards will work out whether to charge you per journey, for a return or for a day travelcard.

➡ You need to pay a £5 deposit per Oyster card, which you will get back, along with any remaining credit, when you return the card.

➡ If you're staying for more than just a few days, consider getting a weekly or monthly pass (which can be loaded on to the Oyster card).

➡ Paper tickets are still available but are more expensive than Oyster fares.

For much more on **getting around** see p400

Top Itineraries

Day One

The West End (p84)

First stop, **Trafalgar Square** for its architectural grandeur and photo-op views down Whitehall to **Big Ben**. Art lovers will make an instant break for the **National Gallery** and its unrivalled collection of European paintings. Alternatively, if you're here during **Buckingham Palace's** summer opening, visit the royal residence.

Lunch Portrait (p125) for views or Inn the Park (p119) for leafy surroundings.

South Bank (p168)

Walk across the pedestrian Hungerford Bridge to the South Bank and, with your pre-booked ticket for the **London Eye**, enjoy a revolution in the city skies and astronomical views. Sashay along the river and head down the ramp into the bowels of the **Tate Modern** for some grade-A art. Aim your camera at **St Paul's Cathedral** on the far side of the elegant **Millennium Bridge**.

Dinner Fish at Applebee (p180) or elaborate Italian at Zucca (p181).

South Bank (p168)

Depending what mood you're in, you could watch a performance at Shakespeare's Globe, a very faithful reconstruction of an Elizabethan outdoor theatre. Standing tickets can be bought last minute (but book in advance for seats). Otherwise join the post-work crowds in the pubs around London Bridge for real ales and historical surroundings.

Day Two

The City (p146)

London's finance-driven Square Mile is home to the **Tower of London**. Get here early to witness the **Ceremony of the Keys** and spend the rest of the morning following the **Beefeaters** and marvelling at the **Crown Jewels**. When you're finished, take a minute to admire the iconic **Tower Bridge** on the Thames.

Lunch The Wine Library (p165) for good wine and platters.

The City (p146)

If you have the energy, walk to **St Paul's**: the City is the oldest neighbourhood in London and has history at every turn. If not, hop on a bus and save yourself for the glorious cathedral. Wrap up the afternoon with a drink at **Madison** and sumptuous views of St Paul's.

Dinner Yauatcha (p123) for excellent Chinese food in the heart of Soho.

The West End (p84)

There are literally dozens of pubs, bars and cocktail bars to choose from. If you fancy soaking up the atmosphere, stroll through **Chinatown** and **Soho** and make your way to **Leicester Sq** for some people watching.

Day Three

Greenwich (p277)

Hop on a boat in central London and make your way down to Greenwich with its world-renowned architecture. Start your visit at the legendary **Cutty Sark**, a star clipper during the tea-trade years.

Lunch Greenwich Market (p291) for a culinary tour of world cuisine.

Greenwich (p277)

Stroll through **Greenwich Park** all the way up to the **Royal Observatory**. The views of **Canary Wharf**, the business district across the river, are stunning. Inside the Observatory, straddle the **Greenwich Meridian** and find out about the incredible quest to solve the longitude problem. At the **planetarium**, join another quest: finding extra-terrestrial life. Walk back down to Greenwich and settle down for a pint at the **Trafalgar Tavern**.

Dinner St John (p212) for high-brow British cuisine.

Clerkenwell, Shoreditch & Spitalfields (p206)

Head back to central London on the DLR from Greenwich and treat yourself to dinner in one of the fine restaurants dotting this part of town. There are plenty of clubs if you fancy a boogie after dinner; otherwise have a game of table football (and a beer) at **Bar Kick** or **Cafe Kick**.

Day Four

North London (p238)

Start the day with an invigorating stroll through **Hampstead Heath** at the top of which is the beautiful 18th-century **Kenwood House**, with its grand collection of art. Amble down to **Parliament Hill** for sweeping views of the city. Head to **Camden** for lunch: have a takeaway on the scooter seats and browse the many market stalls for cool T-shirts and accessories.

Lunch Camden Market (p245) for street food; Market (p251) for gourmet.

Kensington & Hyde Park (p186)

Hop on the tube to **Kensington**. Keen shoppers will want to stroll along Old Brompton Rd and pop into **Harrods**, the famous department store. Culture vultures should save their energy for the **Victoria & Albert Museum**: you could spend your entire afternoon browsing the design collections.

Dinner Dinner by Heston Blumenthal (p201) for theatrical English cuisine.

Notting Hill (p263)

If the pubs around Kensington are too staid for you, hop over to **Notting Hill** where the crowds are livelier and the nightlife more eclectic. If you just fancy sitting down with a good film, you're in luck: Notting Hill has some of the coolest independent **cinemas** in London.

If You Like...

Royalty

Tower of London Castle, tower, prison, medieval execution site and home of the dazzling Crown Jewels. (p148)

Buckingham Palace The Queen Mother of all London's royal palaces, with lovely gardens and – the popular drawcard – the Changing of the Guard. (p93)

Hampton Court Palace Magnificent Tudor palace, located within beautiful grounds on the Thames. (p302)

Kensington Palace Princess Diana's former home, this stately and stunning royal palace is the highlight of Kensington Gardens. (p196)

Windsor Castle Magnificent and ancient royal fortress within easy reach of London. (p317)

Views

London Eye For gently rotating, tip-top views of London – but choose a fair-weather day. (p173)

View from the Shard The highest – and most expensive – views one can get in London. (p177)

Parliament Hill Skyscraping views across London from Hampstead Heath. (p246)

Greenwich Park Clamber up to the statue of General Wolfe for superlative views of Canary Wharf, the Thames and the O2. (p280)

Duck & Waffle Fabulous city views served with food and drink around the clock. (p165)

London Eye (p173), designed by David Marks and Julia Barfield, and County Hall (p173)

Madison For a full-frontal view of St Paul's elegant dome in alfresco settings, you can't beat this cocktail bar. (p167)

Parks & Gardens

Hampstead Heath Woods, hills, meadows and top scenic views, all rolled into one sublime sprawl. (p246)

Richmond Park Europe's largest urban parkland has everything from herds of deer to tranquil pockets of woodland, seemingly infinite wild tracts and beautiful vistas. (p308)

St James's Park Feast on some sublime views in one of London's most attractive royal parks. (p107)

Kew Gardens A botanist's paradise, a huge expanse of greenery and a great day out with the kids. (p306)

Chelsea Physic Garden Tranquil and particularly tidy botanical enclave just a stone's throw from the Thames. (p198)

Victoria Park This is party central every weekend in spring and summer, with East Londoners enjoying a picnic or revelling at the park's many events. (p227)

Animals & Wildlife

London Wetland Centre Birds, bats, dragonflies, otters and much more: this is proper wildlife in the heart of London. (p311)

London Zoo One of the world's oldest and most famous zoos now has an impressive new tiger enclosure. (p242)

London Sea Life Aquarium A tremendous collection of creatures from the world's saltwater depths on display next to the Thames. (p173)

Mudchute Park & Farm A lovely city farm on the Isle of Dogs: cows, sheep and llamas with a Canary Wharf backdrop. (p230)

Kensington Roof Gardens Not many rooftop bars come equipped with their own pink flamingos. (p272)

Cemeteries

Highgate Cemetery Gothic and sublimely overgrown 20-hectare Victorian place of the dead, including Karl Marx. (p247)

Abney Park Cemetery Tangled with weeds, reclaimed by nature, with moments of magic. (p247)

Brompton Cemetery Some of this cemetery's dead found immortality in the names of Beatrix Potter's animal characters. (p266)

Tower Hamlets Cemetery Park Another specialist in the wild and sublime Victorian ruin look. (p227)

Kensal Green Cemetery Distinctive Greek Revival architecture and illustrious residents including Isambard Brunel and Charles Babbage. (p266)

Squares

Trafalgar Square London's iconic central square, lorded over by Lord Nelson – and four magnificent felines. (p102)

Soho Square Serene spot for a sandwich in the sun at the heart of the West End. (p110)

Trinity Square Gardens Picturesque and well-tended one-time location of the notorious Tower Hill scaffold. (p157)

Squares of Bloomsbury Elegant, historic and tranquil squares dotted around literary Bloomsbury. (p105)

For more top London spots, see the following:

- Museums & Galleries (p42)
- Eating (p47)
- Drinking & Nightlife (p57)
- Gay & Lesbian (p63)
- Entertainment (p65)
- Shopping (p71)
- Sports & Activities (p76)

Covent Garden Piazza Fine-looking West End square originally laid out in the 17th century, and now popular with street performers. (p111)

Leicester Square Unbeatable for people-watching and celebrity-spotting on film premiere nights. (p112)

Music

Wireless Music Festival London's flagship music festival rocks, especially now that it's moved to its new home in the Queen Elizabeth Olympic Park. (p30)

Wigmore Hall One of the most active classical-music concert venues in the capital. (p137)

Royal Festival Hall Fantastic acoustics and an excellent program of music across the aural spectrum. (p184)

Church recitals Take a pew at one of the many free afternoon church recitals around town. (p41)

Indie rock gigs Playing in one of North London's numerous grungy bars is a rite of passage for aspiring acts. (p259)

Royal Opera House London's world-famous opera in Covent Garden is second to none for lavish productions. (p136)

Cultural Diversity

Chinatown At the heart of London and the place to be for dim sum dining or the Chinese New Year. (p110)

Dalston The heartland of the Turkish and Kurdish communities – you need not look further for outstanding kebabs. (p248)

Brick Lane Take a wander and a gander and go shopping around this vibrant London outpost of the Bangladeshi community. (p209)

Brixton Village Great dining and shopping converge in South London's most famous multicultural neighbourhood. (p285)

Whitechapel Road Lively, vibrant and cacophonous tangle of cultures and languages. (p224)

Rivers & Canals

Regent's Canal Amble along the historic trade route and take a shortcut across North London at the same time. (p251)

Richmond Home to some spectacular views of the Thames with enchanting pastoral shade in Petersham Meadows. (p308)

Greenwich Pop into a riverside pub and toast the fine views of the river with a pint. (p294)

South Bank Hop on our South Bank Walk and walk from County Hall to City Hall past some outstanding waterside sights. (p174)

Hampton Court Palace Take a riverboat up the Thames to Henry VIII's spectacular palace. (p302)

Village Charms

Primrose Hill With lovely restaurants, boutiques and pubs, this North London village has genuine appeal (and celebrity-spotting ops). (p244)

Richmond Perhaps the archetypal London village, with village green, a river perspective, a fabulous bridge and gorgeous parkland. (p308)

Dulwich Village After viewing the Dulwich Picture Gallery, wander around Dulwich Village with its towering horse chestnut trees to experience some of London's easy-going and tranquil charms. (p287)

Blackheath Nestled in a small vale south of Greenwich Park, Blackheath looks more rural chic than London suburb. (p292)

Walking

Hampstead Heath Wild, hilly, carefree heathland and woodland with some excellent views from London's highest open space. (p246)

Regent's Canal Take a canalside hike across North London. (p251)

Putney to Barnes Amble along the delightful riverside on this do-able segment of the Thames Path. (p315)

The West End Jump on our highlights tour from Covent Garden to Trafalgar Sq. (p118)

Wimbledon Common Follow nature trails or just branch off in any direction for woodland, heath, grassland and bracing exploration. (p311)

Churches

St Paul's Cathedral Sir Christopher Wren's 300-year-old domed masterpiece and London's most iconic historic church. (p154)

Westminster Abbey Ancient and sublime site of coronation for English monarchs since William the Conqueror. (p86)

Westminster Cathedral The interior sparkles fitfully with dazzling Byzantine mosaics. (p199)

Brompton Oratory Sublime, incense-wreathed Catholic church in dapper Knightsbridge. (p197)

St Stephen Walbrook Sir Christopher Wren's finest City church, and his first experience with a dome, a precursor to St Paul's. (p158)

Modern Architecture

Velodrome Nicknamed 'the Pringle', it's the most striking and dramatic masterpiece of the Olympic Park. (p228)

30 St Mary Axe Colloquially dubbed 'the Gherkin', this is the City's most iconic modern edifice. (p157)

Shard A crystalline spike dominating the South Bank, with views of the city to die for. (p177)

London Eye Unsurprisingly visible from many remote parts of town. (p173)

City Hall Does it look like a woodlouse or Darth Vader's helmet? Your call. (p178)

Month by Month

TOP EVENTS

Notting Hill Carnival, August

Chelsea Flower Show, May

Trooping the Colour, June

Guy Fawkes Night, November

Wimbledon Lawn Tennis Championships, June

January

January in London kicks off with a big bang at midnight. London is in the throes of winter, with short days: light appears at 8am and is all but gone by 4pm.

New Year's Celebration

On 31 December, the famous countdown to midnight with Big Ben is met with terrific fireworks from the London Eye and massive crowds.

London Art Fair

Over 100 major galleries participate in this contemporary art fair (www.londonartfair.co.uk), now one of the largest in Europe, with thematic exhibitions, special events and the best emerging artists.

London International Mime Festival

Held in the last two weeks of January, this festival (www.mimefest.co.uk) is a must for lovers of originality, playfulness, physical talent and the unexpected.

February

February is usually chilly, wet and even snow-encrusted. The Chinese New Year (Spring Festival) is fun, and Londoners lark about with pancakes on Shrove Tuesday.

Chinese New Year

In late January or early February, Chinatown fizzes, crackles and pops in this colourful street festival, which includes a Golden Dragon parade, eating and partying.

BAFTAs

The British Academy of Film and Television Arts (BAFTA; www.bafta.org) rolls out the red carpet on Leicester Sq in early February to hand out its annual cinema awards, the BAFTAs (the British Oscars if you will). Expect plenty of celebrity glamour.

Pancake Races

On Shrove Tuesday, in late February/early March, you can catch pancake races and associated silliness at various venues around town (Spitalfields Market, Covent Garden and Lincoln's Inn Fields).

March

March sees spring in the London air and trees beginning to flower, most colourfully in parks and gardens. London is getting in the mood to head outdoors again.

Head of the River Race

Some 400 crews take part in this colourful annual boat race (www.horr.co.uk) held over a 7km course on the Thames, from Mortlake to Putney.

Kew Gardens Spring Festival

For flower aficionados, this is the best time (continuing through April) to see Kew Gardens.

St Patrick's Day Parade & Festival

Top festival for the Irish in London, held on the Sunday

closest to 17 March, with a colourful parade through central London and other festivities in and around Trafalgar Sq.

April

April sees London in bloom with warmer days and a spring in everyone's step. British summer time starts late March, so it's now light until 7pm. Some sights previously shut for winter reopen.

London Marathon

Some 35,000 runners – most running for charity – pound through London in one of the world's biggest road races (www.virginlondonmarathon.com), heading from Greenwich Park to The Mall.

Oxford & Cambridge Boat Race

Crowds line the banks of the Thames for the country's two most famous universities going oar-to-oar from Putney to Mortlake. Dates vary, due to each university's Easter breaks, so check the website (www.theboatrace.org).

May

A delightful time to be in London: days are warming up and Londoners begin to start lounging around in parks, popping sunshades on and enjoying two bank holiday weekends (the first and the last in May).

Chelsea Flower Show

The world's most renowned horticultural event (www.rhs.org.uk/chelsea) attracts the cream of London's green-fingered and flower-mad gardeners.

Museums at Night

For one weekend in May, numerous museums across London open after-hours (www.culture24.org.uk/museumsatnight), with candle-lit tours, spooky atmospheres, sleep-overs and special events such as talks and concerts.

London Literature Festival

For two weeks in late May/early June, the written word takes centre stage at the Southbank Centre, with readings, lectures and live poetry from prize-winning authors and emerging talents.

June

The peak season begins with long, warm days (it's light until 10pm) and the arrival of Wimbledon and other alfresco events.

Trooping the Colour

The Queen's official birthday (www.trooping-the-colour.co.uk) is celebrated with much flag-waving, parades, pageantry and noisy flyovers.

Wimbledon Lawn Tennis Championships

For two weeks a year the quiet South London village of Wimbledon falls under a sporting spotlight as the world's best tennis players gather to battle for the championships (p312).

London Festival of Architecture

This month-long celebration of London's built environment (www.lfa2010.org) became annual in 2013. It explores the significance of architecture and design and how London has become a centre for innovation in those fields.

Open Garden Squares Weekend

Over one weekend, more than 200 gardens in London that are usually inaccessible to the public fling open their gates for exploration (www.opensquares.org).

July

July features the capital's major gay parade and a host of outdoor festivities, with the music calendar in full swing.

Royal Academy Summer Exhibition

Beginning in June and running through August, this exhibition at the Royal Academy of Arts (p108) showcases works submitted by artists from all over Britain, distilled to a thousand or so pieces.

Pride London

The gay community paints the town pink in this annual extravaganza (www.londoncommunitypride.org) featuring a morning parade and a huge afternoon event on Trafalgar Sq (locations frequently change).

Wireless

One of London's flagship music festivals, with an emphasis on R&B, Wireless (www.wirelessfestival.co.uk)

(Top) Fireworks over the River Thames
(Bottom) Chelsea Flower Show

DOUG ARMAND / GETTY IMAGES ©

DANIELA WHITE IMAGES / GETTY IMAGES ©

moved from Hyde Park to its new home at the Olympic Park in 2013. It is extremely popular so book in advance.

☆ Lovebox

This three-day music extravaganza (www.mamacolive.com/lovebox) in Victoria Park in East London was created by DJ band Groove Armada in 2002. Although its raison d'être is dance music, there are plenty of other genres, too, including indie, rock and pop.

August

Schools have broken up for summer, families are holidaying and the hugely popular annual Caribbean carnival dances into Notting Hill.

☆ BBC Promenade Concert (the Proms)

Starting in mid-July and ending in early September, the Proms offer two months of outstanding classical concerts (www.bbc.co.uk/proms) at various prestigious venues, centred on the Royal Albert Hall.

Great British Beer Festival

Organised by CAMRA (Campaign for Real Ale), this boozy festival (www.gbbf.org.uk) cheerfully cracks open casks of ale from the UK and abroad at Earls Court Exhibition Centre.

Notting Hill Carnival

Europe's biggest – and London's most vibrant – outdoor carnival (p265) is a celebration of Caribbean London, featuring music, dancing and costumes over the summer bank-holiday weekend.

Live by the Lake Concerts

Summer evenings don't get much better than this: good music (www.livebythelake.co.uk), in the stunning grounds of Kenwood House in Hampstead Heath, with a picnic and a bottle of rosé. Last weekend of August and first weekend of September.

September

The end of summer and start of autumn is a lovely time to be in town, with comedy festivals and a chance to look at London properties normally shut to the public.

The Mayor's Thames Festival

Celebrating the River Thames, this cosmopolitan festival (www.thamesfestival.org) sees fairs, street theatre, music, food stalls, fireworks and river races culminating in the superb Night Procession.

Greenwich Comedy Festival

At the time of writing, this week-long laugh fest – London's largest comedy festival (www.greenwich-comedyfestival.co.uk) – was looking for new digs. Check the website for updates.

London Open House

For a weekend in late September, the public is invited in to see over 700 heritage buildings throughout the capital that are normally off-limits (www.londonopenhouse.org).

Great Gorilla Run

It looks bananas, but this gorilla-costume charity run (www.greatgorillarun.org/london) along a 7km route from the City to Bankside and back again is all in aid of gorilla conservation.

October

The weather is getting colder, but London's parkland is splashed with gorgeous autumnal colours. Clocks go back to winter time the last weekend of the month.

Dance Umbrella

London's annual festival of contemporary dance (www.danceumbrella.co.uk) features five weeks of performances by British and international dance companies at venues across London.

London Film Festival

The city's premier film event (www.bfi.org.uk/lff) attracts big overseas names and you can catch over 100 British and international films before their cinema release. Masterclasses are given by world-famous directors.

November

London nights are getting longer, but they crackle with fireworks in the first week of November.

Guy Fawkes Night (Bonfire Night)

Bonfire Night commemorates Guy Fawkes' foiled attempt to blow up Parliament in 1605. Bonfires and fireworks light up the night on 5 November. Primrose Hill, Highbury Fields, Alexandra Palace, Clapham Common and Blackheath all have the best firework displays.

Lord Mayor's Show

In accordance with the Magna Carta of 1215, the newly elected Lord Mayor of the City of London travels in a state coach from Mansion House to the Royal Courts of Justice to take an oath of allegiance to the Crown. The floats, bands and fireworks that accompany the Mayor were added later (www.lordmayorsshow.org).

London Jazz Festival

Musicians from around the world swing into town for 10 days of jazz (www.londonjazzfestival.org.uk). World influences are well represented, as are more conventional strands.

December

London may see snow and a festive mood reigns as Christmas approaches and shops are dressed up to the nines. Days are increasingly shorter.

Lighting of the Christmas Tree & Lights

A celebrity is normally carted in to switch on all the festive lights that line Oxford, Regent and Bond streets, and a towering Norwegian spruce is set up in Trafalgar Sq.

With Kids

London is a fantastic place for children. The city's museums will fascinate all ages, and you'll find theatre, dance and music performances ideal for older kids. Playgrounds and parks, city farms and nature reserves are perfect for either toddler energy-busting or relaxation.

RAY WISE / GETTY IMAGES ©

anada geese goslings, Kew Gardens (p306)

Central London Kid Picks

Hyde Park & St James's Park

Open spaces, playgrounds, water and wildlife. (p195 & p107)

West End

Museum and gallery activities.

London Transport Museum

Drive the tube, trains and buses and then have a London Underground–themed smoothie in the upstairs cafe (p112).

Coram's Fields

Sandpits, swings, animals, and areas for all kinds of acrobatics. See www.coramsfields.org.

Kensington Gardens

A ship-shaped playground and wonderful paddling fountain (p195).

East London Kid Picks

V&A Museum of Childhood

Active and gregarious fun in the numerous play areas (p225).

Hackney City Farm

Best combined with a nearby market (Columbia Rd or Broadway Market) for teens (p37).

Mudchute Park & Farm

The biggest city farm (p230) in town.

South London Kid Picks

Southbank Centre

This area is car-free and full of fun. There are also music and theatre events at the Royal Festival Hall (p184) for teens, toddlers and those in between.

Battersea Park

Leafy spot that has its own zoo (p286).

Horniman Museum

Has an array of free-to-touch objects, such as puppets and masks, and interactive exhibits in the Nature Base. The Music

Gallery is a true highlight, with 1600 instruments on display; not only can the little ones listen to the instruments' sounds, they can also bash on a selection in the Hands On room (p287).

Vauxhall City Farm

Animal petting and picnicking on the grass. See www.vauxhallcityfarm.org.

Imperial War Museum

Older kids learn about history and check out battle aeroplanes. The whole family can then picnic on the vast green outside while the little ones play at the adjacent playground (p285).

North London Kid Picks

London Zoo

Where the wild things are (p242).

Hampstead Heath

The closest your child will get to a real forest within the city (p246).

Kentish Town City Farm

A lovely place to get in touch with the gentle beasts (p37).

Best Museums

London's museums are nothing if not child friendly. You'll find storytelling at the National Gallery (p97) (three years and over), art and craft workshops at the Victoria & Albert Museum (p188), train-making workshops at the Transport Museum (p112), tons of finger-painting opportunities at Tate Modern (p170) and Tate Britain (p100), or performance, art and craft at Somerset House (p115). And, what's better, they're all free (check websites for details). You'll also find that many arts and cultural festivals aimed at adults also cater to children – for example the annual Opera Holland Park (p274) has performances aimed at children.

Get Behind the Wheel at the London Transport Museum

Twenty London Transport buses and trains are on display and available for touching, climbing on and general child-handling, while also providing valuable learning opportunities on the history of the development of London and its transport. There is a modest picnic area too. Check the website for workshop information (p112).

Meet the Mummies at the British Museum

London's, and Britain's, best museum (p89) has hours of fun for all the family, but plan your visit in advance since the place is vast. The mummies are a favourite with children over three.

Interact till You Drop at the Science Museum

This is the definitive children's museum (p193), with interactive exhibits and fascinating learning and educational displays, as well as a basement garden play area. There are also great storytelling sessions and a fantastic cafe for families.

Gawp at the Dinosaurs at the Natural History Museum

The weekend and half-term-time queues attest to this museum's immense popularity with families, thanks to its fascinating permanent display of around 70 million plant, animal, fossil, rock and mineral specimens, a wildlife garden, and excellent temporary exhibitions. Activities are marvellous with themes such as building a five-star bee 'hotel' or making your very own volcano (p192).

NEED TO KNOW

- ➡ Under-16s travel free on buses, under-11s travel free on the tube and under-5s go free on the trains.
- ➡ Get a babysitter or nanny at Greatcare (www.greatcare.co.uk).
- ➡ The best way to see London is to walk – public transport can be crowded and hot in the summer months.
- ➡ If you are a new London resident, check your local council for information on child-friendly activities in your area.

FEARGUS COONEY / GETTY IMAGES ©

Mammals Gallery, Natural History Museum (p192)

See Stars at the Peter Harrison Planetarium

London's only planetarium (p280) has state-of-the-art HD projection technology, fascinating visualisations of space and real astronomers – plus a journey across the universe. What else could you wish for?

Museum Sleepovers

What better fun than to spend the night curled up with the mummies (of the ancient kind) or next to a dinosaur's foot?

British Museum

Bed down in the Egyptian and Mesopotamian galleries, but not before storytelling and activities relating to the museum's current exhibitions (p89). Quarterly only.

Natural History Museum

Dino-snore in the grand Central Hall under the watchful eye of the 150-million-year-old diplodocus, having first explored the museum's darkest nooks and crannies with only a torch to light your way (p192).

Science Museum

Running for nearly 20 years, this is the young Londoners' favourite, with IMAX 3D film screenings and science workshops to lull you to sleep (p193).

Museum Ice Skating

In winter months (November to January), a section by the East Lawn of the Natural History Museum is transformed into a glittering and highly popular ice rink. Book your slot well ahead (www.ticketmaster.co.uk).

Eating with Kids

OK, it's not Italy, Spain or France with their uber-relaxed approach to small diners, but most of London's restaurants and cafes are child friendly and offer baby-changing facilities and high chairs. Pick your places with some awareness – avoid high-end and quiet, small restaurants and cafes if you have toddlers or small babies (and those with the 'No Children' signs on the doors!). Go for noisier restaurants and more relaxed cafes, and you'll find that you'll be welcomed and probably even given that hardest of London's currencies to come by – a smile.

London is a great opportunity for your kids to taste all the world's cuisines in

NOT FOR PARENTS

For an insight into London aimed directly at kids, pick up a copy of Lonely Planet's *Not for Parents: London*. Perfect for children aged eight and up, it opens up a world of intriguing stories and fascinating facts about London's people, places, history and culture.

close proximity to each other, so pick from good-quality (and MSG-free) Chinese, Italian, French, Mexican, Japanese and Indian restaurants. Many places have kids' menus, but ask for smaller portions of adult dishes if your children have a more adventurous palate; you'll find that most places will be keen to oblige. Kids' menus cover the usual burgers, pastas (tomato/bolognese sauce), sausage and mash, and so on, and cost anything from £3.50 to £6.

Best Kid-Friendly Eateries

Wagamama

This chain is much loved by kids for its noodles and general buzz. Fresh juices and sugar-free ice lollies are favourites, and your little ones get to master the chopsticks. See wagamama.com.

That Place on the Corner

Great food and tons of workshops and classes and birthday party catering. See www.thatplaceonthecorner.co.uk.

Frizzante@City Farm

Great cafe (p232) for a big lunch before or after animal sightings at Hackney City Farm.

Parks & Playgrounds

Great parks abound in London and, within them, an abundance of playgrounds and wildlife. Here are some favourites.

St James's Park

Admiring the ducks and squirrels and watching the pelicans' teatime is a must at St James's Park (p107), followed by running around the rocky playground and sandpit. Finish up with a break at Inn the Park (p119).

Coram's Fields

Almost 3 hectares of lawns, sandpits, a shallow pool, an animal yard, swings and other contraptions are all yours at Coram's Fields, a local favourite. See www.coramsfields.org.

Hyde Park

Row your boat on the Serpentine lake or hire a pedalo and go out onto the water en famille (p195). You can also cycle (hire a 'Boris bike' in the park) or hit the ship-shaped playground at the Diana, Princess of Wales Memorial Fountain in Kensington Gardens.

Battersea Park

A leafy haven (p286) that contains its own zoo and provides some great playing opportunities.

Regent's Park

A truly wonderful park (p244) with lots of peaceful green spaces that your child can enliven – and it is home to London Zoo (p242), which makes it cool without even trying.

Off-Beat Activities

If you're a London resident, or if you're just after a bit of off-beat fun for your children, take them to one of these courses:

Children's Cookery Classes

Try **La Cucina Caldesi** (www.caldesi.com) in Marylebone who aim their courses from six-year-olds to teens, or **Kiddy Cook** (www.kiddycook.co.uk) in Twickenham, who will let a two-year-old get busy with the raw ingredients.

Circus Skills

Get those unicycling skills up to scratch at **Albert & Friends Instant Circus** (www.albertandfriendsinstantcircus.co.uk).

Children & Youth Dance

The Place (p137) has great term-time courses for young people between the ages of 6 and 15. Some toddler classes too. Best for London residents.

Mushroom Hunting

Fungi to Be With (www.fungitobewith.org) runs trips to Hampstead Heath, Epping Forest and Wimbledon Common.

City Farms, Wildlife & Nature Reserves

City kids need a regular fix of their animal buddies, and London obliges with the UK's most diverse pick of the animal kingdom through its city farms, zoos and nature reserves.

Freightliners City Farm

A fantastic working **farm** (www.freightliners farm.org.uk) in the inner city that's home to cows, sheep, pigs and giant Flemmish rabbits. It's also a community centre with an own-built cafe and opportunities to buy eggs and veggies grown on the farm.

Hackney City Farm

A retreat from the urban East London surroundings, the **Hackney City Farm** (Map p454; www.hackneycityfarm.co.uk) has goats, sheep, pigs and a donkey named Larry. It also has a vegetable and herb garden and sells eggs. The on-site Frizzante@City Farm (p232) has won awards for its excellent food.

Greenwich Peninsula Ecology Park

The perfect place to meander on the marshland paths and bird watch. Lose yourself in nature in the midst of industrial London. See www.urbanecology.org.uk.

Kentish Town City Farm

London's oldest city **farm** (Map p459; www.ktcityfarm.org.uk) has been going since 1972 and was the example for the rest of the capital's farms. Apart from petting the animals, kids can get involved in feeding and cleaning; there are popular pony-riding and pottery-throwing workshops too.

Highgate Wood & Queen's Wood

Once part of the ancient Forest of Middlesex, **Highgate Wood** (Map p459; Archway Rd; ⏲7.30am-sunset; ⊖Highgate) is a huge woodland area that feels worlds away from the traffic-laden streets of London. The entire place is just heavenly for kids with its carefully thought-out playground and outdoor storytelling sessions and treasure hunts.

Mudchute Park & Farm

This is the largest city farm (p230) in town, though the view of the nearby Canary Wharf skyscrapers denies the farm the chance to imagine itself a bucolic idyll. There's a 9am duck walk and other daily activities, as well as a great picnic area.

Epping Forest

Twelve miles in length and nearly as many across, **Epping Forest** (www.visiteppingforest.org) is popular for horse riding, cycling and walking, and is also the place to spot a grazing cow. Best for older kids and their families, and those keen on getting plenty of exercise.

Like a Local

Local life envelops you in London, but you might notice it only in snatches. Londoners know how to avoid the tourist crowds – waiting till late-opening nights before slipping into museums or galleries, swarming to parks as soon as the sun pops out – so go where they go and be surprised.

SCOTT E BARBOUR / GETTY IMAGES ©

Summer in Green Park (p109)

Drinking Like a Local

Londoners, and the British in general, get bad press for binge drinking. But most drinking in London is actually warmly sociable, gregarious and harmless fun. Londoners drink at the 'local', shorthand for the 'pub around the corner'. It's a community mainstay and a local haven. Prices may be high but generosity is commonplace and drinkers always step up to buy the next round. Aim for pubs with a sense of quirky history and a great range of ales and you can't go wrong.

Dining Like a Local

Londoners can be found queuing for seats or reserving tables at stylish restaurants across the city. As a rule of thumb, they'll dine at their local fish and chip shop rather than trek across town, but once a week they'll don their glad rags and blow their savings on a treat. You'll find them stocking up at Borough Market (p180) and picking up organic vegetables at farmers markets across town. But you'll also find them piling on the peri-peri sauce at Nando's, downing bowls of noodles at Wagamama or grabbing a sandwich from Marks & Spencer to lunch outside in Hyde Park. Sunday roast in a pub is a local weekend institution.

Shopping Like a Local

They are on home turf, so Londoners know precisely where to shop. They'll be in charity shops hunting for overlooked first editions and hard-to-find clothing, skimming market stalls for vintage togs off Brick Lane (p209), browsing along Portobello Rd (p267), rifling through Brixton Village (p285) or retreating to small, independent bookshops for peace, quiet and old-school service. But you'll also find them in well-heeled Mayfair, and bargain hunting along Kensington High St and Oxford St.

Taking to the Park

Despite being urban creatures, Londoners have a very, very low tolerance for concrete.

They also have access to some of the world's most beautiful urban green spaces and swarm en masse to the park the minute the sun pops out to read a book, play football, lord over a picnic or just chat with friends on the grass. Join them at lunch time when office workers come out for their fix of sunlight or at weekends for fun and games.

Sightseeing Like a Local

Londoners habitually get off the beaten track, taking the back route into their local park, exploring the city's wilder fringes or making short cuts like following Regent's Canal across North London. Go exploring in zones 2 and 3 and see what you find. Many Londoners bide their time till late-night openings for central London museums, when there are smaller crowds.

Local Obsessions

Property

Owning a property is a national obsession in the UK but is made particularly difficult in London where prices are stratospheric. Talk of unaffordable housing, renting versus buying, mortgage deals, putting in an offer and being gazumped, DIY and grand renovations are classic Sunday lunch fodder.

North vs South

The existential divide between 'Norff' and 'Saff' of the river remains as wide as ever. Each camp swears by its side. For Londoners, the main difference is that South London lacks access to the tube (which means that house prices are lower). But for visitors, the debate is moot: London is London, with the same amazing array of sights, restaurants, bars and markets.

The Weather (& Whether It'll Hold Out for Saturday's Barbecue)

More than wet, cold or grey, London's weather is unpredictable, which causes Londoners any amount of angst about their barbecue/picnic/beer garden plans from April to September, when it's supposed to be spring/summer but you may still get hit by unseasonable showers/cold snaps/high winds.

> **NEED TO KNOW**
>
> Everyone's getting about town on two wheels these days, so why not hop on a Barclays Bike (p405): it's fun, cheap, practical, definitively local and there are docking stations everywhere. All Londoners who travel by public transport invest in an Oyster card, which nets excellent discounts and avoids queues for tickets. On the buses, Routemaster heritage lines 9 and 15 are excellent for sightseeing, so grab a seat upstairs.

Public Transport

London has a world-class public transport network but Londoners like nothing more than a good old moan about their commute to work. Grievances range from delays due to improbably long red lights/signal failure/leaves on track/the wrong kind of snow (these are all real-life examples by the way) to the horribly high fares and the inexplicable fact that in a city where you can party all night, the tube clocks out at 12.30am.

Politics

Traditional rabble-rousers, the British always talk about politics. Once their teeth are truly stuck in, they won't let a political debate go; so if you like politics, you'll find company. Head to Speakers' Corner (p197) to find out what bees are in whose bonnets.

Football

If you are a football supporter, you should check how the land lies before revealing your allegiance. Passions run high when it comes to the beautiful game and rivalries between London's three major teams (Arsenal, Chelsea and Tottenham) are real. The capital has many more clubs in the Premier League and Championship, each with equally devoted supporters.

For Free

London may be one of the world's most expensive cities, but it won't always cost the earth. Many sights and experiences are free, gratis, complimentary, thrown in or won't cost you a penny (or very little). Become a London freeloader for the day and cash in on some tip-top freebies.

Southwark Cathedral (p176)

Free Sights

Houses of Parliament

When parliament is in session, it's free to attend and watch UK parliamentary democracy in action (p95).

Changing of the Guard

London's most famous open-air freebie, the Changing of the Guard at Buckingham Palace (p93) takes place at 11.30am from April to July (and alternate days, weather permitting, August to March). Grab your spot early. Alternatively, catch the changing of the mounted guard at Horse Guard's Parade (p114) at 11am (10am on Sundays). For further pomp and pageantry, Windsor Castle has its own version.

Unlocking of the Tower of London

Daily ritual performed at the Tower (p148) at 9am (10am on Sundays). The more elaborate evening Ceremony of the Keys is also free, but you'll have to apply in writing well in advance.

Architecture & Interiors

For one weekend in September, **London Open House** (www.londonopenhouse.org) opens the doors to more than 700 private buildings for free.

Free Museums & Galleries

All state-funded museums and galleries are free, except their temporary exhibitions.

Victoria & Albert Museum

The spectacular V&A (p188) can easily consume a day of complimentary exploration.

National Gallery

The Trafalgar Sq corner shops charge a king's ransom but this magnificent art collection (p97) is on the house.

Tate Modern

The art at this gallery (p170) may have a larger combined value than the GDP of a small nation, but it won't cost you a penny.

Saatchi Gallery
Exceptionally well-presented displays of contemporary art works, all for nothing (p198).

Free Activities

Guided Tours
Some museums, galleries and churches, such as the National Gallery (p97), Tate Britain (p100), Brompton Cemetery (p266) and All Hallows-by-the-Tower (p157), offer free guided tours (on top of free admission). Other attractions such as the Churchill War Rooms (p103) or St Paul's Cathedral (p154) offer free audio guides, but general admission might not be free.

A number of attractions, such as the Courtauld Gallery (p115) and the Natural History Museum (p192), host free talks and lectures.

Walking in London
Walking around town is possibly the best way to get a sense of the city and its history. Try our walking tours (see the neighbourhood chapters) or check **London Footprints** (www.london-footprints.co.uk) for further suggestions.

Picnicking in Hyde Park
Few pastimes can beat lying around on the grass or hurling a frisbee in one of London's parks. And the alfresco views are five-star.

Free Music
A number of churches in London offer free lunchtime classical-music concerts.

St Martin-in-the-Fields
This magnificent church (p112) hosts free concerts at 1pm on Monday, Tuesday and Friday.

St James's Piccadilly
Free 50-minute recitals (donation suggested) on Monday, Wednesday and Friday at 1.10pm (p108).

NEED TO KNOW

- **Websites** Click on **London for Free** (www.londonforfree.net) for budget ideas.
- **Discount cards** The London Pass (p409) can be a good investment.
- **Wi-fi access** Many cafes and bars offer free wi-fi to customers.
- **Newspapers** The *Evening Standard* and *Metro* are both free.
- **Children** Under-16s travel free on buses, under-11s travel free on the tube, under-5s go free on the trains.

Chapel at the Old Royal Naval College, Greenwich
Days vary but the offering is fabulous, from classical to slightly jazzier (p281).

St Alfege Church, Greenwich
Free recital at 1.10pm on Thursdays courtesy of the students from Trinity Laban Conservatoire of Music and Dance (p283).

Free Films
Snoop around and you'll find pubs and cafes showing free films – although they'd expect you to buy a drink perhaps. Try Garrison Public House (p181), which offers free films every Sunday at 7pm in its basement cinema, or check Scootercaffe (p181) for free screenings every other Sunday.

Shopping Discounts
Wedge Card (www.wedgecard.co.uk; per card £10) encourages people to shop locally by giving them a discount in shops that have signed up to the scheme.

Low-Cost Transport
Barclays Cycle Hire Scheme access fee is £2 for 24 hours; bike hire is then free for the first 30 minutes. Use a one-day Travel Card or an Oyster Card to travel as much as you can on London Transport.

British Library (p240)

Museums & Galleries

London's museums and galleries top the list of the city's must-see attractions – and not just for rainy days. Many display incomparable collections that make them acknowledged leaders in their field. A big constellation of top-name museums awaits in South Kensington, and there is a similar concentration in the West End, especially around Trafalgar Sq.

Hayward Gallery, Southbank Centre (p175)

NEED TO KNOW

Tickets

➡ Permanent collections at national museums (eg British Museum, National Gallery, Victoria & Albert Museum) are free; temporary exhibitions cost extra.

➡ Smaller museums will charge an entrance fee, typically £5 to £8.

➡ Private galleries are usually free or have a small admission fee.

➡ Book online at some museums (eg the British Music Experience) for discounted tickets.

Opening Hours

National collections are generally open 10am to about 6pm, with one or two late nights a week; evenings are an excellent time to visit museums as there are far fewer visitors.

Dining

Many of the top museums also have fantastic restaurants, worthy of a visit in their own right.

Useful Websites

Most London museums – especially the most visited ones like the British Museum, the National Gallery and the Victoria & Albert Museum – have sophisticated and comprehensive websites.

Culture 24 (www.culture24.org.uk) Reams of museum and gallery info.

London Galleries (www.london-galleries.co.uk) A to Z list of all London's galleries, with links.

The Big Hitters

London's most famous museums are all central, easy to get to and – best of all – free! The National Gallery on Trafalgar Sq displays masterpieces of Western European art from the 13th to the early 20th centuries, ranging from Leonardo da Vinci to Turner and Van Gogh. Just behind the gallery, the National Portrait Gallery celebrates famous British faces through a staggering collection of paintings, sculptures and photographs from the 16th century to the present day. A short tube or bus trip north is the British Museum in Bloomsbury, housing an astonishing assembly of antiquities.

Affluent South Kensington is the home of three of London's leading museums: the Victoria & Albert Museum, with its vast range of historical exhibits from the decorative arts, and the kid-friendly Natural History and Science Museums.

Modern and contemporary art lovers will enjoy the Tate Modern on the South Bank. The Tate Britain, venue of the annual Turner Prize, is home to British artworks across the centuries.

Private Art Galleries

London's vibrant artistic scene finds expression in private galleries across the city. Despite these challenging financial times, art remains a major cultural commodity and can be viewed in many London neighbourhoods. Mayfair has long been strong on private galleries in the more highbrow, traditional schools of painting, while more contemporary art finds its way into Spitalfields.

Museums at Night

Many museums open late once or twice a week, but several museums organise special nocturnal events to extend their range of activities and to present the collection in a different mood. Some museums arrange night events only once a year, in May.

Museums with special nocturnal events or late-night opening hours:

Sir John Soane's Museum (p104) Evenings (6pm to 9pm) of the first Tuesday of each month are illuminated by candlelight.

National Portrait Gallery (p101) Open till 9pm Thursday and Friday.

ALEX SEGRE / ALAMY ©

Top: Victoria & Albert Museum (p188)

Bottom: Egyptian mummies, British Museum (p89)

Natural History Museum (p192)

Tate Modern (p170) Open till 10pm Friday and Saturday.

Tate Britain (p100) Open till 10pm some Fridays.

British Museum (p89) Open till 8.30pm on Friday.

Natural History Museum (p192) Organises night safaris and sleepovers once a month.

British Library (p240) Talks, music and film on selected evenings throughout the year.

Courses, Talks & Lectures

Museums and galleries are excellent places to pick up specialist skills from qualified experts in their field. If you'd like to learn a new skill, brush up on an old one, or attend a fascinating lecture, there are many to choose from. Venues include the British Museum, Dulwich Picture Gallery, National Gallery, National Portrait Gallery, Tate Britain, Tate Modern and Victoria & Albert Museum.

Museums & Galleries by Neighbourhood

➡ **The West End** British Museum, National Gallery, National Portrait Gallery, Tate Britain, Charles Dickens Museum and many smaller museums and galleries. (p89)

➡ **The City** Museum of London, Barbican, Bank of England Museum. (p161)

➡ **The South Bank** Tate Modern, Hayward Gallery, Design Museum, Fashion & Textile Museum and small art galleries. (p170)

➡ **Kensington & Hyde Park** Victoria & Albert Museum, Natural History Museum, Science Museum and others. (p188)

➡ **Clerkenwell, Shoreditch & Spitalfields** Geffrye Museum, Dennis Severs' House. (p208)

➡ **The East End & Docklands** Museum of London Docklands, Ragged School Museum, Whitechapel Gallery. (p224)

➡ **Hampstead & North London** Wellcome Collection, London Canal Museum, Kenwood House, British Library. (p244)

➡ **Notting Hill & West London** Museum of Brands, Packaging & Advertising, Linley Sambourne House. (p265)

➡ **Greenwich & South London** National Maritime Museum, Royal Observatory, Imperial War Museum, Fan Museum, Horniman Museum, Dulwich Picture Gallery. (p282)

Lonely Planet's Top Choices

British Museum (p89) Supreme collection of international artefacts and an inspiring testament to human creativity over seven millennia.

Victoria & Albert Museum (p188) Very eclectic collection of decorative arts and design in what is affectionately known as 'the nation's attic'.

National Portrait Gallery (p101) Put a face to a name in this shrine to British portraiture.

Tate Modern (p170) A feast of modern and contemporary art, housed within a transformed riverside power station.

Museum of London (p161) Get a firm handle on the history of the city at this fantastic museum.

Wellcome Collection (p244) Brings the sciences, medicine, art and life together with an astonishing collection arranged A to Z.

Best Large Museums & Galleries

National Gallery (p97) Treasury of European artwork from the 13th to 20th centuries.

Tate Britain (p100) The best of British: Turner, Constable, Reynolds, Gainsborough.

Churchill War Rooms (p103) The nerve centre of Britain's war effort during WWII.

Museum of London Docklands (p229) The story of the river and the trade that made London prosper.

Natural History Museum (p192) A cathedral to the natural world.

Wallace Collection (p117) An aristocrat's collection in a stunning mansion.

Best Small Museums

Geffrye Museum (p208) A fascinating journey through British households from the 16th century on.

Old Operating Theatre Museum & Herb Garret (p177) Delve into the pre-anaesthetic, pre-antiseptic days of modern medicine.

London Canal Museum (p243) Once essential, then neglected, now quaint, London's canals live on.

Shakespeare's Globe (p172) As much as you'll ever need to know about the Bard and his work.

Brunel Museum (p183) Discover how the world's first-ever underwater tunnel was built.

Best Small Galleries

Guildhall Art Gallery (p160) Eclectic City of London collection above a Roman amphitheatre.

Courtauld Gallery (p115) Probably the best collection of Impressionist art in London.

Kenwood House (p248) Stunning collection of 19th-century greats in equally stunning settings.

Whitechapel Gallery (p231) A groundbreaking gallery that continues to challenge with excellent exhibitions.

Saatchi Gallery (p198) Cutting-edge, ultra-cool shrine to contemporary art.

Photographers' Gallery (p111) Photography as an art form in a splendid new building.

Best House Museums

Charles Dickens Museum (p106) The Victorian novelist's only London house.

Dennis Severs' House (p210) A quirky time capsule that sends you back to an 18th-century Huguenot house.

Carlyle's House (p199) Victorian essayist's home and workspace frozen in time.

Apsley House (p194) No 1 London: home to the Iron Duke of Wellington for 35 years.

Leighton House (p265) Byzantine gem on the cusp of Holland Park.

Danson House (p291) Exquisite 18th-century mansion, delightful park and a top-notch cafe in South London.

Best Specialist Museums

Fan Museum (p283) Tortoiseshell, ivory, bone, feather and paper – fans in all their glory.

Ragged School Museum (p227) Reading, writing and 'rithmatic in an original Victorian setting.

Hunterian Museum (p116) Vast collection of innards, both grisly and educational.

Wimbledon Lawn Tennis Museum (p312) Everything tennis, with ace views of centre court.

Museum of Brands, Packaging & Advertising (p265) Brimful with nostalgia from television, radio and print.

Science Museum (p193) Spellbinding A to Z of gizmos, devices, contraptions and thingamabobs.

National Maritime Museum (p283) Model ships, a real ship simulator and a pirate gallery. Arrr!

Borough Market (p180)

Eating

Once the laughing stock of the cooking world, London has got its culinary act together in the last 20 years and is now an undisputed dining destination. There are plenty of fine, Michelin-starred restaurants, but it is the sheer diversity on offer that is extraordinary: from Afghan to Vietnamese, London is a virtual A to Z of world cuisine.

NEED TO KNOW

Opening Hours

As a rule, most restaurants serve lunch between noon and 2.30pm and dinner between 6pm and 11pm. Brasserie-type establishments and chains tend to have continuous service from noon to 11pm.

Price Ranges

These symbols indicate the average cost per main course at the restaurant in question.

£	less than £10
££	£10 to £20
£££	more than £20

Reservations

➡ Make reservations for weekends if you're keen on a particular place or if you're in a group of more than four people.

➡ Top-end restaurants often run multiple sittings, with allocated time slots (generally two hours); pick a late slot if you don't want to be rushed.

Tipping

Most restaurants automatically tack a 'discretionary' service charge (usually 12.5%) onto the bill; this should be clearly advertised. If you feel the service wasn't adequate, you can tip separately (or not tip at all). If there is no service charge on your bill and you would like to tip, 10% is about right.

Haute Cuisine, Low Prices

➡ Top-end restaurants offer set lunch menus that are great value. À la carte prices are also sometimes cheaper for lunch than dinner.

➡ Many West End restaurants offer good-value pre- or post-theatre menus.

➡ The reliable internet booking service Top Table (www.toptable.co.uk) offers substantial discounts (up to 50% off the food bill) at selected restaurants.

BYO

➡ BYO is common among budget establishments; some charge corkage (£1 to £1.50 per bottle of wine).

➡ See Wine Pages (www.wine-pages.com) for a useful directory of BYO restaurants.

Fresh berry cupcakes

Specialities

ENGLISH FOOD

England might have given the world beans on toast, mushy peas and chip butties (French fries between two slices of buttered and untoasted white bread), but that's hardly the whole story. When well prepared – be it a Sunday lunch of roast beef and Yorkshire pudding (light batter baked until fluffy, eaten with gravy) or a cornet of lightly battered fish and chips sprinkled with salt and malt vinegar – English food can have its moments. And nothing beats a fry-up (or full English breakfast) with bacon, sausages, beans, eggs and mushrooms the morning after a big night out.

Modern British food has become a cuisine in its own right, by championing traditional (and sometimes underrated) ingredients such as root vegetables, smoked fish, shellfish, game, sausages and black pudding (a kind of sausage stuffed with oatmeal, spices and blood). Dishes can be anything from game served with a traditional vegetable such as Jerusalem artichoke, to seared scallops with orange-scented black pudding, or roast pork with chorizo on rosemary mash.

SEAFOOD

Many who travel to England comment on the fact that for an island, Brits seem to make surprisingly little of their seafood, with the exception of the ubiquitous fish and chips. Modern British restaurants have started catching up, though, and many now offer local specialities such as Dover sole, Cornish oysters, Scottish scallops, smoked Norfolk eel, Atlantic herring and

Top: Oxo Tower Restaurant (p180)

Bottom: Traditional British roast dinner

ROSS WOODHALL / GETTY IMAGES ©

Eating by Neighbourhood

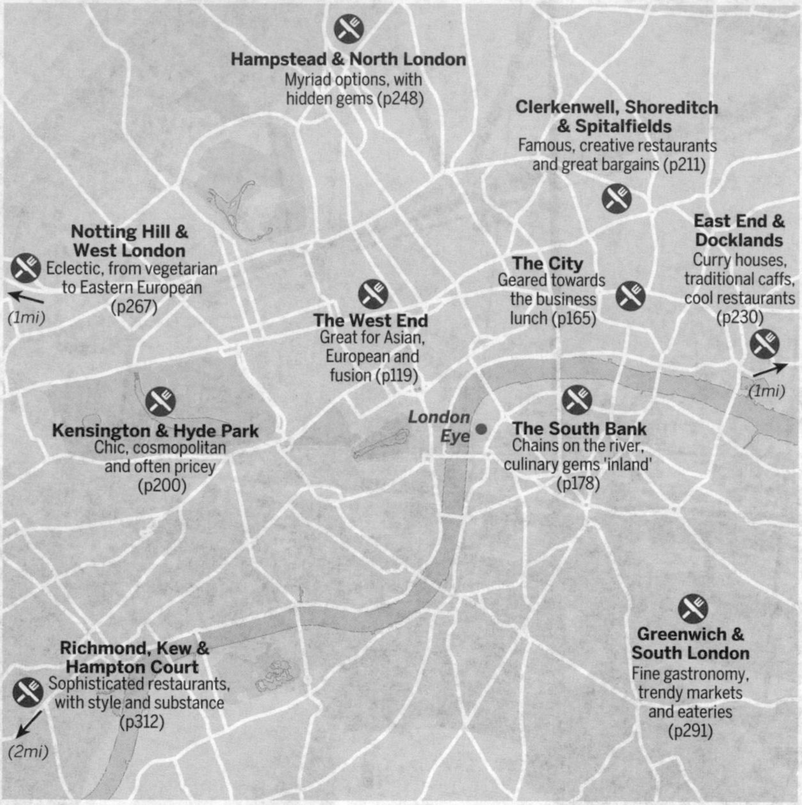

mackerel. There are some excellent restaurants specialising in seafood, as well as fish-and-chips counters trading in battered cod, haddock and plaice.

WORLD FOOD

One of the joys of eating out in London is the profusion of choice. For historical reasons Indian cuisine is widely available (curry has been labelled a national dish), but Asian cuisines in general are very popular: you'll find dozens of Chinese, Thai, Japanese and Korean restaurants, as well as elaborate fusion establishments blending flavours from different parts of Asia.

Food from continental Europe – French, Italian, Spanish, Greek, Scandinavian – is another favourite, with many classy modern European establishments. Restaurants serving these cuisines tend to congregate where their home community is based: Eastern European in Shepherd's Bush, Turkish in Dalston etc.

DESSERTS

England does a mean dessert, and establishments serving British cuisine revel in these indulgent treats. Among our favourites are bread-and-butter pudding, sticky toffee pudding (a steamed pudding that contains dates and is topped with a divine caramel sauce), the alarmingly named spotted dick (a steamed suet pudding with currants and raisins), Eton mess (meringue, cream and strawberries mixed into a gooey, heavenly mess), and seasonal musts such as Christmas pudding (a steamed pudding with candied fruit and brandy) and fruity crumbles (rhubarb, apple etc).

Gastropubs

While not so long ago the pub was where you went for a drink, with maybe a packet of potato crisps to soak up the alcohol, the birth of the gastropub in the 1990s means that today just about every establishment serves full meals. But the quality varies widely, from defrosted-on-the-premises to Michelin-star worthy.

Breakfast

The Brits were always big on breakfast – they even invented one, the full English breakfast. It's something of a protein overload but there's nothing quite like it to mop up the excesses of the night before. A typical plate will include bacon, sausages, baked beans in tomato sauce, eggs (fried or scrambled), mushrooms, tomatoes and toast (maybe with Marmite). You'll find countless grotty cafes – nicknamed 'greasy spoons' – serving these monster plates. They're also a must in gastropubs.

Making a comeback on the breakfast table is porridge, boiled oats in water or milk, served hot, sweet or savoury. Top-end restaurants serving breakfast, such as the **Wolseley** (Map p440; ☎020-7499 6996; www.thewolseley.com; 160 Piccadilly, W1; cream/afternoon tea £9.75/22.50 (£32.50 with Champagne); ⊙3.30-6.30pm Sun-Fri, to 5.30pm Sat; ⊖Green Park), have played a big part in glamming up what was essentially poor folk's food. We love it with banana and honey, fruit compote or even plain with some chocolate powder.

Vegetarians & Vegans

London has been one of the best places for vegetarians to dine out since the 1970s, initially due mostly to its many Indian restaurants, which, for religious reasons, always cater for people who don't eat meat. A number of dedicated vegetarian restaurants have since cropped up, offering imaginative, filling and truly delicious meals. Most nonvegetarian places generally offer a couple of dishes for those who don't eat meat; vegans, however, will find it harder outside Indian or dedicated restaurants.

Celebrity Chefs

London's food renaissance was partly led by a group of telegenic chefs who built food empires around their names and their TV programs. Gordon Ramsay is the most (in) famous of the lot but his London venues are still standard-bearers for top-quality cuisine. Other big names include Jamie Oliver, whose restaurant Fifteen trains disadvantaged young people, and Heston Blumenthal, whose mad-professor-like experiments with food (molecular gastronomy, as he describes it) have earned him rave reviews.

PIE & MASH

From the middle of the 19th century until just after WWII, the staple lunch for many Londoners was a spiced-eel pie (eels were once plentiful in the Thames) served with mashed potatoes and liquor (a parsley sauce). Pies have been replaced by sandwiches nowadays, although they remain popular in the East End. A popular modern-day filling is beef and mashed potato (curried meat is also good), with eel served smoked or jellied as a side dish.

Cafes

While tea remains a quintessential English beverage, Londoners long ago adopted espresso and steamy latte as the hot drinks de rigueur. There are Starbucks and other coffee chains seemingly at every corner, but plenty of smaller cafes fly the independent flag too. Many sell pastries for breakfast and sandwiches for lunch and are great for a quick bite on the go or a break from pounding the pavement.

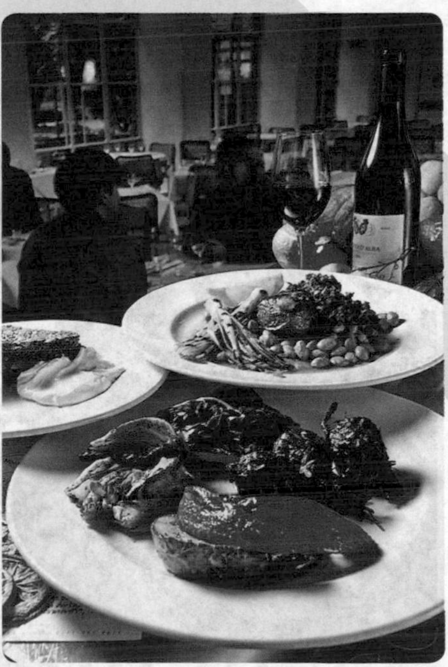
TONY ROBINS / GETTY IMAGES ©

River Café (p271)

Food Markets

The boom in London's eating scene has extended to its markets, which come in three broad categories: food stalls that are part of a broader market and appeal to visitors keen to soak up the atmosphere (eg Spitalfields (p220), Borough (p180) or Camden (p245)); farmers markets, which sell pricey local and/or organic products (check out www.lfm.org.uk for a selection of the best, such as Broadway (p237) and Marylebone (p124)); and the many colourful food markets, where the oranges and lemons come from who knows where and the barrow boys and girls speak with perfect Cockney accents (Brixton (p298), Ridley Rd (p248), Berwick St (p124)).

For something a little different you could also pay a visit to London's wholesale markets, where retailers and restaurants get their supplies, such as **Billingsgate Fish Market** (Map p453; Trafalgar Way, E14; ⌚4-9.30am Tue-Sat; DLR Blackwall, Canary Wharf) for seafood and Smithfield Market (p162) for meat.

Food Trends

Just like with fashion and music, Londoners like to keep up with the Joneses when it comes to eating. Here are some of the current food obsessions in the capital:

Burgers Everyone loves a burger, but none more so than Londoners who have several chains devoted to meat-and-bun combos.

Food trucks Whether part of a market or just occupying a chain-free corner, food trucks have become a feature of the capital's eating scene. Office workers in particular love them.

Brunch The new Sunday lunch? It's not quite at US proportions yet but an increasing number of restaurants offer brunch on weekends and Londoners lap it up.

Peruvian food Having come out of left field, ceviche and Peruvian food is now all the rage.

Supper Clubs

If you think restaurants are so last season, you'll love supper clubs. Half-restaurant, half-dinner-party, they combine the quality of the former with the informality of the latter. They're run by average Joes with a penchant for cooking and generally cater

Spitalfields Market (p220)

for 10 to 20 people. Meals are set three- or four-course menus (£20 to £40), and the clientele couldn't be more eclectic.

The difficulty is that these underground restaurants are rarely permanent (the cook might move or decide that his/her day job is quite enough) and so recommending a supper club can be tricky. The following will help:

Ms Marmite (www.supperclubfangroup.ning.com) An excellent directory of London supper clubs set up by a supper club host.

London Foodie (www.thelondonfoodie.co.uk) This food blog features regular supper club reviews.

Facebook Hosts post details of forthcoming events on their pages.

Chain Gang

While the usual bleak offerings of US-based chain restaurants are to be found all over the capital, London also boasts some excellent chains of inventive and interesting restaurants, which locals patronise frequently. They're all good value and made even cheaper by regular voucher offers: check out www.vouchercodes.co.uk and www.myvouchercodes.co.uk for the latest offers.

The following are some of our favourites; check their websites for a full list of outlets.

Benugo (www.benugo.com) Deli chain serving good but expensive sandwiches.

Busaba Eathai (www.busaba.com) Divine Thai food, served without fuss among beautiful, modern Asian decor.

Byron (www.byronhamburgers.com) Simple but excellent burgers accompanied by the bare essentials (lettuce, tomato, red onion).

Jamie's Italian (www.jamieoliver.com) Good (but not gastronomic) Italian food in modern settings.

Le Pain Quotidien (www.lepainquotidien.com) A simple, French-style chain of cafes that serves salads, baguettes and cakes.

Masala Zone (www.masalazone.com) An excellent Indian chain that specialises in *thalis* (a meal made of several small dishes).

Pret a Manger (www.pret.com) Affordable sandwich chain, with a good selection of sandwiches and chunky soups.

Top: Afternoon tea at the Orangery (p200)

Middle: Dinner by Heston Blumenthal restaurant (p201)

Bottom: Gerrard St, Chinatown (p110)

Look Mum No Hands cafe-bar (p211)

Real Greek (www.therealgreek.com) Beautifully presented meze and souvlaki, perfect for sharing between friends.

Tas (www.tasrestaurant.com) An established chain of good Turkish restaurants with a roll-call of stews, grills and meze.

Wagamama (www.wagamama.com) Fusion noodle place with rapid turnover, ideal for a quick meal.

Wahaca (www.wahaca.com) Working the Mexican street-food angle in fresh, colourful settings.

Food Festivals

Because just eating never seems enough, London has whole festivals dedicated to food. They generally have tastings galore and are always good for inspiration.

Feast London (www.wefeast.co.uk; ⌚Mar) A tip-top event bringing together top chefs and the best street-food stalls in the capital for four days, with music and entertainment on the side.

London Chocolate Festival (www.festivalchocolate.co.uk; ⌚Mar/Apr) Everyone's favourite, for obvious reasons, generally in time for Easter.

London Coffee Festival (www.londoncoffeefestival.com; ⌚Apr) If you know your robusta from your arabica, this is the place for you. Host of the UK Barista Championship.

Taste of London (www.tastefestivals.com/london; Regent's Park, NW1; ⌚Jun) Celebrating its 10th edition in 2013, this festival turns Regent's Park into a haze of Michelin stars, with top chefs rivalling for your palate's attention.

BBC Good Food Show (www.bbcgoodfoodshowlondon.com; London Olympia, Hammersmith Rd, W14; ⌚Nov) Masterclasses, recipes, tastings – this is very hands-on and very delicious.

Lonely Planet's Top Choices

Providores & Tapa Room (p128) Fusion food at its best.

Gordon Ramsay (p202) Three Michelin stars and a celebrity chef.

Newman Street Tavern (p120) Lovely new West End brasserie with superb wine list.

Towpath (p231) A simple but sumptuous cafe and restaurant by Regent's Canal.

Viajante (p233) Super fusion cuisine in an Edwardian dining room in the East End.

Best by Budget

£

Dirty Burger (p249) Succulent, messy, no-nonsense burger shack. Great milkshakes too.

Busaba Eathai (p120) Mini-chain with communal seating serving reliable Thai.

Ceviche (p121) Colourful Soho arrival serves Peruvian street food.

Princi (p122) Excellent value pizzas and Italian pastries.

Kerbisher & Malt (p270) Classic fish and chips.

Lardo (p232) Excellent pizzas with seasonal Mediterranean offerings.

££

10 Greek St (p124) Top-quality British produce with a Med accent.

Duke's Brew & Que (p254) Barbequed ribs smoked on the premises.

Gauthier Soho (p124) Probably the best set-lunch deal currently in London.

Angels & Gypsies (p293) Authentic Spanish products and cuisines, with a Mexican wild card thrown in.

Buenos Aires Café (p292) Fine Argentinian meat, pasta and wood-fired pizzas.

£££

Medlar (p201) Faultless culinary panache along the King's Rd.

Greenhouse (p129) Amongst the most imaginative menus in Mayfair.

Le Boudin Blanc (p130) For ace French food, this place has no rival.

Chez Bruce (p293) Timeless elegance and gastronomy on the edge of Wandsworth Common.

Best by Cuisine

Modern European

Ledbury (p269) Still causing a gastronomic stir in Notting Hill.

Andrew Edmunds (p123) Perennial favourite with a handwritten menu.

Abbeville Kitchen (p294) Pocket-sized restaurant in Clapham, with large dishes to share.

Green Man & French Horn (p126) Relaxed bistro serving Modern European with a British twist.

Giaconda Dining Room (p127) European staples with a decent wine list in Soho.

Indian

Tayyabs (p231) Long-standing Punjabi favourite in the East End.

Potli (p269) Steeping Hammersmith in authentic Indian aromas.

Dishoom (p125) Bombay caff food as it really is served and eaten.

La Porte des Indes (p129) Exotic French-influenced dishes from Pondicherry.

Tamarind (p130) Award-winning curry house serving Moghul classics and new creations.

Chinese

Yauatcha (p123) Glamorous dim sum and great for people watching.

Bar Shu (p123) Very authentic Szechuan that will blow your mind.

Baozi Inn (p122) Excellent steamed dumplings amid communist pop décor.

Vegetarian

Gate (p270) Meat-free but full of flavours.

Mildreds (p121) Soho stalwart with vegan dishes too.

Manna (p253) Outstanding vegan and vegetarian address in rarefied Primrose Hill.

Orchard (p119) Excellent-value lunch spot with above-average soups.

Sagar (p120) South Indian vegetarian food as light as it is tasty.

Italian

Trullo (p252) Northern Italy should be proud: this is Italian gastronomy at its finest.

Bar Trattoria Semplice (p129) Lovely little trattoria with excellent-value set lunch.

Polpo (p121) *Ciccheti* 'tapas' as the Venetians make them – in casual surrounds.

Lardo (p232) Hackney pizzeria that celebrates the seasonal and the art of the aromatic Italian lardo.

British

St John (p212) The restaurant that inspired the revival of British cuisine.

Launceston Place (p200) Magnificent food, presentation and service.

Rules (p127) London's oldest restaurant serves classic game dishes.

Market (p251) Simple, elegant modern British fare in brash Camden.

Best for Eating Like a Local

Mangal Ocakbasi (p253) Succulent Turkish kebabs cooked on a charcoal BBQ. And it's BYO.

F. Cooke (p232) Grab a pie with a serving of mash: this is how it was done in the East End before gentrification.

Stag (p252) Order Sunday roast, buy the Sunday papers and your afternoon is gone.

Rosie's Deli Café (p293) Grab lunch or a slice of cake after a morning pottering about Brixton Village.

Yauatcha (p123) See and be seen eating dim sum at this swanky Soho address.

Best Gastropubs

Anchor & Hope (p180) Flying the gastropub flag on the South Bank for the best part of a decade.

White Swan Pub & Dining Room (p166) Wonderful City venue open during the week only.

Bear (p293) Comfort food given a gourmet makeover in Camberwell.

Gun (p234) So good it is more of a restaurant than a pub.

Best for Views

Duck & Waffle (p165) Hearty British dishes from the top of Heron Tower round the clock.

Skylon (p179) River views and fine dining on the South Bank.

Min Jiang (p201) Breathtaking panoramas over Kensington Gardens.

Drawing Room Cafe (p202) Delectable views across the Fulham Palace lawn.

Best Afternoon Teas

Dean Street Townhouse (p335) Old-world cosy is on the menu at teatime here.

Orangery (p200) Sit with tea and cake in the shadow of Kensington Palace.

Wolseley (p51) Viennese-style brasserie hosts an opulent afternoon tea.

Portrait (p125) The tea and accompaniments are second to the views over Trafalgar Sq.

Delaunay (p126) New brasserie offering afternoon tea with Champagne.

Best Food Markets

Borough Market (p180) Foodscapes, free tastings and glorious takeaways.

Portobello Road Market (p267) A global atlas of street food.

Maltby Street Market (p179) Perfect for lazing an afternoon away at quirky food stalls.

Broadway Market (p237) The East End foodies' weekly event.

Marylebone Farmers Market (p124) A posh offering reflecting the neighbourhood make-up.

Best Gourmet Shops

Fortnum & Mason (p138) Elegant Piccadilly shop with no end of fine comestibles.

Algerian Coffee Stores (p140) Beans and more beans for sale at this historic Soho shop.

Vintage House (p141) Some 1400 types of Scotch whisky available.

Lina Stores (p141) Yummy-looking prewar delicatessen selling Italian goods.

Best Celebrity-Chef Restaurants

Dinner by Heston Blumenthal (p201) Molecular gastronomy at its very best.

Gordon Ramsay (p202) A must for discerning diners.

Nobu (p129) Nobuyuki Matsuhisa's Japanese eatery still reigns supreme.

Dabbous (p120) The latest from favourite chef Ollie Dabbous.

HIX (p123) Seasonal British food is Mark Hix's speciality.

Best Ice Cream

Chin Chin Labs (p251) Liquid nitrogen ice cream: weird and utterly wonderful.

Gelupo (p122) All natural ingredients, right in central London.

Gelato Mio (p267) Thick, low-fat Italian gelati to cool the summers in Notting Hill.

Gelateria Danieli (p313) Handmade ice cream with seasonal flavours such as Christmas pudding.

Golden Heart (p219)

Drinking & Nightlife

There's little Londoners like to do more than party. From Hogarth's 18th-century Gin Lane prints to Mayor Boris Johnson's decision to ban all alcohol on public transport in 2008, the capital's history has been shot through with the population's desire to imbibe as much alcohol as possible and party into the night.

NEED TO KNOW

Opening Hours

Unless otherwise stated all pubs and bars reviewed in this book open at 11am and close at 11pm from Monday to Saturday and close at 10.30pm on Sunday. Thanks to a change in the law in 2005, some pubs and bars now stay open longer, although most close around 2am or 3am at the latest.

Clubs generally open at 10pm and close between 4am and 7am.

Costs

Midweek prices are reasonable, and there are plenty of student nights or other budget nights. If you want to go to a big club on a Saturday night (*the* night for clubbing), expect to pay at least £20.

Tickets & Guest Lists

Queuing in the cold at 11pm can be frustrating; get there early and/or book tickets for bigger events if you can't bear being left in line.

Some clubs will require you to sign up on their guest list beforehand; check ahead.

Dress Code

London's clubs are generally relaxed. Posh clubs in areas such as Kensington will want a glam look, so dress to impress (no jeans or trainers); the further east, the more laid-back and edgy the fashion.

What's On?

Check the listings in *Time Out* or the *Evening Standard* – part of the charm of London's nightlife is that it's always changing, so keep your eyes peeled.

Ale on tap

The Pub

The pub (public house) is at the heart of London's existence and is one of the capital's great social levellers. Virtually every Londoner has a 'local' and looking for your own is one of the highlights of any visit to the capital.

Pubs in central London are mostly drinking dens, busy from 5pm onwards with the postwork crowd during the week and revellers at weekends. But in more residential areas in East, South, West and North London, pubs come into their own at weekends, when long lunches turn into afternoons and groups of friends settle in for the night. Many also run popular quizzes on week nights.

You'll be able to order almost anything you like in a pub, from beer to wine, soft drinks, spirit and mixer (whisky and cola etc) and sometimes hot drinks too. Some specialise in beer and real ales, offering drinks from local microbreweries, fruit beers, organic ciders and other rarer beverages; others have invested in a good wine list (often the case in gastropubs serving good food).

In winter a number of pubs offer mulled wine; in summer the must-have drink is Pimms and lemonade (if it's properly done it should have fresh mint leaves, citrus, strawberries and cucumber).

Beer

The raison d'être of a pub is first and foremost to serve beer – be it lager, ale or stout in a glass or a bottle. On draught (drawn from the cask) it is served by the pint (570mL) or half-pint (285mL) and, more occasionally, third-of-a-pint for real ale tasting.

Pubs generally serve a good selection of lager (what most people would refer to as 'beer': highly carbonated and drunk cool or cold) and a smaller selection of real ales or 'bitter' (slightly gassy or still, drunk at room temperature, with strong flavours). In London the best-known British brands are Tennent's and Carling, although you'll find everything from Fosters to San Miguel.

Top: Rooftop burgers, Queen of Hoxton (p218)

Bottom: Loungelover (p217)

LOUNGE LOVER ©

Drinking by Neighbourhood

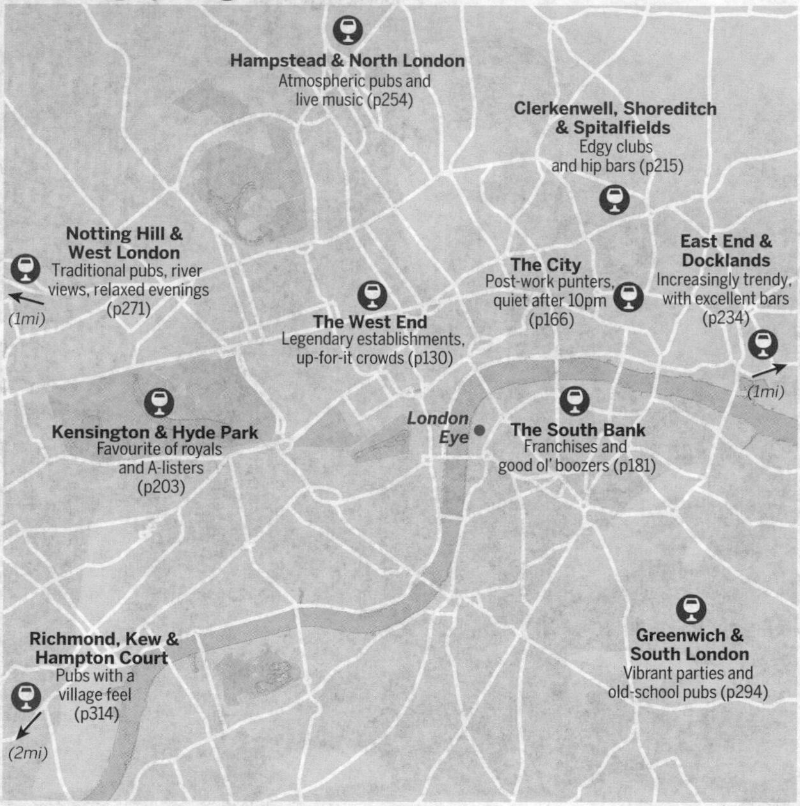

Among the multitude of ales on offer in London pubs, London Pride, Courage Best, Burton Ale, Adnams, Theakston (in particular Old Peculier) and Old Speckled Hen are among the best.

Stout, the best known of which is Irish Guinness, is a slightly sweet, dark beer with a distinct flavour that comes from malt that is roasted before fermentation.

Once considered something of an old man's drink, real ale is enjoying a renaissance among young Londoners keen to sample flavours from the country's brewing tradition. Staff at bars serving good selections of real ales are often hugely knowledgeable, just like a sommelier in a restaurant with a good cellar, so ask them for recommendations if you're not sure what to order.

Clubbing

When it comes to clubbing, London's where it's at. You'll probably know what you want to experience – it might be big clubs such as Fabric or the Ministry of Sound, or sweaty shoebox clubs with the latest DJ talent – but there's plenty to tempt you to branch out from your usual tastes and try something new. From thumping techno, rock, nu rave, Latin, ska, pop, country, grime, minimal electro or hip hop, there's something going on every night.

Thursdays are loved by those who want to have their fun before the office workers mob the streets on Friday. Saturdays are the busiest and best if you're a serious clubber, and Sundays often see surprisingly good events throughout London.

There are clubs across town, though it has to be said that good clubs are moving further out of the centre by the year, so be prepared to take a hike on a night bus. East

London is the top area for cutting-edge clubs, especially Shoreditch; Dalston is popular for makeshift clubs in restaurant basements and former shops – so great for night-fun hunters, while Camden still favours the indie crowd.

Bars

In the small party space left by pubs and clubs, bars have managed to grow into a popular alternative for a London night out. Generally staying open later than pubs but closing earlier than clubs, they tempt those keen to skip bedtime at 11pm but not keen enough to go clubbing. They generally have DJs (sometimes a small dance floor too), door charges after 11pm (sometimes), more modern decor than pubs and fancier (and pricier) drinks. Cocktail bars are undergoing a renaissance, so you'll find lots of signature bars and excellent concoctions.

Cabaret Craze

After years of low-profile parties with high-glitter gowns, the cabaret scene burst into the mainstream in the noughties, showering London with nipple tassels, top hats, sexy lingerie and some of the best parties in town. Subsequently, the 'alternative' cabaret scene became overwhelmingly mainstream, and some club-night organisers raised prices to ward off those who wouldn't buck up and dress up. So prepare to pay an average of £25 for some (but not all) of the city's best cabaret nights, and make sure you look like a million dollars.

Expect anything from male burlesque contests to girls on roller skates hosting tea parties on a good burlesque night. Venues and events to look out for:

Volupté (p167) The queen of London cabaret and burlesque, with shows, parties, dinners and much more.

Bethnal Green Working Men's Club (p235) A true working men's club that hosts great and quirky cabaret nights.

Last Tuesday Society (www.thelasttuesday society.org) Runs fantastic masked balls on various occasions (St Valentine's Day, summer party, Halloween etc).

Cabaret performance

Lonely Planet's Top Choices

Jerusalem Tavern (p215) Tiny but delightful, with original beers from a Norfolk brewery.

Book Club (p216) A modern temple to good times, with great off-beat events.

Draft House (p296) A standout watering hole, popular with high-flyers and families alike.

Princess Louise (p134) Stunner of a Victorian pub with snugs and a riot of etched glass.

Corsica Studios (p295) A fantastic electronic music venue for true electro buffs.

Best Pubs

Princess Louise (p134) Beautifully decorated and perfect for settling in all evening.

Lamb & Flag (p133) Just about everyone's favourite so expect a scrum.

French House (p131) Not exactly a pub, but still Soho's best boozer, with a steady supply of local eccentrics.

Edinboro Castle (p255) With a huge beer garden in a refined Primrose Hill atmosphere, this is the perfect place for long summer evenings.

Golden Heart (p219) A great local pub where you can mix with the hipsters and the drinkers.

Best Cocktail Bars

Worship St Whistling Shop (p217) Molecular cocktails at a Victorian-style drinking den.

LAB Soho (p131) Bespoke cocktails at a long-standing Soho favourite.

Happiness Forgets (p217) Mixed drinks and mischief in Shoreditch.

Opium (p131) There's no smoke but fire in this brothel-like Chinatown boozer.

London Cocktail Club (p131) Most inventive concoctions in town in a basement bar.

Best Clubs

Fabric (p215) The ultimate club and the top stop on the London scene for international electronic music fans.

Dalston Superstore (p257) An upstairs-downstairs industrial club that sends clubbers into a frenzy with its basement parties.

Passing Clouds (p257) One for lovers of all-nighters with a world-music twist and renowned jam sessions.

Corsica Studios (p295) A not-for-profit, underground club that hosts some of the best electronic music nights.

XOYO (p218) Excellent and varied gigs and club nights, plus art exhibitions.

Best for Views

Galvin at Windows (p135) Stunning views (and cocktails) west across Hyde Park.

Madison (p167) Look into the heart of St Paul's and beyond from One New Change.

Paramount (p134) Atop Centre Point it's as high as you'll get in central London.

Skylon (p181) Glorious views of the north bank of the Thames from this South Bank beauty.

Best Bars

Drink, Shop & Do (p254) Breakfast, cultural events, afternoon tea, DJs and dancing – a bar to cater to all needs.

Bar Pepito (p254) A delightful, pocket-sized Andalucian bar dedicated to lovers of *jerez* (sherry).

BrewDog (p217) Bespoke beer is brought to London from a Scottish brewery.

Lost Society (p296) Lavish decadence is paired with burlesque performances and killer cocktails in this beautiful venue.

Gordon's Wine Bar (p134) A classic and long-standing London institution in darkened vaults.

Best Beer Gardens

Spaniard's Inn (p256) A 16th-century beauty with a dreamy garden to booze in.

Garden Gate (p256) Perfect for Sunday roasts and homemade BBQ burgers amid the lush greenery.

Edinboro Castle (p255) One of London's biggest beer gardens, where you can enjoy a hog roast on a sunny Sunday.

Britannia (p236) Summer barbecues in the sunny garden near Victoria Park

Gay & Lesbian

The city of Oscar Wilde, Quentin Crisp and Elton John does not disappoint its queer visitors, proffering a fantastic mix of brash, camp, loud and edgy parties, bars, clubs and events year-round. A world gay capital on par with New York and San Francisco, London's gay and lesbian communities have turned good times into an art form.

Gay Rights

Protection from discrimination is enshrined in law. Civil partnerships have allowed gay couples the same rights as straight ones since 2005, and in 2013 both houses of parliament passed a bill to allow bona fide gay marriage in England and Wales. That's not to say homophobia does not exist.

Drinking

The queer drinking scene in London is wonderfully varied. Whether you fancy a quiet pint in a traditional boozer that just happens to be gay, or want a place to wet your whistle before going out dancing, you'll be spoiled for choice.

Clubbing

London has some exciting and varied gay clubs, including **Pulse** (Map p444; www.pulseclub.co.uk; 1 Invicta Plaza, Blackfriars Bridge, SE1; ⊖Blackfriars or Southwark) and **Scala** (Map p456; ☎020-7833 2022; www.scala-london.co.uk; 275 Pentonville Rd, N1; ⊙10pm-5am Fri & Sat; underground rail King's Cross). But it's a moveable feast, as the clubbing scene is about club nights rather than venues, meaning a club that was fantastic and full of hunks one night might well be straight and full of goths the next.

Lesbian

The lesbian scene in London is far less in your face than the flamboyant gay one, though there are a couple of excellent lesbian bars in Soho, notably Candy Bar (p132). Certain areas of the capital are well known to have thriving lesbian communities and are worth a visit in their own right – particularly Hackney and Stoke Newington in northeast London. Check out the **Ginger Beer** (www.gingerbeer.co.uk) website for the full low-down.

Gay & Lesbian Events

The **Lesbian & Gay Film Festival** (www.bfi.org.uk/llgff) is a renowned film festival in March, now well into its third decade, hosted by the British Film Institute, with screenings, premieres, awards and talks.

In June, **London Gay Pride** (www.londongaypride.co.uk), one of the world's largest gay parades, complete with floats, stalls and performers, parties across town. The smaller, more intimate **Soho Pride** (www.sohopride.net) in mid-August has less activism but just as much fun.

Gay & Lesbian by Neighbourhood

➡ **Shoreditch** Fashionable Shoreditch is home to London's more alternative gay scene, often very well mixed in with local straights. Here you'll find arty parties and the hipper bars and clubs. (p216)

➡ **Soho** The long-established gay village of Soho in the West End, once so central to any gay experience here, has somewhat lost its pre-eminence to the edgy East End. (p131)

➡ **Vauxhall** The erstwhile bleak concrete jungle that was Vauxhall is now home to London's mainstream muscle boys. (p296)

NEED TO KNOW

Free Listings

London has a lively gay online press charting the ever-changing scene. Check out any of these publications online; their listings are the most up-to-date available.

Boyz (www.boyz.co.uk)

QX (www.qxmagazine.com)

AXM (www.axm-mag.com)

Magazines

Available at most newsagents in Soho.

➡ *Gay Times* (www.gaytimes.co.uk)

➡ *Diva* (www.divamag.co.uk)

➡ *Attitude* (www.attitude.co.uk)

➡ *Out in the City* (www.outmag.co.uk)

Blogs & Other Resources

Ginger Beer (www.gingerbeer.co.uk)

Me Me Me (www.me-me-me.tv)

Jake (www.jaketm.com)

With Richard (www.withrichard.com)

Time Out London LGBT (www.timeout.com/london/lgbt)

Help

➡ Always report homophobic crimes to the **police** (☎999).

➡ **London Lesbian & Gay Switchboard** (☎0300 330 0630; www.llgs.org.uk; ⏰ 10am-11pm) offers free advice, counselling and other help to anyone who needs a sympathetic ear.

Best Gay Bars

George & Dragon (p216) The epicentre of the gay Hackney scene for over a decade has just got better.

Edge (p132) London's largest gay bar, with something for everybody on four floors.

Two Brewers (p296) Bar, cabaret venue, club – it's many things to South London's gay community.

Black Cap (p255) Camden's longstanding gay bar, complete with roof top and packed events listing.

Duke of Wellington (p136) Friendly Soho boozer with a nonscene gay clientele.

Nelsons Head (p235) Small laid-back pub in Hackney with a friendly mixed crowd.

Best Gay Clubs

Area (p297) A stalwart for great shows and good times.

RVT (p297) Cabaret, drag shows, open stage, crazy bingo, and never a dull night.

Fire (p296) Vauxhall's leading light, with regular all-nighters and big names.

Heaven (p135) The point on the map for most gay weekend clubbers.

XXL (p63) Saturday night has never felt so manly.

Best Gay Club Nights

XXL at Pulse (p63) Weekend all-nighter by Blackfriars Bridge bursting with testosterone.

Popcorn at Heaven (p135) A fun and cheap night out, Popcorn is an Ibiza-style club night with a great selection of music on offer and refreshingly priced drinks offers. Monday.

Orange at Fire (p296) Regularly hosting some of the best gay club nights in London, Fire is best known for its infamous Sunday all-nighter, Orange. Pure hedonism.

G-A-Y at Heaven (p135) Love it or hate it, G-A-Y is a centre of gravity for the gay scene and seemingly where half of Soho is headed on a Saturday night. Bring your tight T-shirt.

Horsemeat at Eagle (p136) One of the biggest Sunday nights in town, especially popular at bank holidays, when you can expect to queue for at least an hour.

Popstarz at Scala (p63) Unashamed mix of pop and indie on Friday. Normally at Scala but the venue does change every now and then so worth checking the website.

London's West End (p135)

Entertainment

London's cultural pizazz is the most exciting and varied in the English-speaking world. Whatever soothes your soul, flicks your switch or floats your boat, from inventive theatre to dazzling musicals, comedy venues, dance, opera or live music, London has an energetic and innovative answer. In fact, you could spend several lifetimes in London and only skim the surface of the astonishing entertainment choices on offer.

NEED TO KNOW

Tickets

➡ Book well ahead for live performances.

➡ Cut-price standby tickets are sometimes available at several theatrical venues, including the National Theatre, the Barbican, the Royal Court Theatre and the Southbank Centre.

➡ Student standby tickets are sometimes available one hour or so before performances start. Other theatres may have cheap tickets or cheap student/youth tickets on certain days. Shakespeare's Globe offers 700 standing tickets (£5) for each performance. A handful of 10p standing tickets are available for each performance at the Jerwood Theatre Downstairs at the Royal Court Theatre.

➡ Midweek matinees at such venues as the Royal Opera House are usually much cheaper than evening performances; restricted-view seats can be cheap.

➡ At gigs, be wary of touts outside the venue on the night.

➡ Most mainstream and art-house cinemas offer discounts all day Monday (or Tuesday) and most weekday afternoon screenings. Annual membership of the Prince Charles (p136) nets you tickets as low as £4 (membership £10).

➡ On the day of performance, you can buy discounted tickets, sometimes up to 50% off, for West End productions from **Tkts Leicester Sq** (www.tkts.co.uk/leicester-square).

➡ If you can, buy direct from the venue. Events sell out rapidly and agencies tend to have tickets after the venue has sold out. **Ticketmaster** (www.ticketmaster.co.uk) and **Stargreen** (www.stargreen.com) have 24-hour telephone and online booking services.

Useful Magazines

The free weekly *Time Out* (www.timeout.com/london) has current theatre and entertainment listings.

Useful Websites

London Theatre (www.londontheatre.co.uk) Comprehensive theatre overview.

London Dance (www.londondance.com) Handy listing for dance events.

Shakespeare's Globe (p172)

Theatre

A night out at the theatre is as much a must-do London experience as a trip on the top deck of a double-decker bus or a whirl on the London Eye. London's Theatreland in the dazzling West End – from Aldwych in the east, past Shaftesbury Ave to Regent St in the west – has a concentration of English-speaking theatres rivalled only by New York's Broadway. London drama is also the world's most diverse, from Shakespeare's classics performed with old-school precision to controversially edgy productions, raise-the-roof musicals and some of the world's longest-running shows.

With over 40 theatres in the West End alone, more theatre tickets sell here than anywhere else on Earth, many for musicals and shows that have run for decades. But the West End is just the brightest facet of London's sparkling theatre world, where productions range from highbrow theatrical institutions to tiny fringe stages stuffed away above pub.

London's cosmopolitan DNA and multicultural roots nourish a great flowering of theatrical creativity: even Hollywood stars have abandoned their pampered lives for a season treading the boards in London. The celebrated National Theatre is the regular home of innovative new shows, creative directing and much-loved classics that often migrate to other West End theatres. The Barbican hosts foreign drama companies to massive acclaim. Traditional stagecraft is also on offer, particularly at the lovely old-school Shakespeare's Globe, where the focus is on Shakespearian traditionalism.

Top: Up the Creek comedy club (p297)
Bottom: O2 Academy Brixton (p297)

MICK HUTSON / REDFERNS / GETTY IMAGES ©

Theatrical edges are busy with peripheral, subsidised shows from experimental groups, where conceptual ideas find expression to sometimes bewildered audiences. In summer, open-air theatres avail themselves of balmy days (punctuated with sudden showers) to entertain crowds in parks, most famously in Regent's Park.

Classical Music

With four world-class symphony orchestras, two opera companies, various smaller ensembles, quality venues (and reasonable ticket prices) and the whole musical gamut from traditional crowd-pleasers to innovative compositions, London will satisfy even the fussiest classical-music buff. The Southbank Centre, Barbican and Royal Albert Hall all maintain an alluring program of performances, further gilding London's outstanding reputation as a cosmopolitan venue for classical music. The Proms is the festival calendar's biggest event.

Opera

With one of the world's leading opera companies at the Royal Opera House in Covent Garden, and inspiring direction from Edward Gardner at the English National Opera (the Coliseum), as well as other operatic venues and events, London will keep opera-lovers busy. It's not just the classics that get attention, as operatic productions grapple with a host of modern-day themes. Holland Park is the summer opera venue. Opera is expensive to produce and, consequently, tickets can be pricey.

Dance

London is home to five major dance companies and a host of small and experimental ones. The **Royal Ballet** (Map p430; www.roh.org.uk), the best classical-ballet company in the land, is based at the Royal Opera House (p136) in Covent Garden. The English National Ballet (p386) often performs at the London Coliseum (p138), especially at Christmas and in summer. Sadler's Wells (p219) is excellent for experimental dance.

The annual contemporary dance event in London is **Dance Umbrella** (www.danceumbrella.co.uk) from early October.

Live Rock, Pop, Jazz & Blues

Musically diverse and defiantly different, London is a natural point of gravitation for musical innovation and talent. Local bands and singers attest to world-beating musical flair: soulful Adele, Lily Allen, the late Amy Winehouse, folk rockers Mumford & Sons, South London rapper Tinie Tempah, Jessie J and Coldplay all wave the London flag. Monster acts worldwide see London as an essential stop on their trans-global stomps, so be prepared for tickets selling out faster than you can find your credit card. Tickets for (London band) The Rolling Stones' July 2013 concert in Hyde Park vanished in three minutes after going on sale. If jazz or blues is your thing, London has some truly excellent clubs and pubs where you can catch classics and contemporary tunes. The city's major jazz event is the **London Jazz Festival** (www.londonjazzfestival.org.uk) in November.

Comedy

They look a miserable bunch on the underground, and the winter drizzle, summer wash-outs and double-dip blues don't help, but Londoners have a solid sense of humour. And despite – or because of – the recession, comedy is still flourishing in the capital. You can pitch up at any one of the 20-plus major comedy clubs or countless other venues (including pubs) to roll in the aisles or snort your drink down the wrong way.

Most comedy acts have both eyes on the critical Edinburgh Festival season: April to July, new acts are being tried out on audiences; August is the cruellest month for comedy in London, because everyone's shifted up north for the festival itself; winter has comedians doing the stuff that went down well at the festival. Check **Edinburgh Comedy Awards** (www.comedyawards.co.uk) for the new bright stars.

Some of the world's most famous modern comedians hail from, or made their names in, London, including Ben Elton, Alexei Sayle, Victoria Wood, Julian Clary, Rowan Atkinson, Reeves & Mortimer, Eddie Izzard, Jo Brand, Sacha Baron Cohen (aka Ali G, Borat and Brüno), Ricky Gervais, Matt Lucas, David Walliams, Russell Brand, Josie Long, Paul Sinha, Tiernan Douieb, Russell Howard and Alan Carr.

London's leading comedy event is the **Greenwich Comedy Festival** (www.greenwichcomedyfestival.co.uk) and Union Chapel (p258) is a wonderful venue that hosts a monthly **Live at the Chapel** (http://liveat-

CHRISTER FREDRIKSSON / GETTY IMAGES ©

oyal Albert Hall (p203)

thechapel.co.uk), with big names and live music.

Film

Londoners have a passion for film, from the vast BFI IMAX (p185) in Waterloo, to the huge screen at the Empire Leicester Sq, small 40-seater cinemas, a host of art-house and independent cinemas and local pub film clubs that cram in beer-quaffing film buffs. For back-catalogue classics, turn to the BFI (p185) at South Bank, but keep an eye out for film festivals at independent cinemas, which bring in reels of foreign movies.

For further eclectic tastes, shorts, foreign cinema as well as mainstream movies, London's independent cinemas (p273) allow you to put your feet up, sip a glass of wine and feel right at home. You can catch monthly seasons and premieres, as well as actors and directors chatting about their work and answering questions. Cinemas such as the Prince Charles (p136) have cheap tickets, run mini-festivals and screen popular singalong classics. Many major premieres are held in Leicester Sq, the priciest part of London for cinema tickets. Look out also for the Summer Screen at Somerset House (p115), Movies on the Lawn at Fulham Palace (p199) and other open-air cinema screenings.

Entertainment by Neighbourhood

- **The West End** Packed with theatres, musicals, opera, classical-music concert halls, small live-music venues and cinemas. (p135)
- **The City** Barbican Arts Centre and church concerts. (p167)
- **The South Bank** Major theatre concentration: the National Theatre, Royal Festival Hall, Shakespeare's Globe and the Old Vic. (p183)
- **Kensington & Hyde Park** Royal Albert Hall and the Royal Court Theatre. (p203)
- **Clerkenwell, Shoreditch & Spitalfields** Sadler's Wells, live-music bars and comedy. (p219)
- **The East End & Docklands** Cabaret and theatre. (p236)
- **Hampstead & North London** The works: indie rock, open-air live music, comedy, theatre, jazz and opera. (p257)
- **Notting Hill & West London** Tremendous independent cinemas, live music, summer opera. (p273)
- **Greenwich & South London** Live music, dance, theatre and cinema. (p297)
- **Richmond, Kew & Hampton Court** Open-air concerts in Kew Gardens and live-music pubs. (p306)

Lonely Planet's Top Choices

12 Bar Club (p135) Indie-rock venue with solo acts/bands performing nightly.

Southbank Centre (p184) Concerts, recitals, musicals – you name it – the Southbank Centre has it.

Royal Opera House (p136) London's preeminent stage for opera and classical dance.

Barbican (p167) A powerhouse of culture, from music and dance to theatre and film.

Vortex Jazz Club (p258) All things jazz in up-and-coming Dalston.

Best Mainstream Theatre

Shakespeare's Globe (p184) Shakespeare, as it would have been 400 years ago.

National Theatre (p183) Contemporary theatre at its best.

Royal Court Theatre (p203) Forward-thinking, promoting new voices.

Old Vic (p185) Kevin Spacey's theatre, a heavy-hitter in London's drama scene.

Best Fringe Theatre

Arcola Theatre (p259) East London cutting-edge powerhouse of the visual arts.

Bush Theatre (p273) Provocative and contemporary slant.

Donmar Warehouse (p138) London's most popular theatre, with strong, thought-provoking productions.

Young Vic (p185) Dramatic directions from new writers, actors and directors.

Best for Classical Music

Wigmore Hall (p137) London's most important chamber-music venue.

Royal Albert Hall (p203) The Grand Dame of classical-music venues.

Royal Festival Hall (p184) Classical music from around the world in this stunning 1950s auditorium.

Cadogan Hall (p204) Chelsea Home of the Royal Philharmonic Orchestra.

Best Church Venues for Music

St Martin-in-the-Fields (p112) Excellent classical music concerts, many by candlelight.

St Paul's Cathedral (p154) Evensong at its most evocative.

Westminster Abbey (p86) Organ concerts at the abbey are the city's finest.

Best Dance Performance Venues

London Coliseum (p138) Home to the English National Ballet.

Sadler's Wells (p219) Top-drawer international and UK dance.

Southbank Centre (p184) From break-dancing to Bolly-wood, and all in between.

Trinity Laban Conservatoire of Music & Dance (p298) A pioneering dance school hosting new and emerging talent.

Place (p137) The very birthplace of modern English dance.

Best Live Rock & Pop Venues

Barfly (p259) North London's seminal indie-rock venue, as grotty and brilliant as ever.

O2 Arena (p297) Temple of pop and rock.

Royal Albert Hall (p203) Imposing venue for big-name acts.

KOKO (p258) Fabulously glitzy venue, with original indie-rock programming.

Best for Live Jazz

606 Club (p203) Legendary Chelsea basement jazz outfit.

Ronnie Scott's (p137) Still the best jazz club in Britain.

Pizza Express Jazz Club (p137) Top-class jazz in the basement of a chain restaurant.

Vortex Jazz Club (p258) Tiny but packs a punch with superb programming.

Best Pubs for Live Music

Old Blue Last (p219) Hip Hoxton pub with top gigs and a rocking jukebox.

Blues Kitchen (p258) Blues on a plate, straight from America.

Best for Comedy

Comedy Store (p136) Hosts the most famous improvisation outfit in town.

Up the Creek (p297) Long-standing comedy favourite south of the river.

Amused Moose Soho (p137) Comedy routines without the heckling.

Soho Theatre (p137) Attracts local and foreign new comedy-writing talent.

Harrods department store (p204)

Shopping

From charity-shop finds to designer 'it bags', there are thousands of ways to spend your hard-earned cash in London. Many of the big-name shopping attractions, such as Harrods, Hamleys and Camden and Spitalfields Markets, have become must-sees in their own right. Chances are that with so many temptations, you'll give your wallet a full workout.

NEED TO KNOW

Opening Hours

- Shops generally open from 9am or 10am to 6pm or 7pm Monday to Saturday.
- The majority of shops in the West End (Oxford St, Soho and Covent Garden), Chelsea, Knightsbridge, Kensington, Greenwich, Hampstead and Islington also open on Sunday, typically from noon to 6pm but sometimes 10am to 4pm.
- Shops in the West End open late (to 9pm) on Thursday; those in Chelsea, Knightsbridge and Kensington open late on Wednesday.
- If there's a major market on a certain day – say, Columbia Road Flower Market on a Sunday morning – it's a good bet that neighbouring stores will also fling their doors open.

Taxes & Refunds

In certain circumstances visitors from non-EU countries are entitled to claim back the 20% value-added tax (VAT) they have paid on purchased goods. The rebate applies only to items purchased in stores displaying a 'tax free' sign (there are plenty of these along Bond St).

Selfridges department store (p144)

Markets

Perhaps the biggest draw for visitors is the capital's famed markets. A treasure trove of small designers, unique jewellery pieces, original framed photographs and posters, colourful vintage pieces and bric-a-brac, they are the antidote to impersonal, carbon-copy shopping centres.

The most popular markets are Camden, Spitalfields and Portobello Road, which are in full swing at the weekend. Although they're all more or less outdoors (Spitalfields is now covered, as are the Stables in Camden), they are always busy, rain or shine.

Designers

British designers are well established in the fashion world and a visit to Stella McCartney, Matthew Williamson, Burberry or Mulberry is an experience in its own right.

Vintage Fashion

The realm of vintage apparel has moved from being sought out by those looking for something off-beat and original, to an all-out mainstream shopping habit. So much so, that nearly every chain store has a 'vintage' corner or at least a rail, with sometimes astounding prices. Go to a few old, reliable places for the best offers.

Vintage designer pieces from Chanel, Dior, Miu Miu, Vivienne Westwood, you name it – and odd bits and pieces from the 1920s to the 1980s – are all busting the rails in shops that are often as extravagant as the clothes they stock.

Charity shops in areas such as Chelsea, Notting Hill and Kensington usually have cheap designer wear (usually, the richer the area, the better the secondhand shops).

Chain Stores

Many bemoan the fact that chains have taken over the main shopping centres, leaving independent shops struggling to balance the books. But since they're cheap, fashionable and always conveniently located, Londoners (and others) keep going back for more. As well as familiar overseas retailers, such as Gap, H&M, Urban Outfitters and Zara, you'll find a number of home-grown chains, including luxury womenswear brand Karen Millen (p143) and global giant Topshop (p140). For a full list of outlets, check the websites listed below.

Top: Liberty department store (p141)
Bottom: Carnaby St, Soho

Shopping by Neighbourhood

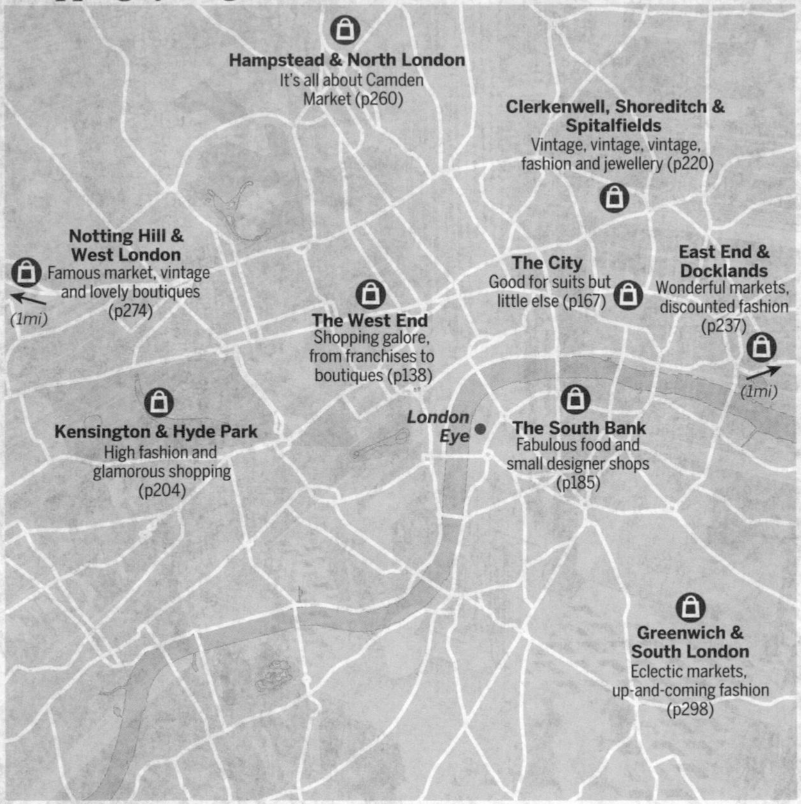

French Connection UK (Map p438; www.frenchconnection.com; 396 Oxford St, W1; ⌚10am-8pm Mon-Sat, noon-6pm Sun; ⊖Bond St) Good for party outfits, girly frills and cool men's clothing.

Jigsaw (Map p430; www.jigsaw-online.com; 21 Long Acre, WC2; ⌚10am-8pm Mon-Sat, noon-6pm Sun; ⊖Covent Garden) Classic yet slightly boho women's clothes, with an emphasis on tweeds and knits. A menswear section opened in 2012.

Marks & Spencer (Map p438; www.marksandspencer.co.uk; 458 Oxford St, W1; ⌚8am-10pm Mon-Sat, noon-6pm Sun; ⊖Bond St) After years of being synonymous with 'quality knickers', M&S continues to produce some fabulous fashion lines.

Oasis (Map p430; www.oasis-stores.com; 13 James St, WC2; ⌚10am-8pm Mon-Sat, 11am-7pm Sun; ⊖Covent Garden) Good catwalk copies that are sure to keep you on trend.

Reiss (Map p432; www.reiss.co.uk; 14-17 Market Pl, W1; ⌚10am-7pm Mon, Tue, Fri & Sat, to 8pm Wed & Thu, 11.30am-6pm Sun; ⊖Oxford Circus) A classic English label of understated fashion with a good dose of class.

Lonely Planet's Top Choices

London Silver Vaults (p167) The world's largest collection of silver, from cutlery to jewellery.

Harrods (p204) Garish, stylish, kitsch, yet perennially popular department store.

John Sandoe Books (p204) A treasure trove of literary gems, with excellent staff recommendations.

Sister Ray (p142) A top independent music shop, with an ever-changing collection of vinyls and CDs.

Darkroom (p139) Stylish, sleek and carefully chosen designer jewellery, accessories and handbags.

Best Fashion Shops

Folk (p139) Simple but striking Scandinavian style.

Dover Street Market (p145) An indoor market that's a shrine to fine fashion labels.

Selina Blow (p205) Bright, full-colour, period-inspired threads.

Start (p221) Denim fittings, directional designer labels and personal tailoring.

Best Markets

Spitalfields (p220) One of London's best for young fashion designers.

Portobello Road Market (p267) Classic Notting Hill sprawl, perfect for vintage everything.

Brixton Market (p298) It's bright, fun and keeps evolving and getting better all the time.

Camden Market (p245) Authentic antiques to tourist tat – and everything in between.

Greenwich Market (p291) Food, food, glorious food, with shopping to be had, too.

Best Vintage

Absolute Vintage (p220) Vintage shoes of all kinds.

Bang Bang Clothing Exchange (p139) On-trend vintage designer pieces.

Rellik (p275) Fashionista favourite retro store.

Beyond Retro (p237) London vintage empire with a rock 'n' roll heart.

Best Bookshops

Village Books (p298) A small independent bookshop with expert knowledge.

Daunt Books (p140) Guides, maps and tales from every corner of the world.

Slightly Foxed (p204) Well-stocked bibliophile's hunting ground in Gloucester Rd.

Books for Cooks (p275) As the name suggests, plus a cafe and cookery classes.

Best Music Shops

Rough Trade East (p220) Excellent choice of vinyl, CDs and in-store gigs.

Honest Jon's (p276) For reggae, jazz, funk, soul, dance and blues junkies.

Sounds of the Universe (p142) Soul, reggae, funk and dub CDs and vinyl and some original 45s.

Best Department Stores

Harvey Nichols (p204) Fashion, food, beauty and lifestyle over eight floors.

Selfridges (p144) Over 100 years of retail innovation.

Harrods (p204) Enormous, overwhelming and indulgent, with a world-famous food hall.

Fortnum & Mason (p138) A world of food in luxuriously historic surroundings.

Sports & Activities

Third place for Team GB in the Olympic Games medals table put a spring into London's step and the sporting event left the city with a sudden embarrassment of world-class sports facilities in the east of town. The rest of London boasts a well-developed infrastructure for participatory and spectator sports to get your heart racing and the endorphins flowing.

Health & Fitness

London parks and commons swarm with joggers, but when the skies open overhead they hit the treadmill. For a rather large organised run, check out the **London Marathon** (www.london-marathon.co.uk) in spring.

Fitness First (Map p464; ☎0844 571 3400; www.fitnessfirst.co.uk) Branches all over the city.

La Fitness (www.lafitness.co.uk) With 25 gyms in town.

Virgin Active (☎020-7717 9000; www.virginactive.co.uk) One of the largest chains in the UK; top end.

Football

Football is at the very heart of English culture, and there are a dozen league teams in London with usually around five or six in the Premier League. Attending a game should be one of the highlights of any visit to the city, but tickets for Premier League fixtures (August to mid-May) can be impossible to secure. Stadiums where you can watch matches (or, more realistically, take tours) include the city's landmark national stadium, **Wembley** (☎0844 980 8001; www.wembleystadium.com; tours adult/child £16/9); Arsenal Emirates Stadium (p246); **Chelsea** (Map p464; ☎0871 984 1955; www.chelseafc.com; Stamford Bridge, Fulham Rd, SW6; tours adult/child £18/12; museum 9.30am-5pm; Fulham Broadway); and **West Ham United** (www.whufc.com; Boleyn Ground, Green St, Upton Park, E13; Upton Park), who will be making the Olympic Stadium their new ground from 2016.

Athletics

London has a rich history in athletics and continues to produce world champions. Major international athletics events will be staged at the Olympic Stadium in the Queen Elizabeth Olympic Park (p228), the site of the Olympic Games in 2012. Other athletics meets are staged at the Crystal Palace National Sports Centre in Crystal Palace Park.

Cricket

On a long summer's day, you could do a lot worse than packing up a picnic and spending a day enjoying the thwack of leather on willow. The **English Cricket Board** (☎020-7432 1200; www.ecb.co.uk) has complete details of match schedules and tickets. Test matches are regularly played at Lord's (p244) and the Oval (p299).

Cycling

Apart from their ingenious practicality, Barclays Bikes (p405) are a sloth-busting inducement to pedal your way around London. The city is carpeted with dedicated cycle paths and the choice of cycle routes around London is breathtaking, from breezy canalside towpaths to criss-crossing parks and commons.

Horse Racing

If you fancy a flutter, several racecourses are within striking distance of London. The flat racing runs from April to September, while you can see the gee-gees jumping fences from October to April. Famous venues include

Ascot (☎0844 346 3000; www.ascot.co.uk; admission from £10; 🚉Ascot), **Epsom** (☎01372-726 311; www.epsomdowns.co.uk; admission from £10; 🚉Epsom Downs), **Royal Windsor Racecourse** (☎01753-498400; www.windsor-racecourse.co.uk; admission from £9; 🚉Windsor) and **Sandown Park** (☎01372-464348; www.sandown.co.uk; admission from £16; 🚉Esher).

Ice Skating

A combined ice rink and bowling venue, Queen's Ice & Bowl (p276) has skating year-round and disco nights on ice. In winter months, outside ice rinks sparkle at Somerset House (p115), the Natural History Museum (p192), the Tower of London (p148) and other venues.

Rugby Union

Between January and March, England competes against Scotland, Wales, Ireland, France and Italy in the Six Nations Championship. Three games take place at Twickenham Stadium (p315).

Swimming

With two 50m pools and a 25m diving pool, the London Aquatics Centre at the Queen Elizabeth Olympic Park (p228) will be a magnet for swimmers when it opens to the public in spring 2014. London also has some lovely 1930s art-deco lidos, while swimming pools and public baths can be found across town. For something different, head to Hampstead Heath for a dip in the ponds (p261) or to Porchester Spa (p276) where you can indulge in some post-exercise pampering.

THAMES BOAT RACES

The top event on the Thames rowing calendar is the **Oxford & Cambridge Boat Race** (www.theboatrace.org) – otherwise known as the Boat Race – usually held in late March or early April. Surging upstream between Putney and Mortlake, the race is watched by huge crowds along the river. The other major date on the rowing calendar is the **Head of the River Race** (www.horr.co.uk), held along the same course (but in the opposite direction and with international crews) in March.

NEED TO KNOW

Opening Hours

As a rule, most gyms open very early, usually from 6.30am, to ensure early risers get their workout on time. Equally, they are open until at least 9pm. Parks are generally open dawn to dusk.

Tickets

Finding tickets for Premier League matches during the August to mid-May football season in London is tricky, as seats are snapped up by season-ticket holders. Tickets for all other enclosed sporting events need to be booked well in advance. The free entertainment weekly *Time Out* (www.timeout.com/london) has the best information on fixtures, times, venues and ticket prices.

Tennis

Wimbledon (www.wimbledon.com) becomes the centre of the sporting universe for a fortnight in June/July when the world-famous tennis tournament takes place, but obtaining tickets (p312) is far from straightforward. To look out over centre court at other times of the year, head to the Wimbledon Lawn Tennis Museum (p312). Numerous parks around London have tennis courts, many free.

Explore London

LONDON'S TOP SIGHTS

Neighbourhoods at a Glance

❶ The West End p84

With many of London's premier postcodes, and superlative restaurants, hotels and shops, the West End should be your first port of call. Iconic sights (Trafalgar Sq, Piccadilly Circus), buildings and museums (Buckingham Palace, Westminster Abbey, British Museum), nightlife (Soho), shopping (Covent Garden, Regent St), parks (St James's Park) and theatres – they are all here.

❷ The City p146

London's historic core is a tale of two cities: all go during the week and deserted at weekends. But there are ancient streets and spectacular architecture, and history waits at every turn. St Paul's Cathedral and the Tower of London are hallmark sights.

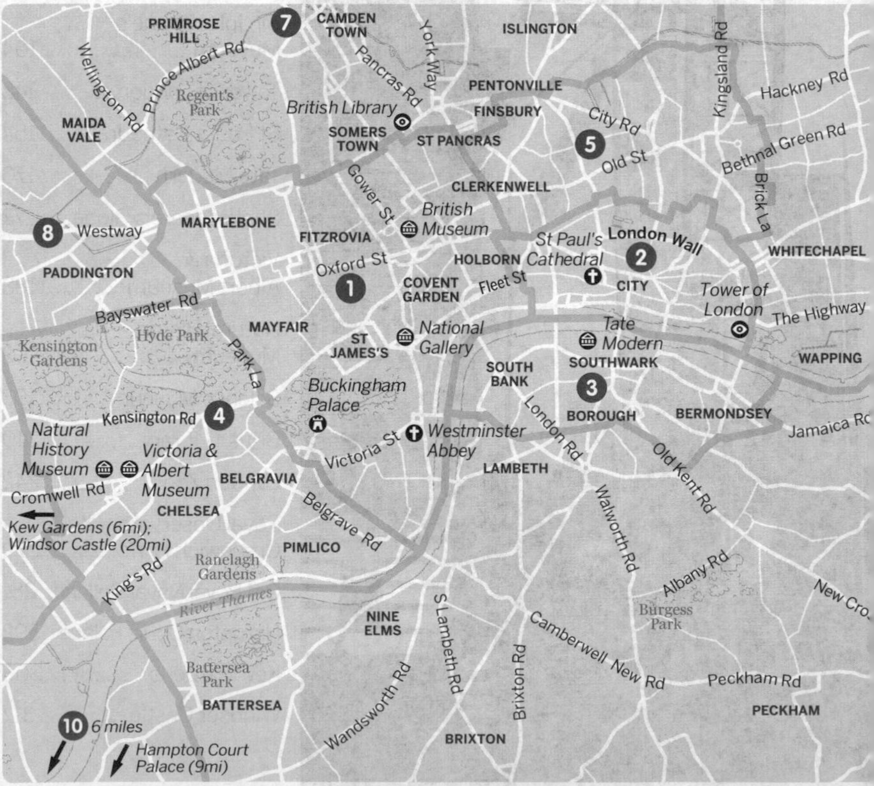

❸ The South Bank p168

The Tate Modern effect has done much to re-energise the South Bank, a must-visit area for art lovers, theatre-goers, culture hounds and iconic Thames views. There are also great food markets, first-rate pubs, dollops of history, striking examples of modern architecture and a sprinkling of fine gastropubs and restaurants.

❹ Kensington & Hyde Park p186

Splendidly well groomed, Kensington is one of London's most pleasant neighbourhoods. You'll find three fine museums here: the V&A, the Natural History Museum and the Science Museum, as well as excellent dining and shopping and graceful parklands.

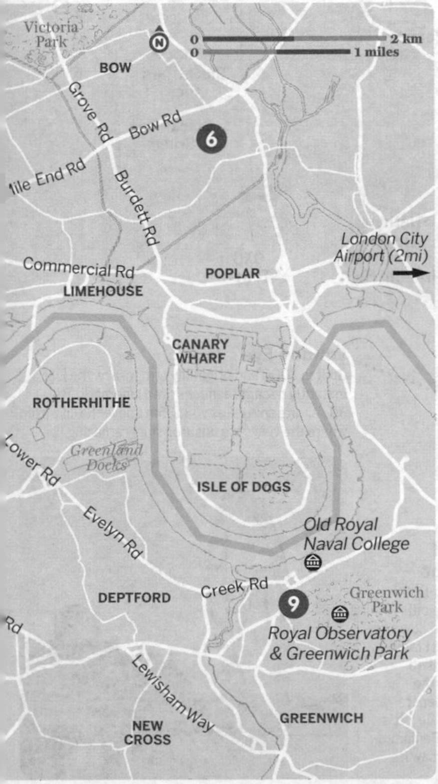

❺ Clerkenwell, Shoreditch & Spitalfields p206

This redeveloped area boasts top sights (Geffrye Museum, Georgian Spitalfields), excellent markets (Exmouth, Spitalfields, Brick Lane) and a creative frisson, but truly comes alive at night.

❻ The East End & Docklands p222

Anyone with an interest in multicultural London needs to visit the East End. There's top Asian cuisine, great museums, excellent pubs, canalside eating, and the slowly unfurling Queen Elizabeth Olympic Park.

❼ Hampstead & North London p238

Leafy Hampstead, Primrose Hill, Islington and Highgate are splendidly upmarket, but there's also diamond-in-the-rough Dalston, wild parkland, markets, Victorian cemeteries and a huge zoo. With top-notch nightlife, this area is a round-the-clock experience.

❽ Notting Hill & West London p263

Portobello Market, fabulous cinemas, swish parkland and mansions, canalside charms, superb pubs and clubs, varied shopping and ethnic eats all make Notting Hill and West London an eclectic must-see.

❾ Greenwich & South London p277

Regal Greenwich complements its village feel with some grand architecture, grassy parkland and riverside pubs. Brixton has the creative edge in its revitalised market, Clapham and Battersea are full of hidden gems, while Dulwich Village is all leafy charm.

❿ Richmond, Kew & Hampton Court p300

Wander by the Thames, get lost in beautiful Kew Gardens, explore haunted Tudor palaces, go deer-spotting in Richmond Park and down a pint by the riverside at sunset.

The River Thames

A FLOATING TOUR

London's history has always been determined by the Thames. The city was founded as a Roman port nearly 2000 years ago and over the centuries since then many of the capital's landmarks have lined the river's banks. A boat trip is a great way to experience the attractions.

There are piers dotted along both banks at regular intervals where you can hop on and hop off the regular services to visit places of interest. The best place to board is Westminster Pier, from where boats head downstream, taking you from the City of Westminster, the seat of government, to the original City of London, now the financial district and dominated by a growing band of skyscrapers. Across the river, the once shabby and neglected South Bank now bristles with as many top attractions as its northern counterpart, including the slender Shard.

In our illustration we've concentrated on the top highlights you'll enjoy from a

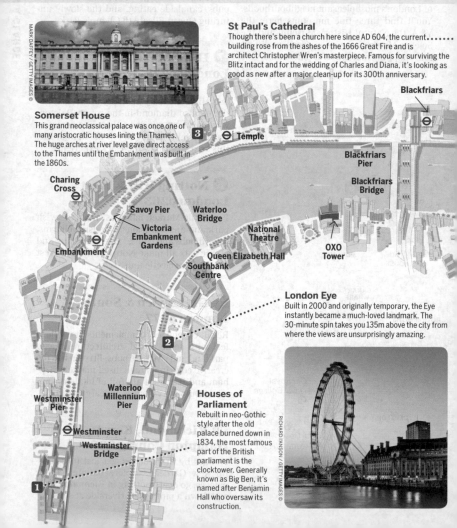

MARK DAFFEY / GETTY IMAGES ©

Somerset House
This grand neoclassical palace was once one of many aristocratic houses lining the Thames. The huge arches at river level gave direct access to the Thames until the Embankment was built in the 1860s.

St Paul's Cathedral
Though there's been a church here since AD 604, the current building rose from the ashes of the 1666 Great Fire and is architect Christopher Wren's masterpiece. Famous for surviving the Blitz intact and for the wedding of Charles and Diana, it's looking as good as new after a major clean-up for its 300th anniversary.

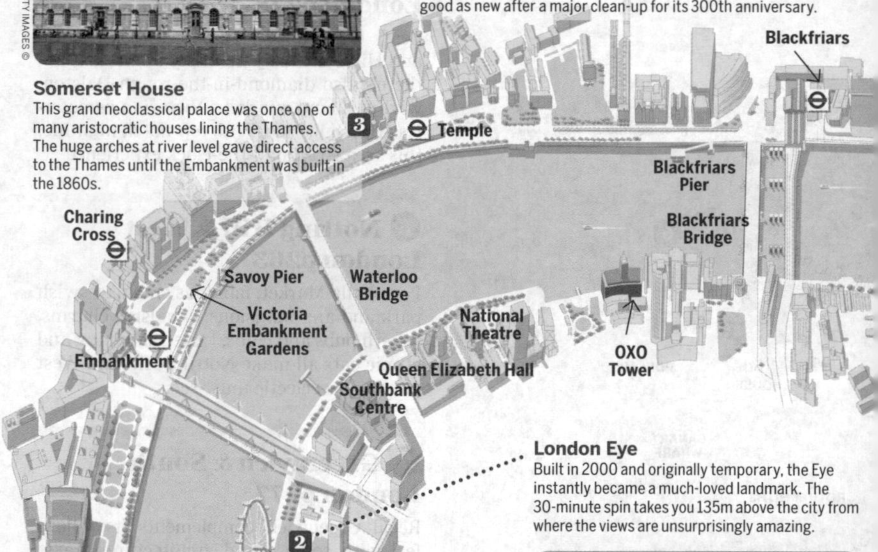

London Eye
Built in 2000 and originally temporary, the Eye instantly became a much-loved landmark. The 30-minute spin takes you 135m above the city from where the views are unsurprisingly amazing.

RICHARD I'ANSON / GETTY IMAGES ©

Houses of Parliament
Rebuilt in neo-Gothic style after the old palace burned down in 1834, the most famous part of the British parliament is the clocktower. Generally known as Big Ben, it's named after Benjamin Hall who oversaw its construction.

waterborne vessel. These are, from west to east, the **Houses of Parliament** 1, the **London Eye** 2, **Somerset House** 3, **St Paul's Cathedral** 4, **Tate Modern** 5, **Shakespeare's Globe** 6, the **Tower of London** 7 and **Tower Bridge** 8.

Apart from covering this central section of the river, boats can also be taken upstream as far as Kew Gardens and Hampton Court Palace, and downstream to Greenwich and the Thames Barrier.

BOAT HOPPING

Thames Clippers hop-on/hop-off services are aimed at commuters but are equally useful for visitors, operating every 15 minutes on a loop from piers at Embankment, Waterloo, Blackfriars, Bankside, London Bridge and the Tower. Other services also go from Westminster. Oyster cardholders get a discount off the boat ticket price.

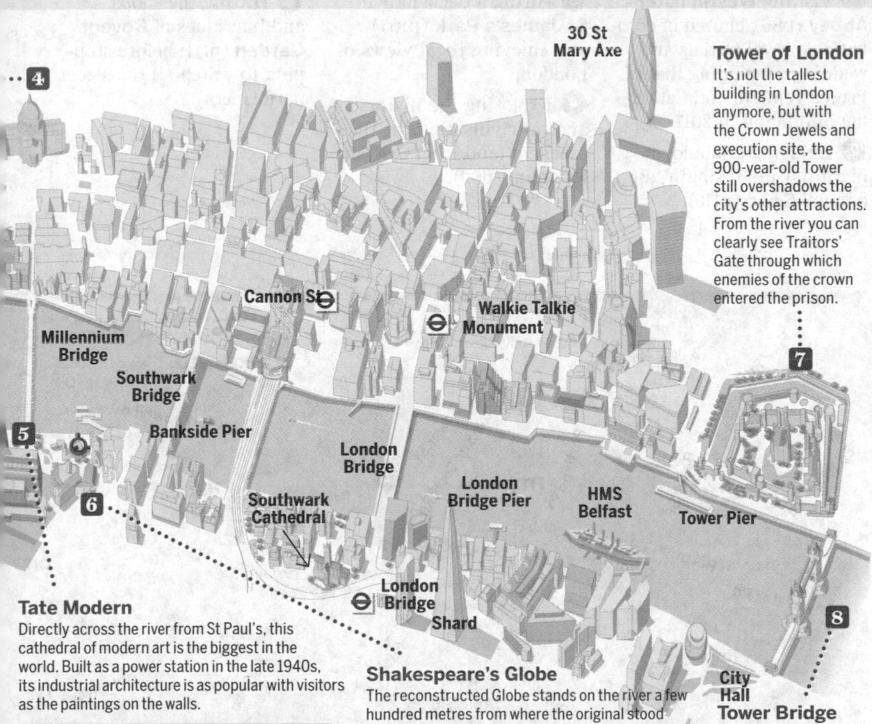

Tower of London
It's not the tallest building in London anymore, but with the Crown Jewels and execution site, the 900-year-old Tower still overshadows the city's other attractions. From the river you can clearly see Traitors' Gate through which enemies of the crown entered the prison.

Tate Modern
Directly across the river from St Paul's, this cathedral of modern art is the biggest in the world. Built as a power station in the late 1940s, its industrial architecture is as popular with visitors as the paintings on the walls.

DOUG MCKINLAY / GETTY IMAGES ©

Shakespeare's Globe
The reconstructed Globe stands on the river a few hundred metres from where the original stood (and burnt down in 1613 during a performance). The life's work of American actor Sam Wanamaker, the theatre runs a hugely popular season from April to October each year.

DOUG MCKINLAY / GETTY IMAGES ©

Tower Bridge
It might look as old as its namesake neighbour but one of the world's most iconic bridges was only completed in 1894. Not to be confused with London Bridge upstream, this one's famous raising bascules allowed tall ships to dock at the old wharves to the west and are still lifted up to 1000 times a year.

The West End

WESTMINSTER | BLOOMSBURY | FITZROVIA | ST JAMES'S | SOHO | CHINATOWN | COVENT GARDEN | LEICESTER SQUARE | WHITEHALL | HOLBORN | THE STRAND | MARYLEBONE | MAYFAIR

Neighbourhood Top Five

❶ Visiting **Westminster Abbey** (p86), church of coronations, royal burials and weddings, including that of Prince William and Catherine Middleton in 2011.

❷ Enjoying a fabulous night out in all singin', all dancin' **Soho** (p110).

❸ Hiring a deckchair in **St James's Park** (p107) and enjoying regal views of London.

❹ Exploring the history of ancient civilisations at the excellent (and free) **British Museum** (p89).

❺ Hitting the shops and boutiques of **Covent Garden** (p111) before stopping to watch all the street performers.

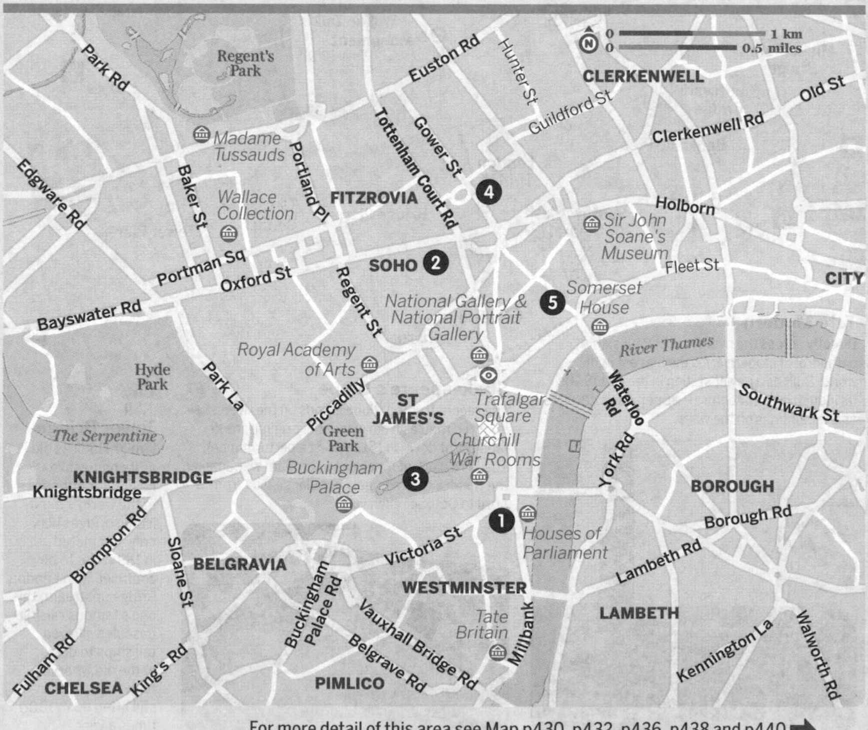

For more detail of this area see Map p430, p432, p436, p438 and p440

Explore: The West End

It may be a compact area, but the West End packs in a lot when it comes to sights. You'll need to allow half a day for each of the big museums (such as the British Museum or the National Gallery) and at least a couple of hours for places like Westminster Abbey and Buckingham Palace.

One of the delights of the West End is its energy and there is no better way to enjoy it than by walking around and taking it all in. Atmospheric places for a breather include Covent Garden, Trafalgar Sq and St James's Park.

Westminster and Whitehall are deserted in the evenings, with little in the way of bars and restaurants. The same goes for St James's. Instead head to vibrant Soho for fantastic bars and restaurants, or the streets surrounding Covent Garden.

Local Life

➡ **Eating out** Soho is unrivalled when it comes to eating out. Andrew Edmunds (p123) and Mildreds (p121) never seem to go out of fashion, while new, hip places such as Polpo (p121) and 10 Greek St (p124) open all the time.

➡ **Late-night openings** Be it for catching the latest exhibition or simply enjoying the permanent collections without the weekend crowds, many Londoners make the best of late-night openings at the National Gallery (p97), the National Portrait Gallery (p101) and the British Museum (p89).

➡ **Shopping** Love it or loathe it, most Londoners will hit Oxford St at some stage to shop; it's smack bang in the centre of town and has every franchise under the sun as well as good department stores such as Selfridges (p144) and John Lewis (p144).

Getting There & Away

➡ **Underground** Every tube line goes through the West End, so wherever you're staying in London, you'll have no difficulty getting there. The tube is also good for getting from one end of the West End to the other (Russell Sq to Green Park or Baker St to Embankment).

➡ **Walking** The West End is relatively compact so it'll be cheaper and generally more enjoyable to walk from one place to another rather than take public transport.

➡ **Barclays Bikes** There are docking stations everywhere within the West End and cycling is your best bet for short journeys.

Lonely Planet's Top Tip

London – the West End especially – can be expensive but there are plenty of tricks to make your pennies last. Many of the top museums are free, so give them priority. The West End is compact, so walk or take the bus (cheaper than the tube).

Best Places to Eat

- Brasserie Zédel (p123)
- Newman Street Tavern (p120)
- Dishoom (p125)
- Dabbous (p120)
- Bar Shu (p123)
- Bar Trattoria Semplice (p129)

For reviews, see p119 ➡

Best Places to Drink

- Lamb & Flag (p133)
- Opium (p131)
- London Cocktail Club (p131)
- Holborn Whippet (p134)
- Gordon's Wine Bar (p134)
- Queen's Larder (p130)

For reviews, see p130 ➡

Best Free Sights

- British Museum (p89)
- National Gallery (p97)
- National Portrait Gallery (p101)
- Houses of Parliament (p95)
- Wallace Collection (p117)
- Sir John Soane's Museum (p104)

For reviews, see p89 ➡

TOP SIGHT
WESTMINSTER ABBEY

FEARGUS COONEY / GETTY IMAGES ©

Westminster Abbey is such an important commemoration site that it's difficult to overstress its symbolic value or imagine its equivalent anywhere else in the world. With the exception of Edward V (murdered) and Edward VIII (abdicated), every English sovereign has been crowned here since William the Conqueror in 1066, and most of the monarchs from Henry III (died 1272) to George II (died 1760) – a total of 17 – are buried here.

There is an extraordinary amount to see at the Abbey. The interior is chock-a-block with small disused chapels, elaborate tombs of monarchs, and monuments to various luminaries down through the ages. Be warned: it can get intolerably busy.

A Regal History

Though a mixture of architectural styles, the Abbey is considered the finest example of Early English Gothic (1190–1300). The original church was built in the 11th century by King (later St) Edward the Confessor, who is buried in the chapel behind the sanctuary and main altar. Henry III (r 1216–72) began work on the new building but didn't complete it; the French Gothic nave was finished by Richard II in 1388. Henry VII's huge and magnificent Lady Chapel was added in 1519.

The Abbey was initially a monastery for Benedictine monks, and many of the building's features attest to this collegial past (the octagonal Chapter House, the Quire and four cloisters). In 1536, Henry VIII separated the Church of England from the Roman Catholic Church and

DON'T MISS...

- Coronation Chair
- Henry VII's Lady Chapel
- Cosmati marble pavement
- College Garden
- Chapter House
- Poets' Corner

PRACTICALITIES

- Map p440
- 020-7222 5152
- www.westminster-abbey.org
- 20 Dean's Yard, SW1
- adult/child £18/8, verger tours £3
- 9.30am-4.30pm Mon, Tue, Thu & Fri, to 7pm Wed, to 2.30pm Sat
- Westminster

dissolved the monastery. The king became head of the Church of England and the Abbey acquired its 'royal peculiar' status, meaning it is administered directly by the Crown and exempt from any ecclesiastical jurisdiction.

North Transept, Sanctuary & Quire

Individual visitors enter the Abbey by the Great North Door. The North Transept is often referred to as Statesmen's Aisle: politicians and eminent public figures are commemorated by large marble statues and imposing marble plaques.

At the heart of the Abbey is the Sanctuary (or sacrarium), a kind of stage for coronations, royal weddings and funerals. George Gilbert Scott designed the ornate **high altar** in 1873. In front of the altar is the **Cosmati marble pavement** dating back to 1268. It has intricate designs of small pieces of marble inlaid into plain marble, which predicts the end of the world in AD 19,693!

The Quire, a sublime structure of gold, blue and red Victorian Gothic by Edward Blore, dates back to the mid-19th century. It sits where the original choir for the monks' worship would have been but bears no resemblance to the original. Nowadays, the Quire is still used for singing but its regular occupants are the Westminster Choir – 22 boys and 12 'lay vicars' (men) who sing the daily services.

Chapels & Chair

The Sanctuary is surrounded by chapels. **Henry VII's Lady Chapel**, in the easternmost part of the Abbey, is the most spectacular with its fan vaulting on the ceiling, colourful banners of the Order of the Bath and dramatic oak stalls. Behind the chapel's altar is the elaborate sarcophagus of Henry VII and his queen, Elizabeth of York.

Beyond the chapel's altar is the **Royal Air Force Chapel**, with a stained-glass window commemorating the force's finest hour, the Battle of Britain, and 1500 RAF pilots who died. A stone plaque on the floor marks the spot where Oliver Cromwell's body lay for two years until the Restoration, when it was disinterred, hanged and beheaded. The bodies believed to be those of the two child princes allegedly murdered in the Tower of London in 1483 were buried here almost two centuries later.

There are two small chapels either side of Lady Chapel with the tombs of famous monarchs: on the left (north) is where **Elizabeth I** and her half-sister **Mary I** (aka Bloody Mary) rest. On the right (south) is the tomb of **Mary Queen of Scots**, beheaded on the orders of her cousin Elizabeth.

REFRESHMENTS

You can get drinks and snacks at the Coffee Club in the Cloister. For a proper sit-down meal, head for the new **Cellarium** (☎020-7222 0516; www.cellariumcafe.com; mains £9.50-14.50; ⏲9am-6pm Mon-Fri, to 4.30pm Sat), part of the original 14th-century Benedictine monastery with stunning views of the Abbey's architectural details.

On 29 April 2011, Prince William married his fiancée Catherine Middleton at Westminster Abbey. The couple had chosen the Abbey for the relatively intimate setting of the Sanctuary. Unusually, the couple decided to decorate the Abbey with trees; less controversial was the bride's decision to opt for a gown by a British designer, Sarah Burton (of Alexander McQueen). And in a tradition started by the future Queen Mother in 1923, Kate left her bridal bouquet on the Tomb of the Unknown Warrior.

The vestibule of the Lady Chapel is the usual place for the rather ordinary-looking Coronation Chair, upon which every monarch since the early 14th century has been crowned.

Shrine of St Edward the Confessor

The most sacred spot in the Abbey lies behind the high altar; access is generally restricted to protect the 13th-century flooring. St Edward was the founder of the Abbey and the original building was consecrated a few weeks before his death. His tomb was slightly altered after the original was destroyed during the Reformation but still contains Edward's remains – the only complete saint's body in Britain.

Outer Buildings & Gardens

The oldest part of the cloister is the East Cloister (or East Walk), dating to the 13th century. Off the cloister are three museums. The octagonal **Chapter House** has one of Europe's best-preserved medieval tile floors and retains traces of religious murals on the walls. It was used as a meeting place by the House of Commons in the second half of the 14th century. To the right of the entrance to Chapel House is what is claimed to be the oldest door in Britain – it's been there 950 years.

The adjacent **Pyx Chamber** is one of the few remaining relics of the original Abbey and holds the Abbey's treasures and liturgical objects. It contains the pyx, a chest with standard gold and silver pieces for testing coinage weights in a ceremony called the Trial of the Pyx.

Next door, the **Abbey Museum** exhibits the death masks of generations of royalty, wax effigies representing Charles II and William III (who is on a stool to make him as tall as his wife, Mary II), armour and stained glass.

To reach the 900-year-old **College Garden** (⌚10am-6pm Tue-Thu Apr-Sep, to 4pm Tue-Thu Oct-Mar), enter Dean's Yard and the Little Cloisters off Great College St.

Nave & South Transept

The south transept contains **Poets' Corner**, where many of England's finest writers are buried and/or commemorated by monuments or memorials.

In the nave's north aisle is **Scientists' Corner**, where you will find **Sir Isaac Newton's tomb**. Just ahead of it is the north aisle of the quire, known as **Musicians' Aisle**, where baroque composers Henry Purcell and John Blow are buried as well as more modern music-makers like Benjamin Britten and Edward Elgar.

The two towers above the west door are the ones through which you exit. These were designed by Nicholas Hawksmoor and completed in 1745. Just above the door, perched in 15th-century niches, are the additions to the Abbey unveiled in 1998: 10 stone statues of international 20th-century martyrs who died for their Christian faith. These include American pacifist Dr Martin Luther King and the Polish priest St Maximilian Kolbe, who was murdered by the Nazis at Auschwitz.

ROCCO FASANO / GETTY IMAGES ©

TOP SIGHT
BRITISH MUSEUM

Still London's most visited attraction, the British Museum draws an average of five and a half million punters each year. The museum was founded in 1753 when royal physician Hans Sloane sold his 'cabinet of curiosities' for the then-princely sum of £20,000, raised by national lottery. The collection opened to the public for free in 1759, and the museum has since kept expanding its collection through judicious acquisitions, bequests and the controversial plundering of imperialism. It's an exhaustive and exhilarating stampede through world cultures over 7000 years, with galleries devoted to ancient civilisations, from Egypt to western Asia, the Middle East, Rome and Greece, India, Africa, prehistoric and Roman Britain and medieval antiquities.

The museum is huge, so make a few focused visits if you have time, and consider the tours. There are 15 free 30- to 40-minute **eyeOpener tours** of individual galleries per day. The museum also has excellent **multimedia iPad tours** (adult/child £5/3.50), offering six themed one-hour tours, and eight 35-minute children's trails. Highlights tours (adult/child £12/free) depart at 11.30am and 2pm Saturday and Sunday.

Great Court

Covered with a spectacular glass-and-steel roof designed by Norman Foster in 2000, the Great Court is the largest covered public square in Europe. In its centre is the world-famous **Reading Room**, formerly the British Library, which

DON'T MISS...

- Rosetta Stone
- Mummy of Katebet
- Parthenon Sculptures
- Winged Bulls from Khorsabad
- Sutton Hoo Ship-Burial artefacts
- Mildenhall Treasure
- Lewis Chessmen

PRACTICALITIES

- Map p436
- 020-7323 8000
- www.britishmuseum.org
- Great Russell St, WC1
- 10am-5.30pm Sat-Thu, to 8.30pm Fri
- Russell Sq, Tottenham Court Rd

A HALF-DAY TOUR

The British Museum, with almost eight million items in its permanent collection, is so vast and comprehensive that it can be daunting for the first-time visitor. To avoid a frustrating trip – and getting lost on the way to the Egyptian mummies – set out on this half-day exploration, which takes in some of the museum's most important sights. If you want to see and learn more, join a tour or hire a multimedia iPad.

A good starting point is the **Rosetta Stone** **1**, the key that cracked the code to ancient Egypt's writing system. Nearby treasures from Assyria – an ancient civilisation centred in Mesopotamia between the Tigris and Euphrates Rivers – including the colossal **Khorsabad Winged Bulls** **2**, give way to the **Parthenon Sculptures** **3**, highpoints of classical Greek art that continue to influence us today. Be sure to see both the sculptures and the monumental

Winged Bulls from Khorsabad
This awesome pair of alabaster winged bulls with human heads once guarded the entrance to the palace of Assyrian King Sargon II at Khorsabad in Mesopotamia, a cradle of civilisation in present-day Iraq.

Parthenon Sculptures
The Parthenon, a white marble temple dedicated to Athena, was part of a fortified citadel on the Acropolis in Athens. There are dozens of sculptures and friezes with models and interactive displays explaining how they all once fitted together.

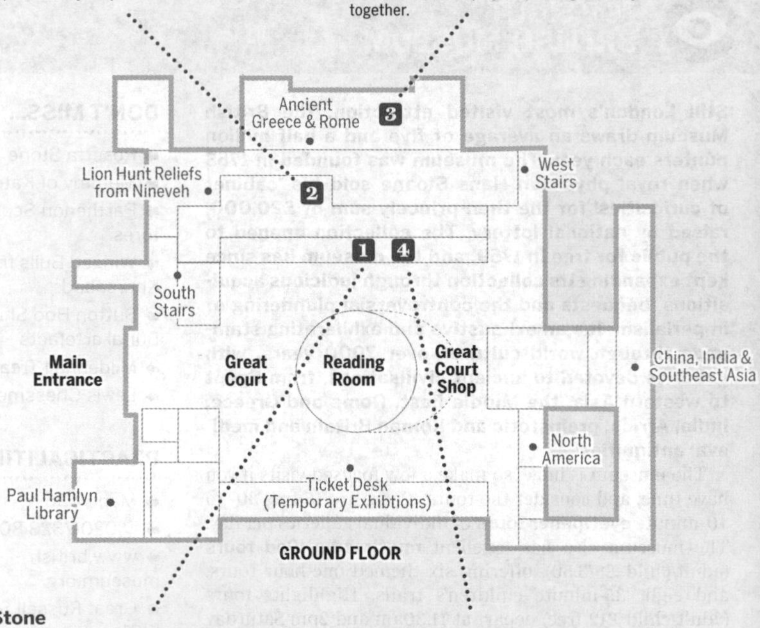

Rosetta Stone
Written in hieroglyphic, demotic (cursive ancient Egyptian script used for everyday use) and Greek, the 762kg stone contains a decree exempting priests from tax on the first anniversary of young Ptolemy V's coronation.

Bust of Ramesses the Great
The most impressive sculpture in the Egyptian galleries, this 7.5-tonne bust portrays Ramesses II, scourge of the Israelites in the Book of Exodus, as great benefactor.

JAMES MCCORMICK, VISITBRITAIN / GETTY IMAGES ©

NORTH LIGHT IMAGES / GETTY IMAGES ©

frieze celebrating the birth of Athena. En route to the West Stairs is a huge bust of **Pharaoh Ramesses II** **4**, just a hint of the large collection of **Egyptian mummies** **5** upstairs. (The earliest, affectionately called Ginger because of wispy reddish hair, was preserved simply by hot sand.) The Romans introduce visitors to the early Britain galleries via the rich **Mildenhall Treasure** **6**. The Anglo-Saxon **Sutton Hoo Ship Burial** **7** and the medieval **Lewis Chessmen** **8** follow.

EATING OPTIONS

➡ **Court Cafes** At the northern end of the Great Court; takeaway counters with salads and sandwiches; communal tables

➡ **Gallery Cafe** Slightly out of the way near Room 12; quieter; offers hot dishes

➡ **Court Restaurant** Upstairs overlooking the former Reading Room; sit-down meals

Lewis Chessmen
The much-loved 78 chess pieces portray faceless pawns, worried-looking queens, bishops with their mitres turned sideways and rooks as 'warders', gnawing away at their shields.

Egyptian Mummies
Among the rich collection of mummies and funerary objects is 'Ginger', who was buried at the site of Gebelein, in Upper Egypt, more than 5000 years ago, and Katebet, a one-time chantress (ritual performer) at the Amun temple in Karnak.

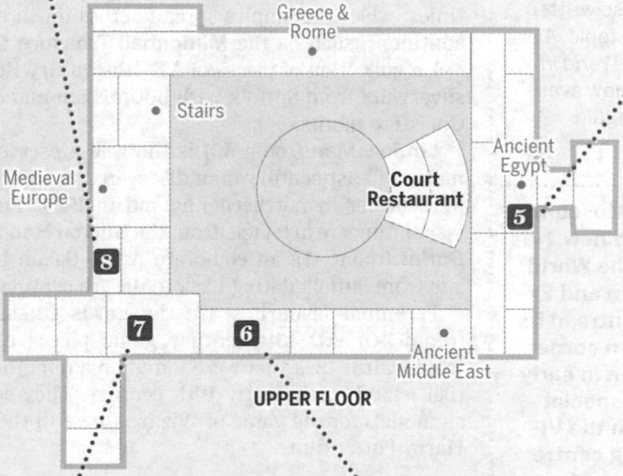

Sutton Hoo Ship Burial
This unique grave of an important (but unidentified) Anglo-Saxon royal has yielded drinking horns, gold buckles and a stunning helmet with face mask.

Mildenhall Treasure
Roman gods such as Neptune and Bacchus share space with early Christian symbols like the *chi-rho* (short for 'Christ') on the find's three dozen silver bowls, plates and spoons.

A HISTORY OF THE WORLD IN 100 OBJECTS

In 2010, the British Museum launched an outstanding radio series on BBC Radio 4 called *A History of the World in 100 Objects*. The series, presented by British Museum director Neil MacGregor, retraces two million years of history through 100 objects from the museum's collections. Each object is described in a 15-minute program, its relevance and significance analysed. Anyone with access to an MP3 player would be encouraged to download the podcasts, available from www.bbc.co.uk/podcasts/series/ahow. Neil MacGregor has also written a book on the topic, *A History of the World in 100 Objects*, now available from Penguin.

The British Museum's long-awaited new extension, the World Conservation and Exhibitions Centre in its northwestern corner, is set to open in early 2014 with a special exhibition on the Vikings. Taking centre stage will be a 36m-long Danish warship from the 11th century that may have helped King Canute conquer the seas.

has been frequented by all the big brains of history, from Mahatma Gandhi to Karl Marx. It is currently used for temporary exhibits.

Ancient Egypt, Middle East & Greece

The star of the show is the Ancient Egypt collection. It comprises sculptures, fine jewellery, papyrus texts, coffins and mummies, including the beautiful and intriguing **Mummy of Katebet** (room 63). The most prized item in the collection (and the most popular postcard in the shop) is the **Rosetta Stone** (room 4), the key to deciphering Egyptian hieroglyphics. In the same gallery is the enormous bust of the pharaoh **Ramesses the Great** (room 4).

Assyrian treasures from ancient Mesopotamia include the 16-tonne **Winged Bulls from Khorsabad** (room 10), the heaviest object in the museum. Behind it are the exquisite **Lion Hunt Reliefs from Ninevah** (room 10) from the 7th century BC, which influenced Greek sculpture.

A major highlight of the museum is the **Parthenon sculptures** (room 18). The marble frieze is thought to be the Great Panathenaea, a blow-out version of an annual festival in honour of Athena.

Roman & Medieval Britain

Upstairs are finds from Britain and the rest of Europe (rooms 40 to 51). Many go back to Roman times, when the empire spread across much of the continent, such as the **Mildenhall Treasure** (room 49), a collection of pieces of AD 4th-century Roman silverware from Suffolk with both pagan and early-Christian motifs.

Lindow Man (room 50) is the well-preserved remains of a 1st-century man discovered in a bog near Manchester in northern England in 1984. Equally fascinating are artefacts from the **Sutton Hoo Ship-Burial** (room 41), an elaborate Anglo-Saxon burial site from Suffolk dating back to the 7th century.

Perennial favourites are the **Lewis Chessmen** (room 40), AD 13th-century game pieces carved from walrus tusk that were found on a remote Scottish island in the early 19th century. They served as models for the game of Wizard Chess in the first Harry Potter film.

Enlightenment Galleries

Formerly known as the King's Library, this stunning neoclassical space (room 1) was built between 1823 and 1827 and was the first part of the new museum building as it is seen today. The collection traces how such disciplines as biology, archaeology, linguistics and geography emerged during the Enlightenment of the 18th century.

RICHARD I'ANSON / GETTY IMAGES ©

TOP SIGHT
BUCKINGHAM PALACE

Built in 1705 as Buckingham House for the duke of the same name and purchased by George III, the palace has been the Royal Family's London lodgings only since 1837, when Queen Victoria moved in from her childhood home at Kensington Palace. St James's Palace was judged too old-fashioned and insufficiently impressive, although Buckingham underwent a number of modifications until it was deemed fit.

The palace's first resident is commemorated in great pomp outside the palace with the 25m-high **Queen Victoria Memorial** (Map p440; Queen's Gardens; ⊖St James's Park) by Thomas Brock on a spot where Marble Arch once stood. The memorial was dedicated by her grandson George V in 1911 and got a nose job for the Royal Wedding a century later. Commoners now get a peek of the State Rooms, a mere 19 of the palace's 775 rooms, and only during August and September, when Her Majesty is holidaying in Scotland. The Queen's Gallery is open year-round, and the Royal Mews from April to December.

State Rooms

The tour starts in the Grand Hall at the foot of the monumental Grand Staircase, commissioned by George IV in 1828. It takes in John Nash's Italianate Green Drawing Room, the State Dining Room (all red damask and Regency furnishings), the Blue Drawing Room (which has a gorgeous fluted ceiling by Nash) and the White Drawing Room, where foreign ambassadors are received.

The Ballroom, where official receptions and state banquets are held, was built between 1853 and 1855 and opened

DON'T MISS...

- Picture Gallery
- Royal Mews
- Palace Gardens
- Changing of the Guard
- Queen's Gallery
- Throne Room

PRACTICALITIES

- Map p440
- ☎020-7766 7300
- www.royalcollection.org.uk
- Buckingham Palace Rd, SW1
- adult/child £19/10.85
- ⏲9.30am-7pm late Jul-Aug, to 6.30pm Sep
- ⊖St James's Park, Victoria, Green Park

CHANGING OF THE GUARD

At 11.30am daily from April to July, and on alternate days, weather permitting, from August to March, the old guard (Foot Guards of the Household Regiment) comes off duty to be replaced by the new guard on the forecourt of Buckingham Palace. Crowds come to watch the carefully choreographed marching and shouting of the guards in their bright red uniforms and bearskin hats. It lasts about 40 minutes and is very popular so arrive early if you want to get a good spot.

At the centre of Royal Family life is the Music Room, where four royal babies have been christened: the Prince of Wales (Prince Charles), the Princess Royal (Princess Anne), the Duke of York (Prince Andrew) and the Duke of Cambridge (Prince William) with water brought from the River Jordan.

with a ball a year later to celebrate the end of the Crimean War. The Throne Room is rather anticlimactic, with his-and-hers pink chairs initialled 'ER' and 'P', sitting under a curtained theatre arch.

Picture Gallery & Gardens

The most interesting part of the tour is the 47m-long Picture Gallery, featuring splendid works by such artists as Van Dyck, Rembrandt, Canaletto, Poussin, Claude Lorrain, Rubens, Canova and Vermeer.

Wandering the 18 hectares of gardens is another highlight – as well as admiring some of the 350 or so species of flowers and plants and listening to the many birds, you'll get beautiful views of the palace and a peek of its famous lake.

Queen's Gallery

Since the reign of Charles I, the Royal Family has amassed a priceless collection of paintings, sculpture, ceramics, furniture and jewellery. The splendid **Queen's Gallery** (Map p440; southern wing, Buckingham Palace; adult/child £9.50/4.80, with Royal Mews £16.25/9.10; ⏲10am-5.30pm) showcases some of the palace's treasures on a rotating basis.

The gallery was originally designed as a conservatory by John Nash. It was converted into a chapel for Queen Victoria in 1843, destroyed in a 1940 air raid and reopened as a gallery in 1962. A £20-million renovation for Elizabeth II's Golden Jubilee in 2002 added three times as much display space.

Royal Mews

Southwest of the palace, the **Royal Mews** (Map p440; adult/child £8/5, with Queen's Gallery £16.25/9.10; ⏲10am-5pm Apr-Oct, to 4pm Mon-Sat Nov-Dec) started life as a falconry but is now a working stable looking after the royals' three dozen immaculately groomed horses, along with the opulent vehicles – motorised and horse-driven – the monarch uses for transport. The Queen is well known for her passion for horses; she names every horse that resides at the mews and still rides every weekend. Nash's 1820 stables are stunning.

Highlights for visitors include the enormous and opulent Gold State Coach of 1762, which has been used for every coronation since that of George III; the 1911 Glass Coach used for royal weddings and the Diamond Jubilee in 2012; Queen Alexandra's State Coach (1893), used to transport the Imperial State Crown to the official opening of Parliament, and a Rolls-Royce Phantom VI from the royal fleet.

CHRIS HEPBURN / GETTY IMAGES ©

TOP SIGHT
HOUSES OF PARLIAMENT

Both the House of Commons and the House of Lords sit in the sumptuous Palace of Westminster, a neo-Gothic confection dating from the mid-19th century. The House of Commons is where Members of Parliament (MPs) meet to propose and discuss new legislation and to grill the prime minister and other ministers. The House of Lords contains Lords Spiritual, linked with the established church, and Lords Temporal, who are both appointed and hereditary.

When Parliament is in session, visitors are allowed to attend the debates in the **House of Commons** (⌚2.30-10pm Mon & Tue, 11.30am-7.30pm Wed, 10.30am-6.30pm Thu, 9.30am-3pm Fri) and the **House of Lords** (www.parliament.uk/business/lords; ⌚2.30-10pm Mon & Tue, 3-10pm Wed, 11am-7.30pm Thu, 10am to close of session Fri). Enter via **St Stephen's Entrance** (Map p440). It's not unusual to have to wait up to two hours to access the chambers. The best time to watch a debate is during Prime Minister's Question Time at noon on Wednesday, but it's also the busiest.

DON'T MISS...

- Westminster Hall's hammer-beam roof
- Palace's 'Tudor Gothic' interior
- Big Ben
- Sovereign's Entrance
- Jewel Tower

PRACTICALITIES

- Map p440
- www.parliament.uk
- Parliament Sq, SW1
- ⊖Westminster

Towers

The most famous feature of the Houses of Parliament is the Clock Tower, officially named Elizabeth Tower to mark the Queen's Diamond Jubilee in 2012 but commonly known as **Big Ben**. Ben is actually the 13-tonne bell hanging inside and is named after Benjamin Hall, the rotund commissioner of works when the tower was completed in 1858. At the base of the taller **Victoria Tower** at the southern end is the Sovereign's Entrance, which is used by the Queen.

DEBATES

To find out what's being debated on a particular day, check the notice board beside the entrance, or check online at www.parliament.uk. The debating style in the Commons is quite combative but not all debates are flamboyant argumentative duelling matches. In fact, many are rather boring and long-winded, although they are an essential feature of British democracy.

After the campaign group Fathers 4 Justice lobbed a condom full of purple powder at Tony Blair in May 2004, a bulletproof screen was placed between members of the public and the debating chamber.

Westminster Hall

One of the most stunning features of the Palace of Westminster, seat of the English monarchy from the 11th to the early 16th centuries, is Westminster Hall. Originally built in 1099, it is the oldest surviving part of the complex; the awesome hammer-beam roof was added around 1400. It has been described as 'the greatest surviving achievement of medieval English carpentry'. The only other part of the original palace to survive the devastating 1834 fire is the **Jewel Tower** (Map p440; ☎020-7222 2219; www.english-heritage.org.uk/daysout/properties/jewel-tower; Abingdon St, St James's Park, SW1; adult/child £4/2.50; ⌚10am-5pm daily Apr-Oct, 10am-4pm Sat & Sun Nov-Mar; ⊖Westminster), built in 1365 and used to store the monarch's valuables.

Westminster Hall was used for coronation banquets in medieval times, and also served as a courthouse until the 19th century. The trials of William Wallace (1305), Thomas More (1535), Guy Fawkes (1606) and Charles I (1649) all took place here. In the 20th century, monarchs and Winston Churchill lay in state here after their deaths.

House of Commons

The layout of the Commons Chamber is based on St Stephen's Chapel in the original Palace of Westminster. The chamber, designed by Giles Gilbert Scott, replaced the one destroyed by a 1941 bomb.

Although the Commons is a national assembly of 650 MPs, the chamber has seating for only 437. Government members sit to the right of the Speaker and Opposition members to the left.

House of Lords

The House of Lords is visited via the amusingly named Strangers' Gallery. The intricate 'Tudor Gothic' interior led its poor architect, Pugin (1812–52), to an early death from overwork and nervous strain.

Most of the 760-odd members of the House of Lords are life peers (appointed for their lifetime by the monarch); there is also a small number – 92 at the time of research – of hereditary peers and a group of 'crossbench' members (not affiliated to the main political parties).

Tours

On Saturdays year-round and when Parliament is in summer recess (mid-July to early September), visitors can join a 75-minute **guided tour** (☎0844 847 1672; www.parliament.uk/guided-tours; adult/child £16.50/7) of both chambers, Westminster Hall and other historic buildings conducted by qualified Blue Badge Tourist Guides in six languages. Tour schedules change with every recess, so check ahead. It's best to book.

TOP SIGHT
NATIONAL GALLERY

With some 2300 European paintings on display, this is one of the richest art galleries in the world. There are seminal paintings from every important epoch in the history of art from the mid-13th to the early 20th century, including works by Leonardo da Vinci, Michelangelo, Titian, Van Gogh and Renoir.

The modern Sainsbury Wing on the gallery's western side houses paintings from 1260 to 1510. Here you will find largely religious paintings commissioned for private devotion (eg the *Wilton Diptych*) as well more unusual masterpieces such as Botticelli's *Venus & Mars* and Van Eyck's *Arnolfini Portrait.*

The High Renaissance (1510–1600) is covered in the West Wing where Michelangelo, Titian, Raphael, Correggio, El Greco and Bronzino hold court; Rubens, Rembrandt and Caravaggio can be found in the North Wing (1600–1700). Notable are two self-portraits of Rembrandt (age 34 and 63) and the beautiful *Rockeby Venus*, by Velázquez.

The most popular part is the East Wing (1700–1900), with great works by 18th-century British artists such as Gainsborough, Constable and Turner, and highbrow Impressionist and post-Impressionist masterpieces by Van Gogh and Monet.

The comprehensive audioguides (£3.50) are highly recommended, as are the free one-hour introductory guided tours that leave from the information desk in the Sainsbury Wing daily at 11.30am and 2.30pm, and at 7pm Friday. There are also special trails and activity sheets for children.

The National Dining Rooms (p125) have high-quality British food and an all-day bakery.

DON'T MISS...

- *Sunflowers*, by Van Gogh
- *Venus & Mars*, by Botticelli
- *The Arnolfini Portrait*, by Van Eyck
- *Wilton Diptych*
- *Rockeby Venus*, by Velázquez
- *Rain, Steam & Speed – The Great Western Railway*, by Turner

PRACTICALITIES

- Map p430
- www.nationalgallery.org.uk
- Trafalgar Sq, WC2
- 10am-6pm Sat-Thu, to 9pm Fri
- Charing Cross

THE ART GALLERY COLLECTION / ALAMY ©

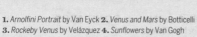

1. *Arnolfini Portrait* by Van Eyck **2.** *Venus and Mars* by Botticelli
3. *Rockeby Venus* by Velázquez **4.** *Sunflowers* by Van Gogh

2

ERSOY EMIN / ALAMY ©

4

National Gallery Masterpieces

The National Gallery's collection spans seven centuries of European painting. It's a whirl of 2000-odd tableaux displayed in sumptuous, airy galleries. All are masterpieces, but some stand head and shoulders above the rest.

Arnolfini Portrait, Van Eyck

This is history's first bourgeois portrait, an early example of the use of oils and a revolutionary way to create space by painting light. It shows a rich Bruges merchant and his wife, who, despite looking pregnant, is actually making a fashion statement.

Venus & Mars, Botticelli

Venus, goddess of love, upright and alert, stares intently at Mars, god of war, fast asleep after they've made love. The message: make love not war.

Rockeby Venus, Velázquez

A rare subject during the Spanish Inquisition, a self-absorbed Venus is gazing at herself – and us – in a mirror held by her son Cupid.

Sunflowers, Van Gogh

This instantly recognisable masterpiece, one of four by the great Dutch Impressionist, depicts 14 sunflowers at different stages of life. The one colour – yellow – is applied thickly, a bold new 'sculptural' approach to painting.

Hay Wain, Constable

A horse-drawn wagon in the middle of a river is a romantic portrayal of England on the eve of the Industrial Revolution. Flecks of white paint reflect and create movement – a foretaste of Impressionism.

Fighting Temeraire, Turner

Britain's favourite painting shows the sailing ship Temeraire, a hero of Trafalgar, being towed to a ship-breaking yard. The sun goes down, the moon comes up; her world is ending and the age of steam and industrialisation approaches.

VULTURE LABS / GETTY IMAGES ©

TOP SIGHT
TATE BRITAIN

You'd think that Tate Britain might have suffered since its lavish, sexy sibling, Tate Modern, took half its collection and all of the limelight across the river at its millennium opening. On the contrary, the venerable Tate Britain, built in 1897 by Henry Tate (the man who invented the sugar cube), stretched its definitive collection of British art from the 16th to the late 20th centuries out splendidly, while Tate Modern devoted its space to modern art.

The star of the show at Tate Britain is JMW Turner. After he died in 1851, his estate was settled by a decree declaring that whatever had been found in his studio – 300 oil paintings and about 30,000 sketches and drawings – would be bequeathed to the nation. You'll find such classics as *The Scarlet Sunset* and *Norham Castle, Sunrise*.

As well as Turner's art, there are seminal works by such artists as Constable, Gainsborough and Reynolds as well as pre-Rahaelites (Rossetti, Holman Hunt, Millais), but also more modern artists, such as Lucian Freud, Francis Bacon and Tracey Emin. Tate Britain also hosts the prestigious and often controversial Turner Prize for contemporary art from October to early December every year.

There are free 45-minute **thematic tours** (11am, noon, 2pm & 3pm), along with free 15-minute **Art in Focus** (1.15pm Tue, Thu & Sat) talks on specific works. Audioguides (£3.50) are also available.

DON'T MISS...

- *The Scarlet Sunset*, by JMW Turner
- *Three Studies for Figures at the Base of a Crucifixion*, by Francis Bacon
- *Ophelia*, by John Everett Millais
- *O the Roast Beef of Old England*, by William Hogarth
- *Flatford Mill*, by John Constable
- *Carnation, Lily, Lily, Rose*, by John Singer Sargent

PRACTICALITIES

- Map p440
- www.tate.org.uk
- Millbank, SW1
- 10am-6pm daily, 6-10pm some Fri
- Pimlico

DOUG MCKINLAY / LONELY PLANET ©

TOP SIGHT
NATIONAL PORTRAIT GALLERY

What makes the National Portrait Gallery, the only such museum in Europe, so compelling is its familiarity; in many cases you'll have heard of the subject (royals, scientists, politicians, celebrities) or the artist (Andy Warhol, Annie Leibovitz, Sam Taylor-Wood).

The collection is organised chronologically (starting with the early Tudors on the 2nd floor), and then by theme. A highlight is the famous 'Chandos portrait' of William Shakespeare, the first artwork the gallery acquired (in 1856); believed to be the only one to have been painted during the playwright's lifetime. Other highlights include the 'Ditchley' portrait of Queen Elizabeth I displaying her might by standing on a map of England, and a touching sketch of novelist Jane Austen by her sister.

The 1st-floor portraits illustrate the rise and fall of the British Empire through the Victorian era and the 20th century. Don't miss the high-kitsch statue of Victoria and Albert in Anglo-Saxon dress in room 21.

The ground floor is dedicated to modern figures, using a variety of media (sculpture, photography, video etc). Among the most popular are the iconic Blur portraits by Julian Opie; Sam Taylor-Wood's *David,* a video-portrait of David Beckham asleep after football training; and Stuart Pearson Wright's slightly distorted *JK Rowling*.

The excellent audioguide (£3) highlights 200 portraits and allows you to hear the voices of some of the subjects. The Portrait restaurant (p125) has superb views towards Westminster and does wonderful food.

DON'T MISS...

- Blur portraits by Julian Opie
- Shakespeare 'Chandos Portrait', attributed to John Taylor
- *Queen Elizabeth II*, by Andy Warhol
- *Jane Austen*, by Cassandra Austen
- *Queen Elizabeth I*, by Marcus Gheeraerts the Younger

PRACTICALITIES

- Map p430
- www.npg.org.uk
- St Martin's Pl, WC2
- 10am-6pm Sat-Wed, to 9pm Thu & Fri
- Charing Cross, Leicester Sq

TOP SIGHT
TRAFALGAR SQUARE

In many ways Trafalgar Sq is the centre of London, where tens of thousands congregate for anything from communal open-air cinema and Christmas and New Year celebrations to political protests.

The great square was neglected over many years, ringed with traffic and given over to flocks of feral pigeons fed by tourists and locals alike. In 2000 newly elected Mayor Ken Livingstone embarked on a scheme to transform the square into the kind of space John Nash had intended when he designed it in the early 19th century. Traffic was banished from the northern flank in front of the National Gallery and a new pedestrian plaza built.

DON'T MISS...

- Nelson's Column
- Bronze lions
- Fourth Plinth
- Admiralty Arch
- Nelson's 'nose'

PRACTICALITIES

- Map p430
- WC2
- Charing Cross

Square

The square commemorates the victory of the British navy at the Battle of Trafalgar against the French and Spanish navies in 1805 during the Napoleonic wars. The main square contains two beautiful fountains, which are dramatically lit at night. At each corner of the square is a plinth, three topped with statues of military leaders and the fourth, in the northeast corner, now a ubiquitous art space called the Fourth Plinth (p113).

The plaza at the north, in front of the National Gallery, is a favourite of buskers and street performers.

Nelson's Column

Standing in the centre of the square since 1843, the 52m-high Nelson's Column honours Admiral Lord Horatio Nelson, who led the fleet's victory over Napoleon. If you look closely you can see the good admiral surveying his fleet of 'ships' atop the lampposts along the Mall to the southwest. The column is flanked by four enormous bronze statues of lions sculpted by Sir Edwin Landseer. The battle plaques at the base of the column were cast with seized Spanish and French cannons.

Buildings around Trafalgar Square

The splendid buildings ringing the square are, clockwise from 12 o'clock: National Gallery (and National Portrait Gallery behind it); St Martin-in-the-Fields; and three commissions – South Africa House, Malaysia House and Canada House, designed by Robert Smirke in 1827. If you look southwest down Whitehall, past the statue of Charles I, you'll also get a glimpse of Big Ben at the Houses of Parliament.

Admiralty Arch

To the southwest of Trafalgar Sq stands Admiralty Arch, from where the ceremonial Mall leads to Buckingham Palace. It is a grand Edwardian monument, a triple-arched stone entrance designed by Aston Webb in honour of Queen Victoria in 1910 and soon to be transformed into an Armani-branded hotel. The large central gate is opened only for royal processions and state visits. About 2m up the wall of the northernmost (right) arch is a curious porcelain nose. Local lore says it is Nelson's (he had a big one apparently) and guards would stroke it for luck as they rode by.

ALEX SEGRE / ALAMY ©

TOP SIGHT
CHURCHILL WAR ROOMS

In late August 1939, with war seemingly imminent, the British cabinet and chiefs of the armed forces decided to move underground into a converted basement below what is now the Treasury. On 3 September Britain was at war.

The bunker served as nerve centre of the war cabinet until the end of WWII in 1945: here chiefs of staff ate, slept and plotted Hitler's downfall, believing they were protected from Luftwaffe bombs (turns out the 3m slab of cement above them would have crumpled had the area taken a direct hit).

Cabinet War Rooms

The Cabinet War Rooms have been left much as they were on 15 August 1945. Many rooms have been preserved, including the room where the War Cabinet met 115 times; the Transatlantic Telegraph Room, with a hotline to President Roosevelt; the converted broom cupboard that was Churchill's office-bedroom (though he slept here only three times), and the all-important Map Room, which was the operational centre.

The free audioguide is very informative and entertaining and features plenty of anecdotes, including some from people who worked here in the war.

Churchill Museum

This superb multimedia museum doesn't shy away from its hero's fallibilities – it portrays Churchill as having a legendary temper, being a bit of a maverick and, on the whole, a pretty lousy peace-time politician. It does focus on his strongest suit: his stirring speeches. Churchill's orations are replayed for each goose-bumped visitor who steps in front of the interactive displays.

DON'T MISS...

- Map Room
- Cabinet Room
- Anecdotes from former War Rooms staff
- Extracts from Churchill's famous speeches
- Churchill's office/bedroom

PRACTICALITIES

- Map p440
- www.iwm.org.uk/visits/churchill-war-rooms
- Clive Steps, King Charles St, SW1
- adult/child £17/free
- 9.30am-6pm
- Westminster

NIGEL DICKINSON / ALAMY ©

TOP SIGHT
SIR JOHN SOANE'S MUSEUM

This little museum is one of the most atmospheric and fascinating in London. The building is the bewitching home of architect Sir John Soane (1753–1837), which he left brimming with surprising personal effects and curiosities, and the museum represents his exquisite and eccentric taste.

Soane was a country bricklayer's son, most famous for designing the Bank of England. In his work and life, he drew on ideas picked up while on an 18th-century grand tour of Italy. He married a rich woman and used the wealth to build this house and the one next door at No 12, which now serves as an exhibition and education space. The 2nd floor of No 13, including Soane's private apartment and model room, was being restored at press time and will be open to the public for the first time in history.

The heritage-listed house is largely as it was when Soane died and is itself a main part of the attraction. It has a canopy dome that brings light right down to the crypt, a colonnade filled with statuary and a picture gallery where paintings are stowed behind each other on folding wooden panes. This is where Soane's choicest artwork is displayed, including *Riva degli Schiavoni, looking West*, by Canaletto, architectural drawings by Christopher Wren and Robert Adam, and the original *Rake's Progress*, William Hogarth's set of satirical cartoons of late-8th-century London lowlife. Among Soane's more unusual acquisitions are an Egyptian hieroglyphic sarcophagus, a mock-up of a monk's cell and slaves' chains.

The first Tuesday evening of each month is the choice time to visit as the house is lit by candles and the atmosphere is even more magical (it is very popular and there are always long queues).

DON'T MISS...

- *Rake's Progress*, by William Hogarth
- Sarcophagus of King Seti I
- *Riva degli Schiavoni, looking West*, by Canaletto
- Candlelit tours

PRACTICALITIES

- Map p430
- www.soane.org
- 13 Lincoln's Inn Fields, WC2
- 10am-5pm Tue-Sat, 6-9pm 1st Tue of month
- Holborn

SIGHTS

The West End is a vague term – any Londoner you meet will give you their own take on which neighbourhoods it does and doesn't include – but what is striking is its variety: from reverentially quiet in Bloomsbury and Holborn to bustling with revellers and shoppers 24/7 in Soho, Piccadilly Circus and Oxford St. The best way to get to know the West End is on foot. Most sights are within walking distance of one another and you'll get a much better sense of the area's atmosphere that way.

Westminster

WESTMINSTER ABBEY — CHURCH

See p86.

HOUSES OF PARLIAMENT — HISTORIC BUILDING

See p95.

CHURCHILL WAR ROOMS — MUSEUM

See p103.

SUPREME COURT — LANDMARK

Map p440 (www.supremecourt.gov.uk; Parliament Sq, SW1; admission free; 9.30am-4.30pm Mon-Thu ; Westminster) FREE The Supreme Court, the highest court in the UK, was the Appellate Committee of the House of Lords until as recently as 2009. It is now housed in the neo-Gothic Middlesex Guildhall (1913), and members of the public are welcome to observe cases when the court is sitting four days a week.

For who or what's on trial, ask for a list at reception or go to the Current Cases page of the court's website. On the lower ground floor there's a permanent exhibition looking at the work and history of the UK's highest court as well as the history of the building.

ST JOHN'S, SMITH SQUARE — HISTORIC BUILDING

Map p440 (020-7222 1061; www.sjss.org.uk; Smith Sq, Westminster, SW1; Westminster, St James's Park) In the heart of Westminster, this eye-catching church was built by Thomas Archer in 1728 under Queen Anne's Fifty New Churches Act (1711), which aimed to build that many new churches for London's rapidly growing metropolitan area. After receiving a direct hit during WWII, it was rebuilt in the 1960s as a classical-music venue, and is renowned for its excellent acoustics.

Though they never did build all 50 churches, St John's, along with about a dozen others, saw the light of day. Unfortunately, with its four corner towers and monumental facades, the structure was much maligned for the first century of its existence thanks to rumours that Queen Anne likened it to a footstool. In any case it's generally agreed now that the church is a masterpiece of English baroque. The brick-vaulted **Smith Square Cafe & Restaurant** in the crypt is open from 8am to 5pm daily.

LITERARY BLOOMSBURY

Bloomsbury's beautiful squares were once colonised by the so-called Bloomsbury Group, a collection of artists and writers who included Virginia Woolf and EM Forster, and the stories of their many intricate love affairs are as fascinating as their books. Charles Dickens, Charles Darwin, William Butler Yeats and George Bernard Shaw also lived in this district, as attested by the many blue plaques dotted around.

Bedford Sq was home to many London publishing houses until the 1990s, when they were swallowed up by multinational conglomerates and relocated. They included Jonathan Cape, Chatto and the Bodley Head (set up by Woolf and her husband Leonard), and were largely responsible for perpetuating the legend of the Bloomsbury Group by churning out seemingly endless collections of associated letters, memoirs and biographies.

Today Bloomsbury contains some excellent bookshops and cafes, while remaining relatively uncommercial.

Bloomsbury & Fitzrovia

BRITISH MUSEUM — MUSEUM

See p89.

SQUARES OF BLOOMSBURY — SQUARE

The Bloomsbury Group, they used to say, lived in squares, moved in circles and loved in triangles. It's the squares – Russell, Gordon and Bedford primarily – that have the most fascinating histories.

LOCAL KNOWLEDGE

BT TOWER

Visible from virtually everywhere in central London, the 189m-tall **BT Tower** (Map p436; 60 Cleveland St, W1) was the highest structure in the city when it opened in 1966 (St Paul's Cathedral was No 2 at the time). It was closed to the public 15 years later for security reasons. Incongruously for such a conspicuous structure, the building was officially a 'secret' and didn't appear on official maps until 1993.

The tower is still used as a communications hub and for air-pollution monitoring. It is also a listed building, which meant getting special permission to remove the defunct circular antennas in 2011. The BT Tower reopened to the public for one day in 2010 and again in 2011 as part of Open House London (p375). See the website for any plans to reopen it as part of this annual event.

At the very heart of the district is **Russell Square** (Map p436). Originally laid out in 1800 by Humphrey Repton, it was dark and bushy until a striking facelift a decade ago pruned the trees, tidied up the plants and gave it a 10m-high fountain.

The centre of literary Bloomsbury was **Gordon Square** (Map p436) where, at various times, Bertrand Russell (No 57), Lytton Strachey (No 51) and Vanessa and Clive Bell, Maynard Keynes and the Woolf family (No 46) lived. Strachey, Dora Carrington and Lydia Lopokova (the future wife of Maynard Keynes) all took turns living at No 41. Some of the buildings are marked with blue plaques.

Lovely **Bedford Square** (Map p436) is the only completely Georgian square still surviving in Bloomsbury.

NEW LONDON ARCHITECTURE — EXHIBITION

Map p436 (www.newlondonarchitecture.org; Building Centre, 26 Store St, WC1; ⌚9am-6pm Mon-Fri, 10am-5pm Sat; ⊖Goodge St) FREE This is an excellent place to see which way London's architectural development is going, and the frequently changing exhibitions will capture the imagination of anyone who loves the city. A large, constantly updated model of the capital highlights the planned and new buildings as well as various neighbourhood regeneration programs. There's an excellent Royal Institute of British Architects bookshop and cafe here too.

CHARLES DICKENS MUSEUM — MUSEUM

(www.dickensmuseum.com; 48 Doughty St, WC1; adult/child £8/4; ⌚10am-5pm; ⊖Chancery Lane, Russell Sq) After a £3.5 million year-long renovation, this museum in a handsome four-storey house – the great Victorian novelist's sole surviving residence in London – is bigger and better than ever. A period kitchen in the basement and a nursery in the attic have been added, and newly acquired 49 Doughty St increases the exhibition space substantially.

Not that he stayed here very long – a mere 2½ years (1837–39) – but this is where his work really flourished: he dashed off *The Pickwick Papers, Nicholas Nickleby* and *Oliver Twist,* despite worry over debts, the death of his beloved sister-in-law, Mary Hogarth, and his ever-growing family. The house was saved from demolition and the museum opened in 1925, showcasing the family drawing room (restored to its original condition) and a dozen rooms containing various memorabilia. An audioguide costs £3.

POLLOCK'S TOY MUSEUM — MUSEUM

Map p436 (www.pollockstoymuseum.com; 1 Scala St, enter from 41 Whitfield St, W1; adult/child £6/3; ⌚10am-5pm Mon-Sat; ⊖Goodge St) Aimed at adults as much as kids, this museum is simultaneously creepy and mesmerising. You walk in through its shop, laden with excellent wooden toys and various games, and start your exploration by climbing up a rickety narrow staircase, where displays begin with mechanical toys, puppets and framed dolls from Latin America, Africa, India and Europe.

Upstairs is the museum's collection of toy theatres, many made by Benjamin Pollock himself, the leading Victorian manufacturer of the popular sets, as well as tin toys, teddy bears and weird-looking dolls in cotton nighties.

PETRIE MUSEUM OF EGYPTIAN ARCHAEOLOGY — MUSEUM

Map p436 (UCL; www.petrie.ucl.ac.uk; University College London, Malet Pl, WC1; ⌚1-5pm Tue-Sat; ⊖Goodge St) FREE Counting some 80,000 artefacts, this is one of the most impressive collections of Egyptian and Sudanese archaeology in the world. The old-fashioned dusty displays in glass cases don't really do much to highlight them, though. The museum is named after Professor William Flinders Petrie (1853–1942), who uncovered many of the items during his excavations and donated them to the university in 1933.

ST GEORGE'S, BLOOMSBURY CHURCH

Map p436 (www.stgeorgesbloomsbury.org.uk; Bloomsbury Way, WC1; ⌚9.30am-5.30pm Mon-Fri, 10.30am-12.30pm Sun; ⊖Holborn, Tottenham Court Rd) This superbly restored church designed by Nicholas Hawksmoor (1731) is distinguished by its classical portico of Corinthian capitals and a steeple that was inspired by the Mausoleum of Halicarnassus and can be seen in William Hogarth's satirical painting *Gin Lane*. The statue at the top is of King George I in Roman dress.

BROADCASTING HOUSE TV LOCATION

Map p438 (☎0370 901 1227; www.bbc.co.uk/showsandtours; Portland Pl, W1; ⌚tour days & times vary; ⊖Oxford Circus) This is the iconic building from which the BBC began radio broadcasting in 1932 and from where all TV and radio broadcasting in London has taken place since early 2013. You can visit Broadcasting House on a 1½-hour tour; tours depart up to nine times per day but check the website for details.

The tour will take you to the radio theatre where you can take part in a radio play, have you anchoring the main news or weather and give you a peek behind the scenes at the studios (and live recordings) of the various BBC channels.

ALL SOULS CHURCH CHURCH

Map p438 (www.allsouls.org; 2 All Souls Pl, off Langham Pl, W1; ⌚9.30am-5.30pm Mon-Fri; ⊖Oxford Circus) Designed by John Nash in golden-hued Bath stone, All Souls features a circular columned porch and distinctive needle-like spire, reminiscent of an ancient Greek temple. But the church was not very popular when completed in 1824 – a contemporary cartoon by George Cruikshank shows Nash rather painfully impaled on the spire through the bottom with the words 'Nashional Taste!!!' below it.

St James's

BUCKINGHAM PALACE PALACE

See p93.

TATE BRITAIN GALLERY

See p100.

ST JAMES'S PARK PARK

Map p440 (www.royalparks.gov.uk; The Mall, SW1; deckchairs per hr/day £1.50/7; ⌚5am-midnight, deckchairs Mar-Oct daylight hours; ⊖St James's Park, Green Park) At just 23 hectares, St James's is one of the smallest but most groomed of London's royal parks. It has brilliant views of the London Eye, Westminster, St James's Palace, Carlton Tce and Horse Guards Parade; the sight of Buckingham Palace from the footbridge spanning the central lake is photo-perfect and the best you'll find.

The lake is full of different types of ducks, geese, swans and general fowl, and the rocks on its southern side serve as a rest stop for a half-dozen pelicans (fed at 2.30pm daily). Some of the technicolour flowerbeds were modelled on John Nash's original 'floriferous' beds of mixed shrubs, flowers and trees. You can rent deckchairs to make lounging around more comfortable.

GETTING HIGH IN LONDON

Not so long ago, getting a good view of London was a near-impossible endeavour. There was the London Eye (p173), to be sure, but been-there-done-that, yeah? And Vertigo 42 (p166) involved a lot of forward planning.

Now things are a lot more democratic and, well, the sky's the limit. The 72nd-floor open-air platform of the Shard (p177) is as high as you'll get in the EU. For nibbles and views, head for the 40th-floor location of Duck & Waffle (p165) or to Madison (p167). For drinks we love Galvin at Windows (p135). Dirty windows notwithstanding, Paramount (p134) at Centre Point is fabulously placed. The 5th View (p123) atop Waterstones bookshop in Piccadilly is admittedly low on the totem pole but, having taken afternoon tea there, you can legitimately use the ultimate intellectual's chat-up line: 'I get high on books'.

TOP SIGHT
ROYAL ACADEMY OF ARTS

Britain's oldest society devoted to fine arts was founded in 1768 and the organisation moved to Burlington House exactly a century later. The collection contains drawings, paintings, architectural designs, photographs and sculptures by past and present Academicians such as Joshua Reynolds, John Constable, Thomas Gainsborough, JMW Turner, David Hockney and Norman Foster. Highlights are displayed in the **John Madejski Fine Rooms** on the 1st floor, which are accessible on **free guided tours** (1pm & 3pm Wed-Fri, 1pm Tue, 11.30am Sat).

The famous **Summer Exhibition** (Jun–mid-Aug), which has showcased contemporary art for sale by unknown as well as established artists for nearly 250 years, is the academy's biggest annual event.

Burlington House's courtyard features a stone-paved piazza with choreographed lights and fountains arranged to display the astrological star chart of Joshua Reynolds, the RA's first president, on the day he was born. His statue stands in the centre.

DON'T MISS...

- Summer Exhibition
- John Madejski Fine Rooms
- Forecourt piazza

PRACTICALITIES

- Map p432
- www.royalacademy.org.uk
- Burlington House, Piccadilly, W1
- admission from adult/child £10/6
- 10am-6pm Sun-Thu, to midnight Fri, 9am-midnight Sat
- Green Park

On the Mall's park edge stands the **National Police Memorial** (Map p440), one column of marble and another of glass. Conceived by film director Michael Winner *(Death Wish)* and designed by architect Norman Foster and artist Per Arnoldi, it pays tribute to 1600 policemen and women who have lost their lives in the line of duty.

BURLINGTON ARCADE — SHOPPING ARCADE

Map p440 (www.burlington-arcade.co.uk; 51 Piccadilly, W1; 10am-9pm Mon-Fri, 9am-6.30pm Sat, 11am-5pm Sun; Green Park) Flanking Burlington House, home to the Royal Academy of Arts, is this delightful arcade, built in 1819. Today it is a shopping precinct for the wealthy, and is most famous for the Burlington Berties, uniformed guards who patrol the area keeping an eye out for such offences as running, chewing gum or whatever else might lower the tone.

The fact that the arcade once served as a brothel isn't mentioned. Running perpendicular to it between Old Bond and Albermarle Sts is the more recent (1880) **Royal Arcade** (Map p432; between 28 Old Bond & 12 Albemarle Sts, W1; Green Park).

ST JAMES'S PICCADILLY — CHURCH

Map p432 (www.st-james-piccadilly.org; 197 Piccadilly, W1; 8am-8pm; Piccadilly Circus) The only church Christopher Wren (1684) built from scratch and on a new site (most of the other London churches are replacements for ones razed in the Great Fire), this simple building is exceedingly easy on the eye and substitutes what some might call the pompous flourishes of Wren's most famous churches with a warm and elegant user-friendliness.

This is a particularly sociable church; it houses a counselling service, stages lunchtime and evening concerts, provides shelter for an antiques market (10.30am to 5pm Tuesday) and an arts and crafts fair (10am to 6pm Wednesday to Saturday). The baptismal font portraying Adam and Eve on the shaft and the altar reredos are by Grinling Gibbons.

ST JAMES'S PALACE — PALACE

Map p440 (www.royal.gov.uk/theroyalresidences/stjamesspalace/stjamesspalace.aspx; Cleveland Row, SW1; Green Park) The striking Tudor gatehouse of St James's Palace, the only surviving part of a building initiated by the palace-mad Henry VIII in 1530, is best approached from St James's St to the north of St James's Park. This was the official residence of kings and queens for more than three centuries.

Foreign ambassadors are still formally accredited to the Court of St James, although they are actually received at Buckingham Palace. Princess Diana, who hated this place, lived here until her divorce from Charles in 1996, when she moved to Kensington Palace. Prince Charles and his sons stayed on at St James's until 2004, before decamping next door to Clarence House, leaving St James's Palace as the London residence of his sister Anne, the Princess Royal, and nieces the Princesses Beatrix and Eugenie.

CLARENCE HOUSE — PALACE

Map p440 (☎020-7766 7300; www.royalcollection.org.uk; Cleveland Row, SW1; adult/child £9/5; ⏲10am-4pm Mon-Fri, to 5.30pm Sat & Sun Aug; ⊖Green Park) Five rooms of Clarence House, the official residence of Charles, the Prince of Wales, Camilla, the Duchess of Cornwall, and Prince Harry, are open to the public on guided tour for one month in summer.

The highlight of the 45-minute tour is the late Queen Mother's small art collection, including one painting by playwright Noël Coward and others by WS Sickert and Sir James Gunn. The house was originally designed by John Nash in the early 19th century, but has been modified much since. Book in advance.

SPENCER HOUSE — HISTORIC BUILDING

Map p440 (☎020-7514 1958; www.spencerhouse.co.uk; 27 St James's Pl, SW1; adult/child £12/10; ⏲10.30am-5.45pm Sun Feb-Jul & Sep-Dec; ⊖Green Park) Just outside Green Park is Spencer House, completed in the Palladian style in 1766 for the first Earl Spencer, an ancestor of Princess Diana. The Spencers moved out in 1927 and their grand family home was used as an office, until Lord Rothschild stepped in and returned it to its former glory in 1987 with an £18-million restoration.

Visits to the eight lavishly furnished rooms of the house are by guided tour only. The 18th-century gardens are open only between 2pm and 5pm on a couple of Sundays in summer.

QUEEN'S CHAPEL

Map p440 (Marlborough Rd, SW1; [illegible] only, 8.30am & 11.15am Sun Easter-[illegible] Park) This small chapel is wh[illegible] porary royals such as Princess [illegible] the Queen Mother have lain in their coffins in the run-up to their funerals. The church was originally built by Inigo Jones in the Palladian style for the French wife of Charles I and was the the first post-Reformation Roman Catholic church erected in England.

The simple interior, illuminated by light streaming through the large windows above the altar, has exquisite 17th-century fittings. It was once part of St James's Palace but was separated after a fire.

GREEN PARK — PARK

Map p440 (www.royalparks.gov.uk; ⏲24hr; ⊖Green Park) Less manicured than adjoining St James's, 19-hectare Green Park has huge oaks and hilly meadows, and it's never as crowded as St James's. It was once a duelling ground and, like Hyde Park, served as a vegetable garden during WWII.

It famously has no flowers beds as they were banned by Queen Catherine of Braganza after she learned her philandering husband Charles II had been picking posies for his mistresses. Or so the story goes...

GUARDS MUSEUM — MUSEUM

Map p440 (www.theguardsmuseum.com; Wellington Barracks, Birdcage Walk, SW1; adult/child £5/free; ⏲10am-4pm; ⊖St James's Park) Learn the the history of the five regiments of foot guards and their role in military campaigns from Waterloo onwards at this little museum in Wellington Barracks. There are uniforms, oil paintings, medals, curios and memorabilia that belonged to the soldiers. Perhaps the biggest draw is the huge collection of toy soldiers for sale in the shop.

If you found the crowds at the Changing of the Guards tiresome and didn't see a thing, get here 10.50am on any day from April to July (alternate days the rest of the year) to see the soldiers of the new guard get into formation outside the museum, be inspected 20 minutes later, and depart just before 11.30am for their march over to Buckingham Palace to relieve the old guard.

INSTITUTE OF CONTEMPORARY ARTS — ARTS CENTRE

Map p440 (ICA; ☎020-7930 9493; www.ica.org.uk; Nash House, The Mall, SW1; ⏰11am-11pm Tue-Sun, exhibition times vary; 📶; ⊖Charing Cross) **FREE** Housed in a John Nash building along the Mall, the untraditional ICA is where Picasso and Henry Moore had their first UK shows. Since then the ICA has been on the cutting (and controversial) edge of the British arts world, with an excellent range of experimental and progressive films, music nights, photography, art, lectures, multimedia works and book readings.

There's also the licensed **ICA Cafe Bar**. The complex includes an excellent bookshop.

Soho & Chinatown

SOHO — NEIGHBOURHOOD

Map p432 (⊖Tottenham Court Rd, Leicester Sq) Soho's reputation as the epicentre of nightlife and a proud gay neighbourhood is legendary and well deserved. It definitely comes into its own in the evenings, but during the day you'll be charmed by the area's bohemian side and the sheer energy of the place.

At Soho's northern end, leafy **Soho Square** (Map p432) is the area's back garden. It was laid out in 1681, and originally named King's Sq; a statue of Charles II stands in its northern half. In the centre is a tiny mock-Tudor house – the gardener's shed – whose lift was a passage to underground shelters during WWII.

South of the square is **Dean Street**, lined with bars and restaurants. No 28 was the home of Karl Marx and his family from 1851 to 1856; they lived here in extreme poverty as Marx researched and wrote *Das Kapital* in the Reading Room of the British Museum.

Old Compton Street is the epicentre of Soho's gay village. It's a street loved by all, gay or other, for its great bars, risqué shops and general good vibes.

Seducer and heart-breaker Casanova and opium-addicted writer Thomas de Quincey lived on nearby Greek St, while the parallel **Frith Street** housed Mozart at No 20 for a year from 1764.

CHINATOWN — NEIGHBOURHOOD

Map p432 (www.chinatownlondon.org; ⊖Leicester Sq) Immediately north of Leicester Sq – but a world away in atmosphere – are Lisle and Gerrard Sts, the focal point for London's Chinese community. Although not as big as Chinatowns in many other cities – it's just two streets really – this is a lively quarter with fake oriental gates, Chinese street signs, red lanterns, many restaurants and great Asian supermarkets.

London's original Chinatown was further east at Limehouse but moved here after heavy bombardments in WWII. To see it at its effervescent best, time your visit for Chinese New Year in late January/early February. Do be aware that the quality of food here varies enormously.

PICCADILLY CIRCUS — SQUARE

Map p432 (⊖Piccadilly Circus) John Nash had originally designed Regent St and Piccadilly in the 1820s to be the two most elegant streets in town but, curbed by city planners, couldn't realise his dream to the full. He would certainly be disappointed with what Piccadilly Circus has become: swamped with visitors, flanked by flashing advertisement panels and surrounded by shops flogging tourist tat.

But despite the crowds and traffic, Piccadilly Circus has become a postcard for the city, buzzing with the liveliness that makes it exciting to be in London. It was named in the 17th century for the stiff collars (picadils) that were the sartorial staple of the time (and were the making of a nearby tailor's fortune).

At the centre of the circus is the famous aluminium statue, Anteros, twin brother of Eros, dedicated to the philanthropist and child-labour abolitionist Lord Shaftesbury. The sculpture was at first cast in gold, but it was later replaced by newfangled aluminium, the first outdoor statue in that

> **ARCADE FUN**
>
> Just east of Piccadilly Circus is **London Trocadero** (Map p432; www.londontrocadero.com; 1 Piccadilly Circus, W1; ⏰10am-midnight Sun-Thu, to 1am Fri & Sat; ⊖Piccadilly Circus), a huge indoor amusement arcade that has six levels of high-tech, high-cost fun for youngsters, along with cinemas, US-themed restaurants and bowling alleys. Good to know in case the kids need a break from sightseeing.

metal. Down the years the angel has been mistaken for Eros, the God of Love, and the misnomer has stuck (you'll even see signs for 'Eros' from the Underground).

REGENT STREET STREET

Map p432 (⊖Piccadilly Circus, Oxford St) Regent St is the border separating the hoi polloi of Soho and the well heeled of Mayfair. It was designed by John Nash as a ceremonial route linking the Prince Regent's long-demolished city dwelling with the 'wilds' of Regent's Park, and was envisaged as a grand thoroughfare. Nash had to downscale his plan but it is today a well-subscribed shopping street.

The street's most famous retail outlet is undoubtedly Hamleys, London's premier toy and game store. Regent St is also famous for its Christmas light displays, which are turned on with great pomp earlier and earlier (or so it seems) each year. Last year it was mid-November.

PHOTOGRAPHERS' GALLERY GALLERY

Map p432 (www.photonet.org.uk; 16-18 Ramillies St, W1; ⏲10am-6pm Mon-Wed, Fri & Sat, to 8pm Thu, 11.30am-6pm Sun; ⊖Oxford Circus) FREE With seven galleries over three floors, an excellent cafe and a shop brimming with prints and photography books, the Photographers' Gallery has risen phoenix-like from a massive refurbishment. It awards the prestigious Deutsche Börse Photography Prize annually, which is of major importance for contemporary photographers; past winners include Richard Billingham, Luc Delahaye, Andreas Gursky, Boris Mikhailov and Juergen Teller.

Covent Garden & Leicester Square

NATIONAL GALLERY GALLERY

See p97.

NATIONAL PORTRAIT GALLERY GALLERY

See p101.

TRAFALGAR SQUARE SQUARE

See p102.

COVENT GARDEN PIAZZA SQUARE

Map p430 (www.coventgardenlondonuk.com/-/covent-garden-piazza; ⊖Covent Garden) London's first planned square is now the exclusive preserve of tourists who flock here to shop in the quaint old arcades, pay through the nose for refreshments at outdoor cafes and bars and watch street performers pretend to be statues.

On the square's west side is **St Paul's Church** (Map p430; www.actorschurch.org; Bedford St, WC2; ⏲8.30am-5pm Mon-Fri, varies Sat, 9am-1pm Sun; ⊖Covent Garden), built in 1633. When the Earl of Bedford, the man who had commissioned Inigo Jones to design the piazza, asked for the simplest church, basically no more than a barn, the architect responded by producing 'the handsomest barn in England'. It has long been regarded as the actors' church for its associations with all the nearby theatres, and contains memorials to the likes of Charlie Chaplin, Noël Coward and Vivien Leigh. The first Punch and Judy show took place in the square in 1662.

ST GILES-IN-THE-FIELDS, A LITANY OF MISERIES

Built in what used to be countryside between the City of London and Westminster, **St Giles-in-the-Fields** (Map p430; 60 St Giles High St, WC2; ⏲9am-4pm Mon-Fri; ⊖Tottenham Court Rd) isn't much to look at but its history is a chronicle of London's most miserable inhabitants.

The current structure (1733) is the third to stand on the site of an original chapel built in the 12th century to serve as a hospital for lepers. Until 1547, when the hospital closed, prisoners on their way to be executed at Tyburn stopped at the church gate and sipped a large cup of soporific ale – their last refreshment – from St Giles's Bowl. From 1650 the prisoners were buried in the church grounds. It was also within the boundaries of St Giles that the Great Plague of 1665 took hold.

In Victorian times it was London's worst slum, often mentioned in Dickens' novels. Today the drug users who hang out around the area make it feel like things haven't changed much.

An interesting relic in the church (north side) is the plain white pulpit that was used for 40 years by John Wesley, the founder of Methodism.

ROYAL OPERA HOUSE HISTORIC BUILDING

Map p430 (www.roh.org.uk; Bow St, WC2; adult/child general tour £9.50/7.50, backstage tour £12/8.50; ⏱general tour 4pm daily, backstage tour 10.30am, 12.30pm, 2.30pm Mon-Fri, 10.30am, 11.30am, 12.30pm & 1.30pm Sat; ⊖Covent Garden) On the northeastern flank of Covent Garden piazza is the gleaming Royal Opera House. The 'Velvet, Gilt & Glamour Tour' is a general 45-minute turn around the auditorium; more distinctive are the 1¼-hour backstage tours taking you through the venue – a much better way to experience the planning, excitement and hissy fits happening before a performance.

LONDON TRANSPORT MUSEUM MUSEUM

Map p430 (www.ltmuseum.co.uk; Covent Garden Piazza, WC2; adult/child £15/free; ⏱10am-6pm Sat-Thu, 11am-6pm Fri; ⊖Covent Garden) One of our favourite 'other' museums, this one looks at how London developed as a result of better transport and contains everything from horse-drawn omnibuses, early taxis, underground trains you can drive yourself and everything in between. Check out the museum shop for original and interesting souvenirs, including a great selection of historical tube posters.

LEICESTER SQUARE SQUARE

Map p430 (⊖Leicester Sq) Although Leicester Sq was very fashionable in the 19th century, the last few decades have had it synonymous with antisocial behaviour, rampant pickpocketing and outrageous cinema ticket prices (a whopping £16!). As part of the Diamond Jubilee and 2012 Olympics celebrations, the square was given an extensive £15.5 million makeover to turn it once again into a lively plaza.

Today a sleek, open-plan design replaces the once-dingy little park. It retains its many cinemas and nightclubs, and as a glamorous premiere venue it still attracts celebrities and their spotters. At the time of writing the much beloved Shakespeare Fountain (1874) was getting a facelift.

ST MARTIN-IN-THE-FIELDS CHURCH

Map p430 (www.stmartin-in-the-fields.org; Trafalgar Sq, WC2; ⏱8.30am-6pm Mon, Tues, Thu & Fri, 8.30am-5pm Wed, 9.30am-6pm Sat, 3.30-5pm Sun, usually shuts 1hr at lunch; ⊖Charing Cross) The 'royal parish church' is a delightful fusion of classical and baroque styles that was completed by James Gibbs in 1726 and serves as a model for many churches in New England. The church is well known for its excellent classical-music concerts, many by candlelight, and its links to the Chinese community (services in English, Mandarin and Cantonese).

The wonderful Cafe in the Crypt hosts jazz evenings at 8pm on Wednesday, there's brass rubbing in the shop for kids and you can visit the church with an audioguide (£3.50). Refurbishment excavations in the

COVENT GARDEN IN A NUTSHELL

Covent Garden was originally pastureland that belonged to a 'convent' associated with Westminster Abbey in the 13th century. The site became the property of John Russell, the first Earl of Bedford, in 1552. His descendants employed the architect Inigo Jones to convert a vegetable field into a square in the 17th century. He built the elegant Italian-style piazza, and its tall terraced houses soon started to draw rich socialites who coveted the central living quarters. The bustling fruit and veg market – immortalised in *My Fair Lady* where it was a flower market – dominated the piazza. London society, including such writers as Pepys, Fielding and Boswell, gathered here in the evenings looking for some action among the coffee houses, theatres, gambling dens and brothels.

Lawlessness became commonplace, leading to the formation of a volunteer police force known as the Bow Street Runners. In 1897 Oscar Wilde was charged with gross indecency in the now-closed Bow St Magistracy. A flower market designed by Charles Fowler was added at the spot where London's Transport Museum now stands.

During the 1970s the city traffic made it increasingly difficult to maintain the fruit and veg market so it was moved to Nine Elms in South London in 1974. Property developers loomed over the space and there was even talk of the market being demolished for a road but, thanks to the area's dedicated residential community who demonstrated and picketed for weeks, the piazza was saved.

FOURTH PLINTH

Three of the four plinths at Trafalgar Sq's corners are occupied by notables: King George IV on horseback, and military men General Sir Charles Napier and Major General Sir Henry Havelock. One, originally intended for a statue of William IV, has largely remained vacant for the past 150 years. The Royal Society of Arts conceived the unimaginatively titled **Fourth Plinth Project** (Map p430; www.london.gov.uk/fourthplinth) in 1999, deciding to use the empty space for works by contemporary artists. They commissioned three works: *Ecce Homo* by Mark Wallinger (1999), a life-size statue of Jesus, which appeared tiny in contrast to the enormous plinth; Bill Woodrow's *Regardless of History* (2000) and Rachel Whiteread's *Monument* (2001), a resin copy of the plinth, turned upside down, and Marc Quinn's controversial marble nude sculture of a heavily pregnant disabled woman called Alison Lapper.

The Mayor's office has since taken over what's now called the Fourth Plinth Commission, continuing with the contemporary-art theme. One of the most memorable commissions so far was Antony Gormley's *One & Other* (2009), which featured no inanimate object but simply a space for individuals to occupy – each person spent an hour on the plinth, addressing the crowds on any chosen subject, performing or simply sitting quietly. The project ran 24 hours a day for 100 days, and the rules specified that the participants spent their hour on the plinth alone, could do what they wanted as long as it wasn't illegal and were allowed to take with them anything they could carry.

Following Yinka Shonibare's *MBE Nelson's Ship in a Bottle* (2011), a wink to the square's dominant figure, Mayor Boris Johnson announced in early 2011 that artist duo Elmgreen & Dragset would present *Powerless Structures, Fig 101*, a golden boy astride a rocking horse, in 2012. It was replaced by Katharina Fritsch's *Hahn/Cock*, a huge, bright blue sculpture of a cockerel. Each artwork will be exhibited for 18 months.

last decade unearthed a 1.5-tonne limestone Roman sarcophagus in the churchyard; the yard also holds the graves of 18th-century artists Joshua Reynolds and William Hogarth.

BENJAMIN FRANKLIN HOUSE — MUSEUM

Map p430 (www.benjaminfranklinhouse.org; 36 Craven St, WC2; adult/concession £7/5; ⏲10.30am-5pm Wed-Mon; ⊖Charing Cross, Embankment) Because the house is effectively empty – there are only a few items associated with Franklin on display – the tour is conducted by a costumed guide playing Polly Stevenson, daughter of Franklin's landlord Margaret. Billed as 'museum as theatre', it's all a bit plodding and overly dramatic, though the introductory film is quite instructive. About the most interesting things in the house are the human bones discovered during conservation work in 1998, now on display in the basement. Apparently Polly's husband, William Hewson, ran his own anatomy school from here in the late 18th century.

Whitehall

NO 10 DOWNING STREET — HISTORIC BUILDING

Map p440 (www.number10.gov.uk; 10 Downing St, W1; ⊖Westminster) The official office of British leaders since 1732, when George II presented No 10 to Robert Walpole, this has also been the Prime Minister's London residence since refurbishment in 1902. For such a famous address, No 10 is a small-looking building on a plain-looking street, hardly warranting comparison with the White House, for example.

The street was cordoned off with a rather large iron gate during Margaret Thatcher's time so you won't see much. Breaking with tradition when he came to power, Tony Blair and his family (he has four children) swapped houses with the then-unmarried Chancellor Gordon Brown, who traditionally occupied the larger flat at No 11. Current Prime Minister David Cameron did the same with his three children in the summer of 2011 after extensive refurbishment of the flat.

HORSE GUARDS PARADE HISTORIC SITE

Map p440 (www.changing-the-guard.com/london-programme.html; Horse Guards Parade, off Whitehall, W1; ⏲11am Mon-Sat, 10am Sun; ⊖Westminster, St James's Park) In a more accessible version of Buckingham Palace's Changing of the Guard, the mounted troops of the Household Cavalry change guard here daily, at the official vehicular entrance to the royal palaces. A slightly less pompous version takes place at 4pm when the dismounted guards are changed. On the Queen's official birthday in June, the Trooping of the Colour is staged here.

The parade ground and its buildings were built in 1745 to house the Queen's so-called Life Guards. During the reigns of Henry VIII and his daughter Elizabeth, jousting tournaments were staged here.

BANQUETING HOUSE PALACE

Map p440 (www.hrp.org.uk/BanquetingHouse; Whitehall, SW1; adult/child £5/free; ⏲10am-5pm; ⊖Westminster) This is the only surviving part of the Tudor Whitehall Palace (1532), which once stretched most of the way down Whitehall and burned down in 1698. Designed by Inigo Jones in 1622, Banqueting House was England's first purely Renaissance building and looked like no other structure in the country at the time. Apparently, the English hated it for more than a century.

A bust outside commemorates 30 January 1649, when Charles I, accused of treason by Oliver Cromwell after the Civil War, was executed on a scaffold built against a 1st-floor window here. When the monarchy was reinstated with his son, Charles II, it inevitably became something of a royalist shrine. Look to the clock tower opposite at Horse Guards Parade. The number 2 (the time of the execution) is blacked out. In a huge, virtually unfurnished hall on the 1st floor there are nine ceiling panels painted by Peter Paul Rubens in 1635. They were commissioned by Charles I and celebrate the 'benefits of wise rule' and the Union of England and Scotland Act (1603).

INNS OF COURT

Clustered around Holborn and Fleet Sts are the Inns of Court, with quiet alleys, open spaces and a serene atmosphere. All London barristers work from within one of the four inns, and a roll-call of former members ranges from Oliver Cromwell and Charles Dickens to Mahatma Gandhi and Margaret Thatcher. It would take a lifetime working here to grasp the intricacies of the protocols of the inns; they're similar to the Freemasons – both are 13th-century creations with centuries of tradition. It's best to just soak in the dreamy atmosphere and relax.

Lincoln's Inn (Map p430; www.lincolnsinn.org.uk; Lincoln's Inn Fields, Newmans Row, WC2; ⏲grounds 7am-7pm Mon-Fri, chapel noon-2.30pm Mon-Fri; ⊖Holborn) The most attractive of the four inns has a chapel, pleasant square and picturesque gardens that invite a stroll, especially early or late in the day. The court itself, although closed to the public, is visible through the gates and is relatively intact, with original 15th-century buildings, including the Tudor Lincoln's Inn Gatehouse on Chancery Lane. Inigo Jones helped plan the well-preserved chapel, which was built in 1623.

Inner Temple (Map p430; www.innertemple.org.uk; King's Bench Walk, EC4; ⏲grounds 10am-4pm Mon-Fri, gardens 12.30-3pm Mon-Fri; ⊖Temple) and **Middle Temple** (Map p430; www.middletemple.org.uk; Middle Temple Lane, EC4; ⏲grounds 10-11.30am & 3-4pm Mon-Fri; ⊖Temple) From the Strand, look for a studded black door labelled 'Middle Temple Lane', opposite the Royal Courts building, and you'll find yourself in the sprawling complex surrounding the Temple Church and the Elizabethan Middle Temple Hall. The church was originally planned and built by the secretive Knights Templar in the mid-12th century; the hall was pieced together bit by bit after being blown to smithereens during WWII. There are wonderful gardens and courtyards at every turn. At the weekend enter from the Victoria Embankment.

Gray's Inn (www.graysinn.org.uk; Gray's Inn Rd, WC1; ⏲grounds 10am-4pm Mon-Fri, chapel 10am-6pm Mon-Fri; ⊖Chancery Lane) This inn – destroyed during WWII, rebuilt and expanded – is less interesting than the others, although the peaceful gardens are still something of a treat. The original hall saw the first-ever performance of Shakespeare's *Comedy of Errors*.

TOP SIGHT
SOMERSET HOUSE

Passing beneath the arched entrance before this splendid Palladian masterpiece, it's hard to believe that the magnificent Safra Courtyard, with its 55 dancing fountains, was a car park for tax collectors of the IRS until a spectacular refurbishment in 2000. William Chambers designed the house in 1775 for royal societies – the first purpose-built office block – and it now contains two galleries.

The **Courtauld Gallery** (Map p430; www.courtauld.ac.uk; adult/child £6/free Tue-Sun, £3/free Mon; ⌚10am-6pm; ⊖Charing Cross, Embankment or Temple) is near the Strand entrance. Have an uncrowded stroll among masterpieces by Rubens, Botticelli, Cézanne, Degas, Renoir, Manet and Monet. There are free, 15-minute talks on specific works or themes from the collection at 1.15pm every Monday and Friday and sometimes Wednesday. The **Embankment Galleries** focus on contemporary fashion, architecture, photography and design. Somerset House hosts **London Fashion Week** in February and September.

The courtyard is transformed into a popular **ice rink** in winter and used for concerts and events in summer. Particularly popular is the **Film4 Summer Screen**, an outdoor cinema in the Great Court in early August. Behind the house, there's a cafe overlooking the embankment.

DON'T MISS...

- Courtauld Gallery
- Skating in winter
- Movies in summer
- London Fashion Week

PRACTICALITIES

- Map p430
- www.somersethouse.org.uk
- The Strand, WC2
- ⌚galleries 10am-6pm, Safra Courtyard 7.30am-11pm
- ⊖Charing Cross, Embankment, Temple

CENOTAPH MEMORIAL

Map p440 (Whitehall, SW1; ⊖Westminster, Charing Cross) The Cenotaph (from the Greek *kenos taphos* for 'empty tomb'), completed in 1920 by Edwin Lutyens, is Britain's main memorial to the men and women of Britain and the Commonwealth killed during the two world wars. The Queen and other public figures lay poppies at its base on Remembrance Sunday, the second Sunday in November.

Holborn & the Strand

SIR JOHN SOANE'S MUSEUM MUSEUM

See p104.

STRAND STREET

Map p430 (⊖Charing Cross, Temple) Built in the 12th century, the Strand (from the Old English word for 'shore') runs by the Thames. Over the centuries its grandiose stone houses counted as some of the most prestigious places to live, sitting as they did on a street that connected the City and Westminster. Some of these buildings are now the Savoy Hotel, Simpson's, King's College and Somerset House.

But modern times haven't treated the Strand with much respect; the street is overrun by offices, cheap restaurants and odd souvenir shops, though the Savoy and wonderful Somerset House still grace it with their presence. Other interesting addresses include **Twinings** (Map p430) at No 216 – a teashop opened by Thomas Twining in 1706 and thought to be the oldest company in the capital still trading on the same site and owned by the same family – and the stamp- and coin-collectors' mecca **Stanley Gibbons** (Map p430) at No 339.

ROYAL COURTS OF JUSTICE HISTORIC BUILDING

Map p430 (www.justice.gov.uk; 460 The Strand, WC2; ⌚9am-4.30pm Mon-Fri; ⊖Temple) FREE Where the Strand joins Fleet St, you'll see the entrance to this gargantuan melange of Gothic spires, pinnacles and burnished Portland stone, built in 1874. It is a public building and you're allowed to sit in on court proceedings; the list of cases to be heard is both on the website and available at reception in the Great Hall.

TOP SIGHT
MADAME TUSSAUDS

It may be kitschy and terribly overpriced (a family ticket will set you back £108), but Madame Tussauds still makes for a fun-filled day. There are photo ops with your dream celebrity at the A-List Party (Daniel Craig, Lady Gaga, George Clooney, the Beckhams), the Bollywood gathering (studs Hrithik Roshan and Salman Khan) and the Royal Appointment (the Queen, Harry, William and Kate). If you're into politics, get up close and personal with Barack Obama, Vladimir Putin or even London Mayor Boris Johnson with his signature mop haircut.

The whole place is pretty commercial, with shops and spending opportunities in every room, but the Spirit of London taxi ride through the city's history is educational fun, the Chamber of Horrors as scary as ever and the 3-D Super Heroes extravaganza very high-tech.

The museum has a long and interesting history since the French artist and model-maker Marie Tussaud (1761–1850) started making death masks of people guillotined during the French Revolution. She came to London in 1803 and exhibited around 30 wax models in nearby Baker St, providing visitors with their only glimpse of the famous and infamous before photography was widespread.

DON'T MISS...

- Lady Gaga
- The Queen
- David & Victoria Beckham
- Barack Obama
- Daniel Craig

PRACTICALITIES

- Map p438
- ☎0870 400 3000
- www.madame-tussauds.co.uk
- Marylebone Rd, NW1
- adult/child £30/26
- 9/10am-5/7pm (seasonal)
- Baker St

The building was designed in 1874 by aspiring cathedral builder GE Street; apparently it took so much out of him that he died of a stroke shortly before its completion. The statues at the top represent Christ in Majesty, King Solomon and King Alfred the Great.

ST CLEMENT DANES CHURCH

Map p430 (www.raf.mod.uk/stclementdanes; The Strand, WC2; 9am-4pm; Temple) Christopher Wren designed the original church in 1682 but only the walls and a steeple added by James Gibbs in 1719 survived WWII bombing, and the church was rebuilt as a memorial to Allied airmen. Today it is the chapel of the Royal Air Force (RAF), and there are some 800 slate badges of different squadrons set into the pavement of the nave.

The statue in front of the church quietly and contentiously commemorates the RAF's Sir Arthur 'Bomber' Harris, who led the bombing raids that obliterated Dresden and killed up to 25,000 civilians during WWII. Should you pass the church at 9am, noon or 3pm, you may hear the bells chiming a distantly familiar tune. It's the 18th-century English nursery rhyme that incorporates the names of London churches starting: 'Oranges and lemons, say the bells of St Clements', with the soothing final lines: 'Here comes a chopper to chop off your head/Chop, chop, chop, chop, the last man's dead!'

TWO TEMPLE PLACE GALLERY

Map p430 (www.twotempleplace.org; 2 Temple Pl, WC2 ; 10am-4.30pm Mon & Thu-Sat, to 9pm Wed, 11am-4.30pm Sun; Temple) FREE This neo-Gothic house built in the late 1890s for William Waldorf Astor, of hotel fame and once the richest man in America, is now the only gallery in London devoted to showcasing art from outside the capital. Visit as much to see the opulent house as the collections on display. Check the website to see what's being exhibited.

HUNTERIAN MUSEUM MUSEUM

Map p430 (www.rcseng.ac.uk/museums/hunterian; Royal College of Surgeons, 35-43 Lincoln's Inn Fields, WC2; 10am-5pm Tue-Sat; Holborn) FREE The collection of anatomical specimens of pioneering surgeon John Hunter (1728–93) inspired this fascinating, slightly morbid, little-known, yet fantastic London museum. Among the more bizarre items on display are the skeleton of a 2.3m Irish giant named Charles Byrne, half of mathematician Charles Babbage's brain (the other part is in the Science Museum) and, incongruously, Winston Churchill's dentures.

The atmosphere is less gory than it used to be and allows clear viewing of such things as animal digestive systems (forensically documented in formaldehyde) and the 'hearing organ' of a blue whale. The art gallery contains Hunter's own paintings of 'exotics': Chinese with queues, Cherokee Indians with tomahawks and the original Siamese twins, Chang and Eng, with, well, each other. Upstairs there's a display on surgery techniques, which will impress and disgust in equal measure. There's a free curator-led guided tour at 1pm on Wednesday. The excellent audioguide costs £3.50.

STAPLE INN HISTORIC BUILDING

Map p430 (www.stapleinn.co.uk; Staple Inn, off Holborn, WC1; ⊖Chancery Lane) The 16th-century half-timbered shopfront facade is the main interest at Staple Inn (1580), the last of eight Inns of Chancery whose functions were superseded by the Inns of Court in the 18th century. The buildings, mostly postwar reconstructions, are now occupied by offices and aren't open to the public, although you can have a look around the courtyard.

Marylebone

SHERLOCK HOLMES MUSEUM MUSEUM

Map p438 (www.sherlock-holmes.co.uk; 221b Baker St, NW1; adult/child £8/5; ⏲9.30am-6pm; ⊖Baker St) Fans of Arthur Conan Doyle's classic detective novels will enjoy examining the three floors of reconstructed Victoriana, complete with deerstalkers, burning candles and flickering grates, but may baulk at the dodgy waxworks of Professor Moriarty and 'the Man with the Twisted Lip' at the top. It's a pity too that there is so little information on the author himself.

For years there was a dispute over the famous address, since the occupant of 221b Baker St, the fictional abode of Sherlock Holmes, was the Abbey National Bank. A

TOP SIGHT
WALLACE COLLECTION

Arguably London's finest smaller gallery, the Wallace Collection is an enthralling glimpse into 18th-century aristocratic life. The sumptuously restored Italianate mansion shelters a treasure-trove of 17th- and 18th-century paintings, porcelain and furniture collected by one family. It was bequeathed to the nation by the widow of Sir Richard Wallace (1818–90) on condition it should always be on display in the centre of London and the paintings hung as specified in his will.

Among the many highlights are paintings by Rembrandt, Delacroix, Titian, Rubens, Poussin, Velázquez and Gainsborough in the stunning **Great Gallery**. Particularly rich is its collection of Rococo paintings and furniture and porcelain that belonged to Queen Marie-Antoinette of France. There's also a spectacular array of medieval and Renaissance armour and a sweeping staircase – deemed one of the best examples of French interior architecture anywhere. The excellent audioguide costs £3.

The fabulous glass-roofed courtyard restaurant Wallace (p125) is in the heart of the museum.

DON'T MISS...

- Great Gallery
- Marie-Antoinette's bric-a-brac
- Furniture by André-Charles Boulle
- Boucher's *Madame de Pompadour*
- Medieval and Renaissance armour

PRACTICALITIES

- Map p438
- www.wallacecollection.org
- Hertford House, Manchester Sq , W1
- ⏲10am-5pm
- ⊖Bond St

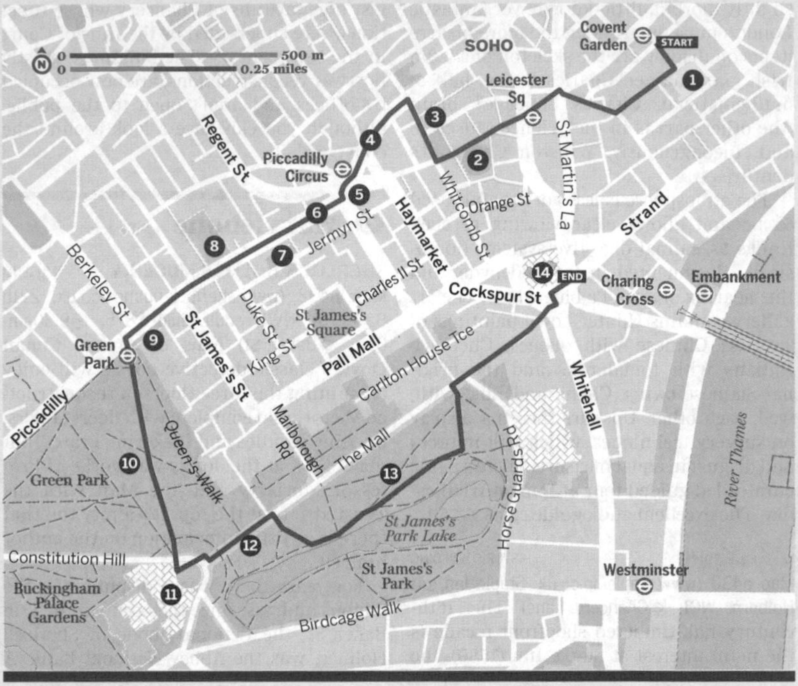

Neighbourhood Walk
The West End

START COVENT GARDEN TUBE STATION
END TRAFALGAR SQ
LENGTH 2.5 MILES; 1½ HOURS

This walk takes you through the heart of the West End, from Covent Garden's chic shopping streets to Trafalgar Sq via Chinatown and leafy St James's Park.

First, head to busy **1 Covent Garden Piazza** (p111) and enjoy the street performers outside St Paul's Church. Continue along King and Garrick Sts; turn left on Long Acre and you'll arrive at renovated **2 Leicester Square** (p112), where many international blockbuster films premiere. Turn right on Wardour St; you'll soon come to the Oriental gates of **3 Chinatown** (p110) on your right. The area is especially attractive around Chinese New Year, when hundreds of lanterns adorn the streets.

Turn left on **4 Shaftesbury Ave**, where you'll find some of the West End's most prestigious theatres. At the end of the avenue is hectic **5 Piccadilly Circus** (p110), 'London's Times Square', full of flashing ads, shops and tourists.

Make your way west along **6 Piccadilly**; this avenue gives just a hint of the aristocratic St James's and Mayfair neighbourhoods. Pop into **7 St James's Piccadilly** (p108), Wren's only original church. Further along on the right, you'll see stately Burlington House, home of the **8 Royal Academy of Arts** (p108), before passing the famous **9 Ritz Hotel** (p338).

Turn left into **10 Green Park** (p109), a quiet space with stunning oak trees and old-style street lamps. **11 Buckingham Palace** (p93) is at the bottom of the park, past the beautiful Canada Gates.

Walk down the grandiose **12 Mall**; on the right is the lovely **13 St James's Park** (p107). Views of Buckingham Palace and Whitehall are stunning from the footbridge over the lake. At the end of the Mall is **14 Trafalgar Square** (p102), dominated by Nelson's Column and the National Gallery. There are also great views of Big Ben and the Houses of Parliament from its south side.

bank secretary even had the full-time job of responding to fan mail. When the bank moved out in 2005, the Royal Mail recognised the museum's exclusive right to receive post addressed to 'Sherlock Holmes'.

Mayfair

HANDEL HOUSE MUSEUM MUSEUM

Map p438 (www.handelhouse.org; 25 Brook St, W1; adult/child £6/2; 10am-6pm Tue, Wed, Fri & Sat, 10am-8pm Thu, noon-6pm Sun; Bond St) George Frederick Handel lived in this 18th-century Mayfair building for 36 years until his death in 1759; this is where he composed some of his finest works, including *Water Music, Messiah, Zadok the Priest* and *Fireworks Music*. Following extensive restorations the house looks as it would have when the great German-born composer was in residence. Enter from Lancashire Court.

Early editions of Handel's operas and oratorios, portraits of musicians and singers who worked with Handel and musical instruments are on the 1st floor; musicians regularly come to practise so you may be treated to a free concert. On the 2nd floor there are more exhibits and quite a good film with music. The staff attending the rooms are all Handel enthusiasts and wonderfully knowledgeable.

Funnily enough, the house at No 23 (now part of the museum) was home to a musician as different from Handel as could be imagined: American guitarist Jimi Hendrix (1942–70), who lived there from 1968 until his death. A blue plaque on the exterior attests to his and Handel's residencies; there's a small exhibition on Hendrix's life and music on the 2nd floor.

EATING

Many of the city's most eclectic, fashionable and, quite simply, best restaurants are dotted around the West End. As with most things in London, it pays to be in the know: while there's a huge concentration of mediocre places to eat along the main tourist drags, the best eating experiences are frequently tucked away on backstreets and not at all obvious.

Westminster & St James's

VINCENT ROOMS MODERN EUROPEAN £

Map p440 (020-7802 8391; www.thevincentrooms.com; Westminster Kingsway College, Vincent Sq, SW1; mains £8-12; noon-2pm Mon-Fri, 6-8pm Wed & Thu; Victoria) Care to be a guinea pig for student chefs at Westminster Kingsway College, where celebrity chef Jamie Oliver was trained? Service is eager to please, the atmosphere in both the Brasserie and the Escoffier Room smarter than expected, and the food (including veggie options) ranges from wonderful to exquisite – at prices that put other culinary stars to shame.

INN THE PARK BRITISH ££

Map p440 (020-7451 9999; www.innthepark.com; St James's Park, SW1; mains £14.50-22.50; 8am-6pm Oct-Mar, 8am-11pm Apr-Sep; Charing Cross, St James's Park) This stunning wooden cafe and restaurant in St James's Park is run by Irish wonderchef Oliver Peyton and offers cakes and tea as well as excellent British food, with the menu changing monthly. The terrace, which overlooks one of the park's fountains with views of Whitehall's grand buildings, is wonderful in warm weather.

MINT LEAF INDIAN ££

Map p432 (020-7930 9020; www.mintleafrestaurant.com; Suffolk Pl, Haymarket, SW1; mains £16-23; noon-3pm Mon-Fri, 5.30-11pm daily; Piccadilly) This large, very central place just up from Trafalgar Sq represents a new breed of Indian restaurant – all sleek design with a highly inventive menu. Dishes come in large and small sizes – a boon for a couple anxious to sample a few – and the vegetarian options are bountiful. Set lunch of two/three courses is £14/18.

Bloomsbury

ORCHARD VEGETARIAN £

Map p430 (www.orchard-kitchen.co.uk; 11 Sicilian Ave, WC1; mains £6.50-7; 8am-8pm Mon-Sat, 10am-7pm Sat; Holborn) A boon for vegetarians in central London is this delightful retro-style cafe on a quiet pedestrian street. Mains include specialities like broccoli and Yorkshire blue-cheese pie, a sarnie (that's a sandwich to Londoners) and mug of soup is just £4.95 and desserts are unusual – try the toasted oat and currant cake with Horlicks icing.

LADY OTTOLINE
GASTROPUB ££

(☎020-7831 0008; www.theladyottoline.com; 11a Northington St, WC1; mains £12-20; ⏰noon-11pm Mon-Sat, to 10.30pm Sun; ⊖Chancery Lane) Bloomsbury can sometimes feel like a culinary wasteland, but the arrival of this buzzy gastropub named after a patron of the Bloomsbury Set has helped change that. You can eat in the noisy pub downstairs but the cosy dining room above is much nicer. Favourites like Welsh rarebit and steak pies are way above average.

ABENO
JAPANESE ££

Map p436 (www.abeno.co.uk; 47 Museum St, WC1; mains £9.50-21; ⏰noon-10pm Mon-Sat; ⊖Tottenham Court Rd) This Japanese restaurant specialises in *okonomiyaki,* a savoury pancake from Osaka. The pancakes consist of cabbage, egg and flour combined with the ingredients of your choice (there are more than two dozen varieties, including anything from sliced meats and vegetables to egg, noodles and cheese) and they're cooked on the hotplate at your table. There's also more familiar teppanyaki and yakisoba dishes.

NORTH SEA FISH RESTAURANT
FISH & CHIPS ££

Map p436 (www.northseafishrestaurant.co.uk; 7-8 Leigh St, WC1; mains £10-20; ⏰noon-2.30pm & 5.30-11pm Mon-Sat; ⊖Russell Sq) The North Sea sets out to cook fresh fish and potatoes – a simple ambition in which it succeeds admirably. Look forward to jumbo-sized plaice or halibut fillets, deep-fried or grilled, and a huge serving of chips. There's takeaway next door if you can't face the rather austere dining room.

Fitzrovia

BUSABA EATHAI
THAI £

Map p436 (www.busaba.com; 22 Store St, WC1; mains £7-12.50; ⏰noon-11pm Mon-Thu, to 11.30pm Fri & Sat, to 10pm Sun; ⊖Goodge St) The Store St premises of this hugely popular mini-chain is slightly less hectic than some of the other West End outlets, but it retains all the features that have made it a roaring success: sleek Asian interior, large communal wooden tables and heavenly cheap and tasty Thai dishes like *pad thai* noodles, green and red curries and fragrant noodle soups.

SAGAR
VEGETARIAN £

Map p436 (www.sagarveg.co.uk; 17a Percy St, W1; mains £5-8.50; ⏰noon-3pm & 5.30-11pm Mon-Thu, noon-11pm Fri & Sat, to 10pm Sun; 🖉; ⊖Tottenham Court Rd) This branch of a mini-chain specialises in vegetarian dishes from the southern Indian state of Karnataka. It's cheap, filling and of a standard; try the paper masala dosa, an enormous lentil pancake with spicy potato filling. Thalis – steel trays with a selection of small dishes – are £14 to £17.

★NEWMAN STREET TAVERN
BRASSERIE ££

Map p436 (☎020-3667 1445; www.newmanstreettavern.co.uk; 48 Newman St, W1; mains £12-20; ⏰noon-11pm Mon-Sat, 10.30am-5pm Sun; ⊖Goodge St) A branch of a prosaic dim-sum restaurant chain has metamorphosed into one of the loveliest new brasseries in the West End. As you'll gather from the tray of large crabs and other briny things on display in the front window, the emphasis here is on seafood, with Colchester oysters, Devon crab and local cod in profusion.

But fish-fearing carnivores need not worry; they're accommodated with the likes of venison and mushroom stew and the signature hay-baked black-faced-lamb breast. The wine list appears overwhelming but is broken down into some original headings and the staff are incredibly knowledgeable and helpful.

DABBOUS
MODERN EUROPEAN ££

Map p436 (☎020-7323 1544; www.dabbous.co.uk; 39 Whitfield St, W1; mains £12-16; ⏰noon-3pm & 5.30-11.30pm Tue-Sat; ⊖Goodge St) This award-winning eatery is the creation of Ollie Dabbous, everyone's favourite new chef, so book ahead for dinner or come for lunch (four courses £28). The combination of flavours is inspired – squid with buckwheat, pork with mango, rhubarb with lavender – and at first seems at odds with the industrial, hard-edged decor. But it all works exceedingly well.

FINO
SPANISH ££

Map p436 (☎020-7813 8010; www.finorestaurant.com; 33 Charlotte St, enter from Rathbone St, W1; tapas £4-19; ⏰noon-2.30pm Mon-Fri, 6-10.30pm Mon-Sat; ⊖Goodge St) Set in a glamorous basement with a fabulous bar, Fino is a tapas restaurant with a difference (in a city overwhelmed with dreary and uninventive examples of same). Try the salt cod fritters, piquilla peppers with mushrooms and prawns, and the squid a la plancha with fennel for a feast of innovative and delightful Spanish cooking.

ROKA JAPANESE ££

Map p436 (☎020-7580 6464; www.rokarestaurant.com; 37 Charlotte St, W1; mains £12-37; ⊙noon-3.30pm & 5.30-11.30pm Mon-Sat, to 10.30pm Sun; ⊖Goodge St) This stunner of a Japanese restaurant mixes casual dining (wooden benches) with savoury titbits from the *robatayaki* (grill) kitchen in the centre. It has modern decor, the dominating materials being grey steel and floor-to-ceiling windows.

VILLANDRY BRASSERIE ££

Map p438 (☎020-7631 3131; www.villandry.com; 170 Great Portland St, W1; mains £9-19.50; ⊙8am-10pm Mon-Sat, 9am-5pm Sun; ; ⊖Great Portland St) This excellent brasserie has moved away from its strong Gallic slant and gone more international. It has an attractive market/delicatessen attached so freshness and quality of ingredients is guaranteed. Try the confit of duck leg or one of the several daily fish dishes.

HAKKASAN CHINESE £££

Map p436 (☎020-7927 7000; www.hakkasan.com; 8 Hanway Pl, W1; mains £11-61; ⊙noon-12.30am Mon-Wed, to 1.30am Thu-Sat, to midnight Sun; ⊖Tottenham Court Rd) This basement restaurant – hidden down a back alleyway – successfully combines celebrity status, stunning design, persuasive cocktails and sophisticated Chinese food. The low, nightclub-style lighting makes it a good spot for dating or a night out with friends (the bar serves seriously creative cocktails). Book far in advance or come for lunch (three courses for £29, also available from 6pm to 7pm).

Soho & Chinatown

★**NORDIC BAKERY** SCANDINAVIAN £

Map p432 (www.nordicbakery.com; 14a Golden Sq, W1; snacks £4-5; ⊙8am-8pm Mon-Fri, 9am-7pm Sat, 10am-7pm Sun; ⊖Piccadilly Circus) This is the perfect place to escape the chaos that is Soho and relax in the dark-wood-panelled space on the south side of a delightful 'secret' square. Lunch on Scandinavian smoked-fish sandwiches, goat's cheese and beetroot salad or have an afternoon break with coffee and rustic oatmeal cookies.

MILDREDS

Map p432 (www.mildreds.co.uk; 45 Lexington St, W1; mains £8-10.50; ⊙noon-11pm Mon-Sat; ; ⊖Oxford Circus, Piccadilly Circus) Central London's most inventive vegetarian restaurant, Mildred's heaves at lunchtime so don't be shy about sharing a table in the sky-lit dining room. Expect the likes of Sri Lankan sweet potato and cashew nut curry, pumpkin and ricotta ravioli, Middle Eastern meze, wonderfully exotic (and filling) salads and delicious stir-fries. There are also vegan and gluten-free options.

CEVICHE PERUVIAN £

Map p432 (www.cevicheuk.com; 17 Frith St, W1; mains £5-11; ⊙noon-11.30pm Mon-Sat, to 10.30pm Sun; ⊖Leicester Sq) Peruvian food is the new black in London, and this colourfully decorated *bodega* serves some of the most authentic. Start with *cancha* (large crunchy corn kernels) and move onto one of the signature dishes of *ceviche* (fish or shellfish marinated in lime juice with chillies, onion and coriander). Salads made with quinoa (a type of grain) and palm hearts are excellent.

SPUNTINO AMERICAN £

Map p432 (www.spuntino.co.uk; 61 Rupert St, W1; mains £6-10; ⊙11am-midnight Mon-Sat, noon-11pm Sun; ⊖Piccadilly Circus) Offering an unusual mix of speakeasy decor and surprisingly creative fusion American–Italian food, Spuntino is a delight at every turn. Try old favourites such as macaroni cheese, cheese burger with jalapeno chillis and, as a dessert, peanut butter and jelly sandwich. Seating is at the bar or counters at the back.

KOYA NOODLES £

Map p432 (www.koya.co.uk; 49 Frith St, W1; dishes £7-15; ⊙noon-3pm & 5.30-10.30pm Mon-Sat, to 10pm Sun; ⊖Tottenham Court Rd, Leicester Sq) Arrive early or late if you don't want to queue at this excellent Japanese eatery. Londoners come for their fill of authentic udon noodles (served hot or cold, in soup or with a cold sauce), the efficient service and very reasonable prices.

POLPO ITALIAN £

Map p432 (www.polpo.co.uk; 41 Beak St, W1; ⊙dishes £6-9.50; ⊖Oxford Circus, Piccadilly Circus) OK, we hadn't heard of them either

... apparently *cicchetti* – 'Italian tapas', for want of a better word – are all the rage in backstreet *bàcari* in Venice. Polpo serves a lovely selection, including such unusual pairings as grilled fennel with white anchovy. More substantial are the half-dozen types of flavourful meatballs and the mini pizzette. The Venetian painter Canaletto lived here.

PRINCI ITALIAN £

Map p432 (www.princi.co.uk; 135 Wardour St, W1; mains £7.50-12.50; ⌚8am-11.30pm Mon-Sat, 8.30am-10pm Sun; 📶; ⊖Tottenham Court Rd, Piccadilly Circus) Most people come to Princi by accident rather than design; they were just walking by and suddenly noticed a mouth-watering array of breads and Italian pastries through the restaurant's huge bay windows. Before they know it, they're tucking into focaccia, authentic pizzas or a hearty salad with a slice of tiramisu.

JEN CAFÉ CHINESE £

Map p430 (4-8 Newport Pl, WC2; mains £5-10; ⌚10.30am-8.30pm Mon-Wed, to 9.30pm Thu-Sun; ⊖Leicester Sq) This is the best place to come for homemade wonton soup and dumplings – bar none. And you can be assured of their freshness by looking through the plate glass window where they're in the process of being made.

BONE DADDIES RAMEN BAR NOODLES £

Map p432 (www.bonedaddiesramen.com; 21 Peter St, W1; dishes £8-11; ⌚noon-3pm Mon-Fri & 5.30-10pm Mon, to 11pm Tue & Wed, to midnight Thu & Fri, noon-midnight Sat, noon-9pm Sun; ⊖Tottenham Court Rd) For a bowl of sustaining ramen noodles you couldn't do better than Bone Daddies (and we'll come back just for the name). Choose your 'foundation' – be it noodles in broth or a salad – and then add a topping or two (*chāshū* pork, pulled chicken, bean sprouts etc).

GELUPO ICE CREAM £

Map p432 (www.gelupo.com; 7 Archer St, W1; pot £3-5; ⌚noon-11pm Mon-Thu, to midnight Fri & Sat, to 10pm Sun; ⊖Piccadilly Circus) The queue outside Gelupo can stretch down the street on summer weekends, and it's no wonder: this is central London's most authentic gelateria. All the ingredients are natural and the servings are generous. Go for traditional flavours such as pistachio or bitter chocolate or try original creations such as *marron glacé* (candied chestnut) or bergamot.

FERNANDEZ & WELLS CAFE £

Map p432 (www.fernandezandwells.com; 73 Beak St, W1; dishes £4.50-6; ⌚7.30am-6pm Mon-Fri, from 9am Sat & Sun; ⊖Piccadilly Circus) A wonderful taste of Spain in Soho, Fernandez serves simple lunches of *jamón* (ham) and cured meats and cheese platters. Grilled chorizo sandwiches are perfect for quick lunchtime bites. The place is usually busy, with a relaxed atmosphere. Excellent coffee.

KULU KULU JAPANESE £

Map p432 (www.kulukulu.co.uk; 76 Brewer St, W1; sushi £2-4; ⌚noon-2.30pm & 5-10pm Mon-Sat; ⊖Piccadilly Circus) This simple, bustling place just off Piccadilly Circus is one of the best and most affordable conveyor-belt Japanese places in town. The offerings are pretty standard (tuna and salmon *maki* rolls, prawn tempura, teriyaki chicken etc) but it's all really tasty and fresh. At busy times, you'll be expected to leave as soon as you put your chopsticks down.

BAOZI INN CHINESE £

Map p430 (25 Newport Ct, WC2; mains £5-7.50; ⌚noon-10.30pm Sun-Thu, to 11pm Fri & Sat; ⊖Leicester Sq) Decorated in a vintage style that plays at kitsch communist pop (complete with old Chinese communist military marches tinkling out of the speakers), Baozi Inn serves quality Beijing- and Chengdu-style street food, such as dan dan noodles with spicy pork and baozi buns (steamed buns with stuffing) handmade daily. It's authentic, delicious and cheap food in often-unreliable Chinatown.

LONGJI CHINESE £

Map p430 (47-49 Charing Cross Rd, WC2; mains £7-10; ⌚11.30am-11pm Mon-Sat, 11am-10.30pm Sun; ⊖Leicester Sq) Longji is as authentic a Hong Kong canteen as you'll find in Chinatown. Chinese students flock here for the tasty Cantonese food served double fast. Order any of the various noodle or rice dishes (fried ho fun noodles with beef in black bean sauce is great) and swish it down with taro bubble tea.

NUDE ESPRESSO CAFE £

Map p432 (www.nudeespresso.com; 19 Soho Sq, W1; dishes £3.50-7.50; ⌚8am-5pm Mon-Fri, 10am-6pm Sat & Sun; ⊖Tottenham Court Rd) It's not just the name – we live in hope – that keeps us coming back to this cafe enviably positioned in the northeast corner of delightful Soho Sq. We also like the hearty breakfasts, the enlightened lunches (try the pesto mushroom burger) and the wonderful cakes.

★ BRASSERIE ZÉDEL FRENCH ££

Map p432 (☎020-7734 4888; www.brasseriezedel.com; 20 Sherwood St, W1; mains £8-20; ⏲8am-11pm Mon-Fri, noon-11pm Sat, noon-8pm Sun; ⊖Piccadilly Circus) This brasserie in the renovated art deco ballroom of a former Piccadilly hotel is the French-est eatery west of Calais. Choose from among the usual favourites, including *choucroute alsacienne* (sauerkraut with sausages and charcuterie, £14) and duck-leg confit with Puy lentils. The set menus (£8.25/11.75 for two/three courses) and plats du jour (£12.95) offer excellent value.

ANDREW EDMUNDS MODERN EUROPEAN ££

Map p432 (☎020-7437 5708; www.andrewedmunds.com; 46 Lexington St, W1; mains £11.50-19.50; ⏲noon 3.30pm & 5.30-10.45pm Mon-Fri, 12.30-3.30 & 5.30-10.45pm Sat, 1-4pm & 6-10.30pm Sun; ⊖Oxford Circus, Piccadilly Circus) This cosy little place, in situ since 1986, is exactly the sort of restaurant you wish you could find everywhere in Soho. Two floors of wood-panelled bohemia with a hand-written menu of French (confit of duck) and European (beetroot and goat's cheese tart) country cooking – it's a real find and reservations are essential.

YAUATCHA CHINESE ££

Map p432 (☎020-7494 8888; www.yauatcha.com; 15 Broadwick St, W1; dishes £4-17; ⏲noon-11.30pm Mon-Sat, to 10.30pm Sun; ⊖Piccadilly Circus, Oxford Circus) This most glamorous of dim sum restaurants is divided into two: the upstairs dining room offers a delightful blue-bathed oasis of calm from the chaos of Berwick St Market, while downstairs has a smarter, more atmospheric feel with constellations of 'star' lights. Both serve exquisite dim sum and have a fabulous range of teas.

BOCCA DI LUPO ITALIAN ££

Map p432 (☎020-7734 2223; www.boccadilupo.com; 12 Archer St, W1; mains £8-27.50; ⏲12.30-3.45pm & 5.30-11pm Mon-Sat, to 9pm Sun; ⊖Piccadilly Circus) Hidden in a dark Soho backstreet, Bocca radiates elegant sophistication. The menu has dishes from across Italy (and informs you which region they're from) and every main course can be ordered as a large or small portion. There's a good choice of Italian wines and fantastic desserts. It's often full, so make sure to book.

5TH VIEW INTERNATIONAL ££

Map p432 (☎020-7851 2433; www.5thview.co.uk; 5th fl, Waterstone's Piccadilly, 203-205 Piccadilly, W1; mains £9-15; ⏲9am-10pm Mon-Sat, noon-5pm Sun; ⊖Piccadilly Circus) The views of Westminster from the top floor of Waterstone's on Piccadilly are just the start. Add a relaxed, sophisticated dining room and some lovely food, and you have a gem of a place. We love the Greek meze and antipasti platters (small/large £9/15) to share, and the larger-than-average breakfast selection.

BAR SHU CHINESE ££

Map p432 (☎020-7287 8858; www.bar-shu.co.uk; 28 Frith St, W1; mains £10-31; ⊖Piccadilly Circus, Leicester Sq) This is the restaurant that introduced London to the joys of fiery Szechuan cuisine and it remains more authentic than much of the competition. Dishes are redolent of smoked chillies and the all-important (and ubiquitous) peppercorn. Service can be a little brusque, but the food is delicious and the portions huge.

HIX MODERN BRITISH ££

Map p432 (☎020-7292 3518; www.hixsoho.co.uk; 66-70 Brewer St, W1; mains £17.50-24; ⏲noon-11.30pm; ⊖Piccadilly Circus) Celebrity chef Mark Hix's flagship restaurant is all about seasonal British food. You'll find such classics as fish-fingers and chips and sticky toffee pudding given an elaborate makeover, as well as more unusual fare: hake with Kentish fava beans or goat curry. The decor is an eclectic collection of artworks from such British artists as Tracey Emin and Damien Hirst.

ARBUTUS MODERN EUROPEAN ££

Map p432 (☎020-7734 4545; www.arbutusrestaurant.co.uk; 63-64 Frith St, W1; mains £18-20; ⏲noon-2.30pm & 5-11pm Mon-Sat, noon-3pm & 5.30-10.30pm Sun; ⊖Tottenham Court Rd) This Michelin-starred brainchild of Anthony Demetre does great British food, focusing on seasonal produce. Try such inventive dishes as pigeon, sweet onion and beetroot tart, squid and mackerel 'burger' or *pieds et paquets* (lamb tripe parcels with pig trotters). Don't miss the bargain set 'working lunch' menu at £17.95 for two courses and £19.95 for three. Booking essential.

WEST END FRUIT & VEG MARKETS

Berwick Street Market (Map p432; Berwick St, W1; ⏲9am-6pm Mon-Sat; ⊖Piccadilly Circus, Oxford Circus) South of Oxford St and running parallel to Wardour St, this fruit-and-vegetable market has managed to hang onto its prime location since about 1830. It's a great place to put together a picnic or shop for a prepared meal, and to hear Cockney accents straight out of central casting.

Marylebone Farmers Market (Map p438; www.lfm.org.uk/markets/marylebone; Cramer St, W1; ⏲10am-2pm Sun; ⊖Baker St) This weekly farmers market is the largest in town with 30 to 40 producers coming from within a 100-mile radius of the M25. It's expensive but charming, reflecting the local demographic.

GAY HUSSAR
HUNGARIAN ££

Map p432 (☎020-7437 0973; www.gayhussar.co.uk; 2 Greek St, W1; mains £13-18; ⏲12.15-2.30pm & 5.30-10.45pm Mon-Sat; ⊖Tottenham Court Rd) This is the Soho of the 1950s, when dining was still done grand style in wood-panelled rooms with brocade and sepia prints on the walls. Portions are huge; try the crispy roast duck with all the trimmings or the 'Gypsy quick dish' of pork medallions, onions, green peppers and paprika. A two-/three-course lunch is £19.50/23.50.

BARRAFINA
SPANISH ££

Map p432 (☎020-7813 8016; www.barrafina.co.uk; 54 Frith St, W1; tapas £5-18.50; ⏲noon-3pm & 5-11pm Mon-Sat, 1-3.30pm & 5.30-10pm Sun; ⊖Tottenham Court Road) Tapas are always better value in Spain, but the quality of this food justifies the prices. Along with *gambas al ajillo* (prawns in garlic, £8.50), there are more unusual things such as tuna tartare and grilled quail with aioli. Customers sit along the bar so it's not a good choice for groups.

10 GREEK ST
MODERN EUROPEAN ££

Map p432 (☎020-7734 4677; www.10greekst.com; 10 Greek St, W1; mains £12-19; ⏲noon-11.30pm Mon-Sat; ⊖Tottenham Court Rd) This understated bistro, which takes bookings at lunch but not dinner, is making quite a splash with a menu that takes top-quality British produce and puts a Mediterranean spin on it (hake with pickled grapes, lamb with roasted artichokes). Puddings are especially fine and service is seamless.

GAUTHIER SOHO
FRENCH ££

Map p432 (☎020-7494 3111; www.gauthiersoho.co.uk; 21 Romilly St, W1; 2-/3-course set lunch £18/25, with wine £26/33; ⏲noon-2.30pm & 5.30-10.30pm Tue-Sat; ⊖Leicester Sq) Alexis Gauthier's temple of gastronomy – a find if there ever was one – is housed over two floors of a discreet Georgian town house where you have to buzz to be let in. Evening meals are a delight but pricey at £40/50/60 for three/four/five courses. Do what we do and treat yourself to a luxurious weekday lunch for half the price.

BURGER & LOBSTER SOHO
AMERICAN ££

Map p432 (www.burgerandlobster.com; 36 Dean St, W1; mains £20; ⏲noon-10.30pm Mon-Sat, to 10pm Sun; ⊖Leicester Sq, Piccadilly Circus) London's seemingly insatiable appetite for burgers has taken a slight detour at this branch of an award-winning mini chain. The concept is simple: £20 gets you a burger, a 1.5lb lobster or a lobster roll as well as a carton of chips and salad. Seating is in bright-red banquettes and the atmosphere buzzing, almost party-like.

GOLDEN DRAGON
CHINESE ££

Map p432 (www.goldendragonlondon.com; 28-29 Gerrard St, W1; mains £8-20; ⏲noon-11.30pm Mon-Thu, to midnight Fri & Sat; 11am-11pm Sun; ⊖Leicester Sq) If we had to choose one Chinese restaurant in Chinatown for a sitdown meal, this would probably be it. It's one of the more reliable eateries, both for quality and value and is usually at least half-full with Chinese diners (always a sign of quality). Dim sum is available until about 5pm.

PITT CUE
BARBECUE ££

Map p432 (www.pittcue.co.uk; 1 Newburgh St, W1; mains £11.50-16.50; ⏲noon-3pm & 5.30-10.30pm Mon-Sat, noon-5pm Sun; ⊖Oxford Circus) This one-time food truck selling American-style barbecue and other meaty dishes has parked permanently and moved into funny little digs with seating up and downstairs just around the corner from Carnaby St. Choose from pulled pork, beef ribs or smoked chipotle wings, add pickles and slaw then wash it all down with a Sam Adams or (for the abstemious) A&W root beer.

POLLEN STREET SOCIAL MODERN EUROPEAN £££

Map p432 (☎020-7290 7600; www.pollenstreet-social.com; 8-10 Pollen St, W1; mains £29-37; ⏲noon-2.45pm & 6-10.45pm Mon-Sat; ⊖Oxford Circus) Jason Atherton's cathedral to haute cuisine would be out of reach to anyone not on a hefty expense account, but the excellent-value set lunch (£26/29.50 for two/three courses) makes it accessible to all. A generous two-hour slot allows ample time to linger over such delights as lime-cured salmon, braised ox 'tongue 'n' cheek' and a choice from the dessert bar.

Covent Garden & Leicester Square

★DISHOOM INDIAN £

Map p430 (☎020-7420 9320; www.dishoom.com; 12 Upper St Martin's Lane, WC2; £4-12.50; ⏲8am-11pm Mon-Thu, 8am-midnight Fri, 10am-midnight Sat, 10am-10pm Sun; ⊖Covent Garden) This laidback eatery takes the fast-disappearing old-style 'Bombay cafe' and gives it the kiss of life. It's distressed with a modern twist – all ceiling fans and Bollywood photos. The yummy dishes include caff favourites like lamb raan bun, a spicy pulled lamb 'sandwich', okra fries and snack foods like bhel, Bombay mix and puffed rice with pomegranate and lime.

CANELA PORTUGUESE £

Map p430 (www.canelacafe.com; 33 Earlham St, WC2; mains £9-13; ⏲9am-10pm Mon, to 10.30pm Tue-Sat, 8am-8pm Sun; ✎; ⊖Covent Garden) This small cafe in the heart of Covent Garden next to thc Donmar Warehouse theatre serves tasty Portuguese and Brazilian dishes. Try the delicious *pão de queijo,* a bread and cheese roll with one of the filling salads, or opt for the Portuguese national dish *feijoada,* a bean stew with smoked meat. There's a good selection of vegetarian dishes too.

MONMOUTH COFFEE COMPANY CAFE £

Map p430 (www.monmouthcoffee.co.uk; 27 Monmouth St, WC2; pastry & cakes from £2.50; ⏲8am-6.30pm Mon-Sat; ⊖Tottenham Court Rd, Leicester Sq) Essentially a shop selling beans from just about every coffee-growing country, Monmouth, here since 1978, has a few wooden alcoves at the back where you can squeeze in and savour blends from around the world as well as cakes from local patisseries.

MUSEUM RESTAURANTS

National Dining Rooms (Map p430; ☎020-7747 2525; www.peytonandbyrne.co.uk; 1st fl, Sainsbury Wing, National Gallery, Trafalgar Sq, WC2 ; mains £15.50-20.50; ⏲10am-5.30pm Sat-Thu, till 8.30pm Fri; ⊖Charing Cross) Chef Oliver Peyton's restaurant at the National Gallery styles itself as 'proudly and resolutely British', and what a great idea. The menu features an extensive and wonderful selection of British cheeses for a light lunch. For something more filling, go for the monthly changing County Menu, honouring regional specialities from across the British Isles. Set lunch is £19.50/23.50 for two/three courses.

Portrait (Map p430; ☎020-7312 2490; www.npg.org.uk/visit/shop-eat-drink.php; 3rd fl, National Portrait Gallery, St Martin's Pl, WC2; mains £18.50; ⏲11.45am-2.45pm daily, 5.30-8.15pm Thu-Sat; ⊖Charing Cross) This stunningly located restaurant above the excellent National Portrait Gallery – with views over Trafalgar Sq and Westminster – is a great place to relax after a morning or afternoon at the gallery. The brunch (10am to 11.30am) and afternoon tea (3.30 to 4.45pm) come highly recommended; set meals are £25/30 for two/three courses. Booking is advisable.

Wallace (Map p438; ☎020-7563 9505; www.wallacecollection.org/visiting/thewallacerestaurant; Hertford House, Manchester Sq, W1; mains £15.50-22.50; ⏲10am-5pm Sun-Thu, to 11pm Fri & Sat; ⊖Bond St) There are few more idyllically placed restaurants than this brasserie in the enclosed courtyard of the Wallace Collection. The emphasis is on seasonal French-inspired dishes, with the daily menu offering two- or three-course meals for £22/26. Afternoon tea is £17.

MISHKIN'S AMERICAN £

Map p430 (www.mishkins.co.uk; 25 Catherine St, WC2; dishes £8-13; ⌚11.15am-11.15pm Mon-Sat, 8am-11pm Sun; ⊖Covent Garden) A welcome addition to the dining scene just round the corner from frenetic Covent Garden is this modern American diner with Jewish (not kosher) favourites such as chicken matzo ball soup, chopped chicken livers and salmon and cream cheese on a bagel. The baked cheesecake is the real deal.

WAHACA MEXICAN £

Map p430 (www.wahaca.com; 66 Chandos Pl, WC2; mains £7-10; ⌚noon-11pm Mon-Sat, to 10.30pm Sun; ⊖Covent Garden) This delightful cantina, a branch of an ever-expanding chain, styles itself as a 'Mexican market eating' experience. You can choose to share a selection of street snacks (tacos, tostadas, *quesadillas*) or go for more traditional mains such as grilled fish with chilli or a seafood salad. Wash it down with one of a dozen tequilas.

ROCK & SOLE PLAICE FISH & CHIPS £

Map p430 (47 Endell St, WC2; mains £10-11.50; ⌚11.30am-10.30pm Mon-Sat, noon-9.30pm Sun; ⊖Covent Garden) The approach at this no-nonsense fish-and-chip shop dating back to Victorian times is simplicity itself: basic wooden tables under the trees in summer (downstairs in the cooler months), simple decor inside and delicious cod, haddock or skate in batter served with a generous portion of chips. You can eat in or take away.

SALT CAFE £

Map p430 (www.saltwc2.co.uk; 34 Great Queen St, WC2; dishes £4.50-7; ⌚7.30am-7pm Mon-Fri, from 10am Sun; ⊖Holborn) This new kid on the block southeast of Holborn – an 'espresso lunch and tea bar', if you will – is all white walls and furnishings made from recycled wood. It's good for breakfast, lunch (try the daily stew on offer) and something sweet when tea time rolls around.

FOOD FOR THOUGHT VEGETARIAN £

Map p430 (www.foodforthought-london.co.uk; 31 Neal St, WC2; mains £5-8.50; ⌚noon-8.30pm Mon-Sat, to 5pm Sun; ✎; ⊖Covent Garden) This tiny vegetarian cafe, in situ for four decades, is big on sociability and flavour, and small on price and space. Food ranges from soups and salads to stews and stir-fries with brown rice. Dishes might be vegan, organic and/or gluten-free. Food for Thought is earthy, unpretentious and deservedly packed.

NOTES CAFE £

Map p430 (www.notes-uk.co.uk; 31 St Martin's Lane, WC2; dishes £5-8; ⌚7.30am-9pm Mon-Wed, to 10pm Thu & Fri, 9am-10pm Sat, 10am-6pm Sun; ⊖Charing Cross) An authentic place in a tourist ghetto, Notes has great coffee, tea and wine. Come for the lunchtime range of salads, sandwiches, soups and tarts. In the evening there are cheese and meat platters. The place also sells jazz CDs and DVDs

GREEN MAN & FRENCH HORN MODERN EUROPEAN ££

Map p430 (☎020-7836 2645; www.greenmanfrenchhorn.co; 54 St Martin's Lane, WC2; £11.50-25; ⌚noon-3pm & 5.30-11pm Mon-Sat; ⊖Leicester Sq, Charing Cross) Set in a long narrow space that was once a Victorian pub but has now been given a postmodern patina, this new eatery does some wonderful new things with class-A British produce (eg squid and black pudding). More bistro than restaurant, it's very relaxed and service is seamless.

DELAUNAY BRASSERIE ££

Map p430 (☎020-7499 8558; www.thedelaunay.com; 55 Aldwych, WC2; mains £6.50-27.50; ⌚7am-midnight Mon-Sat, to 11pm Sun; ⊖Temple, Covent Garden) This flashy new brasserie across from Bush House is a kind of Franco-German hybrid, where schnitzels and wieners sit happily beside croque-monsieurs and *choucroute alsacienne*. Even more relaxed is the adjacent **Counter** (Map p430; ⌚7am-7.30pm Mon-Fri, from 10.30am Sat), where you can drop in for a nosh of chicken noodle soup and a New York–style hot dog.

Brunch is from 11am to 5pm at the weekend and tea (£22.50, or £32.50 with Champagne) is daily from 3pm.

GREAT QUEEN STREET BRITISH ££

Map p430 (☎020-7242 0622; 32 Great Queen St, WC2; mains £12-16; ⌚noon-2.30pm & 6-10.30pm Mon-Sat, noon-3pm Sun; ⊖Holborn) The menu at what is one of Covent Garden's best places to eat is seasonal (and changes daily), with an emphasis on quality, hearty dishes and good ingredients – there are always delicious stews, roasts and simple fish dishes. The atmosphere is lively, with a small bar downstairs. The staff are knowledgeable about the food and wine they serve and booking is essential.

GIACONDA DINING ROOM MODERN EUROPEAN ££

Map p430 (☎020-7240 3334; www.giacondadining.com; 9 Denmark St, WC2; mains £15-19.50; ⌚noon-2.30pm Tue-Fri, 5.30-9.30pm Mon-Sat; ⊖Tottenham Court Rd) A tiny room in a 17th-century building off Charing Cross Rd hides some of the best food around, with European staples such as duck confit, baked gnocchi, great steak tartare, vitello tonnato and good fresh fish of the day. The wine list is decent and you'll be greeted by friendly staff with a carafe of sparkling water.

J SHEEKEY SEAFOOD £££

Map p430 (☎020-7240 2565; www.j-sheekey.co.uk; 28-32 St Martin's Ct, WC2; mains £16-42; ⌚noon-3pm daily, 5.30pm-midnight Mon-Sat, 6-11pm Sun; ⊖Leicester Sq) A jewel of the local dining scene, this incredibly smart restaurant, whose pedigree stretches back to 1896, has four elegant, discreet and spacious wood-panelled rooms in which to savour the riches of the sea, cooked simply and exquisitely. The oyster bar, popular with pre- and post-theatre punters, is another highlight. The three-course weekend lunch is £26.50.

BALTHAZAR BRASSERIE £££

Map p430 (☎020-3301 1155; www.balthazar.com; 8 Russell St, WC2; mains £18-43; ⌚7.30am-midnight Mon-Fri, 8am-1am Sat, 8am-midnight Sun; ⊖Covent Garden) The opening of the London branch of this pricey New York–based restaurant (and its yummy boulangerie adjacent) was the culinary event of early 2013. Few have been disappointed by the mostly French fare on offer (moules frites, bouillabaisse, duck confit) with the odd nod to *les rosbifs* ('roast beefs', or Britons) in the way of shepherd's pie.

RULES BRITISH £££

Map p430 (☎020-7836 5314; www.rules.co.uk; 35 Maiden Lane, WC2; mains £19-29; ⌚noon-11.30pm Mon-Sat, to 10.30pm Sun; ⊖Covent Garden) Established in 1798, this very posh and very British establishment is London's oldest restaurant. The menu is inevitably meat-oriented – Rules specialises in classic game cookery, serving up tens of thousands of birds between mid-August an[d] from its own estate – but fish d[ishes are] also available. Puddings are tra[ditional] crumbles, sticky toffees and trea[cle ...] lashings of custard.

CANTINA LAREDO MEXICAN £££

Map p430 (☎020-7420 0630; www.cantinalaredo.co.uk; 10 Upper St Martin's Lane, WC2; mains £14-27; ⌚noon-11.30pm Mon-Thu, to midnight Fri & Sat, to 10.30pm Sun; ⊖Covent Garden) Mexican food might not be quite the new Thai in London but its popularity has grown and this cantina serves modern, enlightened versions of all the favourites (fajitas, chile relleno) as well as some more inspired dishes like lamb rump in a pumpkin-seed crust with pistachio pipian sauce. Colourful and very upbeat surrounds.

Holborn

KIMCHEE KOREAN £

Map p430 (www.kimchee.uk.com; 71 High Holborn, WC1; mains £7-8.50; ⌚11.30am-11pm; ⊖Holborn) Named after Korea's signature dish (pickled spicy cabbage), Kimchee has combined a zen-like interior with neutral colours and the soft glow of dozens of enormous lampshades with the buzz of an open kitchen and vast dining room. The food is good, and excellent value: try sharing a few dishes from the charcoal barbecue and the many sides, as Koreans do.

FLEET RIVER BAKERY CAFE £

Map p430 (www.fleetriverbakery.com; 71 Lincoln's Inn Fields, WC2; dishes £6-10; ⌚7am-7pm Mon-Wed, to 9pm Thu & Fri, 9am-6pm Sat; ⊖Holborn) Our favourite new cafe in London has gained even a few more points now it has extended its hours on Thursday and Friday. Good for lunch (quiche, soup, sandwiches), great for coffee, wi-fi that always works and some supper club events. But Saturday brunch is our favourite: heavenly eggs benedict.

ASADAL KOREAN ££

Map p430 (www.asadal.co.uk; 227 High Holborn, WC1; mains £8-20; ⌚noon-2.30pm & 6-10.30pm

…-Sat, 6-10pm Sun ; ⊖Holborn) If you fancy Korean but want a bit more style thrown into the act, head for this spacious basement restaurant next to the Holborn tube station. The *kimchi* (pickled Chinese cabbage with chillies) is searing and the barbecues (£8 to £14) are done on your table.

The *bibimbab* – rice served in a sizzling pot topped with thinly sliced beef, preserved vegetables and chilli-laced soybean paste – is the best in town.

SHANGHAI BLUES CHINESE £££

Map p430 (☎020-7404 1668; www.shanghaiblues.co.uk; 193-197 High Holborn, WC1; mains £14-52; ⏱noon-midnight; ⊖Holborn) A former Victorian library now houses one of London's most stylish Chinese restaurants. The dark and atmospheric interior – think black and blue tables and chairs punctuated by bright red screens – recalls imperial China with a modern twist. The menu is just as arresting, particularly the 'new style' dim sum served as appetisers, the roast duck and the twice-cooked pork belly.

On Friday and Saturday nights, you can also enjoy live jazz till 11pm.

Marylebone

GOLDEN HIND FISH & CHIPS £

Map p438 (73 Marylebone Lane, W1; mains £5-11; ⏱noon-3pm & 6-10pm Mon-Fri; ⊖Bond St) This 90-year-old chippie has a classic interior, chunky wooden tables and builders sitting alongside folks in suits. And from the vintage fryer come ace fish and chips.

FISHWORKS SEAFOOD ££

Map p438 (☎020-7935 9796; www.fishworks.co.uk; 89 Marylebone High St, W1; mains £12.50-38; ⏱noon-10pm; ⊖Baker St) The emphasis is on the freshest seafood and, just to get the point home, you enter the restaurant via the fishmongers! There are some nice English specialities to try such as Dover sole, Dartmouth crab and Colchester oysters, but you'll also find seafood delights from across the pond or on the Mediterranean, including lobster, tuna steak and fish soup.

LOCANDA LOCATELLI ITALIAN ££

Map p438 (☎020-7935 9088; www.locandalocatelli.com; 8 Seymour St, W1; mains £12.50-32; ⏱noon-3pm daily, 6.45-11pm Mon-Sat, 6.45-10.15pm Sun; ⊖Marble Arch) This dark but quietly glamorous restaurant in an otherwise unremarkable Marble Arch hotel remains one of London's hottest tables, and you're likely to see some famous faces being greeted by celebrity chef Giorgio Locatelli. The restaurant is renowned for its pasta dishes, and the mains include five fish and five meat dishes. Booking is essential.

IL BARETTO ITALIAN ££

Map p438 (www.ilbaretto.co.uk; 43 Blandford St, W1; mains £11-32; ⏱noon-3pm Mon-Fri, 12.30-4pm Sat & Sun, 6.30-10.30pm daily; ⊖Baker St, Bond St) An unpretentious trattoria that seems to be winning local custom, Il Baretto specialises in good, wood-fired-oven pizza and such simple Italian dishes as penne with tomato sauce and sausage, while sometimes venturing into exciting territory with its delicious langoustine grill.

LA FROMAGERIE CAFE ££

Map p438 (www.lafromagerie.co.uk; 2-6 Moxon St, W1; mains £7-16.50; ⏱8am-7.30pm Mon-Fri, 9am-7pm Sat, 10am-6pm Sun; ⊖Baker St) This deli-cafe has bowls of delectable salads, antipasto, peppers and beans scattered about the long communal table. Huge slabs of bread invite you to tuck in, and all the while the heavenly waft from the cheese room beckons. Cheese boards come in small and large (£8.75 and £13.50).

REUBENS JEWISH ££

Map p438 (☎020-7486 0035; www.reubensrestaurant.co.uk; 79 Baker St, W1; mains £10-24; ⏱11.30am-4pm & 5.30-10pm Sun-Thu, to 2hr before sunset Fri; ⊖Baker St) This glatt kosher cafe-restaurant has all the Ashkenazi favourites: gefilte fish, latkes and the famous salt beef as well as more complicated (and filling) main courses. It's pricey for what you get, but if you answer to a higher authority, it's of course money well spent.

PROVIDORES & TAPA ROOM FUSION £££

Map p438 (☎020-7935 6175; www.theprovidores.co.uk; 109 Marylebone High St, W1; 2/3/4/5 courses £33/47/57/63; ⏱9am-10.30pm Mon-Fri, 10am-10pm Sat & Sun; ⊖Baker St) This place is split over two levels: tempting tapas (£2.50 to £17) on the ground floor (no bookings); and outstanding fusion cuisine in the elegant and understated dining room above. The food at Providores is truly original and tastes divine: try the Sri Lankan spiced short ribs, the Cajun pork belly with Puy lentils or the beef fillet with Szechuan-pickled shiitake mushrooms.

There is also a fantastic brunch on Saturdays and Sundays.

Mayfair

BRICIOLE ITALIAN £

(☎020-7723 0040; www.briciole.co.uk; 20 Homer St, W1; mains £6-12; ⊖Edgware Rd) This trattoria fronted by a cafe and a deli is tiny but perfectly formed. It serves pretty basic stuff: Palermo-style sweet-and-sour meatballs, Tuscan barbecue, all kinds of pasta. But it's very tasty and excellent value, especially for this part of town.

SAKURA JAPANESE £

Map p432 (www.sakuramayfair.com; 23 Conduit St, W1; mains £7-13.50; ⊖Oxford Circus) This very authentic Japanese restaurant has something for everyone throughout the day – from sushi and sashimi (£2 to £7.50) to tempura, sukiyaki and a host of sets (£9 to £16).

BAR TRATTORIA SEMPLICE ITALIAN ££

Map p438 (☎020-7491 8638; www.bartrattoriasemplice.com; 22 Woodstock St, W1; mains £15-23; ⏲noon-2.30pm & 7-10pm Mon-Sat; ⊖Bond St) A lovely little authentic trattoria opposite a higher-end Italian restaurant with the same name offering superb pasta dishes (try the lasagne) and charcuterie boards. The excellent two-course lunch (£19.50) is worth a trip in itself.

EL PIRATA SPANISH ££

(☎020-7491 3810; www.elpirata.co.uk; 5-6 Down St, W1; tapas £3.75-7; ⏲noon-11.30pm Mon-Fri, from 6pm Sat; ⊖Green Park) Rather silly name notwithstanding, this is a good Spanish restaurant with a great list of tapas and traditional mains such as paella (from £19). There are two set menus (£16.50 and £21) if you can't decide which tapas to have. The selection of Spanish wines is one of the best in London.

LA PORTE DES INDES INDIAN ££

Map p438 (☎020-7224 0055; www.laportedesindes.com; 32 Bryanston St, W1; mains £15-25; ⊖Marble Arch) 'Indian cuisine with a difference' might sound like hyberbole but it's a fact: 'Gateway to the Indies' serves the food of Pondicherry (now Puducherry), a French colony on the southeast coast until 1962. Gallic-inspired dishes include *kari de mouton* (actually a goat curry) and *magret de canard pulivaar* (Barbary duck breast fillets with tamarind).

The decor is a riot of colour and kitsch that works. If you really can't make up your mind, order a thali (£25), a tray with a selection of the best Franco-Indian dishes, either meat-based or vegetarian.

GREENHOUSE MODERN EUROPEAN £££

Map p438 (☎020-7499 3331; www.greenhouserestaurant.co.uk; 27a Hay's Mews, W1; 2-/3-course set lunch £25/29, dinner £65/75; ⏲noon-2.30pm Mon-Fri, 6.30-11pm Mon-Sat; ⊖Green Park) Located at the end of a wonderful sculpted 'garden', Greenhouse offers some of the best food in Mayfair served with none of the attitude commonly found in restaurants of this class. The tasting menu (£90) is only for the intrepid and truly hungry. Greenhouse doles out so many dishes, from *amuses-gueule* (appetisers) and inter-course sorbets to petits fours, you'll never get up.

MOMO MOROCCAN £££

Map p432 (☎020-7434 4040; www.momoresto.com; 25 Heddon St, W1; mains £18-28; ⏲noon-2.15pm Mon-Sat, 6.30-11.30 daily; ⊖Piccadilly Circus) This atmospheric Moroccan restaurant is stuffed with cushions and lamps, and staffed by tambourine-playing waiters. Service is very friendly and the dishes are as exciting as you dare to be, so after the meze eschew the traditional and ordinary *tajine* (stew cooked in a traditional clay pot) and couscous, and tuck into the splendid Moroccan speciality *pastilla* (pigeon pie).

There's outside seating in this quiet backstreet in the warmer months.

NOBU JAPANESE £££

(☎020-7447 4747; www.noburestaurants.com; 1st fl, Metropolitan Hotel, 19 Old Park Lane, W1; mains £13-48; ⏲noon-2.15pm Mon-Fri, 12.30-2.30pm Sat & Sun, 6-10pm Mon-Thu & Sun, 6-11pm Fri & Sat; ⊖Hyde Park Corner) You'll have to book a month in advance to eat here (or resign yourself to 6pm or 10pm if you book just a few days before), but you'll get to chew at and view the greatest celebrity restaurant magnet in town. Signature dishes include the black cod with miso at a whopping £42. Decor understated, service discreet and efficient.

LE BOUDIN BLANC FRENCH £££

Map p438 (☑020-7499 3292; www.boudinblanc. co.uk; 5 Trebeck St, W1; mains £17-26; ⊙noon-2.30pm & 7-11pm; ⊕Green Park) This has to be one of the best French restaurants in the capital: the meat is cooked to perfection, the sauces mouth-wateringly good and the portions huge. The *frites* (French fries) are the best you'll find this side of La Manche. And there is, of course, a whopping 500 wines to choose from. No wonder it's always full.

WILD HONEY MODERN EUROPEAN £££

Map p438 (☑020-7758 9160; www.wildhoneyrestaurant.co.uk; 12 St George St, W1; mains £24-30; ⊙noon-2.30pm daily, 6-11pm Mon-Sat, 6-10pm Sun; ⊕Oxford Circus) Wild Honey receives consistently good reviews for its food and wine, stunning wood-panelled dining room and professional service. The menu is seasonal, so surprises await; you'll generally find a combination of inventive dishes, such as salad of Dorset crab with avocado and leaves, and classic mains like grilled rib-eye of beef with bone marrow and young spring vegetables, cooked to perfection.

TAMARIND INDIAN £££

Map p438 (☑020-7629 3561; www.tamarindrestaurant.com; 20 Queen St, W1; mains £18.50-24.50; ⊙noon-2.45pm Sun-Fri, 5.30-11pm Mon-Sat, 6-10.30pm Sun; ⊕Green Park) A mix of spicy Moghul classics and new creations have earned this northwest Indian restaurant plaudits and a loyal clientele. The set lunches are a good deal (two/three courses £19.50/22.50).

🍷 DRINKING & NIGHTLIFE

Over the last decade or so, the East End has trumped the West End as the coolest place in town. But this is still a wonderful place for a night out – Friday and Saturday nights are buzzing with excitement and decadence, particularly the areas around Soho, Leicester Sq and Covent Garden where you'll find people, booze and rickshaws in the streets till the early hours, and bars and clubs that range from the swanky to the skanky – with everything in between.

🍷 Bloomsbury & Fitzrovia

★LAMB PUB

(www.thelamblondon.com; 94 Lamb's Conduit St, WC1; ⊙noon-11pm Mon-Wed, to midnight Thu-Sat, to 10.30pm Sun; ⊕Russell Sq) The Lamb's central mahogany bar with beautiful Victorian dividers (also called 'snob screens' as they allowed the well-to-do to drink in private) has been a favourite with locals since 1729. Nearly three centuries later, its popularity hasn't waned, so come early to bag a booth. It has a decent selection of Young's bitters and a genial atmosphere perfect for unwinding.

QUEEN'S LARDER PUB

Map p436 (www.queenslarder.co.uk; 1 Queen Sq, WC1; ⊙11.30am-11pm Mon-Sat, noon-10.30pm Sun; ⊕Russell Sq) In a lovely square southeast of Russell Sq is this pub, so called because Queen Charlotte, wife of 'Mad' King George III, rented part of the pub's cellar to store special foods for her husband while he was being treated nearby. It's a tiny but wonderfully cosy pub; there are benches outside for fair-weather fans and a dining room upstairs.

DUKE PUB

(www.dukepub.co.uk; 7 Roger St, WC1; ⊙noon-11pm Mon-Sat, to 10.30pm Sun; ⊕Chancery Lane) As unexpected as sunshine in November, this secluded little pub in the heart of Bloomsbury is like a step back in time to the inter-war years. Original art-deco decor and furnishings are everywhere (burl wood bar, Bakelite phone, pink walls) with Vera Lynn crooning somewhere in the background. Couple of real ales on offer.

NEWMAN ARMS PUB

Map p436 (www.newmanarms.co.uk; 23 Rathbone St, W1; ⊙noon-11.30pm Mon-Fri; ⊕Goodge St) A lovely local that is one of the few family-run pubs in central London, this is a one-tiny-room affair with a 150-year history of providing great beer to thirsty locals. George Orwell and Dylan Thomas were regulars, and Michael Powell's *Peeping Tom* was filmed here in 1960. There's also an excellent pie (from £10) room upstairs.

MUSEUM TAVERN PUB

Map p436 (www.taylor-walker.co.uk/pub/museum-tavern-bloomsbury/c0747; 49 Great Russell St, WC1; ⊙11am-11.30pm Mon-Thu, to midnight Fri &

Sat, 10am-10pm Sun; ⊖Holborn, Tottenham Court Rd) This is where Karl Marx used to retire for a well-earned pint after a hard day inventing communism in the British Museum's Reading Room, and where George Orwell boozed after his literary musings. A lovely traditional pub set around a long bar, it has friendly staff and is popular with academics and students alike.

BRADLEY'S SPANISH BAR BAR

Map p436 (www.bradleysspanishbar.co.uk; 42-44 Hanway St, W1; ⌚noon-11pm Mon-Sat, 3-10.30pm Sun; ⊖Tottenham Court Rd) Bradley's is only vaguely Spanish in decor, but much more authentic in its choice of booze: San Miguel, Cruzcampo, *tinto de verano* (red wine with rum and lemonade) and that teen favourite, sangria. Punters are squeezed under low ceilings in the nooks of the basement, while a vintage vinyl jukebox plays rock tunes of their choice.

LONDON COCKTAIL CLUB COCKTAIL BAR

Map p436 (www.londoncocktailclub.co.uk; 61 Goodge St, W1; ⌚4.30pm-midnight Mon-Fri, from 5pm Sat; ⊖Goodge St) There are cocktails and then there are cocktails. The guys in this slightly tatty subterranean bar will shake, stir, blend and smoke (yes, smoke) you some of the most inventive, colourful and punchy concoctions in creation. Try the smoked apple martini or the squid ink sour. And relax. You'll be staying a lot longer than you thunk (errr, make that thought).

FITZROY TAVERN PUB

Map p436 (16 Charlotte St; ⌚noon-11pm Mon-Sat, to 10.30pm Sun; ⊖Goodge St) In the years before and after WWII, the Fitzroy was the hangout of literary giants like George Orwell and Dylan Thomas. Today it's a typical downtown boozer – though a bit rough round the edges – and part of the popular Sam Smith's chain, which means plenty of ales and specialist beers at rock-bottom prices.

Soho & Chinatown

★OPIUM COCKTAIL BAR

Map p432 (☎020-7734 7276; www.opiumchinatown.com; 15-16 Gerrard St, W1; ⌚5pm-midnight Mon-Wed, to 2am Thu-Sat, noon-midnight Sun) Towering above Chinatown's main drag, what touts itself as a 'cocktail and dim sum parlour' could easily pass as an opium den-cum-brothel with Suzie Wong as host. Everything is in various shades of scarlet, there's a bartender's table with unmarked bottles (surprise, surprise) and the dim sum (£7 to £11) is made with ingredients available at the moment. Call ahead.

Look for the jade-coloured door just west of Macclesfield St. And if you can't choose your poison, let us help: it's the signature Opium Cocktail No 1, with rum, absinthe, kaffir lime syrup and mandarin and ginger juice poured over dry ice. You'll be smoking.

LAB SOHO COCKTAIL BAR

Map p432 (www.labbaruk.com; 12 Old Compton St, W1; ⌚4pm-midnight Mon-Sat, to 10.30pm Sun; ⊖Leicester Sq, Tottenham Court Rd) A long-standing Soho favourite for over a decade, the London Academy of Bartenders (to give it its full name) has some of the best cocktails in town. The list is the size of a small book but, fear not, if you can't make your way through it, just tell the bartenders what you feel like and they'll concoct something divine.

EXPERIMENTAL COCKTAIL CLUB COCKTAIL BAR

Map p432 (www.experimentalcocktailclublondon.com; 13a Gerrard St, W1; ⌚6pm-3am Mon-Sat, to midnight Sun; ⊖Leicester Sq, Piccadilly Circus) The Experimental is a sensational cocktail bar in Chinatown with an unmarked door (it's next to the Four Seasons restaurant). The interior, with its soft lighting, mirrors, bare brick wall and elegant furnishings, matches the sophistication of the cocktails: rare and original spirits, vintage Champagne and homemade fruit syrups. Booking not essential; there's a £5 cover charge after 11pm.

WHITE HORSE PUB

Map p432 (45 Rupert St, W1; ⌚noon-11pm Mon-Sat, to 10.30pm Sun; ⊖Piccadilly Circus, Leicester Sq) A lovely pub in a very busy corner of Soho, the White Horse ticks all the boxes: friendly staff, cheap drinks (it's part of the Sam Smith brewery empire) and a great traditional interior with etched glass and wood panels. The upstairs area is particularly cosy and usually quieter than downstairs.

FRENCH HOUSE BAR

Map p432 (www.frenchhousesoho.com; 49 Dean St, W1; ⌚noon-11pm Mon-Sat, to 10.30pm Sun;

SEX, DRUGS & ROCK 'N' ROLL – THE HISTORY OF SOHO

Soho's character was formed by many waves of immigration. Residential development started in the 17th century, after the Great Fire of 1666 had levelled much of the city. Greek and Huguenot refugees and, later, the 18th-century influx of Italian, Chinese and other artisans and radicals into Soho replaced the bourgeois residents, who moved out of the area and into Mayfair. During the following century Soho was no more than a slum, with cholera frequently attacking the impoverished residents. Despite its difficulties, the cosmopolitan vibe attracted writers and artists, and the overcrowded area became a centre for entertainment, with restaurants, taverns and coffee houses springing up.

The 20th century was even more raucous, when a fresh wave of European immigrants settled in, making Soho a bona fide bohemian enclave for two decades after WWII. Ronnie Scott's famous jazz club, originally in Gerrard St, provided Soho's soundtrack from the 1950s, while the likes of Jimi Hendrix, the Rolling Stones and Pink Floyd had early gigs at the legendary Marquee club, which used to be on Wardour St. Soho had long been known for its seediness but when the hundreds of prostitutes who served the Square Mile were forced off the streets and into shop windows, it became the city's red-light district and a centre for porn, strip joints and bawdy drinking clubs. Gay liberation soon followed, and by the 1980s Soho was the hub of London's gay scene, as it remains today. The neighbourhood has a real sense of community, best absorbed on a weekend morning when Soho almost feels like a village.

⊖Leicester Sq) French House is Soho's legendary boho boozer with a history to match: this was the meeting place of the Free French Forces during WWII, and De Gaulle is said to have drunk here often, while Dylan Thomas, Peter O'Toole and Francis Bacon all ended up on the wooden floor at least once.

Come to sip on Ricard, French wine or Kronenbourg and check out the quirky locals. Be warned: beer is served by the half-pint only. Above-average pub grub (mains £6.50 to £12) is served upstairs noon to 4pm weekdays.

EDGE
GAY

Map p432 (www.edgesoho.co.uk; 11 Soho Sq, W1; ⌚3pm-1am Mon-Thu, to 3am Fri & Sat, to 11.30pm Sun; ⊖Tottenham Court Rd) Overlooking Soho Sq in all its four-storey glory, the Edge is London's largest gay bar and heaves every night of the week: there are dancers, waiters in skimpy outfits, good music and a generally super friendly vibe. There's a heavy straight presence, as it's so close to Oxford St. So much the better.

CANDY BAR
LESBIAN

Map p432 (www.ku-bar.co.uk; 4 Carlisle St, W1; ⌚3pm-3am Mon & Wed-Fri, from 1pm Sat, 1-9.30pm Sun; ⊖Tottenham Court Rd) AKA Ku Bar Girls, this brilliant watering hole has been the centre of London's small but active lesbian scene for years. Busy most nights of the week, this is very much a girls' space (though one male guest per two women is allowed) and this should definitely be your first port of call on the London lesbian scene.

VILLAGE
GAY

Map p432 (www.village-soho.co.uk; 81 Wardour St, W1; ⌚4pm-1am Mon-Sat, to 11.30pm Sun; ⊖Piccadilly Circus) The Village is always up for a party, whatever the night of the week. There are karaoke nights, 'discolicious' nights, go-go dancer nights – take your pick. And if you can't wait to strut your stuff until the clubs open, there is a dance floor downstairs, complete with pole, of course.

NORMAN'S COACH & HORSES
PUB

Map p432 (www.coachandhorsessoho.co.uk; 29 Greek St, W1; ⌚11am-11.30pm Mon-Thu, to midnight Fri & Sat, noon-10.30pm Sun; ⊖Leicester Sq) Oh, the times they are a-changing. Once famous as the unreconstructed boozer where *Spectator* columnist Jeffrey Bernard drank himself to death amidst a regular clientele of soaks, writers, hacks, tourists and those too drunk to lift their heads off the counter, this is now London's first vegetarian pub (mains £7.50 to £9). We wish them all the luck in the world.

YARD GAY

Map p432 (www.yardbar.co.uk; 57 Rupert St, W1; ⏲4-11.30pm Mon-Wed, 3-11.30pm Thu, 2pm-midnight Fri & Sat, 2-10.30pm Sun; ⊖Piccadilly Circus) This old Soho favourite attracts a cross-section of the great and the good. It's fairly attitude-free, perfect for pre-club drinks or just an evening out. There are DJs upstairs in the Loft most nights as well as a friendly crowd in the al fresco (heated in season) Courtyard Bar below.

LOOP BAR BAR

Map p438 (www.theloopbar.co.uk; 19 Dering St, W1; admission £10 after 10pm Fri & Sat; ⏲noon-11pm Mon, to midnight Tue, to 1am Wed, to 3am Thu & Fri, 5pm-3am Sat; ⊖Oxford Circus) Just off Oxford Circus, Loop has three floors of fun: a street-level bar, a sleek basement bar with leather booths and chandeliers and, on the level below that, Groovy Wonderland, a disco-style club with flashing dancefloors, platform shoes on the walls and mirror balls everywhere. Fun, fun, fun.

JOHN SNOW PUB

Map p432 (39 Broadwick St, W1; ⏲noon-11pm; ⊖Oxford Circus, Piccadilly Circus) Named after the doctor who established that cholera was a waterborne disease (the site of the culprit water pump, the key to his discovery, is marked by a granite slab outside), this is a classic Victorian pub, with no music, just plenty of chat and cheap ale, lager, bitter and stout from British brewery Sam Smith's.

ENDURANCE PUB

Map p432 (www.theendurance.co.uk; 90 Berwick St, W1; ⏲12.30-11pm Mon-Sat; ⊖Oxford Circus, Piccadilly Circus) A Soho favourite, the Endurance has a retro jukebox full of indie hits, there's good wine and draught ales to be savoured, and decent food courtsey of the Wild Game Company (such a boar!). Often the crowd spills outside in the evening, and daytime drinks afford good views of the Berwick St Market buzz.

KU BAR FRITH ST GAY

Map p432 (www.ku-bar.co.uk; 25 Frith St, W1; ⏲noon-11pm Mon-Thu, to midnight Fri & Sat, to 10.30pm Sun; ⊖Leicester Sq) This venue is not quite the party place that Ku Bar Lisle St is and it therefore tends to be popular with a slightly older, smarter gay crowd. It's within easy reach of all the other bars that line the gay strip that is Old Compton St.

Covent Garden & Leicester Square

★LAMB & FLAG PUB

Map p430 (www.lambandflagcoventgarden.co.uk; 33 Rose St, WC2; ⏲11am-11pm Mon-Sat, noon-10.30pm Sun; ⊖Covent Garden) Pocket-sized but packed with charm and history, the Lamb & Flag is still going strong after three and a half centuries (indeed, the poet John Dryden was mugged outside in 1679). Rain or shine, you'll have to elbow your way to the bar through the merry crowd drinking outside. Inside, it's all brass fittings and creaky wooden floors.

The main entrance is on top of a tiny cobbled street, but you can also reach it from the backstreet donkey path called Lazenby Court that'll make you think of Victorian England.

SALISBURY PUB

Map p430 (www.taylor-walker.co.uk/pub/salisbury-covent-garden/c3111; 90 St Martin's Lane, WC2; ⏲11am-11pm Mon-Wed, to 11.30pm Thu, to midnight Fri & Sat, noon-10.30pm Sun; ⊖Leicester Sq) Brave the crowds at this centrally located pub established in 1898 just to see the beautifully etched and engraved windows and other Victorian features that have somehow escaped the developer's hand. It has a vast range of beers, including lots of cask ales and rarer continental lagers.

SPORTS CAFE BAR

Map p440 (www.thesportscafe.com; 80 Haymarket, SW1; ⏲noon-3am Mon-Sat, to midnight Sun; ⊖Piccadilly Circus) For those keen to watch the latest ice hockey, American football, baseball or even soccer matches, this is the place to be. It's huge, with four bars over two floors, giant screens everywhere and sports posters and memorabilia on the walls. The late licence means it's often raucous in the evenings, although it's pretty quiet during the day.

KU BAR LISLE ST GAY

Map p430 (www.ku-bar.co.uk; 30 Lisle St, WC2; ⏲noon-3am Mon-Sat, to midnight Sun; ⊖Leicester Sq) With its smart interior, geometric black-and-white patterns on the walls and busy events schedule (disco, cabaret, DJ sets etc) in the basement, the Lisle St branch of this gay mini-chain attracts a young, fun-loving crowd. It's student night on Mondays. And all the noodles of Chinatown are to hand.

CROSS KEYS PUB

Map p430 (www.crosskeyscoventgarden.com; 31 Endell St, WC2; ⏲11am-11pm Mon-Sat, noon-10.30pm Sun; ⊖Covent Garden) Covered in ivy and frequented by loyal locals who come for pints and spicy fry-ups, the Cross Keys is Covent Garden's tourist-free local pub. Eccentric landlord Brian has displayed his pop purchases as bar decorations (such as his £500 Elvis Presley napkin), and punters spill onto the pavement and outside tables on summer days.

FREUD BAR BAR

Map p430 (198 Shaftesbury Ave, WC2; ⏲11am-11pm Mon-Wed, to 1am Thur & Sat, to 2am Fri, noon-10.30pm Sun; ⊖Covent Garden) Make this the first stop on your crawl because there's no way you'll make it down the stairs (not much more than a ladder) after a few drinks. It's a small basement bar/gallery with works from up-and-coming artists on the walls. The decor and punters are suitably scruffy and the cocktail list (40-plus) extensive.

PARAMOUNT BAR

Map p430 (☎020-7420 2900; www.paramount.uk.net; 33rd fl, Centre Point, 101-103 New Oxford St, WC1; ⏲8am-1.30am Mon-Wed, to 2.30am Thu-Sat, noon-4pm Sun; ⊖Tottenham Court Rd) The second best thing about sipping a cocktail from the top of Centre Point, taking in the 360-degree view, is not having to look at the godawful 1960s listed monstrosity you're sitting in. This is probably the best view you'll get in central London; pity they don't keep the windows cleaner. Booking essential.

There is a restaurant with a complete menu (mains £16.50 to £27.50).

Holborn & the Strand

★HOLBORN WHIPPET PUB

Map p430 (www.holbornwhippet.com; Sicilian Ave, WC1; ⏲11am-1am; ⊖Holborn) This new breed of pub – tiny, all wood, at the end of a pedestrian-only street – stocks a commendable range of ales (we counted two dozen) from small craft breweries. Staff are more than keen to offer a taste from the spouts on the 'brick wall' to help you decide.

It must be the only pub in London that sells only draft beer. Food is of the sandwich/salad variety (£5.50 to £8).

★PRINCESS LOUISE PUB

Map p430 (208 High Holborn, WC1; ⏲11.30am-11pm Mon-Fri, noon-11pm Sat, to 10.30pm Sun; ⊖Holborn) This late-19th-century Victorian pub is spectacularly decorated with a riot of fine tiles, etched mirrors, plasterwork and a stunning central horseshoe bar. The old Victorian wood partitions give punters plenty of nooks and alcoves to hide in. Beers are Sam Smith's only but cost just under £3 a pint, so it's no wonder many elect to spend the whole evening here.

GORDON'S WINE BAR BAR

Map p430 (www.gordonswinebar.com; 47 Villiers St, WC2; ⏲11am-11pm Mon-Sat, noon-10pm Sun; ⊖Embankment) Gordon's is a victim of its own success; it is relentlessly busy and unless you arrive before the office crowd does (generally around 6pm), you can forget about getting a table. It's cavernous and dark, and the French and New World wines are heady and reasonably priced. You can nibble on bread, cheese and olives. Outside garden seating in summer.

SEVEN STARS PUB

Map p430 (53-54 Carey St, WC2; ⏲11am-11pm Mon-Fri, noon-11pm Sat, to 10pm Sun ; ⊖Holborn, Temple) Even though it's packed with lawyers in the after-office booze rush hour, the tiny Seven Stars is still a relative secret to many Londoners. Sitting between Lincoln's Inn Fields and the Royal Courts of Justice and originally a sailors' hang-out, this is the place to come for real ale and ravishing game dishes.

The eccentric landlady and chef, Roxy Beaujolais, is a former TV chef and raconteur.

POLSKI BAR BAR

Map p430 (11 Little Turnstile, WC1; ⏲4-11pm Mon, 12.30-11pm Tue-Thu, 12.30-11.30pm Fri, 6-11pm Sat; ⊖Holborn) With around 60 different types of vodka, from hazelnut to wheat-flavoured, simple old *slivowica* (plum brandy) to kosher, everyone should find something that tickles their taste buds. There's great Polish food like *bigos* (hunter's stew) and *pierogis* (dumplings), too, but the bare and cold interior leaves something to be desired.

Marylebone

PURL COCKTAIL BAR

Map p438 (020-7935 0835; www.purl-london.com; 50-54 Blandford St, W1; 5-11.30pm Mon-Thu, to midnight Fri & Sat; Baker St) A 'purveyor of fine matches and alcoholic libations', Purl is a fabulous underground drinking den. Decked out in vintage furniture, it serves original and intriguingly named cocktails (What's Your Poison? or Mr Hyde's No 2) and a punch of the day. It's all subdued lighting and hushed-tone conversations, which only adds to the mysterious air. Booking recommended.

PRINCE REGENT PUB

Map p438 (www.theprinceregentw1.co.uk; 71 Marylebone High St, W1; noon-11pm Mon-Fri, 11am-11pm Sat, noon-10.30pm Sun; Baker St) With rich upholstered furniture, regal colours on the walls and gold-framed mirrors, the Prince Regent has pulled out the stops on decor. Drinks are pretty good too, with changing ales, a good selection of draught beers and wines. There's a new emphasis on food, which is very good indeed, and there's a small street terrace open in the warmer months.

Mayfair

PUNCH BOWL PUB

Map p438 (www.punchbowllondon.com; 41 Farm St, W1; noon-11pm Mon-Sat, to 5pm Sun; Bond St) Partly owned by film director Guy Ritchie *(Lock, Stock & Two Smoking Barrels; Snatch),* the Punch Bowl attracts a young and happening crowd sipping cask ales, fine wines and whisky rather than run-of-the-mill pints. The pub retains many of its original 18th-century features (wood panels, cornicing etc), although the dining room at the back has a more modern feel.

GUINEA PUB

Map p438 (www.theguinea.co.uk; 30 Bruton Pl, W1; 11.30am-11pm Mon-Fri, from 5.30pm Sat; Green Park, Bond St) This quiet, friendly pub in London's most exclusive neighbourhood has something of a gentlemen's club feel about it, with its shiny brass fittings, heavy upholstery and good selection of ales. There are very few places to sit but if you do manage to bag a seat, you could order one of the famous pies (£15) from the rear restaurant.

GALVIN AT WINDOWS BAR

(www.galvinatwindows.com; London Hilton on Park Lane, 28th fl, 22 Park Lane, W1; 11am-1am Mon-Wed, to 3am Thu-Sat, to 11pm Sun; Hyde Park Corner) This swish bar on the edge of Hyde Park opens onto stunning views, especially at dusk. Cocktail prices reach similar heights (£11.50 to £15.25) but the leather seats are comfortable and the marble bar is gorgeous. The restaurant (same views, one Michelin star) offers a giveaway two- and three-course lunch menu for £25 and £29.

ENTERTAINMENT

HEAVEN GAY

Map p430 (www.heavennightclub-london.com; Villiers St, WC2; 11pm-5am Mon, Thu & Fri, 10pm-5am Sat; Embankment, Charing Cross) This long-standing, perennially popular gay club under the arches beneath Charing Cross station has always been host to good club nights. Monday's Popcorn (mixed dance party, all-welcome door policy) has to be one of the best weeknight's clubbing in the capital. The celebrated G-A-Y takes place here on Thursday (G-A-Y Porn Idol), Friday (G-A-Y Camp Attack) and Saturday (plain ol' G-A-Y).

MADAME JO JO'S CLUB

Map p432 (www.madamejojos.com; 8 Brewer St, W1; 8pm-3am Tue, from 10pm Wed-Sat, from 9.30pm Sun ; Leicester Sq, Piccadilly Circus) The renowned subterranean crimson cabaret bar and all its sleazy fun comes into its own with Kitsch Cabaret on Saturday and Burlesque Idol on the last Friday of the month. Andy Smith's Lost & Found club night on Saturdays is legendary, attracting a cool crew of breakdancers, jazz dancers and party people. It's Tranny Shack (drag queen night) on Wednesdays.

★12 BAR CLUB LIVE MUSIC

Map p430 (www.12barclub.com; Denmark St, WC2; admission £6-10; 7pm-3am Mon-Sat, to 12.30am Sun; Tottenham Court Rd) Small, intimate, with a rough-and-ready feel, the 12 Bar is a favourite live-music venue, with anything from solo acts to bands performing nightly. The emphasis is on songwriting and the music is very much indie rock, with anything from folk and jazzy influences to full-on punk and metal sounds.

LOCAL KNOWLEDGE

GAY TIMES IN LONDON

Freelance journalist Stephen Unwin gives us the lowdown on his favourite places for gay good times in London. Stephen contributes to mainstream publications as well *Attitude* and *Gay Times*, edits the luxury gay travel magazine WithRichard.com and runs Jake, Europe's most influential networking community for high-flying gay men.

For Weeknights & Weekend Afternoons

Sunday afternoons at **Boheme Kitchen & Bar** (Map p432; ☎020-7734 5656; www.bohemekitchen.co.uk; 19-21 Old Compton St, W1; ⏲11am-1pm Mon-Wed, to 3am Thu-Sat, to midnight Sun; ⊖Leicester Sq) are brilliant for people watching in Soho. Grab a cocktail (or three) and a seat outside, and buckle down for the evening. Dean Street Townhouse (p335) is great for dinner – British grub, a smart-for-town crowd, beautifully cosy, and there's often a famous face on the next table.

For After-Work Drinks

The **Duke of Wellington** (Map p432; 77 Wardour St, W1; ⏲noon-11pm Mon-Wed, to midnight Thu-Sat, to 10.30pm Sun; ⊖Leicester Sq) is a slightly ratty pub off Old Compton St that attracts a beardy, pint-drinking, friendly crowd intent on fun. On a sunny day the crowd outside meshes with the after-work punters from the **Rupert Street Bar** (Map p432; www.rupert-street.com; 50 Rupert St, W1; ⏲noon-midnight; ⊖Leicester Sq) next door. I also love the **Club at the Ivy** (Map p430; www.the-ivy.co.uk/the-club-at-the-ivy; 1-5 West St, WC2; ⊖Leicester Sq) in Covent Garden. It's members only, but if you can tag along with one, Friday nights are particularly same-sex oriented. Fancy, and full of theatre types. The vodka martinis are delicious and very strong.

Partying until the Wee Hours

Horse Meat Disco at the **Eagle** (Map p468; 349 Kennington Lane, Vauxhall, SE11; ⊖Vauxhall) in Vauxhall comes over all Studio 54 on Sunday nights, with clever disco music and a very cool crowd (that isn't snooty about it). Prepare to queue on bank holiday weekends. I love **XXL** (Map p444; www.xxl-london.com; 51-53 Southwark St, SE1; ⏲10pm-6am Sat) by Blackfriars Bridge: it's the 'everyman' all-nighter on Saturdays that's fit-to-bursting with testosterone. And you can't beat the George & Dragon (p216) in Shoreditch, a tiny, eccentric pub rammed with East End hipsters. As for summer Sundays at **Shoreditch House** (Map p450; www.shoreditchhouse.com; Ebor St, off Bethnal Green Rd, E1; overground Shoreditch High St, ⊖Liverpool St) by the rooftop pool… they may as well rename them 'Gayday'.

ROYAL OPERA HOUSE OPERA

Map p430 (☎020-7304 4000; www.roh.org.uk; Bow St, WC2; tickets £7-175; ⊖Covent Garden) The £210 million redevelopment for the millennium gave classic opera a fantastic setting in London, and coming here for a night is a sumptuous – if pricey – affair. Although the program has been fluffed up by modern influences, the main attractions are still the opera and classical ballet – all are wonderful productions and feature world-class performers.

Midweek matinees are usually much cheaper than evening performances and restricted-view seats cost as little as £7. There are same-day tickets (one per customer available to the first 67 people in the queue) from 10am for £8 to £44 and student standby tickets for £10. Half-price stand-by tickets four hours before the performance are only occasionally available.

COMEDY STORE COMEDY

Map p432 (☎0844 871 7699; www.thecomedystore.co.uk; 1a Oxendon St, SW1; admission £15-22.50; ⊖Piccadilly Circus) This was one of the first (and is still one of the best) comedy clubs in London. Wednesday and Sunday night's Comedy Store Players is the most famous improvisation outfit in town, with the wonderful Josie Lawrence; on Thursdays, Fridays and Saturdays Best in Stand Up features the best on London's comedy circuit.

PRINCE CHARLES CINEMA

Map p432 (www.princecharlescinema.com; 7 Leicester Pl, WC2; ⊖Leicester Sq) Ticket prices at Leicester Sq cinemas are highway robbery, so wait until the first-runs have moved to the Prince Charles, central London's cheapest cinema. This is where non-members pay only £8 to £10 for new releases. There are also mini-festivals, Q&As with film directors, old classics and, most famously, sing-along screenings of *Grease, The Sound of Music* and *Rocky Horror Picture Show*.

PIZZA EXPRESS JAZZ CLUB JAZZ

Map p432 (☎0845 602 7017; www.pizzaexpresslive.com; 10 Dean St, W1; admission £15-20; ⊖Tottenham Court Rd) Believe it or not, Pizza Express is one of the best jazz venues in London. It's a bit of a strange arrangement, in a basement beneath the main chain restaurant, but it seems to work. Lots of big names perform here and such promising artists as Norah Jones, Jamie Cullum and the late Amy Winehouse played here in their early days.

RONNIE SCOTT'S JAZZ

Map p432 (☎020-7439 0747; www.ronniescotts.co.uk; 47 Frith St, W1; ⊙6.30pm-3am Mon-Sat, to midnight Sun; ⊖Leicester Sq, Tottenham Court Rd) Ronnie Scott originally opened his jazz club on Gerrard St in 1959 under a Chinese gambling den. The club moved to its current location six years later and became widely known as Britain's best jazz club. Gigs are at 8.30pm (8pm Sunday) with a second one at 11.15pm Friday and Saturday, and are followed by a late show until 2am. Expect to pay between £20 and £50.

Ronnie Scott's has hosted such luminaries as Miles Davis, Charlie Parker, Thelonious Monk, Ella Fitzgerald, Count Basie and Sarah Vaughan. The club continues to build upon its formidable reputation by hosting a range of big names and new talent. The atmosphere is great, but talking during music is a big no-no.

SOHO THEATRE COMEDY

Map p432 (☎020-7478 0100; www.sohotheatre.com; 21 Dean St, W1; ⊖Tottenham Court Rd) The Soho Theatre has developed a superb reputation for showcasing new comedy-writing talent and comedians. It's also hosted some top-notch stand-up or sketch comedians including Alexei Sayle and Doctor Brown. Tickets cost between £10 and £20.

BORDERLINE CONCERT VENUE

Map p432 (www.mamacolive.com/theborderline; Orange Yard, off Manette St, W1; ⊖Tottenham Court Rd) Through the Tex-Mex entrance off Orange Yard and down into the basement you'll find a packed, 275-capacity venue that really punches above its weight. Read the gig list: Crowded House, REM, Blur, Counting Crows, PJ Harvey, Lenny Kravitz, Debbie Harry, plus many anonymous indie outfits, have all played here. The crowd's equally diverse but full of music journos and record-company talent spotters.

PLACE DANCE

Map p436 (www.theplace.org.uk; 17 Duke's Rd, WC1; ⊖Euston Sq) One of London's most exciting cultural venues, this was the birthplace of modern British dance; it still concentrates on challenging and experimental choreography. Behind the late-Victorian facade you'll find a 300-seat theatre, an arty, creative cafe atmosphere and a dozen training studios. The Place sponsors an annual Place Prize, which awards new and outstanding dance talent. Tickets cost £12 to £25.

CURZON SOHO CINEMA

Map p432 (www.curzoncinemas.com; 99 Shaftesbury Ave, W1; ⊖Leicester Sq, Piccadilly Circus) The Curzon Soho is one of London's best cinemas. It has a fantastic program lineup with the best of British, European, world and American indie films; regular Q&As with directors; shorts and mini-festivals; a Konditor & Cook cafe upstairs; cakes to die for; and an ultracomfortable bar. Tickets are between £8 and £14.

★WIGMORE HALL CLASSICAL MUSIC

Map p438 (www.wigmore-hall.org.uk; 36 Wigmore St, W1; ⊖Bond St) This is one of the best and most active (400 events a year) classical-music venues in town, not only because of its fantastic acoustics, beautiful art nouveau hall and great variety of concerts and recitals, but also because of the sheer standard of the performances. Built in 1901, it has remained one of the world's top places for chamber music.

The Sunday coffee concerts at 11.30am and the lunchtime ones at 1pm on Monday (both adult/concession £12/10) are excellent value. Evening concerts cost between £15 and £35.

AMUSED MOOSE SOHO COMEDY

Map p432 (www.amusedmoose.com; Moonlighting Nightclub, 17 Greek St , W1; ⊖Tottenham Court Rd) One of the city's best clubs, the peripatetic

Amused Moose (Moonlighting is just one of its hosting venues) is popular with audiences and comedians alike, perhaps helped along by the fact that heckling is 'unacceptable' and all of the acts are 'first-date friendly' (ie unlikely to humiliate the front row).

LONDON COLISEUM OPERA

Map p430 (☎020-7845 9300; www.eno.org; St Martin's Lane, WC2; ⊖Leicester Sq) The London Coliseum is home to the English National Opera (ENO), celebrated for making opera modern and more relevant, as all productions are sung in English. The building, built in 1904 and lovingly restored 100 years later, is very impressive. The English National Ballet also does regular performances at the Coliseum. Tickets range from £12 to £99.

After several years in the wasteland, the ENO has been receiving better reviews and welcoming much bigger audiences under the tutelage of music director Edward Gardner.

100 CLUB LIVE MUSIC

Map p436 (☎020-7636 0933; www.the100club.co.uk; 100 Oxford St, W1; admission £8-15; ⊖Oxford Circus, Tottenham Court Rd) This legendary London venue has always concentrated on jazz, but it's also spreading its wings to swing and rock. It once showcased Chris Barber, BB King and the Stones, and was at the centre of the punk revolution and the '90s indie scene. It hosts dancing swing gigs and local jazz musicians, as well as the occasional big name.

DONMAR WAREHOUSE THEATRE

Map p430 (☎0844 871 7624; www.donmarwarehouse.com; 41 Earlham St, WC2; ⊖Covent Garden) The cosy Donmar Warehouse is London's 'thinking person's theatre'. The new artistic director, Josie Rourke, has staged some interesting and unusual productions such as the Restoration comedy *The Recruiting Officer*, by George Farquhar, and a restaging of Conor McPherson's *The Weir*.

But some think it has taken a step back from the days when Nicole Kidman administered 'theatrical Viagra' nightly by peeling off her clothes in Sam Mendes' production of *The Blue Room*, and Michael Grandage framed blue-eyed Jude Law as *Hamlet*.

ICA CINEMA CINEMA

Map p440 (www.ica.org.uk; Nash House, The Mall, SW1; ⊖Charing Cross, Piccadilly Circus) The Institute of Contemporary Arts (ICA) is a treasure for lovers of indie cinema – its program always has material no one else is showing, such as the latest independents from the developing world, films showing out of season, all-night screenings and rare documentaries. The two cinemas are quite small, but comfortable enough. Tickets usually cost £10 (concessions £8).

SHOPPING

The West End's shopping scene hardly needs a formal introduction. Oxford St is heaven or hell, depending on what you're after; it's all about chains, from Marks & Spencer to H&M, Top Shop to Gap. Covent Garden is also beset with run-of-the-mill outlets, but they tend to be smaller and counterbalanced by independent boutiques, vintage ones in particular. As well as fashion, the West End is big on music. There are some great independent record shops, especially in Soho.

Westminster & St James's

PENHALIGON'S ACCESSORIES

Map p440 (www.penhaligons.com; 16-17 Burlington Arcade, W1; ⏲10am-6pm Mon-Fri, to 6.30pm Sat, 11am-5pm Sun; ⊖Piccadilly Circus, Green Park) Penhaligon's is the antidote to buying your favourite scent at airport duty-free. Here attendants ask about your favourite smells, take you on an exploratory tour of the shop's signature range and help you discover new scents. There is a range of products, from traditional perfumes to home fragrances and bath and body products. Everything is made in Cornwall.

FORTNUM & MASON DEPARTMENT STORE

Map p440 (www.fortnumandmason.com; 181 Piccadilly, W1; ⏲10am-8pm Mon-Sat, 11.30am-6pm Sun; ⊖Piccadilly Circus) London's oldest grocery store, now into its fourth century, refuses to yield to modern times. Its staff are still dressed in old-fashioned tailcoats and it keeps its glamorous food hall supplied with hampers, cut marmalade, speciality teas and so on. Downstairs is an elegant wine bar as well as elegant kitchenware, luxury gifts and perfumes.

TAYLOR OF OLD BOND STREET BEAUTY

Map p440 (www.taylorOldbondst.co.uk; 74 Jermyn St, SW1; ⌚9am-6pm Mon-Sat; ⊖Green Park) This shop has been plying its trade since the mid-19th century and has much contributed to the expression 'well-groomed gentleman'. It stocks every sort of razor, shaving brush and scent of shaving soap imaginable – not to mention oils, soaps and other bath products.

SHEPHERDS GIFTS

Map p440 (www.bookbinding.co.uk; 76 Rochester Row, SW1; ⌚10am-7pm Tue-Fri, to 8pm Sat; ⊖Victoria) Suckers for fine stationery, leather boxes, elegant albums and exquisite paper will get their fix at this tiny shop in a wonderful bookbindery.

MINAMOTO KITCHOAN FOOD

Map p432 (www.kitchoan.com; 44 Piccadilly; ⌚10am-7pm Sun-Fri, to 8pm Sat; ⊖Piccadilly Circus) Walking into this Japanese sweet shop is a mind-blowing experience. *Wagashi* – Japanese sweets – are made out of all sorts of rice and sweet red-bean paste *(anko)* and shaped into glazed red cherries, green-bean bunches or spiky kidney-bean rolls. Order a couple, sit down and enjoy with a complimentary green tea, or buy a box as an unusual gift.

Bloomsbury & Fitzrovia

BANG BANG CLOTHING EXCHANGE VINTAGE

Map p436 (www.bangbangclothingexchange.co.uk; 21 Goodge St, W1; ⌚10am-6.30pm Mon-Fri, 11am-6pm Sat; ⊖Goodge St) Got some designer or high-street or vintage pieces you're tired of? Bang Bang exchanges, buys and sells. As they say, 'think of Alexander McQueen cocktail dresses rubbing shoulders with Topshop shoes and 1950s jewellery'.

GAY'S THE WORD BOOKS

Map p436 (www.gaystheword.co.uk; 66 Marchmont St, WC1; ⌚10am-6.30pm Mon-Sat, 2-6pm Sun; ⊖Russell Sq) This London gay institution has been selling books nobody else stocks for 35 years and still has a great range of gay- and lesbian-interest books and magazines as well as a real community spirit. Used books available as well.

JAMES SMITH & SONS ACCESSORIES

Map p430 (www.james-smith.co.uk; 53 New Oxford St, WC1; ⌚10am-6pm Mon-Fri, to 5.30pm Sat; ⊖Tottenham Court Rd) 'Outside every silver lining is a big black cloud', claim the cheerful owners of this quintessential English shop. Nobody makes and stocks such elegant umbrellas, walking sticks and canes as this traditional place does. They've been here since 1857 and, thanks to London's notoriously bad weather, they'll hopefully do great business for years to come.

DARKROOM JEWELLERY

(www.darkroomlondon.com; 52 Lamb's Conduit St, WC1; ⌚11am-7pm Mon-Fri, to 6pm Sat, noon-5pm Sun; ⊖Holborn, Russell Sq) This, well, very dark room on one of London's top shopping streets displays and sells stylish, carefully chosen designer jewellery, accessories and handbags. There's also glassware and ceramics and its own line of prints and cushions.

BLADE RUBBER STAMPS ARTS & CRAFTS

Map p436 (www.bladerubberstamps.co.uk; 12 Bury Pl, WC1; ⌚10.30am-6pm Mon-Sat, 11.30am-4.30pm Sun; ⊖Holborn) Just south of the British Museum, this shop stocks just about every wooden-handled rubber stamp you care to imagine: from London icons like post boxes, Beefeaters and the Houses of Parliament to cartoon characters and Christmas stamps. They can make you one to your design or you can have a go yourself with a stamp-making kit.

FOLK FASHION

(www.folkclothing.com; 49 & 53 Lamb's Conduit St, WC1; ⌚11am-7pm Mon-Sat, noon-5pm; ⊖Holborn) Simple but strikingly styled casual clothes, often in bold colours and with a hand-crafted feel. Head for No 49 for Folk's own line of menswear and to No 53 for womenswear.

Soho & Chinatown

JOY FASHION

Map p432 (www.joythestore.com; 162-170 Wardour St, W1; ⌚10am-7pm Mon-Fri, to 8pm Sat, noon-7pm Sun; ⊖Tottenham Court Rd, Oxford Circus) Joy is an artistic blend of mainstream and vintage: there are excellent clothes, from silk dresses for women, fabulous shirts for men and timeless T-shirts for both, as well as funky gadgets such as moustache clocks and lip-shaped ice-cube trays. Conventional shoppers abstain!

BOOKWORM PARADISE: THE WEST END'S BEST BOOKSHOPS

Daunt Books (Map p438; www.dauntbooks.co.uk; 83 Marylebone High St, W1; ⌚9am-7.30pm Mon-Sat, 11am-6pm Sun; ⊖Baker St) An original Edwardian bookshop, with oak panels and gorgeous skylights, Daunt is one of London's loveliest travel bookshops. It has two floors and stocks general fiction and nonfiction titles as well.

London Review Bookshop (Map p436; www.lrb.co.uk; 14 Bury Pl, WC1; ⌚10am-6.30pm Mon-Sat, noon-6pm Sun; ⊖Holborn) The flagship bookshop of the *London Review of Books* literary magazine doesn't believe in piles of books, taking the clever approach of stocking wide-ranging titles in one or two copies only. It often hosts high-profile author talks (tickets £7), and there is a charming **cafe** where you can peruse your new purchases.

Foyle's (Map p432; www.foyles.co.uk; 113-119 Charing Cross Rd, WC2; ⌚9.30am-9pm Mon-Sat, 11.30am-6pm Sun; ⊖Tottenham Court Rd) This is London's most legendary bookshop, where you can bet on finding even the most obscure of titles. The lovely **cafe** is on the 1st floor where you'll also find **Grant & Cutler** (Map p432; www.grantandcutler.com; 113-119 Charing Cross Rd, WC2; ⊖Oxford Circus), the UK's largest foreign-language bookseller. Ray's Jazz (p142) is on the 3rd floor.

Stanford's (Map p430; www.stanfords.co.uk; 12-14 Long Acre, WC2; ⌚9am-8pm Mon-Fri, from 10am Sat, noon-6pm Sun; ⊖Leicester Sq, Covent Garden) As a 150-year-old seller of maps, guides and literature, the grand-daddy of travel bookshops is a destination in its own right. Ernest Shackleton and David Livingstone and, more recently, Michael Palin and Brad Pitt have all popped in here.

Waterstone's (Map p432; www.waterstones.com; 203-206 Piccadilly, W1; ⌚9am-10pm Mon-Sat, noon-6pm Sun; ⊖Piccadilly Circus) The chain's megastore is the largest bookshop in Europe, boasting knowledgeable staff and regular author readings and signings. The store spreads across four floors, and there is a cafe in the basement and a fabulous rooftop bar–restaurant, 5th View (p123).

Gosh! (Map p432; www.goshlondon.com; 1 Berwick St, W1; ⌚10.30am-7.30pm; ⊖Piccadilly Circus) Draw up here for graphic novels, manga, newspaper-strip collections and children's books, such as the Tintin and Asterix series. It's also perfect for finding presents for kids and teenagers.

Skoob Books (Map p436; www.skoob.com; 66 The Brunswick, off Marchmont St, WC1; ⌚10.30am-8pm Mon-Sat, to 6pm Sun; ⊖Russell Sq) Skoob (you work out the name) has got to be London's largest secondhand bookshop, with some 60,000 titles spread over 2500 sq ft of floor space. If you can't find it here, it probably doesn't exist.

TOPSHOP — CLOTHING

Map p432 (www.topshop.co.uk; 36-38 Great Castle St, W1; ⌚9am-9pm Mon-Sat, 11.30am-6pm Sun; ⊖Oxford Circus) The 'It'-store when it comes to clothes and accessories, venturing boldly into couture in recent years, it encapsulates London's supreme skill at bringing catwalk fashion to the youth market affordably and quickly.

URBAN OUTFITTERS — FASHION

Map p432 (www.urbanoutfitters.co.uk; 200 Oxford St, W1; ⌚10am-8pm Mon-Wed, Fri & Sat, to 9pm Thu, noon-6pm Sun; ⊖Oxford Circus) Probably the trendiest of all chains, this cool US-based store serves both men and women and has the best young designer T-shirts, an excellent designer area (stocking Vanessa Bruno Athé, Vivienne Westwood, Something Else and See by Chloé, among others), 're-newed' secondhand pieces, saucy underwear, silly homewares and quirky gadgets.

PROWLER — GAY, ACCESSORIES

Map p432 (www.prowler-stores.co.uk; 5-7 Brewer St, W1; ⌚11am-9.30pm Mon-Wed, to 10pm Thu & Fri, 10.30am-10pm Sat, 1-8pm Sun; ⊖Piccadilly Circus) Prowler's flagship Soho store is a gay shopping mecca selling books, magazines, clothes and 'lifestyle accessories' (with or without batteries). There's also a discreet 'adult' section with the usual array of DVDs and magazines, but the overall feel is of a respectable (kinda) gay department store.

ALGERIAN COFFEE STORES — COFFEE

Map p432 (www.algcoffee.co.uk; 52 Old Compton St, W1; ⌚9am-7pm Mon-Wed, to 9pm Thu & Fri, to

8pm Sat; ⊖Leicester Sq) Stop and have a shot of espresso while you select your freshly ground coffee beans. Choose among dozens of varieties of coffees and teas at this 125-year-old shop.

VINTAGE HOUSE DRINK

Map p432 (http://freespace.virgin.net/vintage-house.co; 42 Old Compton St, W1; ⌚9am-11pm Mon-Fri, 10am-11pm Sat, noon-10pm Sun; ⊖Leicester Sq) A whisky connoisseur's paradise, this shop stocks more than 1400 single-malt Scotches, from smooth Macallan to peaty Lagavulin. It also offers a huge array of spirits and liqueurs that you wouldn't find in your average off-licence.

AGENT PROVOCATEUR LINGERIE

Map p432 (www.agentprovocateur.com; 6 Broadwick St, W1; ⌚11am-7pm Mon-Wed, Fri & Sat, noon-5pm Sun; ⊖Oxford Circus) For women's lingerie that is to be worn and seen, certainly *not* hidden, pull up to wonderful Agent Provocateur, originally set up by Joseph Corré, son of Vivienne Westwood. Its sexy and saucy corsets, bras and nighties for all shapes and sizes exude confident and positive sexuality.

HAMLEYS TOYS

Map p432 (www.hamleys.com; 188-196 Regent St, W1; ⌚10am-8pm Mon-Fri, 9.30am-8pm Sat, noon-6pm Sun; ⊖Oxford Circus) Said to be the largest toy store in the world, Hamleys is a layer cake of playthings. Spread over five floors are computer games next to preschool toys, girls' playthings opposite model cars and science kids next to the latest playground trends. The confection is topped off with Lego world and a cafe on the 5th floor.

LIBERTY DEPARTMENT STORE

Map p432 (www.liberty.co.uk; Great Marlborough St, W1; ⌚10am-8pm Mon-Sat, noon-6pm Sun; ⊖Oxford Circus) An irresistible blend of contemporary styles in an old-fashioned mock-Tudor atmosphere, Liberty has a huge cosmetics department and an accessories floor, along with a breathtaking lingerie section, all at very inflated prices. A classic London souvenir is a Liberty fabric print especially in the form of a scarf.

LINA STORES FOOD

Map p432 (www.linastores.co.uk; 18 Brewer St, W1; ⌚8.30am-7.30pm Mon & Tue, to 8.30pm Wed-Fri, 10am-7.30pm Sat, 11am-5pm Sun ; ⊖Piccadilly Circus) This delightful Italian delicatessen in the heart of Soho, here since 1944, is so gorgeous in its cream and pastel greeness that you could almost imagine eating it. Come here for picnic cheeses, charcuterie, bread and olives.

BEYOND RETRO VINTAGE

Map p432 (www.beyondretro.com; 58-59 Great Marlborough St, W1; ⌚10.30am-7.30pm Mon-Wed & Sat, to 8.30pm Fri & Sat, 11am-6pm Sun; ⊖Oxford Circus) A more central basement outlet of an enormous warehouse just off Brick Lane in East London, Beyond Retro sells vintage and some vintage repro clothes for men and women, with the requisite stilettos, bowler and top hats and satin wedding dresses.

Covent Garden & Leicester Square

NEAL'S YARD DAIRY FOOD

Map p430 (www.nealsyarddairy.co.uk; 17 Shorts Gardens, WC2; ⌚10am-7pm Mon-Sat; ⊖Covent Garden) A fabulous, fragrant cheese house that would fit in rural England, this place is proof that the British can do just as well as the French when it comes to big rolls of ripe cheese. There are more than 70 varieties that the shopkeepers will let you taste, including independent farmhouse brands. Condiments, pickles, jams and chutneys are also on sale.

MOLTON BROWN BEAUTY

Map p430 (www.moltonbrown.co.uk; 18 Russell St, WC2; ⌚10am-7pm Mon-Fri, to 6pm Sat, 11am-5pm Sun; ⊖Covent Garden) A fabulously fragrant British natural beauty range, Molton Brown is *the* choice for boutique hotel, posh restaurant and 1st-class airline bathrooms. Its skin-care products offer plenty of pampering for both men and women. In this store you can also have a facial as well as pick up home accessories.

APPLE STORE ELECTRONICS

Map p430 (www.apple.com/uk/retail/coventgarden; 1-7 The Piazza, Covent Garden, WC2; ⌚9am-9pm Mon-Sat, noon-6pm Sun; ⊖Covent Garden) Mac geeks of the world unite! Here's your temple, so come and warm your faces on the soft glow emanating from iPads to iPods, laptops to desktops, inside this white and airy emporium.

INDEPENDENT MUSIC STORES

Britons buy more music per head than any other nation. Independent music stores find it difficult to keep going, especially in central London, but they still exist and here are the West End's best.

Sister Ray (Map p432; www.sisterray.co.uk; 34-35 Berwick St, W1; ⌚10am-8pm Mon-Sat, noon-6pm Sun; ⊖Oxford Circus, Tottenham Court Rd) If you were a fan of the late, great John Peel on the BBC/BBC World Service, this specialist in innovative, experimental and indie music is just right for you.

Ray's Jazz (Map p432; www.foyles.co.uk; 113-119 Charing Cross Rd, WC2; ⌚9.30am-9pm Mon-Sat, 11.30am-6pm Sun; ⊖Tottenham Court Rd) Quiet and serene with friendly and helpful staff, this shop on the 3rd floor of Foyles bookshop has one of the best jazz selections in London.

Sounds of the Universe (Map p432; www.soundsoftheuniverse.com; 7 Broadwick St, W1; ⌚11am-7.30pm; ⊖Oxford Circus, Tottenham Court Rd) The outlet of the Soul Jazz Records label (responsible for so many great soul, reggae, funk and dub albums), this place stocks CDs and vinyl plus some original 45s.

Harold Moore's Records (Map p432; www.hmrecords.co.uk; 2 Great Marlborough St, W1; ⌚10am-6.30pm Mon-Sat; ⊖Oxford Circus, Tottenham Court Rd) London's finest classical-music store stocks an extensive range of vinyl, CDs and DVDs, plus jazz in the basement, and can source hard-to-find music for you.

Reckless Records (Map p432; www.reckless.co.uk; 30 Berwick St, W1; ⌚10am-7pm; ⊖Oxford Circus, Tottenham Court Rd) Despite numerous name changes, this outfit hasn't really changed in spirit. It still stocks new and secondhand records and CDs, from punk, soul, dance and independent to mainstream.

Phonica (Map p432; www.phonicarecords.co.uk; 51 Poland St, W1; ⊖Tottenham Court Rd, Oxford Circus) A cool and relaxed shop that stocks a lot of house, electro and hip hop, but you can find just about anything from reggae to dub, jazz and rock.

On the Beat (Map p436; 22 Hanway St, W1; ⌚11am-7pm; ⊖Tottenham Court Rd) Mostly '60s and '70s retro – along with helpful staff – in a tiny room plastered with posters.

There are daily workshops and talks to help make the best of your Apple ware, and the banks of iMacs are a free-for-all internet-surfing base.

TED BAKER — FASHION

Map p430 (www.tedbaker.com; 9-10 Floral St, WC2; ⌚10.30am-7.30pm Mon-Wed & Fri, to 8pm Thu, 10am-7pm Sat, noon-6pm Sun; ⊖Covent Garden) The one-time Glasgow-based tailor shop has grown into a superb brand of clothing with elegant men's and womenswear. Ted's forte is its formal wear, with beautiful dresses for women (lots of daring prints and exquisite material) and sharp tailoring for men. The casual collections (denim, beachwear etc) are excellent too.

FORBIDDEN PLANET — COMICS

Map p430 (www.forbiddenplanet.com; 179 Shaftesbury Ave, WC2; ⌚10am-7pm Mon & Tue, to 7.30pm Wed, Fri & Sat, to 8pm Thu, noon-6pm Sun; ⊖Tottenham Court Road) A trove of comics, sci-fi, horror and fantasy literature, this is an absolute dream for anyone into manga comics or off-beat genre titles.

PAUL SMITH — FASHION

Map p430 (www.paulsmith.co.uk; 40-44 Floral St, WC2; ⌚10.30am-6.30pm Mon-Wed, to 7pm Thu & Fri, 10am-7pm Sat, noon-6pm Sun ; ⊖Covent Garden) Paul Smith represents the best of British classics with innovative twists. Super-stylish menswear, suits and tailored shirts are all laid out on open shelves in this walk-in closet of a shop. Smith also does womenswear with sharp tailoring for an androgynous, almost masculine, look.

SPACE NK — BEAUTY

Map p430 (www.spacenk.co.uk; 32 Shelton St, WC2; ⌚10am-7pm Mon-Wed, Fri & Sat, to 7.30pm Thu, 11.30am-7.30pm Sun; ⊖Covent Garden) Space NK specialises in skincare products and stocks such brands as Eve Lom, Chantecaille, Kiehl's and Phyto, as well as anti-ageing products from the likes of Dr

Sebagh. Men's products range from Anthony to Kiehl's.

BENJAMIN POLLOCK'S TOY SHOP TOYS

Map p430 (www.pollocks-coventgarden.co.uk; 1st fl, 44 Market bldg, Covent Garden, WC2; 10.30am-6pm Mon-Sat, 11am-4pm Sun; Covent Garden) Here's a traditional toyshop stuffed with the things that kids of all ages love. There are Victorian paper theatres, wooden marionettes and finger puppets, and antique teddy bears that might be too fragile to play with.

KAREN MILLEN FASHION

Map p430 (www.karenmillen.com; 32-33 James St, WC2; 10.30am-7pm Mon-Sat, noon-6pm Sun; Covent Garden) An upmarket womenswear store, with glam suit-trousers, voluptuous knits, shiny trench coats and evening frocks.

POSTE MISTRESS SHOES

Map p430 (www.sevendials.co.uk/component/stores/store/7-shoes-and-accessories/25-poste-mistress; 61-63 Monmouth St, WC2; 10am-7pm Mon-Wed, Fri & Sat, to 8pm Thu, 11am-6pm Sun; Leicester Sq, Covent Garden) This is where all shoe fetishists should head for the wonderful collection of women's shoes from Vivienne Westwood, Dries Van Noten and Chie Mihara. They're discounted from their original price, but this is still for shoppers for whom money is no object.

OPENING CEREMONY FASHION

Map p430 (www.openingceremony.us; 35 King St, WC2; 11am-8pm Mon-Sat, noon-6pm Sun; Covent Garden) This is the fashion child of Chloë Sevigny and has great street cred among the fashion crowd stocking the likes of Kenzo and Mishka. The prices are atrociously high. King St was redone for the Olympics in 2012 and now has loads of high-end clothing shops.

DO SHOP HOMEWARES

Map p430 (www.do-shop.com; 34 Shorts Gardens, WC2; 10am-6.30pm Mon-Wed, Fri & Sat, to 8pm Thu, noon-6pm Sun; Covent Garden) A great collection of always functional furniture, kitchenware and home accessories from independent designers, including students at the Royal College of Art. Check out the versatile tables that double as bookshelves, the neon bento boxes or scrunched-up paper cups that are made of porcelain (for real). Perfect for presents (to self, as well).

MOOMIN SHOP

Map p430 (www.themoomins bldg, Covent Garden, WC2; 1 11am-7pm Sun; Covent Gar shop in Covent Garden's building is a temple to all t that weird hippo-like charac Finnish artist Tove Jansson. T coasters, towels, lunchboxes – it has everything (and Little My stuff too).

GALLERY ONE ART

Map p430 (www.g-1.com; 20 Market bldg, Covent Garden, WC2; Covent Garden) This gallery stocks an excellent and quite diverse collection of contemporary art, both paper and canvas, framed or unframed, as well as some cutting-edge photography. It's all pretty decorative stuff but a world apart from the usual designer art sold to fill in the gaps on the wall.

Marylebone

CATH KIDSTON HOMEWARES, CLOTHING

Map p438 (www.cathkidston.co.uk; 51 Marylebone High St, W1; 10am-7pm Mon-Wed, Fri & Sat, to 8pm Thu, 11am-6pm Sun; Baker St) If you favour the preppy look, you'll love Cath Kidston with her signature floral prints and 1950s fashion (dresses above the knee and cinched at the waist, cardigans, shawls and old-fashioned pyjamas). There is also a range of homewares.

MONOCLE SHOP ACCESSORIES

Map p438 (www.monocle.com; 2a George St, W1; 11am-7pm Mon-Sat, noon-5pm Sun; Bond St) Run by the people behind the design and international current affairs magazine *Monocle,* whose publisher is the enviably named Tyler Brûlé, this shop is pure understated heaven. Costly stuff but if you're a fan of minimalist quality design across the board (clothes, bags, umbrellas and so on), you won't regret dropping in. Beautifully bound first editions too.

BEATLES STORE SOUVENIRS

Map p438 (www.itsonlyrocknrolllondon.co.uk; 230 Baker St, NW1; 10am-6.30pm; Baker St) Anything and everything to do with the Fab Four – wallets, bags, T-shirts, posters – as well as every other rock star or group who ever appeared on stage in the '60s, '70s and (maybe just) '80s.

...ayfair

...STING FASHION

Map p432 (www.thesting.nl; 55 Regent St, W1; ⌚10am-10pm Mon-Sat, noon-6pm Sun; ⊖Piccadilly Circus) This Dutch chain is a 'network of brands': most of the clothes it stocks are European labels that are little known in the UK. Spread over three floors are anything from casual sweatpants and fluoro T-shirts to elegant dresses, frilly tops and handsome shirts.

ABERCROMBIE & FITCH FASHION

Map p432 (www.abercrombie.com; 7 Burlington Gardens, W1; ⌚10am-7pm Mon-Sat, noon-6pm Sun; ⊖Piccadilly Circus) Abercrombie's wholesome look (denims, jersey tops, cosy knitwear, perfectly tailored cotton shirts) hasn't waned in popularity. This shop is busy from the minute it opens its doors, and at weekends queues snake through the ground floor. And why not? With loud dance music, dark, moody lighting, musky scents and topless hunks ready and willing to serve, who's complaining?

SELFRIDGES DEPARTMENT STORE

Map p438 (www.selfridges.com; 400 Oxford St, W1; ⌚9.30am-8pm Mon-Wed, to 9pm Thu-Sat, 11.30am-6.15pm Sun; ⊖Bond St) Selfridges loves innovation – it is famed for its inventive window displays by international artists, gala shows and, above all, its amazing range of products. It's the trendiest of London's one-stop shops, with labels such as Boudicca, Luella Bartley, Emma Cook, Chloé and Missoni; an unparalleled food hall; and Europe's largest cosmetics department.

MULBERRY ACCESSORIES

Map p438 (www.mulberry.com; 41-42 New Bond St, W1; ⌚10am-7pm Mon-Sat, 11am-5pm Sun; ⊖Bond St) Is there a woman in the world who doesn't covet a Mulberry bag? They are voluptuous, soft and a massive style statement. The brand has followed in the footsteps of its other British design titans like Burberry and Pringle and modernised itself in recent years.

POSTE SHOES

Map p438 (www.office.co.uk/brand/poste/50; 10 South Molton St, W1; ⌚10am-7pm Mon-Wed, Fri & Sat, to 8pm Thu, 11.30am-6pm Sun; ⊖Bond St) Sitting on one of London's most fashionable streets, this very cool shop is aimed at boys who like good shoes, and stocks everything from vintage street labels to razor-sharp Italian imports.

VIVIENNE WESTWOOD FASHION

Map p432 (www.viviennewestwood.com; 44 Conduit St, W1; ⌚10am-6pm Mon-Wed, Fri & Sat, to 7pm Thu, noon-5pm Sun; ⊖Bond St, Oxford Circus) The ex-punk who created the punk look has always had a reputation for being controversial (she flashed her privates to the paparazzi after receiving her OBE). Thankfully, though, La Westwood continues to design clothes as bold, innovative and provocative as ever, featuring 19th-century-inspired bustiers, wedge shoes, tartan and sharp tailoring.

BURBERRY FASHION

Map p432 (www.burberry.com; 21-23 New Bond St, SW1; ⌚10am-8pm Mon-Sat, 12.30-6pm Sun; ⊖Bond St) The first traditional British brand to reach the heights of fashion, Burberry is known for its innovative take on classic pieces (eg bright-coloured trench coats, khaki pants with large and unusual pockets), its brand check pattern and a tailored, groomed look.

JOHN LEWIS DEPARTMENT STORE

Map p438 (www.johnlewis.co.uk; 300 Oxford St, W1; ⌚9.30am-8pm Mon-Wed, Fri & Sat, to 9pm Thu, 11.30am-6pm Sun; ⊖Oxford Circus) 'Never knowingly undersold' is the motto of this store, whose range of household goods, fashion and luggage is better described as reliable rather than cutting edge. And for that reason it's some people's favourite store in the whole wide world.

STELLA MCCARTNEY FASHION

Map p438 (www.stellamccartney.co.uk; 30 Bruton St, W1; ⌚11am-7pm Mon-Sat; ⊖Bond St) Her sharp tailoring, floaty designs, accessible style and 'ethical' approach to fashion (no leather or fur) is very of-the-moment. This three-storey terraced Victorian home is a minimalist showcase for the designer's current collections. Depending on your devotion and wallet, you'll feel at ease or like an intruder.

WRIGHT & TEAGUE JEWELLERY

Map p440 (www.wrightandteague.com; 27 Burlington Arcade, W1; ⌚10am-8pm Mon-Fri, to 5pm

Sat; ⊖Green Park) The Wright & Teague gold charm bracelets are absolutely ravishing, as are its elegant silver and gold bangles, long necklaces and rings for men and women. What's more, many are very affordable.

BUTLER & WILSON JEWELLERY

Map p438 (www.butlerandwilson.co.uk; 20 South Moulton St, Mayfair, W1; ⏲10am-6pm Mon-Wed, Fri & Sat, to 7pm Thu, noon-6pm Sun; ⊖Bond St) There's a sybaritic 1920s Shanghai vibe to Butler & Wilson's central branch, where costume jewellery, handbags, T-shirts and knick-knacks are sold ... painted with giant red C...

DOVER STREET MARKET

Map p432 (www.doverstree... Dover St, W1; ⏲11am-6.30pm ... Thu-Sat, noon-5pm Sun; ⊖Gree... ing the colourful creations o... darlings Comme des Garçons (among other labels), Dover St Market is the place to come for that shirt you only wear on special occasions. There are four floors of clothing for men and women, all artfully displayed.

The City

Neighbourhood Top Five

❶ Walking through a head-spinning wealth of history past the colourful Yeoman Warders (or Beefeaters), the spectacular Crown Jewels, the soothsaying ravens and armour fit (!) for a king at the unmissable **Tower of London** (p148).

❷ Eavesdropping on whispering neighbours in the dome of **St Paul's** (p154), before enjoying its far-reaching views.

❸ Getting below the surface – literally – of the city at the extensive **Museum of London** (p161).

❹ Imagining the tragedy of medieval London ablaze as you climb the **Monument** (p159) to the Great Fire.

❺ Marvelling at the City's ultramodern new buildings like **30 St Mary Axe** (p157), aka 'the Gherkin'.

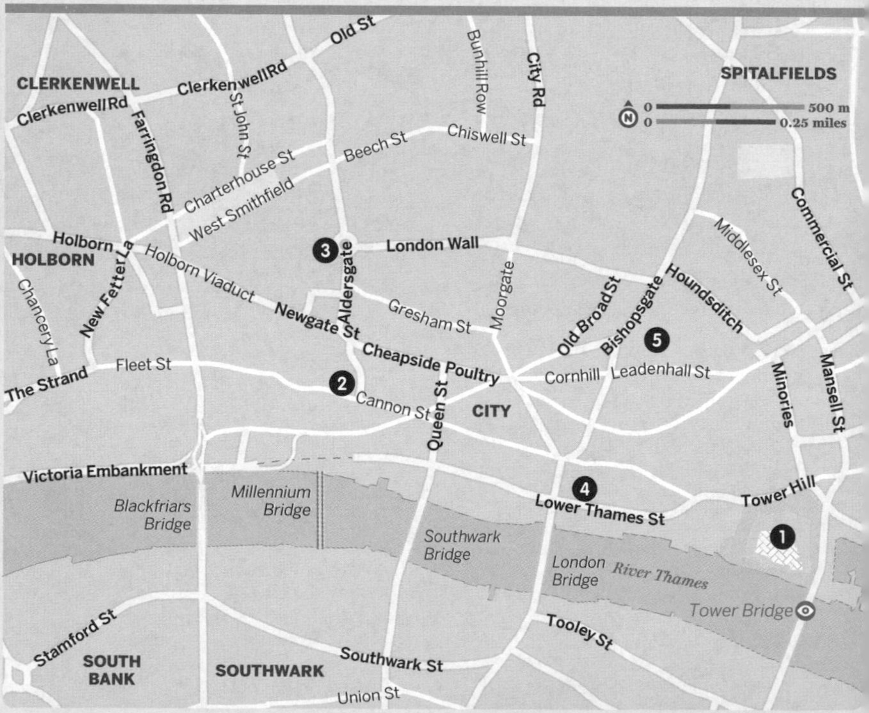

For more detail of this area see Map p442

Explore: The City

For its size – a mere square mile (about 2.6 sq km) – the City punches well above its weight for sightseeing attractions. Start with the heavyweights – the Tower of London and St Paul's – and try to allow at least a half day for each. It's worth arriving early to avoid the queues in high season. You can combine the other top sights with explorations of the City's lesser-known delights and quieter corners; Christopher Wren's scores of churches make peaceful stops along the way.

While about 330,000 people work in the City of London, fewer than 8000 actually live here. To appreciate its frantic industry and hum, you're best to come during the week, which is when you'll find everything open. It empties quickly in the evening, though, as its workers retreat to the suburbs. Weekends have a very different appeal, giving you a lot more space for quiet contemplation. Although you'll find most places shut tight until Monday, the City is trying to reverse this by opening such places as One New Change.

Local Life

➡ **Barbican** A powerhouse of culture, people flock to the Barbican (p161) for its innovative dance, theatre, music and art, stopping to enjoy lunch or a coffee in its excellent food hall.

➡ **Meals with a View** There's nothing like getting a taste of the high life, trying to spot your hotel and watching the sun go down over the capital at the Heron Tower's Duck & Waffle (p165).

➡ **Old-Style Drinking** Though they tend to keep banker's hours, the City's pubs are some of the most atmospheric and historic; the Hoop and Grapes (p167) even claims to be the oldest in town.

Getting There & Away

➡ **Underground** There's a veritable tangle of tube lines under the City and you're never too far away from one of them. Handiest are Bank (Central, Northern, DLR and Waterloo & City) and St Paul's (Central Line), but Blackfriars (Circle and District), Barbican (Circle, Metropolitan and Hammersmith & City) and Tower Hill (Circle & District) are useful for sights farther afield.

➡ **Bus** For a west-to-east sweep from Oxford Circus through St Paul's, Bank and Liverpool St, hop on the 8; and from Piccadilly Circus via Fleet St and the Tower, the 15. The 11 sets off from Liverpool St and passes Bank and Mansion House on its way to Chelsea. The 26 follows the same route through the City but branches off for Waterloo.

Lonely Planet's Top Tip

Designed by Jean Nouvel, **One New Change** – called the Stealth Bomber by some because of its distinctive shape – is a shopping mall housing mainly run-of-the-mill, high-street brands, but take the lift to its 6th floor and a great open viewing platform will reward you with up-close views of the dome of St Paul's Cathedral and out over London.

Best Places to Eat

- Duck & Waffle (p165)
- Sweeting's (p166)
- Bread Street Kitchen (p165)
- Camino Monumento (p166)
- Wine Library (p165)

For reviews, see p165 ➡

Best Places to Drink

- Madison (p167)
- Vertigo 42 (p166)
- Blackfriar (p166)
- Folly (p166)
- Ye Olde Cheshire Cheese (p167)

For reviews, see p166 ➡

Best Churches

- St Bartholomew-the-Great (p162)
- St Stephen Walbrook (p158)
- Temple Church (p165)

For reviews, see p157 ➡

ANDREA PISTOLESI / GETTY IMAGES ©

TOP SIGHT
TOWER OF LONDON

The absolute kernel of London, with a history as bleak and bloody as it is fascinating, the Tower of London should be very near the top of anyone's list of London's sights. Begun during the reign of William the Conqueror (1066–87), the Tower is in fact a castle containing 22 towers, and has served over the years as a palace, observatory, storehouse, mint and even a zoo but most famously as a prison and site of execution.

Plan to spend at least half a day in this incredible complex. Having a plan of attack is highly appropriate here and ours starts with one of the excellent Yeoman Warder's tours.

Tower Green

The buildings to the west and the south of this verdant patch have always accommodated Tower officials. Indeed, the current Tower constable has a flat in Queen's House built in 1540. But what looks at first glance like a peaceful, almost village-y slice of the Tower's inner ward is actually one of its bloodiest.

Scaffold Site

Those 'lucky' enough to meet their fate here (rather than suffering the embarrassment of execution on Tower Hill observed by tens of thousands of jeering and cheering onlookers) numbered but a handful and included Henry VIII's wives (and alleged adulterers) Anne Boleyn and Catherine Howard; 16-year-old Lady Jane Grey, who fell foul of Henry's daughter Mary I by attempting to have herself crowned queen; and Robert Devereux, Earl of Essex,

DON'T MISS...

- Crown Jewels
- Tower Green scaffold site
- White Tower and armour collection
- A Yeoman Warder's tour
- Ravens
- Medieval Palace

PRACTICALITIES

- Map p442
- ☎0844 4827777
- www.hrp.org.uk/toweroflondon
- Tower Hill, EC3
- adult/child £21.45/10.75, audioguide £4/3
- 9am-5.30pm Tue-Sat, from 10am Sun & Mon, to 4.30pm Nov-Feb
- Tower Hill

once a favourite of Elizabeth I. Just west of the scaffold site is brick-faced **Beauchamp Tower**, where high-ranking prisoners have left behind unhappy inscriptions and other graffiti.

Chapel Royal of St Peter ad Vincula

Just north of the site is the Chapel Royal of St Peter ad Vincula (St Peter in Chains), a rare example of ecclesiastical Tudor architecture and the burial place of those beheaded on the scaffold outside, most notably Anne Boleyn, Catherine Howard and Lady Jane Grey. The church can be visited on a Yeoman Warder tour or during the first and last hour of normal opening hours.

Crown Jewels

To the east of the chapel and north of the White Tower is **Waterloo Barracks**, the home of the Crown Jewels, which are said to be worth up to £20 billion but are in a very real sense priceless. Here, you file past footage film clips of the jewels and their role through through history and of Queen Elizabeth II's coronation in 1953 before you reach the vault itself.

Once inside you'll be greeted by lavishly bejewelled sceptres, plates, orbs and, naturally, crowns. A travelator takes you past the dozen or so crowns and other coronation regalia, including the platinum crown of the late Queen Mother, Elizabeth, which is set with the 105-carat Koh-i-Noor (Mountain of Light) diamond, and the State Sceptre with the Cross topped with the 530-carat First Star of Africa (or Cullinan I) diamond. A bit father on is the centrepiece: the Imperial State Crown, set with diamonds (including the 317-carat Second Star of Africa, or Cullinan II), sapphires, emeralds, rubies and pearls and worn by the Queen at the State Opening of Parliament. Note the bizarrely shaped boxes at the exit used to transport the jewels from the Tower to state functions.

White Tower

Begun in 1078, this was the original 'Tower' of London, built as a palace and fortress; its name arose after Henry III whitewashed it in the 13th century. Standing just 30m, it's not exactly tall by modern standards. But in the the Middle Ages it would have dwarfed the wooded huts surrounding the castle walls and intimidated the peasantry.

Apart from St John's Chapel, most of its interior is given over to a **Royal Armouries** collection of cannons, guns and suits of mail and armour for men and horses. Among the most remarkable exhibits on the entrance floor are Henry VIII's two suits of armour, one made for him when he was a dashing

YEOMAN WARDERS

A true icon of the city, the Yeoman Warders have been guarding the tower since the late 15th century. There can be up to 40 – they number 37 at present – and, in order to qualify for the job, they must have served a minimum of 22 years in any branch of the British Armed Forces. They all live within the tower walls and are known affectionately as 'Beefeaters', a nickname they dislike. The origin of this name is unknown, although it's thought to be due to the large rations of beef – then a luxury food – given to them in the past. There is currently just one female Yeoman Warder, Moira Cameron, who in 2007 became the first ever woman to be given the post. While officially they guard the Tower and Crown Jewels at night, their main role is as tour guides (and to pose for photographs with curious foreigners). Tours leave from the Middle Tower every 30 minutes from 10am to 3.30pm (2.30pm in winter).

The red-brick New Armouries Cafe, in the southeastern corner of the inner courtyard, offers hot meals, sandwiches and drinks.

TACKLING THE TOWER

Although it's usually less busy in the late afternoon, don't leave your assault on the Tower until too late in the day. You could easily spend hours here and not see it all. Start by getting your bearings on one of the Yeoman Warder (Beefeater) tours; they are included in the cost of admission, entertaining and the easiest way to access the **Chapel Royal of St Peter ad Vincula** **1**, which is where they finish up.

When you leave the chapel, the **Tower Green Scaffold Site** **2** is directly in front. The building immediately to your left is Waterloo Barracks, where the **Crown Jewels** **3** are housed. These are the absolute highlight of a Tower visit, so keep an eye on the entrance and pick a time to visit when it looks relatively quiet. Once inside, take things at your own pace. Slow-moving travelators shunt you past the dozen or so crowns that are the treasury's centrepiece, but feel free to double-back for a second or even third pass – particularly if you ended up on the rear travelator the first time around. Allow plenty of time for the **White Tower** **4**, the core of the whole complex, starting with the exhibition of royal armour. As you continue onto the 1st floor, keep an eye out for **St John's Chapel** **5**. The famous **ravens** **6** can be seen in the courtyard south of the White Tower. Head next through the towers that formed the **Medieval Palace** **7**, then take the **East Wall Walk** **8** to get a feel for the castle's mighty battlements. Spend the rest of your time poking around the many other fascinating nooks and crannies of the Tower complex.

BEAT THE QUEUES

➡ **Buy** your fast-track ticket in advance online or at the City of London Information Centre in St Paul's Churchyard.

➡ **Become a member** An annual Historic Royal Palaces membership allows you to jump the queues and visit the Tower (and four other London palaces) as often as you like.

MIKE BOOTH / ALAMY ©

Chapel Royal of St Peter ad Vincula
This chapel serves as the resting place for the royals and other members of the aristocracy who were executed on the small green out front. Several other historical figures are buried here too, including Thomas More.

Tower Green Scaffold Site
Seven people, including three queens (Anne Boleyn, Catherine Howard and Jane Grey), lost their heads here during Tudor times, saving the monarch the embarrassment of public executions on Tower Hill. The site now features a sculpture by Brian Catling.

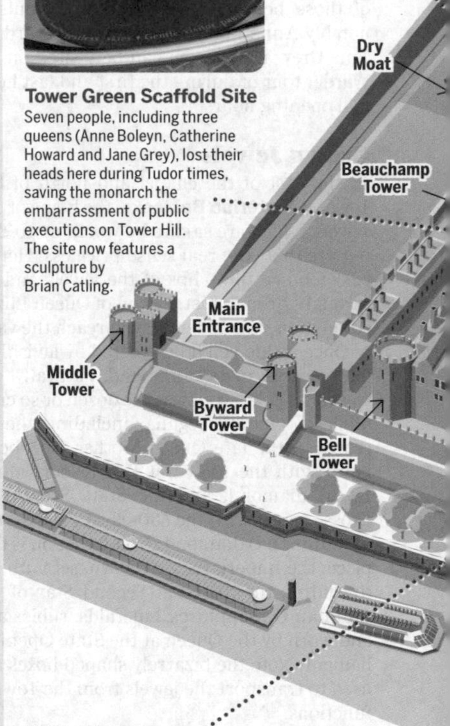

White Tower
Much of the White Tower is taken up with an exhibition on 500 years of royal armour. Look for the virtually cuboid suit made to match Henry VIII's bloated body, complete with an oversized armoured pouch to protect, ahem, the crown jewels.

PAWEL LIBERA IMAGES / ALAMY ©

St John's Chapel

Kept as plain and unadorned as it would have been in Norman times, the White Tower's 1st-floor chapel is the oldest surviving church in London, dating from 1080.

TOM HANLEY / ALAMY ©

Crown Jewels

When they're not being worn for ceremonies of state, Her Majesty's bling is kept here. Among the 23,578 gems, look out for the 530-carat Cullinan I diamond at the top of the Sovereign's Sceptre with cross, the largest part of what was then the largest diamond ever found.

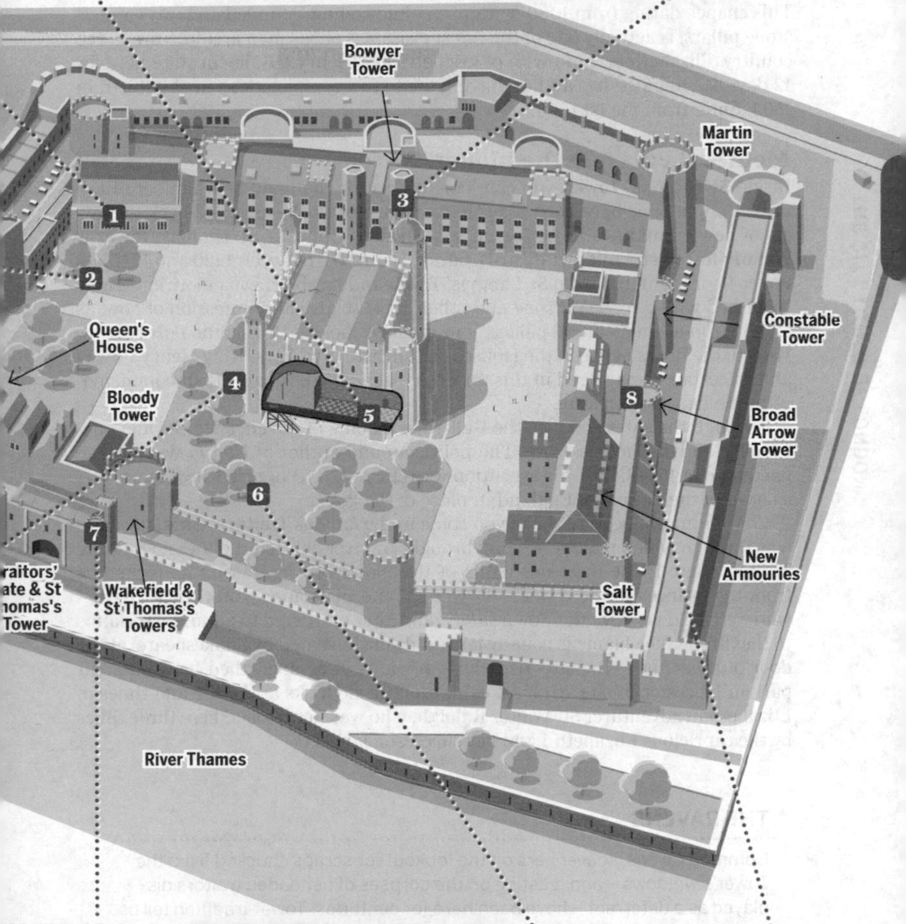

Medieval Palace

This part of the Tower complex was begun around 1220 and was home to England's medieval monarchs. Look for the recreations of the bedchamber of Edward I (1272–1307) in St Thomas's Tower and the throne room of his father, Henry III (1216–72) in the Wakefield Tower.

ENIGMA / ALAMY ©

Ravens

This stretch of green is where the Tower's half dozen ravens are kept, fed on raw meat and blood-soaked bird biscuits. According to legend, if the birds were to leave the Tower, the kingdom would fall.

East Wall Walk

Follow the inner ramparts, starting from the 13th-century Salt Tower, passing through the Broad Arrow and Constable Towers, and ending at the Martin Tower, where the Crown Jewels were stored till the mid-19th century.

24-year-old and the other when he was a bloated 50-year-old with a waist measuring 51 inches (129cm). On the 1st floor, check out the 2m suit of armour once thought to have been made for the giant-like John of Gaunt and, alongside it, a tiny child's suit of armour designed for James I's young son, the future Charles I. Up on the 2nd floor you'll find the block and axe used to execute Simon Fraser at the last public execution on Tower Hill in 1747.

St John's Chapel

This chapel, dating from 1080, with its vaulted ceiling, rounded archways and 12 stone pillars, is actually one of the finest examples of Norman architecture in the country. Elizabeth of York, wife of grief-stricken Henry VII, lay in state here for 12 days, surrounded by candles, having died after complications in childbirth in 1503. Enter from the 1st floor.

Medieval Palace & the Bloody Tower

Inside **St Thomas' Tower**, you can look at what the hall and bedchamber of Edward I might once have been like. Here archaeologists have peeled back the layers of newer buildings to find what went before. Opposite St Thomas' Tower is **Wakefield Tower**, built by Edward's father, Henry III, between 1220 and 1240. Its upper floor is entered from St Thomas' Tower and has been even more enticingly furnished with a replica throne and other decor to give an impression of how, as an ante-room in a medieval palace, it might have looked. During the 15th-century Wars of the Roses between the Houses of Lancaster and York, King Henry VI was almost certainly murdered in this tower. A plaque on the chapel floor commemorates the Lancastrian king.

Through the gates you face the **Bell Tower**, home of the curfew bells and one-time lock-up of Thomas More. The politician and author of *Utopia* was imprisoned here in 1534 before his execution for refusing to recognise King Henry VIII as head of the Church of England in place of the Pope.

Continuing along Water Lane you come to the famous **Traitors' Gate**, the gateway through which prisoners being brought by river entered the tower. Opposite Traitors' Gate is the huge portcullis of the Bloody Tower, taking its nickname from the 'princes in the tower' – Edward V and his younger brother, Richard – who were held here 'for their own safety' and later murdered to annul their claims to the throne. The blame is usually laid (and substantiated by Shakespeare) at the door of their uncle, Richard III, whose remains were unearthed beneath a car park in Leicester in late 2012. An exhibition inside looks at the life and times of Elizabethan adventurer Sir Walter Raleigh, who was imprisoned here three times by the capricious Elizabeth I and her successor James I.

THE RAVENS

Common ravens, scavengers on the lookout for scraps chucked from the Tower's windows – and feasting on the corpses of beheaded traitors displayed as a deterrent – have been here for centuries. Tower tradition tell us that when it was proposed they be culled, someone remembered the old legend that should the ravens depart, a great calamity would befall England. Having lived through the plague, the Great Fire *and* the execution of his father, Charles II clearly wasn't going to take any chances and let the birds stay. There are always at least six ravens in residence at the Tower, and their wing feathers are clipped to keep them around. The birds are all named and live charmed, well-fed (6oz of raw beef, biscuits soaked in blood, the odd egg etc) lives.

East Wall Walk

East Wall Walk

The huge inner wall of the Tower was added to the fortress in 1220 by Henry III to improve the castle's defences. It is 36m wide and is dotted with towers along its length. The East Wall Walk allows you to climb up and tour its eastern edge, beginning in the 13th-century **Salt Tower,** probably used to store saltpetre for gunpowder. The walk also takes in **Broad Arrow Tower** and **Constable Tower**, each containing small exhibits. It ends at the **Martin Tower**, which houses an exhibition about the original coronation regalia. Here you can see some of the older crowns, whose jewels have been removed. The oldest surviving crown (1715) is that of George I, which is topped with the ball and cross from James II's crown. It was from the Martin Tower that Colonel Thomas Blood attempted to steal the Crown Jewels in 1671, disguised as a clergyman. Surprisingly Charles II gave him a full pardon.

CEREMONY OF THE KEYS

The elaborate locking of the main gates has been performed daily without fail for more than 700 years. The ceremony begins at 9.53pm precisely, and it's all over by 10pm. Even when a bomb hit the Tower of London during the Blitz, the ceremony was only delayed by 30 minutes – the essence of the famed British stiff upper lip. Entry to the ceremony begins at 9.30pm and is free but, in a suitably antiquated style, you have to apply for tickets by post as demand is so high; see the Tower website.

The official unlocking of the Tower takes place every day at 9am. The keys are escorted by a military guard and the doors are unlocked by a Yeoman Warder. With fewer visitors around, this is a great time to arrive. And everyone can see the Ceremony of the Word at 2.45pm daily when the Queen's Guard on duty at Waterloo Barracks marches to the Byward Tower to collect the secret password for after-hours entry to the Tower from the Chief Yeoman Warder.

CHRISTER FREDRIKSSON / GETTY IMAGES ©

TOP SIGHT
ST PAUL'S CATHEDRAL

Towering over Ludgate Hill, one of just three hills in the pancake-flat City, in a superb position that has been a place of Christian worship for over 1400 years, St Paul's Cathedral is one of London's most majestic and iconic buildings. For Londoners the vast dome, which still manages to dominate the skyline despite the far higher skyscrapers of the Square Mile, is a symbol of resilience and pride, standing tall for over 300 years (in this incarnation).

Officially completed in 1711 and sporting the capital's largest church dome, this is the fifth Christian church to stand on this site.

The most painless way to explore the cathedral is by joining a free 1½-hour guided tour, which grants you access to the Geometric Staircase, the Chapel of St Michael and St George and the quire. These *usually* take place a half-dozen times a day (10.30am, 10.45am, 11.15am, 1pm, 1.30pm and 2pm); head to the desk just past the entrance to check times and book a place. You can also inquire here about the shorter introductory talks of 15 to 20 minutes. Or pick up one of the free 1½-hour iPod tours at the entrance.

DON'T MISS...

- Climbing the dome
- Quire ceiling mosaics
- Tombs of Admiral Nelson and Duke of Wellington
- American Memorial Chapel

PRACTICALITIES

- Map p442
- www.stpauls.co.uk
- St Paul's Churchyard, EC4
- adult/child £15/6
- 8.30am-4.30pm Mon-Sat, last entry 4pm
- St Paul's

Dome

Despite the cathedral's rich history and impressive (and uniform) English Baroque interior, many visitors are more interested in climbing the dome for one of the best views of London. It actually consists of two domes, a brick inner one, a nonstructural outer one visible on the skyline and a brick cone between them holding it all together, one inside the other. This unique structure, the first triple dome ever built and second only to St Peter's in the Vatican in size, made the cathedral Christopher Wren's tour de force.

Exactly 528 stairs take you to the top, but it's a three-stage journey. Through a door on the western side of the southern transept and some 30m and precisely 257 steps above, you reach the interior walkway around the dome's base. This is the **Whispering Gallery**, so called because if you talk close to the wall it really does carry your words around to the opposite side, 32m away. Climbing even more steps (another 119) you reach the **Stone Gallery**, an exterior viewing platform at 53m obscured by pillars and other suicide-preventing measures. The remaining 152 iron steps to the **Golden Gallery** are steeper and narrower than below but are really worth the effort. From here, 85m above London, you can enjoy superb 360-degree views of the city.

Interior

Just beneath the dome is an **epitaph** written for Wren by his son: *Lector, si monumentum requiris, circumspice* (Reader, if you seek his monument, look around you). In the north aisle you'll find the grandiose **Duke of Wellington Memorial** (1912), which took 54 years to complete; the Iron Duke's horse Copenhagen originally faced the other way but it was deemed unfitting that a horse's rear end should face the altar.

In the north transept chapel is Holman Hunt's celebrated painting, *The Light of the World*, which depicts Christ knocking at an overgrown door that, symbolically, can only be opened from within. Beyond, in the cathedral's heart, are the particularly spectacular **quire** (or chancel) – its ceilings and arches dazzling with green, blue, red and gold mosaics telling the story of creation – and the **high altar**. The ornately carved choir stalls by Dutchman Grinling Gibbons on either side of the quire are exquisite, as are the ornamental wrought-iron gates, separating the aisles from the altar, by French Huguenot Jean Tijou (both men also worked on Hampton Court Palace).

Walk around the altar, with its massive gilded oak **baldacchino**, a kind of canopy with barley-twist columns, to the **American Memorial Chapel**, a memorial to the 28,000 US Citizens based in Britain who lost their lives during WWII. Note the Roll of Honour book turned daily, the state flags in the stained glass and American flora and fauna in the carved wood panelling.

In the south quire aisle is an **effigy of John Donne** (1573–1631), metaphysical poet and one-time dean of Old St Paul's, that survived the Great Fire.

REFRESHMENTS & FACILITIES

In the crypt you'll find the **Crypt Café** (dishes £5.65-8.25; ⏲9am-5pm Mon-Sat, noon-4pm Sun) for light meals, and the excellent **Restaurant at St Paul's** (Map p442; ☎020-7248 2469; www.restaurantatstpauls.co.uk; 2-/3-course lunch £21.50/25.95; ⏲noon-5pm; 📶), in addition to a **shop** (⏲8.30am-5pm Mon-Sat, 10am-4.30pm Sun). Anyone is welcome to use the facilities in the cathedral crypt (for free), entering via the side door under the north transept.

As part of its 300th-anniversary celebrations, St Paul's underwent a £40-million, decade-long renovation project that cleaned the cathedral inside and out – a painstakingly slow process that has been likened to carefully applying and removing a face mask. To the right as you face the enormous Great West Door (opened only on special occasions), there is a section of unrestored wall under glass that shows the effects of centuries of pollution and failed restoration attempts in the past. How dark and gloomy St Paul's had become!

Crypt

On the eastern side of both the north and south transepts are stairs leading down to the crypt and **OBE Chapel**, where services are held for members of the Order of the British Empire. The crypt has memorials to some 300 heroes and military demigods, including Florence Nightingale, Lord Kitchener and Winston Churchill, while both the Duke of Wellington and Admiral Nelson are actually buried here. On the surrounding walls are plaques in memory of those from the Commonwealth who died in various conflicts during the 20th century, including Gallipoli and the Falklands War.

Wren's tomb is also in the crypt, and many others, notably artists (Joshua Reynolds, John Everett Millais, JMW Turner; William Holman Hunt), are remembered here too.

The **Oculus** in the former treasury projects four short films onto its walls (you'll need to have picked up the iPod to hear the commentary).

Exterior

Just outside the north transept, there's a simple **monument to the people of London**, honouring the 32,000 civilians killed (and another 50,000 seriously injured) in the city during WWII. Also to the north at the entrance to Paternoster Square is **Temple Bar**, one of the original gateways to the City of London. This medieval stone archway once straddled Fleet St at a site marked by a silver dragon but was removed to Middlesex in 1877. It was moved here in 2004.

ST PAUL'S CATHEDRAL

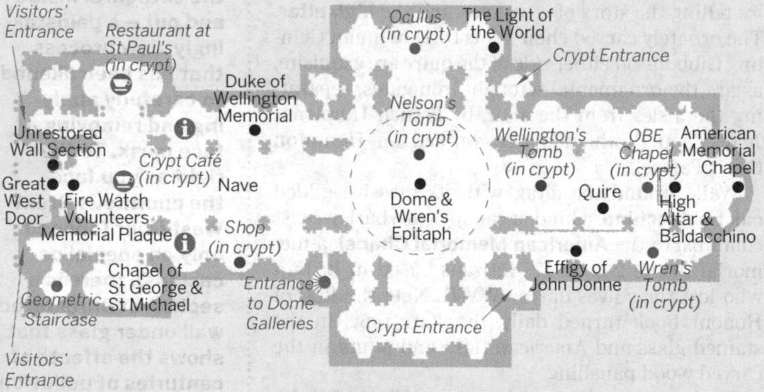

Cathedral Floor & Crypt

◉ SIGHTS

TOWER OF LONDON CASTLE
See p148.

ST PAUL'S CATHEDRAL CHURCH
See p154.

ALL HALLOWS-BY-THE-TOWER CHURCH
Map p442 (www.ahbtt.org.uk; Byward St, EC3; ⊙8am-6pm Mon-Fri, 10am-5pm Sat, 10am-1pm Sun; ⊖Tower Hill) **FREE** A church by this name (meaning 'all saints') has stood here since AD 675. Despite its proximity to the spot where the Great Fire started (Samuel Pepys watched the blaze from the brick tower), All Hallows survived virtually unscathed, only to be hit by German bombs in 1940.

In the atmospheric Saxon undercroft (crypt) you'll find a pavement of 2nd-century Roman tiles and walls of the 7th-century Saxon church. In the nave note the pulpit taken from a Wren church on Cannon St destroyed in WWII and the beautiful 17th-century font cover decorated by the master woodcarver Grinling Gibbons. The church has a strong American connection: William Penn, founder of Pennsylvania, was baptised here in 1644, and John Quincy Adams, sixth president of the USA, was married here in 1797. Free 20-minute tours depart daily at 2pm from April to October.

TRINITY SQUARE GARDENS GARDENS
Map p442 (⊖Tower Hill) Trinity Square Gardens, just west of Tower Hill tube station, was once the site of the Tower Hill scaffold where many met their fate, the last in 1747. Now it's a much more peaceful place, ringed with important buildings and bits of the Roman wall.

To the north is **Trinity House** (1795), topped with a ship weather vane and housing the General Lighthouse Authority for England and Wales. To the west is the massive former **Port of London Authority building** (1922) lorded over by Father Thames; it's now being converted into a residential block and hotel. To the south is Edwin Lutyens' **Tower Hill Memorial** (1928), dedicated to the 24,000 merchant sailors who died in both world wars and have no known grave. On a grassy area next to the tube's main exit there's a stretch of the **medieval wall** built on Roman foundations, with a modern **statue of Emperor Trajan** (r AD 98–117) standing in front of it. You can see more of the 2nd-century Roman wall around the corner from the tube station, in the forecourt of the Grange Hotel.

ST OLAVE'S CHURCH
Map p442 (www.sanctuaryinthecity.net; 8 Hart St, EC3; ⊙9am-5pm Mon-Fri, closed Aug; ⊖Tower Hill) **FREE** Tucked at the end of quiet Seething Lane, St Olave's was built in the mid-15th century and survived the Great Fire. It was bombed in 1941 and restored in the 1950s. The diarist Samuel Pepys worshipped and is buried here; see the tablet on the south wall. Dickens called the place 'St Ghastly Grim' because of the skulls above its entrance.

30 ST MARY AXE NOTABLE BUILDING
Map p442 (Gherkin; www.30stmaryaxe.co.uk; 30 St Mary Axe, EC3; ⊖Aldgate) ✔ Nicknamed 'the Gherkin' for its odd shape, 30 St Mary Axe remains the City's most distinctive skyscraper, dominating the skyline though actually being slightly smaller than the neighbouring NatWest Tower. Built in 2003 by award-winning Norman Foster, the phallic Gherkin's futuristic exterior has become an emblem of modern London and as recognisable as Big Ben or the London Eye.

LLOYD'S OF LONDON NOTABLE BUILDING
Map p442 (www.lloyds.com/lloyds/about-us/the-lloyds-building; 1 Lime St, EC3; ⊖Aldgate or Monument) While the world's leading insurance brokers are inside underwriting everything from cosmonauts' lives to film stars' legs, people outside still stop to gawp at the stainless-steel external ducting and staircases of this 1986 building. Designed by Richard Rogers, one of the architects of the Pompidou Centre in Paris, its brave-new-world postmodernism strikes a particular contrast with the olde-worlde Leadenhall Market next door.

LEADENHALL MARKET MARKET
Map p442 (www.leadenhallmarket.co.uk; Whittington Ave, EC3; ⊙public areas 24hr, shop times vary; ⊖Bank) Like stepping into a small slice of Victorian London, a visit to this covered mall off Gracechurch St is a step back in time. There's been a market on this site since the Roman era, but the architecture that survives is all cobblestones and late-19th-century ironwork; even modern restaurants and chain stores decorate their facades in period style here.

TOP SIGHT
TOWER BRIDGE

One of London's most recognisable sights, Tower Bridge doesn't disappoint up close. There's something about its neo-Gothic towers and blue suspension struts that make it quite enthralling. Built in 1894 as a much-needed crossing point in the east, it was equipped with a then revolutionary bascule (see-saw) mechanism that could clear the way for oncoming ships in three minutes. Although London's days as a thriving port are long over, the bridge still does its stuff, lifting around 1000 times a year and as often as 10 times a day in summer.

Housed within is the **Tower Bridge Exhibition** (Map p442; www.towerbridge.org.uk; adult/child £8/3.40; ⌚10am-6pm Apr-Sep, 9.30am-5.30pm Oct-Mar), which explains the nuts and bolts of it all. If you're not technically minded, it's still fascinating to get inside the bridge and look along the Thames from its two walkways. A lift takes you to the top of the structure, 42m above the river, from where you can walk along the east- and west-facing walkways, lined with information boards. There are a couple of stops on the way down before you exit and continue on to the Engine Rooms, which provide the real mechanical detail, and also house a few interactive exhibits and a couple of short films.

DON'T MISS...

- Bridge lifting
- Victorian Engine Rooms
- View from top

PRACTICALITIES

- Map p442
- ⊖Tower Hill

The market appears as Diagon Alley in *Harry Potter and the Philosopher's Stone* and an optician's shop was used for the entrance to the Leaky Cauldron wizarding pub in *Harry Potter and the Goblet of Fire*.

BANK OF ENGLAND MUSEUM — MUSEUM

Map p442 (www.bankofengland.co.uk/museum; Bartholomew Lane, EC2; ⌚10am-5pm Mon-Fri; ⊖Bank) FREE The centrepiece of this museum, which explores the evolution of money and the history of the venerable Bank of England founded in 1694, is a reconstruction of architect John Soane's original Bank Stock Office, complete with original mahogany counters. A series of rooms leading off the office are packed with exhibits ranging from silverware and coins to a 13kg gold bar you can lift up.

ROYAL EXCHANGE — HISTORIC BUILDING

Map p442 (www.theroyalexchange.co.uk; Royal Exchange, EC3; ⌚shops 10am-6pm, restaurants 8am-11pm; ⊖Bank) Founded by Thomas Gresham in 1564, this imposing, colonnaded building at the juncture of Threadneedle St and Cornhill is the third building on the site; the first was officially opened by Elizabeth I in 1571. It has not had a role as a financial institution since the 1980s and now houses a posh shopping centre, a cafe and restaurant.

MANSION HOUSE — HISTORIC BUILDING

Map p442 (☎020-7626 2500; www.cityoflondon.gov.uk; btwn King William St & Walbrook; guided tour adult/concession £7/5; ⌚2pm Tue; ⊖Bank) Opposite the Bank of England stands porticoed Mansion House, the official residence of the Lord Mayor of London. Built in 1752 by George Dance the Elder, its magnificent interiors, including an impressive art collection and stunning banqueting hall, can be visited on a weekly tour, which leaves from the porch entrance on Walbrook. The 40 tickets are sold on a first-come-first-served basis.

ST STEPHEN WALBROOK — CHURCH

Map p442 (www.ststephenwalbrook.net; 39 Walbrook, EC4; ⌚10am-4pm Mon-Fri; ⊖Bank) FREE Just south of Mansion House, St Stephen Walbrook (1672) is considered to be the finest of Wren's City churches and, as it was his first experiment with a dome, a forerunner to St Paul's Cathedral. Some 16 pillars with Corinthian capitals rise up to support the dome; the modern travertine marble altar nicknamed 'the Camembert' is by sculptor Henry More.

The late rector Chad Varah founded the Samaritans here to befriend and assist the suicidal and desperate. The original 'hotline' telephone from 1953 is on display in a glass box inside.

TEMPLE OF MITHRAS RUIN

Map p442 (Btwn Queen Victoria St & Walbrook EC4; ⊖Bank) A site not visible at the time of research is the 3rd-century Temple of Mithras. It was first uncovered in the 1950s during the construction of Bucklersbury House, an office block on Walbrook St, and the temple was then moved to Queen St where it remained until 2010. The peripatetic house of worship is now under wraps while work on Walbrook Square, future headquarters of the financial media giant Bloomberg, continues and it will be relocated to its original site when complete. In the meantime if you're interested in this Persian god, artefacts found in the temple are on display at the Museum of London (p161).

ST MARY-LE-BOW CHURCH

Map p442 (☎020-7248 5139; www.stmarylebow.co.uk; Cheapside, EC2; ⏱7.30am-6pm Mon-Wed, to 6.30pm Thu, to 4pm Fri; ⊖St Paul's or Bank) FREE Another of Wren's great churches, St Mary-le-Bow (1673) is famous as the church with the medieval curfew bells that still dictate who is – and who is not – a true cockney; it's said that a true cockney has to have been born within earshot of Bow Bells. The church's delicate steeple is one of Wren's finest works.

GUILDHALL HISTORIC BUILDING

Map p442 (☎020-7606 3030; www.guildhall.cityoflondon.gov.uk; Gresham St, EC2; ⊖Bank) Bang in the centre of the Square Mile, the Guildhall has been the City's seat of government for more than 800 years. The present building dates from the early 15th century, making it the only secular stone structure to have survived the Great Fire of 1666, although it was severely damaged both then and during the Blitz of 1940.

Check in at reception to visit the impressive **Great Hall** (⏱9am-5pm, closed Sun Oct-Apr) where you can see the banners and shields of London's 12 principal livery companies, or guilds, which used to wield absolute power throughout the city. The lord mayor and two sheriffs are still elected annually in the vast open hall.

TOP SIGHT MONUMENT

Sir Christopher Wren and Dr Robert Hooke's huge 1677 column, known simply as the Monument, is a memorial to the Great Fire of London of 1666, whose impact on London's history cannot be overstated. Tens of thousands of Londoners were left homeless and much of the city was destroyed (though only a handful of people died).

An immense Doric column made of Portland stone, the 'Fish St Pillar' (as Hooke called it) is 4.5m wide, and 60.6m tall – the exact distance it stands from the bakery in Pudding Lane where the fire reputedly started – and is topped with a gilded bronze urn of flames that some think looks like a big gold pincushion. Although Lilliputian by today's standards, the Monument would have been gigantic when built, and towered over London.

Climbing up the column's 311 spiral steps rewards you with some of the best 360-degree views over London (due to its central location as much as to its height). And after your descent, you'll also be the proud owner of a certificate that commemorates your achievement.

DON'T MISS...

- Fantastic views
- Claiming your certificate

PRACTICALITIES

- Map p442
- www.themonument.info
- Fish Street Hill, EC3
- adult/child £3/1
- ⏱9.30am-5.30pm
- ⊖Monument

LOCAL KNOWLEDGE

GOG & MAGOG

According to the 12th-century *Historia Regum Britanniae* (History of the Kings of Britain) by Geoffrey of Monmouth, Britain was once inhabited by giants who were conquered by Brutus the Trojan and his compatriot, Corineus. Brutus founded Troia Nova (New Troy), or London, while Corineus established Cornwall after hurling the last of the great giants, the 3.5m-tall chieftain, Gogmagog, into the sea. By the 18th century Gog and Magog were thought to have been the last two surviving giants, forced to work for Brutus in his palace on the site of today's Guildhall. The pair of effigies of the giants there is the third since the reign of Henry V.

Among the monuments to look out for are statues of Winston Churchill, Admiral Nelson, the Duke of Wellington, the two prime ministers Pitt the Elder and Younger and William Beckford, father of the similarly named author and a former lord mayor. In the upper gallery at the western end are statues of the biblical giants Gog and Magog, traditionally considered to be guardians of the city; today's figures replaced similar 18th-century statues destroyed in the Blitz. The Guildhall's stained glass was also blown out during the Blitz but a modern window in the southwestern corner depicts the city's history; look out for a picture of London's most famous lord mayor, Richard 'Dick' Whittington, with his famous cat, a scene of the Great Fire and even the Lloyd's of London building.

The modern buildings to the west house Corporation of London offices and the **Guildhall Library** (Map p442; Aldermanbury, EC2; ⏲9.30am-5pm Mon-Sat), founded in 1425 under the terms of Dick Whittington's will. It specialises in the history of London and contains a large collection of cookery books by Elizabeth David. Also here is the **Clockmakers' Museum** (Map p442; www.clockmakers.org; ⏲9.30am-4.45pm Mon-Sat) FREE, which has a collection of more than 700 clocks and watches dating back some 500 years.

GUILDHALL ART GALLERY & ROMAN AMPHITHEATRE — GALLERY

Map p442 (www.guildhallartgallery.cityoflondon.gov.uk; Guildhall Yard, EC2; admission free, special exhibits £5; ⏲10am-5pm Mon-Sat, noon-4pm Sun; ⊖Bank) FREE The gallery of the City of London provides a fascinating look at the politics of the Square Mile over the past few centuries, with a great collection of paintings of London in the 18th and 19th centuries. Below the gallery is a Roman amphitheatre dating back to the early 2nd century AD.

Among paintings by Thomas Lawrence, George Frederick Watts and Lawrence Alma-Tadema is *The Defeat of the Floating Batteries* (1791) by the American John Singleton Copley, which depicts the British victory at Gibraltar in 1782. This huge oil painting was removed to safety just a month before the gallery was hit by a German bomb in 1941 – it spent 50 years rolled up before a spectacular restoration in 1999.

The archaeological remains of Roman London's amphitheatre (or coliseum) were only discovered in 1988 when work finally began on a new gallery after the original's destruction in the Blitz. They were immediately declared an ancient monument, and the new gallery was built around them. While only a few remnants of the stone walls lining the eastern entrance still stand, they're imaginatively fleshed out with a black-and-fluorescent-green *trompe l'oeil* of the missing seating, and computer-meshed outlines of spectators and gladiators. Markings on the square outside the Guildhall indicate the original extent and scale of the amphitheatre, which could seat up to 6000 spectators.

ST LAWRENCE JEWRY — CHURCH

Map p442 (www.stlawrencejewry.org.uk; Gresham St, EC2; ⏲8am-4pm; ⊖Bank) FREE To look at the Corporation of London's well-preserved official church, you'd barely realise that it was almost completely destroyed during WWII bombing. Instead it does Sir Christopher Wren, who built it in 1677, and its subsequent restorers, proud with its immaculate alabaster walls and gilt trimmings.

The arms of the City of London can be seen on the north wall and the Commonwealth Chapel is bedecked with the flags of member nations. Free piano recitals are held each Monday at 1pm; organ recitals at the same time on Tuesday.

The first part of the church's name refers to a 3rd-century Christian martyr executed on a sizzling gridiron (see a copy of same atop the spire). As the second part suggests this was once part of the Jewish quarter – the centre being Old Jewry, the street to the southeast. The Jews were expelled from England by Edward I in 1290 and did not return until the late 17th century.

BARBICAN HISTORIC BUILDING

Map p442 (☎0845-1216823; www.barbican.org.uk; Silk St, EC2; architectural tours £8; ⊙arts centre 9am-11pm Mon-Sat, noon-1pm Sun, architectural tours 4pm Wed, 7pm Thu, 11am & 2pm Sat & 2pm Sun; 📶; ⊖Barbican or Moorgate)

Londoners remain fairly divided about the architectural legacy of this vast complex but the Barbican remains the City's preeminent cultural centre, boasting the main Barbican Hall, two theatres, a new cinema complex and two well-regarded art galleries, the **Barbican Gallery** (⊙11am-8pm Fri-Tue, to 6pm Wed, to 10pm Thu), and the **Curve** (⊙11am-8pm Fri-Wed, to 10pm Thu). It also has three restaurants, including the highly recommended canteen-style **Barbican Foodhall** (⊙9am-8.30pm Mon-Sat, 11am-8pm Sun).

Built on a huge bomb site abandoned since WWII and opened progressively between 1969 and 1982, this vast housing and cultural complex is named after a Roman fortification that may once have stood here protecting ancient Londinium. It's fair to say that its austere concrete isn't everyone's cup of tea. Yet, although it has topped several polls as London's ugliest building, many Londoners see something very beautiful about its cohesion and ambition – it incorporates John Milton's parish church, **St Giles Cripplegate** (Map p442; www.stgilescripplegate.com; Fore St, EC2; ⊙11am-4pm Mon-Fri), into its avant-garde (for the time) design and embellishes its public areas with lakes and ponds ringed with benches. Apartments in the three high-rise towers that surround the cultural centre are some of the city's most sought-after living spaces. Guided architectural tours are fascinating and the best way to make sense of the purpose and beauty of the estate.

Getting around the Barbican can be frustratingly difficult. There are stairs from the Barbican tube station that take you up onto the highwalks, from where a yellow line on the floor guides you to the arts complex.

TOP SIGHT
MUSEUM OF LONDON

One of the capital's best museums, this is a fascinating walk through the various incarnations of the city from Anglo-Saxon village to 21st-century metropolis.

The first gallery, **London Before London**, brings to life the ancient settlements that predated the capital and is followed by the Roman era, full of excellent displays, models and archaeological finds. The rest of the floor takes you through the Saxon, medieval (don't miss the 1348 Black Death video), Tudor and Stuart periods, culminating in the Great Fire of 1666. After a glimpse of the real Roman wall from the window, head down to the modern galleries where, in **Expanding City**, you'll find exquisite fashion and jewellery, the graffitied walls of a prison cell (1750) and the *Rhinebeck Panorama*, an incredibly detailed watercolour of London in 1806–7. After a quick spin through the recreated Georgian Pleasure Gardens, you emerge onto a glorious re-creation of a Victorian street. Highlights of the galleries leading up to the present day include a 1908 taxi cab, an art-deco 1928 lift from Selfridges and costumes worn by East End Pearly Kings and Queens. The testimonies of ordinary people from WWII are particularly moving. Highlights tours depart daily at 11am, noon, 3pm and 4pm.

DON'T MISS...

- Victorian walk
- *Rhinebeck Panorama*
- Wellclose Square prison cell
- Roman London
- 1348 Black Death video

PRACTICALITIES

- Map p442
- www.museumoflondon.org.uk
- 150 London Wall, EC2
- ⊙10am-6pm
- ⊖Barbican

More straightforward is to walk through the Beech St road tunnel to the Silk St entrance.

ST BARTHOLOMEW-THE-GREAT CHURCH

Map p442 (www.greatstbarts.com; West Smithfield, EC1; adult/concession £4/3.50; ⌚8.30am-5pm Mon-Fri, to 4pm mid-Nov–mid-Feb, 10.30am-4pm Sat, 8.30am-8pm Sun; ⊖Farringdon or Barbican) Dating from 1123 and adjoining one of London's oldest hospitals, St Bartholomew-the-Great is worth more than a fleeting visit. The authentic Norman arches and other details lend this holy space an ancient calm; approaching from nearby Smithfield Market through the restored 13th-century archway is like walking back in time.

The church was originally part of the monastery of Augustinian Canons, but became the parish church of Smithfield in 1539 when King Henry VIII dissolved the monasteries. It sits on the corner of the grounds of St Bart's Hospital, on the side closest to Smithfield Market. William Hogarth was baptised here and the American statesman Benjamin Franklin worked on-site in his youth as an apprentice printer. The church has been used as the setting for many films and TV productions, including *Four Weddings and a Funeral*, *Shakespeare in Love*, *Sherlock Holmes* and that hysterical T-Mobile advertisement satirising the royal wedding of Prince William and Kate Middleton in 2011. The **Cloister Cafe** (⌚10am-4pm Mon-Fri, 9.30am-1.30pm & 5.15-6.30pm Sun, closed Sat) is great for a meal or snack.

SMITHFIELD MARKET MARKET

Map p442 (www.smithfieldmarket.com; West Smithfield, EC1; ⌚3am-noon Mon-Fri; ⊖Farringdon) Smithfield is central London's last surviving meat market. Its name derives from 'smooth field' where animals could graze, although its history is far from pastoral as this was once a place where public executions were held. Visit the market before 7am to see it in full swing.

Built on the site of the notorious St Bartholomew's Fair, where witches were traditionally burned at the stake, this is where Scottish independence leader William Wallace was executed in 1305 (there's a plaque on the wall of St Bart's Hospital south of the market ending with the Gaelic words 'Bas agus Buaidh' or 'Death and Victory'), as well as the place where one of the leaders of the Peasants' Revolt, Wat Tyler, met his end in 1381. Described in terms of pure horror by Dickens in *Oliver Twist*, this was once the armpit of London, where animal excrement and entrails created a sea of filth. Today the surrounding area is a very smart annexe of Clerkenwell and full of bars and restaurants, while the market itself is a wonderful building designed in 1868 by Horace Jones (who also did Leadenhall Market and Tower Bridge).

GOLDEN BOY OF PYE CORNER MONUMENT

Map p442 (cnr Cock Lane & Giltspur St, EC1; ⊖St Paul's or Barbican) This small statue of a corpulent boy opposite St Bartholomew's Hospital has a somewhat odd dedication: 'In memory put up for the fire of London occasioned by the sin of gluttony 1666'. All becomes clear, however, when you realise the Great Fire started in a busy bakery on Pudding Lane and finally burned itself out in what was once called Pye (Pie) Corner.

This was interpreted by many as a sign that the fire was an act of God as punishment for the gluttony of Londoners. On this site the Fortune of War pub once stood, gathering place of the 'resurrection men' – bodysnatchers who sold freshly exhumed corpses to surgeons for study at St Barts.

POSTMAN'S PARK PARK

Map p442 (btwn King Edward & St Martin's-le-Grand Sts, EC1; ⊖St Paul's) This peaceful patch of greenery just north of what was once London's General Post Office on St Martin's-le-Grand St would not rate special mention if it were not for the **Memorial to Heroic Self-Sacrifice**, a loggia with 54 ceramic plaques describing deeds of bravery by ordinary people who died saving the lives of others and who might otherwise have been forgotten.

The memorial was the brainchild of the artist George Frederic Watts and unveiled in 1900. His wife, Mary, oversaw the project after his death in 1904 but the memorial was all but abandoned when she died in 1938. Only two plaques have been added since that time, most recently in 2009. That one is dedicated to Leigh Pitt, a print technician who died two years before while trying to rescue a nine-year-old boy who was drowning in a canal in southeast London.

CENTRAL CRIMINAL COURT (OLD BAILEY) HISTORIC BUILDING

Map p442 (www.cityoflondon.gov.uk; cnr Newgate & Old Bailey Sts; ⌚approx 10am-1pm & 2-4pm Mon-Fri; ⊖St Paul's) FREE Just as fact is often better than fiction, taking in a trial in what's nicknamed Old Bailey leaves watching a TV courtroom drama for dust. Even if you end up sitting in on a fairly run-of-the-mill trial, simply being in the court where such people as the Kray brothers and Oscar Wilde (in an earlier building on this site) once appeared is memorable.

The entrance is on Old Bailey St opposite Limeburner Lane and the daily register of cases is outside to the right of the doorway. Choose from 18 courts, of which the oldest – courts one to four – usually have the most interesting cases. As cameras, video equipment, mobile phones, large bags and food and drink are all forbidden inside, and there are no cloakrooms or lockers, it's important not to take these with you. Take a cardigan or something to cushion the hard seats though, and if you're interested in a high-profile trial, get there early.

The Central Criminal Court gets its nickname from the street on which it stands: *baillie* was Norman French for 'enclosed courtyard'. The current building opened in 1907 on the combined site of a previous Old Bailey and Newgate Prison. Intriguingly the figure of justice holding a sword and scales in her hands above the building's copper dome is not blindfolded (against undue influence, as is traditionally the case).

HOLBORN VIADUCT — BRIDGE

Map p442 (⊖St Paul's or Farringdon) This fine iron bridge was built in an effort to smarten up the area, as well as to link Holborn and Newgate St above what had been a valley created by the River Fleet. The four bronze statues represent commerce and agriculture (on the southern side) and science and fine art (on the north).

When Queen Victoria opened it in 1869 she was booed by onlookers because of her relationship with her Scottish servant John Brown.

ST ANDREW HOLBORN — CHURCH

Map p442 (www.standrewholborn.org.uk; Holborn Viaduct, EC4; ⌚9am-5pm Mon-Fri; ⊖Chancery Lane) **FREE** This church on the southeastern corner of Holborn Circus, first mentioned in the 10th century, was rebuilt by Wren in 1686 and is the largest of his parish churches. Even though the interior was bombed to smithereens during WWII, much of what you see inside today is original 17th century, as it was brought from other churches.

DR JOHNSON'S HOUSE — MUSEUM

Map p442 (www.drjohnsonshouse.org; 17 Gough Sq, EC4; adult/child £4.50/1.50, audioguide £2; ⌚11am-5.30pm Mon-Sat May-Sep, to 5pm Mon-Sat Oct-Apr; 👪; ⊖Chancery Lane) This house, built in 1700, is a rare surviving example of a Georgian city mansion. It has been well preserved, as it was the home of the great Georgian wit Samuel Johnson – the author of the first serious dictionary of the English language and the man who proclaimed 'When a man is tired of London, he is tired of life'.

Filled with antique furniture and artefacts from Johnson's life, the house is an atmospheric and worthy place to visit. The numerous paintings of Dr Johnson and his associates, including his black manservant Francis Barber and his clerk and biographer James Boswell, are, sadly, not particularly revealing of the great minds who would have considered the building a home away from home. A more revealing object in the parlour is a chair from Johnson's local pub, the Old Cock Tavern on Fleet St. On display in the 2nd-floor library is a copy of the first edition of the dictionary from 1755.

There are leaflets describing how the lexicographer and six clerks (Boswell wasn't among them, yet) developed the first English dictionary in the house's attic during the period he lived here from 1748 to 1759. Children will love the Georgian dress-up clothes on the top floor, and there are also temporary exhibits (mostly facsimile dictionaries) in the attic.

Out in Gogh Sq fronting the house is a modern statue of Johnson's cat, Hodge, haughtily eating oysters. Below him is the full quote explaining why a man who is tired of London is also tired of life: 'For there is in London all that life can afford'.

ST BRIDE'S, FLEET STREET — CHURCH

Map p442 (☎020-7427 0133; www.stbrides.com; Bride Lane, EC4; admission free, £2 donation requested; ⌚8am-6pm Mon-Fri, hrs vary Sat, 10am-6.30pm Sun; ⊖St Paul's or Blackfriars) Printing presses fell silent on Fleet St in the 1980s, but St Bride's, designed by Christopher Wren in 1671 and his tallest (and most expensive) church after St Paul's, is still referred to as 'the journalists' church'. There's quite a moving chapel in the north aisle honouring journalists who have died or been injured in the course of their work.

The add-on spire (1703) is said to have inspired the design of the tiered wedding

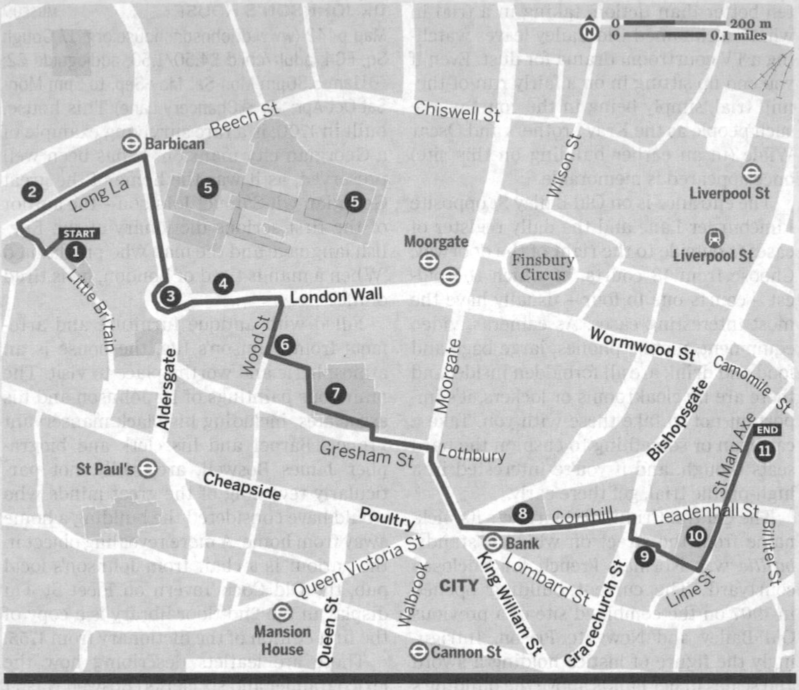

Neighbourhood Walk
A Taste of the City

START ST BARTHOLOMEW-THE-GREAT
END 30 ST MARY AXE
LENGTH 1.5 MILES; THREE HOURS

The City of London has as much history in its Square Mile as the rest of London put together, and this walk picks out just a few of its highlights. Start by exploring the 12th-century **1 St Bartholomew-the-Great** (p162), whose atmospheric interior has been used frequently as a film set. Head out through the Tudor gatehouse and turn right towards the Victorian arches of **2 Smithfield Market** (p162). Take a right down Long Lane and again at Aldersgate St. Follow the roundabout to the right and nip up the stairs to the **3 Museum of London** (p161). Explore the museum's excellent galleries or head to the right to admire the ruins of the **4 Roman city walls** and behind them the distinctive towers and balconies of the **5 Barbican** (p161). Turn right at Wood St to find the remaining tower of **6 St Alban's**, a Wren-designed church destroyed in WWII bombing in 1940. Turn left into Love Lane and right into Aldermanbury – the 15th-century **7 Guildhall** (p159) is on your left. Crossing its paved courtyard – note the black outline of the Roman amphitheatre – continue east onto Gresham St, taking a right into Prince's St and emerging onto the busy Bank intersection lined with neoclassical temples to commerce. Behind the equestrian statue of the Duke of Wellington is a metal pyramid detailing the many significant buildings here. From the **8 Royal Exchange** (p158), follow Cornhill and take a right down Gracechurch St. Turn left and into wonderful **9 Leadenhall Market** (p157), roughly where the Roman forum once stood. As you wander out the far end of the market, **10 Lloyd's of London** (p157) displays its innards for all to see. Once you turn left onto Lime St, **11 30 St Mary Axe** (p157), or 'the Gherkin', looms proudly before you. Built nearly 900 years after St Bartholomew-the-Great, it's a testimony to the city's ability to constantly reinvent itself.

cake. The church was hit by bombs in December 1940, and the interior layout is wood-panelled, modern and not particularly attractive.

In the 11th-century crypt, however, there's a well-presented history of the church, its surrounding areas and the printing industry; don't miss the Roman pavement from the 2nd century AD. Guided tours (£6), which allow access to the charnel house, depart at 3pm on Tuesdays on selected dates (check the website for details).

TEMPLE CHURCH CHURCH

Map p430 (☎020-7353 8559; www.templechurch.com; adult/concession £4/2; ⏰11am-1pm & 2-4pm Mon-Fri, hrs vary) This magnificent church was built by the secretive Knights Templar, an order of crusading monks founded in the 12th century to protect pilgrims travelling to and from Jerusalem. Today the sprawling oasis of fine buildings and pleasant, traffic free green space is home to two Inns of Court: Inner Temple and Middle Temple.

The Temple Church has a distinctive design and is in two parts: the Round (consecrated in 1185 and modelled after the Church of the Holy Sepulchre in Jerusalem) adjoins the Chancel (built in 1240), which is the heart of the modern church. Both parts were severely damaged by a bomb in 1941 and have been completely reconstructed. Its most obvious points of interest are the life-size stone effigies of nine 13th-century knights lying on the floor of the Round. Some of them are cross-legged but contrary to popular belief this doesn't necessarily mean they were crusaders. In recent years the church has become a must-see for readers of *The Da Vinci Code* because a key scene was set here.

Check opening times in advance as they change frequently. During the week the easiest access to the church is via Inner Temple Lane, off Fleet St. At weekends you'll need to enter from Victoria Embankment.

EATING

The financial heart of London unsurprisingly caters for a well-heeled crowd and it can be a tough place to find a meal at the weekend, if not on a weekday evening. You'll find plenty of places to choose from in the One New Change shopping mall, however. During the week, Leadenhall Market (p157) stalls offer a delicious array of food, from steaming noodles to mountains of sweets (11am to 4pm).

CAFÉ BELOW CAFE £

Map p442 (www.cafebelow.co.uk; St Mary-le-Bow Church, Cheapside, EC2; mains £6.50-10; ⏰7.30am-2.30pm Mon-Fri; ✎; ⊖Mansion House) This atmospheric cafe-restaurant, in the crypt of one of London's most famous churches, is breakfast and lunch only these days but offers excellent value and such tasty dishes as fish pie and Moroccan slow roast lamb in focaccia. There are always as many vegetarian choices as meat and fish ones. In summer there are tables outside on the shady courtyard.

★**DUCK & WAFFLE** BRASSERIE ££

Map p442 (☎020-3640 7310; www.duckandwaffle.com; 40th fl, Heron Tower, 110 Bishopsgate, EC2; mains £7-32; ⏰24hr; ⊖Liverpool St) If you like your views with sustenance round the clock, this is the place for you. Perched atop Heron Tower just down from Liverpool St Station, it offers hearty British dishes (lots of offal, some unusual seafood concoctions like pollack meatballs and chip-shop cod tongues) in small and large sizes by day, waffles by night and drinks any time.

BREAD STREET KITCHEN BRASSERIE ££

Map p442 (☎020-3030 4050; www.breadstreetkitchen.com; 10 Bread St, EC4; mains £12-19; ⏰7am-midnight Mon-Fri, from noon Sat & Sun; ⊖St Paul's) Gordon Ramsay's latest foray into the City makes us wonder whether he thinks he's in East London. It's a huge warehouse-like space in One New Change with a raw bar, wine balcony and open kitchen that produces mostly Modern British favourites like mutton and potato pie and roasted cod. 'Lazy Loaf' brunch just might lure the crowds to the City on a Sunday.

WINE LIBRARY MODERN EUROPEAN ££

Map p442 (☎020-7481 0415; www.winelibrary.co.uk; 43 Trinity Sq, EC3; set meal £17.50; ⏰11.30am-3pm Mon, to 8pm Tue-Fri; ⊖Tower Hill) This is a great place for a light but boozy lunch in the City. Buy a bottle of wine at retail price (no mark-up, £7.50 corkage fee) from the large selection on offer at the vaulted-cellar restaurant and then snack on a set plate of delicious pâtés, cheeses and salads. Reservations recommended for lunch.

CAMINO MONUMENTO SPANISH ££

Map p442 (☎020-7841 7335; www.camino.uk.com; 15 Mincing Lane, EC3; mains £13.50-22; ⊙7.30am-11pm Mon-Fri; ⊖Monument) With an enormous map of the Iberian peninsula on one wall and its illustrative name, there's no doubt where you are: in a Spanish restaurant just west of the Monument. Stick with the tapas (£2.25 to £12.75), which might be *del asador* (from the grill) like Rioja chorizo with roasted *piquillo* peppers or the more prosaic *bodega* (cellar) ones like *manchega* cheese.

WHITE SWAN PUB & DINING ROOM GASTROPUB ££

Map p442 (☎020-7242 9696; www.thewhiteswanlondon.com; 108 New Fetter Lane, EC4; mains £13-19.50; ⊙11am-11pm Mon, to midnight Tue-Thu, to 1am Fri; 📶; ⊖Chancery Lane) Though it may look like just another City pub from the street, the White Swan is anything but typical – a smart downstairs bar that serves excellent pub food under the watchful eyes of animal prints and trophies, and an upstairs dining room with a classic, meaty British menu (two-/three-course meal £27/31).

LONDON WALL BAR & KITCHEN BRASSERIE ££

Map p442 (☎020-7600 7340; www.londonwallbarandkitchen.com; 150 London Wall, EC2; mains £9.50-15; ⊙11am-11pm Mon-Fri; ⊖Barbican or St Paul's) Located right at the entrance of the Museum of London above London Wall, this brasserie makes inventive use of its meat supplies from nearby Smithfield Market, with everything from Spanish charcuterie to lamb *kofta* with apricots and *harissa* yoghurt on offer.

ROYAL EXCHANGE GRAND CAFÉ & BAR MODERN EUROPEAN ££

Map p442 (☎020-7618 2480; www.royalexchange-grandcafe.co.uk; Royal Exchange, Bank, EC3; mains £13.50-22; ⊙8am-11pm Mon-Fri; ⊖Bank) This lovely cafe-restaurant sits in the middle of the covered courtyard of the beautiful Royal Exchange building and is a good place to people-watch. The food runs the gamut from breakfast, salads and sandwiches to oysters (from £11 a half-dozen) and rabbit *cassoulet* (£13.50).

SWEETING'S SEAFOOD £££

Map p442 (☎020-7248 3062; www.sweetingsrestaurant.com; 39 Queen Victoria St, EC4; mains £13.50-35; ⊙11.30am-3pm Mon-Fri; ⊖Mansion House) Sweeting's is a City institution, having been around since 1889. It hasn't changed much, with its small sit-down dining area, mosaic floor and narrow counters, behind which stand waiters in white aprons. Dishes include sustainably sourced fish of all kinds (grilled, fried or poached), potted shrimps, eels and Sweeting's famous fish pie (£13.50).

DRINKING & NIGHTLIFE

FOLLY BAR

Map p442 (www.thefollybar.com; 41 Gracechurch St, EC3; ⊙7.30am-late Fri, from 10am Sat & Sun; ⊖Monument) Love, love, love this 'secret garden' bar-cum-cafe on two levels filled with greenery (both real and faux) and picnic-table seating. The aptly named Folly has a full menu on offer, with a strong emphasis on burgers and steaks, but we come for the excellent wine and champagne selection.

VERTIGO 42 BAR

Map p442 (☎020-7877 7842; www.vertigo42.co.uk; Tower 42, 25 Old Broad St, EC2; ⊙noon-3.45pm & 5-11pm Mon-Fri, 5-11pm Sat; ⊖Liverpool St) On the 42nd floor of a 183m-high tower, this circular bar has expansive views over the city that stretch for miles on a clear day. The classic drinks list is, as you might expect, pricier than average – wine by the glass starts from £9.50 and champagne and cocktails from £14, and there's also a limited food menu. Reservations essential; minimum spend £10.

BLACKFRIAR PUB

Map p442 (174 Queen Victoria St, EC4; ⊙10am-11.30 Mon-Thu, to midnight Fri & Sat, to 11pm Sun; ⊖Blackfriars) It may look like the corpulent friar just stepped out of this 'olde pub' just north of Blackfriars station, but the interior is actually an Arts and Crafts makeover dating back to 1905. Built on the site of a monastery of Dominicans (who wore black), the theme is appealingly celebrated throughout the pub. There's a good selection of ales.

SHIP PUB

Map p442 (3 Hart St, EC3; ⌚11.30am-11pm Mon-Fri; ⊖Tower Hill) This small 'old school' pub with a nautical theme is a short walk from Tower Hill and an oasis of calm away from the hubbub of the Tower. Note the neckties above the bar left behind by forgetful imbibers.

COUNTING HOUSE PUB

Map p442 (50 Cornhill, EC3; ⌚11am-11pm Mon-Fri; 📶; ⊖Bank or Monument) With its counters and basement vaults this award-winning pub certainly looks and feels comfortable in the former headquarters of NatWest Bank with its domed skylight and beautifully appointed main bar. This is a favourite of City boys and girls – they come for the good range of real ales and the speciality pies (from £9.25).

MADISON COCKTAIL BAR

Map p442 (www.madisonlondon.net; Roof Terrace, One New Change, EC4; ⌚10am-midnight Mon-Sat, to 8pm Sun; ⊖St Paul's) Perched atop One New Change with a full-frontal view of St Paul's and beyond, Madison offers one of largest public open-air roof terraces you'll ever encounter. There's a full restaurant on one side and a cocktail bar with outdoor seating on the other; we come for the latter and inventive tapas (£4 to £14) like popcorn squid.

YE OLDE CHESHIRE CHEESE PUB

Map p442 (Wine Office Court, 145 Fleet St, EC4; ⌚11am-11pm Mon-Fri, from noon Sat; ⊖Chancery Lane) The entrance to this historic pub is via a narrow alley off Fleet St. Over its long history locals have included Dr Johnson, Thackeray and Dickens. Despite (or possibly because of) this, the Cheshire feels today like a bit of a museum. Nevertheless it's one of London's most famous pubs and it's well worth popping in for a pint.

HOOP AND GRAPES PUB

Map p442 (www.thehoopandgrapes.co.uk; 47 Aldgate High St, EC3; ⌚10am-11pm Mon-Fri; ⊖Aldgate) It's not our favourite watering hole in the City but how can you not do business with a pub claiming to be the oldest in town, with foundations dating to the 13th century? It's a Shepherd Neame–tied pub so you'll find Spitfire and Bishop's Finger on the menu. The cellars are said to contain a closed-off tunnel that led to the Tower of London.

☆ ENTERTAINMENT

BARBICAN PERFORMING ARTS

Map p442 (☎0845 1216823; www.barbican.org.uk; Silk St, EC2; ⊖Barbican) Home to the wonderful London Symphony Orchestra and its associate orchestra, the lesser-known BBC Symphony Orchestra, the arts centre hosts scores of other leading musicians each year as well, focusing in particular on jazz, folk, world and soul artists. Dance is another strong point here.

The centre's multidisciplinary **Barbican International Theatre Events**, which takes place year-round, showcases some great performances, as well as the work of exciting overseas drama companies alongside local fringe-theatre troupes. It's also a dream to watch a film here, with an interesting line-up and brilliant sloping seating that ensures a full-screen view wherever you sit.

VOLUPTÉ CABARET

Map p442 (☎020-7831 1622; www.volupte-lounge.com; 9 Norwich St, EC4; ⌚4.30pm-1am Tue & Wed, to 3am Thu & Fri, noon-3am Sat; ⊖Chancery Lane) A gorgeous little cabaret venue north of Fleet St, Volupté offers a real variety of burlesque, vaudeville, comedy and live music. During the week, Baby Grand Burlesque offers cabaret stars complete with live music; there's often comedy or a gay club night on Thursday. At the weekend sit down to Afternoon Tease, with live music, cabaret or burlesque performances.

SHOPPING

LONDON SILVER VAULTS SILVER

Map p442 (www.thesilvervaults.com; 53-63 Chancery Lane, WC2; ⌚9am-5.30pm Mon-Fri, to 1pm Sat; ⊖Chancery Lane) The 30 shops that work out of these incredibly secure subterranean vaults make up the largest collection of silver under one roof in the world. Everything from cutlery sets and picture frames to jewellery and tableware is on offer.

HATTON GARDEN JEWELLERY

Map p450 (www.hatton-garden.net; Hatton Garden, EC1; ⊖Chancery Lane) If you're in the market for classic settings and unmounted stones, stroll along Hatton Garden – it's chock-a-block with gold, diamond and jewellery shops, especially at the southern end.

The South Bank

WATERLOO | BANKSIDE | SOUTHWARK | LONDON BRIDGE | BERMONDSEY

Neighbourhood Top Five

❶ Finding out what all the fuss is about by exploring the magnificent modern-art collection at the peerless **Tate Modern** (p170).

❷ Revolving in leisurely fashion above London's panoramic cityscape in the iconic **London Eye** (p173).

❸ Stimulating your taste buds on a gastronomic tour of discovery at **Borough Market** (p180).

❹ Stopping by **Skylon** (p179) for riveting views of the Thames and the city.

❺ Getting a Bard's-eye view of Elizabethan theatrics as a groundling at the magnificent **Shakespeare's Globe** (p172).

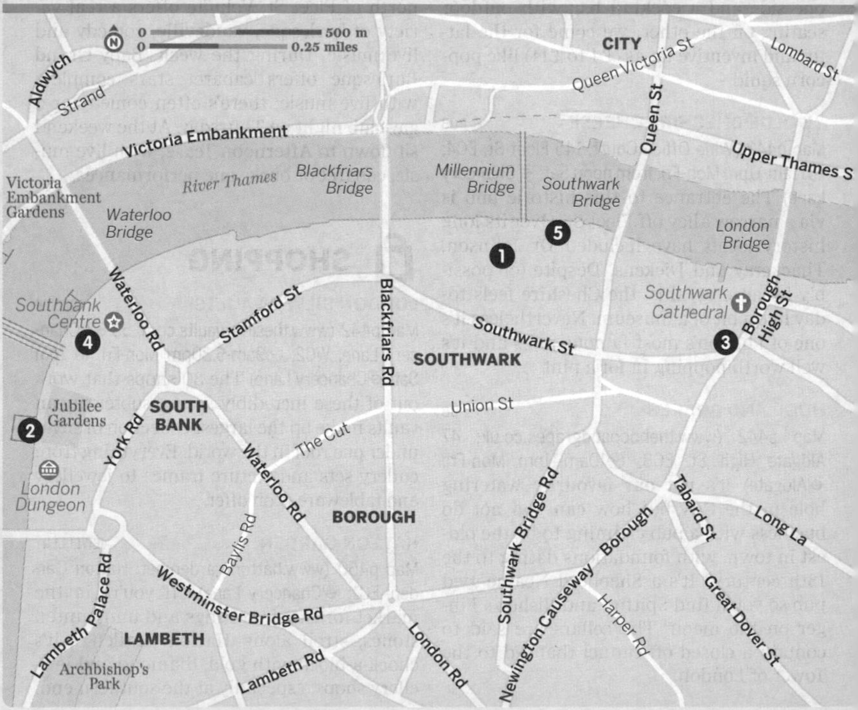

For more detail of this area see Map p444

Explore: The South Bank

Once neglected beyond its arts venues, the South Bank today has transformed into one of London's must-see neighbourhoods. A roll call of riverside sights stretches along the Thames, commencing with the London Eye, running past the cultural enclave of the Southbank Centre and on to the Tate Modern, the Millennium Bridge and Shakespeare's Globe. It continues: waterside pubs, a cathedral, one of London's most-visited food markets, London's tallest building, a handful of fun diversions for kids and irrepressible kidults and the hippest neighbourhood in which to hang out, Bermondsey. A stunning panorama unfolds on the far side of the Thames, as head-swivelling architecture rises up on either bank.

The drawcard sights stretch west-east in a manageable riverside melange, so doing it on foot is the best way. Located roughly halfway between the London Eye and Tower Bridge, the Tate Modern is by far the most time-intensive sight, and can easily hollow out a day's sightseeing; two to three days for the South Bank is optimum but if you're in a rush, one day may do for a (frazzling) whistle-stop look at the main sights.

Local Life

➡ **Hang-outs** Cool Londoners love Maltby Street Market (p179) for its gourmet sandwiches, crazy cocktails and rollicking atmosphere.

➡ **Museums** Locals earmark Friday and Saturday late-night opening (till 10pm) at the Tate Modern (p170), when the art crowds have thinned.

➡ **Theatre** Londoners applaud Shakespeare's Globe (p184) and seats are stuffed with locals at impressive theatre venues such as the National Theatre (p183), the Old Vic (p185) and the Young Vic (p185).

Getting There & Away

➡ **Underground** The South Bank is lashed into the tube system by stations at Waterloo, Southwark, London Bridge and Bermondsey, all on the Jubilee Line; the Northern Line runs through London Bridge and Waterloo (the Bakerloo line runs through the latter).

➡ **On Foot** Cross to South Bank from the City over Tower Bridge or the Millennium Bridge, or from the West End across Waterloo Bridge. Each offers sublime views of the city.

➡ **Bicycle** Jump on a Barclays bike and wheel it!

➡ **Bus** The Riverside RV1 runs around the South Bank and Bankside, linking all the main sights (running between Covent Garden and Tower Gateway).

Lonely Planet's Top Tip

To collect the main sights, trace the Silver Jubilee Walk and the South Bank section of the Thames Path along the southern riverbank, but do venture further inland for the best eating and drinking.

Best Places to Eat

➡ Skylon (p179)
➡ Market Gourmet (p179)
➡ Baltic (p179)
➡ Anchor & Hope (p180)
➡ Magdalen (p181)

For reviews, see p178 ➡

Best Places to Drink

➡ Little Bird Gin (p179)
➡ 40 Maltby Street (p182)
➡ Rake (p182)
➡ Scootercaffe (p181)
➡ Skylon (p181)

For reviews, see p181 ➡

Best Theatres

➡ Shakespeare's Globe & Sam Wanamaker Playhouse (p184)
➡ National Theatre (p183)
➡ Young Vic (p185)
➡ Old Vic (p185)

For reviews, see p183 ➡

JOHN HARPER / GETTY IMAGES ©

TOP SIGHT
TATE MODERN

The public's love affair with this phenomenally successful modern-art gallery shows no sign of cooling more than a decade after it opened. In fact, so enraptured are art goers with the Tate Modern that over 50 million visitors flocked to the former power station in its first 10 years. To accommodate this exceptional popularity, the Tate is expanding: the museum is converting the power station's three huge subterranean oil tanks and building a daring 11-storey geometric extension at the back. Grand opening planned for 2016.

Power Station

The 200m-long Tate Modern is an imposing sight. The conversion of the empty Bankside Power Station – all 4.2 million bricks of it – to an art gallery in 2000 was a masterstroke of design. The 'Tate Modern effect' is clearly as much about the building and its location as the mostly 20th-century art inside. The new Tate Modern Project extension will similarly be constructed of brick, but artistically devised as a lattice through which interior lights will be visible at eventide.

DON'T MISS...

- Turbine Hall
- *The Snail* by Matisse
- Mark Rothko canvases
- *Whaam!* by Roy Lichtenstein

PRACTICALITIES

- Map p444
- www.tate.org.uk
- Queen's Walk, SE1
- 10am-6pm Sun-Thu, to 10pm Fri & Sat
- Southwark

Turbine Hall

The first thing to greet you as you pour down the ramp off Holland St (the main entrance) is the cavernous 3300-sq-metre Turbine Hall. Originally housing the power station's humungous turbines, this vast space is the commanding venue for large-scale, temporary exhibitions; the sense of scale is astounding (enter from the river entrance and you'll end up on more-muted level 2). Some art critics swipe at its populism, particularly the 'participatory art' (Carsten Höller's funfair-like slides *Test Site;* Doris Salcedo's enormous *Shibboleth* fissure in the floor; and Robert Morris' climbable geometric sculpture), but others insist this makes art more accessible. Originally visitors were invited to trample over Ai Weiwei's thoughtful and compelling *Sunflower Seeds* – a huge carpet of hand-painted ceramic seeds – until it was discovered people were making off with them in their shoes and turn-ups (to later appear on eBay) and the dust emitted by the 'seeds' was diagnosed a health risk.

Permanent Collection

Tate Modern's permanent collection is arranged by both theme and chronology on levels 2, 3 and 4. More than 60,000 works are on constant rotation, which can be frustrating if you'd like to see one particular piece, but is thrilling for repeat visitors.

The curators have at their disposal paintings by Georges Braque, Henri Matisse, Piet Mondrian, Andy Warhol, Mark Rothko and Jackson Pollock, as well as pieces by Joseph Beuys, Damien Hirst, Rebecca Horn, Claes Oldenburg and Auguste Rodin.

Level 2: Poetry & Dream

This collection submerges the viewer in the world of surrealism and the dreamlike mindscapes of Yves Tanguy, Max Ernst and other artists. Search out *Sleeping Venus* by Paul Delvaux, a haunting, erotic work.

Level 3: Transformed Visions

After WWII, many artists channelled their emotions about war and violence in their works. One such manifestation was a new kind of expressive, contemplative abstraction, as exemplified by Mark Rothko's *The Seagram Murals*.

Level 4: Evolution of Abstraction & Radical Art

Focussing on the evolution of abstract art since the beginning of the 20th century, including cubism, geometric abstraction and minimalism, **Structure & Clarity** includes work by early adopters such as Matisse and Picasso *(Seated Nude)*. **Energy & Process** highlights Arte Povera, a revolutionary Italian art movement from the 1960s, as its main focus.

Special Exhibitions

Special exhibitions (levels 2 and 3, subject to admission charge) have included retrospectives on Edward Hopper, Frida Kahlo, Roy Lichtenstein, August Strindberg, Nazism and 'Degenerate' Art, and Joan Miró. Highlights for 2014 include exhibitions on Matisse, JMW Turner and Piet Mondrian.

FURTHER INFORMATION

Audioguides (in five languages) are available for £4 – they contain explanations about 50 artworks across the galleries and offer suggested tours for adults or children. Free guided highlights tours depart at 11am, noon, 2pm and 3pm daily.

Swiss architects Herzog & de Meuron scooped the prestigious Pritzker Prize for their transformation of empty Bankside Power Station, which closed in 1981. Leaving the building's single central 99m-high chimney, adding a two-storey glass box onto the roof and employing the cavernous Turbine Hall as a dramatic entrance space were three strokes of genius. They also designed the new Tate extension, opening in 2016.

TATE TO TATE BOAT

For the most scenic of culture trips, take the **Tate Boat** (Map p444; www.tate.org.uk/visit/tate-boat; adult/child £5/2.80; ⏲every 40min 10am-6pm) between the Bankside Pier at Tate Modern and the Millbank Pier at its sister-museum, Tate Britain (p100).

PETER PHIPP / GETTY IMAGES ©

TOP SIGHT
SHAKESPEARE'S GLOBE

Unlike other venues for Shakespearean plays, the new Globe was designed to resemble the original as closely as possible, painstakingly constructed with 600 oak pegs (not a nail or a screw in the house), specially fired Tudor bricks and thatching reeds from Norfolk that pigeons supposedly don't like. Even the plaster contains goat hair, lime and sand, as it did in Shakespeare's time. It even means having the arena open to the fickle London skies and roar of passing aircraft, leaving the 700 'groundlings' to stand in London's notorious downpours.

Despite the worldwide popularity of Shakespeare over the centuries, the Globe was almost a distant memory when American actor (and, later, film director) Sam Wanamaker came searching for it in 1949. Undeterred by the fact that the theatre's foundations had vanished beneath a row of heritage-listed Georgian houses, Wanamaker set up the Globe Playhouse Trust in 1970 and began fundraising for a memorial theatre. Work started only 200m from the original Globe site in 1987, but Wanamaker died four years before it opened in 1997.

At the time of writing, the Globe was also applying the finishing touches to the new **Sam Wanamaker Playhouse**, an indoor Jacobean theatre (the first plays were due to open in January 2014). Shakespeare wrote for both outdoor and indoor theatre and the playhouse had always been part of the Globe's ambitions.

Visits include tours of the Globe and the playhouse (which depart half-hourly, generally in the morning so as not to clash with performances) as well as access to the exhibition space beneath the theatre, which has fascinating exhibits about Shakespeare and theatre in the 17th century (including costumes and props) and fun live talks and demonstrations. Or you can of course take in a play (p184).

DON'T MISS...

- Exhibition Hall and Tour
- Interior of the Globe Theatre
- Sam Wanamaker Playhouse

PRACTICALITIES

- Map p444
- www.shakespearesglobe.com
- 21 New Globe Walk, SE1
- adult/child £13.50/8
- 9am-5.30pm
- London Bridge

SIGHTS

Waterloo

ROUPELL ST
STREET

Map p444 (Roupell St, SE1; ⊖Waterloo) Waterloo station isn't exactly scenic but wander round the back of this transport hub and you'll be amazed by the architecture you'll find. Roupell St is an astonishingly pretty row of workers' cottages, all dark bricks and coloured doors, dating back to the 1820s. The street is so uniform it looks like a film set.

The same architecture extends to Theed St and Whittlesey St (which run parallel to Roupell St to the north). The terraced houses were developed by John Palmer Roupell, a gold refiner, from the 1820s to the 1840s for artisan workers and have survived the many developments of the area intact.

NATIONAL THEATRE
THEATRE

Map p444 (☎020-7452 3000; www.nationaltheatre.org.uk; South Bank, SE1; ⊖Waterloo) The nation's flagship theatre complex comprises three auditoriums for performances (p183): the Olivier, the Lyttelton and the Cottesloe. Fantastic **backstage tours** (adult/child £8.50/free), lasting 1¼ hours, are available. Every tour is different but you're likely to see rehearsals or changes of sets or bump into actors in the corridors. There are generally a couple of tours a day, sometimes more. Consult the website for exact times and make sure you book.

COUNTY HALL
HISTORIC BUILDING

Map p444 (Riverside Bldg, Westminster Bridge Rd, SE1; ⊖Westminster or Waterloo) Begun in 1909 but not completed until 1922, this grand building with its curved, colonnaded facade contains a vast aquarium and a museum devoted to the local film industry.

The excellent **London Sea Life Aquarium** (Map p444; www.visitsealife.com; adult/child £20.70/15; ⏲10am-6pm Mon-Fri, to 7pm Sat & Sun; ⊖Westminster or Waterloo) is one of the largest in Europe. Fish and other creatures from the briny deep are grouped in 14 zones according to their geographic origin, from the Pacific to the Atlantic Ocean and from temperate waters to tropical seas. There are over 40 sharks, a colony of gentoo penguins and other Antarctic

TOP SIGHT
LONDON EYE

It's hard to remember what London looked like before the landmark London Eye (officially the EDF Energy London Eye) began twirling at the southwestern end of Jubilee Gardens in 2000. Not only has it fundamentally altered the South Bank skyline but, standing 135m tall in a fairly flat city, it is visible from many surprising parts of the city (eg Kennington, Mayfair or Honor Oak Park).

A ride – or 'flight', as it is called here – in one of the wheel's 32 glass-enclosed eye pods holding up to 28 people draws 3.5 million visitors annually. At peak times (July, August and school holidays) it may seem like they are all in the queue with you; save money and shorten queues by buying tickets online, or cough up an extra £10 to showcase your fast-track swagger. Alternatively, visit before 11am or after 3pm to avoid peak density.

It takes a gracefully slow 30 minutes and, weather permitting, you can see 25 miles in every direction from the top of the eye.

DID YOU KNOW?

- The London Eye is the northern hemisphere's tallest Ferris wheel.
- The hub of the eye and 23m-tall spindle weigh 20 times more than Big Ben.

PRACTICALITIES

- Map p444
- ☎0871 7813000
- www.londoneye.com
- adult/child £19.20/12.30
- ⏲10am-8pm
- ⊖Waterloo

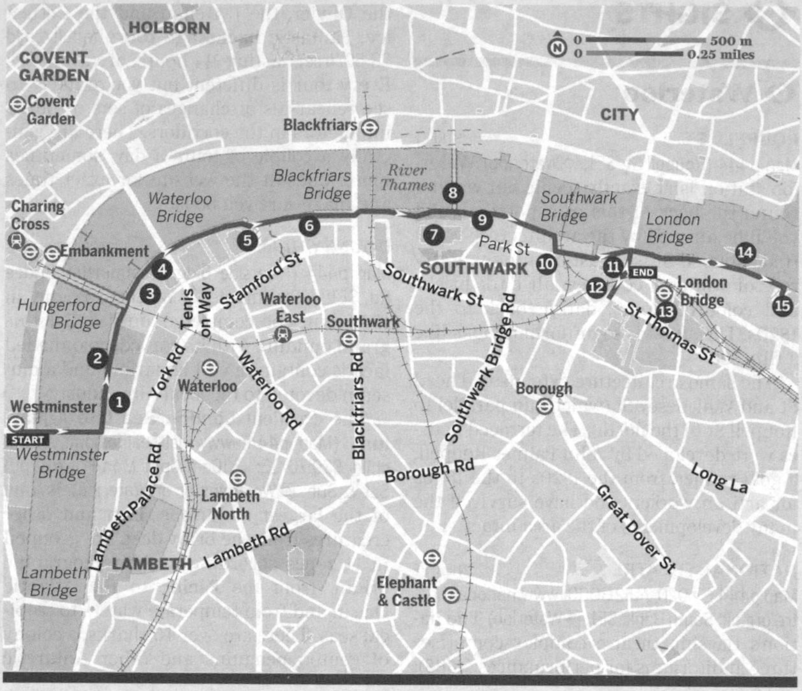

Neighbourhood Walk
South Bank Stroll

START WESTMINSTER TUBE STATION
END LONDON BRIDGE TUBE STATION
LENGTH 2.8 MILES, 3½ HOURS

From Westminster tube station, cross the river on Westminster Bridge and admire the views of Big Ben. As you reach the South Bank, the first building you'll walk past is the sombre **1 County Hall** (p173), the seat of London's local government from 1922 until Margaret Thatcher dissolved the Greater London Council in 1986.

The **2 London Eye** (p173) gracefully rotates next to it and the atmosphere on this stretch of the river is always party-like, with ice-cream vans, street performers, dozens of visitors and Londoners on their lunch-time run. Push on east past the **3 Southbank Centre** (p175) and pause to admire the acrobatics of local teenagers at the graffitied skatepark underneath **4 Queen Elizabeth Hall** (p184).

Carry on strolling along the river, past the boutiques of **5 Gabriel's Wharf** and the **6 Oxo Tower**. After 20 to 30 minutes you'll emerge in front of the imposing **7 Tate Modern** (p170). Opposite is the **8 Millennium Bridge** (p175), Sir Norman Foster's 'blade of light'.

Just 100m past the Tate is the magnificently rebuilt **9 Shakespeare's Globe** (p172). Walk under Southwark Bridge, which is beautifully lit at night, past the perennially busy **10 Anchor** (p182) pub and down the maze of streets leading to **11 Southwark Cathedral** (p176).

Spreading around the railway arches is **12 Borough Market** (p180), London's premier gourmet products market (and one of its oldest), at its busiest on Fridays and Saturdays. Lording over this area is the **13 Shard** (p177), th EU's tallest building. Pass London Bridge, and the intimidating **14 HMS Belfast** (p177), for glorious views of Tower Bridge. You'll also see **15 City Hall** (p178) on your right, nicknamed 'the egg' (or, more cheekily, 'the testicle'). Then retrace your steps to the London Bridge tube station.

creatures, ever-popular clownfish and a rewarding rainforests section. There are talks and feeding sessions throughout the day. Online tickets are cheaper.

The **London Film Museum** (Map p444; ☎020-7202 7040; www.londonfilmmuseum.com; adult/student/child £13.50/11.50/9.50; ⏰10am-5pm Mon-Wed & Fri, from 11am Thu & Sun; 📶) is a British film industry retrospective; it looks at the history of the main studios (Pinewod, Elstree etc) and iconic films shot there such as *Star Wars* and the Indiana Jones films. There are plenty of costumes, props, set drawings and scripts to look at. The only downside is the noise, with half a dozen videos constantly playing, which makes it hard to focus on what you want to hear.

Bankside & Southwark

TATE MODERN MUSEUM

See p170.

SHAKESPEARE'S GLOBE HISTORIC BUILDING

See p172.

BANKSIDE GALLERY GALLERY

Map p444 (☎020-7928 7521; www.bankside gallery.com; 48 Hopton St, SE1; ⏰11am-6pm; ⊖St Paul's, Southwark or London Bridge) **FREE** Home of the Royal Watercolour Society and the Royal Society of Painter-Printmakers, this friendly, upbeat place has no permanent collection, but there are frequently changing exhibitions of watercolours, prints and engravings (many for sale).

MILLENNIUM BRIDGE BRIDGE

Map p444 The elegant Millennium Bridge staples the south bank of the Thames, in front of Tate Modern, with the north bank, at the steps of Peter's Hill below St Paul's Cathedral. The low-slung frame designed by Sir Norman Foster and Antony Caro looks spectacular, particularly lit up at night with fibre optics.

The Millennium Bridge got off on the wrong footing when it was closed just three days after opening in June 2000 due to an alarming swing; a costly 18-month refit put things right.

The view of St Paul's from the South Bank is one of London's iconic images.

TOP SIGHT
SOUTHBANK CENTRE

The flagship venue of the Southbank Centre, Europe's largest centre for performing and visual arts, is the **Royal Festival Hall**. Its gently curved facade of glass and Portland stone is more humane than its 1970s brutalist neighbours. It is one of London's leading music venues (p184) and the epicentre of life on this part of the South Bank, hosting cafes, restaurants, shops and bars.

Just north, the austere **Queen Elizabeth Hall** is a brutalist icon, the second-largest concert venue in the centre, hosting chamber orchestras, quartets, choirs, dance performances and sometimes opera. Underneath its elevated floor is a long-term, graffiti-decorated **skateboarders' hang-out**.

The opinion-dividing 1968 **Hayward Gallery** (Map p444; ⏰10am-6pm Sat-Wed, to 8pm Thu & Fri), another brutalist beauty, is a leading contemporary-art exhibition space.

The QEH and Hayward Gallery are about to receive a major overhaul. Works are due to start in 2014 and will temporarily dampen the buzz of the area. The finished result however, with a floating glass box on top of the brutalist buildings and brand new art space, will be worth the wait.

DON'T MISS...

- Street artists
- Views of Wesminster and St Paul's
- Hayward Gallery exhibitions
- Skatepark

PRACTICALITIES

- Map p444
- ☎020-7960 4200
- www.southbankcentre.co.uk
- Belvedere Rd, SE1
- ⊖Waterloo

TOP SIGHT SOUTHWARK CATHEDRAL

The earliest surviving parts of this relatively small cathedral are the **retrochoir** at the eastern end, which contains four chapels and was part of the 13th-century Priory of St Mary Overie, some ancient arcading by the southwest door, 12th-century wall cores in the north transept and an arch that dates to the original Norman church. But most of the cathedral is Victorian.

Enter via the southwest door and immediately to the left is a length of arcading dating to the 13th century; nearby is a selection of intriguing **medieval roof bosses** from the 15th century. Walk up the north aisle of the nave and on the left you'll see the **tomb of John Gower**, the 14th-century poet who was the first to write in English. Cross into the choir to admire the 16th-century **Great Screen** separating the choir from the retrochoir.

In the south aisle of the nave have a look at the green alabaster **monument to William Shakespeare**. Beside the monument is a **plaque to Sam Wanamaker** (1919–93); nearby hangs a splendid **icon** of Jesus Christ illuminated by devotional candles. Do hunt down the exceedingly fine **Elizabethan sideboard** in the north transept.

DON'T MISS...

- Retrochoir
- Ancient arcading
- Great Screen

PRACTICALITIES

- Map p444
- 020-7367 6700
- cathedral.southwark.anglican.org
- Montague Close, SE1
- admission free, donations welcome
- 8am-6pm Mon-Fri, from 9am Sat & Sun
- London Bridge

CLINK PRISON MUSEUM MUSEUM

Map p444 (020-7403 0900; www.clink.co.uk; 1 Clink St, SE1; adult/child £7.50/5.50; 10am-6pm Mon-Fri, to 7.30pm Sat & Sun; London Bridge) This one-time private jail in the park of Winchester Palace, a 32-hectare area known as the Liberty of the Clink and under the jurisdiction of the bishops of Winchester and not the City, was used to detain debtors, prostitutes, thieves and numerous Protestants and Catholics during the Reformation.

GOLDEN HINDE SHIP

Map p444 (020-7403 0123; www.goldenhinde.com; St Mary Overie Dock, Cathedral St, SE1; adult/child £7/5; 10am-5.30pm; London Bridge) Okay, it looks like a dinky theme-park ride and kids love it, but stepping aboard this replica of Sir Francis Drake's famous Tudor ship will inspire genuine admiration for the admiral and his rather short (average height: 1.6m) crew, which counted between 40 and 60. It was in a tiny five-deck galleon just like this that Drake and his crew circumnavigated the globe from 1577 to 1580.

London Bridge

LONDON BRIDGE EXPERIENCE & LONDON TOMBS HISTORIC ATTRACTION

Map p444 (www.thelondonbridgeexperience.com; 2-4 Tooley St, SE1; adult/child £23/17; 10am-5pm Mon-Fri, to 6pm Sat & Sun; London Bridge) Stuffed away in the vaults beneath so-called New London Bridge (dating back to 1831), this historical attraction takes you on a whistle-stop tour of London's most famous span – from the Romans to Peter de Colechurch's 'Old London Bridge' (1209) lined with shops, to the American Robert McCulloch, who bought the bridge in 1967 for US$2.50 and transported it to Arizona.

It's essentially for kids, so the roll call includes 'the Keeper of the Heads', who preserved (mummified) the severed heads of the executed for display on the bridge. Things ratchet up as you descend into a series of tombs and plague pits dating as far back as the 14th century, where darkness, rodents (animatronics) and claustrophobia meet zombies-from-nowhere (actors). It's all great, occasionally heart-in-the-mouth entertainment and you save up to 20% (and the queues) by buying tickets online.

OLD OPERATING THEATRE MUSEUM & HERB GARRET MUSEUM

Map p444 (www.thegarret.org.uk; 9a St Thomas St, SE1; adult/child £6/3.50; ⏲10.30am-5pm; ⊖London Bridge) This unique museum, 32 steps up the spiral stairway in the tower of St Thomas Church (1703), is the unlikely home of Britain's oldest operating theatre. Rediscovered in 1956, the garret was used by the apothecary of St Thomas's Hospital to store medicinal herbs. The museum looks back at the horror of 19th-century medicine – all pre-ether, pre-chloroform and pre-antiseptic.

You can browse the natural remedies, including snail water for venereal disease and bladderwrack for goitre and tuberculosis. A fiendish array of amputation knives and blades is a presage to operating conditions at the time: surgeons had to be snappy; one minute for an amputation was judged about right. A box of sawdust beneath the table caught the blood, and contemporary accounts record the surgeons wearing frock coats 'stiff and stinking with pus and blood'.

There's a demonstration on Victorian speed surgery at 2pm Saturday and one on how drugs were made at 2pm Sunday. If you're wondering how they forced patients up the constricted spiral staircase, the original entrance was upstairs.

SHARD NOTABLE BUILDING

Map p444 (www.the-shard.com; 32 London Bridge St, SE1; adult/child £29.95/23.95; ⏲9am-10pm; ⊖London Bridge) Puncturing the skies above London, the dramatic splinter-like form of the Shard has rapidly become an icon of the town. The viewing platforms on floors 68, 69 and 72 are open to the public and the views are, as you'd expect from a 244m vantage point, sweeping, but they come at a hefty price – book online to save £5.

As well as the viewing platform, the Shard will be home to flats, hotels, and restaurants: the first three of which opened over the summer in 2013.

HMS BELFAST SHIP

Map p444 (hmsbelfast.iwm.org.uk; Queen's Walk, SE1; adult/child £14.50/free; ⏲10am-5pm; 👪; ⊖London Bridge) White ensign flapping on the Thames breeze, HMS *Belfast* is a magnet

TOP SIGHT
LONDON DUNGEON

In a brand new home on the Thames since March 2013, this attraction has been milking it since 1974, spawning six other 'dungeons' in the UK and Europe. It's a highly entertaining whirlwind through London's most famous historical anecdotes – the Gunpowder plot, the Great Plague, Jack the Ripper, Sweeney Todd and his cronies – narrated through a combination of rides, actors and special effects. There is great audience participation, but prepare to be scared and startled at every corner!

The best bits are the vaudevillian delights of being sentenced by a mad, bewigged judge on trumped-up charges, the utterly disorientating Whitechapel labyrinth, the unnervingly sweet Mrs Lovett, and the Drop Dead Drop Ride that has you 'plummeting' to your death by hanging from the gallows.

It takes about 90 minutes to work your way through the gory dungeon. Buy tickets online to avoid the mammoth queues and save a few pounds too. Note that children younger than eight might find some of the attractions too scary.

DON'T MISS...

- Jack the Ripper
- Sweeney Todd
- The Judge
- Drop Dead Drop Ride

PRACTICALITIES

- Map p444
- www.thedungeons.com/london
- County Hall, Westminster Bridge Rd, SE1
- adult/child £24.60/19.20
- ⏲10am-5pm, extended hrs holidays
- ⊖Westminster or Waterloo

for naval-gazing kids of all ages. This large, light cruiser – launched in 1938 – served in WWII, helping to sink the German battleship *Scharnhorst,* shelling the Normandy coast on D Day and later participating in the Korean War. Her 6in guns could bombard a target 14 land miles distant.

Ranging over five decks and four platforms, HMS *Belfast* is surprisingly interesting – even for landlubbers – as an insight into the way of life on board a cruiser, from boiler room to living quarters. The operations room has been reconstructed to show its role in the 1943 Battle of North Cape off Norway, which ended in the sinking of the *Scharnhorst.* On the bridge you can visit the admiral's cabin and sit in his chair, peer through the sights of the 4in HA/LA guns on the open deck, or sink a coffee in the aptly named Walrus cafe.

The excellent audio guide takes you on a 1½-hour tour of the ship, only available until 3.30pm.

Bermondsey

CITY HALL NOTABLE BUILDING

Map p444 (www.london.gov.uk; Queen's Walk, SE1; London Bridge) Home to the Mayor of London, bulbous City Hall was designed by Foster and Partners and opened in 2002. The 45m, glass-clad building has been compared to a host of objects – from an onion, to Darth Vader's helmet, a woodlouse and a 'glass gonad'.

The scoop amphitheatre outside the building is the venue for a variety of free entertainment in warmer weather, from music to theatre. Free exhibitions relating to London are also periodically held at City Hall.

FASHION & TEXTILE MUSEUM MUSEUM

Map p444 (020-7407 8664; www.ftmlondon.org; 83 Bermondsey St, SE1; adult/student/child £8/5.50/free; 11am-6pm Tue-Sat; London Bridge) This brainchild of designer Zandra Rhodes has no permanent collection, just quarterly temporary exhibitions, which have included retrospectives on Swedish fashion, the evolution of underwear and royal fashion.

WHITE CUBE BERMONDSEY GALLERY

Map p444 (www.whitecube.com; 144-152 Bermondsey St, SE1; 10am-6pm Tue-Sat, noon-6pm Sun; London Bridge) FREE The newest and largest of the White Cube galleries – the brainchild of Jay Jopling, dealer to the stars of the Brit Art movement who made his reputation in the 1990s by exhibiting then-unknown artists such as Damien Hirst and Antony Gormley – this gallery impresses by its large exhibition spaces, which lend themselves to monumental pieces or expansive installations using several mediums.

DESIGN MUSEUM MUSEUM

Map p444 (www.designmuseum.org; 28 Shad Thames, SE1; adult/child £8.50/5; 10am-5.45pm; ; Tower Hill) Housed in a 1930s-era warehouse, the rectangular galleries of the Design Museum stage a revolving programme of special exhibitions devoted to contemporary design. Both populist and popular, past shows have ranged from Manolo Blahnik shoes to Formula One racing cars. The museum encourages visitors, children in particular, to get creative too.

The museum plans to move to a new site in the former Commonwealth Institute in West London in 2015.

LOCAL KNOWLEDGE

DICKENSIAN HISTORY

One of the old brick walls of Marshalsea Prison, where Charles Dickens' father and family were interred for debts, still stands along Angel Pl, an alley off Borough High St.

EATING

Waterloo

The area around the Southbank Centre is full of chains – head 'inland' to discover authentic gastronomic gems.

KONDITOR & COOK BAKERY £

Map p444 (www.konditorandcook.com; 22 Cornwall Rd, SE1; cakes £2-3, hot food £3-6; 7.30am-6.30pm Mon-Fri, 8.30am-3pm Sat; ; Waterloo) This elegant cake shop and bakery produces wonderful cakes – lavender and orange, lemon and almond – massive raspberry meringues, cookies and loaves of warm bread with olives, nuts and spices. It also serves hot take-away food such as quiches or risottos, popular with local office workers.

TOP SIGHT
MALTBY STREET MARKET

We would have loved to keep Maltby Street Market to ourselves but the cat has been slowly coming out of the bag, so we thought we'd share the love! This rollicking little market, nicknamed the Ropewalk, is a true gem: started as an alternative to the juggernaut that is Borough Market, it is a small, rough-on-the-edges, bunting-lined gathering of small producers and boutique food stalls.

Among the outstanding pop-up restaurants and bars, don't miss **Market Gourmet** (Map p444; mains £4-10; ⏲10am-4pm Sat), which makes the best sandwiches you'll ever eat. Fact. The brisket, horseradish, rarebit and onion on a brioche brings new meaning to the term 'convenience food'.

For drinks, look no further than **Life's a Bottle** (Map p444; www.lifesabottle.com; ⏲10am-3pm Sat), run by the inimitable Marty (and his giant hat), for affordable wine by the glass. Or go to **Little Bird Gin's bar** (Map p444; www.littlebirdgin.com; ⏲10am-4pm Sat), who use their eponymous gin (a small batch, citrusy gin distilled in London) to make eye-poppingly good cocktails served in jam jars or apothecary's glass bottles.

DON'T MISS

- Sipping a Little Bird Gin cocktail
- Tucking into a brisket brioche

PRACTICALITIES

- Map p444
- www.maltby.st
- Maltby St, SE1
- ⏲10am-4pm Sat
- ⊖London Bridge

MASTERS SUPER FISH FISH & CHIPS £
Map p444 (191 Waterloo Rd, SE1; mains £8-12; ⏲noon-3pm & 4.30-10.30pm Mon-Sat; ⊖Waterloo) This popular place serves excellent fish (brought in fresh daily from Billingsgate Market and grilled rather than fried if desired); low on charm but full marks for flavour.

CUT BRITISH £
Map p444 (www.thecutbar.com; Young Vic, The Cut, SE1; mains £7-12; ⏲9am-11pm Mon-Fri, 10am-11pm Sat; 📶✍; ⊖Waterloo) 🍃 This all-day brasserie at the front of the Young Vic theatre has put sustainability at the heart of its menu: organic beef burgers, free-range chicken breast in spices and lime, sustainably sourced pan-fried sea bass – and freshly made salads and cakes every day. The Triple Cut lunch deal (Monday to Thursday) with burger and drink for £8.95 is a snip.

★**SKYLON** MODERN EUROPEAN ££
Map p444 (☎020-7654 7800; www.skylonrestaurant.co.uk; 3rd fl, Royal Festival Hall, Southbank Centre, Belvedere Rd, SE1; grill mains £13-25, restaurant 2-/3-course menu £42/47.50; ⏲grill noon-11pm; restaurant noon-2.30pm & 5.30-10.30pm Mon-Sat, noon-4pm Sun; ⊖Waterloo) Named after the defunct 1950s tower, this excellent restaurant on top of the refurbished Royal Festival Hall is divided into grill and fine-dining sections by a large bar (p181) (open until 1am). The decor is cutting-edge 1950s: muted colours and period chairs (trendy then, trendier now) while floor-to-ceiling windows bathe you in magnificent views of the Thames and the City.

Weekday lunch is a bargain at £18/25 in the grill/restaurant. Dress smart casual (no sportswear). Booking is advised, especially for the restaurant.

BALTIC EASTERN EUROPEAN ££
Map p444 (www.balticrestaurant.co.uk; 74 Blackfriars Rd; mains £9.50-18.50; ⏲noon-3pm & 5.30-11.15pm Mon-Sat, to 10.30pm Sun; ⊖Southwark) In a bright and airy, high-ceilinged dining room with glass roof and wooden beams, Baltic is travel on a plate: dill and beetroot, dumplings and blini, pickle and smoke, rich stews and braised meat. From Poland to Georgia, the flavours are authentic and the dishes beautifully presented. The wine and vodka lists are equally diverse.

ANCHOR & HOPE PUB ££

Map p444 (36 The Cut, SE1; mains £12-20; ⏲noon-2.30pm Tue-Sat, 6-10.30pm Mon-Sat, from 2pm Sun; ⊖Southwark) The hope is that you'll get a table without waiting hours because you can't book at this quintessential gastropub. The anchor is gutsy, British food. Critics love this place inside out and despite the menu's heavy hitters (pork shoulder, salt marsh lamb shoulder cooked for seven hours and soy-braised shin of beef), vegetarians aren't completely stranded.

OXO TOWER RESTAURANT & BRASSERIE FUSION £££

Map p444 (☎020-7803 3888; www.harveynichols.com/restaurants/oxo-tower-london; Barge House St, SE1; mains £21.50-35; ⏲restaurant noon-2.30pm & 6-11pm, brasserie noon-11pm; ✎; ⊖Waterloo) The iconic Oxo Tower's conversion, with this restaurant on the 8th floor, helped spur much of the local dining renaissance. In the stunning glassed-in terrace you have a front-row seat for the best view in London, and you pay for this handsomely in the brasserie and stratospherically in the restaurant.

Fish dishes – grilled sardines, squid with chorizo, sea bass with smoked aubergine purée – usually comprise half the fusion menu, but vegetarians will feel at home. Strong wine list. Booking essential.

London Bridge

APPLEBEE'S FISH CAFE SEAFOOD ££

Map p444 (☎020-7407 5777; www.applebeesfish.com; 5 Stoney St, SE1; mains £15.50-25.50; ⏲noon-3.30pm & 6-11pm Tue-Sat; ⊖London Bridge) Tempted by the seafood bounty of Borough Market? Then head for this excellent fishmonger with a cafe-restaurant attached: all manner of fresher-than-fresh fish and shellfish dishes are on the ever-changing chalkboard. And if nothing takes your fancy on the menu, the chef will happily cook the fish of your choice from the counter.

Bermondsey

M MANZE BRITISH £

Map p444 (www.manze.co.uk; 87 Tower Bridge Rd, SE1; ⏲11am-2pm Mon-Thu, 10am-2.30pm Fri

TOP SIGHT
BOROUGH MARKET

Located here in some form or another since the 13th century, 'London's Larder' has enjoyed an astonishing renaissance in the past decade. Always overflowing with food lovers, inveterate gastronomes, wide-eyed newcomers, guidebook-toting visitors and all types in between, this fantastic market has become firmly established as a sight in its own right.

Along with a section devoted to quality fresh fruit, exotic vegetables and organic meat, there's a fine-foods retail market, with the likes of home-grown honey and homemade bread plus loads of free samples. Throughout, takeaway stalls supply sizzling gourmet sausages, chorizo sandwiches and quality burgers in spades, filling the air with meaty aromas.

The market simply heaves on Saturdays so get here early for the best pickings or enjoy the craze at lunch time: if you'd like some elbow space to enjoy your takeaway, head to Southwark Cathedral (p176) gardens or walk five minutes in either direction along the Thames for river views.

DON'T MISS...

- Free samples
- Takeaway in Southwark Cathedral gardens
- Foodscapes (really!)

PRACTICALITIES

- Map p444
- www.boroughmarket.org.uk
- cnr Southwark & Stoney Sts, SE1
- ⏲11am-5pm Thu, noon-6pm Fri, 8am-5pm Sat
- ⊖London Bridge

& Sat; ⊖Borough) Dating to 1902, M Manze (Italian roots) started off as an ice-cream seller before moving on to selling its legendary staples: pies. It's a classic operation, from the lovely tile work to the traditional working-man's menu: pie and mash (£3.40), pie and liquor (£2.40) and you can take your eels jellied or stewed (£3.50).

MAGDALEN MODERN BRITISH ££

Map p444 (☎020-7403 1342; www.magdalenrestaurant.co.uk; 152 Tooley St, SE1; mains £17-18, lunch 2-/3-course £15.50/18.50; ⊙noon 2.30pm Mon-Fri, 6.30-10pm Mon-Sat; ⊖London Bridge) You can't go wrong with this formal dining room. The Modern British fare adds its own appetising spin to familiar dishes (grilled calves' kidneys, creamed onion and sage, smoked haddock *choucroute*); the desserts and English cheese selection are another delight. The welcome is warm and the service excellent.

ZUCCA ITALIAN ££

Map p444 (☎020-7873 6809; www.zuccalondon.com; 184 Bermondsey St; mains £15-18; ⊙noon-3pm Tue-Sun, 6-10pm Tue-Sat; ⊖London Bridge) In a crisp, minimalist dining room with wrap-around bay windows and an open kitchen, an (almost) all-Italian staff serves contemporary Italian fare. The pasta is made daily on the premises and the menu is kept deliberately short to promote freshness.

JOSE SPANISH ££

Map p444 (www.josepizarro.com; 104 Bermondsey St; tapas £4-12; ⊙noon-10.30pm Mon-Sat, to 5.30pm Sun; ⊖London Bridge) From the tiled bar counter to the barrel table, leg of ham on its stand and espresso machine behind the bar, Jose looks straight out of the streets of Madrid or Valencia. The food too is authentic: exquisitely tender *pluma ibérica* (grilled pork), garlic-rubbed *pan con tomate* (toasted bread with puréed tomatoes) and of course, *jamón* (ham) and chorizo.

The wine (and sherry) list is exclusively Spanish, with every wine available by the glass or bottle (a rare thing in London).

GARRISON PUBLIC HOUSE GASTROPUB ££

Map p444 (www.thegarrison.co.uk; 99-101 Bermondsey St, SE1; mains £8.50-17; ⊙8-11am, 12.30-3pm & 6-10pm; ⊖London Bridge) The Garrison's traditional green-tiled exterior and rather distressed, beach-shack interior are both appealing. It boasts an actual cinema (free films every Sunday at 7pm, intermissions for drinks provided) in its basement, but it's the food – razor clams, black-face lamb gigot with roast squash, and pumpkin, chickpea and courgette cake – that lures punters to this evergreen Bermondsey gastropub.

DRINKING & NIGHTLIFE

The South Bank is a strange combination of good, down-to-earth boozers, which just happen to have been here for hundreds of years, and modern bars – all neon and alcopops – patronised by a younger, trendier crowd.

Waterloo

★SKYLON BAR

Map p444 (www.skylon-restaurant.co.uk; Royal Festival Hall, Southbank Centre, Belvedere Rd, SE1; ⊙noon-1am Mon-Sat, to 10.30pm Sun; ⊖Waterloo) With its ravishing 1950s decor and show-stopping views, Skylon is a memorable place to come for a drink or meal (p179). You'll have to come early to bag the tables at the front with plunging views of the river however. Drinks-wise, just ask: from superb seasonal cocktails to infusions and a staggering choice of whiskys (and whiskeys!), you'll finish the night in high spirits.

★SCOOTERCAFFE CAFE-BAR

Map p444 (132 Lower Marsh, SE1; ⊙8am-11pm Mon-Thu, to midnight Fri & Sat; 📶; ⊖Waterloo) A real find in the elephants' graveyard we like to call Waterloo, this funky cafe-bar and former scooter repair shop with a Piatti scooter in the window serves killer hot chocolates, coffee and decadent cocktails. Unusually, you're allowed to bring takeaway food. The tiny patio at the back is perfect to soak up the sun.

There are films screenings every other Sunday.

BALTIC BAR

Map p444 (www.balticrestaurant.co.uk; 74 Blackfriars Rd, SE1; ⊙noon-midnight Mon-Sat, to 10.30pm Sun; ⊖Southwark) This stylish Eastern European bar specialises – not surprisingly – in vodkas; some 60-plus, including bar-infused concoctions, served straight in frozen glasses or long in fantastic cocktails.

KING'S ARMS PUB

Map p444 (www.windmilltaverns.com; 25 Roupell St, SE1; 11am-11pm Mon-Fri, noon-midnight Sat, noon-10.30pm Sun; Waterloo or Southwark) Relaxed and charming when not crowded, this award-winning neighbourhood boozer at the corner of a terraced Waterloo backstreet was a funeral parlour in a previous life. The large traditional bar area, serving up a good selection of ales and bitters, gives way to a fantastically odd conservatory bedecked with junk-store eclectica of local interest and serving decent Thai food.

CONCRETE CAFE-BAR

Map p444 (www.southbankcentre.co.uk; Hayward Gallery, Southbank Centre, Belvedere Rd, SE1; 10am-6pm Sun & Mon, to 11pm Tue-Thu, to 1am Fri & Sat; ; Waterloo) By day this outlet in the Hayward Gallery (p175) is a trendy cafe serving tea, cake and light meals to an earnest, art-loving crowd. By night this Cinderella transforms into a wicked stepsister, with DJs, neon-pink cement mixers as props, chilled absinthe and tapas. Happy hour is 5pm to 7pm Tuesday to Saturday.

QUEEN ELIZABETH ROOF GARDEN CAFE-BAR

Map p444 (Queen Elizabeth Hall, Southbank Centre, Belvedere Rd; 10am-10pm Apr-Sep; Waterloo) Amidst the concrete jungle of the Queen Elizabeth Hall and the Hayward Gallery is this unexpected rooftop garden cafe-bar. The AstroTurf, colourful metal chairs, potted trees and planted 'wild meadows' make a disarming contrast with the surroundings and the river views just add to the sense of wonder. It's just a shame the drinks are so expensive...

Bankside & Southwark

SWAN AT THE GLOBE BAR

Map p444 (www.swanattheglobe.co.uk; 21 New Globe Walk, SE1; 7.30am-11.30pm Mon-Thu, to 12.30am Fri & Sat, to 10.30pm Sun; London Bridge) At Shakespeare's Globe this fine pub-bar at the piazza level, with brasserie, is open for lunch and dinner (lunch only on Sunday) and has simply glorious views of the Thames and St Paul's from the 1st floor.

REFINERY BAR

Map p444 (www.therefinerybar.co.uk; 110 Southwark St, SE1; 9am-1am Mon-Fri, 10am-2am Sat, 10am-6pm Sun; ; Southwark) This cafe-bar, located just a stone's throw from the Tate Modern, is the South Bank's most handsome venue. The decor is a hit, with its long trestle tables, fresh herbs growing on every table and colourful plaids in which to wrap yourself on the outdoor deck chairs. Everything from the coffee to the cocktails is spot-on. Good food is also available.

ANCHOR PUB

Map p444 (34 Park St, SE1; 11am-11pm Sun-Wed, to midnight Thu-Sat; London Bridge) Firmly anchored in many guidebooks (including this one) – and with good reason – this riverside boozer dates to the early 17th century (subsequently rebuilt after the Great Fire and again in the 19th century). Trips to the terrace are rewarded with superb views across the Thames but brace for a constant deluge of drinkers.

Dictionary writer Samuel Johnson, whose brewer friend owned the joint, drank here, as did diarist Samuel Pepys.

London Bridge

★RAKE PUB

Map p444 (www.uttobeer.co.uk; 14 Winchester Walk, SE1; noon-11pm Mon-Sat, to 8pm Sun; London Bridge) The Rake offers more than 100 beers at any one time. The selection of bitters, real ales, lagers and ciders (with one-third pint measures) changes constantly. It's a tiny place yet always busy; the bamboo-decorated decking outside is especially popular.

GEORGE INN PUB

Map p444 (www.nationaltrust.org.uk/george-inn; 77 Borough High St, SE1; 11am-11pm; London Bridge) This magnificent old boozer is London's last surviving galleried coaching inn, dating from 1676 and mentioned in Dickens' *Little Dorrit*. It is on the site of the Tabard Inn, where the pilgrims in Chaucer's *Canterbury Tales* gathered before setting out (well lubricated, we suspect) on the road to Canterbury, Kent.

Bermondsey

★40 MALTBY STREET WINE BAR

Map p444 (www.40maltbystreet.com; 40 Maltby St, SE1; 5.30-10pm Wed & Thu, 12.30-2pm & 5.30-10pm Fri, 11am-5pm Sat) This tunnel-like wine-bar-cum-kitchen sits under the railway arches taking trains in and out of London Bridge. It is first and foremost a wine importer focusing on organic vintages but its hospitality venture has become incredibly popular. The wine recommendations are obviously top-notch (most of them by the glass) and the food – simple, gourmet bistro fare – is spot on.

STREET COFFEE CAFE

Map p444 (www.streetcoffee.co.uk; 163-167 Bermondsey St; ⌚7am-7pm Mon-Fri, 8am-8pm Sat & Sun; 📶; ⊖London Bridge) With its distressed sofas, house music and punk-meets-vintage-chic decor, Coffee Street is no ordinary cafe: the crowd is young, cool, all equipped with smartphones or laptops, and keen to be seen enjoying the lattes, smoothies, hot soups and sandwiches.

WOOLPACK PUB

Map p444 (www.woolpackbar.com; 98 Bermondsey St; ⌚11am-11pm Mon-Sat, to 10.30pm Sun; ⊖London Bridge) This lovely free house (a pub that doesn't belong to a brewery) is a crowdpleaser: the British food is good, the decor lovely – dark-wood panels downstairs, sumptuous Victorian wallpaper upstairs – the garden spacious, and they show football and rugby games.

ENTERTAINMENT

The South Bank of London is home to some heavy hitters when it comes to London's theatre scene. Music and performing arts are big generally at the Southbank Centre.

NATIONAL THEATRE THEATRE

Map p444 (☎020-7452 3000; www.nationaltheatre.org.uk; South Bank, SE1; ⊖Waterloo) England's flagship theatre (p173) showcases a mix of classic and contemporary plays performed by excellent casts in three theatres (Olivier, Lyttelton and Cottesloe). Outstanding artistic director Nicholas Hytner (who will step down in March 2015) has overseen a golden decade at the theatre, with landmark productions such as *War Horse*, and there are constant surprises in the program.

Travelex tickets costing just £12 are available to certain performances during the peak period; otherwise, standby tickets (around £20) are sometimes available 90 minutes before the performance. Students can wait until just 45 minutes before the curtain goes up to purchase £10 standby tickets. Under-18s pay half price.

WORTH A DETOUR

ROTHERHITHE

Nestled in a bend of the River Thames east of Bermondsey, the neighbourhood of Rotherhithe makes for a fascinating detour. The area was an important port along the river and had working docks until the 1970s, an architectural heritage that is still in evidence today in the shape of converted warehouses and preserved wharves.

Rotherhithe also happens to be the place where the world's first underwater tunnel was built, which is celebrated at the **Brunel Museum** (www.brunel-museum.org.uk; Railway Ave, SE16; adult/child £3/free; ⌚10am-5pm; ⊖Rotherhithe). The tunnel was the brainchild of engineer Marc Isambard Brunel (father of Isambard Kingdom Brunel, another famous structural engineer – he also worked on the tunnel), who came up with the idea of a tunnel as an alternative to a bridge to allay congestion on the Thames. Works started in 1825 and the tunnel, initially designed for pedestrians (it is now used by trains of the East London line), opened to great fanfare in 1843.

The museum, housed in the old engine house, is small but has fascinating exhibits retracing Isambard's life, the history of the project, its financial (mis)fortunes and the pioneering technology used to dig the tunnel. Guided tours that include access to the tunnel shaft, the former Grand Entrance, meet at Bermondsey tube station Tuesdays at 6.15pm and Sundays at 10.45am.

Once you've had enough exploring, plump yourself down at the **Mayflower** (www.themayflowerrotherhithe.com; 117 Rotherhithe St, SE16; ⌚11am-11pm; ⊖Rotherhithe), a 15th-century pub named after the vessel that took the pilgrims to America in 1620. The ship set sail from Rotherhithe, and Captain Christopher Jones supposedly charted out its course here while supping schooners. There's seating on a small back terrace, from which you can view the Thames.

LOCAL KNOWLEDGE

ALL LONDON'S A STAGE

Tom Bird is executive producer at Shakespeare's Globe (p172) theatre. As well as working on productions in London (including international plays), his main responsibility is to take the Globe to the world, on tours, festivals and off-beat locations.

Seating or Standing at the Globe?

Standing! I absolutely love it. You can sit down in every other theatre but there is nowhere in the world where standing offers the best seats in the house. And for just £5.

North or South of the river?

I lived in Hackney (North London) for years and have just moved to New Cross (South London). There are a lot of people who seem to be making that journey and I think southeast London is becoming very exciting.

Weekend plans?

I love swimming in the ponds (p261) in Hampstead Heath. It is so unique – there is nowhere else in the world like this and it's a totally new way to discover the city.

My favourite pub isn't far from the ponds; it's the **Southampton Arms** (Map p459; www.thesouthamptonarms.co.uk; 139 Highgate Rd, NW3; 11am-midnight; Gospel Oak). It's a proper London pub, without any kind of pretension, with good ales, lagers and ciders. There's a piano in the corner and an old bloke regularly comes and plays. And they make their own pork pies!

For dinner, I am obsessed with Mangal Ocakbasi (p253) in Dalston. I feel like I need to move on and discover somewhere new! **Palmers** (Map p454; www.palmersrestaurant.net; 238 Roman Rd, E2; mains £9.50-17.50; 6-10.30pm Mon-Sat, noon-9pm Sun; Bethnal Green or Mile End) in Bow is another good find: the decor isn't great but the food is to die for and very reasonable.

Top tip for visitors?

My advice would be to get out of Zone 1 (the West End and the South Bank) and to explore areas on the edge of the centre, like Hackney, Hampstead or East London: they're so interesting and very authentic.

SOUTHBANK CENTRE CONCERT HALL

Map p444 (020-7960 4200; www.southbankcentre.co.uk; Belvedere Rd, SE1; Waterloo) The overhauled **Royal Festival Hall** (Map p444; 020-7960 4242; admission £6-60) is London's premier concert venue (p175) and seats 3000 in a now-acoustic amphitheatre. It's one of the best places for catching world and classical music artists. The sound is fantastic, the programming impeccable and there are frequent free gigs in the wonderfully expansive foyer.

There are more eclectic gigs at the smaller **Queen Elizabeth Hall** (QEH; Map p444) and **Purcell Room** (Map p444), including talks and debates, dance performances, poetry readings and so forth.

Numerous festivals take place across the three venues; our favourites include London **Wonderground** (dedicated to circus and cabaret), **Udderbelly** (a festival of comedy in all its guises – stand up, music, mime etc) and **Meltdown** (a music event curated by the best and most eclectic names in music – Yoko Ono in 2013, Massive Attack in 2008, etc).

SHAKESPEARE'S GLOBE THEATRE

Map p444 (020-7401 9919; www.shakespearesglobe.com; 21 New Globe Walk, SE1; seats £15-42, standing £5; St Paul's or London Bridge) If you love Shakespeare and the theatre, the Globe (p172) will knock you off your feet. This authentic Shakespearean theatre is a wooden O without a roof over the central stage area, and although there are covered wooden bench seats in tiers around the stage, many people (there's room for 700) do as 17th-century 'groundlings' did, standing in front of the stage.

The theatre season runs from late April to mid-October and includes works by Shakespeare and his contemporaries such as Christopher Marlowe. The theatre's artistic director, Dominic Dromgoole, has decided to introduce a couple of new plays each season.

Because the building is quite open to the elements, you may have to wrap up. No umbrellas are allowed, but cheap raincoats are on sale. A warning: two pillars holding up the stage canopy (the so-called Heavens) obscure much of the view in section D; you'd almost do better to stand.

From January 2014 onwards, you'll also get the chance to watch candle-lit plays in the new **Sam Wanamaker Playhouse**, a Jacobean indoor theatre similar to the one Shakespeare would have used in winter.

BFI SOUTHBANK — CINEMA

Map p444 (020-7928 3232; www.bfi.org.uk; Belvedere Rd, SE1; tickets £9; 11am-11pm; Waterloo) Tucked almost out of sight under the arches of Waterloo Bridge is the British Film Institute, containing four cinemas that screen thousands of films each year (mostly arthouse), a gallery devoted to the moving image and the mediatheque, where you watch film and TV highlights from the BFI National Archive.

There's also a gallery space with shows relating to film, a film store for books and DVDs, a restaurant and a gorgeous cafe. Largely a repertory or art-house theatre, the BFI runs regular retrospectives and is the major venue for the **BFI London Film Festival**, which screens 300 films from 60 countries in October every year.

OLD VIC — THEATRE

Map p444 (0844 8717628; www.oldvictheatre.com; The Cut, SE1; Waterloo) Never has there been a London theatre with a more famous artistic director. American actor Kevin Spacey took the theatrical helm in 2003, looking after this glorious theatre's program. The theatre does both new and classic plays, and its cast and directors are consistently high-profile.

YOUNG VIC — THEATRE

Map p444 (020-7922 2922; www.youngvic.org; 66 The Cut, SE1; Waterloo) This groundbreaking theatre is as much about showcasing and discovering new talent as it is about people discovering theatre. The Young Vic showcases actors, directors and plays from across the world, many of which tackle contemporary political or cultural issues such as the death penalty, racism or corruption, often blending dance and music with acting.

Discounts are available for children, students and over 60s.

SOUTH BANK BOOK MARKET

The **South Bank Book Market** (Map p444; Riverside Walk, SE1; 11am-7pm, shorter hours in winter; Waterloo) is great for secondhand books long out of print, and is held in (almost) all weather in front of the BFI Southbank, under the arches of Waterloo Bridge.

BFI IMAX CINEMA — CINEMA

Map p444 (www.bfi.org.uk/bfi-imax; 1 Charlie Chaplin Walk, SE1; adult/child from £9/5.75; Waterloo) The British Film Institute IMAX Cinema screens 2-D and IMAX 3-D documentaries about travel, space and wildlife, lasting anywhere from 40 minutes to 1½ hours, as well as recently released blockbusters à la IMAX.

SHOPPING

Along with the following, check out the cute boutiques at Gabriel's Wharf and the Oxo Tower.

LOVELY & BRITISH — DESIGN

Map p444 (132a Bermondsey St; 11.30am-6pm Mon-Fri, 10am-5.30pm Sat, noon-4pm Sun; London Bridge) As the name suggests, this gorgeous Bermondsey boutique prides itself on stocking prints, jewellery and home furnishings from British designers. It's an eclectic mix of vintage and new, with very reasonable prices.

SOUTHBANK CENTRE SHOP — DESIGN

Map p444 (www.southbankcentre.co.uk; Festival Tce; 10am-9pm Mon-Fri, to 8pm Sat, noon-8pm Sun; Waterloo) This is the place to come for quirky London books, '50s-inspired homewares, original prints and creative gifts for children. The shop is rather eclectic but you're sure to find unique gifts or souvenirs to take home.

BERMONDSEY MARKET — MARKET

Map p444 (Bermondsey Sq; 5am-3pm Fri; Borough or Bermondsey) Reputedly it's legal to sell stolen goods here before dawn, but late risers will find this market altogether upright and sedate, with cutlery and other old-fashioned silverware, antique porcelain, paintings and some costume jewellery.

Kensington & Hyde Park

KNIGHTSBRIDGE | KENSINGTON | HYDE PARK | CHELSEA | BELGRAVIA | VICTORIA | PIMLICO | FULHAM

Neighbourhood Top Five

❶ Thumbing through an encyclopaedic A–Z of decorative and design works from across the globe in the **Victoria & Albert Museum** (p188).

❷ Becoming hypnotised by the awe-inspiring stonework and inexhaustible collection of the world-leading **Natural History Museum** (p192).

❸ Getting your ultimate retail fix – and indulging in the grand food court – at **Harrods** (p204).

❹ Nurturing a wide-eyed fascination for the perplexities of the world and the cosmos in the electrifying **Science Museum** (p193).

❺ Dining out at some of London's best-loved and most mouth-watering restaurants, such as **Medlar** (p201).

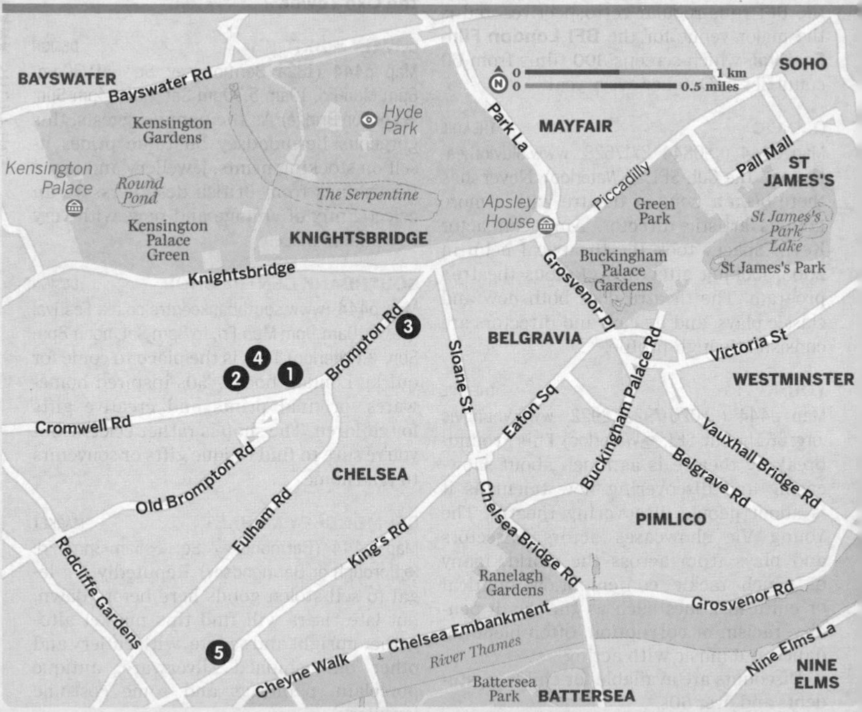

For more detail of this area see Map p448 ➡

Explore: Kensington & Hyde Park

You can navigate a serious learning curve or at least gen up on all you forgot since high school at South Kensington's magnificent museums of the arts and sciences. You'll need several days – and considerable calorific reserves – to do them all justice. Museums open at 10am, so you don't have to set your alarm too early, but being near the front of the queue when the doors open gives useful elbow room.

Shoppers will make an eager beeline for Knightsbridge, Harrods and Harvey Nichols, but there are tranquil shopping escapes – such as John Sandoe Books – to sidestep the maddening crowds.

Earmark a sight-packed day for a visit to Hyde Park and conjoined Kensington Gardens – crucial to see why Londoners love their green spaces. Begin by exploring the opulence of Apsley House before walking across the park, via the Serpentine, to the Albert Memorial, Royal Albert Hall and Kensington Palace.

Outstanding restaurants will be with you every step of the way: Kensington, Knightsbridge and Chelsea take their dining particularly seriously, so some of your fondest memories could well be gastronomic, whether you're grazing, snacking or plain feasting.

Local Life

➡ **Hang-outs** Join Londoners swooning before the lawn of Fulham Palace (p199) beyond the Drawing Room Cafe (p202) or snap your fingers with local jazz hounds at the swinging 606 Club (p203).

➡ **Museums** Late-night Fridays at the Victoria & Albert (p188) mean fewer crowds and locals can get a look-in.

➡ **Parks** When the sun's out, Londoners dust off their shades, get outdoors to expanses of green like Hyde Park (p195) and lie on the grass reading chunky novels.

Getting There & Away

➡ **Underground** Kensington and Hyde Park are excellently connected to the rest of London via stations at South Kensington, Sloane Square, Victoria, Knightsbridge and Hyde Park Corner. The main lines are Circle, District, Piccadilly and Victoria.

➡ **Bus** Handy routes include 74 from South Kensington to Knightsbridge and Hyde Park Corner; 52 from Victoria to High St Kensington; 360 from South Kensington to Sloane Square and Pimlico; and 11 from Fulham Broadway to the King's Road, Sloane Square and Victoria.

➡ **Bicycle** The Barclays Cycle Hire Scheme (p405) is very handy for pedal-powering your way in, out and around the neighbourhood.

Lonely Planet's Top Tip

Catch the Queen's Life Guard (Household Cavalry) departing for Horse Guards Parade at 10.28am (9.28am Sundays) from Hyde Park Barracks for the daily Changing of the Guard, performing a ritual that dates to 1660. They troop via Hyde Park Corner, Constitution Hill and The Mall.

Best Places to Eat

➡ Gordon Ramsay (p202)
➡ Medlar (p201)
➡ Kazan (p202)
➡ Launceston Place (p200)
➡ Pimlico Fresh (p202)

For reviews, see p200 ➡

Best Places to Drink

➡ Zuma (p203)
➡ Queen's Arms (p203)
➡ Drayton Arms (p203)
➡ Anglesea Arms (p203)
➡ 606 Club (p203)

For reviews, see p203 ➡

Best Museums

➡ Victoria & Albert Museum (p188)
➡ Natural History Museum (p192)
➡ Science Museum (p193)

For reviews, see p188 ➡

MAURICE CROOKS / ALAMY ©

TOP SIGHT
VICTORIA & ALBERT MUSEUM

The Museum of Manufactures, as the V&A was known when it opened in 1852, was part of Prince Albert's legacy to the nation in the aftermath of the successful Great Exhibition of 1851, and its original aims – which still hold today – were the 'improvement of public taste in design' and 'applications of fine art to objects of utility'. It's done a fine job so far.

Collection
Through 146 galleries, the museum houses the world's greatest collection of decorative arts, from ancient Chinese ceramics, to modernist architectural drawings, Korean bronze and Japanese swords, cartoons by Raphael, gowns from the Elizabethan era, ancient jewellery, a Sony Walkman – and much, much more.

Entrance
Entering under the stunning blue-and-yellow blown glass **chandelier** by Dale Chihuly, you can grab a museum map (free; £1 donation requested) at the information desk. (If the 'Grand Entrance' on Cromwell Rd is too busy, there's another around the corner on Exhibition Rd or you can enter from the tunnel in the basement, if arriving by tube.)

Level 1
The street level is mostly devoted to art and design from India, China, Japan, Korea and Southeast Asia, as well as European art. One of the museum's highlights is the **Cast Courts** in room 46a, containing staggering plaster casts collected in the Victorian era, such as Michelangelo's *David*, acquired in 1858.

DON'T MISS...
- Tipu's Tiger
- Jewellery Gallery
- Raphael cartoons
- Ardabil Carpet
- Hereford Screen

PRACTICALITIES
- V&A
- Map p448
- www.vam.ac.uk
- Cromwell Rd, SW7
- 10am-5.45pm Sat-Thu, to 10pm Fri
- South Kensington

The **T.T. Tsui China collection** (rooms 44 and 47e) displays lovely pieces, including a beautifully lithe wooden statue of Guanyin seated in *lalitasana* pose from AD 1200; also check out a leaf from the 'Twenty views of the Yuanmingyuan Summer Palace' (1781–86), revealing the Haiyantang and the 12 animal heads of the fountain (now ruins) in Beijing. Within the subdued lighting of the **Japan Gallery** (room 45) stands a fearsome suit of armour in the Domaru style. More than 400 objects are within the **Islamic Middle East Gallery** (room 42), including ceramics, textiles, carpets, glass and woodwork from the 8th century up to the years before WWI. The exhibition's highlight is the gorgeous mid-16th-century **Ardabil Carpet**.

For fresh air, the landscaped **John Madejski Garden** is a lovely shaded inner courtyard. Cross it to reach the original **Refreshment Rooms** (Morris, Gamble and Poynter Rooms), dating from the 1860s and redesigned by McInnes Usher McKnight Architects (MUMA), who also renovated the **Medieval and Renaissance galleries** (1350–1600) to the right of the Grand Entrance.

Levels 2 & 4

The **British Galleries**, featuring every aspect of British design from 1500 to 1900, are divided between levels 2 (1500–1760) and 4 (1760–1900). Level 4 also boasts the **Architecture Gallery** (rooms 127–128a), which vividly describes architectural styles via models and videos, and the spectacular brightly illuminated **Contemporary Glass Gallery** (room 131).

Level 3

The **Jewellery Gallery** (rooms 91–93) is outstanding; the mezzanine level – reached via the glass-and-perspex spiral staircase – gleams and glitters with jewel-encrusted swords, watches and gold boxes. The **Photographs Gallery** (room 100) is one of the nation's best, with access to over 500,000 images collected since the mid-19th century. **Design Since 1946** (room 76) celebrates design classics from a Sony credit-card radio from 1985 to Katherine Hamnett T-shirts, a Nike 'Air Max' shoe from 1992, the once-iconic Apple flatscreen iMac from the late '90s and Peter Ghyczy's Garden Egg Chair from 1968.

Level 6

Among the pieces in the **Ceramics Gallery** – the world's largest – are standout items from the Middle East and Asia. The **Dr Susan Weber Gallery** celebrates furniture design over the past six centuries.

V&A ARCHITECTURE

Look around you at the fabric of the Victoria & Albert Museum – tiled staircases and floors, painted, vaulted ceilings and the astonishing frescoes in the Leighton Corridor – the museum is a work of art in itself.

When militant suffragettes threatened to damage exhibits at public museums in 1913, the V&A considered denying women entry to the museum, but instead opted for scrapping admission charges to the museum to boost visitor numbers and so help protect the V&A's collection.

V&A TOURS

Free one-hour guided tours leave the main reception area at 10.30am, 12.30pm, 1.30pm and 3.30pm. Check the website for details.

The V&A's temporary exhibitions are compelling and fun (note admission fees apply). There are also talks, workshops, events and one of the best museum shops around.

HALF-DAY HIGHLIGHTS TOUR

The art- and design-packed V&A is vast: we have devised an easy-to-follow tour of the museum highlights to help cover some signature pieces while also allowing you to appreciate some of the grandeur of the museum architecture.

Enter the V&A by the Grand Entrance off Cromwell Rd and immediately turn left to explore the Islamic Middle East Gallery and to discover the sumptuous silk-and-wool **Ardabil Carpet** **1**. Among the pieces from South Asia in the adjacent gallery is the terrifying automated **Tipu's Tiger** **2**. Continue to the outstanding **Fashion Room** **3** with its displays of clothing styles through the ages. The magnificent gallery opposite, which houses the Raphael Cartoons, offers a shortcut via stairs on its far side to Level 2 and the Britain 1500–1760 Gallery; turn left in the gallery to find the **Great Bed of Ware** **4**, beyond which rests the exquisitely crafted artistry of **Henry**

DAMIAN HARPER ©

Fashion Gallery

With clothing from the 18th century to the present day, this circular and chronologically arranged gallery showcases evening wear, undergarments and iconic fashion milestones, such as 1960s dresses designed by Mary Quant.

The Great Bed of Ware

Created during the reign of Queen Elizabeth I, its headboard and bedposts etched with ancient graffiti, the 16th-century oak Great Bed of Ware is famously name-dropped in Shakespeare's *Twelfth Night*.

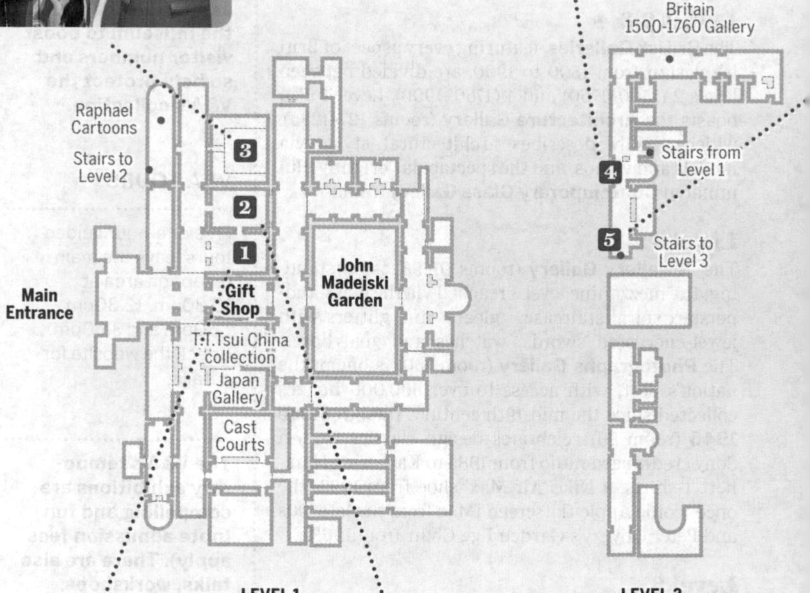

The Ardabil Carpet

One of the world's most beautiful carpets, the Ardabil was completed in 1540, one of a pair commissioned by Shah Tahmasp, ruler of Iran. The piece is most astonishing for the artistry of the detailing and the subtlety of design.

Tipu's Tiger

This disquieting 18th-century wood-and-metal mechanical automaton depicts a European being savaged by a tiger. When a handle is turned, an organ hidden within the feline mimics the cries of the dying man, whose arm also rises.

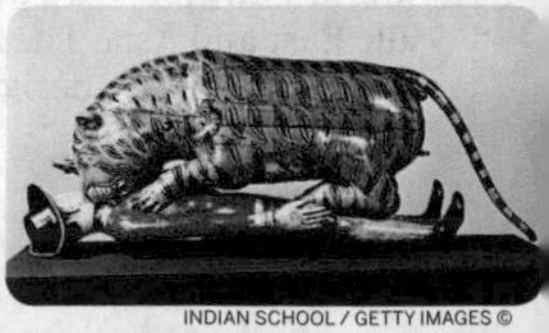

INDIAN SCHOOL / GETTY IMAGES ©

VIII's writing box 5. Head up the stairs into the Metalware Gallery on Level 3 for the **Hereford Screen** 6. Continue through the Ironwork and Sculpture Galleries and through the Leighton Corridor to the glittering **Jewellery Gallery** 7, from where a succession of galleries bordering the John Madejski Garden lead you to the **Design Since 1946** 8 gallery, opposite the 20th Century Gallery (at the end of which are stairs and a lift to the rest of the museum).

TOP TIPS

- **More Info** Museum attendants are always at hand along the route.
- **Photography** Allowed in most galleries, except the Jewellery Gallery, the Raphael Cartoons and the China Gallery.
- **Evening Exploration** Avoid daytime crowds: visit the V&A till 10pm on Friday.

Henry VIII's Writing Box

This exquisitely ornate walnut and oak 16th-century writing box has been added to over the centuries, but the original decorative motifs are superb, including Henry's coat of arms, flanked by Venus (holding Cupid) and Mars.

Design Since 1946

Weigh up some innovative classics that defined much of the late 20th century, when mobile phones were seriously chunky and portable audio cassette players were the latest must-have gadget.

DAMIAN HARPER ©

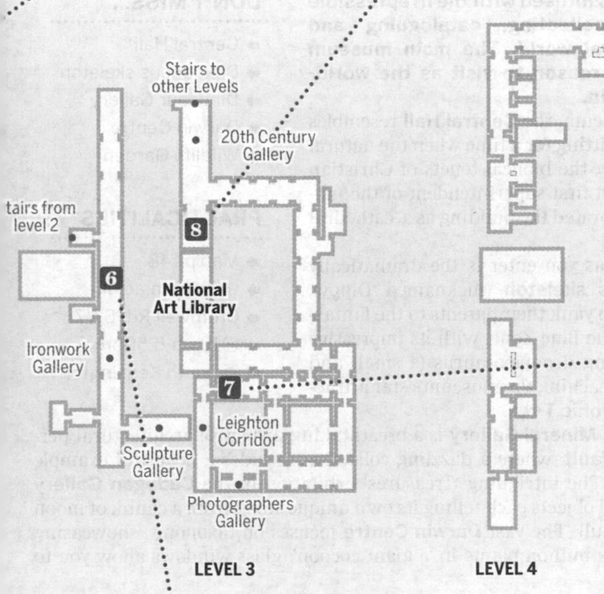

Jewellery Gallery

The beautifully illuminated Jewellery Gallery has a stunning collection of items from ancient Greece to the modern day, including a dazzling gold Celtic breastplate, art-nouveau jewellery and animals fashioned by Fabergé.

DAMIAN HARPER ©

The Hereford Screen

Designed by Sir George Gilbert Scott, this awe-inspiring choir screen is a labour of love, originally fashioned for Hereford Cathedral. An almighty conception of wood, iron, copper, brass and hardstone, there were few parts of the V&A that could support its great mass.

TOP SIGHT
NATURAL HISTORY MUSEUM

This colossal building is infused with the irrepressible Victorian spirit of collecting, cataloguing and interpreting the natural world. The main museum building is as much a reason to visit as the world-famous collection within.

A highlight of the museum, the **Central Hall** resembles a cathedral nave – quite fitting for a time when the natural sciences were challenging the biblical tenets of Christian orthodoxy. Naturalist and first superintendent of the museum Richard Owen celebrated the building as a 'cathedral to nature'.

Your first impression as you enter is the dramatically over-arching **diplodocus skeleton** (nicknamed Dippy), which inspires children to yank their parents to the fantastic **dinosaur gallery** in the Blue Zone, with its impressive overhead walkway passing dromaeosaurus (a small and agile meat eater) before reaching the museum's star attraction: the roaring **animatronic T-rex**.

In the Green Zone, the **Mineral Gallery** is a breathtaking display of architectural perspective leading to the **Vault**, where a dazzling collection includes a beautiful example of butterscotch crystals. The intriguing 'Treasures' exhibition in the **Cadogan Gallery** houses a host of unrelated objects each telling its own unique story, from a chunk of moon rock to a Barbary lion skull. The vast **Darwin Centre** focuses on taxonomy, showcasing 28 million insects and six million plants in 'a giant cocoon'; glass windows allow you to watch scientists at work.

Sensational Butterflies (adult/family £4.50/16; ⌚10am-5.50pm mid-Apr–mid-Sep), a tunnel tent on the East Lawn, swarms with what must originally have been called 'flutter-bys'.

A slice of English countryside in SW7, the beautiful **Wildlife Garden** (⌚Apr-Oct) encompasses a range of British lowland habitats, including a meadow with farm gates and a bee tree where a colony of honey bees fills the air.

DON'T MISS...

- Central Hall
- Diplodocus skeleton
- Dinosaur Gallery
- Darwin Centre
- Wildlife Garden

PRACTICALITIES

- Map p448
- www.nhm.ac.uk
- Cromwell Rd, SW7
- ⌚10am-5.50pm
- South Kensington

TOP SIGHT

SCIENCE MUSEUM

With seven floors of interactive and educational exhibits, this scientifically spellbinding museum will mesmerise adults and children alike. Some children insist on making a beeline for the ground floor shop voice-warpers, lava lamps, boomerangs, bouncy globes and alien babies, and largely stay put.

The **Energy Hall**, on the ground floor, displays machines of the Industrial Revolution, including Stephenson's innovative **rocket** (1829), beyond which rises a further rocket, the German **V-2** from WWII. Nostalgic adults will delight in the **Apollo 10 command module** in the **Making the Modern World Gallery**. Temporary exhibitions are held on the **Bridge**.

The **History of Computing** on the 2nd floor displays some intriguing devices, from Charles Babbage's radical analytical engine to hulking valve-based computers such as hefty Pegasus from 1959.

The 3rd-floor **Flight Gallery** (free tours 1pm most days) is a favourite place for children, with its gliders, hot-air balloon and aircraft, including the *Gipsy Moth*, which Amy Johnson flew to Australia in 1930. There are also fascinating insights into the pre–Wright brothers era of flight attempts, including Henson's hopefully-named *Aerial Steam Carriage* of 1847. This floor also features a **Red Arrows 3D flight simulation theatre** (adult/children £6/5) and **Fly 360 degree flight simulator capsules** (£12 per capsule). **Launchpad** on the same floor is stuffed with hands-on gadgets exploring physics and the properties of liquids.

The hi-tech **Wellcome Wing** has an **IMAX Cinema** (adult/child £10/8) that shows the usual crop of travelogues, space adventures and dinosaur attacks in stunning 3D.

If you've kids under the age of five, pop down to the basement and the **Garden**, where there's a fun-filled play zone, including a water-play area, besieged by tots in red waterproof smocks.

DON'T MISS...

- Apollo 10 command module
- V-2
- Stephenson's rocket
- Flight Gallery

PRACTICALITIES

- Map p448
- www.sciencemuseum.org.uk
- Exhibition Rd, SW7
- 10am-6pm
- South Kensington

SIGHTS

Knightsbridge, Kensington & Hyde Park

VICTORIA & ALBERT MUSEUM MUSEUM
See p188.

NATURAL HISTORY MUSEUM MUSEUM
See p192.

SCIENCE MUSEUM MUSEUM
See p193.

WELLINGTON ARCH MUSEUM
Map p448 (www.english-heritage.org.uk; Hyde Park Corner, W1; adult/child 5-15 £4/2.40, with Apsley House £8.20/4.90; 10am-5pm Wed-Sun Apr-Oct, 10am-4pm Wed-Sun Nov-Mar; ; Hyde Park Corner) Dominating the green space throttled by the Hyde Park Corner roundabout, this imposing neoclassical 1826 arch originally faced the Hyde Park Screen, but was shunted here in 1882 for road widening. The same year saw the removal of the disproportionately large equestrian statue of the duke crowning it, making space for Europe's largest bronze sculpture: *Peace Descending on the Quadriga of War* (1912), three years in the casting.

Until the 1960s part of the monument served as a tiny police station (complete with pet moggy), but the arch was restored and opened up to the public as a three-floor exhibition space; today it contains the Quadriga Gallery (for temporary exhibitions) and an exhibition tracing the history of the arch. The open-air balconies (accessible by lift) afford unforgettable views of Hyde Park, Buckingham Palace and the Houses of Parliament; the views get even better during the annual Trooping the Colour pageantry in June with its RAF fly-past.

SERPENTINE GALLERY ART GALLERY
Map p448 (www.serpentinegallery.org; 10am-6pm; ; Lancaster Gate or Knightsbridge) FREE Resembling an unprepossessing 1930s tearoom in the midst of leafy Kensington Gardens, this is one of London's most important contemporary art galleries. Damien Hirst, Andreas Gursky, Louise Bourgeois, Gabriel Orozco, Tomoko Takahashi and Jeff Koons have all exhibited here. A leading architect (who has never

TOP SIGHT
APSLEY HOUSE

This stunning house, containing exhibits about the Duke of Wellington, was once the first building to appear when entering London from the west and was therefore known as 'No 1 London'. Still one of London's finest, Apsley House was designed by Robert Adam for Baron Apsley in the late 18th century, but later sold to the first Duke of Wellington, who lived here until he died in 1852.

In 1947 the house was given to the nation, which must have come as a surprise to the duke's descendants, who still live in a flat here; 10 of its rooms are open to the public. Wellington memorabilia, including his death mask, fills the basement gallery, while there's an astonishing collection of china and silver, including a dazzling Egyptian service: a divorce gift (call it a golden handshake) from Napoleon to Josephine, which she declined.

The stairwell is dominated by Antonio Canova's staggering 3.4m-high statue of a fig-leafed Napoleon with titanic shoulders, adjudged by the subject as 'too athletic'. The 1st-floor Wellington Gallery contains paintings by Velasquez, Rubens, Van Dyck, Brueghel, Murillo and Goya. A highlight is the elaborate Portuguese silver service, presented to Wellington in honour of his triumph over 'Le Petit Caporal'.

DON'T MISS...

- Egyptian service
- Canova's statue of Napoleon
- Wellington Gallery paintings

PRACTICALITIES

- Map p448
- www.english-heritage.org.uk
- 149 Piccadilly, W1
- adult/child £6.30/3.80, with Wellington Arch £8.20/4.90
- 11am-5pm Wed-Sun Apr-Oct, to 4pm Wed-Sun Nov-Mar
- Hyde Park Corner

TOP SIGHT
HYDE PARK

London's largest royal park spreads itself over 142 hectares of neatly manicured gardens, wild expanses of overgrown grass and glorious trees.

Henry VIII expropriated the park from the church in 1536, after which it emerged as a hunting ground for kings and aristocrats; later it became a popular venue for duels, executions and horse racing. It was the first royal park to open to the public in the early 17th century, the famous venue of the Great Exhibition in 1851, and during WWII it became a vast potato bed.

West of the **Queen Elizabeth Gate** (Map p448) is the **Holocaust Memorial Garden** (Map p448), a simple stone marker in a grove of trees. Hyde Park is separated from Kensington Gardens by the L-shaped **Serpentine**, a small lake once fed with waters from the River Westbourne; the lake hosted the Olympic triathlon and marathon swimming events in 2012. Rent a paddle boat from the **Serpentine boathouse** (Map p448; 020-7262 1330; adult/child per 30min £10/4, per 1hr £12/5). The **Serpentine solar shuttle boat** (020-7262 1330; www.solarshuttle.co.uk; adult/child £5/3) harnesses solar power to ferry you from the boathouse to the Diana, Princess of Wales Memorial Fountain (p195).

DON'T MISS...

- Serpentine
- Serpentine solar shuttle boat

PRACTICALITIES

- Map p448
- 5.30am-midnight
- Marble Arch, Hyde Park Corner or Queensway

built in the UK) is annually commissioned to build a new 'Summer Pavilion' nearby, open from May to October.

Readings, talks and open-air cinema screenings take place here as well. Admission to the gallery is free but a £1 donation is appreciated. A new 880-sq-metre exhibition space, the **Serpentine Sackler Gallery** (Map p448; www.serpentinegallery.org; West Carriage Drive; open daily; Lancaster Gate), was poised to open in 2013 within the Magazine, a former Palladian villa-style gunpowder depot on the far side of the Serpentine Bridge. Built in 1805, the depot has been augmented with an undulating extension designed by Pritzker Prize–winning architect Zaha Hadid. The new gallery will aim to 'present the stars of tomorrow in art, architecture, dance, design, fashion, film, literature, music, performance and technology'.

DIANA, PRINCESS OF WALES MEMORIAL FOUNTAIN — MEMORIAL

Map p448 (Kensington Gardens, W2; Knightsbridge) This memorial fountain is dedicated to the late Princess of Wales. Envisaged by the designer Kathryn Gustafson as a 'moat without a castle' and draped 'like a necklace' around the southwestern edge of Hyde Park near the Serpentine Bridge, the circular double stream is composed of 545 pieces of Cornish granite, its waters drawn from a chalk aquifer more than 100m below ground.

KENSINGTON GARDENS — GARDENS

Map p448 (dawn-dusk; High St Kensington) Immediately west of Hyde Park and across the Serpentine lake, these picturesque 275-acre gardens are technically part of Kensington Palace. The **Diana, Princess of Wales Memorial Playground** (Map p448; Queensway), in the northwest corner of the gardens, has some pretty ambitious attractions for children. Next to the playground stands the delightful **Elfin Oak** (Map p448), a 900-year-old tree stump carved with elves, gnomes, witches and small creatures.

George Frampton's celebrated **Peter Pan statue** (Map p448; Lancaster Gate) is close to the lake. On the opposite side is a statue of **Edward Jenner** (Map p448), who developed a vaccine for smallpox. The recently restored water gardens of the elegant **Italian Gardens** (Map p448) can be found at the head of the Long Water, not far from Bayswater Road.

TOP SIGHT
KENSINGTON PALACE

Built in 1605, the palace became the favourite royal residence under William and Mary of Orange in 1689, and remained so until George III became king and relocated to Buckingham Palace.

The palace underwent a recent refit and the last of the new turf in the garden was being rolled out at the time of writing. As many of the rooms are quite empty, a narrative employing visual effects, props, paper cuts and textual notes accompanies the visitor, but the effect is frequently more baffling than illuminating.

Venue for evenings of music and dance, the beautiful **Cupola Room** in the **King's State Apartments** is arranged with gilded statues and a gorgeous painted ceiling. The **Drawing Room** is beyond, where the king and courtiers would entertain themselves with cards. The **King's Grand Staircase** is a dizzying feast of trompe l'oeil while the **King's Gallery** displays some of the royal art collection. Queen Mary entertained her visitors in the **Queen's Apartments**; an exhibition displaying items from the Royal Ceremonial Dress Collection was due to be unveiled in 2013.

DON'T MISS...

➡ Cupola Room
➡ Drawing Room
➡ King's Grand Staircase
➡ King's Gallery
➡ Queen's Apartments

PRACTICALITIES

➡ Map p448
➡ www.hrp.org.uk/kensingtonpalace
➡ Kensington Gardens, W8
➡ adult/child £14.50/free
➡ ⊙10am-6pm
➡ ⊖High St Kensington

ALBERT MEMORIAL MONUMENT

Map p448 (☑020-7936 2568; 45min tours adult/concession £6/5; ⊙tours 2pm & 3pm 1st Sun of month Mar-Dec; ⊖Knightsbridge or Gloucester Rd) FREE This splendid Victorian confection on the southern edge of Kensington Gardens, facing the Royal Albert Hall, is as ostentatious as the subject was purportedly humble. Queen Victoria's German husband Albert (1819–61) explicitly insisted he did not want a monument; ignoring the good prince's wishes, the Lord Mayor instructed George Gilbert Scott to build the 53m-high, gaudy Gothic memorial in 1872.

An eye-opening blend of mosaic, gold leaf, marble and Victorian bombast, the renovated monument is topped with an ornate cross. The 4.25m-tall gilded statue of the prince, surrounded by 187 figures representing the continents (Asia, Europe, Africa and America), the arts, industry and science, was erected in 1876. The statue was painted black for 80 years, originally – some say – to disguise it from WWI Zeppelins (nonetheless, the memorial was selected by German bombers during WWII as a landmark). To step beyond the railings for a close-up of the 64m-long *Frieze of Par-*

nassus along the base, hop on one of the 45-minute tours.

ROYAL ALBERT HALL HISTORIC BUILDING

Map p448 (☑box office 0845-4015045; www.royalalberthall.com; Kensington Gore, SW7; ☎; ⊖South Kensington) Built in 1871, this huge, domed, red-brick amphitheatre, adorned with a frieze of Minton tiles, is Britain's most famous concert venue and home to the BBC's Promenade Concerts (the Proms) every summer. Book a one-hour front-of-house **guided tour** (☑0845-4015045; adult/concession £11.50/9.50; ⊙tours hourly 10am-4.30pm), operating most days, from the box office at door 12. Check the website for dates for far less frequent 90-minute **backstage tours** (☑0845-4015045; adult £16) and other tours.

The hall was never intended as a concert venue but as a 'Hall of Arts and Sciences', so it spent the first 133 years of its existence tormenting everyone with shocking acoustics. The huge mushroom-like acoustic reflectors first dangled from the ceiling in 1969 and a further massive refurbishment was completed in 2004.

ROYAL COLLEGE OF MUSIC MUSEUM MUSEUM

Map p448 (Prince Consort Road; ⌚11.30am-4.30pm Tue-Fri term time & summer; ⊖South Kensington) If you've a musical ear and the vast museums of South Kensington have left your head spinning, a far smaller and more manageable collection can be discovered downstairs at the illustrious Royal College of Music. The museum presentation is dated but there are some fascinating instruments on display, dating from the 15th century.

There's a 1615 spinet, a replica of a clavichytherium, a barrel organ from 1815, old musical scores, a *bin* from Northern India, a German toy piano and a host of Eastern European plucked instruments. Guided tours of the museum cost £5. If you find this interesting, consider a trip to the outstanding Horniman Museum (p287) in Forest Hill, which has a superlative collection of instruments from around the world.

BROMPTON ORATORY CHURCH

Map p448 (☎020-7808 0900; www.bromptonoratory.com; 215 Brompton Rd, SW7; ⌚7am-8pm; ⊖South Kensington) Also known as the London Oratory and the Oratory of St Philip Neri, this Roman Catholic church is second in size only to the incomplete Westminster Cathedral. It was built in Italian baroque style in 1884. The impressive interior is swathed in marble and statuary; much of the decorative work predates the church and was imported from Italian churches.

Intriguingly the church was employed by the KGB during the Cold War as a dead-letter box. If you want to get married here, apply six months in advance. The incense-infused services are spellbinding, especially the Solemn Mass in Latin on Sundays (11am). There are five daily Masses on weekdays, four on Saturday and seven on Sunday between 8am and 7pm.

MICHELIN HOUSE HISTORIC BUILDING

Map p448 (81 Fulham Rd, SW3; ⊖South Kensington) FREE Built for Michelin between 1905 and 1911 by François Espinasse, and completely restored in 1985, the building blurs the stylish line between art nouveau and art deco. The iconic roly-poly Michelin Man (Bibendum) appears in the exquisite modern stained glass (the originals were removed at the outbreak of WWII and subsequently vanished), while the lobby is decorated with tiles showing early-20th-century cars.

SPEAKERS' CORNER LANDMARK

Map p448 (Park Lane; ⊖Marble Arch) Frequented by Karl Marx, Vladimir Lenin, George Orwell and William Morris, Speakers' Corner in the northeastern corner of Hyde Park is traditionally the spot for oratorical acrobatics and soapbox ranting. If you've got something to get off your chest, do so on Sunday, although you'll mainly have fringe dwellers, religious fanatics and hecklers for company.

It's the only place in Britain where demonstrators can assemble without police permission, a concession granted in 1872 after serious riots 17 years before when 150,000 people gathered to demonstrate against the Sunday Trading Bill before Parliament only to be unexpectedly ambushed by police concealed within Marble Arch.

MARBLE ARCH MONUMENT

Map p438 (⊖Marble Arch) Designed by John Nash in 1827, this huge white arch was moved here from its original spot in front of Buckingham Palace in 1851, when adjudged too unimposing an entrance to the royal manor. If you're feeling anarchic, walk through the central portal, a privilege reserved by (unenforced) law for the Royal Family and the ceremonial King's Troop Royal Horse Artillery.

Lending its name to the entire area, the arch contains three rooms (inaccessible to the public) and was employed as a police hideout (two doors open to the interior). A plaque on the traffic island at Marble Arch indicates the spot where the infamous Tyburn Tree, a three-legged gallows, once stood. An estimated 50,000 people were executed here between 1571 and 1783, many having been dragged from the Tower of London. During the 16th century many Catholics were executed for their faith and it later became a place of Catholic pilgrimage. The arch stands at the axis between two Roman roads (one of which is Watling Street which runs along Edgware Road, the start of the A5). To the west of the arch stands a magnificent outsize bronze sculpture of a horse's head called *Still Water*, created by Nic Fiddian-Green.

TYBURN CONVENT CONVENT

Map p462 (☎020-7723 7262; www.tyburnconvent.org.uk; 8 Hyde Park Pl, W2; ⌚6.30am-8.30pm; ⊖Marble Arch) FREE A convent was established here in 1903, close to the site of the Tyburn Tree gallows. The crypt contains the relics of 105 martyrs, along with paintings commemorating their lives and recording their deaths. Crypt tours run at 3.30pm, but phone to check. A closed order of Benedictine sisters still forms a community here. The brick building at No 10 next door is considered by some to be the smallest house in London, with a width of a mere three foot six inches.

Chelsea & Belgravia

SAATCHI GALLERY GALLERY

Map p448 (www.saatchi-gallery.co.uk; Duke of York's HQ, King's Rd; 10am-6pm; Sloane Sq) FREE This enticing gallery hosts temporary exhibitions of experimental and thought-provoking work across a variety of media. The white and sanded bare-floorboard galleries are magnificently presented, but save some wonder for Gallery 15, where Richard Wilson's *20:50* is on permanent display. Mesmerising, impassive and ineffable, it's a riveting tour de force. A cool bookshop chips in down in the basement.

KING'S ROAD STREET

Map p448 (Sloane Sq) At the counter-cultural forefront of London fashion during the technicolour '60s and anarchic '70s, the King's Road today is more a stamping ground for the leisure-class shopping set. The last green-haired Mohawk punks – once tourist sights in themselves – shuffled off sometime in the 1990s. Today it's all Bang & Olufsen, Kurt Geiger and a sprinkling of specialist shops; even pet canines are slim and snappily-dressed.

In the 17th century Charles II fashioned a love nest here for himself and his mistress Nell Gwyn, an orange seller turned actress at the Drury Lane Theatre. Heading back to Hampton Court Palace at eventide, Charles would employ a farmer's track that inevitably came to be known as the King's Road.

RIVER WESTBOURNE

One of London's many underground rivers, the River Westbourne flows secretly through a highly visible steel conduit above the platform of Sloane Square tube station on its underground journey to the Thames. The watercourse is also the source of the name Knightsbridge, a former crossing point of the river.

ROYAL HOSPITAL CHELSEA HISTORIC BUILDINGS

Map p448 (www.chelsea-pensioners.co.uk; Royal Hospital Rd, SW3; grounds 10am-noon & 2-4pm Mon-Sat, museum 10am-noon & 2-4pm Mon-Fri; ; Sloane Sq) FREE Designed by Christopher Wren, this superb structure was built in 1692 to provide shelter for ex-servicemen. Since the reign of Charles II it has housed hundreds of war veterans, known as Chelsea Pensioners. They're fondly regarded as national treasures, and cut striking figures in the dark-blue greatcoats (in winter) or scarlet frock coats (in summer) that they wear on ceremonial occasions.

The museum contains a huge collection of war medals bequeathed by former residents and you'll get to peek at the hospital's Great Hall refectory, Octagon Porch, chapel and courtyards.

NATIONAL ARMY MUSEUM MUSEUM

Map p448 (020-7881 2455, 7730 0717; www.nam.ac.uk; Royal Hospital Rd, SW3; 10am-5.30pm; ; Sloane Sq) FREE This museum's four levels tell the history of the British army from the perspective of its servicemen and servicewomen. Standout pieces include the life and times of the 'Redcoat', the tactical battle at Waterloo between victor and vanquished and the skeleton of Marengo, Napoleon's horse.

In the fascinating and more modern Conflicts of Interest, 1969–Present section on level 4, hunt down the distinctly Darth Vaderish 'Fedayeen' helmet from 2003, worn by members of a paramilitary unit loyal to Saddam Hussein. At the time of writing, a dramatic and inspiring exhibition on horses in war called 'War Horse: Fact & Fiction' was on the ground floor. The museum makes inventive efforts to woo children, with lively activities and performances.

CHELSEA PHYSIC GARDEN GARDEN

Map p448 (www.chelseaphysicgarden.co.uk; 66 Royal Hospital Rd, SW3; adult/child £9/6; 11am-6pm Tue-Fri, to 10pm Wed Jul & Aug, 11am-6pm Sun Apr-Oct; ; Sloane Sq) This walled pocket of botanical enchantment was established by the Apothecaries' Society in 1676 for students working on medicinal plants and healing. One of Europe's oldest of its kind, the small grounds are a compendium of botany from carnivorous pitcher plants to rich yellow flag irises, a cork oak from Portugal, delightful ferns, rare trees and shrubs.

The fascinating pharmaceutical garden grows plants used in contemporary Western medicine; the world medicine garden has a selection of plants used by indigenous peoples in Australia, China, India, New Zealand and North America; and there's a heady perfume and aromatherapy garden. Enter from Swan Walk. Free tours are held three times daily and a host of courses and lectures detail plant remedies.

CARLYLE'S HOUSE HISTORIC BUILDING

Map p448 (☎020-7352 7087; www.nationaltrust.org.uk; 24 Cheyne Row, SW3; adult/child £5.10/2.60; ⏲11am-5pm Wed-Sun Mar-Oct; ⊖Sloane Sq) From 1834 until his death in 1881, the eminent Victorian essayist and historian Thomas Carlyle dwelt in this three-storey terrace house, bought by his parents when it was surrounded by open fields in what was then a deeply unfashionable part of town. The lovely Queen Ann house – built in 1708 – is magnificently preserved as it looked in 1895, when it became London's first literary shrine.

It's not big but has been left much as it was when Carlyle was living here and Chopin, Tennyson and Dickens came to call.

Carlyle unsuccessfully soundproofed his attic room from the hullabaloo of street criers, organ grinders and Italian ice-cream sellers and against this acoustic backdrop penned his famous history of the French Revolution. The first chapter was inadvertently tossed onto the fire by John Stuart Mill's maid; the stoic Carlyle took up his quill and wrote it again.

The family managed to get through 32 maids in as many years (one was an old soak who collapsed comatose in the hall, blocking the door, while another went into labour in the China room).

CHELSEA OLD CHURCH CHURCH

Map p448 (☎020-7795 1019; www.chelseaoldchurch.org.uk; cnr Cheyne Walk & Old Church St, SW3; ⏲during church services & 2-4pm Tue, Wed & Thu; 📶; ⊖South Kensington or Sloane Sq) This church stands behind a bronze monument to Thomas More (1477–1535), who had a close association with it. At the western end of the south aisle don't miss the only chained books in a London church.

The central tome is a 'Vinegar Bible' from 1717 (so-named after an erratum in Luke, chapter 20), alongside a 'Book of Common Prayer' from 1723 and a 1683 copy of 'Homilies'. The books were gifts from Sir Hans Sloane; to read them, scholars must apply in writing to the vicar. Original features of the largely rebuilt church (it was badly bombed in 1941) include the Tudor More Chapel; also look out for fragments of 17th century Flemish stained glass, of exceptional clarity and artistry.

⊙ Victoria & Pimlico

WESTMINSTER CATHEDRAL CHURCH

Map p440 (www.westminstercathedral.org.uk; Victoria St, SW1; tower adult/child £5/2.50; ⏲7am-7pm; 📶; ⊖Victoria) With its distinctive candy-striped red-brick and white-stone tower features, John Francis Bentley's 19th-century cathedral, the mother church of Roman Catholicism in England and Wales, is a splendid example of neo-Byzantine architecture. Although construction started here in 1896 and worshippers began attending services seven years later, the church ran out of money and the gaunt interior remains largely unfinished.

The application of colour is a painfully slow process. The **Chapel of the Blessed Sacrament** and elsewhere are ablaze with Eastern Roman mosaics and ornamented with 100 types of marble; the arched ceiling of the **Lady Chapel** is also richly presented, while other areas of the church remain just bare brick.

The highly regarded stone bas-reliefs of the **Stations of the Cross** (1918) by Eric Gill and the marvellously sombre atmosphere make this a welcome haven from the traffic outside. The views from the 83m-tall **bell tower** (⏲9.30am-5pm Mon-Fri, 9.30am-6pm Sat & Sun) – thankfully, accessible by lift – are impressive, the **Treasures of the Cathedral exhibition** is rewarding and there's a cafe near the Baptistry. Six Masses are said daily from Sunday to Friday and five on Saturday.

⊙ Fulham

FULHAM PALACE HISTORIC BUILDING

(www.fulhampalace.org; Bishop's Ave; ⏲palace & museum 1-4pm Sat-Wed, gardens dawn-dusk daily; 📶; ⊖Putney Bridge) Within stumbling distance of the Thames, this summer home of the bishops of London from 704 to 1975 is an appealing blend of architectural styles immersed in beautiful gardens. It was originally enclosed by the longest moat in England until, in 1924, the ditch was filled with rubble. The oldest surviving palace chunk is the little red-brick Tudor gateway, while the main building dates from the mid-17th century and was remodelled in the 19th century.

The lovely courtyard draws watercolourists on sunny days and the genteel drawing room cafe (p202) at the rear, looking out onto the gorgeous lawn, is a superlative spot for some carrot cake and a coffee. There's also a pretty **walled garden** (Sun tours per person £5; ⏲10.15am-4.15pm Mon-Fri, 10.15am-3.45pm Sat) and, detached from the main house, a Tudor Revival **chapel** designed by Butterfield in 1866.

You can learn about the history of the palace and its inhabitants in the museum. Guided **tours** (☎020-7610 7164; tickets £5; ⏲2pm 2nd & 4th Sun, 1st Wed & 3rd Tue of month), usually take in the Great Hall, the Victorian chapel, Bishop Sherlock's Room and the museum and last about 1¼ hours; private tours cost £8. There are also garden tours (£5); check the website for details on evening walks (for a nightfall perspective).

The surrounding land, once totalling almost 15 hectares but now reduced to just over five, forms **Bishop's Park**, and consists of a shady promenade along the river, a bowling green, tennis courts, a rose garden, a cafe and even a paddling pond with fountain. Hiking around the long moat of the palace makes for an excellent walk, while summer sees a popular **art fair** and **music festivals** at the palace. Check the website for details of children's and adults' activities and events – including crowd-pleasing open-air summer **film screenings** and theatre.

Located by the Thames a short walk northwest of Putney Bridge, the palace can be easily reached from Putney Bridge underground station.

EATING

Quality and cashola being such easy bedfellows, you'll find some of London's finest establishments in the smart hotels and ritzy mews of Chelsea, Belgravia and Knightsbridge, but there's choice in all budget ranges. Chic and cosmopolitan South Kensington has always been reliable for pan-European options.

Knightsbridge, Kensington & Hyde Park

GESSLER AT DAQUISE — POLISH £

Map p448 (20 Thurloe St, SW7; mains £5-12, set lunch £9; ⏲noon-late; ⊖South Kensington) With an unassuming yet wholesome interior, this popular Polish restaurant welcomes diners with a heart-warming range of vodkas and a reasonably priced, regularly varying menu, where you can usually find the oft-seen *bigos* (a 'hunter's stew' of cabbage and pork) and an abundance of soups. The Monday to Saturday espresso lunch (£9) is attractively priced.

★LAUNCESTON PLACE — MODERN BRITISH ££

Map p448 (☎020-7937 6912; www.launcestonplace-restaurant.co.uk; 1a Launceston Pl, W8; 3-course lunch/Sun lunch/dinner £25/29.50/30; ⏲closed lunch Mon; ⊖Gloucester Rd or High St Kensington) This exceptionally handsome Michelin-starred restaurant hidden away on a picture-postcard Kensington street of Edwardian houses is super-chic. Prepared by Yorkshire chef Tim Allen, the food belongs within the acme of gastronomic pleasures, accompanied by an award-winning wine list. The adventurous will aim for the six-course tasting menu (£65; vegetarian version available).

TOM'S KITCHEN — MODERN EUROPEAN ££

Map p448 (☎020-7349 0202; www.tomskitchen.co.uk; 27 Cale St; breakfast £4-15, mains £13.90-30; ⏲8-11.30am, noon-2.30pm & 6.30-10.30pm Mon-Fri, 10am-3.30pm, 6-9.30pm Sat & Sun; ⊖South Kensington) Celebrity chef Tom Aikens' restaurant serves excellent food (including award-winning breakfasts and pancakes).

ORANGERY — TEAHOUSE ££

Map p448 (☎020-3166 6112; www.hrp.org.uk/kensingtonpalace/foodanddrink/orangery; Kensington Palace, Kensington Gardens, W8; tea £22.65, with Champagne £32.50; ⏲10am-6pm Mar-Sep, to 5pm Oct-Feb; ⊖Queensway, Notting Hill Gate or High St Kensington) The Orangery, housed in an 18th-century conservatory on the grounds of Kensington Palace, is lovely for lunch, especially if the sun is beaming. But the standout experience here is afternoon tea.

RACINE
FRENCH ££

Map p448 (☎020-7584 4477; www.racine-restaurant.com; 239 Brompton Rd, SW3; mains £15.75-29.75, 2-/3-course set lunch £15.50/17.75; ⊙noon-3pm & 6-10.30pm Mon-Fri, noon-10pm Sat & Sun; ⊖Knightsbridge or South Kensington) Regional French cooking is the vehicle at this good-looking brasserie. Expect the likes of *tête de veau* (the classic French veal dish; £17.75) and grilled rabbit with mustard (£16.75). Being French and very classic, dishes might feel heavy to some, but the sauces and the desserts are all spot on.

DINNER BY HESTON BLUMENTHAL
MODERN BRITISH £££

Map p448 (☎020-7201 3833; www.dinnerby-heston.com; Mandarin Oriental Hyde Park, 66 Knightsbridge; set lunch £36, mains £26-38; ⊙noon-2.30pm & 6.30-10.30pm; ⊖Knightsbridge) Sumptuously presented Dinner is a gastronomic tour de force, taking diners on a journey through British culinary history (with inventive modern inflections). Dishes carry historical dates to convey context, while the restaurant interior is a design triumph, from the glass-walled kitchen and its overhead clock mechanism to the large windows onto the park.

The broth of lamb (c 1730) is a lovingly prepared infusion of flavour, and the cod in cider (c 1940) is a joy, but unless you order the set lunch (Monday to Friday), your bill may quickly spiral out of control. Book ahead.

ZUMA
JAPANESE £££

Map p448 (☎020-7584 1010; www.zumares-taurant.com; 5 Raphael St, SW7; mains £15-75; ⊙6-11pm daily & noon-2.30pm Mon-Fri, 12.30-3.30pm Sat & Sun; 📶; ⊖Knightsbridge) A modern-day take on the traditional Japanese *izakaya* ('a place to stay and drink sake'), where drinking and eating harmonise, Zuma oozes style. Traditional Japanese materials – wood and stone – combine with a modern sensibility for a highly contemporary feel. The private *kotatsu* rooms are the place for large dinner groups, or dine alongside the sushi-counter, open-plan kitchen.

Ultimately it's the sushi, sashimi and *robata* (char-grilled) dishes, all excellent and outstandingly presented, that steal the show. With more than 40 different types of sake at the bar drinkers will find themselves in capable hands.

MIN JIANG
CHINESE £££

Map p448 (www.minjiang.co.uk; 2-24 Kensington High St, 10th fl, Royal Garden Hotel, W8; mains £12-68; ⊙noon-3pm & 6-10.30pm; ⊖High St Kensington) Min Jiang serves up seafood, excellent wood-fired Peking duck (half/whole £32/58) and sumptuously regal views over Kensington Palace and Gardens. The menu is diverse, with a sporadic accent on spice (the Min Jiang is a river in Sichuan).

RIB ROOM
BRITISH £££

Map p448 (☎020-7858 7250; www.theribroom.co.uk; Jumeirah Carlton Tower, Cadogan Place SW1; mains from £24, 2/3-course set lunch £24/29; ⊙7-11am, noon-2.30pm & 6.30-10pm Mon-Fri, 8-11am, 12.30-3.30pm & 6.30-10.15pm Sat & Sun; 📶; ⊖Knightsbridge) Head chef Ian Rudge's faultless preparation is the cornerstone of the much-lauded carnivorous menu at the restyled Rib Room, which has been busy satiating Knightsbridge diners on steaks, cutlets, roast rib of beef and oysters since the swinging '60s. Prices may give pause for thought, but the food is superlative (set lunches soften the assault on your wallet) and service is outstanding.

Chelsea & Belgravia

PENNY BLACK
BRITISH ££

Map p464 (☎020-7349 9901; www.thepenny-black.com; 212 Fulham Rd, SW10; mains £12-30; ⊙noon-3pm & 6-11pm Tue-Sat, 10am-10.30pm Sun; ⊖West Brompton or Gloucester Rd) Led by head chef Jan Chanter, this contemporary and stylish SW10 restaurant is a stimulating blend of fresh, locally sourced ingredients, culinary excellence and highly appetising presentation. The beef Wellington and the Penny Black's other roasts are standout experiences and you can't go wrong with the seafood menu. Service is top notch.

★MEDLAR
MODERN EUROPEAN £££

Map p448 (☎020-7349 1900; www.medlarrestaurant.co.uk; 438 King's Rd, SW10; 3-course lunch £26-30, dinner £30-42; ⊙noon-3pm & 6.30-10.30pm; ⊖South Kensington, Fulham Broadway or Sloane Sq) With its uncontrived yet crisply modern green-on-grey design, immaculate and Michelin star–rated Medlar has quickly become a King's Rd sensation. With no à la carte menu and scant pretentiousness, the prix fixe modern European cuisine is delightfully assured, with kitchen magic devised by chef Joe Mercer Nairne (from Chez Bruce); prices are equally appetising and service is exemplary.

★**GORDON RAMSAY** FRENCH £££

Map p448 (☎020-7352 4441; www.gordonramsay.com; 68 Royal Hospital Rd, SW3; 3-course lunch/dinner £55/95; ⏲noon-2.30pm & 6.30-11pm Mon-Fri; ⊖Sloane Sq) One of Britain's finest restaurants and London's longest-running with three Michelin stars, this is hallowed turf for those who worship at the altar of the stove. It's true that it's a treat right from the taster to the truffles, but you won't get much time to savour it all. The blowout tasting Menu Prestige (£135) is seven courses of absolute perfection.

Bookings are made in specific sittings and you dare not linger; book as late as you can to avoid that rushed feeling.

Victoria & Pimlico

★**PIMLICO FRESH** CAFE £

Map p448 (86 Wilton Road; mains from £6; ⏲7.30am-7.30pm Mon-Fri, 9am-6pm Sun & Sat; ⊖Victoria) A wholesome choice for a healthy breakfast or lunch, this friendly two-room cafe cooks up fine homemade dishes from pies, soups, baked beans on toast and lasagne to warming bowls of porridge laced with honey, maple syrup, banana, yoghurt or sultanas, while making regular forays into creative cuisine. There's an invigorating choice of fresh fruit juices, and steaming glasses of spicy apple winter warmer fend off the cold in chillier months.

★**KAZAN** TURKISH ££

Map p448 (☎020-7233 7100; www.kazan-restaurant.com; 93-94 Wilton Rd; mains £5.95-21; ⏲noon-3pm & 5.30-10.30pm; ⊖Victoria) Aromatic Kazan gets repeated thumbs up for its set Turkish mezze, shish kebabs and *kulbasti* (rosemary-rubbed grilled fillet of lamb). Flavours are rich and faultless, service is attentive and the Ottoman ambience alluring, but not over the top. Seafood and vegetarian options available. Booking ahead is recommended.

DAYLESFORD ORGANIC DELI ££

Map p448 (☎020-7881 8060; www.daylesfordorganic.com; 44b Pimlico Rd; mains £11-15; ⏲8am-8pm Mon-Sat, 10am-4pm Sun; ⊖Sloane Sq) A chomping ground for the Chelsea and Pimlico set, with a deli upstairs and a modernist downstairs cafe serving delicious light lunches.

HUNAN CHINESE ££

Map p448 (☎020-7730 5712; www.hunanlondon.com; 51 Pimlico Rd; set lunch/dinner £29.80/45.80; ⏲12.30-2.30pm & 6.30-11pm Mon-Sat; ⊖Sloane Sq) In business for over three decades, this understated Chinese restaurant imaginatively exercises a no-menu policy: just present your preferences and let the *dachu* (chef) get cracking. If you need inspiration, however, staff assist with ideas, such as the appetising slow-cooked belly pork with Chinese spices and preserved vegetables. Dishes – many with a pronounced Taiwanese accent – arrive tapas-style to encourage a spectrum of colour and flavour. Vegetarian tasting menu available.

Fulham

DRAWING ROOM CAFE CAFE £

(www.fulhampalace.org; Fulham Palace, Bishop's Avenue; ⏲9.30am-4pm; 📶; ⊖Putney Bridge) This adorable cafe enjoys a divine setting within the elegant drawing room (the former Bishop's living room) at the rear of Fulham Palace (p199). Sink into a deep sofa or perch by a table with an almond croissant and a cup of tea, pinky aloft. If the sun obliges, nab a table on the terrace facing the gorgeous lawn outside. The kitchen also whips up a range of hot dishes.

LOTS ROAD PUB & DINING ROOM GASTROPUB ££

(www.lotsroadpub.com; 114 Lots Rd, SW10; mains £10.50-18; ⏲11am-11pm Mon-Sat, 12.30-10.30pm Sun; ⊖Fulham Broadway) Even this charmingly tucked-away gastropub's affectation of listing prices in hundreds of pence is forgiven as light floods through the windows into the high-ceilinged, wood-lined, curved dining area and onto the black-and-chrome bar, where choice wines are sold by the glass. Service is tip-top and the regularly changing menu may read as standard fare – beef, salmon, lamb – but it's all delicious.

Sunday roasts are deservedly popular and don't miss the sticky toffee pudding.

DRINKING & NIGHTLIFE

ZUMA BAR

Map p448 (www.zumarestaurant.com; 5 Raphael St; ⌚noon-11.30pm; 📶; ⊖Knightsbridge) After the hectic shopping swirl of Knightsbridge, the stylish simplicity and muted elegance of Zuma is refreshingly soothing. As are the ambitious 40-plus varieties of sake and exquisitely presented cocktails (many blended with Japanese spirits) served to the assorted high-rollers at the bar. If your taste buds warm to the occasion, the fantastic restaurant (p201) awaits (book ahead).

QUEEN'S ARMS PUB

Map p448 (www.thequeensarmskensington.co.uk; 30 Queen's Gate Mews, SW7; ⌚noon-11pm Mon-Sat, noon-10.30pm Sun; ⊖Gloucester Rd) Just around the corner from the Royal Albert Hall, this godsend of a blue-grey painted pub in an adorable cobbled mews setting off bustling Queen's Gate beckons with a cosy interior and a right royal selection of ales and ciders on tap.

DRAYTON ARMS PUB

Map p448 (www.thedraytonarmssw5.co.uk; 153 Old Brompton Rd, SW5; ⌚noon-11pm Mon-Sat, noon-10.30pm Sun; 🚌430, ⊖Gloucester Road or South Kensington) This vast, comely Victorian corner boozer is delightful inside and out, with some bijou art-nouveau features (sinuous tendrils and curlicues above the windows and the doors), contemporary art on the walls, fabulous coffered ceiling and heated beer garden. The crowd is both hip and down-to-earth; great beer and wine selection.

BUDDHA BAR BAR

Map p448 (www.buddhabarlondon.com; 145 Knightsbridge; cocktails from £10.50; ⌚noon-midnight Mon-Sat, noon-11.30pm Sun; 📶; ⊖Knightsbridge) When you've shopped your legs off in Knightsbridge, this serene Pan-Asian zone welcomes you into a world of Chinese bird-cage lanterns, subdued lighting, tucked-away corners and booths, perfect for sipping on a raspberry saketini and chilling out. Live DJ nightly; restaurant downstairs.

ANGLESEA ARMS PUB

Map p448 (www.capitalpubcompany.com/our-pubs/the-anglesea-arms; 15 Selwood Tce; ⌚11am-11pm Mon-Sat, noon-10.30pm Sun; ⊖South Kensington or Gloucester Road) Seasoned with age and decades of ale-quaffing patrons (including Charles Dickens, who lived on the same road, and DH Lawrence), this old-school pub boasts a haunted cellar and a strong showing of beers, while the terrace out front swarms with punters in warmer months.

ENTERTAINMENT

ROYAL ALBERT HALL CONCERT HALL

Map p448 (☎020-7589 8212; www.royalalberthall.com; Kensington Gore, SW7; ⊖South Kensington) This splendid Victorian concert hall hosts classical-music, rock and other performances, but is most famously the venue for the BBC-sponsored Proms. Booking is possible, but from mid-July to mid-September Proms punters also queue for £5 standing (or 'promenading') tickets that go on sale one hour before curtain-up. Otherwise the box office and prepaid ticket collection counter are both through door 12 (south side of the hall).

606 CLUB BLUES, JAZZ

(☎020-7352 5953; www.606club.co.uk; 90 Lots Rd, SW10; music fee Mon-Thu £10, Fri & Sat £12, Sun £10; ⌚7pm-late Mon-Thu, 8pm-late Fri & Sat, 7-11.15pm Sun; ⊖Fulham Broadway) Named after its old address on King's Road which cast a spell over jazz lovers London-wide back in the '80s, this fantastic, tucked-away basement jazz club and restaurant gives centre stage to contemporary British-based jazz musicians nightly. Hidden behind a nondescript brick wall, the club frequently opens until 2am, although at weekends you have to dine to gain admission (booking is advised).

There is no entry charge, but a music fee will be added to your food/drink bill at the end of the evening; open occasional Sunday lunches.

ROYAL COURT THEATRE THEATRE

Map p448 (☎020-7565 5000; www.royalcourttheatre.com; Sloane Sq, SW1; ⊖Sloane Sq) Equally renowned for staging innovative new plays and old classics, the Royal Court is among London's most progressive theatres and has continued to foster major writing talent across the UK.

Tickets for concessions are £6 to £10, and it's £10 for everyone on Monday (four 10p standing tickets sold at the Jerwood Theatre Downstairs); tickets for under 26s are £8. Check the theatre's Facebook page for the lastest on cheap tickets.

Standby tickets are sold an hour before performances, but normally at full price.

CADOGAN HALL CONCERT VENUE

Map p448 (☎020-7730 4500; www.cadoganhall.com; 5 Sloane Tce, SW1; tickets £10-40; ⊖Sloane Sq) Home of the Royal Philharmonic Orchestra, Cadogan Hall is a major venue for classical music, opera and choral music, with occasional dance, rock, jazz and family concerts.

CINÉ LUMIÈRE CINEMA

Map p448 (☎020-7073 1350; www.institut-francais.org.uk; 17 Queensberry Pl, SW7; ⊖South Kensington) Ciné Lumière is attached to South Kensington's French Institute, and its large art-deco 300-seat *salle* (cinema) screens great international seasons (including the London Spanish Film Festival) and French and other foreign films subtitled in English.

SHOPPING

Frequented by models and celebrities and awash with new money (much from abroad) and Russian oligarchs, this well-heeled part of town is all about high fashion, glam shops, groomed shoppers and iconic top-end department stores. Even the charity shops along the chic King's Road resemble fashion boutiques.

HARRODS DEPARTMENT STORE

Map p448 (www.harrods.com; 87 Brompton Rd, SW1; ⌚10am-8m Mon-Sat, 11.30am-6pm Sun; ⊖Knightsbridge) Both garish and stylish at the same time, perennially crowded Harrods is an obligatory stop for London's tourists, from the cash strapped to the big, big spenders. The stock is astonishing and you'll swoon over the spectacular food hall.

High on kitsch, the 'Egyptian Elevator' with its ex-owner Mohammed Al Fayed's sphinxes, resembles something hauled in from an Indiana Jones epic, while the memorial fountain to Dodi and Di merely adds surrealism. Piped opera will be thrown at you as you recoil from the price tags: after an hour of browsing, you may just want to lie down on one of the doubles in the 2nd-floor bedroom department. Serious shoppers can download the handy Harrods app.

HARVEY NICHOLS DEPARTMENT STORE

Map p448 (www.harveynichols.com; 109-125 Knightsbridge, SW1; ⌚10am-8pm Mon-Sat, 11.30am-6pm Sun; ⊖Knightsbridge) At London's temple of high fashion, you'll find Chloé and Balenciaga bags, the city's best denim range, a massive make-up hall with exclusive lines, great jewellery and the fantastic restaurant, Fifth Floor.

JOHN SANDOE BOOKS BOOKS

Map p448 (www.johnsandoe.com; 10 Blacklands Tce; ⌚9.30am-6.30pm Mon-Sat, 11am-5pm Sun; ⊖Sloane Sq) The perfect antidote to impersonal book superstores, this atmospheric little bookshop is a treasure trove of literary gems and hidden surprises. In business for decades, loyal customers swear by it and the knowledgeable booksellers spill forth with well-read pointers.

SLIGHTLY FOXED BOOKS

Map p448 (www.foxedbooks.com; 123 Gloucester Rd; ⌚10am-7pm Mon-Sat, 11am-5pm Sun; ⊖Gloucester Rd) Once owned by a nephew of Graham Green and run by the namesake literary quarterly, this delightfully calming two-floor oasis of literature has a strong lean towards second-hand titles (in good condition) plus new cloth-bound and hardback books. Reasonably priced first editions peek from the shelves, luring collectors and there's a slab or two of Slightly Foxed's own publications, plus a showing of titles from other small presses.

LIMELIGHT MOVIE ART FILM POSTERS

Map p448 (☎020-7751 5584; www.limelightmovieart.com; 313 King's Rd, SW3; ⌚11.30am-6pm Mon-Sat; ⊖Sloane Sq or South Kensington) This spiffing poster shop is a necessary stop for collectors of vintage celluloid memorabilia, nostalgic browsers or film buffs. Ageing mods and Sting fans can swoon before *Quadrophenia* (£750), Ridley Scott purists will go wide-eyed before *Alien* (£475) while 007 aficionados can be shaken and stirred by the price tag of an original *Diamonds are Forever* (£1000), or swept away by *Skyfall* (£125).

PETER JONES DEPARTMENT STORE

Map p448 (020-7730 3434; www.peterjones.co.uk; Sloane Sq, SW1; 9.30am-7pm Mon, Tue & Thu-Sat, to 8pm Wed, 11am-5pm Sun; Sloane Sq) The slightly more upmarket brother of John Lewis, Peter Jones is now competitive with Selfridges and Harvey Nicks. Upmarket china, furnishings and gifts are its forte, though it stocks accessories and cosmetics, too. The Top Floor (and that's where it's at) is a restaurant-cafe-bar with stunning views.

SELINA BLOW CLOTHING

Map p448 (www.selinablow.com; 1 Ellis St; 10am-6pm Mon-Fri, 11am-6pm Sat; Sloane Sq) Individual, sensuous, dapper, colourful and expertly stylish garbs for men and women, fashioned with a feel for period elegance and finished with a splash of imagination and exuberance.

SHANGHAI TANG CLOTHING

Map p448 (www.shanghaitang.com; 6a/b Sloane St; 10am-7pm Mon-Sat, noon-6pm Sun; Knightsbridge) Traditionally Chinese inspired and super-swish silk scarves, *qipao* (*cheongsam*), elegant Chinese jackets, delicious tops, exquisite cardigans, gorgeous handbags and clutches, many served up in trademark vibrant colours.

CHOCODELI FOOD

Map p448 (www.chocodeli.co.uk; 24 Upper Tachbrook St ; 9am-6pm Mon-Sat, to 7pm summer; Victoria) When the sweet-toothed munchies come calling, this small and traditional-style chocolatier can load you up with macaroons and over 300 varieties of multicoloured sweets, lovingly presented in crispy cellophane bags, handmade chocolate in all forms as well as cooling servings of organic ice cream.

RIPPON CHEESE STORES FOOD

Map p448 (020-7931 0628; 26 Upper Tachbrook St, SW1; 8am-5.30pm Mon-Fri, 8.30am-5pm Sat; Victoria or Pimlico) A potently inviting pong greets you as you near this cheesemonger with its 500 varieties of English and European cheeses. The list is sensational, from black bomber to *idiazabal*, Isle of Mull truckle, Cornish yarg, Kilree goat's cheese and beyond, all ripened on site (if in doubt, taste before you buy).

LULU GUINNESS FASHION

Map p448 (020-7823 4828; www.luluguinness.com; 3 Ellis St, SW1; 10am-6pm Mon-Sat; Sloane Sq) Quirky, whimsical and eye-catching British designs (the Japanese love them), from small evening bags resembling bright lips to fun umbrellas and cosmetic bags.

PENHALIGON'S ACCESSORIES

Map p448 (www.penhaligons.com; 132 Kings Rd, SW3; 9.30am-6.30am Mon, Tue, Thu & Fri, 9.30am-7pm Wed, noon-6pm Sun; Sloane Sq) Stepping through the door of this cute branch of the famous perfumery, sitting cosily on the corner of Bywater St, is like walking into a floral spray of hyacinths, roses and peonies.

Clerkenwell, Shoreditch & Spitalfields

CLERKENWELL | SHOREDITCH | SPITALFIELDS | HOXTON

Neighbourhood Top Five

❶ Wandering through wonderfully preserved Georgian **Spitalfields** (p209) and soaking up the crowds, cacophony, colour and vibrantly exuberant multicultural mix.

❷ Donning your trendiest outfit and heading to **Shoreditch** (p216) for cocktails and carousing.

❸ Joining the bargain hunters and heading out for a spot of market crawling on a sunny Sunday at the **Spitalfields Market** (p220).

❹ Tasting all the exciting foodie options in **Exmouth Market** (p211), from authentic Spanish tapas to old-school British favourites.

❺ Stepping back through the living rooms of time at the **Geffrye Museum** (p208).

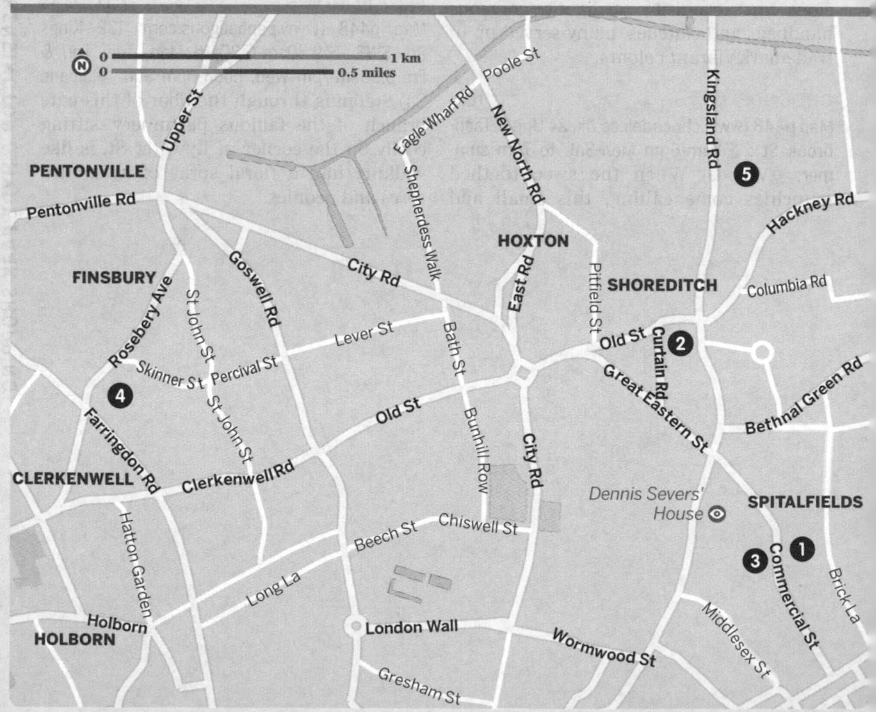

For more detail of this area see Map p450

Explore: Clerkenwell, Shoreditch & Spitalfields

These three redeveloped post-industrial areas northeast of the city contain a few key sights and shops that you'll want to explore in the daytime, but none get too overrun so there's no compulsion to head out particularly early. Which isn't a bad thing, given this is a haven for night owls. All three neighbourhoods have a glut of excellent cafes, restaurants, bars and clubs catering to Londoners' desires at all hours. There are plenty of options sprinkled throughout Clerkenwell and Spitalfields, but Shoreditch remains the centre of the late-night activity. Sunday is a great day to join the crowds shrugging off their hangovers with a leisurely stroll through Spitalfields.

Local Life

➡ **Nights Out with a Difference** Mingle amongst London's trendiest at DreamBagsJaguarShoes (p217), learn to life draw or play ping pong at the Book Club (p216), or take in a moonlit flick on the roof of the Queen of Hoxton (p218).

➡ **Coffee Crawl** The area has so many excellent cafes that it'd be a shame not to walk around hands trembling from too much caffeine. Get a creamy flat white or a shotgun espresso at the Shoreditch Grind (p211), Look Mum No Hands (p211) or Allpress Espresso (p213).

➡ **The Pho Mile** Spend some time working out which is your favourite Vietnamese eatery on the Kingsland Rd.

➡ **Shopping Strip** Sashay down Redchurch St and check out the designer shops for what the cool kids are wearing this season.

Getting There & Away

➡ **Underground** Farringdon and Barbican are the stopping-off points for Clerkenwell, on the Circle, Hammersmith & City and Metropolitan Lines. Old St is on the Bank branch of the Northern Line. Liverpool St, on the Central Line, gives you access to the City and the West End, as well as Bethnal Green and Stratford in the east.

➡ **Overground** Shoreditch High St and Hoxton are handy stops on the overground, running north to Dalston and Highbury & Islington, and south to Wapping.

➡ **Bus** Clerkenwell and Old St are connected with Oxford St by the 55 and with Waterloo by the 243. The 38 runs up Rosebery Ave, handy for Exmouth Market, on its way from Victoria to Islington. The 8 and 242 zip through the city and up Shoreditch High St.

Lonely Planet's Top Tip

Fancy a late one? Clubs Aquarium and Fabric stay open until at least dawn. Brick Lane Beigel Bake will serve you munchies throughout the night, and for breakfast with a pint, the Fox & Anchor throws back its doors at 7am (Monday to Friday). Night buses run on all the major routes, and tubes from Old St, Farringdon and Liverpool St start running between 5am and 6am (7am to 7.30am Sunday).

Best Places to Eat

➡ Moro (p211)
➡ St John (p212)
➡ Morito (p211)
➡ Coach & Horses (p212)
➡ Les Trois Garçons (p214)

For reviews, see p211 ➡

Best Places to Drink

➡ Jerusalem Tavern (p215)
➡ Book Club (p216)
➡ Golden Heart (p219)
➡ Worship St Whistling Shop (p217)
➡ BrewDog (p217)

For reviews, see p215 ➡

Best Places to Dance

➡ Fabric (p215)
➡ Cargo (p218)
➡ XOYO (p218)
➡ Plastic People (p218)
➡ DreamBagsJaguarShoes (p217)

For reviews, see p215 ➡

SIGHTS

Clerkenwell & Shoreditch

CHARTERHOUSE HISTORIC BUILDING

Map p450 (www.thecharterhouse.org; Charterhouse Sq, EC1; tours £10; guided tours 2.15pm Wed Apr-Aug; Barbican or Farringdon) You need to book well in advance to visit this former Carthusian monastery, where the centrepiece is a Tudor hall with a restored hammerbeam roof. Its incredibly popular two-hour guided tours begin at the 14th-century gatehouse on Charterhouse Sq, before going through to the Preachers' Court, the Master's Court, the Great Hall and the Great Chamber, where Queen Elizabeth I stayed on numerous occasions.

The monastery was founded in 1371 by the Carthusians, the strictest of all Roman Catholic monastic orders, refraining from eating meat and taking vows of silence, broken only for three hours on Sunday. During the Reformation the monastery was oppressed, with at least three priors hanged at Tyburn and a dozen monks sent to Newgate, where they were chained upright and died of starvation. King Henry VIII confiscated the monastery in 1537, and it was purchased in 1611 by Thomas Sutton, known at the time as the 'richest commoner in England'. Sutton opened an almshouse for 'destitute gentlemen'; some three-dozen pensioners (known as 'Brothers') live here today and lead the tours.

Tickets must be prebooked either online (see website) or by post – most tours take place between April and August, although there are dates throughout the year.

ST JOHN'S GATE HISTORIC BUILDING

Map p450 (St John's Lane; guided tours suggested donation £5; priory church 10am-3pm Mon-Sat, guided tours 11am & 2.30pm Tue, Fri & Sat; Farringdon) FREE This surprisingly out-of-place medieval gate cutting across St John's Lane is no modern folly, but the real deal. During the 12th century, the crusading Knights of St John of Jerusalem (a religious and military order with a focus on providing care to the sick) established a priory on this site that originally covered around 4 hectares.

TOP SIGHT GEFFRYE MUSEUM

This beautiful series of 18th-century ivy-clad almshouses, with its extensive and well-presented herb garden, was first opened as a museum in 1914, in a spot that was then in the centre of the furniture industry. The museum inside is devoted to domestic interiors, with each room of the main building furnished to show how the homes of the relatively affluent middle class would have looked from Elizabethan times right through to the end of the 19th century. A postmodern extension completed in 1998 contains several 20th-century rooms (a flat from the 1930s, a room in the contemporary style of the 1950s and a 1990s converted warehouse complete with IKEA furniture) as well as a gallery for temporary exhibits, a shop and restaurant. The garden is also organised by era, mirroring the museum's exploration of domesticity through the centuries.

Be sure to time your visit to see the exquisite restoration of a historic **almshouse interior**. It's the absolute attention to detail that impresses, right down to the vintage newspaper left open on the breakfast table. The setting is so fragile, however, that **tours** (admission £2.50; hourly tours 11am-4pm Sat, Tue & Wed) run only a few times a month; check the website for up-to-date tour dates.

DON'T MISS...

- Herb garden (Apr-Oct)
- Almshouse interior

PRACTICALITIES

- Map p450
- www.geffrye-museum.org.uk
- 136 Kingsland Rd, E2
- 10am-5pm Tue-Sat, noon-5pm Sun
- Hoxton or Old St

The gate was built in 1504 as a grand entrance to the priory and although most of the buildings were destroyed when Henry VIII dissolved every monastery in the country between 1536 and 1540, the gate lived on. It had a varied afterlife, not least as a Latin-speaking coffee house run, without much success, by William Hogarth's father during Queen Anne's reign. Restored in the 19th century, it also housed the Old Jerusalem Tavern where writers and artists, including Charles Dickens, met. Inside is the small **Museum of the Order of St John** (Map p450; www.museumstjohn.org.uk; St John's Lane, EC1; ⏲10am-5pm Mon-Sat) FREE, which covers the history of the order (including rare examples of the knights' armour), as well as the foundation of St John Ambulance, set up in the 19th century to promote first aid and revive the order's ethos of caring for the sick.

Across the road from the gate is the fine Norman crypt of the original priory church, which houses a sturdy alabaster effigy of a Castilian knight (1575) and a battered monument portraying the last prior, William Weston, as a skeleton in a shroud. There are also further displays on the history of the area and a lovely secluded garden.

Try to time your visit with one of the comprehensive guided tours of the gate and the restored church. You'll also be shown the sumptuous 1902 Chapter Hall and council chamber that are still used by the order to this day.

BUNHILL FIELDS CEMETERY

Map p450 (Bunhill Row, EC1; ⏲7.30am-7pm Mon-Fri, 9.30am-7pm Sat & Sun Apr-Sep, closed 4pm Oct-Mar; ⊖Old St) This cemetery, just outside the City walls, has been a burial ground for over 1000 years ('Bunhill' supposedly comes from the area's macabre historical name – 'Bone Hill'). You'll see the graves of such literary giants as Daniel Defoe and William Blake. It's a lovely place for a stroll, and a rare green space in this built-up area.

Bunhill Fields is probably the best-known 'dissenters' (ie non-Church of England) cemetery in the country. Across City Rd, to the east of the cemetery, is **Wesley's Chapel** (Map p450), built in 1778. It was the home and place of work and worship for John Wesley, the founder of Methodism.

⊙ Spitalfields

BRICK LANE STREET

Map p450 (⊖Shoreditch High St or Liverpool St) Full of noise, colour and life, Brick Lane is a vibrant mix of history and modernity, and a palimpsest of cultures. Today it is the centrepiece of a thriving Bengali community in an area nicknamed Banglatown. The southern part of the lane is one long procession of curry and balti houses intermingled with fabric shops and Indian supermarkets.

Sadly the once-high standard of cooking in the curry houses is a distant memory, so you're probably better off trying subcontinental cuisine in Whitechapel.

Just past Hanbury St is the converted **Old Truman Brewery** (Map p450), a series of buildings on both sides of the lane that was once London's largest brewery. The Director's House on the left harks back to 1740, the old Vat House across the road with its hexagonal bell tower is early 19th century, and the Engineer's House next to it dates

GEORGIAN SPITALFIELDS

Crowded around its eponymous market and the marvellous Hawksmoor Christ Church, Spitalfields is a layer cake of immigration from all over the world. Waves of French Huguenots, Jews, Irish and, more recently, Indian and Bangladeshi immigrants have made Spitalfields home, and it remains one of the capital's most multicultural areas. A walk down Brick Lane is the best way to get a sense of today's Bangladeshi community, but to get a taste of what Georgian Spitalfields was like, branch off to Princelet, Fournier, Elder and Wilkes Sts. Having fled persecution in France, the Huguenots set up shop here from the late 1600s, practising their trade of silk weaving. The attics of these grand town houses were once filled with clattering looms and the area became famous for the quality of its silk – even providing the material for Queen Victoria's coronation gown. To see inside one of these wonderful old buildings, visit Dennis Severs' House, or, if it's open, 19 Princelet St. Also check out the weavers' impressive place of worship, Christ Church Spitalfields.

TOP SIGHT
DENNIS SEVERS' HOUSE

This quirky hotchpotch of a cluttered house is named after the late American eccentric who restored and turned it into what he called a 'still-life drama'. Severs was an artist, and lived in the house (in a similar way to the original inhabitants) until his death in 1999.

Visitors today find they have entered the home of a 'family' of Huguenot silk weavers, who were common to the Spitalfields area in the 18th century. However, while they see the fabulous restored Georgian interiors, with meals and drinks half-abandoned and rumpled sheets, and while they smell cooking and hear creaking floorboards, their 'hosts' always remain tantalisingly just out of reach. Each of the 10 rooms re-creates a specific time in the house's history from 1724 to 1914; and from the cellar to the bedrooms, the interiors demonstrate both the original function and design of the rooms, as well as the highs and lows of the area's history. It's a unique and intriguing proposition by day, but 'Silent Night' tours by candlelight every Monday evening (bookings essential) are even more memorable.

DON'T MISS...

- Silent Night tours
- House cat

PRACTICALITIES

- Map p450
- 020-7247 4013
- www.dennisseivershouse.co.uk
- 8 Folgate St, E1
- Liverpool St

from 1830. The brewery stopped producing beer in 1989, and in the 1990s became home to a host of independent music businesses, small shops and hip clubs and bars. North of here Brick Lane is a very different place, stuffed with eclectic clothing stores, excellent bagel bakeries and plenty of cafes and bars.

BRICK LANE GREAT MOSQUE MOSQUE

Map p450 (Brick Lane Jamme Masjid; www.bricklanejammemasjid.co.uk; 59 Brick Lane, E1; Shoreditch High St or Liverpool St) This is the best example of the historic changes in population in this area. Built in 1743 as the New French Church for the Huguenots, it was a Methodist chapel from 1819 until it was transformed into the Great Synagogue for Jewish refugees from Russia and central Europe in 1898. In 1976 it changed faiths yet again, becoming the Great Mosque.

CHRIST CHURCH SPITALFIELDS CHURCH

Map p450 (www.christchurchspitalfields.org; Commercial St, E1; 11am-4pm Tue, 1-4pm Sun; Shoreditch High St or Liverpool St) Diagonally opposite Spitalfields Market, on the corner of Commercial and Fournier Sts, is this restored church, where many of the area's weavers worshipped. The magnificent English baroque structure, with a tall spire sitting on a portico of four great Tuscan columns, was designed by Nicholas Hawksmoor and completed in 1729.

19 PRINCELET ST MUSEUM

(www.19princeletstreet.org.uk; 19 Princelet St, E1; limited; Shoreditch High St or Liverpool St) FREE This unique Huguenot town house was built in 1719 and housed a prosperous family of weavers, before becoming home to waves of immigrants, including Polish, Irish and Jewish families, the last of which built a synagogue in the back garden in 1869.

In keeping with the house's multicultural past, it's now home to a museum of immigration and diversity, with carefully considered exhibits aimed at both adults and children. Unfortunately the house is in urgent need of repair and, as such, opens only infrequently (usually no more than a dozen times a year). Check the website for dates. Donations are welcome.

EATING

As well as a wealth of fantastic cafes and restaurants, this area also hosts a number of food markets where you can grab a real variety of dishes and cuisines, from deliciously moist chocolate brownies to fiery Thai curries and overflowing burritos. Places to check out include Exmouth Market, Whitecross St Market and Brick Lane and the surrounding streets.

Clerkenwell

★MORITO TAPAS £

Map p450 (☎020-7278 7007; www.morito.co.uk; 32 Exmouth Market, EC1; tapas £4-10; ⌚noon-4pm & 5-11pm Mon-Sat, noon-4pm Sun; 📶; ⊖Farringdon or Angel) This titchy venue is an authentic take on a Spanish tapas bar. Seats are at the bar, along the window, or on one of the small tables inside or out. It's relaxed, convivial and often completely crammed, and the food is excellent.

Try the boiled quail's eggs that are delicate and dipped into salt and cumin, or the spiced lamb with aubergine, yoghurt and pine nuts. You may want more than the recommended three per person because the portions are small, though the true Spanish classic *huevos rotos* – chorizo, potato, peppers and eggs – should be filling enough. You can book at lunch but not in the evening.

LOOK MUM NO HANDS CAFE £

Map p450 (www.lookmumnohands.com; 49 Old St, EC1; dishes £4-8; ⌚7.30am-10pm Mon-Fri, 10am-10pm Sat & Sun; ⊖Old St) Cyclists and noncyclists alike adore this cafe-bar-workshop, set in a light, airy space looking out onto Old St. Excellent homemade pies and wholesome salads are accompanied by a small range of daily specials, cakes, pastries, sarnies and good coffee. There are also a few outdoor tables and they'll loan you a lock if you need to park your wheels.

SHOREDITCH GRIND CAFE £

Map p450 (☎020-7490 7490; www.shoreditchgrind.com; 213 Old St London, EC1V; ⌚7am-11pm Mon-Thu, 7am-1am Fri, 8am-1am Sat, 9am-11pm Sun) Housed in a striking little round building, the Shoreditch Grind has top coffee – and its own espresso blend – breakfasts, lunches and then cocktails after dusk. The interior is simple and stylish with wood and glass dominating, and you can sit at a window and watch the hipsters go by.

CLARK'S BRITISH £

Map p450 (46 Exmouth Market, EC1; mains £3.50-5.50; ⌚10.45am-4pm Mon-Sat; ⊖Farringdon or Angel) One of London's famous pie and mash shops. With old-school booths, benches and tiled walls, Clark's has been serving up this favourite East End staple since 1910.

★MORO FUSION ££

Map p450 (☎020-7833 8336; www.moro.co.uk; 34-36 Exmouth Market, EC1; mains £16.50-21; ⌚noon-2.30pm & 6-10.30pm Mon-Sat, 12.30-2.45pm Sun; ⊖Farringdon or Angel) Still a frequent award-winner 15 years after it launched, Moro serves Moorish cuisine, a fusion of Spanish, Portuguese and Moroccan flavours. The restaurant is always full and buzzing, and the food is divine. Reservations are essential but you can often turn up without a booking and perch at the bar for some tapas, wine and desserts.

Its constantly evolving menu has delicacies such as charcoal grilled sea bass with sprouting broccoli, Seville orange sauce and wrinkled potatoes or grilled lamb chops with pistachio and orange zest pilav. Try the rose-water and cardamom ice cream for a taste of brilliance.

CARAVAN BRASSERIE ££

Map p450 (☎020-7833 8115; www.caravanonexmouth.co.uk; 11-13 Exmouth Market, EC2; small plates £5-8, big plates £12.50-16; ⌚8am-10.30pm Mon-Fri, 10am-10.30pm Sat & Sun; 📶; ⊖Farringdon) Perfect for a sunny day when the sides of the restaurant are opened onto bustling Exmouth Market, this place is a relaxed affair, offering all-day dining and drinking. The menu offers a real variety of dishes to suit your appetite, combining global flavours and carefully sourced ingredients. The coffee, roasted in the basement, is fantastic.

MEDCALF BRITISH ££

Map p450 (☎020-7833 3533; www.medcalfbar.co.uk; 40 Exmouth Market, EC1; mains £10-16; ⌚noon-midnight Mon-Sat, to 4pm Sun; ⊖Farringdon) Medcalf is one of the best-value hang-outs in Exmouth Market. Housed in a beautifully converted butcher shop dating back to 1912, it serves up innovative and well-realised British fare, such as hand-picked Dorset crab and Welsh rarebit.

BISTROT BRUNO LOUBET FRENCH ££

Map p450 (020-7324 4455; www.bistrotbrunoloubet.com; 86-88 Clerkenwell Rd, EC1; mains £12-17; 7.30-10.30am, noon-2.30pm & 6-10pm; ; Farringdon) Overlooking St John's Square, this is an elegant hotel restaurant with much-lauded chef Bruno Loubet at the helm. High-quality ingredients are transformed into hearty dishes full of interesting and gutsy flavour combinations. As you'd expect, there's a well-chosen wine list and the service is impeccable.

★**COACH & HORSES** GASTROPUB ££

Map p450 (www.thecoachandhorses.com; 26-28 Ray St, EC1; mains £10.50-16.50; noon-3pm & 6-10pm Mon-Fri, 6-10pm Sat, 1-4pm Sun; ; Farringdon) One of Clerkenwell's best gastropubs, sacrificing none of its old-world pub charm in attracting a well-heeled foodie crowd for its range of daily changing dishes.

EAGLE GASTROPUB ££

Map p450 (020-7837 1353; 159 Farringdon Rd, EC1; mains £9.50-18; 12.30-3pm & 6.30-10.30pm Mon-Sat, 12.30-4pm Sun; Farringdon) London's first gastropub may have seen its original owners move on, but it's still a great place for a bite to eat and a pint, especially at lunchtime, when it's relatively quiet. The menu is largely Italian and Spanish, and the atmosphere is lively. Watch the chefs work their magic right behind the bar, above which is chalked the menu.

★**ST JOHN** BRITISH £££

Map p450 (020-7251 0848; www.stjohnrestaurant.com; 26 St John St, EC1; mains £17-23; noon-3pm & 6-11pm Mon-Sat, 1-3pm Sun; Farringdon) This London classic is wonderfully simple – its light bar and cafe area giving way to a surprisingly small dining room where 'nose to tail' eating is served up courtesy of celebrity chef Fergus Henderson. This was one of the places that launched Londoners on the quest to rediscover their culinary past.

Don't miss the signature roast bone-marrow salad with parsley and follow it with one of the tasty daily specials – ox tongue, beetroot and horseradish, or roast squash, walnut and goat's curd; snail, sausage and chickpea stew is marvellous, too. The traditional British puddings are similarly superb.

MODERN PANTRY FUSION £££

Map p450 (020-7553 9210; www.themodernpantry.co.uk; 47-48 St John's Sq, EC1; mains £15-22; noon-3pm Mon, noon-3pm & 6-10.30pm Tue-Sat, 11am-4pm Sun; ; Farringdon) This three-floor Georgian town house in the heart of Clerkenwell has a cracking all-day menu, which gives almost as much pleasure to read as to eat from. Ingredients are combined sublimely into unusual dishes such as tamarind miso marinated onglet steak or panko and parmesan crusted veal escalope. The breakfasts are great, too, though sadly portions can be on the small side. Reservations recommended for the evenings.

Shoreditch & Hoxton

LEILA'S SHOP CAFE £

Map p450 (17 Calvert Ave, E2; dishes £5-9; 10am-6pm Wed-Sun; Shoreditch High St) Tucked away on up-and-coming Calvert Ave, Leila's Shop feels like a bohemian country kitchen. For breakfast, go for the eggs and ham, which come beautifully cooked in their own little frying pan. Sandwiches are freshly made with superior produce, and there's homemade lemonade and great coffee – but it's a tad overpriced.

LOCAL KNOWLEDGE

SHOREDITCH DISTINCTIONS

Hoxditch? Shoho? Often confusingly used interchangeably by Londoners, Hoxton and Shoreditch signify the area stretching from the roundabout at Old St tube station, across to the start of Brick Lane. The name Shoreditch first appeared in the 12th century, signifying a settlement that grew up around the junction of two important Roman thoroughfares: Kingsland Rd and Old St. Shoreditch was the name of the parish, within which was the village of Hoxton. These days Hoxton is generally known as the area to the north of Old St, up to the Kingsland Rd, with Shoreditch being the roads to the south, stretching to the east as far as Brick Lane. But switch them around, or get them confused, and no one will bat an eyelid.

LOCAL KNOWLEDGE

MORE THAN A COFFEE

Local musician Chantal Hill lives in Hoxton, and still manages to regularly trip over new favourite hang-outs.

Chantal's Pick

I had assumed the **Bridge** (Map p450; 15 Kingsland Rd, E2; noon-1am Sun-Thu, to 2am Fri & Sat; ; Old St or Hoxton) was just another (albeit very elaborate) coffee shop until I actually went in and discovered the magical truth. It does sell coffee, along with a selection of snacks, but its main draw is the Aladdin's cave upstairs, a rococo salon-cum-boudoir that looks like it has been decorated by the bastard love child of Louis XIV and your eccentric auntie with all the cats. The downstairs bar retains a distinctive Italian theme, with Joe di Maggio slugging it out on a loop above the door, and the most fantastic old-fashioned till you will probably ever see. It also sells beer, wine and spirits. A total find.

ALLPRESS ESPRESSO — CAFE £

Map p450 (www.allpressespresso.com; 58 Redchurch St, E2; dishes £4-6; 9am-5pm Tue-Sun; Shoreditch High St) Neat-as-a-pin roastery and coffee shop, selling superior coffee, pastries and sandwiches.

ALBION — BRITISH ££

Map p450 (020-7729 1051; www.albioncaff.co.uk; 2-4 Boundary St, E2; mains £9-13; 8am-11pm; ; Old St) This is Sir Terence Conran's contribution to the capital's eating scene, with a combination of two eateries, a hotel and a fantastic rooftop terrace. Albion, the ground-floor 'caff' combines a bright and stylish canteen-style restaurant with a terrific deli. The menu features feel-good British food, cooked to perfection, with plenty of attention to detail.

There are accompanying English wines and beers, quirky crockery and some classic British desserts. Bread is baked on site and breakfasts are a little more adventurous than most, with kippers, kidneys and duck eggs on offer. The subterranean Boundary restaurant is the spot for a glamorous meal of French and British cooking, with a focus on seafood, cheese and charcuterie. And the rooftop terrace is an excellent choice for a sunset drink on a sunny evening.

PRINCESS OF SHOREDITCH — PUB ££

Map p450 (020-7729 9270; www.theprincessofshoreditch.com; 76 Paul St; pub mains £10-18.50; kitchen noon-3pm & 6.30-10pm Mon-Sat, noon-9pm Sun; ; Old St) Handsome pub with a buzzy atmosphere, frequented by a mix of City suits and media types. Food is gastropub standard but very well done, with daily specials and polite service. There's a comprehensive wine list and a good ale selection. Head up the spiral staircase to the more refined (and slightly pricier) first-floor dining space (reservations advised).

★ LES TROIS GARÇONS — MODERN FRENCH £££

Map p450 (020-7613 1924; www.lestroisgarcons.com; 1 Club Row, E1; 2/3 courses £39.50/45.50; noon-2pm Thu & Fri, 6-9.30pm Mon-Thu, 6-10.30pm Fri & Sat; Shoreditch High St) The name may prepare you for the French menu, but nothing on Earth could prepare you for the camp decor inside this made-over Victorian pub. A virtual menagerie of stuffed or bronze animals fills every surface, while chandeliers dangle between a set of suspended handbags.

The food is excellent, if a tad overpriced, and the small army of waiters unobtrusively delivers complimentary bread and tasty gifts from the kitchen. Weekday set lunch menus (two/three courses £17.50/22) are good value.

EYRE BROTHERS — SPANISH, PORTUGUESE £££

Map p450 (020-7613 5346; www.eyrebrothers.co.uk; 70 Leonard St, EC2; mains £16-21; noon-3pm & 6.30-10.45pm Mon-Fri, 7-10.45pm Sat; ; Old St) The cuisine at this elegant Shoreditch restaurant is Iberian with a touch of African flair, courtesy of the eponymous brothers' upbringing in Mozambique, and it's every bit as exciting as it sounds. The rare acorn-fed Ibérico pork, in particular, is top-notch. It's all accompanied by an extensive list of Portuguese and Spanish wines.

FIFTEEN — ITALIAN £££

Map p450 (020-3375 1515; www.fifteen.net; 15 Westland Pl, N1; breakfast £2-8.50, trattoria £6-11, restaurant £11-25; noon-3pm & 6-10pm;

THE PHO MILE

Vietnamese refugees first started to arrive in the UK in 1975, after the Vietnam War, with communities setting up in Lewisham, Southwark and throughout the borough of Hackney. Some worked in the clothing industry, others in factories, but families also took over restaurants and started serving traditional Vietnamese cuisine to Londoners. Kingsland Rd has become famous for its string of Vietnamese cafes and restaurants, many of which are BYO and serve authentic and great-value cuisine. Quality varies and most people tend to have a personal favourite. These are ours:

Viet Grill (Map p450; ☎020-7739 6686; www.vietnamesekitchen.co.uk; 58 Kingsland Rd, E2; mains £6.50-10; ⊖Hoxton) One of the more upmarket options along the road, Viet Grill is a low-lit, modern restaurant over two floors with a buzzy atmosphere and colonial decor. On our last visit the mango and squid salad was particularly good, as were sake lamb skewers and the mighty feudal beef.

Sông Quê (Map p450; www.songque.co.uk; 134 Kingsland Rd, E2; mains £6-9; ⊖Hoxton) With the kind of demand for seats that most London restaurants can only dream of, this perennial favourite always has a line of people waiting for a table. Service is frenetic, but the food is great and good value.

Cây Tre (Map p450; ☎020-7729 8662; www.vietnamesekitchen.co.uk; 301 Old St, EC1; mains £7-9; ⊖Old St) Sister to Viet Grill, Cây Tre serves up all the classics to a mix of Vietnamese diners and Hoxton scenesters in a simple but nicely decorated and tightly packed space. Across the road its cafe, **Kêu!** (Map p450; 332 Old St, EC1; baguettes £4.50; ⊙8am-8pm), offers up lip-smacking *banh mi* (baguettes) to eat in or takeaway, as well as soups, salads and specials.

Wi-fi; ⊖Old St) It would be easy to dismiss Jamie Oliver's nonprofit training restaurant as a gimmick, but on our latest visit the kitchen was in fine fettle. Here young chefs from disadvantaged backgrounds train with experienced professionals, creating an ambitious and interesting Italian menu. The ground-floor trattoria is a relaxed venue, while the underground dining room is more formal. Reservations are usually essential.

Spitalfields

NUDE ESPRESSO CAFE £

Map p450 (www.nudeespresso.com; 26 Hanbury St, E1; dishes £2.50-9; ⊙7.30am-5pm Mon-Fri, 10am-6pm Sat & Sun; ⊖Shoreditch High St or Liverpool St) A simply styled, well-run coffee shop serving excellent Australasian-influenced breakfasts and lunches that focus on natural, seasonal ingredients. It roasts and blends its own coffee just round the corner at its roastery, off Brick Lane.

BRICK LANE BEIGEL BAKE BAGELS £

Map p450 (159 Brick Lane, E2; most bagels less than £2; ⊙24hr; ⊖Liverpool St) You won't find fresher (or cheaper) bagels anywhere in London than at this bakery and delicatessen; just ask any taxi driver (it's their favourite nosherie). It's always busy – with market shoppers on Sunday and Shoreditch clubbers by night.

LUXE CAFE, BAR £

Map p450 (☎020-7101 1751; www.theluxe.co.uk; 109 Commercial St, E1; mains £8-10; ⊙8am-late; Wi-fi, ✎; ⊖Liverpool St) Housed in the Old Flower Market building and with a terrace on the edge of Old Spitalfields Market, this is the food baby of celebrity chef John Torode. There's a 1st-floor dining room (reservations advised) with a central kitchen and lovely corner booths, a more relaxed ground-floor cafe and bar, and a basement venue hosting live music and club nights.

The cafe serves a good range of breakfasts, sandwiches and salads and it's a great choice for a weekend brunch.

ROSA'S THAI ££

Map p450 (www.rosaslondon.com; 12 Hanbury St, E1; mains £7-12.50; ⊙noon-10.30pm; ⊖Shoreditch High St or Liverpool St) Red-fronted Rosa's is a cosy Thai restaurant, over two floors, just off Commercial St, simply kitted out with low benches, banquettes and red stools. Go for its signature pumpkin curry, one of the zingy salads or delicious chargrills.

POPPIES FISH & CHIPS ££

Map p450 (www.poppiesfishandchips.co.uk; 6-8 Hanbury St, E1; mains £6-11; ⏲11am-11pm, to 10.30pm Sun; 📶; 🚉Shoreditch High St, ⊖Shoreditch High St) Glorious re-creation of a 1950s East End chippy, complete with waitresses in pinnies and hairnets, and retro memorabilia. As well as the usual fishy suspects, it also does jellied eels, homemade tartare sauce and mushy peas, and you can wash it all down with a glass of wine or beer. Also does a roaring takeaway trade.

ST JOHN BREAD AND WINE BRITISH ££

Map p450 (☎020-7251 0848; www.stjohngroup.uk.com; 94-96 Commercial St, E1; mains £14-19; ⏲9am-10.30pm Mon-Sat, to 9pm Sun; ⊖Liverpool St) Offers 'nose to tail' traditional British fare (potted pork, venison and trotter pie, blood cake) at good prices in a simple, clean and bright space popular with Spitalfields creative types. It also has an excellent selection of British cheeses and puddings.

HAWKSMOOR STEAK £££

Map p450 (☎020-7247 7392; 157 Commercial St, E1; mains £22-30; ⏲noon-2.30pm Mon-Sat, to 4.30pm Sun, 5-10.30pm Mon-Fri, 6-10.30pm Sat; 📶; ⊖Shoreditch High St or Liverpool St) You could easily miss discreetly signed Hawksmoor, on an unlovely stretch of Commercial St, but carnivores will find this impressive steak restaurant worth seeking out. The dark wood, bare bricks and velvet curtains make for a handsome setting in which to gorge yourself on the best of British meat. Make sure you try one of the equally impressive cocktails.

The meaty brunch (11am to 4pm Saturday and Sunday) is a great weekend option.

DRINKING & NIGHTLIFE

Clerkenwell

★JERUSALEM TAVERN PUB

Map p450 (www.stpetersbrewery.co.uk; 55 Britton St, EC1; ⏲11am-11pm Mon-Fri; 📶; ⊖Farringdon) Starting life as one of the first London coffee houses (founded in 1703), with the 18th-century decor of occasional tile mosaics still visible, the JT is an absolute stunner, though sadly it's both massively popular and tiny, so come early to get a seat.

There's good lunch food and, this being the only London outlet of St Peter's Brewery (based in North Suffolk), it has a brilliant range of drinks – organic bitters, cream stouts, wheat and fruit beers – many of which are dispensed in green apothecary-style bottles.

★FABRIC CLUB

Map p450 (www.fabriclondon.com; 77a Charterhouse St, EC1; admission £8-18; ⏲10pm-6am Fri, 11pm-8am Sat, 11pm-6am Sun; ⊖Farringdon) This most impressive of superclubs is still the first stop on the London scene for many international clubbers. The crowd is hip and well dressed without overkill, and the music – electro, techno, house, drum and bass and dubstep – is as superb as you'd expect from London's top-rated club.

A warren of three floors, three bars, many walkways and unisex toilets, room one also contains a kidney-shaking 'bodysonic' dance floor. Superstar DJs often sell out Friday night's FabricLive, when big names such as Goldie or DJ Hype take over. WetYourSelf!, a hedonistic techno and house night, is a real Sunday night treat.

YE OLDE MITRE PUB

Map p450 (1 Ely Ct, EC1; ⏲11am-11pm Mon-Fri; 📶; ⊖Chancery Lane or Farringdon) A delightfully cosy historic pub, tucked away in a backstreet off Hatton Garden (look for a Fullers sign above a low archway on the left), Ye Olde Mitre was built for the servants of Ely Palace. There's still a memento of Elizabeth I – the stump of a cherry tree around which she once danced. There's no music, so the rooms only echo to the sound of amiable chit-chat.

FILTHY MACNASTY'S PUB

Map p450 (www.filthymacnastys.co.uk; 68 Amwell St, EC1; ⏲noon-11pm; 📶; ⊖Angel or Farringdon) The local of 'Amwell Village', tucked between Clerkenwell and Islington, is this stellar Irish music pub and whiskey bar that's every bit as cool as its name suggests. The two-room pub attracts an up-for-it young crowd that comes for live bands in the back room, the great whiskey list and the 'filthy food'.

FOX & ANCHOR PUB

Map p450 (020-7250 1300; www.foxandanchor.com; 115 Charterhouse St, EC1; noon-11pm; ; Farringdon or Barbican) A revamped Victorian pub that has retained its three beautiful snugs at the back of the bar. Fully celebrating its proximity to Smithfield Market, food here is gloriously meaty and the pub opens at 7am during the week. Only the brave will opt for the All Day City Boy Breakfast – a veritable meat feast (£16.95).

THREE KINGS PUB

Map p450 (7 Clerkenwell Close, EC1; noon-11pm Mon-Fri, 5.30-11pm Sat; ; Farringdon) Down-to-earth and welcoming pub, attracting a friendly bunch of relaxed locals for its quirky decor, great music and good times.

VINOTECA WINE BAR

Map p450 (www.vinoteca.co.uk; 7 St John St, EC1; noon-11pm Mon-Sat; ; Farringdon) Simple yet elegant oak decor, an astonishingly comprehensive wine list and amiable service make this a popular choice with suited City workers and local creatives. At the on-site shop you can also buy bottles of all of the wines available in the bar – and the modern European food is very good too.

PRUFROCK CAFE

Map p450 (www.prufrockcoffee.com; 23-25 Leather Lane, EC1; 8am-6pm Mon-Fri, 10am-4pm Sat; ; Chancery Lane or Farringdon) This large, serene space is a temple to coffee. Check out the line of equipment that looks like a lab and ask the helpful staff to advise on your choice of filter coffee, with a method chosen specifically to maximise the qualities of each different variety of bean.

Shoreditch & Hoxton

★BOOK CLUB BAR

Map p450 (020-7684 8618; www.wearetbc.com; 100 Leonard St; 8am-midnight Mon-Wed, 8am-2am Thu & Fri, 10am-2am Sat & Sun; ; Old St) This former Victorian warehouse has been transformed into an innovative temple to good times. Spacious and whitewashed with large windows upstairs and a basement bar below, it hosts a real variety of offbeat events, such as spoken word, dance lessons and life drawing, as well as a varied program of DJ nights.

Table tennis and pool add to the friendly, fun atmosphere. Breakfast is served from 8am, and food is available throughout the day and evening.

★GEORGE & DRAGON PUB

Map p450 (2 Hackney Rd, E2; 6-11pm; Old St) Once a scuzzy local pub, the George was taken over and decorated with the owner's grandma's antiques (antlers, racoon tails, old clocks), cardboard cut-outs of Cher and fairy lights, turning this one-room pub into what has remained the epicentre of the Hoxton scene for more than a decade.

A favourite for the trendy gay crowd, some of the best DJ nights in London are on offer here, with cabaret performances taking place on window sills. It's total fun and mindless hedonism. Expect moustachioed media types and fashion-forward youths. Definitely not a place for a quiet pint, there's a great jukebox, and it tends to get packed out at the weekends.

SHOREDITCH COOL

The Shoreditch phenomenon began in the late 1990s, when creative types chased out of the West End by prohibitive rents began buying warehouses in this then urban wasteland, abandoned after the collapse of the fabrics industry. Within a few years the area was seriously cool, boasting superslick bars, cutting-edge clubs, galleries and restaurants that catered to the new media-creative-freelance squad. Despite the general expectation that the Shoreditch scene would collapse under the weight of its own trucker hats, the regenerated area is flourishing more than ever, with new developments bringing life to some of London's poorest corners, spilling over into nearby Hackney and Bethnal Green. Once the site of one of London's most notorious slums (known as the Old Nichol), the area just to the east of Shoreditch High St, is currently enjoying most of the attention. Redchurch St is lined with a slew of new cafes and trendy shops, with Calvert Ave and Boundary St, just to the north, following suit.

THE COCKTAIL HOUR

While mojitos and caipirinhas are these days two-a-penny in Shoreditch bars, there are some places that take their shaking far more seriously. Here is a list of our favourites. It's worth booking ahead at all of them. Cocktails usually range from £7 to £10.

Worship St Whistling Shop (Map p450; 020-7247 0015; www.whistlingshop.com; 63 Worship St, EC2; Old St) A 'Victorian' drinking den that takes cocktails to a molecular level, the Whistling Shop (as Victorians called a place selling illicit booze) serves expertly crafted and highly unusual concoctions using potions conjured up in its on-site lab. Try a Panacea, Black Cat Martini or the Bosom Caresser (made with formula milk). There's an incredible array of interesting spirits, as well as a Dram Shop for a private party, and an Experience Room for the really adventurous.

Happiness Forgets (Map p450; 020-7613 0325; www.happinessforgets.com; 8-9 Hoxton Sq, N1; 5-11pm Mon-Sat; Hoxton, Old St) The menu promises you mixed drinks and mischief at this low-lit, basement bar with good-value cocktails in a relaxed and intimate setting.

Nightjar (Map p450; 020-7253 4101; www.barnightjar.com; 129 City Rd, EC1; 6pm-1.30am Tue & Wed, to 3.30am Thu-Sat; Old St) Slick, wood-panelled speakeasy offering nightly live music. The well-executed cocktails are divided into four eras: before and during prohibition, postwar and Nightjar signatures.

Zetter Townhouse (Map p450; 020-7324 4545; www.thezettertownhouse.com; 49-50 St John's Sq, EC1; 8am-1am; Farringdon) Cocktail lounge of the Zetter Townhouse, this ground-floor bar is quirkily decorated with plush armchairs, stuffed animal heads and a legion of lamps. The cocktail list takes its theme from the area's distilling history; recipes of yesteryear and homemade ingredients (such as nettle cordial) are used to create interesting and unusual tipples.

Callooh Callay (Map p450; 020-7739 4781; www.calloohcallaybar.com; 65 Rivington St, EC2; 6pm-midnight Sun-Wed, to 1am Thu-Sat; Old St) Given it's inspired by *Jabberwocky*, Lewis Carroll's nonsense poem, this bar's eccentric decor doesn't come as a surprise. Try the Ale of Two Cities, which comes in a half-pint beer mug.

Loungelover (Map p450; 020-7012 1234; www.lestroisgarcons.com; 1 Whitby St, E1; 6pm-midnight Sun-Thu, to 1am Fri & Sat;) The drinks and the look are both faultless at this Shoreditch institution, where it's all about the superb cocktails and the junk-shop chic of the decor.

★ DREAMBAGSJAGUARSHOES — DJ BAR

Map p450 (www.jaguarshoes.com; 32-36 Kingsland Rd, E2; noon-1am; ; Old St or Hoxton) The bar is named after the two shops whose two-floor space it now occupies, and this nonchalance is a typical example of the we-couldn't-care-less Shoreditch chic. The small interior is filled with sofas and formica-topped tables, and art exhibitions deck the walls. You can also order a pizza from the excellent Due Sardi, next door.

There are great DJ nights on weekends, and you'll always find something good going on. Check out the cafe bar the **Old Shoreditch Station** (www.jaguarshoes.com; 1 Kingsland Rd, E2; Mon & Tue 8am-11pm, Wed-Fri 8am-1am, Sat 10am-1am, Sun 10am-11pm) and fashion store JSC Store, both of which are the height of hipster cool.

★ BREWDOG — BAR

Map p450 (020-7729 8476; www.brewdog.com; 51-55 Bethnal Green Rd, EC1; noon-midnight Sun-Thu, noon-1am Fri & Sat; ; Shoreditch High St) A self-titled 'post Punk apocalyptic (too rude to repeat) of a craft brewery,' BrewDog is a beer-lover's paradise. Their eco-brewery sits up in northeast Scotland and everything is done by the company, from getting the hops, to packaging and shipping the beer. The Shoreditch bar is always packed, the atmosphere is great, and the range and quality of the beer is very fine indeed.

BAR KICK — BAR

Map p450 (www.cafekick.co.uk; 127 Shoreditch High St, E1; noon-11pm Sun-Wed, to midnight Thu, to 1am Fri & Sat; ; Old St or Shoreditch High St) Four table-football tables sit on the ground floor, and downstairs is a room with leather sofas and simple tables and chairs. There are tables outside on the street, too, and there's always a lively vibe. Major football games are broadcast on large screens both upstairs and down.

★CARGO CLUB

Map p450 (www.cargo-london.com; 83 Rivington St, EC2; admission free-£16; ⏲6pm-1am Mon-Thu, to 3am Fri & Sat, to midnight Sun; ⊖Old St) Cargo is one of London's most eclectic clubs. Under its brick railway arches you'll find a dance-floor room, bar and outside terrace. The music policy is innovative and varied, with plenty of up-and-coming bands also on the menu. Food is available throughout the day.

★PLASTIC PEOPLE CLUB

Map p450 (www.plasticpeople.co.uk; 147-149 Curtain Rd, EC2; admission £5-10; ⏲10pm-3.30am Fri & Sat, to 2am Sun; ⊖Old St) This is a tiny club with just a dance floor and bar and a booming sound system that experts say easily kicks the butts of bigger clubs. Head here on Fridays and Saturdays for nights that are often given over to one long DJ set by the likes of Kieran Hebden, Kode9 or Mr Scruff, smashing out mainly house and electronica.

★XOYO CLUB

Map p450 (www.xoyo.co.uk; 32-37 Cowper St, EC2; ⏲hours vary; ⊖Old St) Run by a group of music professionals, this lofty venue plays host to a finely chosen selection of gigs and club nights, as well as exhibiting art. The varied program – expect indie bands, hip hop, electro, dubstep and much in between – attracts a mix of clubbers from skinny-jeaned hipsters to more mature hedonists.

QUEEN OF HOXTON BAR

Map p450 (www.queenofhoxton.com; 1-5 Curtain Rd, EC2; ⏲5pm-midnight Mon-Wed, 5pm-2am Thu & Fri, 6pm-2am Sat; 📶; ⊖Liverpool St) Industrial-chic bar with a games room, basement and varied music nights, though the real draw-card is the vast rooftop bar, decked out with flowers, fairy lights and even a fish pond, with fantastic views across the city and a popular **outdoor film club** (www.rooftopfilmclub.com; ⏲Jun-Sep).

RED LION PUB

Map p450 (www.redlionhoxtonst.com; 41 Hoxton St, N1; ⏲5-11pm Mon-Fri, noon-11pm Sat & Sun; ⊖Old St or Hoxton) This stalwart of the scene is well enough tucked away from Hoxton Sq to avoid being overrun by the suburban crowd that now dominates the area at the weekends. Inside it's pure kitsch fun, with a well-balanced mix of down-to-earth and trendy folk. The top-floor roof terrace is a real draw.

CATCH CLUB

Map p450 (www.thecatchbar.com; 22 Kingsland Rd, E2; ⏲6pm-midnight Mon-Wed, to 2am Thu-Sat, 7pm-1am Sun; ⊖Old St or Shoreditch High St) It doesn't look like much, but Catch is one of the best nights out in Shoreditch. Upstairs you'll hear anything from '90s to funk and hip hop, as well as a great selection of new and established bands. Downstairs you get a big house-party vibe with DJs who mix up pretty much anything from current chart hits to electro and techno. Downstairs is free, it's open late and really fun.

HORSE & GROOM PUB, CLUB

Map p450 (www.thehorseandgroom.net; 28 Curtain Rd, EC2; ⏲noon-midnight Mon-Wed, to 2am Thu & Sun; ⊖Liverpool St) A relaxed pub/club, in an underwhelming backstreet location, with two intimate spaces serving up hedonistic nights where you're most likely to hear disco, house, funk or soul.

333 MOTHER BAR CLUB

Map p450 (www.333mother.com; 333 Old St, EC1; ⏲7pm-2am; ⊖Old St) Hoxton's true old-timer, the 333 Mother Bar just keeps going, despite not being what it once was in terms of pulling power. The club still hosts great nights that are simultaneously scruffy and innovative, covering indie, electro, dubstep and hip hop. Check the website for the latest club nights.

MACBETH PUB

Map p450 (www.themacbethuk.co.uk; 70 Hoxton St, N1; ⏲11am-1am Mon-Thu, 5pm-2am Fri-Sun; 📶; ⊖Hoxton) This enormous old boozer on a still-to-be-yuppified street, just a short walk north of Hoxton Sq, is an established stop on the ever-changing Hoxton scene. Run by musicians and providing a great platform for up-and-coming talent, as well as the occasional big name on its downstairs stage, Macbeth is an intimate venue, with a second bar upstairs and a large roof terrace as well.

OLD BLUE LAST PUB

Map p450 (www.theoldbluelast.com; 38 Great Eastern St, EC2; ⌚noon-midnight Sun-Thu, to 1.30am Fri & Sat; wi-fi; ⊖Old St or Shoreditch High St) Frequently crammed with a hip teenage-and-up crowd of Hoxtonites, this beautiful old corner pub's trendy credentials are courtesy of *Vice* magazine, the bad-boy rag that owns the place. It hosts some of the best Shoreditch parties and has a rocking jukebox.

EAST VILLAGE CLUB

Map p450 (www.eastvillageclub.co.uk; 89 Great Eastern St, EC2; ⌚hours vary; ⊖Old St) Basement club that sees house lovers flocking from all over London, especially for one-off nights featuring some of New York's finest. Other events range from disco to dancehall and dubstep to drum and bass.

AQUARIUM CLUB

Map p450 (www.clubaquarium.co.uk; 256-264 Old St, EC1; ⌚hours vary; ⊖Old St) The real attraction at this big and brash club is the swimming pool and Jacuzzi (towels provided) and the often very-late opening hours (selected nights until 9am). DJs play mainly house and techno to a mainstream, dressed-up crowd. Trainers are not welcome here.

Spitalfields

★**GOLDEN HEART** PUB

Map p450 (110 Commercial St, E1; ⌚11am-11pm Mon-Sat, noon-10.30pm Sun; ⊖Liverpool St) It's an unsurprisingly trendy Hoxton crowd that mixes in the surprisingly untrendy interior of this brilliant Spitalfields boozer. While it's famous as the watering hole for the cream of London's art crowd, our favourite part about any visit is a chat with Sandra, the landlady-celebrity who talks to all comers and ensures the bullshit never outstrips the fun.

TEN BELLS PUB

Map p450 (cnr Commercial & Fournier Sts, E1; ⌚11am-11pm Mon-Sat, noon-10.30pm Sun; ⊖Liverpool St) This landmark Victorian pub, with its large windows and beautiful tiles, is perfect for a pint after a wander round Spitalfields Market. It's famous for being one of Jack the Ripper's pick-up joints, although these days it attracts a rather more salubrious and trendy clientele.

93 FEET EAST CLUB

Map p450 (www.93feeteast.co.uk; 150 Brick Lane, E2; ⌚5-11pm Mon-Thu, to 1am Fri & Sat, 3-10.30pm Sun; ⊖Liverpool St or Shoreditch High St) This great venue has a courtyard, three big rooms and an outdoor terrace that gets crowded on sunny afternoons, packed with a cool East London crowd.

VIBE BAR DJ BAR

Map p450 (www.vibe-bar.co.uk; Old Truman Brewery, 91-95 Brick Lane, E1; ⌚11am-11.30pm Sun-Thu, 11am-late Fri & Sat; ⊖Liverpool St or Shoreditch High St) Once the epicentre of the Hoxton scene, the Vibe is part bar, part club, part outdoor drinking arena complete with fast-food stalls. While its '90s time in the sun is long past, it's still popular and good fun outside in summer. There are live acts most nights, and DJs at other times in the spacious interior.

☆ ENTERTAINMENT

SADLER'S WELLS DANCE

Map p450 (☎0844 412 4300; www.sadlerswells.com; Rosebery Ave, EC1; tickets £10-49; ⊖Angel) The theatre site dates from 1683 but was completely rebuilt in 1998; today it is the most eclectic and modern dance venue in town, with experimental dance shows of all genres and from all corners of the globe. The Lilian Baylis Studio stages smaller productions.

AUBIN CINEMA CINEMA

Map p450 (☎0845 604 8486; www.aubincinema.com; 64-66 Redchurch St, E2) Run by Shoreditch House, this is cinema-going to impress your date with, with space for an intimate 50 on the comfy velvet sofas and armchairs. There is a full bar and some food too, and tickets go like crazy, so book well ahead (and that's despite the astronomic prices – between £23 and £32 per person).

COMEDY CAFÉ COMEDY

Map p450 (☎020-7739 5706; www.comedycafe.co.uk; 68 Rivington St, EC2; admission free-£15; ⌚Wed-Sat; ⊖Old St) A major venue, the Comedy Café is purpose built for, well, comedy, hosting some good comedians. It can be a little too try-hard and wacky, but it's worth seeing the Wednesday night try-out spots for some wincing entertainment.

SHOPPING

This is a great area for discovering cool boutiques and market stalls for vintage clothes and up-and-coming designers. There are tonnes of shops off Brick Lane, especially in burgeoning Cheshire St, Hanbury St and the Old Truman Brewery on Dray Walk. Each December there's a major showcase of the latest products, clothes, jewellery and art at Shoreditch Town Hall; see www.eastlondondesignshow.co.uk. Clerkenwell is mostly known for its jewellery. For classic settings and unmounted stones, visit London's traditional jewellery and diamond trade area, Hatton Garden.

★SPITALFIELDS MARKET — MARKET

Map p450 (www.oldspitalfieldsmarket.com; Commercial St btwn Brushfield & Lamb Sts, E1; ⏲10am-4pm Sun-Fri; ⊖Liverpool St) One of London's best markets, with traders hawking their wares here since the early 17th century. The covered market that you see today was built in the late 19th century, with the more modern development added in 2006. It is open six days a week, but Sundays are best and filled with fashion, jewellery, food and music stalls.

It's also good to come on Thursdays when traders flog antiques and Fridays for independent-label fashion.

★ROUGH TRADE EAST — MUSIC

Map p450 (www.roughtrade.com; Dray Walk, Old Truman Brewery, 91 Brick Lane, E1; ⏲8am-8pm Mon-Fri, 11am-7pm Sat & Sun; ⊖Liverpool St) This vast record store has an impressive selection of CDs and vinyl across all genres, as well as an interesting offering of books. There are stacks of knowledgeable recommendations and staff are happy to help. It also sells good coffee and stages great gigs.

TATTY DEVINE — JEWELLERY

Map p450 (www.tattydevine.com; 236 Brick Lane, E2; ⏲11am-6pm Tue-Sun; ⊖Shoreditch High St) Harriet Vine and Rosie Wolfenden make hip and witty jewellery that's become the favourite of many young Londoners. Their original designs feature all manner of fauna-and-flora inspired necklaces, as well as creations sporting moustaches, dinosaurs and bunting. Perspex name necklaces (made to order; £27.50) are also a treat.

LABOUR & WAIT — HOMEWARES

Map p450 (www.labourandwait.co.uk; 85 Redchurch St, E2; ⏲11am-6pm Tue-Sun; ⊖Liverpool St or Shoreditch High St) Dedicated to simple and functional, yet scrumptiously stylish, traditional British homewares, Labour & Wait specialises in items by independent manufacturers who make their products the old-fashioned way. There are school tumblers, enamel coffee pots, luxurious lambswool blankets, elegant ostrich-feather dusters and even kitchen sinks.

ABSOLUTE VINTAGE — VINTAGE

Map p450 (www.absolutevintage.co.uk; 15 Hanbury St, E1; ⏲11am-7pm; ⊖Liverpool St or Shoreditch High St) Check out the mammoth vintage shoe collection here – there are colours and sizes for all, with footwear ranging from designer vintage to something out of your grandma's storage. Clothes for men and women line the back of the shop.

SUPER MARKET SUNDAY

Head out east on a Sunday and it might feel that you can't move for markets. Starting at Columbia Road Flower Market (p237) and working your way south makes for a colourful and thrifty retail crawl. Spilling out into its surrounding streets, **Brick Lane Market** (Map p454; www.visitbricklane.org; Brick Lane, E1; ⏲8am-2pm Sun; ⊖Liverpool St) takes over a vast area with household goods, bric-a-brac, secondhand clothes and cheap fashion. You can even stop off and play carrom. Just off Brick Lane, you'll find the **Backyard Market** (Map p450; www.backyardmarket.co.uk; ⏲11am-5pm Sat & Sun; ⊖Shoreditch High St), with stalls full of vintage clothes, ceramics and furniture. A little further south, on the other side of the lane, is the **Sunday UpMarket** (Map p450; www.sundayupmarket.co.uk; Old Truman Brewery, Brick Lane, E1; ⏲10am-5pm Sun; ⊖Liverpool St), where young designers sell wonderful clothes, music and crafts, and the excellent food hall has worldwide grub, from Ethiopian veggie dishes to Japanese delicacies. If you've got the stamina, top it all off with a browse round Spitalfields.

MAGMA BOOKS

Map p450 (www.magmabooks.com; 117-119 Clerkenwell Rd, EC1; ⏲10am-7pm Mon-Sat; ⊖Farringdon) This much-loved shop sells books, magazines, T-shirts and almost anything on the design cutting edge. Great for present shopping.

MAISON TROIS GARÇONS HOMEWARES

(www.lestroisgarcons.com/shop; 45 Redchurch St, E2; ⊖Shoreditch High St) Antique, vintage and contemporary furniture and ceramics are sourced from around Europe. The garçons offer a search and find service, as well as an interior design service, and a cafe, part of the shop, was being added at the time of writing.

ECONE JEWELLERY

Map p450 (www.econe.co.uk; 41 Exmouth Market, EC1; ⏲10am-6pm Mon-Sat; ⊖Farringdon or Angel) Husband-and-wife team Jos and Alison Skeates sell gorgeous contemporary collections by British and international jewellery designers on funky Exmouth Market.

START CLOTHING

Map p450 (www.start-london.com; 42-44 Rivington St, EC2; ⏲10.30am-6.30pm Mon-Sat, noon-6pm Sun; ⊖Old St) 'Where fashion meets rock n roll' is the appropriate tagline to this group of three boutiques brought to you by former Fall guitarist Brix Smith, a cult rocker who loves girly clothes. Designer labels such as Mulberry and Helmut Lang dominate, and Smith prides herself on her selection of flattering jeans, for which the store offers a fitting service.

A similarly excellent store, **Start Menswear** (Map p450; 59 Rivington St; ⏲10.30am-6.30pm Mon-Sat, noon-6pm Sun), is over the road, and there's a third location, **Mr Start** (Map p450; 40 Rivington St; ⏲10.30am-6.30pm Mon-Sat, noon-6pm Sun), which is a men's tailoring shop.

PRESENT CLOTHING

Map p450 (www.present-london.com; 140 Shoreditch High St, E1; ⏲10.30am-7pm Mon-Sat, 11am-5pm Sun; ⊖Old St) Everything for the hip gentleman, including designer gear, shoes, books and bike accessories. You can also grab a great cup of coffee here.

NO-ONE FASHION

Map p450 (www.no-one.co.uk; 1 Kingsland Rd, E2; ⏲10am-7pm; ⊖Old St or Shoreditch High St) This fun boutique can be found inside the Old Shoreditch station bar. It's all ultrahip, with fashion magazines, quirky accessories and shoes, and stocks Cheap Monday, House of Dagmar and new labels for women and men.

123 BETHNAL GREEN ROAD FASHION

Map p450 (www.123bethnalgreenroad.co.uk; 123 Bethnal Green Rd, E2; ⏲11.30am-7pm; ⊖Old St or Shoreditch High St) Housed in a grand, corner building that dates to the late 19th century, this three-floor store brings together designs by Dr Noki and the house collection 123, both of which comprise original and striking pieces using recycled materials. You'll find further rails on the ground floor along with homewares, and there's a cafe and bar in the basement.

LESLEY CRAZE GALLERY JEWELLERY

Map p450 (www.lesleycrazegallery.co.uk; 33-35a Clerkenwell Green, EC1; ⏲11am-5pm Tue-Sat; ⊖Farringdon) Considered one of Europe's leading centres for arty, contemporary jewellery, this gallery has exquisitely understated and sometimes pricey designs.

The East End & Docklands

WHITECHAPEL | BETHNAL GREEN | HACKNEY | MILE END | VICTORIA PARK | HACKNEY WICK | STRATFORD | WAPPING | LIMEHOUSE | DOCKLANDS

Neighbourhood Top Five

❶ Stopping to smell the roses at London's most fragrant market, **Columbia Road** (p237).

❷ Seeing the latest brilliant exhibition at the groundbreaking **Whitechapel Gallery** (p224).

❸ Taking in the landscaped majesty, incredible architecture and fauna-filled wetlands of East London's mighty **Queen Elizabeth Olympic Park** (p228).

❹ Having a summertime supper by the Regent's Canal at **Towpath** (p231).

❺ Heading to **Whitechapel** (p224) for a burst of multicultural London and authentic Bangladeshi cuisine.

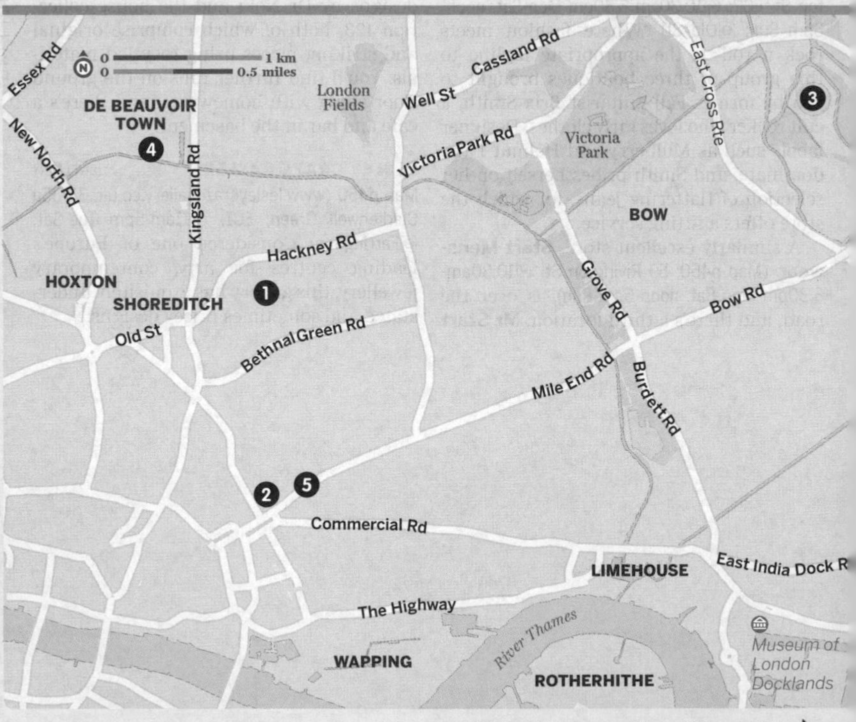

For more detail of this area see Map p453 and p454 ➡

Explore: The East End & Docklands

A vast area, the East End and Docklands has a few standout sights but will really repay those happy to wander and soak up the unique character of each of its neighbourhoods. Handily, the opening of the overground lines has made East London much easier to traverse. The three main areas to head for are the Queen Elizabeth Olympic Park (and neighbouring Hackney), the Docklands (and adjoining waterside Limehouse and Wapping) and Whitechapel (from which Bethnal Green is just a short hop away). Each of these has a few don't-miss attractions, but also plenty of places to linger over a coffee, lazy lunch or a few jars of ale.

Local Life

➡ **Picnics** On a sunny Saturday, East Enders of all ages grab some goodies from Broadway Market (p237) and head to London Fields (p225) for a picnic and a dip in the lido.

➡ **Gallery** With no permanent collection, there's always something new to check out at Whitechapel Gallery (p224), before heading to Tayyabs (p231) for the daily special.

➡ **Hang-outs** Mix with the local art cognoscenti, sip a cocktail and take in the views at the arts hub Platform Cafe, Bar & Terrace (p235).

➡ **Cabaret** From lip-synching trannies to trashy burlesque, Bistrotheque (p237) and the Bethnal Green Working Men's Club (p235) always provide a fun reason to get your glad rags on.

Getting There & Away

➡ **Underground** Central Line runs from the West End and the City to Bethnal Green, Mile End and Stratford.

➡ **Overground** From Camden and Highbury, the overground affords a quick link to Hackney, Hackney Wick and Stratford. A separate branch connects Dalston and the southerly stops of Whitechapel and Wapping.

➡ **DLR** Starting at Tower Gateway or Bank, the DLR provides a scenic link to Limehouse and Docklands, as well as joining the dots with Stratford Domestic and International stations further north.

➡ **Bus** The 55 from Oxford St is a handy route to Hackney, as is the 38 from Victoria via Islington. The 277 runs from Hackney to the Docklands, via Victoria Park.

➡ **Train** A quick ride to London Fields, Cambridge Heath or Stratford from Liverpool St. The high-speed link from St Pancras whisks you to Stratford International in just seven minutes.

Lonely Planet's Top Tip

The most genial way to get around the East End is along the water. Cyclists and pedestrians can drop down to Regent's Canal at the bottom of Broadway Market and follow the waterway to Limehouse. Branching east of this at Victoria Park, the Hertford Union Canal will deliver you to Hackney Wick and Queen Elizabeth Olympic Park. From Limehouse Basin you can also pick up the Thames Path and follow it along the river to St Katharine Docks.

Best Places to Eat

➡ Wapping Food (p234)
➡ Formans (p234)
➡ Viajante (p233)
➡ Towpath (p231)
➡ Whitechapel Gallery Dining Room (p231)

For reviews, see p230 ➡

Best Places to Drink

➡ Dove Freehouse (p235)
➡ Grapes (p236)
➡ Carpenter's Arms (p235)
➡ Royal Inn on the Park (p236)
➡ Palm Tree (p236)

For reviews, see p234 ➡

Best Places for East End History

➡ Museum of London Docklands (p229)
➡ Sutton House (p225)
➡ Ragged School Museum (p227)
➡ House Mill (p227)

For reviews, see p224 ➡

SIGHTS

Whitechapel

WHITECHAPEL BELL FOUNDRY — HISTORIC BUILDING

Map p454 (www.whitechapelbellfoundry.co.uk; 32-34 Whitechapel Rd, E1; tours per person £11; ⏲tours 10am & 1.30pm selected Wed & Sat, shop 9.30am-4.15pm Mon-Fri; ⊖Aldgate East, Whitechapel) The Whitechapel Bell Foundry has been standing on this site since 1738, although an earlier foundry nearby is known to have been in business in 1570. Both Big Ben (1858) and the Liberty Bell (1752) in Philadelphia were cast here, and the foundry also cast a new bell for New York City's Trinity Church, damaged in the terrorist attacks of 11 September 2001.

The 1½-hour guided tours (maximum 25 people) are conducted on particular Saturdays and Wednesdays (check the website) but are often booked out a year in advance. During weekday trading hours you can view a few small but informative exhibits in the foyer and buy bell-related items from the shop.

WHITECHAPEL ROAD — STREET

Map p454 (⊖Whitechapel) The East End's main thoroughfare, Whitechapel Rd hums with a cacophony of Asian, African and Middle Eastern languages, its busy shops and market stalls selling everything from Indian snacks to Nigerian fabrics and Turkish jewellery, as the East End's multitudinous ethnic groupings rub up against each other more or less comfortably.

It's a chaotic and poor place, but it's full of life. Within a few minutes' walk of Whitechapel tube station you'll find the large East London Mosque and, behind it, the Great Synagogue, built in 1899. Further down Fieldgate St, the enormous Tower House was once a hostel and then a doss-house but is now a redeveloped apartment block. Past residents include Joseph Stalin and authors Jack London and George Orwell. The latter describes it in detail in *Down and Out in Paris and London* (1933).

North along Whitechapel Rd sits the Blind Beggar, where the notorious gangster Ronnie Kray shot George Cornell dead in 1966, in a turf war over control of the East End's organised crime. He was jailed for life and died in 1995. After the intersection

TOP SIGHT WHITECHAPEL GALLERY

This ground-breaking gallery, which moved into its main art-nouveau building in 1899, extended into the library next door in 2009, doubling its exhibition space to 10 galleries. Founded by the Victorian philanthropist Canon Samuel Barnett at the end of the 19th century to bring art to the people of East London, it has made its name by putting on exhibitions by both established and emerging artists, cartoonists and architects, including Jackson Pollock (his first UK show), Gary Hume, Robert Crumb, Mies van der Rohe and Picasso (whose *Guernica* was exhibited here in 1939). The gallery's ambitiously themed shows change every couple of months – check the program online – and there's also live music, poetry readings, talks and films till late on Thursday. Don't miss the phenomenal 'social sculptures' in various (and ephemeral) spaces throughout – there's even one on the roof of the building. Ask at the front desk about Janet Cardiff's *The Missing Voice (Case Study B)*, an audio walk that takes you into the surrounding streets – a surreal but exciting interaction of art and context (you need to leave a bank card as security). Other features are an excellent bookshop, the Whitechapel Gallery Dining Room and an uberdesigned cafe on the mezzanine level.

DON'T MISS...

- Social sculptures
- Bookshop
- A meal in the Dining Room

PRACTICALITIES

- Map p454
- ☎020-7522 7888
- www.whitechapelgallery.org
- 77-82 Whitechapel High St, E1
- admission free
- ⏲11am-6pm Wed-Sun, to 9pm Thu
- ⊖Aldgate East

CABLE STREET

Cable St, just south of Commercial Rd, takes its name from the use of the length of the thoroughfare to twist hemp rope into ships' cables. Similarly named, but shorter and narrower, Twine Ct runs south from here. Cable St is most famous for the Battle of Cable St (1936), in which the British fascist Oswald Mosley led a bunch of his blackshirts into the area, supposedly as a celebration of the fourth anniversary of the British Union of Fascists. Although pockets of fascist supporters existed in the East End, the march was ferociously repelled by local people – thousands of Jews, communists, dockers, trade unionists and other East Enders turned out in solidarity against them. At No 236 you'll find St George's Town Hall building, its west wall sporting a large mural commemorating the riots. The church just behind this building is **St George-in-the-East** (Map p454; www.stgite.org.uk; 16 Canon St Rd, E1), erected by Nicholas Hawksmoor in 1729 and badly damaged in the Blitz of WWII; all that now remains is a shell enclosing a smaller modern core.

with Cambridge Heath Rd, this traditionally poor area's history takes a more philanthropic turn, with a statue of **William Booth** (Map p454) (1829–1912), who established his Salvation Army Christian Mission here in 1865, and the **Trinity Green Almshouses** (Map p454), poorhouses built for injured or retired sailors in 1695. The two rows of almshouses run at right angles away from the street, facing a village-type green and a chapel with a clock tower.

Bethnal Green & Hackney

V&A MUSEUM OF CHILDHOOD — MUSEUM

Map p454 (www.vam.ac.uk/moc; cnr Cambridge Heath & Old Ford Rds, E2; 10am-5.45pm; ; Bethnal Green) FREE Housed in a renovated Victorian-era building moved from South Kensington in 1866, this branch of the Victoria & Albert Museum is aimed at both kids (with activity rooms and interactive exhibits, including a dressing-up box and sandpit) and nostalgic grown-ups who come to admire the antique toys.

From teddies, doll's houses and dolls (one dating from 1300 BC) to Meccano, Lego and computer games, it's a wonderful toy-cupboard trip down memory lane. There's a good cafe on the ground floor too.

SUTTON HOUSE — HISTORIC BUILDING

Map p454 (www.nationaltrust.org.uk/suttonhouse; 2 & 4 Homerton High St, E9; adult/child £3/1; 10am-5pm Thu & Fri, noon-5pm Sat & Sun, closed Jan; 394, Hackney Central) Sutton House was originally known as Bryk Place when it was built in 1535 by a prominent courtier of Henry VIII, Sir Ralph Sadleir. Abandoned and taken over by squatters in the 1980s, it could have been tragically lost to history, but it's since been put under the care of the National Trust and magnificently restored.

The first historic room you enter, the Linenfold Parlour, is the highlight, where the Tudor oak panelling on the walls has been carved to resemble draped cloth. Other notable rooms include the panelled Great Chamber, the Victorian study, the Georgian parlour and the intriguing mock-up of a Tudor kitchen. There's a shop and pleasant cafe on site.

West of Sutton House, in the restored St John's Churchyard Gardens, is 13th-century St Augustine's Tower, all that remains of a church that was demolished in 1798. On the last Sunday of the month (2.30pm to 4.30pm) you can climb the tower's 135 steps for fantastic views across Hackney (free).

LONDON FIELDS — PARK

Map p454 (www.hackney.gov.uk/cp-londonfields; ; 55 or 277, London Fields) A strip of green amid a popular residential area of Hackney, London Fields is where locals hang out after a meander up Broadway Market. Built in the 1930s, and abandoned by the '80s, **London Fields Lido** (Map p454; www.hackney.gov.uk/c-londonfields-lido; London Fields Westside, E8; adult/child £4.10/2.45; usually 6.30am-8pm) reopened to local delight in 2006. It gets packed with swimmers and sunbathers during the summer months.

The park also has two children's play areas and a decent pub.

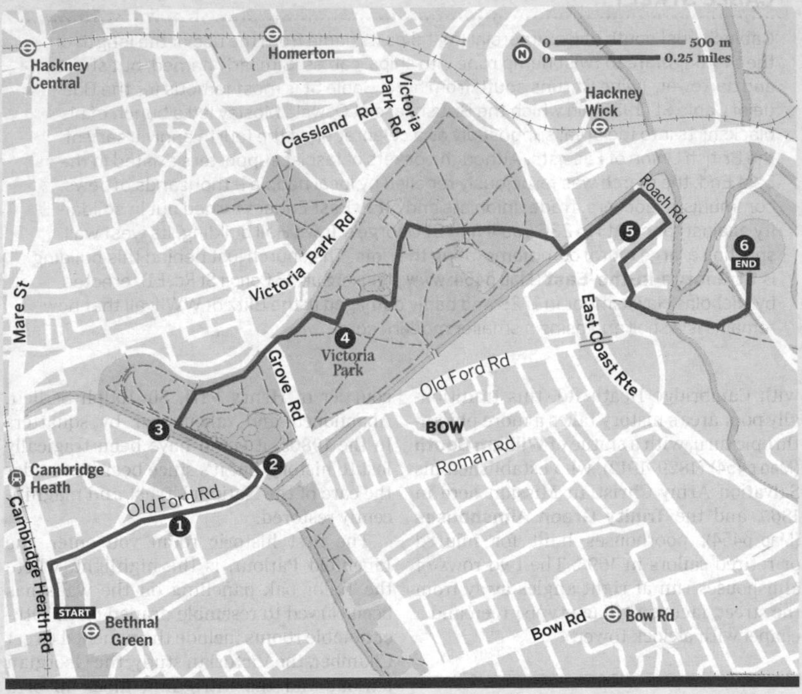

Neighbourhood Walk
East End Eras

START BETHNAL GREEN TUBE STATION
END QUEEN ELIZABETH OLYMPIC PARK
LENGTH 3 MILES; TWO HOURS

This easy stroll offers an insightful view into the old and new of the East End. Exit the tube station towards the Museum of Childhood and head north. Take the first right and continue until you can take a right into Cyprus Pl. The surrounding area was heavily bombed during WWII (due to its industry and proximity to the docks) and the tower blocks you can see if you raise your eyes skyward are a product of postwar redevelopment. But beautifully preserved **1 Cyprus St** gives a taste of what Victorian Bethnal Green would have looked like. Continue left down Cyprus St and back onto Old Ford Rd.

Just over Regent's Canal lies **2 Victoria Park** (p227), built in the 1840s to improve the quality of life of East Enders. Take the path down to the road around the lake and head left to the **3 Dogs of Alciabiades** howling on plinths, replicas of the originals that stood here from 1912. Turn right here and then again at the end of the road and continue to the grand Royal Inn on the Park. Cross the road into the eastern section of the park and take a right towards the recently restored **4 Burdett-Coutts Memorial** (1862), a gift of Angela Burdett-Coutts, once the richest woman in England and a prominent philanthropist.

From here, ramble on to the east lake and exit at the park's southeastern tip. Cross the road and pick up the canal path next to the Top O' the Morning pub, crossing the canal at the first bridge you come to. **5 Hackney Wick** is home to a warren of warehouses and a community of artists, and was extensively redeveloped for the 2012 Olympics. Stop off at the Counter Cafe or Formans for views of the stadium, and check out their latest art exhibits. From here you're a mere shot-put from the **6 Queen Elizabeth Olympic Park** (p228), marking a whole new era for the East End.

Mile End & Victoria Park

VICTORIA PARK PARK

Map p454 (www.towerhamlets.gov.uk; dawn-dusk; 277 or 425, Mile End) The 'Regent's Park of the East End', Victoria Park is an 86-hectare leafy expanse opened in 1845 – the first public park in the East End that came about after a local MP presented Queen Victoria with a petition of 30,000 signatures. In the early 20th century it was known as the Speaker's Corner of the East End.

During WWII the park was largely closed to the public and was used as an anti-aircraft shelling site as well as an internment camp for Italian and then German prisoners of war. Victoria Park has undergone a £12-million revamp, and the work was finished in April 2012, improving both the lakes, introducing a skate park and creating a hub building housing a cafe, community room and park offices in the eastern section of the park.

RAGGED SCHOOL MUSEUM MUSEUM

Map p454 (www.raggedschoolmuseum.org.uk; 46-50 Copperfield Rd, E3; 10am-5pm Wed & Thu, 2-5pm 1st Sun of month; Mile End) FREE Both adults and children are inevitably charmed by this combination of mock Victorian schoolroom – with hard wooden benches and desks, slates, chalk, inkwells and abacuses – re-created East End kitchen and social history museum below. 'Ragged' was a Victorian term used to refer to pupils' usually torn, dirty and dishevelled clothes.

The museum celebrates the legacy of Dr Thomas Barnardo, who founded this school for destitute East End children in the 1870s. The school closed in 1908 but you can experience what it would have been like: on the first Sunday of the month there is a Victorian lesson in which 'pupils' (adults and children alike) are taught reading, writing and 'rithmetic by a strict school ma'am, called Miss Perkins, in full Victorian regalia. It takes place at 2.15pm and 3.30pm (suggested donation £2). There's also a tiny towpath cafe and shop where you can pick up your own slate and chalk. Friendly staff are on hand to pass on plenty of local information and background.

HOUSE MILL HISTORIC BUILDING

(www.housemill.org.uk; Three Mill Lane, E3; adult/concession £3/1.50; 11am-4pm Sun May-Oct, 1st Sun only Mar, Apr & Dec; Bromley-by-Bow) The House Mill (1776) operated as a sluice tidal mill, grinding grain for a nearby distillery until 1941. Tours, which run according to demand and last about 45 minutes, take visitors to all four floors of the mill and offer a fascinating look at traditional East End industry.

This is one of two remaining mills from a trio that once stood on this small island in the River Lea. There's a small cafe and shop on site. To get to House Mill, exit the tube and head down the steps to the left. Continue into the underpass and at the top of the stairs turn right, down the hill. Take a right towards Tesco and right again into Three Mill Lane.

TOWER HAMLETS CEMETERY PARK CEMETERY

Map p454 (www.towerhamletscemetery.org; Southern Grove, E3; 8am-dusk; Mile End or Bow Rd) Opened in 1841 this 13-hectare cemetery was the last of the 'Magnificent Seven', then-suburban cemeteries – including Highgate and Stoke Newington's Abney Park – created by an act of Parliament in response to London's rapid population growth and overcrowded burial grounds.

Some 270,000 souls were laid to rest here until the cemetery was closed for burials in 1966 and turned into a park and local nature reserve in 2001. Today it is a quiet, restful site, its Victorian monuments slowly being consumed by vines. There are usually two-hour guided tours at 2pm on the third Sunday of the month.

MILE END PARK PARK

Map p454 (www.towerhamlets.gov.uk; Mile End) The 36-hectare Mile End Park is a long, narrow series of interconnected green spaces wedged between Burdett and Grove Rds and Regent's Canal. Landscaped to great effect during the millennium year, it incorporates a go-kart track, a children's centre, areas for public art, an ecology area, an indoor climbing wall and a sports stadium.

The centrepiece, though, is architect Piers Gough's 'green bridge' linking the northern and southern sections of the park over busy Mile End Rd and planted with trees and shrubs.

A HERO RISES IN THE EAST

Daniel Mendoza (1764–1836), the father of 'scientific boxing' who billed himself as 'Mendoza the Jew', was the first bare-knuckle boxer to employ strategy and speed in the ring. Mendoza was born in Aldgate and left school at age 13, taking odd jobs as a porter, being taunted as an 'outsider' and getting into scrapes. He was eventually discovered by 'gentleman boxer' Richard Humphreys, 20 years his senior, who took him under his wing and started him training. Mendoza developed a style of fighting in direct opposition to the norm of the day, where two fighters would stand face to face and slug it out until one collapsed.

Mendoza began a highly successful career in the ring, but eventually fell out with his mentor. His most infamous fight came during a grudge match in 1788 with Humphreys. Just as Mendoza was about to administer the coup de grâce, Humphreys' second grabbed Mendoza's arm, a moment caught in a contemporary print called *Foul Play* on display in the National Portrait Gallery. Mendoza went on to fight Humphreys fairly two more times, emerging the victor and moral superior.

Mendoza was the first sportsman in Britain to achieve cult status – a veritable David Beckham of 18th-century London. He made (and lost) a fortune, wrote his memoirs and a how-to book called *The Art of Boxing,* mixed with the high and mighty (including royalty) and sold branded trinkets and images of himself. Most importantly he advanced the cause of Jews in a country that had only allowed them back the century before. People learned for the first time that a Jew could and would fight back – and win.

⊙ Hackney Wick & Stratford

QUEEN ELIZABETH OLYMPIC PARK PARK

(http://noordinarypark.co.uk; ⊖Stratford) Creating world-class sporting facilities for the 2012 Games was, of course, at the forefront of the development, but this was well balanced with the aim of regenerating this area for generations to come. More than 30 new bridges were built to criss-cross the River Lea. Waterways in and around the park were upgraded, with waste cleared and contaminated soil cleaned on a massive scale.

From the mills of Cistercian monks in the 1st century, to the railway hub of the 1880s (from which goods from the Thames were transported all over Britain), the tidal Lower Lea Valley had long been the source of what Londoners required to fuel their industries. But until building work on the Olympic Park began in 2008, this vast area of East London had become derelict, polluted and largely ignored.

The main focal point of the Queen Elizabeth Olympic Park, as it is now known, is the Olympic Stadium, with a Games capacity of 80,000, scaling back to approximately 60,000 seats post-Games. The striking Aquatics Centre is the work of Clerkenwell-based architect Zaha Hadid and houses two 50m swimming pools and a diving pool. The equally impressive and award-winning Velodrome (aka the 'Pringle') has been praised for its aesthetic qualities, as well as its sustainable credentials and functional appeal. The 114m, spiralling red structure is Anish Kapoor's ArcelorMittal Orbit, or the 'Hubble Bubble Pipe', offering a vast panorama from its viewing platform.

The north of the park has been given over to wetlands, which provide a much wilder environment than the gardens and landscaping of the southern half of the park, which is home to the main venues. The developments to transform the park into its promised legacy will take at least another 25 years to complete and are set to open to the public in phases.

⊙ Wapping & Limehouse

WAPPING NEIGHBOURHOOD

Map p454 (⊖Wapping) Once notorious for slave traders, drunk sailors and prostitutes, Wapping's towering warehouses, built at the beginning of the 19th century, still give an atmospheric picture of the area's previous existence. Make sure you take a stroll or cycle ride to the lovely Wapping power station, home to the Wapping Project, an exhibition space, a wonderful bookshop and a great restaurant.

Although there's nothing to actually mark it, down on the riverside below Wapping New Stairs (near the marine police station) was Execution Dock, where convicted pirates were hanged and their bodies chained to a post at low tide, to be left until three tides had washed over their heads. Among the more famous people who died this way was Captain William Kidd, hanged here in 1701, and whose grisly tale you can read about in the nearby Captain Kidd pub.

LIMEHOUSE NEIGHBOURHOOD

Map p454 (DLR Limehouse or Westferry) There isn't much to Limehouse, although it became the centre of London's Chinese community – its first Chinatown – after some 300 sailors settled here in 1890. It gets a mention in Oscar Wilde's *The Picture of Dorian Gray* (1891), when the protagonist passes by this way in search of opium.

The most notable attraction here is St Anne's, Limehouse. This was Nicholas Hawksmoor's earliest church (1725) and still boasts the highest church clock in the city. In fact the 60m-high tower is still a 'Trinity House mark' for identifying shipping lanes on the Thames (thus it flies the Royal Navy's white ensign).

ST KATHARINE DOCKS HARBOUR

Map p454 (Tower Hill) The gateway to the warehouse district of Wapping, built in 1828 after 1250 'insanitary' houses were razed and 11,300 people made homeless, the dock's current incarnation – a marina for luxury yachts surrounded by cafes, restaurants and twee shops – dates from the 1980s. It's the perfect starting point for exploring Wapping and Limehouse.

Docklands

ISLE OF DOGS NEIGHBOURHOOD

Map p453 (DLR Westferry, West India Quay, Canary Wharf) The centrepiece of the Isle of Dogs is Cesar Pelli's 244m-high **Canary Wharf Tower**, which was built in 1991. It's surrounded by more recent towers housing HSBC and Citigroup, and offices for Bank of America, Barclays, Morgan Stanley, Credit

TOP SIGHT
MUSEUM OF LONDON DOCKLANDS

Housed in a converted warehouse dating from 1802, this museum offers a comprehensive overview of the history of the Thames from the arrival of the Romans in AD 43. Well-organised with knowledgeable and helpful staff, it's at its best when dealing with specifics such as the docks during WWII, as well as their controversial transformation into the Docklands during the 1980s.

The tour begins on the 3rd floor with the Roman settlement of Londinium and works its way downwards through the ages. Check out the scale model of old London Bridge. Other highlights include Sailortown – a re-creation of the cobbled streets, bars and lodging houses of a mid-19th-century dockside community and nearby Chinatown – and more detailed galleries such as London, Sugar & Slavery, which examines the capital's role in the transatlantic slave trade.

There's lots for kids, including the hands-on Mudlarks gallery, where children can explore the history of the Thames, tipping the clipper, trying on old-fashioned diving helmets and even constructing a simple model of Canary Wharf. The museum has special exhibitions every few months, for which there is usually a charge. There's also a great cafe on site.

DON'T MISS...

- Sailortown
- London, Sugar & Slavery
- Docklands at War
- New Port New City
- Scale model of London Bridge

PRACTICALITIES

- Map p453
- www.museumoflondon.org.uk/docklands
- Hertsmere Rd, West India Quay, E17
- 10am-6pm
- DLR West India Quay

DOCKLANDS DEVELOPMENT

You'd probably never guess it while gazing up at the ultramodern skyscrapers that dominate the Isle of Dogs and Canary Wharf, but from the 16th century until the mid-20th century this area was the centre of the world's greatest port, the hub of the British Empire and its enormous global trade. At the docks here, cargo from global trade was landed, bringing jobs to a tight-knit working-class community. Even up to the start of WWII this community still thrived, but that all changed when the docks were badly firebombed during the Blitz.

After the war the docks were in no condition to cope with the postwar technological and political changes as the British Empire evaporated. At the same time enormous new bulk carriers and container ships demanded deep-water ports and new loading and unloading techniques. From the mid-1960s, dock closures followed one another as fast as they had opened, and the number of dock workers dropped from as many as 50,000 in 1960 to about 3000 by 1980.

The financial metropolis that exists today was begun by the London Docklands Development Corporation (LDDC), a body established by the Thatcher government in the freewheeling 1980s to take pressure for office space off the City. This rather artificial community had a shaky start. The low-rise toytown buildings had trouble attracting tenants, the Docklands Light Railway – the main transport link – had teething troubles and the landmark Canary Wharf Tower itself had to be rescued from bankruptcy twice. Now, however, news media organisations and financial behemoths have moved in – with Citigroup and HSBC boasting their own buildings.

The Docklands today is both futuristic and rich in history.

Suisse and more. Londoners are divided on their appreciation of this area, though despite its soullessness, it is noteworthy for its radical development.

Pundits can't quite agree on whether this is really an island; strictly speaking it's a peninsula of land on the northern shore of the Thames, though without modern road and transport links it would almost be separated from the mainland at West India Docks. And etymologists are still out to lunch over the origin of the island's name. Some believe it's because the royal kennels were located here during the reign of Henry VIII. Others maintain it's a corruption of the Flemish word dijk (dyke), recalling the Flemish engineers who shored up the area's muddy banks.

MUDCHUTE PARK & FARM FARM

Map p453 (www.mudchute.org; Mudchute, E14; farm 9am-5pm Tue-Sun; ; DLR Mudchute) FREE Entering Mudchute Park from Eastferry Rd through the canopy of trees, you're greeted by a delightfully surprising sight of cows and sheep, roaming freely in this grassy 13 hectares of parkland. The lovely city farm has an array of animals, well kept, in spacious surrounds. Kids will love it.

Looking back to the skyscrapers of Canary Wharf gives you a clear sense of the contrasts of this area of London. There's also a neat cafe, serving excellent breakfasts and wholesome lunch options.

EATING

The East End's multiculturalism has ensured that its ethnic cuisine stretches far and wide, with some fantastic low-key eateries serving authentic and value-for-money fare. But the area's gentrification has introduced a slew of gastropubs and more upmarket restaurants – some even earning a Michelin star. Trendy and excellent coffee shops have sprouted up all over the East End, though you can still – if you must – find plenty of 'greasy spoon' cafes, or a traditional pie with mash and liquor. Places to head if you want to sniff out your own favourites include Columbia Rd, Broadway Market and the streets just to the north of Victoria Park (known to some as Hackney Village).

Whitechapel

KOLAPATA BANGLADESHI £

Map p454 (www.kolapata.co.uk; 222 Whitechapel Rd, E1; mains £4.50-9.95; noon-11.30pm; Whitechapel) This modest restaurant serves up excellent Bangladeshi cuisine. Try the *haleem* (lamb with lentils and spices) and the *sarisha elish* (fish cooked with mustard seed, onion and green chilli).

TAYYABS INDIAN, PAKISTANI £

Map p454 (020-7247 9543; www.tayyabs.co.uk; 83-89 Fieldgate St, E1; mains £6.50-11; noon-midnight; Whitechapel) This buzzing (OK, crowded) Punjabi restaurant is in another league to its Brick Lane equivalents. *Seekh* kebabs, masala fish and other starters served on sizzling hot plates are delicious, as are accompaniments such as dhal, naan and raita. Daily specials are also available. Tayyabs is hugely popular and queues often snake around the restaurant and out of the door.

MIRCH MASALA INDIAN, PAKISTANI £

Map p454 (www.mirchmasalarestaurant.co.uk; 111-113 Commercial Rd, E1; mains £4.50-11; noon-midnight; Whitechapel) 'Chilli and Spice', part of a small chain based in the epicentre of London subcontinental food, Southall, is a less hectic alternative to Tayyabs and the food is almost up to the same level. Order the prawn tikka (£9) as a 'warmer' followed by the *masala karella* (£5), a curry-like dish made from bitter gourd, and a *karahi* (stewed) meat dish.

★WHITECHAPEL GALLERY DINING ROOM MODERN EUROPEAN ££

Map p454 (020-7522 7896; www.whitechapelgallery.org; 77-82 Whitechapel High St, E1; mains £12-17; noon-3pm Tue, noon-3pm & 6-9.30pm Wed-Sat, noon-4pm Sun; Aldgate East) Housed in a small but perfectly formed dining room in the Passmore Edwards Library extension of the Whitechapel Gallery, with high-profile chef Angela Hartnett acting as consultant. The menu offers small or large plates, to suit your appetite. Booking advised.

CAFÉ SPICE NAMASTÉ INDIAN ££

Map p454 (020-7488 9242; www.cafespice.co.uk; 16 Prescot St, E1; mains £14-19, 2-course set lunch £15.95; noon-midnight Mon-Fri, 6.30pm-midnight Sat; DLR Tower Gateway, Tower Hill) Chef Cyrus Todiwala has taken an old magistrates court just a 10-minute walk from Tower Hill and decorated it in carnival colours; the service and atmosphere are as bright as the walls. The Parsi and Goan menu is famous for its superlative *dhansaak* (lamb stew with rice and lentils; £14.95) but just as good are the tandoori dishes and the Goan king-prawn curry.

Bonuses: it makes its own chutneys and there's a little garden behind the dining room open in the warmer months.

Bethnal Green & Hackney

★TOWPATH CAFE £

Map p456 (Regent's Canal towpath, N1, btwn Whitmore Bridge & Kingsland Rd Bridge; mains £3-10; 8am-dusk Tue-Fri, 9am-dusk Sat & Sun, Mar-Nov only; Haggerston rail Bus 67, 149) One of London's most special places to eat – if the weather is fine, that is, since this is a restaurant/cafe on the bank of Regent's Canal. It's a simple affair with four small units looking on to the canal – two serve for sitting 'inside' for shelter from possible drizzle, and the other two are the kitchen and bar.

Most of all, the food is fantastic, with seasonal offers and specials from the Mediterranean – you'll find snails, Catalan *calcots* (a type of grilled leek), or the tenderest of pork loins, depending on the day. The menu changes daily, and is chalked up on the board. The cakes are excellent, and the homemade ice cream, served in a misty tumbler, is scrumptious. Suppertime, with dusk falling on the canal, is magical, as are lively Sunday afternoons, when live music is played on a little barge.

E PELLICI CAFE £

Map p454 (332 Bethnal Green Rd, E2; dishes £5-7.80; 7am-4pm Mon-Sat; 8, Bethnal Green) There aren't many reasons to recommend a stroll down Bethnal Green Rd, but stepping into this diminutive Anglo-Italian cafe is one of them. You're likely to be met by a warmer-than-average greeting as you squeeze onto a table among an amiable collection of East Enders.

Opened in 1900 the wood-panelled caff is bedecked with museum-quality original fittings. Breakfasts are large and sustaining and the traditional English and Italian dishes are certain to satisfy the heartiest of appetites.

COCKNEY RHYMING SLANG

Traditionally cockneys were people born within earshot of the Bow Bells – the church bells of St Mary-le-Bow on Cheapside. Since few people actually live in the City, this definition has broadened to take in those living further east. The term cockney is often used to describe anyone speaking what is also called estuarine English (in which 't' and 'h' are routinely dropped, and glottal stops – what the two 't's sound like in 'bottle' – abound). In fact the true cockney language also uses something called rhyming slang, which may have developed among London's costermongers (street traders) as a code to avoid police attention. This code replaced common nouns and verbs with rhyming phrases. So 'going up the apples and pears' meant going up the stairs, the 'trouble and strife' was the wife, 'telling porky pies' was telling lies and 'would you Adam and Eve it?' was would you believe it? Over time the second of the two words tended to be dropped so the rhyme vanished. Few, if any, people still use pure cockney but a good many still understand it. You're more likely to come across it in residual phrases like 'use your loaf' ('loaf of bread' for head), 'ooh, me plates of meat' (feet) or 'e's me best china' ('china plate' for mate).

CLIMPSON & SONS CAFE £

Map p454 (www.webcoffeeshop.co.uk; 67 Broadway Market, E8; dishes £4-6.50; 8am-5pm; 55 or 277, London Fields) Small and simply decorated, this deservedly popular cafe is housed in what was once a butcher's shop (and has retained the same name). Coffee is superb – it roasts its own just around the corner – and it also does a fine line in sandwiches, pastries and light meals, such as salads and couscous.

LITTLE GEORGIA GEORGIAN £

Map p454 (87 Goldsmith's Row, E2; dishes £4-8; 9am-5pm Mon, to 11pm Tue-Sat, 10am-11pm Sun; 55, Cambridge Heath) A charming slice of the Caucasus in East London, this simple eatery on two floors is an excellent introduction to the cuisine of Georgia; try the mixed meze for two or four. The menu includes such classics as *nigziani* (red pepper or aubergine stuffed with walnuts, herbs and roast vegetables) and the staple *hachapuri* (cheese bread).

The cafe is a good place for breakfast and has a delicious range of salads and sandwiches.

GREEN PAPAYA VIETNAMESE £

Map p454 (191 Mare St, E8; mains £6.50-8.50; 5-11pm Tue-Sun; 55 or 277, London Fields) This simple but friendly neighbourhood restaurant has been serving up high-quality Vietnamese food to Hackney diners for years. The extensive menu is strong on vegetarian and seafood dishes.

F. COOKE BRITISH £

Map p454 (9 Broadway Market, E8; mains £3-4; 10am-7pm; 55, Cambridge Heath) If you want a glimpse of what eating out was like in Broadway Market before the street was gentrified, head to F. Cooke pie and mash shop. This family business has been going strong since 1900, and the shop has the original signage and tiles, along with plenty of family photographs around the walls and sawdust on the floor.

FRIZZANTE@CITY FARM CAFE £

Map p454 (www.frizzanteltd.co.uk; Hackney City Farm, 1a Goldsmith's Row, E2; dishes £4-11; 10am-4.30pm Tue-Sun & 6.30-11pm Wed-Fri; 55, Cambridge Heath) Award-winning restaurant serving excellent Italian food next door to one of London's half-dozen city farms, with a weekly *agroturismo* night offering special country dishes.

GALLERY CAFE CAFE £

Map p454 (www.stmargaretshouse.org.uk; 21 Old Ford Rd, E2; dishes £3.80-5.90; 10am-6pm; Bethnal Green) Tucked around the corner from the Museum of Childhood, the pretty Gallery Cafe is in the basement of a lovely Georgian building. It serves simple but delicious vegan and vegetarian fare to relaxed locals. There's a cute courtyard at the front for sunny days. Check the website for sporadic evening events such as jazz, world and acoustic music, and film nights.

LARDO PIZZERIA ££

Map p454 (020-8985 2683; www.lardo.co.uk; 197-205 Richmond Rd, E8; mains £7-14, pizzas

£5-11; 11am-11pm Mon-Fri, 10am-11pm Sat, 10am-10pm Sun; Hackney Central or London Fields) A simple, one-room affair that celebrates the Italian 'lardo' – the cured back fat of rare-breed pigs scented with aromatic herbs. You'll find it on one of the excellent pizzas, or a platter of cured meats, as well as among the antipasti. Otherwise, the pizza toppings are imaginative: try the goat's curd, anchovy and sprouting broccoli, or clam and peppers.

The wine list carries a good range of European wines, and the gelati are made in-house.

CORNER ROOM MODERN EUROPEAN ££

(020-7871 0460; www.townhallhotel.com/corner_room; Patriot Sq Bethnal Green, E2; lunch 2/3 courses £19/23, mains £13-15; 7-10am, noon-4pm & 6-10.30pm) For a relaxed but creative meal, try this gorgeous restaurant with British and Mediterranean flavours, seasonal food and quality ingredients, on the first floor of the Town Hall Hotel. There is a good wine list, and the decor is simple but attractive. Lunchtime reservations only.

★VIAJANTE FUSION £££

Map p454 (www.viajante.co.uk; Patriot Sq, E2; tasting menu lunch £28-70, dinner £65-90, Corner Room mains £10-12; noon-2pm Fri-Sun & 6-9.30pm Wed-Sun; ; Bethnal Green) Chef Nuno Mendes heads this Michelin-starred restaurant and produces inventive, beautifully put together dishes with an exciting fusion of flavours. The elegant dining room is stylish and modern with the original Edwardian features kept intact. The open kitchen lets you take a peek at what you'll get for your tasting menus. Service is spot on.

The restaurant is part of the Town Hall Hotel & Apartments (but with a separate entrance on Cambridge Heath Rd).

LAXEIRO TAPAS £££

Map p454 (020-7729 1147; www.laxeiro.co.uk; 93 Columbia Rd, E2; tapas £4.50-8.95, paella £21.50-24.50; noon-3pm & 7-11pm Tue-Sat, 9am-3pm Sun; Hoxton) A homely yet stylish and buzzing restaurant with friendly staff providing great service. The menu offers up authentic and robust *raciones* (portions) – the barbecue lamb is a winner. The handful of more ambitious dishes includes paella to be shared. There are tables outside on the picturesque street in summer.

Mile End & Victoria Park

NAMÔ VIETNAMESE £

Map p454 (020-8533 0639; www.namo.co.uk; 178 Victoria Park Rd, E9; dishes £4-6; noon-10.30pm; Mile End then 277) This pretty place serves a carefully chosen selection of punchy Vietnamese dishes in a nicer-than-average setting. There's a lovely garden area with a retractable roof, great for English summers.

LOAFING CAFE £

Map p454 (www.loafing.co.uk; 79 Lauriston Rd, E9; dishes £4-5; 9am-6pm; Mile End then 277) Cute corner cafe with a glorious cake selection, lovingly displayed. Also offers sandwiches, pastries, Monmouth coffee and a great range of teas, served in mismatched fine bone china. The outdoor tables and huge windows make it perfect for people-watching and there's also a tiny garden to relax in out back.

PAVILION CAFE £

Map p454 (www.the-pavilion-cafe.com; cnr Old Ford & Grove Rds, E3; mains £4.50-8; 8.30am-5pm; Mile End then 277) Superb cafe overlooking an ornamental lake in Victoria Park, serving breakfasts and lunches made with locally sourced ingredients, and excellent coffee.

FISH HOUSE FISH & CHIPS ££

Map p454 (www.fishouse.co.uk; 126-128 Lauriston Rd, E9; mains £8.50-12.50; noon-10pm; Mile End then 277) The freshest of fresh fish and crustaceans are dispensed from both a busy takeaway section (where a blackboard tells you from where your fish has come) and a cheerful sit-down restaurant. The lobster bisque and Colchester oysters are always good, while the generous fish pie bursting with goodies from the briny deep is exceptional.

Hackney Wick & Stratford

COUNTER CAFE CAFE £

Map p454 (www.thecountercafe.co.uk; 7 Roach Rd, E3; dishes £4.50-8; 7.30am-5pm Mon-Fri, 9am-5pm Sat & Sun; ; Hackney Wick) Housed within Stour Space (which hosts a variety of art exhibitions) and directly overlooking the Olympic stadium, this friendly local cafe serves up fantastic coffee and breakfasts, sandwiches and pies. The mismatched, thrift-store furniture, painting-clad walls and relaxed atmosphere make this a favourite with the local artist community.

★**FORMANS** BRITISH ££

Map p454 (020-8525 2365; www.formans.co.uk; Stour Rd, Fish Island, E3; mains £11.50-20; 7-11pm Thu & Fri, 10am-2pm & 7-11pm Sat, noon-5pm Sun; ; Hackney) This diminutive restaurant, with unrivalled views over the Olympic stadium, serves a fantastic variety of smoked salmon (the wild smoked salmon is exceptional), as well as an interesting range of dishes with ingredients sourced from within the British Isles. It also has a great selection of English wines and, unusually, spirits.

H Forman & Son has been curing fish here since 1905, and are notable for developing the much-celebrated London cure. Obliged to move to make way for the Olympic developments, they're now housed in appropriately salmon-pink premises that contain their smokery, restaurant, bar and art gallery. Simple sharing platters are available in the bar. Make sure to take a peek into the smokery next door and the art gallery upstairs.

HACKNEY PEARL CAFE ££

Map p454 (www.thehackneypearl.com; 11 Prince Edward Rd, E9; lunch dishes £5-7.50, dinner mains £10-13; 10am-11pm Tue-Sat, to 5pm Sun; ; Hackney Wick) In an unforgiving area, and on an equally unforgiving site, this cafe has created a cheerful and friendly atmosphere where you can enjoy tasty food and delicious coffee. With large windows, outdoor tables and de rigueur salvaged furniture, it's a relaxed place to have breakfast or lunch but is also open into the evening when there is a short but frequently changing menu that includes some good veggie options.

Wapping & Limehouse

★**WAPPING FOOD** MODERN EUROPEAN ££

Map p454 (020-7680 2080; www.thewappingproject.com; The Wapping Project, Wapping Hydraulic Power Station, Wapping Wall, E1; mains £14-21; ; Wapping) Stylish dining room set among the innards of a disused power station, creating a spectacular and unexpectedly romantic atmosphere. The high-quality, seasonal menu changes daily but might include guinea fowl wrapped in pancetta, or onglet with beetroot and horseradish. The owner is Australian, which accounts for the exclusively Australian wine list.

The 'Project' (of which the restaurant is a part) also contains a regularly changing exhibition space (noon to 10pm Monday to Friday, 10am to 10pm Saturday), which is well worth popping into.

Docklands

GUN GASTROPUB, PORTUGUESE £££

Map p453 (020-7515 5222; www.thegundocklands.com; 27 Coldharbour, E14; mains £15-27; ; Canary Wharf) Set at the end of a pretty, cobbled street, this riverside pub has been seriously dolled up, but still manages to ooze history. Previously a local dockers pub, dating from the early 18th century, it is claimed that Lord Nelson had secret assignations with Lady Emma Hamilton here (hence the naming of the toilets).

Inside, the pub is mostly comprised of a dining area but there is a smaller room at the back, as well as a terrace affording expansive views of the Thames. On a separate terrace, during summer months, the pub hosts the completely al fresco A Grelha, grilling up dazzlingly fresh fish from Billingsgate Market, just a few streets away, as well as Portuguese classics such as *cataplana* and *estapada.* Call ahead if the weather's bad.

DRINKING & NIGHTLIFE

Whitechapel

RHYTHM FACTORY CLUB

Map p454 (www.rhythmfactory.co.uk; 16-18 Whitechapel Rd, E1; opening hours vary; Aldgate East) Perennially hip and popular, the Rhythm Factory is a club and venue hosting a variety of bands and DJs of all genres that keep the up-for-it crowd happy until late.

INDO PUB

Map p454 (133 Whitechapel Rd, E1; ⊙to 1am Sun-Thu, to 3am Fri & Sat; ; ⊖Whitechapel) Tiny, narrow pub bang opposite the East London Mosque, with battered old tables, pews and a couple of knackered Chesterfields under the only window. Friendly staff work the beautifully tat-cluttered bar, and serve decent pizzas (£5 to £7) to punters with the munchies. There's art for sale on the walls, DJs on weekend nights and interesting bands on an irregular schedule.

Bethnal Green & Hackney

★DOVE FREEHOUSE PUB

Map p454 (www.dovepubs.com; 24-28 Broadway Market, E8; ⊙noon-11pm Sun-Fri, 11am-11pm Sat; ; 55, Cambridge Heath) This pub attracts at any time with its rambling series of rooms and wide range – 21 on draught – of Belgian Trappist, wheat and fruit-flavoured beers. Drinkers spill out onto the street in warmer weather, or hunker down in the low-lit back room with board games when it's chilly. Decent gastropub fare also on offer.

★CARPENTER'S ARMS PUB

Map p454 (www.carpentersarmsfreehouse.com; 73 Cheshire St, E2; ; Bethnal Green, ⊖Shoreditch High St) After a browse in the shops along Cheshire St, you'll probably end up outside this gorgeous corner pub. Once notorious – the pub was owned in the '60s by the Kray brothers, who gave it over to their mother – it has been well restored to a trendy yet cosy and intimate pub combining traditional pub architecture with contemporary touches.

A back room and small yard provide a little more space for the convivial drinkers. There's a great range of beers and lagers, as well as a menu offering quality drinking food.

PLATFORM CAFÉ, BAR & TERRACE BAR

Map p454 (www.platformlondonfields.com; 2nd Floor, Netil House, 1-7 Westgate St, London Fields, E8; ⊙8.30am-8pm Mon-Wed, to 11pm Thu, to 1am Fri, 2pm-1am Sat) Inside the art studio-filled Netil House, just off London Fields, Platform is one of those places you come across quite accidentally and feel like you've discovered a world. The massive windows and big terrace overlook the train tracks. You can eat from the Persian inspired menu during the day, while evenings are all about DJ sets, film screenings and supper clubs.

> **LAZY MONDAYS**
>
> The East End is peppered with some fascinating and quirky sights, but unfortunately many of them have irregular opening hours, and can be closed on Mondays – as are a number of restaurants, cafes and some shops. There are plenty of parks, waterways and neighbourhoods perfect for exploring, and many a pub in which to rest your feet and grab a bite to eat. Two of the area's best sights, the Museum of Childhood and the Museum of London Docklands, are open daily.

ROYAL OAK PUB

Map p454 (www.royaloaklondon.com; 73 Columbia Rd, E2; ⊙4-11pm Mon-Fri, noon-11pm Sat & Sun; ⊖Hoxton) Lovely wood-panelled pub arranged around a handsome central bar with a good selection of bitter and a better-than-average wine list. There's also a little garden at the back and great food. It really gets into its stride on Sunday when London's famous flower market is just outside the door.

BETHNAL GREEN WORKING MEN'S CLUB CLUB

Map p454 (www.workersplaytime.net; 42-44 Pollard Row, E2; ⊙8pm-2am, days vary; ⊖Bethnal Green) As it says on the tin, this is a true working men's club, which has opened its doors and let in all kinds of off-the-wall club nights, including trashy burlesque, vintage nights of all eras, beach parties and bake offs. Expect sticky carpets, a shimmery stage set and a space akin to a school-hall disco.

NELSONS HEAD GAY

Map p454 (www.nelsonshead.com; 32 Horatio St, E2; ⊙from 4pm Mon-Sat, 9am-11pm Sun; ⊖Hoxton) Small, down-to-earth locals' pub with quirky decor, a fun and friendly mixed clientele, and plenty of camp tunes.

JOINERS ARMS GAY

Map p454 (www.joinershoreditch.com; 116-118 Hackney Rd, E2; ⊙5pm-3am; 55, ⊖Hoxton) Determinedly run-down and cheesy, the Joiners is Hoxton's only totally gay pub-club. It's a crowded, funky old boozer where hip gay boys hang out at the bar, dance and watch people play pool all night.

Mile End & Victoria Park

★ROYAL INN ON THE PARK PUB

Map p454 (www.royalinnonthepark.com; 111 Lauriston Rd, E9; noon-11pm; ; Mile End then 277) On the northern border of Victoria Park, this excellent place, once a poster pub for Transport for London, has a half-dozen real ales and Czech lagers on tap, outside seating to the front and a recently made-over garden at the back. It's always lively and attracts a mixed boho/louche Hackney crowd.

★PALM TREE PUB

Map p454 (127 Grove Rd, E3; to 2am Fri & Sat, to 1am Sun; 277, Mile End) The Palm, the quintessential East End pub on the Regent's Canal, is loved by locals, students and trendies alike, with its comforting gold-flock wallpaper, photos of also-ran crooners and a handful of different guest ales every week. There's jazz on Friday and Saturday from around 9.30pm.

BRITANNIA PUB

Map p454 (www.drinkinlondon.co.uk/britannia; 360 Victoria Park Rd, E9; noon-11pm Sun-Thu, to 1am Fri, to 2am Sat; ; 388, Homerton) A large, rambling old pub with a fabulous beer garden right on the park, with a barbecue running throughout the day on summer weekends. Also serves tasty gastropub dishes and a decent range of drinks.

Stratford

KING EDWARD VII PUB

(www.kingeddie.co.uk; 47 Broadway, E15; noon-11pm Sun-Wed, noon-midnight Thu-Sat; Stratford) Built in the 19th century this lovely old boozer is a series of handsome rooms set around a central bar. The saloon and front bar are the most convivial, and there's a little leafy courtyard at the back. A decent selection of ales and wine, and some great pub grub, make this a real highlight of the area.

Wapping & Limehouse

★GRAPES PUB

Map p454 (www.thegrapes.co.uk; 76 Narrow St, E14; noon-3pm & 5.30-11pm Mon-Wed, noon-11pm Thu-Sun; DRL Limehouse) One of Limehouse's renowned historic pubs – there's apparently been a drinking house here since 1583 – the Grapes is tiny, especially the riverside terrace, which can only really comfortably fit about a half-dozen close friends, but it's cosy inside and exudes plenty of old-world charm.

PROSPECT OF WHITBY PUB

Map p454 (57 Wapping Wall, E1; noon-11pm Sun-Thu, to midnight Fri & Sat; ; Wapping) Once known as the Devil's Tavern, the Whitby is said to date from 1520, making it the oldest riverside pub in London. It's firmly on the tourist trail now, but there's a smallish terrace to the front and the side overlooking the Thames, a decent restaurant upstairs and open fires in winter.

Check out the wonderful pewter bar – Samuel Pepys once sidled up to it to sup.

CAPTAIN KIDD PUB

Map p454 (108 Wapping High St, E1; noon-11pm; ; Wapping) With its large windows, fine beer garden and displays recalling the hanging nearby of the eponymous pirate in 1701, this is a favourite riverside pub in Wapping. Although cleverly done up, it actually only dates back to the 1980s.

WHITE SWAN GAY

Map p454 (www.bjswhiteswan.com; 556 Commercial Rd, E14; 9pm-1am Mon, to 2am Tue-Thur, to 3am Fri & Sat, 5.30pm-midnight Sun; DLR Limehouse) The White Swan is a fun East End kind of place, with a large dance floor as well as a more relaxed pub area. Its legendary amateur strip night takes place every Wednesday and there are also cabaret and karaoke nights. Club classics and cheesy pop predominate.

☆ ENTERTAINMENT

★WILTON'S THEATRE

Map p454 (020-7702 2789; www.wiltons.org.uk; 1 Graces Alley, E1; tour £6; tour 3pm & 6pm Mon, Mahogany Bar 5-11pm Mon-Fri; DLR Tower Gateway, Tower Hill) A gloriously atmospheric example of one of London's Victorian public-house music halls, Wilton's hosts a real variety of shows, from comedy and classical music to literary theatre and opera. You can also take a one-hour guided tour of the building to hear more about its fascinating history.

The hall's Mahogany Bar is a great way to get a taste of the place if you're not attending a performance.

BISTROTHEQUE CABARET, BAR

Map p454 (☎020-8983 7900; www.bistrotheque.com; 23-27 Wadeston St, E2; ⏰5.30pm-midnight Mon-Fri, 11am-midnight Sat, 11am-11pm Sun; Cambridge Heath, Bethnal Green) This converted warehouse offers hilarious transvestite lip-synching in its ground-floor Cabaret Room and high-quality dining in its stylish whitewashed restaurant above. It's also worth coming just for the Napoleon bar, a moody, slightly decadent room with dark walls (the oak panels came from a stately home in Northumberland) and plush seating; the drinks are expertly mixed and the bar staff always friendly.

HACKNEY EMPIRE THEATRE

Map p454 (☎020-8985 2424; www.hackneyempire.co.uk; 291 Mare St, E8; 38 or 277, Hackney Central) The programing at this renovated Edwardian Music Hall (1901) is eclectic to say the least and certainly defines 'something for everyone' – from hard-edged political theatre to opera and comedy. The Empire is definitely one of the best places to catch a pantomime at Christmas.

SHOPPING

The boutiques and galleries lining Columbia Rd (which are usually open at the weekend only) and the shops along Broadway Market and Cheshire St are part of London's up-and-coming independent retail scenes. If you're after something a little more mainstream, Westfield Stratford City, currently Europe's largest urban shopping centre, can't fail to satisfy. There's also a shopping mall beneath the Canary Wharf skyscrapers, with similar shops, bars and restaurants.

★COLUMBIA ROAD FLOWER MARKET MARKET

Map p454 (Columbia Rd, E2; ⏰8am-3pm Sun; Old St) A real explosion of colour and life, this weekly market sells a beautiful array of flowers, pot plants, bulbs, seeds and everything you might need for the garden. A lot of fun, even if you don't buy anything, the market gets really packed so go as early as you can, or later on, when the vendors sell off the cut flowers cheaply. It stretches from Gossett St to the Royal Oak pub.

BROADWAY MARKET MARKET

Map p454 (www.broadwaymarket.co.uk; London Fields, E8; ⏰9am-5pm Sat; Bethnal Green) There's been a market down this pretty street since the late 19th century, the focus of which has these days become artisan food, arty knick-knacks, books, records and vintage clothing. A great place on a Saturday, followed by a picnic at London Fields (p225) park.

JONES DAIRY FOOD

Map p454 (www.jonesdairy.co.uk; 23 Ezra St, E2; ⏰9am-1pm Fri-Sun; Hoxton) This wonderfully preserved shop, set on an atmospheric cobblestoned street, opened in 1902 and was once part of a chain of Welsh dairies across the capital. You can still choose from a quality selection of cheeses, alongside breads, coffees, teas, jams and cakes. Perfect for stocking up on picnic food; there's also a cute little cafe round the back.

BEYOND RETRO VINTAGE

Map p454 (www.beyondretro.com; 110-112 Cheshire St, E2; Bethnal Green, Shoreditch High St) Huge selection of vintage clothes, including wigs, shoes, jackets and lingerie, expertly slung together in a lofty warehouse.

CARHARTT OUTLET STORE FASHION

Map p454 (www.thecarharttstore.co.uk; 18 Ellingfort Rd, E8; London Fields, Hackney Central) You'll find hoodies, sweats and jeans at this outlet of the street-wear label, as well as a small selection of similar brands. It's tucked away on a residential street, under the railway arches just north of London Fields station. Ring the bell to get in.

BURBERRY OUTLET SHOP FASHION

Map p454 (29-31 Chatham Pl, E9; 55, Hackney Central) This outlet shop stocks seconds from the reborn-as-trendy Brit brand's current and last season's collections. Prices are around 30% lower than those in the main shopping centres. Service can be brusque.

Hampstead & North London

KING'S CROSS | EUSTON | REGENT'S PARK | CAMDEN | HAMPSTEAD | HIGHGATE | ARSENAL | ISLINGTON | STOKE NEWINGTON | DALSTON

Neighbourhood Top Five

1. Walking in the gorgeous **Hampstead Heath** (p246): enjoying the sweeping views of London from Parliament Hill, getting a culture fix at the beautiful Kenwood House and slumping in a couch at the Garden Gate pub to recover.

2. Shopping at **Camden Market** (p245): having lunch at one of the food stalls and finishing your day with a leisurely stroll along Regent's Canal.

3. Discovering the treasures of the **British Library** (p240) and marvelling at the sheer amount of knowledge stored within its walls.

4. Enjoying a thought-provoking day exploring the concepts of life, death and art at the **Wellcome Collection** (p244).

5. Going out in **Dalston** (p248) for superb kebabs and an afternoon of vintage shopping.

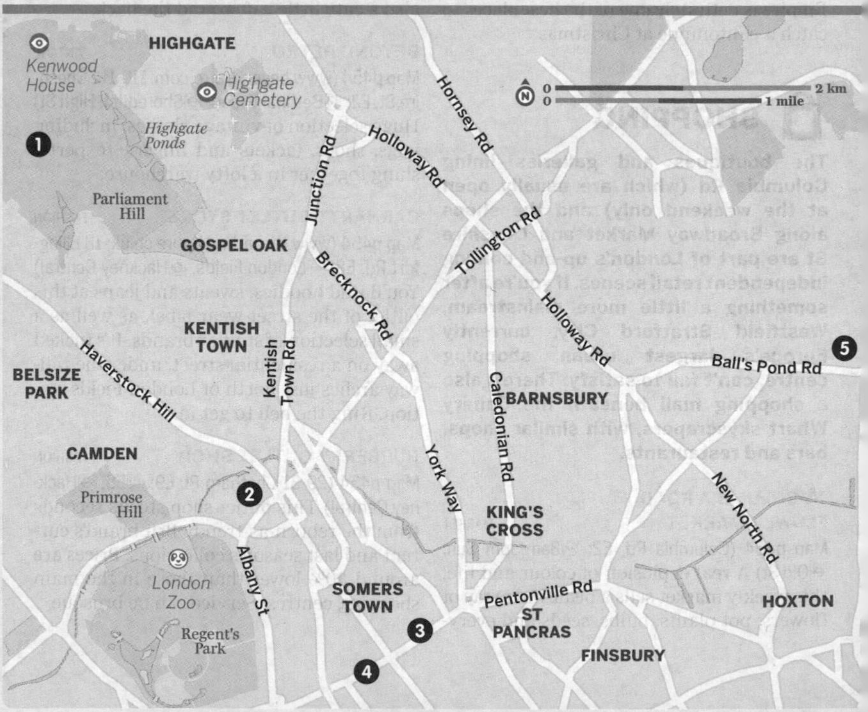

For more detail of this area see Map p456, p459 and p460

Explore: Hampstead & North London

North London is a big place – you could spend a week exploring its parks, checking the sights, lounging in gastropubs and sampling the nightlife. So if you're short on time, you'll have to pick and choose carefully.

Hampstead Heath and Camden Market should be top of your list; Camden is a major sight and its energy is intoxicating, while Hampstead Heath will offer a glorious day out and an insight into how North Londoners spend their weekend. The Wellcome Collection and the British Library are also highly recommended and easily accessible, thanks to their central location.

Because this part of London is predominantly residential, it is at its busiest at the weekend. This means that most sights are relatively quiet during the week, with the exception of the Wellcome Collection and the British Library.

On the whole, North London is a wealthy area, full of 20- or 30-somethings (Camden, Islington, Dalston), young families (Hampstead, Highgate, Stoke Newington) and celebrities (Primrose Hill). The nightlife is excellent wherever you go, with edgy and offbeat bars in Dalston, excellent pubs in Hampstead and Islington and great live music in Camden.

Local Life

➡ **Live music** North London is well known for being the home of indie rock. Music fans flock to Barfly (p259), Forum (p259) and the Bull & Gate (p259) to watch bands aiming for the big time.

➡ **Sunday pub lunch** This institution of English life has been embraced in earnest by gastropubs making a brisk trade. Favourites include the Garden Gate (p256) and the Stag (p252) or brunch at Duke's Brew & Que (p254).

➡ **Swimming** Hampstead Heath's ponds (p261) are open year-round and a small group of hard-core aficionados swim every day, rain or shine.

Getting There & Away

➡ **Underground** Northern Line stops include Camden, Hampstead, Highgate and Angel.

➡ **Overground** The Overground crosses North London from east to west and is useful for areas such as Dalston that are not connected to the tube. The new East London Overground line runs through the east and on to South London.

➡ **Bus** There is a good network of buses in North London connecting various neighbourhoods to each other and the centre of town.

Lonely Planet's Top Tip

North London is all about parks, so make sure you set aside a few hours during your stay to enjoy the greenery. Pack a picnic and do as Londoners do: head to the pub afterwards!

Best Places to Eat

➡ Trullo (p252)

➡ Duke's Brew & Que (p254)

➡ Mangal Ocakbasi (p253)

➡ Ottolenghi (p252)

➡ Market (p251)

For reviews, see p248 ➡

Best Places to Drink

➡ Edinboro Castle (p255)

➡ Bar Pepito (p254)

➡ Drink, Shop & Do (p254)

➡ Garden Gate (p256)

➡ Spaniard's Inn (p256)

For reviews, see p254 ➡

Best for Live Music

➡ Passing Clouds (p257)

➡ Vortex Jazz Club (p258)

➡ Bull & Gate (p259)

➡ Blues Kitchen (p258)

➡ Barfly (p259)

For reviews, see p257 ➡

REX BUTCHER / GETTY IMAGES ©

TOP SIGHT
BRITISH LIBRARY

In 1998 the British Library moved to its new premises between King's Cross and Euston stations. At a cost of £500 million (the original budget was £50 million), it was one of Britain's most expensive buildings, and not one that is universally loved. Colin St John Wilson's exterior of straight lines of red brick, which Prince Charles reckoned was akin to a 'secret-police building', is certainly not to all tastes. But even those who don't like the building from the outside will be won over by the spectacularly cool and spacious interior.

The British Library is the nation's principal copyright library: it contains 180 million items and stocks one copy of every British and Irish publication as well as historic manuscripts, books and maps from the British Museum (the Bodleian Library at Oxford University and the Cambridge University Library fulfil the same functions).

What you can see is the tip of the iceberg. Under your feet, on five basement levels, run some 625 km of shelving (growing by 12 km every year). The library currently contains 14 million books, 920,000 journal and newspaper titles, 58 million patents, 8 million stamps, and 3 million sound recordings.

DON'T MISS...

- King's Library
- Sir John Ritblat Gallery
- Exhibitions
- Philatelic Exhibition

PRACTICALITIES

- Map p456
- www.bl.uk
- 96 Euston Rd, NW1
- exhibition cost varies
- 9.30am-6pm Mon & Wed-Fri, to 8pm Tue, to 5pm Sat, 11am-5pm Sun
- (wi-fi)
- King's Cross/St Pancras

King's Library

At the centre of the building is the wonderful King's Library, the 85,000-volume collection of King George III, displayed in an eerily beautiful six-storey, 17m-high **glass-walled tower**.

The collection is considered one of the most significant of the Enlightenment period, and it was bequeathed to the nation by George III's son, George IV, in 1823. It was decided that the volumes would be kept at the British Museum, in the specially built King's Library

Gallery. But after a bomb fell on the collection during WWII, it was moved to the Bodleian Library in Oxford and only finally moved back to London in 1998 when the new British Library opened.

Sir John Ritblat Gallery

For visitors, the highlight of a visit to the British Library is the Sir John Ritblat Gallery where the library keeps its most precious and high-profile documents. The collection spans almost three millennia and contains manuscripts, religious texts, maps, music scores, autographs, diaries and more.

Rare texts from all the main religions include the **Codex Sinaiticus**, the first complete text of the New Testament, written in Greek in the 4th century; a **Gutenberg Bible** (1455), the first Western book printed using movable type; and the stunningly illustrated **Jain sacred texts**.

There are also historical documents, including one of four remaining copies of **Magna Carta** (1215), the charter credited with setting out the basis of human rights in English law. Not so important but poignant is **Captain Scott's final diary** including an account of fellow explorer Lawrence Oates's death.

Literature is also well represented, with **Shakespeare's First Folio** (1623) and manuscripts by some of Britain's best-known authors (such as Lewis Carroll, Jane Austen, George Eliot and Thomas Hardy). Music fans will love the **Beatles' earliest handwritten lyrics** and original scores by Handel, Mozart and Beethoven.

Exhibitions

As well as hosting excellent permanent collections, the British Library runs regular temporary exhibitions in the PACCAR gallery, all connected to its records. Previous exhibitions included Mughal India: Art, Culture and Empire and an exhibition on international state propaganda over the last two centuries. Admission charges vary from £6 to £9 for adults.

Smaller and free exhibitions also take place in the Folio Society Gallery on various authors, genres and themes (science fiction, the census, crime fiction etc).

The Philatelic Collection

The Philatelic Exhibition, next to the Sir John Ritblat Gallery, is based on collections established in the 19th century and now consists of more than 80,000 items, including postage and revenue stamps and postal stationery from almost every country and all periods. They're not exactly put to their advantage in those sliding racks but it's deliberate – the stamps are fragile and the less they're exposed to light, the better.

LIBRARY CAFES

All the catering at the British Library comes courtesy of the wonderful Peyton & Byrne, the progeny of Irish chef Oliver Peyton. There are three main outfits: the 1st-floor **restaurant** (British Library, 96 Euston Rd, N1; mains £5-10; ⌚9.30am-5pm Mon-Fri, to 4pm Sat; wi-fi), with spectacular views of the King's Library Tower and treats such as made-to-order stir-fries; **Café** (British Library, 96 Euston Rd, NW1; ⌚9.30am-7.30pm Mon-Thu, to 5.30pm Fri, to 4.30pm Sat & Sun; wi-fi) on the ground floor, which serves hot drinks, pastries and sandwiches; and the **Espresso Bar** (96 Euston Rd, NW1; ⌚8am-7pm Mon-Fri, 9am-5.30pm Sat, 10am-4pm Sun) which serves similar fare as Café as well as fresh *churros*.

The British Library has wi-fi throughout the building. You need to register to use it, but it is free of charge.

BEN QUEENBOROUGH / GETTY IMAGES ©

TOP SIGHT
LONDON ZOO

Established in 1828, these zoological gardens are among the oldest in the world, and are where the word 'zoo' originated. The emphasis nowadays is firmly placed on conservation, education and breeding (the zoo is involved in some 130 breeding programs), with fewer species and more spacious conditions.

The newest development is **Tiger Territory**, a little slice of Indonesian forest and new home to the zoo's two endangered Sumatran tigers. The enclosure is much larger than the previous one and allows the animals to climb and bathe as well as wander around more freely.

Penguin Beach, with its cool underwater viewing area, is another popular attraction and is a key element of London Zoo's breeding program of Humboldt, macaroni, black-footed and rockhopper penguins.

London Zoo is also active in gorilla conservation in Gabon and the Democratic Republic of Congo in central Africa. The park has four gorillas who live on their own island, **Gorilla Kingdom**.

For a more inclusive experience, head to the lovely **Clore Rainforest Lookout and Nightzone**, a slice of the South American rainforest complete with marmosets, monkeys, fruit bats and other creatures wandering and flying freely among the visitors inside the humid, tropical-climate room. We love the hot and humid **Butterfly Paradise** where myriad butterflies and moths flutter from flower to flower.

There are feeding sessions or talks throughout the day, which are a great way to learn more about bird-eating spiders, cheeky squirrel monkeys or predatory birds.

There is also plenty to see indoors, with an **aquarium**, a **reptile house** and a building called **Bugs** full of creepy-crawlies.

You can save 20% of the entry fee by booking online.

DON'T MISS...

- Tiger Territory
- Penguin Beach
- Gorilla Kingdom
- Clore Rainforest
- Butterfly Paradise

PRACTICALITIES

- Map p460
- www.londonzoo.co.uk
- Outer Circle, Regent's Park, NW1
- adult/child £25/19
- 10am-5.30pm Mar-Oct, to 4pm Nov-Feb
- Camden Town

SIGHTS

King's Cross & Euston

BRITISH LIBRARY LIBRARY
See p240.

ST PANCRAS CHAMBERS HISTORIC BUILDING
Map p456 (020-7841 3569; Euston Rd, NW1; £20; tours 1½ hrs) Looking at the jaw-dropping Gothic elegance of St Pancras, it's hard to believe that the 1873 Midland Grand Hotel languished empty for years and even faced demolition in the 1960s. Now home to a five-star hotel and 66 luxury apartments, St Pancras has been restored to its former glory and can be visited by guided tour (advanced booking only).

Tours take you on a fascinating journey through the building's history, from its inception as the southern terminus for the Midlands Railway line to its slow fall from grace and eventual revival. The Midland Grand Hotel was incredibly modern when it opened but lack of maintenance meant the building was derelict by the 1930s and the hotel closed. St Pancras was then used for railway offices and finally abandoned in 1988. It was only when plans to use St Pancras as the Eurostar terminal came up in the 1990s that local authorities decided to renovate the building and open a hotel. The Eurostar arrived in 2007 and the hotel opened in 2011.

Royden Stock, the hotel historian, has a long association with the building (St Pancras is a very popular film location and Stock used to work on-site with film crews) and knows it inside out. You'll get to walk up the glorious grand staircase, wander around the exquisitely decorated corridors and visit one of the 30-odd Victorian rooms.

LONDON CANAL MUSEUM MUSEUM
Map p456 (www.canalmuseum.org.uk; 12-13 New Wharf Rd, N1; adult/child £4/2; 10am-4.30pm Tue-Sun & bank holidays; King's Cross/St Pancras) This quirky but fascinating museum is in an old ice warehouse (with a deep well where the frozen commodity was stored) dating from the 1860s. It traces the history of Regent's Canal and the ice business (the ice trade was huge in late Victorian London, with 35,000 tonnes imported from Norway in 1899).

You can access the wharf at the back of the museum where a number of narrow boats are moored. The exhibits in the stables upstairs are dedicated to the history of canal transport in Britain.

Regent's Park

LONDON ZOO ZOO
See p242.

KING'S CROSS' REGENERATION

King's Cross used to be something of a blind spot on London's map, somewhere you only ever went through rather than to. The area was the capital's red light district, and when the British Library first opened here in 1998, drug addicts could regularly be found in the toilets. In fact, it was the area's reputation that had poured cold water on plans to renovate St Pancras into a new hotel in the 1980s and 1990s.

Fast forward a decade or two, and King's Cross' transformation isn't far from the metamorphosis of East London following the 2012 Olympic Games. The two stations, King's Cross and St Pancras, have played a leading role in this rejuvenation, St Pancras first, with the arrival of the Eurostar in 2007 and the opening of the Renaissance St Pancras Hotel in 2011. Ugly duckling King's Cross is now turning into a swan too, with a complete overhaul of the departures concourse, which sits under a magnificent, canopy-like curving roof.

The forecourt of the station is also getting a facelift, with the Victorian, double-arched brick facade being given pride of place, and the back of the station being transformed into desirable real estate. In early 2013, Google announced it would be moving its UK headquarters there in 2016 for the tidy sum of £1 billion.

Expect plenty of new shops, restaurants and bars to pop up along **King's Blvd**, and **Granary Square** to become an increasingly popular space for outdoor events. Check www.kingscross.co.uk for the latest news and developments.

TOP SIGHT
WELLCOME COLLECTION

The Wellcome Collection styles itself as a 'destination for the incurably curious', a pretty accurate tag for an institution that seeks to explore the links between medicine, science, life and art. It's a serious topic but the genius of the museum is that it presents it in an accessible way. The building is light and modern, with varied and interactive displays ranging from interviews with researchers, doctors and patients to art depicting medicine and models of human organs.

The heart of the permanent collection is Sir Henry Wellcome's collection of objects from around the world. Wellcome (1853–1936), a pharmacist, entrepreneur and collector, was fascinated with medicine and amassed more than a million objects from different civilisations associated with life, birth, death and sickness.

The museum also runs outstanding (and free) temporary exhibitions on topics exploring the frontiers of modern medicine, its place in society and its history. Highlights of the last few years include exhibitions on death, dirt, drugs (of the mind-altering kind), the brain, and a controversial series of beautiful black-and-white portraits of individuals before and after their death.

DON'T MISS...

- Temporary exhibitions
- Sir Henry Wellcome's collection

PRACTICALITIES

- Map p460
- www.wellcomecollection.org
- 183 Euston Rd, NW1
- ⌚10am-6pm Tue, Wed, Fri & Sat, 10am-10pm Thu, 11am-6pm Sun
- ⊖Euston Sq

REGENT'S PARK PARK

Map p460 (www.royalparks.org.uk; ⌚5am-dusk; ⊖Regent's Park, Baker St) The most elaborate and ordered of London's many parks, this one was created around 1820 by John Nash, who planned to use it as an estate to build palaces for the aristocracy. Although the plan never quite came off, you can get some idea of what Nash might have achieved from the buildings along the Outer Circle.

Like many of the city's parks, this one was used as a royal hunting ground and then as farmland, before becoming a place for fun and leisure during the 18th century. These days it's a well-organised but relaxed haven in the heart of the city. Among its many attractions are the London Zoo, Regent's Canal along its northern side, an ornamental lake, an open-air theatre in Queen Mary's Gardens where Shakespeare is performed during the summer months, ponds and colourful flowerbeds, rose gardens that look spectacular in June, and sports pitches where Londoners regularly meet to play football, rugby and volleyball.

LORD'S CRICKET GROUND CRICKET GROUND

(www.lords.org; St John's Wood Rd, NW8; tours adult/child £15/9; ⌚tours 11am, noon & 2pm Mon-Fri, 10am & 1pm Sat & Sun; ⊖St John's Wood) The 'home of cricket' is a must for any devotee of this peculiarly English game: book early for the test matches here, but cricket buffs should also take the absorbing and anecdotal 90-minute tour of the ground and facilities.

Tours take in the famous Long Room – where smartly dressed members watch the games surrounded by portraits of cricket's great and good – and a museum featuring evocative memorabilia that will appeal to fans old and new. The famous little urn containing the Ashes, the prize of the most fiercely contested competition in cricket, resides here when in English hands.

Camden

PRIMROSE HILL NEIGHBOURHOOD

Map p460 (⊖Chalk Farm, Camden Town) Wedged between well-heeled Regent's Park and edgy Camden, this little neighbourhood is high on the wish list of most Londoners – but utterly unaffordable. With its independ-

TOP SIGHT
CAMDEN MARKET

Although – or perhaps because – it stopped being cutting-edge several thousand cheap leather jackets ago, Camden market gets a whopping 10 million visitors each year and is one of London's most popular attractions.

What started out as a collection of attractive craft stalls by Camden Lock on the Regent's Canal now extends in various shape or form most of the way from Camden Town tube station to Chalk Farm tube station. There are four main market areas – Buck Street Market (p260), Lock Market (p260), Canal Market (p260) and Stables Market (p260) – although they seem to blend into one with the crowds snaking along and the 'normal' shops lining the streets. You'll find a bit of everything: clothes (of variable quality) in profusion, bags, jewellery, arts and crafts, candles, incense and myriad decorative titbits.

There are dozens of food stalls at the Lock Market and the Stables Market; virtually every type of cuisine is offered, from French to Argentinian, Japanese and Caribbean. Quality varies but is generally pretty good and affordable and you can eat on the big communal tables or by the canal.

DON'T MISS...

- Stables Market
- Lock Market
- Lunch at the food stalls

PRACTICALITIES

- Map p460
- Camden High St, NW1
- 10am-6pm
- Camden Town, Chalk Farm

ent boutiques, lovely restaurants and good pubs, it has a rare village feel. The proximity of the gorgeous, eponymous **park**, with fabulous views of London, is another draw.

On summer weekends the park is absolutely packed with revellers enjoying a picnic with a view, but on weekdays there's mostly dog walkers and nannies and it's a lovely place to enjoy a quiet stroll or an alfresco sandwich.

Famous residents include supermodels Kate Moss and Agyness Deyn, actors Jude Law, Helena Bonham-Carter, Sienna Miller and many more. Part of the fun is to come and celebrity-spot.

ANNROY GALLERY

Map p460 (www.rankin.co.uk; 110-114 Grafton Rd, NW5; 11am-6pm Mon-Fri; Gospel Oak, Kentish Town) FREE This inconspicuous building in Kentish Town is photographer Rankin's studio and editorial headquarters (where legendary titles such as *Dazed & Confused* are published). The ground floor doubles as a small gallery where Rankin's images, most of them the size of a wall, are exhibited. Displays change every few weeks and you might get the chance to peek in the studio.

Hampstead & Highgate

NO 2 WILLOW ROAD HOUSE

Map p459 (www.nationaltrust.org.uk/2-willow-road; 2 Willow Rd, NW3; adult/child £6/3; 11am-5pm Wed-Sun Mar-Oct, tours 11am, noon, 1pm & 2pm; Hampstead Heath, Hampstead) Fans of modern architecture will want to swing past this property, the central house in a block of three, designed by the 'structural rationalist' Ernö Goldfinger in 1939. Many people think it looks uncannily like the sort of mundane 1950s architecture you see everywhere. It may do now, but 2 Willow Rd was in fact a forerunner in this style.

COMBINED TICKET

Visitors interested in seeing both No 2 Willow Rd and Fenton House (highly recommended!) should get a combined ticket (£9) to save a few pounds. The two sights are only about 15 minutes' walk from each other across leafy Hampstead.

The interior has cleverly designed storage space, amazing light (rooms that couldn't have a side window have a skylight) and collection of artworks by Henry Moore, Max Ernst and Bridget Riley. It's accessible to all, thanks to hugely knowledgeable staff. Entry is by guided tour only until 3pm, after which nonguided viewing is allowed.

FENTON HOUSE HISTORIC BUILDING

Map p459 (www.nationaltrust.org.uk/fenton-house; Windmill Hill, Hampstead Grove, NW3; adult/child £6.50/3; ⏲11am-5pm Wed-Sun Mar-Oct; ⊖Hampstead) One of the oldest houses in Hampstead, this late-17th-century merchant's residence has a charming walled garden with roses and an orchard, fine collections of porcelain and keyboard instruments – including a 1612 harpsichord played by Handel. The interior is very evocative thanks to original Georgian furniture and period art, such as 17th-century needlework pictures.

KEATS HOUSE HISTORIC BUILDING

Map p459 (www.keatshouse.org.uk; Wentworth Pl, Keats Grove, NW3; adult/child £5/free; ⏲1-5pm Tue-Sun May-Oct, Fri-Sun Nov-Apr; 🚉Hampstead Heath, ⊖Hampstead) This elegant Regency house was home to the golden boy of the Romantic poets from 1818 to 1820. Never short of generous mates, Keats was persuaded to take refuge here by Charles Armitage Brown, and it was here that he met his fiancée Fanny Brawne, literally the girl next door.

Keats wrote his most celebrated poem, 'Ode to a Nightingale', while sitting under a plum tree in the garden (no longer there), in 1819. The house is sparsely furnished but does a good job of conveying what daily life would have been like in Keats' day.

⊙ Arsenal

ARSENAL EMIRATES STADIUM STADIUM

(www.arsenal.com/tours; 75 Drayton Park, N5; self-guided tour adult/child £17.50/9; ⏲10am-6pm Mon-Sat, to 4pm Sun; ⊖Arsenal, Finsbury Park, Highbury & Islington) When Arsenal's new stadium (named after corporate sponsor Emirates Airlines) opened in 2006, fans claimed it would never be the same again. It's true that the 64,000-seat stadium lacks the bonhomie of the old Highbury grounds, but it's still a sell-out at every game. Visitors

TOP SIGHT HAMPSTEAD HEATH

Sprawling Hampstead Heath, with its rolling woodlands and meadows, feels a million miles away – despite being approximately four – from the City of London. It covers 320 hectares, most of it woods, hills and meadows, and is home to about 180 bird species, 23 species of butterflies, grass snakes, bats and a rich array of flora. It's a wonderful place for a ramble, especially to the top of **Parliament Hill** (Map p459), which offers expansive views across the city and is one of the most popular places in London to fly a kite. Alternatively head up the hill in North Wood or lose yourself in the West Heath.

If walking is too pedestrian for you, another major attraction are the bathing ponds (p261; separate beautiful ones for men and women and a slightly less pleasant mixed pond).

Those of a more artistic bent should make a beeline for Kenwood House (p248) but stop to admire the **sculptures by Henry Moore and Barbara Hepworth** (Map p459) on the way.

Once you've had your fill of fresh air and/or culture, do as Londoners do and head to one of the wonderful nearby pubs for a restorative pint.

DON'T MISS...

- Views from Parliament Hill
- Strolling in the woodlands
- Swimming in the bathing ponds
- Henry Moore and Barbara Hepworth sculptures

PRACTICALITIES

- Map p459
- 🚉Gospel Oak, Hampstead Heath, ⊖Hampstead

TOP SIGHT
HIGHGATE CEMETERY

Most famous as the final resting place of **Karl Marx**, **George Eliot** (pseudonym of Mary Ann Evans) and other notable mortals, Highgate Cemetery is set in 20 wonderfully wild and atmospheric hectares, with dramatic and overdecorated Victorian family crypts. It is divided into two parts on either side of Swain's Lane, with Marx and Eliot on the eastern side.

The real draw is the overgrown western section of this Victorian Valhalla. To visit it, you'll have to take a **tour** (adult/child £12/6; ⊙1.45pm Mon-Fri, hourly from 11am to 3pm Sat & Sun Nov-Mar, to 4pm Apr-Oct). Note that children under eight are not allowed to join and that tours on weekdays must be booked in advance online. A maze of winding paths leads to the **Circle of Lebanon**, rings of tombs flanking a circular path and topped with a majestic cedar of Lebanon tree. Guides will point out the various symbols and the eminent dead occupying the tombs.

Highgate remains a working cemetery – the most recent well-known addition was Russian dissident Alexander Litvinenko, who died under sinister circumstances in 2006, when the radioactive isotope Polonium 210 somehow made it into his tea in a Mayfair hotel.

DON'T MISS...

- Karl Marx's grave
- Tour of the West Cemetery
- Circle of Lebanon

PRACTICALITIES

- Map p459
- www.highgatecemetery.org
- Swain's Lane, N6
- East Cemetery adult/child £4/free
- ⊙10am-5pm Mon-Fri, from 11am Sat & Sun
- ⊖Archway

will struggle to get tickets, so visit the stadium on a tour instead.

Audio self-guided tours are available in eight languages and are very entertaining for anyone with a vague interest in football. Tours take you everywhere from the back entrance used by the players to the entertainment suites where corporate bigwigs watch the game. You'll get to walk to the pitch through 'the tunnel', sit on the team's pitch-side benches and even check out the changing rooms (complete with spa and physio suite on Arsenal's side).

Tours also include entry to the museum, which focuses on the history of the club and the fans, and is therefore likely to only interest the most ardent Arsenal supporters. Visits finish in the stadium's enormous shop where Arsenal merchandise of every guise is available.

Islington

ESTORICK COLLECTION OF MODERN ITALIAN ART GALLERY

Map p456 (www.estorickcollection.com; 39a Canonbury Sq, N1; adult/child £5/free; ⊙11am-6pm Wed-Sat, noon-5pm Sun; ⊖Highbury & Islington) The only gallery in Britain devoted to Italian art, and one of the leading collections of futurist painting in the world, the Estorick Collection is housed in a listed Georgian building and stuffed with works by such greats as Giacomo Balla, Umberto Boccioni, Gino Severini and Amedeo Modigliani.

The collection of paintings, drawings, etchings and sculpture was amassed by American writer and art dealer Eric Estorick and his wife Salome. Well-conceived special exhibitions have included many 20th-century art movements and lesser-known artists from Italy and beyond. The gallery also encompasses an extensive library, cafe and shop.

Stoke Newington

ABNEY PARK CEMETERY CEMETERY

(www.abney-park.org.uk; Stoke Newington Church St, N16; ⊙8am-dusk; 🚌73, 106, 149, 243, 276, 476, ⊖Stoke Newington) This magical place was bought and developed by a private firm in 1840 to provide burial grounds for central London's overflow. It was a dissenters (ie non-Church of England) cemetery and many of the most influential Presbyterians, Quakers and Baptists are buried here, including the Salvation Army founder, William Booth.

Since the 1950s the cemetery has been left to fend for itself and, these days, is as much a bird and plant sanctuary, a gay cruising ground and a hang-out for some of Hackney's least salubrious drug users, as a delightfully overgrown ruin. The derelict chapel at its centre could be right out of a horror film, and the atmosphere of the whole place is nothing short of magical.

Dalston

RIDLEY ROAD MARKET MARKET

Map p456 (Ridley Rd, E8; 6am-6pm Mon-Sat; Dalston Kingsland, Dalston Junction) Massively enjoyed by the ethnically diverse community it serves, this market is best for its exotic fruit and vegetables, specialist cuts of meat and colourful fabrics. You'll also find the usual assortment of plastic tat, cheap clothing and mobile-phone accessories.

EASTERN CURVE GARDENS GARDENS

Map p456 (www.dalstongarden.org; 13 Dalston Lane, E8; 11am-6pm Tue-Sun; Dalston Junction, Dalston Kingsland) This lovely garden is typical of the kind of regeneration happening around Dalston: a project led by the community, for the community, and a roaring success. There are workshops and events almost every day, from gardening sessions to building a greenhouse. It's a nice place to just sit down for a while or to meet friendly locals.

The site used to be a derelict railway line and the garden has used the old sleepers to make a boardwalk and raised beds for the veggie patch.

EATING

North London is full of eating gems. With its historic pubs, smart cafes, market stalls and gastronomic restaurants, this is not a place where you'll be left without options. Islington has the most gourmet addresses; elsewhere you'll find a large choice running from Austrian and Greek to Russian and Turkish.

TOP SIGHT KENWOOD HOUSE

This magnificent neoclassical mansion stands at the northern end of Hampstead Heath in a glorious sweep of landscaped gardens leading down to a picturesque lake.

The house was remodelled by Robert Adam in the 18th century, and rescued from developers by Lord Iveagh Guinness, who donated it and the wonderful collection of art it contains to the nation in 1927. The Iveagh Bequest, as it is known, contains paintings by such greats as Rembrandt (one of his many self-portraits), Constable, Turner, Hals, Vermeer and Van Dyck and is one of the finest small collections in Britain.

Robert Adam's Great Stairs and the library are especially fine. The Suffolk Collection is also noteworthy with Jacobean portraits by William Larkin and royal Stuart portraits by Van Dyck and Lely.

Kenwood House was undergoing substantial refurbishment at the time of writing and planned to reopen in all its glory in late 2013.

Located in what was once the servants' wing of Kenwood House, the **Brew House Café** has delicious food, from light snacks to full meals (mains around £8), and plenty of room on the lovely garden terrace.

DON'T MISS...

- Self-portrait by Rembrandt
- *Hampstead Heath*, by Constable
- Strolling in the landscaped gardens

PRACTICALITIES

- Map p459
- www.english-heritage.org.uk
- Hampstead Lane, NW3
- Gospel Oak, Hampstead Heath

King's Cross & Euston

★PEYTON & BYRNE AT THE WELLCOME COLLECTION
CAFE £

Map p460 (www.peytonandbyrne.co.uk; Wellcome Collection, 183 Euston Rd, NW1; mains £3-7.50; ⏲10am-6pm Fri-Wed, 10am-10pm Thu; ; ⊖Euston, Euston Square) At first sight, this is a museum cafe like any other, with a bright, canteen-like atmosphere. But step closer to the counter and things start looking distinctly gourmet. There are freshly made pies and quiches, soups, mounds of exotic salads, and a mouth-watering array of cakes. Everything is top-notch, copious and unbelievably good value.

KARPO
MODERN BRITISH ££

Map p456 (www.karpo.co.uk; 23-27 Euston Rd, NW1; mains £10-16; ⏲7am-11pm; ; ⊖King's Cross/St Pancras) There is something utterly refreshing about Karpo, with its bright, modern space, its 'living wall', gracious service and delicious, seasonal menu served round the clock. It all looks effortless. Expect plenty of revitalised British classics such as duck eggs, Jerusalem artichokes, purple sprouting broccoli, cod and lamb. The lunch special of sandwich and soup for £5 has to be London's best bargain.

CARAVAN
MEDITERRANEAN ££

Map p456 (020-7101 7661; www.caravankingscross.co.uk; Granary Bldg, 1 Granary Sq, N1C; mains £7-15; ⏲8am-10.30pm Mon-Thu, 8am-midnight Fri, 10am-midnight Sat, 10am-4pm Sun; ; ⊖King's Cross/St Pancras) In the freshly renovated Granary Building on the edge of Regent's Canal, Caravan dishes out tasty fusion Mediterranean food. You can opt for several small plates to share meze-/tapas-style or stick to main-sized plates. The restaurant is huge and has industrial-chic style down to a T. It's popular, so book.

Camden

★DIRTY BURGER
BURGERS £

Map p459 (www.eatdirtyburger.com; Sanderson Cl, 79 Highgate Rd, NW5; burger £5.50; ⏲7am-midnight Mon-Thu, 7am-1am Fri, 9am-1am Sat, 9am-11pm Sun; Gospel Oak, ⊖Kentish Town) The beauty of Dirty Burger, a chic shack rather than a restaurant, is its simplicity: apart from sausages and bacon until 11am, Dirty Burger does nothing but burgers. And what burgers: thick, juicy, horribly messy, with mustard, gherkin and cheese.

They also do delicious fries and the best milkshakes this side of the Atlantic (with just three flavours, to keep it real – vanilla, strawberry and chocolate). You can eat in or take away to the nearby greenery of Hampstead Heath.

WORTH A DETOUR

WILLIAM MORRIS GALLERY

Fans of Victoriana and the Arts & Crafts movement should make time for this sensational little **gallery** (www.wmgallery.org.uk; Lloyd Park, Forest Rd, E17; ⏲10am-5pm Wed-Sun; ⊖Walthamstow Central) FREE. Located in Walthamstow in northeast London, it is the former family home of designer William Morris (1834–96), founder of iconic interior design company Morris & Co, famous far and wide for his patterned wallpaper.

The beautiful Georgian mansion re-opened in August 2012 after two years of extensive renovations and the exhibition inside is truly world class. The gallery gives pride of place to Morris' wide-ranging artistic endeavours, with a fantastic workshop explaining his production processes, and a wonderfully evocative recreation of his shop. But it depicts a much more complete portrait of the artist by also covering his writing (for which he was more famous than his designs in his lifetime) and activism. Morris was appalled by the consequences of industrialisation – on manufacturing processes and quality, on people's living conditions and the environment – and he became a socialist in the 1880s, campaigning tirelessly against capitalism.

The strength of the gallery is its beauty and interactiveness, which children will love (as well as the lovely park at the back, complete with play area). The 1st floor also hosts temporary exhibitions (photographer David Bailey was the star of the show in 2013). The gallery's **shop** sells beautiful, Morris-inspired design objects and the **Tea Room** in the glasshouse is the perfect place for a break or a light lunch.

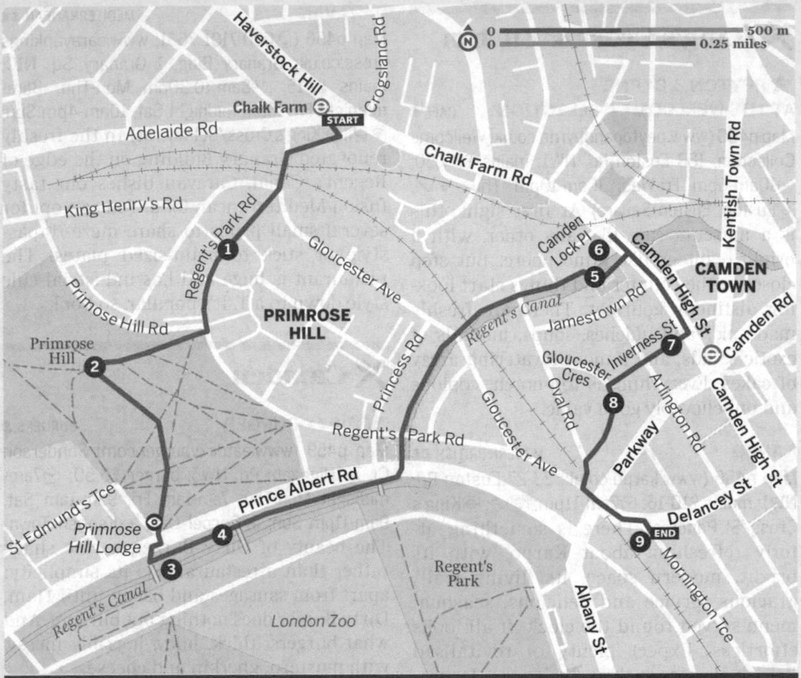

Neighbourhood Walk
A Northern Point of View

START CHALK FARM TUBE STATION
FINISH EDINBORO CASTLE
LENGTH 2.5 MILES; TWO HOURS

This walk takes in some of the big sights of North London – Primrose Hill, Camden – as well as the lesser-known Regent's Canal. When you come out of Chalk Farm tube station, cross the road and walk up Regent's Park Rd, then turn left on the railway bridge and up the southern, boutique-lined, stretch of 1 **Regent's Park Rd**. This is one of London's most affluent neighbourhoods, home to many celebrities, so keep your eyes open for famous faces.

When you reach 2 **Primrose Hill** (p244), walk to the top of the park where you'll be rewarded with a classic view of central London's skyline. On sunny days the park is full of revellers sunbathing, enjoying a picnic or a kickabout.

Walk down the hill through the park bearing right towards Primrose Hill Lodge. Cross the road and join the towpath along 3 **Regent's Canal**, turning left. You'll walk past the huge 4 **London Zoo** (p242) aviary, quaint narrow boats, superb mansions and converted industrial buildings.

At 5 **Camden Lock**, take the footbridge to cross the canal and then turn left on the bridge on Camden High St. Have a mosey at Camden's 6 **Lock Market** (p260). With its original fashion, ethnic art and dozens of food stalls, it is a fun, buzzing place, particularly at weekends. Amble back down Camden High St and turn right onto 7 **Inverness St**, which hosts its own little market and is lined with bars.

When you get to 8 **Gloucester Crescent**, turn left and walk past the glorious Georgian townhouses. At the end of the road, turn left onto Oval Rd, then cross onto Delancey St and make a beeline for the 9 **Edinboro Castle** (p255) where this walk ends, with a well-deserved drink! Warning: if it's a balmy spring or summer day, you may be there awhile. And when you're ready to go home, Camden Town tube station is just a five-minute walk.

★CHIN CHIN LABS ICE CREAM £

Map p460 (www.chinchinlabs.com; 49-50 Camden Lock Pl, NW1; ice-cream from £3.95; ⏲noon-7pm Tue-Sun; ⊖Camden Town, Chalk Farm) This is food chemistry at its absolute best: say hello to the fab liquid-nitrogen ice creams of Chin Chin Labs. Each ice cream is custom-made (chefs prepare the base and freeze it on the spot by adding liquid nitrogen). Flavours change regularly and match the seasons (spiced hot cross bun, mango brûlée, etc). Sauces and toppings are equally creative, from honeycomb to raspberry puree.

To find it, turn towards Camden Lock Market just under the railway bridge – Chin Chin Labs is 100m to the left.

★MARKET MODERN BRITISH ££

Map p460 (☎020-7267 9700; www.marketrestaurant.co.uk; 43 Parkway, NW1; 2-course lunch £10, mains £10-14; ⏲noon-2.30pm & 6-10.30pm Mon-Sat, 1-3.30pm Sun; ⊖Camden Town) This fabulous restaurant is an ode to great, simple British food with a hint of European thrown in. The light and airy space with bare brick walls, steel tables and basic wooden chairs reflects this simplicity. The menu manages to make classic cookery memorable with delights such as roast poussin with baby spring vegetables, and whole plaice with caper butter and chips. Booking advised.

MANGO ROOM CARIBBEAN ££

Map p460 (☎020-7482 5065; www.mangoroom.co.uk; 10-12 Kentish Town Rd, NW1; mains £12-15; ⏲noon-midnight; ⊖Camden Town) With its modern, bright decor and excellent service, Mango Room promises a sophisticated Caribbean experience, with food to match: grilled sea bass with coconut milk and sweet pepper sauce, salt fish with *ackee* (a yellow-skinned Jamaican fruit that has an uncanny resemblance to scrambled eggs), and curried goat with hot pepper and spices, all presented with origami intricacy. Booking recommended.

YORK & ALBANY BRASSERIE ££

Map p460 (www.gordonramsay.com/yorkandalbany; 127-129 Parkway, NW1; mains £14-24, 2-/3-course menu £19/22; ⏲7-11am, noon-3pm & 6-11pm Mon-Sat, 7am-9pm Sun; 📶; ⊖Camden Town) This chic brasserie, part of chef Gordon Ramsay's culinary empire, serves classics with a Mediterranean twist such as roast leg of rabbit with potatoes and lemony anchovies, and confit lamb shoulder with soft polenta. The food is pitch-perfect and the setting informal; you can eat at the bar, in the lounge or the more formal dining room.

The restaurant also does divine pizzas in its wood-fired oven.

LOCAL KNOWLEDGE

WALKING ALONG REGENT'S CANAL

The canals that were once a trade lifeline for the capital have now become a favourite escape for Londoners, providing a quiet walk away from traffic and crowds. For visitors, an added advantage of **Regent's Canal** (Map p460) towpath is that it provides an easy (and delightful) shortcut across North London.

You can, for instance, walk from Little Venice to Camden in less than an hour; on the way, you'll pass Regent's Park, London Zoo, Primrose Hill, beautiful villas designed by architect John Nash as well as redevelopments of old industrial buildings into trendy blocks of flats. Allow 15 to 20 minutes between Camden and Regent's Park, and 25 to 30 minutes between Regent's Park and Little Venice. There are plenty of exits along the way and signposts all along.

If the canals have piqued your curiosity, make a beeline for the London Canal Museum (p243) in King's Cross to learn more about their fascinating history.

NAMAASTE KITCHEN INDIAN ££

Map p460 (www.namaastekitchen.co.uk; 64 Parkway, NW1; mains £7.95-14.95; ⏲noon-2.30pm & 5.30-11pm Mon-Thu, noon-11pm Fri-Sun; 📶; ⊖Camden Town) If there is one thing you should try at Namaaste, it's the kebab platter: although everything is of high standard, the meat and fish coming out of the kitchen grill are beautifully tender and incredibly flavoursome. The bread basket is another hit, with specialities such as Missi Roti (spiced) and Roomali Roti (very thin bread) making a nice change from the usual naans.

Hampstead & Highgate

Most of the pubs listed in the drinking selection for Hampstead & Highgate also do great food.

STAG
GASTROPUB ££

Map p459 (☑020-7722 2646; www.thestag hampstead.com; 67 Fleet Rd, NW3; mains £9.50-15; ☺noon-11pm Mon-Thu, noon-midnight Fri & Sat, noon-10.30pm Sun; ⑭Hampstead Heath) Although the Stag is a pub, it is known far and wide in North London for its outstanding food, its Sunday roast, and its beef-and-ale pie, in particular. The summer BBQ in the garden is another delight. The only bum note is that service can be slow and a little blasé. The trappings of success no doubt. Booking advised.

WELLS TAVERN
GASTROPUB ££

Map p459 (☑020-7794 3785; www.thewells hampstead.co.uk; 30 Well Walk, NW3; mains £12-17; ☺noon-3pm & 7-10pm; ⊜Hampstead) This popular gastropub, with a surprisingly modern interior (given its traditional exterior), is a real blessing in good-restaurant-deprived Hampstead. The menu is proper posh English pub grub – Cumberland sausages, mash and onion gravy, or just a full roast with all the trimmings. At the weekend you'll need to fight to get a table or, more wisely, book.

★GAUCHO GRILL
ARGENTINE £££

Map p459 (☑020-7431 8222; www.gauchores taurants.co.uk; 64 Heath St, NW3; mains £15-52; ☺noon-11pm Mon-Sat, from 10am Sun; ⊜Hampstead) Carnivores, rejoice: this is one of the finest places for steak in London. There are several branches of this Argentinian grill across the capital but this one has the advantage of being less busy than its counterparts, thanks to its residential setting. The Gaucho sampler (£96.40) is well worth sharing to taste different cuts of meat (rump, sirloin, fillet and rib eye).

We love the glitzy modern decor too, although the cowhide chairs are a little spiky.

✕ Islington

CHILANGO
MEXICAN £

Map p456 (www.chilango.co.uk; 27 Upper St, N1; burritos & tacos £6-8; ☺11.30am-10pm; ✐; ⊜Angel) The amazing value and deliciousness of Chilango's Mexican fare is no secret amongst Islington's hungry residents. Burritos come bursting to the seams with your choice of meat (chicken, pork or beef), beans (black or red), salad, rice and sauces. Vegetarians are well catered for too. Eat in the bright, colourful interior or take it away.

LE MERCURY
FRENCH £

Map p456 (☑020-7354 4088; www.lemercury. co.uk; 140a Upper St, N1; mains £7-10; ⊜Highbury & Islington, Angel) An excellent and wildly popular budget French eatery, Le Mercury seems to have a winning formula: romantic atmosphere with candlelit, small tables and plants everywhere combined with superb French food (try the roast duck breast with red wine jus) at unbeatable prices. Londoners have long known about this place, so reservations are advised.

★TRULLO
ITALIAN ££

Map p456 (☑020-7226 2733; www.trullorestau rant.com; 300-302 St Paul's Rd, N1; mains £8.50-25; ☺12.30-3pm & 6-10.30pm Mon-Sat, 12.30-3pm Sun; ✐; ⊜Highbury & Islington) The great thing about Trullo is that it gives pride of place to Italian food that doesn't feature pasta or pizza. There are some exquisite pasta dishes, it must be said, but the star attraction is the charcoal grill, which churns out succulent T-bone steaks or tasty pork chops with baked borlotti beans or polenta.

Dessert could be pannacotta or a selection of Italian cheeses, served, of course, with a fine drop from the all-Italian wine list (with a surprisingly good selection of wines by the carafe). Service is truly fantastic, with great advice on food and wine pairing. Booking is essential.

★OTTOLENGHI
MEDITERRANEAN ££

Map p456 (☑020-7288 1454; www.ottolenghi. co.uk; 287 Upper St, N1; mains £9-12; ☺8am-11pm Mon-Sat, 9am-7pm Sun; ✐; ⊜Highbury & Islington, Angel) This is the pick of Upper Street's many eating options – a brilliantly bright, white space that's worth a trip merely to see the eye-poppingly beautiful cakes in the deli. But get a table at this temple to good food to really appreciate the exquisite fusion Mediterranean cuisine. All this fabulousness means one thing: book or you'll go hungry.

GEORGIAN IBERIAN RESTAURANT
RUSSIAN ££

Map p456 (www.iberiarestaurant.co.uk; 294-296 Caledonian Rd, N1; mains £8.50-16; ☺5-11pm Tue-Fri, 1-11pm Sat, 1-9pm Sun; ✐; ⑭Caledonian Rd & Barnsbury, ⊜Caledonian Rd, Highbury & Islington, King's Cross/St Pancras) There isn't much going on in this part of town but this restaurant alone justifies the 10 minutes' walk from Islington. Georgian food is infused with flavours from neighbouring Russia (smoked ingredients, beans, walnuts, cabbage, dill) and the Middle East (mezes, flatbread and lots of spices). The food is divine and the service is the friendliest you'll find in North London.

KIPFERL
AUSTRIAN ££

Map p456 (www.kipferl.co.uk; 20 Camden Passage, N1; mains £9.50-14.80; ⊗9am-10pm Tue-Sat, from 10am Sun; ⊜Angel) If you like cakes and sausages, Kipferl is for you. This half-cafe, half-restaurant establishment offers the very best of Austrian cuisine. Choose your coffee from the 'colour palette' menu typical of Viennese cafes, and pick from the mouth-watering cakes (Sacher Torte, Apfelstrudel etc). For mains, the Käsekrainer, a

Bradwurst sausage with cheese, is to die for. Alcohol is only served in the evenings.

✕ Dalston

★MANGAL OCAKBASI
TURKISH £

Map p456 (www.mangal1.com; 10 Arcola St, E8; mains £7-12; ⊗noon-midnight; ⛢Dalston Kingsland, Dalston Junction) Mangal is the quintessential Turkish *ocakbasi* (open-hooded charcoal grill, the mother of all BBQs) restaurant: cramped and smoky and serving superb meze, grilled lamb chops, quail and a lip-smacking assortment of kebabs. It's been here for almost 20 years and is always

NORTH LONDON'S BEST VEGETARIAN RESTAURANTS

Not a hint of rabbit food in sight – instead, creative, filling and absolutely delicious vegetarian cuisine to suit all tastes. Of the options listed, Addis is not – strictly speaking – vegetarian but Ethiopian cuisine has a rich vegetarian tradition, well represented in the restaurant's menu.

Manna (Map p460; ☎020-7722 8082; www.mannav.com; 4 Erskine Rd, NW3; mains £14-20; ⊗6.30-10.30pm Tue-Fri, noon-3pm & 6.30-10.30pm Sat, noon-3pm Sun; ☑; ⊜Chalk Farm) Tucked away on a side street in Primrose Hill, this little place does a brisk trade in inventive vegetarian cooking. The menu features such mouthwatering dishes as green korma, wild garlic and pea risotto cake and superb desserts. There are excellent vegan options too and everything comes beautifully presented, from fan-shaped salads to pyramidal mains. Reservations are usually essential.

Diwana Bhel Poori House (Map p460; 121-123 Drummond St, NW1; mains £7-9; ⊗noon-11.30pm Mon-Sat, to 10.30pm Sun; ☑; ⊜Euston, Euston Sq) Arguably one of the best Indian vegetarian restaurants in London, Diwana specialises in Bombay-style *bhel poori* (a sweet-and-sour, soft and crunchy 'party mix' snack) and dosas (filled pancakes made from rice flour). You can try thalis (a meal consisting of lots of small dishes, with a focus on vegetables), which offer a selection of tasty treats (£7 to £9) and the all-you-can-eat lunchtime buffet (£7) is legendary. BYO.

Woodlands (Map p459; www.woodlandsrestaurant.co.uk; 102 Heath St, NW3; mains £7-19; ⊗noon-3pm Tue-Sat, 6-10.45pm Mon-Sat; ☑; ⊜Hampstead) This South Indian vegetarian restaurant, whose rallying cry is 'Let Vegetation Feed the Nation', is determined to prove that South Indian vegetarian food can be as inventive as any meat-based cuisine and it does a pretty convincing job of it.

Addis (Map p456; www.addisrestaurant.co.uk; 40-42 Caledonian Rd, N1; mains £9-12; ⊗noon-midnight; ☑; ⊜King's Cross/St Pancras) Cheery Addis serves pungent Ethiopian dishes such as *ayeb be gomen* (cottage cheese mixed with spinach and spices) and *fuul musalah* (crushed fava beans topped with feta cheese, falafel and sautéed in ghee), which are eaten on a platter-sized piece of soft but slightly elastic *injera* bread. The restaurant is normally full of Ethiopian and Sudanese punters, which is always a good sign.

Rasa (www.rasarestaurants.com; 55 Stoke Newington Church St, N16; mains £4.50-7; ⊗6-11pm Mon-Sun, noon-3pm Sat & Sun; ☑; ⛢73) Flagship restaurant of the Rasa chain, this South Indian vegetarian eatery is Stoke Newington's best-known restaurant. Friendly service, a calm atmosphere, jovial prices and outstanding food from the Indian state of Kerala are its distinctive features. The multicourse Keralan Feast (£16) is for ravenous tummies only.

busy. Takeaway is also available if you can't get a table, and the restaurant itself is BYO.

CAFÉ OTO
CAFE £

Map p456 (www.cafeoto.co.uk; 18-22 Ashwin St, E8; mains £5-9; ☺9.30am-5.30pm Mon-Fri, from 10.30am Sat & Sun; ☎☑; ☐149, 38, ☐Dalston Junction, Dalston Kingsland) This well-known music venue by night is a gorgeous cafe by day. It's run by a Japanese–British couple so you'll find teriyaki wraps cohabiting with traditional soups on the menu. The cafe's latest innovation is its Persian menu, served noon to 4pm Friday to Sunday. There is a fantastic range of teas, artisanal juices and beers from London microbrewery The Kernel.

L'ATELIER
CAFE £

Map p456 (31 Stoke Newington Rd, N16; mains £5-8; ☺8am-6pm Mon-Fri, 10am-6pm Sat & Sun; ☑; ☐Dalston Junction, Dalston Kingsland) One of the newest additions on Dalston's cafe scene, L'Atelier sports the kitsch/vintage decor that is de rigueur in N16: mismatched furniture, retro posters, fresh flowers at every table, with French music and the smell of espresso coffee for ambience. It's a lovely spot to grab a salad or an open sandwich and a cup of something.

★DUKE'S BREW & QUE
AMERICAN ££

Map p456 (☏020-3006 0795; www.dukes-brewandque.com; 33 Downham Rd, N1; mains £10.25-23.50; ☺4-11pm Mon-Fri, 11am-11pm Sat & Sun; ☐Haggerston) There aren't very many restaurants that smoke their meat but Duke's is one, and we whole-heartedly support the effort! The house speciality is ribs, pork or beef, smoked over hickory and various wood and lovingly barbequed until the meat falls off the bone. Washed down with a beer from the nearby Beavertown Brewery, it is lip-smackin' food par excellence.

The weekend brunch is similarly delicious with waffles, pancakes and whopper omelettes filled with BBQ cuts or a heavenly vegetarian combo of cheese and bell peppers. No bookings for brunch but definitely recommended for dinner.

A LITTLE OF WHAT YOU FANCY
BRITISH ££

Map p456 (www.alittleofwhatyoufancy.info; 464 Kingsland Rd, E8; mains £7-18; ☺9am-4pm & 7-11pm Tue-Sat, 11am-5pm Sun; ☑; ☐149, ☐Dalston Junction, Dalston Kingsland) This twee little restaurant in Dalston is a breath of fresh air in an area better known for its kebabs than its cuisine. The decor is simple vintage and the food follows a similar philosophy of 'less is more' (actually the portions are on the 'more' side): risottos, soups, tarts – all simple but divine.

🍷 DRINKING & NIGHTLIFE

Camden Town is one of North London's favoured drinking areas, with more bars and pubs pumping music than you can manage to crawl between. The hills of Hampstead are a real treat for old-pub aficionados, while painfully hip Dalston is currently London's coolest place to drink. As for King's Cross, there are new places opening all the time, including splendid converted Victorian buildings and good places to go dancing.

🍸 King's Cross

★BAR PEPITO
WINE BAR

Map p456 (www.camino.uk.com/pepito; 3 Varnishers Yard, The Regent Quarter, N1; ☺5pm-midnight Mon-Fri, from 6pm Sat; ☐King's Cross/St Pancras) This tiny, intimate *bodega* (Spanish wine bar) specialises in sherry, a wine from the region of Andalucía. Novices fear not: the staff are on hand to advise. They're also experts at food pairings (top-notch ham and cheese selections). To go the whole hog, try a tasting menu, with five selected sherries ranging from dry to sweet.

★DRINK, SHOP & DO
BAR

Map p456 (www.drinkshopdo.com; 9 Caledonian Rd, N1; ☺10.30am-11pm Mon-Wed, 10.30am-midnight Thu, 10.30am-2am Fri & Sat, 10.30am-8pm Sun; ☎; ☐King's Cross/St Pancras) This funky little outlet will not be pigeon-holed. As its name suggests, it is many things to many people: a bar, a cafe, an activities centre, a disco even. But the idea is that there will always be drinking (be it tea or gin), music and activities, anything from dancing to building Lego robots (yes).

HANSOM LOUNGE
CAFE

Map p456 (St Pancras Renaissance London Hotel, Euston Rd, NW1; ☺7am-10pm; ☐King's Cross/St Pancras) Named after the old Hansom cabs (horse-drawn carriages) that once waited in this very place to pick up distinguished guests of the hotel, this elegant cafe occupies the reception area of the Renaissance St Pancras Hotel. The setting is marvellous (brick walls, glass ceilings and those glorious, blue-steel beams) and the perfect place for tea and pastry.

CAMINO BAR

Map p456 (www.camino.uk.com; Regent Quarter, off Caledonian Rd, N1; noon-midnight Mon-Thu, to 1am Fri & Sat, to 11pm Sun; ; King's Cross/St Pancras) Festive Camino is popular with London's Spanish community and therefore feels quite authentic. Drinks too are representative of what you'd find in Spain: *cava*, Estrella on tap, and a long, all-Spanish wine list. It's a brilliant place to watch football, international games in particular. In summer, the courtyard is absolutely crammed. Sadly the food is not as good as the atmosphere.

BIG CHILL HOUSE DJ BAR

Map p456 (www.bigchill.net; 257-259 Pentonville Rd, N1; 9am-midnight Mon-Thu, to 3am Fri & Sat, 11am-midnight Sun; ; King's Cross/St Pancras) A three-floor space with a good selection of live music and DJs, and a great terrace for hanging out, this place is run by the same people behind the popular Big Chill festival and record label. The music choice is always varied and international, the sound system is fantastic and entry is free most nights. Food is also served throughout the day.

BOOKING OFFICE BAR

Map p456 (www.bookingofficerestaurant.com; St Pancras Renaissance London Hotel, Euston Rd, NW1; 6.30am-3am) As the name suggests, this was, in a former life, the booking office of St Pancras train station. The space has been transformed into a show-stopping bar, with dizzyingly high ceilings (and prices). The bar has stayed true to its Victorian origin, using plenty of old-fashioned ingredients in its cocktails such as tea, orange peel, absinthe or gin.

6 ST CHAD'S PLACE BAR

Map p456 (www.6stchadsplace.com; 6 St Chad's Pl, WC1; 8am-11pm Mon-Fri; King's Cross/St Pancras) Once a mechanic's workshop, this Victorian warehouse has scrubbed up well to become one of the shining lights in King's Cross' regeneration. It tends to be favoured by local business people for informal meetings during the day but the same customers let their hair down in the evening with good music and live DJs on Friday nights.

EGG CLUB

Map p456 (www.egglondon.net; 5-13 Vale Royal, N1; admission £8-15; 10pm-8am Fri, 10pm-11am Sat; King's Cross/St Pancras, Caledonian Rd) Egg has the most superb layout with three exposed concrete rooms (across three floors), a garden and two gorgeous tropical roof terraces. It specialises in house, dance, techno and drum and bass. At weekends, Egg runs a free shuttle every 30 minutes between 10pm and 2am from outside American Carwash on York Way.

Camden

★EDINBORO CASTLE PUB

Map p460 (www.edinborocastlepub.co.uk; 57 Mornington Tce, NW1; noon-11pm; ; Camden Town) A reliable Camden boozer, the large and relaxed Edinboro has a refined Primrose Hill atmosphere. It boasts a full menu, gorgeous furniture designed for slumping and a fine bar. Where the pub comes into its own is in its huge beer garden, complete with BBQ and table football and adorned with fairy lights for long summer evenings.

LOCK TAVERN PUB

Map p460 (www.lock-tavern.co.uk; 35 Chalk Farm Rd, NW1; noon-midnight Mon-Thu, to 1am Fri & Sat, to 11pm Sun; Chalk Farm) An institution in Camden, the black-clad Lock Tavern rocks for several reasons: it's cosy inside, has an ace roof terrace from where you can watch the market throngs, the food is good, the beer plentiful and it also has a roll-call of guest bands and DJs at the weekend to spice things up.

BLACK CAP GAY

Map p460 (www.theblackcap.com; 171 Camden High St, NW1; noon-1am Sun-Tue, to 2am Wed & Thu, to 3am Fri & Sat; Camden Town) This friendly, sprawling place is Camden's premier gay venue, and attracts people from all over North London. There's a great outdoor terrace, the pleasantly pub-like upstairs Shufflewick bar and the downstairs club, where you'll find plenty of hilarious camp cabaret as well as decent dance music.

QUEEN'S PUB

Map p460 (www.thequeensprimrosehill.co.uk; 49 Regent's Park Rd, NW1; 11am-11pm Mon-Sat, noon-10.30pm; ; Chalk Farm) Perhaps because this is Primrose Hill, the interior is more cafe than pub. Still, it's a good one, with a nice wine list, ales and lagers and, more importantly, plenty of people-watching to do with your pint; Jude Law and many of Primrose Hill's fashionistas come here for a tipple.

Hampstead & Highgate

Hampstead and Highgate are *the* place to go for historic, charming old pubs where Sunday lunch always seems to turn into an afternoon.

★**GARDEN GATE** PUB

Map p459 (www.thegardengatehampstead.co.uk; 14 South End Rd, NW3; noon-11pm Mon-Fri, 10.30am-midnight Sat, 10.30am-10.30pm Sun; ; Hampstead Heath) At the bottom of the heath hides this gem of a pub, a 19th-century cottage with a gorgeous beer garden. The interior is wonderfully cosy, with dark wood tables, upholstered turquoise chairs and an assortment of distressed sofas. It serves Pimms and lemonade in summer and mulled wine in winter, both ideal after a long walk on the heath.

The pub also does excellent food.

★**SPANIARD'S INN** PUB

Map p459 (www.thespaniardshampstead.co.uk; Spaniards Rd, NW3; noon-11pm Mon-Fri, from 9am Sat, from 11am Sun; 21) This marvellous tavern dates from 1585 and has more character than a West End musical. It was highwayman Dick Turpin's hang-out between robbing escapades, but it's also served as a watering hole for more savoury characters, such as Dickens, Shelley, Keats and Byron. There's a big, blissful garden that is crammed at weekends. The food is overpriced but good.

HOLLY BUSH PUB

Map p459 (www.hollybushhampstead.co.uk; 22 Holly Mount, NW3; noon-11pm Mon-Sat, to 10.30pm Sun; Hampstead) A beautiful pub that makes you envy the privileged residents of Hampstead, the Holly Bush has an antique Victorian interior, a secluded hilltop location, open fires in winter and a knack for making you stay longer than you had intended. Set above Heath St, it's reached via the Holly Bush Steps.

FLASK TAVERN PUB

Map p459 (www.theflaskhighgate.com; 77 Highgate West Hill, N6; noon-11pm Mon-Sat, to 10.30pm Sun; ; Highgate, Archway) This weekend favourite is a brilliant place to end a walk in either Hampstead Heath or Highgate Wood. In the summer months it's all about its large courtyard where delicious burgers are served up along with pints. In the winter, huddle down in the cosy interior and enjoy the much-loved Sunday roast and open fires.

Islington

BULL PUB

Map p456 (www.thebullislington.co.uk; 100 Upper St, N1; noon-midnight Sun-Wed, to 1am Thu-Sat; ; Angel, Highbury & Islington) One of Islington's liveliest pubs, the Bull serves 27 kinds of draught lager, real ales, fruit beers, ciders and wheat beer, plus a large selection of bottled drinks and wine. The mezzanine is generally a little quieter than downstairs, although on weekend nights you'll generally struggle to find a seat.

PUBLIC HOUSE BAR

Map p456 (www.boutiquepubs.com; 54 Islington Park St, N1; 5pm-midnight Sun-Thu, to 1am Fri & Sat; Highbury & Islington) This handsome bar adds a lovely splash of boudoir/burlesque to an area better known for its rowdy pubs than sophisticated drinking dens. Everything is obviously fabulous at Public House, from the carefully prepared cocktails (all seasonal) to the exquisite menu and long list of after-dinner drinks (brandies, whiskies, dessert wines).

CASTLE PUB

Map p456 (www.geronimo-inns.co.uk/thecastle; 54 Pentonville Rd, N1; Sun-Thu noon-11pm, to midnight Fri & Sat; ; Angel) A gorgeous, boutique pub, all wooden floors, designer wallpaper, soft furnishings and bookshelves, with a winning formula of lovely decor, good gastropub food, a rotating selection of ales and lagers and, to top it all off, a roof terrace.

BARRIO NORTH DJ BAR

Map p456 (www.barrionorth.com; 45 Essex Rd, N1; Sun-Wed 5pm-midnight, to 1am Thu, to 3am Fri

& Sat; ⊖Angel, Highbury & Islington) This cocktail/DJ bar is one of the most fun in Islington. The atmosphere, decor and music are a celebration of all things Latino with a hint of London and New York thrown in (if you can, grab a seat in the fairy-lit cut-out caravan). The cocktails are unrivalled with selections from across the Americas. 'Amigo hour' is between 5pm and 8pm.

JUNCTION PUB

Map p456 (2a Corsica St, N5; ⊙noon-11pm; ⊖Highbury & Islington) This warehouse-sized venue isn't exactly full of character but it certainly is fun. It's a favourite of Arsenal fans and is therefore a brilliant place to watch football games, particularly those featuring Arsenal. It's obviously rammed on football nights but the atmosphere is amazing. There is plenty of seating and a beer garden.

The kitchen churns out good pizzas (two for one on Tuesdays).

Stoke Newington

AULD SHILLELAGH PUB

(www.theauldshillelagh.com; 105 Stoke Newington Church St, N16; ⊙11am-11pm Mon-Wed, 11am-1am Thu-Sat, noon-midnight Sun; 73) The Auld Shillelagh is one of the best Irish pubs in London and full of old-style liver pounders. The staff are sharp, the Guinness is good, and the live entertainment is frequent and varied. There is also a beer garden where you can catch some rays.

Dalston

DALSTON SUPERSTORE DJ BAR

Map p456 (www.dalstonsuperstore.com; 117 Kingsland High St, E8; ⊙noon-2am Mon, 10am-2am Tue-Sat; 76, 149, Dalston Kingsland, Dalston Junction) This two-level industrial space, with the feel of New York's meatpacking district, is open all day but really comes into its own after dark when there are club nights in the basement and DJs spinning upstairs.

VIVA COCKTAIL BAR

Map p456 (2 Stoke Newington Rd, N16; ⊙6-11pm Sun-Thu, 4pm-midnight Fri & Sat; Dalston Kingsland, Dalston Junction) It may be a Mexican-themed bar but this being Dalston, there is vintage furniture and kitsch decor rather than sombreros and fake cacti. The sound is positively loungy too, with not a mariachi band in sight. The cocktails – and nibbles – are bang on trend however, with plenty of tequila (*sans* shot) and rum. Ay caramba indeed.

DALSTON ROOF PARK BAR

Map p456 (www.bootstrapcompany.co.uk; Print House, 18 Ashwin St, E8; ⊙5-11pm Tue-Thu, 3pm-midnight Fri & Sat, 3-10pm Sun May-Sep; Dalston Kingsland, Dalston Junction) It is spaces like Dalston Roof Park that make you regret the fact that London ain't sunny year-round. Because when you sit in the colourful chairs, on the bright-green Astroturf, looking over the Dalston skyline and with a drink in your hand, it really is something. The bar puts on an excellent program of arts events and BBQs, too.

DALSTON JAZZ BAR COCKTAIL BAR

Map p456 (4 Bradbury St, N16; ⊙5pm-1am Mon-Thu, to 3am Fri & Sat, to midnight Sun; 76, 149, Dalston Kingsland, Dalston Junction) Hidden just off the chaos of Kingsland High St, Dalston Jazz Bar is a cocktail place where the neighbourhood's hip and friendly inhabitants congregate for a bite to eat, plenty of drinking and a good old romp to hip-hop, R&B and reggae. Strangely, given the name, live jazz only features on Friday and Saturday nights.

★ ENTERTAINMENT

North London is the capital's home of music, so you can be sure to find live music of some kind every night of the week. A number of venues such as KOKO and the Electric Ballroom are multi-purpose, with gigs in the first part of the evening (generally around 7 or 8pm), followed by club nights from 10pm. Check details with the venue before heading out.

★PASSING CLOUDS CLUB

Map p456 (www.passingclouds.org; 1 Richmond Rd, E8; ⊙6pm-12.30am Mon-Thu, to 2.30am Fri & Sat, 2pm-12.30am Sun; 243, 76, ⊖Dalston Junction, Dalston Kingsland) One of those little flickers of nightlife brilliance, Passing Clouds throws legendary parties that go until the early hours of the morning. The music is predominantly world oriented, with a lot of African influence and regular Afrobeat bands, and a reputable jam session on Sunday nights (from 9pm).

The parties are a healthy mix of DJs and live music with a multicultural crowd that really makes you feel you're in London. The decor is makeshift bar, colourful lanterns and tropical titbits, and the atmosphere is just exhilarating.

★VORTEX JAZZ CLUB JAZZ

Map p456 (www.vortexjazz.co.uk; 11 Gillet St, N16; 73, Dalston Kingsland, Dalston Junction) The Vortex has an outstanding program of musicians from the UK, US, Europe, Africa and beyond, and hosts jazz musicians, singers and songwriters. It's a small venue so make sure you book if there is an act you particularly fancy.

LIVE BY THE LAKE LIVE MUSIC

Map p459 (www.livebythelake.co.uk; Hampstead Lane, NW3; 210) Attending an outdoor concert in the grounds of Hampstead's Kenwood House has been a highlight of any good summer in London for years. Programming has been eclectic in the past, with anything from jazz to pop, classical music and opera. Concerts take place over two weekends in late August and early September. Bring a picnic and some bubbly for a brilliant night.

BLUES KITCHEN LIVE MUSIC

Map p460 (www.theblueskitchen.com; 111-113 Camden High St, NW1; free or £4-6; noon-midnight Mon & Tue, to 1am Wed, Thu & Sun, to 3am Fri & Sat; Camden Town) The Blues Kitchen's recipe for success is simple: select brilliant blues bands, host them in a fabulous bar, make it (mostly) free and offer some fabulous food and drink. Which means that the crowds keep on comin'. There are bands every night at 10pm – anything from folk to rock – and jamming sessions at 7.30pm on Sundays. Usually free before 10pm.

PROUD CAMDEN LIVE MUSIC

Map p460 (www.proudcamden.com; Horse Hospital, Stables Market, NW1; free to £15; 11am-1.30am Wed, to 2.30am Thu-Sat; Camden Town, Chalk Farm) Camden's former Horse Hospital, which looked after horses injured pulling barges on nearby Grand Union Canal, is now one of Camden's great music venues. There are live bands, DJs and art exhibitions. It's fantastic in summer, when the terrace is open. The old stables are now drinking booths (although we're not sure about the latest addition of dancing poles).

UNION CHAPEL PERFORMING ARTS

Map p456 (www.unionchapel.org.uk; Compton Tce, N1; Highbury & Islington) One of London's most atmospheric and individual music venues, the Union Chapel is an old church that still holds services, as well as concerts – mainly acoustic – and a monthly comedy night. It was here that Björk performed one of her most memorable concerts to a candlelit audience in 1999.

KOKO CONCERT VENUE

Map p460 (www.koko.uk.com; 1a Camden High St, NW1; 7-11pm Sun-Thu, to 4am Fri & Sat; Mornington Cres) Once the legendary Camden Palace, where Charlie Chaplin, the Goons and the Sex Pistols have all performed, KOKO is keeping its reputation as one of London's better gig venues. The theatre has a dance floor and decadent balconies, and attracts an indie crowd with Club NME on Friday. There are live bands almost every night of the week.

CAFÉ OTO LIVE MUSIC

Map p456 (www.cafeoto.co.uk; 18-22 Ashwin St, E8; tickets £8-10; 8pm-1am; ; 149, 38, Dalston Junction, Dalston Kingsland) Café Oto is one of London's most idiosyncratic and interesting music venues. Set in a converted print warehouse and run by a Japanese-British couple, this place dedicates itself to promoting experimental and alternative international musicians. You'll find lots of Japanese stars of experimental, jazz and pop music, as well as legendary 1960s folk and rock stars.

When there are no gigs on, Café Oto is open as a bar serving an unusually good selection of bottled Belgian beers, whiskies from Scotland and Japan and draught beers from London brewery The Kernel.

ROUNDHOUSE LIVE MUSIC

Map p460 (www.roundhouse.org.uk; Chalk Farm Rd, NW1; Chalk Farm) The Roundhouse was once home to 1960s avant-garde theatre, then was a rock venue, then it fell into oblivion for a while before reopening a few years back. It holds great gigs and brilliant performances, from circus to stand-up comedy, poetry slam and improvisation sessions. The round shape of the building is unique and generally well used in the staging.

RIO CINEMA CINEMA

Map p456 (www.riocinema.org; 107 Kingsland High St, E8; Dalston Kingsland, Dalston Junction) The Rio is Dalston's neighbourhood art-house, classic and new-release cinema, and *the* venue for offbeat festivals, such as the East End Film Festival, the Turkish Film Festival or the Fringe! Queer Film & Arts Fest. It also holds regular Q&A sessions with film directors, such as the East End's very own Asif Kapadia who directed the acclaimed *Senna* documentary about Ayrton Senna.

ARCOLA THEATRE THEATRE

Map p456 (www.arcolatheatre.com; 27 Arcola St, E8; 73, Dalston Kingsland, Dalston Junction) The Arcola's location in Dalston in the East End makes it a bit of a trek, but many still flock to this innovative theatre. The director, Mehmet Ergen, has been staging adventurous and eclectic productions since founding the theatre in 2000. The program focuses on cutting-edge, international productions (such as work by young Turkish, Swedish and Austrian playwrights).

A unique annual feature is **Grimeborn**, a music and opera festival in August/September, the antithesis of the world-famous Glyndebourne opera festival taking place around the same time.

HAMPSTEAD THEATRE THEATRE

(www.hampsteadtheatre.com; Eton Ave, NW3; Swiss Cottage) Not only is this Ewan McGregor's favourite London theatre, the Hampstead is famed for putting on new writing and taking on emerging directors. It staged Harold Pinter's new work way back in the 1960s, which shows it knows a good thing when it sees one.

JAZZ CAFÉ LIVE MUSIC

Map p460 (www.mamacolive.com/thejazzcafe; 5 Parkway, NW1; gigs from £8, club nights £5; 7pm-2am; Camden Town) Though its

ROCK!

North London is the home of indie rock; many a famous band started playing in the area's grungy bars. Here's where to go for some of the best gigs in town. Doors generally open around 7.30pm but bands may not come on until 9pm, sometimes later. Closing time is normally around 2am or 3am, although this can vary depending on the event.

Barfly (Map p460; www.mamacolive.com/thebarfly; 49 Chalk Farm Rd, NW1; gigs from £8, club nights £3-5; 7pm-3am Mon-Sat, to midnight Sun; Chalk Farm) This typically grungy, indie-rock Camden venue is well known for hosting small-time artists looking for their big break. The focus is on indie rock. The venue is small, so you'll feel like the band is just playing for you and your mates. There are club nights most nights of the week: Jubilee on Fridays is probably the best, with a mix of live bands upstairs and DJs downstairs (think Foo Fighters, The Cure, Arctic Monkeys etc). The twice-monthly Casino Royale on Saturdays is another good one with classic guitar sounds upstairs and 1960s soul downstairs.

Forum (Map p459; www.mamacolive.com/theforum; 9-17 Highgate Rd, NW5; tickets from £10; Kentish Town) You can find your way to the Forum – once the famous Town & Country Club – by the ticket touts that line the way from Kentish Town tube. It's a really popular venue to see emerging rock and electronic music acts in a memorable setting (the building is a former art deco cinema and is listed).

Bull & Gate (Map p459; www.bullandgate.co.uk; 389 Kentish Town Rd, NW5; admission £6; noon-11pm, gigs 8pm Tue-Sat; Kentish Town) The best place to see unsigned but promising talent, the legendary Bull & Gate's old-school music venue still pulls in the punters eager to see bands that might just turn out to be the next big thing. Just so you know, Coldplay, Keane, Maximo Park and Bloc Party were all spotted by the club's promoter (Club Fandango), so you are in good hands.

Electric Ballroom (Map p460; www.electricballroom.co.uk; 184 Camden High St, NW1; club nights £7-15, gigs £10-40; Camden Town) One of Camden's historic venues, the Electric Ballroom has been entertaining North Londoners since 1938. Many great bands and musicians have played here, from Blur to Paul McCartney, The Clash and U2. There are club nights on Fridays (Sin City: metal music) and Saturdays (Shake: a crowd pleaser of dance anthems from the '70s, '80s and '90s) from 10pm to 3am.

WHICH CAMDEN MARKET?

Camden Market (p245) comprises four distinct market areas; they tend to sell similar kinds of things although each has its own specialities and quirks.

Stables Market (Map p460; Chalk Farm Rd, NW1; 10am-6pm daily; Chalk Farm) Beyond the railway arches, opposite Hartland Rd, the Stables is the quirkiest part of the market, with antiques, Asian artefacts, rugs and carpets, pine furniture and vintage clothing.

Lock Market (Map p460; www.camdenlockmarket.com; 54-56 Camden Lock Pl, NW1; 10am-6pm; Camden Town, Chalk Farm) The original market, right next to the canal lock, with diverse food, ceramics, furniture, oriental rugs, musical instruments and designer clothes.

Canal Market (Map p460; cnr Chalk Farm Rd & Castlehaven Rd, NW1; 10am-6pm Thu-Sun; Chalk Farm, Camden Town) Just over the canal bridge, Canal Market has bric-a-brac from around the world. This is the part of the market that burnt down in 2008; we love the scooter seats by the canal.

Buck Street Market (Map p460; cnr Camden High & Buck Sts, NW1; 9am-5.30pm Thu-Sun; Camden Town) This covered market houses stalls for fashion, clothing, jewellery and tourist tat. It's the closest to the station but the least interesting.

name would have you think that jazz is this club's main staple, its real speciality is the crossover of jazz into the mainstream. It's a trendy industrial-style restaurant with jazz gigs around once a week, while the rest of the month is filled with Afro, funk, hip hop, R&B and soul styles with big-name acts and a faithful bohemian Camden crowd.

The Saturday club night 'I love the 80s v I love the 90s' is a long-standing favourite for those nostalgic of girl and boy bands, big hair and statement jackets.

KING'S HEAD THEATRE — PERFORMING ARTS

Map p456 (www.kingsheadtheatre.com; 115 Upper St, N1; Angel) This stalwart pub-theatre in Islington has become the home of OperaUpClose, a company determined to offer classical and modern opera in less intimidating settings than London's traditional opera theatres. Its production of *La Bohème* was a runaway success. As well as opera, there are plenty of plays and musicals.

SHOPPING

Shopping in North London is all about vintage and secondhand clothes. Dalston rules in the vintage department; it is also a prime area for pop-up shops. Primrose Hill and Hampstead are the place to go for quality, secondhand designer pieces.

GILL WING — GIFTS

Map p456 (www.gillwing.co.uk; 190 Upper St, N1; 9am-6pm Mon-Sat, from 10am Sun; Highbury & Islington) Gill Wing's gift shop is a staple of Upper St: it is basically impossible to walk past without doing a double-take at the sweet-shop-like window full of colourful glasses, cards, children's toys and other eclectic titbits. Short of ideas? Let the charming staff help you.

TRAID — CLOTHING

Map p456 (www.traid.org.uk; 106-108 Kingsland High St, E8; 10am-6pm Mon-Sat, to 5pm Sun; Dalston Junction, Dalston Kingsland) Banish every preconception you have about charity shops, for Traid is nothing like the ones you have seen before: big, white, bright, with neon light and not a whiff of moth ball. Note that the offering isn't vintage but rather quality, contemporary second-hand clothes for a fraction of the price. The shop also sells its own creations made from offcuts and there are other branches across London.

BEYOND RETRO — VINTAGE

Map p456 (www.beyondretro.com; 92-100 Stoke Newington Rd, N16; 10am-7pm Mon-Wed, Fri & Sat, 10am-8pm Thu, 11.30am-6pm Sun; Dalston Kingsland, Dalston Junction) The latest shop of the vintage empire that is Beyond Retro is a riot of colour, furbelow, frill, feathers and flares. The premises are huge and you'll find every imaginable clothing item for sale, from hats to waistcoats. The owners clearly thought the choice would be overwhelming so they added a (licensed!) cafe to the shop where you can recover from your bargain hunting.

EXCLUSIVO FASHION

Map p459 (2 Flask Walk, NW3; ⊙11.30am-6pm Mon-Fri, noon-6pm Sat & Sun) If you dream of owning a pair of Manolo Blahniks or a Pucci dress but have always balked at the price, Exclusivo might just be your chance. This boutique specialises in secondhand, top-quality designer garments and accessories, and while prices remain high (£300 for a dress, for instance), they are a fraction of the original price tag.

HARRY POTTER SHOP CHILDREN

Map p456 (departure concourse, King's Cross station, N1; ⊙10am-6pm; ⊖King's Cross/St Pancras) Harry Potter fans, unite, this is your very own window into the world of the child wizard. Set up as a wand shop (wands from around £25), with wood panels and plenty of shelves and drawers, it also sells jumpers sporting the colours of Hogwarts' four houses (Gryffindor having pride of place) and assorted merchandise.

ANNIE'S VINTAGE COSTUMES & TEXTILES VINTAGE

Map p456 (www.anniesvintageclothing.co.uk; 12 Camden Passage, N1; ⊙11am-6pm; ⊖Angel) One of London's most enchanting vintage shops, Annie's has costumes to make you look like Greta Garbo. Many a famous designer has come here for inspiration so you might also get to do some celebrity spotting.

HOUSMANS BOOKS

Map p456 (www.housmans.com; 5 Caledonian Rd, N1; ⊙10am-6pm Mon-Sat, noon-6pm Sun; ⊖King's Cross/St Pancras) This long-standing, not-for-profit bookshop, where you'll find books that are unavailable on the shelves of the more mainstream stockists, is a good place to keep up to date with all sorts of progressive, political and social campaigns, and with your more radical reads. The forthcoming owner is a mine of local information.

CAMDEN PASSAGE

Not to be confused with Camden Market, Camden Passage is a series of four arcades selling antiques and curios, located in Islington, at the junction of Upper St and Essex Rd. There is an **antiques market** (Map p456; www.camdenpassageislington.co.uk; Camden Passage, N1; ⊙8am-2pm Wed, to 5pm Sat; ⊖Angel) twice a week; stallholders know their stuff, so bargains are rare.

There are also plenty of vintage, boutique and antique shops along the passage and some great cafes.

SPORTS & ACTIVITIES

★HAMPSTEAD HEATH PONDS SWIMMING

Map p459 (Gordon House Rd, Hampstead Heath, NW5; adult/concession £2/1; 214, C2, 24, Gospel Oak, Hampstead Heath) Set in the midst of the gorgeous heath, the three ponds offer a slightly chilly dip surrounded by wild shrubbery. The men's pond is a bit of a gay cruising area (but it's also a fantastic, beautiful place for a swim), the secluded women's pond is less cruisy. The mixed pond can sometimes get rather crowded and isn't so scenically located.

The men's and women's ponds are open year-round and are supervised by a lifeguard. Opening times vary with the seasons, from 7am or 8am until 3.30pm in the

PLATFORM 9¾

Fans of Harry Potter won't need any explanation about this odd numbering but for the Muggles out there, Platform 9¾ is the platform from which the Hogwarts Express leaves King's Cross to go to Hogwarts School of Witchcraft and Wizardry at the beginning of each term. The platform is located between platforms 9 and 10 and can only be accessed by running into it.

A sign has now been permanently erected, along with a trolley carrying a trunk and an owl cage. You can have your picture taken by the Harry Potter Shop located next door. Find it inside King's Cross station, towards the end of the departure concourse.

WORTH A DETOUR

ALEXANDRA PARK & PALACE

Built in 1873 as North London's answer to Crystal Palace, **Alexandra Palace** (www.alexandrapalace.com; Alexandra Palace Way, N22; Alexandra Palace) suffered the ignoble fate of burning to the ground only 16 days after opening. Encouraged by attendance figures, investors decided to rebuild and it reopened just two years later. During WWI, it housed German prisoners of war and in 1936 was the scene of the world's first TV transmission – a variety show called *Here's Looking at You*. The palace burned down again in 1980 but was rebuilt for the third time and opened in 1988.

Today 'Ally Pally' (as it is affectionately known) is a multipurpose conference and exhibition centre with additional facilities, including an indoor ice-skating rink, the panoramic Phoenix Bar & Beer Garden and fun fairs in summer. It hosts occasional club nights and concerts too.

The park in which it stands sprawls over some 196 hectares. Locals come to enjoy the sweeping views of London, and there is also a farmers market on Sundays.

The fireworks held on Bonfire Night are some of the most spectacular in town, lighting up the city skyline.

winter but until 8.30pm at the height of summer. The mixed pond is open to members only in winter. Despite what you might think from its murky appearance, the water is tested every day and meets stringent quality guidelines.

LORD'S CRICKET GROUND CRICKET GROUND
(www.lords.org; St John's Wood Rd, NW8; St John's Wood) A trip to Lord's, aka 'the home of cricket', is often as much a pilgrimage as anything else. As well as being home to Marylebone Cricket Club, the ground hosts test matches, one-day internationals and domestic finals. International matches are booked months in advance but tickets for county cricket fixtures are reasonably easy to come by.

Notting Hill & West London

NOTTING HILL | WESTBOURNE GROVE | HIGH STREET KENSINGTON | EARL'S COURT | WEST BROMPTON | MAIDA VALE | SHEPHERD'S BUSH | HAMMERSMITH | PADDINGTON | BAYSWATER

Neighbourhood Top Five

❶ Spending a Saturday afternoon browsing the stalls of **Portobello Road Market** (p267).

❷ Easing into early evening with a drink in the relaxing garden of the **Windsor Castle** (p272) pub.

❸ Taking a **boat trip** (p266) between Little Venice and Camden along Regent's Canal.

❹ Blowing the budget with a night out at the sensational **Kensington Roof Gardens** (p272).

❺ Cosying up on a leather sofa for two with a glass of champagne at the **Electric Cinema** (p273).

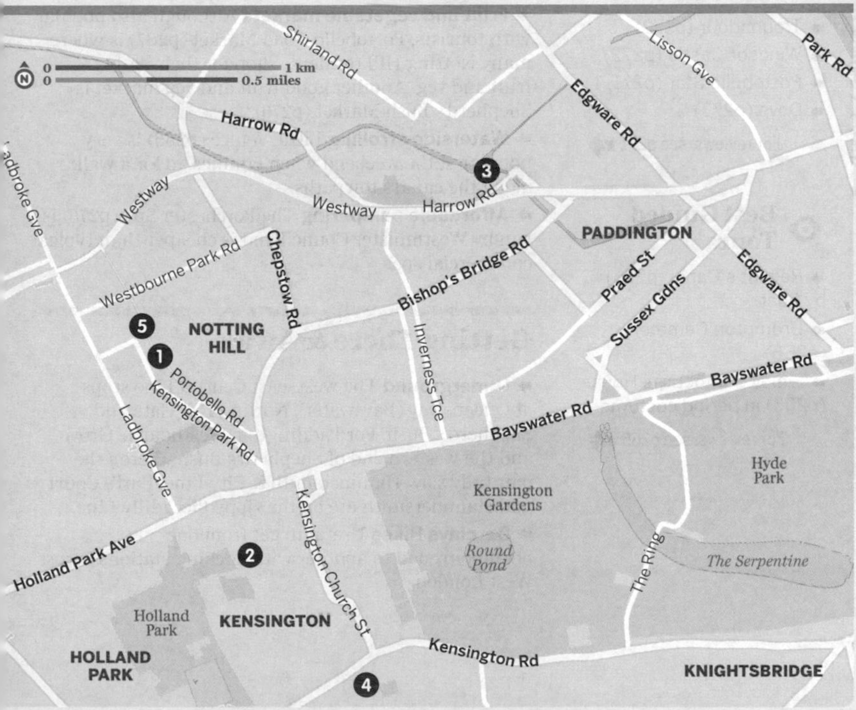

For more detail of this area see Map p462 and p464

Lonely Planet's Top Tip

To make the best of your time at Portobello Road Market, do a one-way circuit between Notting Hill Gate and Ladbroke Rd tube stations. The flow tends to go from Notting Hill to Ladbroke Grove, but either way works fine. Follow our Notting Hill Walk (p268) for a suggested route.

Best Places to Eat

- Potli (p269)
- Ledbury (p269)
- Kerbisher & Malt (p270)
- Taquería (p267)

For reviews, see p267

Best Places to Drink

- Troubadour (p272)
- Windsor Castle (p272)
- Portobello Star (p271)
- Dove (p273)

For reviews, see p271

Best Guided Tours

- Regent's Canal (p276) by boat
- Brompton Cemetery (p266)
- Linley Sambourne House (p265) in period costume

For reviews, see p265

Explore: Notting Hill & West London

Most people come to West London for three reasons: Portobello Road Market, outstanding dining or because they're kipping in one of the area's choice accommodation options.

West London is sight-light, but you should allow half a day for Portobello Road Market and another half day to walk along the Grand Union Canal towards Little Venice, maybe with a pint at one of the waterside pubs en route.

Some excellent restaurant and entertainment options will save those staying in the area from legging it into the West End (although it's close enough to do so if you want). For eating, Notting Hill has a great concentration of good names, but cast your net further and land fantastic pickings in Hammersmith, Shepherd's Bush and Earl's Court.

For nightlife, Notting Hill and Shepherd's Bush are the most vibrant, while Kensington is home to one of the capital's most unique rooftop clubs. Other areas will be pretty quiet once the pubs have rung the 11pm bell.

Local Life

- **Fruit and vegetable markets** Although also popular with tourists, Portobello Road Market (p267) is where many Notting Hill residents shop for their daily fruit and veg. Another good fruit and veg market is Shepherd's Bush Market (p270).
- **Waterside strolling** Little Venice (p266) is very popular at the weekend when families go for a walk along the canal's towpaths.
- **Affordable pampering** The Porchester Spa (p276) is run by Westminster Council and is cheaper than typical commercial spas.

Getting There & Away

- **Underground** The west–east Central Line stops at Queensway (Bayswater), Notting Hill Gate and Shepherd's Bush. For Paddington, Westbourne Grove, and the western end of Shepherd's Bush, there's the painfully slow Hammersmith & City Line. Earl's Court and Hammersmith are on the zippy Piccadilly Line.
- **Barclays Bikes** Useful to get from one neighbourhood to another with docking stations across West London.

SIGHTS

Notting Hill & Westbourne Grove

MUSEUM OF BRANDS, PACKAGING & ADVERTISING
MUSEUM

Map p462 (www.museumofbrands.com; 2 Colville Mews, Lonsdale Rd, W11; adult/child £6.50/2.25; ⌚10am-6pm Tue-Sat, 11am-5pm Sun; ⊖Notting Hill Gate, Ladbroke Grove, Westbourne Park) This shrine to nostalgia is the brainchild of designer Robert Opie, who has amassed advertising memorabilia and packaging since the age of 16. There's early Monopoly sets, the first appearances of Mickey Mouse and Disney, a primitive Cluedo set, Teazie-Weazie powder shampoo, radios, TV sets, and appearances from cultural/consumer icons the Fab Four, Mork & Mindy, Star Wars, Star Trek, Buzz Lightyear, Pokemon *et al.*

High Street Kensington

LEIGHTON HOUSE
HOUSE

Map p464 (www.leightonhouse.co.uk; 12 Holland Park Rd, W14; adult/child £5/3; ⌚10am-5.30pm Wed-Mon; ⊖High St Kensington) Sitting on a quiet street just west of Holland Park and designed in 1866 by George Aitchison, Leighton House was home to the eponymous Frederic, Lord Leighton (1830–96), a painter belonging to the Olympian movement. The ground floor is dished up in an Orientalist style, with the exquisite **Arab Hall** added in 1879 and densely covered with blue and green tiles from Rhodes, Cairo, Damascus, and Iznik in Turkey.

A fountain tinkles away in the centre beneath the golden dome. Even the wooden latticework of the windows and gallery was brought from Damascus. A fireplace upstairs inlaid with Chinese tiles, a stuffed peacock at the foot of the stairs and peacock quills in the fireplace amplify the Byzantine mood. The house contains notable pre-Raphaelite paintings by Burne-Jones, Watts, Millais and Lord Leighton himself. Bombed twice in WWII, the house's recent and lavish refurbishment is detailed in a film upstairs. You can return free of charge within a year if you complete the application form.

LINLEY SAMBOURNE HOUSE
HOUSE

Map p464 (www.rbkc.gov.uk/linleysambournehouse; 18 Stafford Tce, W8; adult/child £8/3; ⌚tours 11.15am & 2.15pm Wed, 11.15am, 1pm, 2.15pm, 3.30pm Sat & Sun mid-Sep–mid-Jun; ⊖High St Kensington) Tucked away behind Kensington High St, this was the home of *Punch* cartoonist and amateur photographer Linley Sambourne and his wife Marion from 1875 to 1914. What you see is pretty much the typical home of a comfortable middle-class Victorian family, with dark wood, Turkish carpets and rich stained glass throughout.

You can visit some nine rooms, by 90-minute guided tour only (on weekends, the guide on all but the first tour is garbed in period costume). A discount of £1 is available with the Leighton House subscription card.

NOTTING HILL CARNIVAL

Every year, for three days over the last weekend of August, Notting Hill echoes to the beats of calypso, ska, reggae and soca during the **Notting Hill Carnival** (www.thenottinghillcarnival.com). Launched in 1964 by the local Afro-Caribbean community keen to celebrate its culture and traditions, it has grown to become Europe's largest street festival (up to one million people) and a highlight of the annual calendar in London.

The carnival includes events highlighting the five main 'arts': the 'mas' (derived from masquerade), which is the main costume parade; pan (steel bands); calypso music; static sound systems (anything goes, from reggae, dub, funk and drum and bass); and the mobile sound systems. The 'mas' is generally held on the Monday and is the culmination of the carnival's celebrations. Processions finish around 9pm, although parties in bars, restaurants and seemingly every house in the neighbourhood go on late into the night.

Another undisputed highlight of the carnival is the food: there are dozens of Caribbean food stands and celebrity chefs such as Levi Roots often make an appearance.

HOLLAND PARK PARK

Map p464 (Ilchester Pl; ⌚7.30am-dusk; ⊖High St Kensington, Holland Park) This handsome park divides into dense woodland in the north, spacious lawns by Holland House for collapsing on under the summer sun, sports fields for the beautiful game and other exertions in the south, and some lovely gardens, including the restful Kyoto Garden. There's also an adventure playground for kids. The park's many splendid peacocks are a gorgeous sight.

Holland House is the venue of Opera Holland Park (p274) in the summer months and the former Commonwealth Institute, just south of the park, is being reinvented as the new Design Museum (due to open in 2015).

Earl's Court & West Brompton

BROMPTON CEMETERY CEMETERY

Map p464 (www.royalparks.org.uk/parks/brompton-cemetery; Old Brompton Rd, SW5; tour £5 donation; ⌚8am-dusk; ⊖West Brompton, Fulham Broadway) While this 19th-century boneyard's most famous resident is Emmeline Pankhurst, the pioneer of women's suffrage in Britain, the cemetery is fascinating as the inspiration for many of Beatrix Potter's characters. A local resident in her youth, Potter may have taken names from headstones for immortalisation in her books, including Mr Nutkin, Mr McGregor, Jeremiah Fisher, Tommy Brock – even a Peter Rabbett.

The chapel and colonnades at one end are modelled on St Peter's in Rome. Two-hour tours depart at 2pm every Sunday from May to August (and two Sundays a month from September to April) from the South Lodge, near the Fulham Rd entrance. The annual summer open day includes rare visits to the catacombs (see www.brompton-cemetery.org for details).

Maida Vale

LITTLE VENICE CANAL

Map p462 It was Lord Byron who dreamed up this evocative phrase to describe the junction between Regent's Canal and the Grand Union Canal, a confluence overseen by beautiful mansions and navigated by colourful narrow boats. The canals go back to the early 19th century when the government was trying to develop new transport links across the country.

The Grand Union Canal actually finishes up in Birmingham (you can journey much of its entire length by bicycle): horse-drawn barges were ideal to carry coal and other bulk commodities such as grain or ice. Little Venice is an important mooring point for narrow boats (many of them permanent homes), which keeps the boating spirit bubbling away.

Shepherd's Bush

KENSAL GREEN CEMETERY CEMETERY

(www.kensalgreencemetery.com; Harrow Rd, W10; tours £7; ⌚9am-5pm Mon-Sat, 10am-5pm Sun, later in summer; ⊖Kensal Green) For many years the most fashionable necropolis in England (you wouldn't be seen dead anywhere else), Kensal Green Cemetery accepted its first occupants in 1833, and the Gothic bone yard is the final resting place of many illustrious names, including Charles Babbage, Isambard Kingdom Brunel, Wilkie Collins, Anthony Trollope, William M Thackeray and the almost comically named Dr Albert Isaiah Coffin.

Supposedly based on the Cimetière du Père-Lachaise in Paris, the cemetery is distinguished by its Greek Revival architecture, arched entrances and the outrageously ornate tombs that bear testimony to 19th-century delusions of grandeur. Two-hour tours of the cemetery are offered on Sundays at 2pm (from March to October; two Sundays per month other times) by the Friends of Kensal Green Cemetery (www.kensalgreen.co.uk); some of these tours also visit the catacombs beneath the Anglican Chapel. The cemetery is laid out alongside the Grand Union Canal, which makes for splendid walks alongside the water, especially if the sun obliges.

Hammersmith

WILLIAM MORRIS SOCIETY MUSEUM

(www.williammorrissociety.org; 26 Upper Mall, W6; ⌚2-5pm Thu & Sat; ⊖Ravenscourt Park) FREE Tucked away in the coach house and basement of Kelmscott House (William Morris' former home), this small riverside museum stages temporary exhibitions on all things William Morris. There's a downstairs shop (with a fireplace designed by Morris) and a still-working printing press (demonstrations given on Saturdays).

Short films on Morris and the house are run and you can also access a small part of the garden, although the rest of the house and the main garden are out of bounds for most of the year.

EATING

Notting Hill & Westbourne Grove

TAQUERÍA MEXICAN £

Map p462 (www.taqueria.co.uk; 139-143 Westbourne Grove; tacos from £4.10; noon-11pm Mon-Fri, 10am-11.30pm Sat, noon-10.30pm Sun; ; Notting Hill Gate) You won't find fresher, softer (they're not supposed to be crispy!) tacos anywhere in London because these ones are made on site. It's a small casual place with a great vibe. Taquería is also a committed environmental establishment: the eggs, chicken and pork are free-range, the meat British, the fish MSC-certified and the milk and cream organic.

GELATO MIO ICE CREAM £

Map p462 (www.gelatomio.co.uk; 37 Pembridge Rd; 10.30am-9pm Mon-Thu, 10.30am-10pm Fri, 9am-10pm Sat, 10am-9pm Sun; ; Notting Hill Gate) Sun-soaked Notting Hill summer days find cooling relief at this trendy ice-cream parlour, where low-fat and dense Italian *gelato* (thicker and less airy than ice cream) is served up in an indulgent range of fruity, nutty and milky sensations. Fine coffee and delicious cake take up the slack on more frigid days.

ELECTRIC DINER AMERICAN £

Map p462 (www.electricdiner.com; 191 Portobello Rd; mains from £7; 8am-midnight Mon-Thu, 8am-1am Fri-Sun) A kitchen fire called in last orders for the Electric Brasserie, ushering in this restaurant's redesign as a slender American-style diner with long counter and red-leather booths, to amplify cinematic associations with the adjacent movie theatre. The French-American menu's breakfasts, burgers, steak frites and hot dogs are

TOP SIGHT
PORTOBELLO ROAD MARKET

Like Camden and Spitalfields, Portobello Road Market is an iconic London attraction with an eclectic mix of street food, fruit and veg, antiques, curios, collectibles, vibrant fashion and trinkets. Although the shops along Portobello Rd open daily and the fruit and veg stalls (from Elgin Cres to Talbot Rd) only close on Sunday, the busiest day by far is Saturday, when antique dealers set up shop (from Chepstow Villas to Elgin Cres). This is also when the fashion market (beneath Westway from Portobello Rd to Ladbroke Rd) is in full swing – although you can also browse for fashion on Friday and Sunday.

Among the vintage and 'first hand' fashion stalls of Westway, you'll also find accessories, shoes, jewellery and CDs. More upmarket, **Portobello Green Arcade** (Map p462; www.portobellodesigners.com; 281 Portobello Rd, W10) is home to some cutting-edge clothing and jewellery designers.

Continue on Portobello Rd towards Golborne Rd (famous for vintage furniture and clothes shops) and you'll hit the 'new goods' section, with kitchenware, bric-a-brac and more fruit and veg stalls – as well as second-hand goods, despite this being the 'new goods' market.

DON'T MISS...

- Fashion market
- Designers at Portobello Green Arcade
- Fruit and veg stalls
- Antiques market

PRACTICALITIES

- Map p462
- www.portobellomarket.org
- Portobello Rd, W10
- 8am-6.30pm Mon-Sat, to 1pm Thu
- Notting Hill Gate, Ladbroke Grove

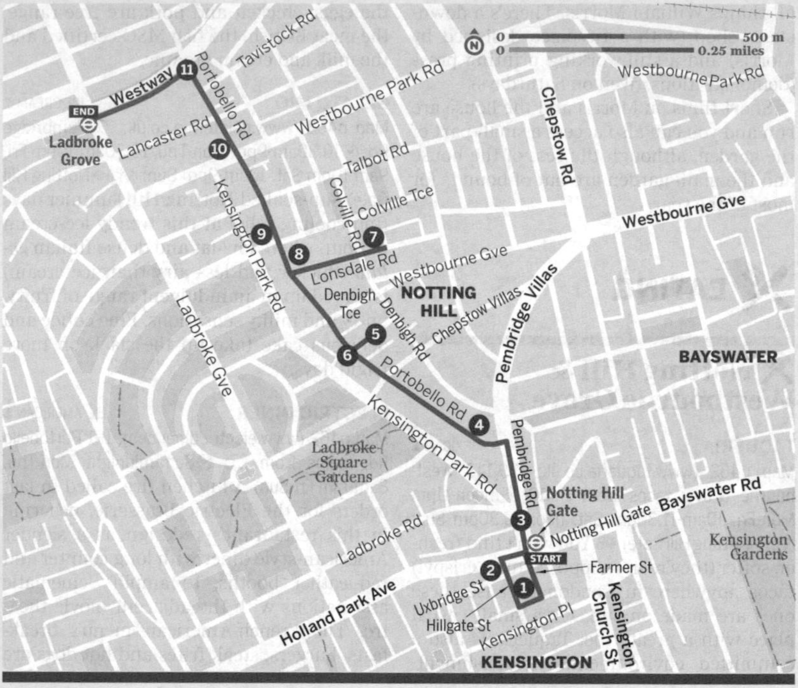

Neighbourhood Walk Notting Hill

START NOTTING HILL GATE STATION
END PORTOBELLO GREEN ARCADE
LENGTH 1.5 MILES; TWO HOURS

A small and manageable neighbourhood, Notting Hill is best visited for Portobello Market (heaving on Saturdays). From Notting Hill Gate tube station, leave the south side exit and take a left down Farmer St into **1 Hillgate Village**, with its picture-postcard painted houses. Callcott St is particularly photogenic. Loop back around and leave Hillgate St by the iconic **2 Coronet** (p273) cinema featured in the rom-com *Notting Hill*. Turn right and cross at the lights to the junction with Pembridge Rd; the tollgate – the 'gate' of Notting Hill Gate – once stood here.

Along Pembridge Rd, at the junction with Kensington Park Rd, was once the main entrance to the huge 19th-century **3 Hippodrome**. The Hippodrome vanished in the 1840s, although its layout survives in the road contours to the west. Bend into Portobello Rd and note the blue plaque high at **4 No 22**, commemorating George Orwell who lived here. Keep walking along Portobello Rd and pop into charming **5 Denbigh Terrace**, with its pastel-coloured houses. Note the steeple of **6 St Peter's Church** to the west on the far side of Portobello Rd.

Continue along Portobello Rd and turn right down Lonsdale Rd to the absorbing **7 Museum of Brands, Packaging & Advertising** (p265), stuffed away down Colville Mews. Backtrack to Portobello Rd and note the **8 shop** named 'Notting Hill' at No 142 on your right: the bookshop of William Thacker (Hugh Grant) in the eponymous film (now a clothes and shoe shop). Further along Portobello Rd, stop outside the historic **9 Electric Cinema** (p273); observe the tiling by the pavement that says 'Electric House' and pop in to take a gander at the classic interior. Down further, cross Westbourne Park Rd, named after the River Westbourne (p198), one of London's underground rivers. The blue front door at **10 No 280 Westbourne Park Rd**, William Thacker's flat in the film *Notting Hill*, still attracts devotees.

At **11 Portobello Green Arcade** (p267), stop to browse a clutch of designer clothes shops and quirky boutiques. Ladbroke Grove tube station is a short walk west.

cooked up in flavoursome fashion while a noteworthy catalogue of draught and bottled beers keeps ale fiends content.

RUM KITCHEN CARIBBEAN £

Map p462 (www.therumkitchen.com; 6-8 All Saints Rd, W11; mains £8.50-16.50; ⏲6-11pm Mon-Wed, 6pm-1am Thu, 6pm-2am Fri, noon-2am Sat, noon-4pm Sun; ⊖Westbourne Park, Ladbroke Grove) This 'Caribbean-inspired beach shack' for Notting Hillbilly landlubbers comes up trumps with its downstairs low-ceiling bar dedicated to rum, running to an eye-watering 100 different varieties, arranged geographically by Caribbean island. The Jamaican breeze isn't quite in your hair but the classic West Indies menu (jerk lamb cutlets, seafood gumbo, chocolate rum cake) and reggae, Afro-funk and calypso get you halfway there.

ARANCINA ITALIAN £

Map p462 (www.arancina.co.uk; 19 Pembridge Rd, W11; dishes £2.20-18.45; ⏲7.30am-10pm; ⊖Notting Hill Gate) A fantastic place to indulge in Sicilian snacks, Arancina stops people dead in their tracks on the way to Portobello Market thanks to the whiffs of freshly baked pizza and the cut-out orange Fiat 500 in the window. Try the *arancine* (fried balls of rice with fillings; £2.20) and the creamy desserts known as *cannoli siciliano* (£2.20). There's another branch not far away at 19 Westbourne Grove.

BUBBLEOLOGY CAFE £

Map p462 (www.bubbleology.co.uk; 45 Pembridge Rd; tea from £3.45; ⏲11am-10pm Mon-Thu, 10am-11pm Fri-Sat, 11am-10pm Sun; ⊖Notting Hill Gate) Originally from Taiwan, bubble tea is a sweet, flavoured (hot or cold) milk or fruit tea loaded with delicious tapioca pearls, hoovered up via a thick straw. Gimmicky, perhaps, but thirst-busting. This popular place transmutes bubble-tea concocting into a science, serving drinks by staff in lab coats.

GEALES SEAFOOD ££

Map p462 (☎020-7727 7528; www.geales.com; 2 Farmer St, W8; 2-/3-course lunch £11.95/14.95, mains £10.95-22.95; ⏲noon-3pm Tue-Sat, 6-10.30pm Mon-Sat, noon-9.30pm Sun; ⊖Notting Hill Gate) Going since 1939, Geales has long enjoyed fame. The quiet location, tucked away on the corner of Hillgate Village, is appetising, and the succulent fish in crispy batter is a fine catch from the menu, although the chips disappointingly cost extra (outside of the set lunch) on what should be a standard sit-down combination.

E&O ASIAN ££

Map p462 (www.rickerrestaurants.com; 14 Blenheim Cres; mains £10-36; ⏲noon-3pm & 6-11pm Mon-Fri, noon-11pm Sat, 12.30-10.30pm Sun; Wi-Fi; ⊖Ladbroke Grove) This Notting Hill hot spot offers Asian fusion fare presented as artfully as an elaborate origami. The decor is equally attractive: black-and-white minimalist. You can do dim sum (£3.50 to £8) at the bar if no tables are available in the evening (it gets busy).

LEDBURY FRENCH £££

Map p462 (☎020-7792 9090; www.theledbury.com; 127 Ledbury Rd; mains £30; ⏲noon-2pm daily plus 6.30-10.15pm Mon-Sat, 7-10pm Sun; ⊖Westbourne Park, Notting Hill Gate) Two Michelin stars and swooningly elegant, Brett Graham's artful French restaurant attracts well-heeled diners in jeans with designer jackets. Dishes – such as roast sea bass with broccoli stem, crab and black quinoa, or saddle of roe deer with beetroot, pinot lees and bone crisp potato – are triumphant. London gastronomes have the Ledbury on speed-dial, so reservations are crucial.

Earl's Court & West Brompton

MR WING CHINESE ££

Map p464 (www.mrwing.com; 242 Old Brompton Rd, SW5; mains £9.50-38; ⏲11am-10pm Sun-Thu, 11am-10.30pm Fri & Sat; ⊖Earl's Court, West Brompton) A smart Chinese restaurant with an ambitiously wide-ranging menu embracing Cantonese dim sum (£3.50 to £12), northern accented aromatic crispy duck and Beijing pork dumplings, as well as piquant Sichuan aubergine. Live jazz gets chopsticks clicking Thursday to Saturday nights from 8pm.

Shepherd's Bush & Hammersmith

POTLI INDIAN £

Map p464 (www.potli.co.uk; 319-321 King St; weekday 1-/2-course set lunch £6.95/9.95, mains from £6.25; ⏲noon-2.45pm & 6-10.30pm Mon-Sat, noon-10.30pm Sun; ⊖Stamford Brook, Raven-

SHEPHERD'S BUSH MARKET

This fruit and veg **market** (Map p464; ⌚9.30am-5pm Mon-Wed, Fri & Sat, to 1pm Thu) stretches underneath the Hammersmith & City and Circle Lines between Goldhawk Rd and Shepherd's Bush tube stations. It's popular with local African and Afro-Caribbean communities and is therefore stockpiled with mangoes, passion fruit, okra, plantains, sweet potatoes and other exotic fare. **Mr Falafel** (Units T4-T5; falafel from £3; ⌚11am-6pm Mon-Sat) is the place for Palestinian falafel wraps, done to a turn.

scourt Park) With its Bollywood posters, scattered pieces from Mumbai's Thieves Market, Indian bazaar cuisine, homemade pickles and spice mixes, and accent on genuine flavour, good-looking Potli deftly captures the aromas of its culinary home. Downstairs there's an open kitchen and service is very friendly, but it's the alluring menu – where flavours are teased into a rich and fully authentic India culinary experience – that's the real crowd-pleaser.

KERBISHER & MALT FISH & CHIPS £

Map p464 (www.kerbisher.co.uk; 164 Shepherd's Bush Rd; mains from £5.80; ⌚noon-2.30pm & 4.30-10pm Tue-Fri, noon-10pm Sat, noon-9pm Sun; ⊖Hammersmith) Every day save Monday is Fry Day at popular, blue-fronted Kerbisher & Malt, where the sustainably sourced, delectable, battered-or-grilled coley, haddock, pollock, cod and plaice have won over scads of partisan diners. The chip butties (crispy servings of whitebait and tasty double-fried chips) have an equally solid fan base, while the white-tile walls and chunky wooden tables casts Kerbisher & Malt as a no-nonsense, but handsome, chippie.

TOSA JAPANESE £

Map p464 (www.tosauk.com; 332 King St; mains from £6; ⊖Stamford Brook) With a welcoming flaming charcoal grill brightening its window, this simple, casual yet pretty-and-precise Japanese restaurant fixes its focus on smaller dishes, as well as delectable skewers of meat, including scrummy *yakitori* (grilled chicken skewers) and *asparamaki* (pork and aubergine).

BUSH THEATRE CAFE & BAR CAFE £

Map p464 (www.bushtheatre.co.uk; 7 Uxbridge Rd; mains from £2.50; ⌚9am-11pm Mon-Fri, 11am-11pm Sat; ⊖Shepherd's Bush Market) Tread the bare wood floorboards of this roomy cafe in this erstwhile library, and reach for a paperback play or two from the dense collection on the shelves. This is a great place to catch breakfast, hang out for pre-threatre snacking or for just taking time out from the vehicular din of Shepherd's Bush.

A COOKES BRITISH £

Map p464 (www.cookespieandmash.com; 48 Goldhawk Rd; mains from £4; ⌚10.30am-4.30pm Mon-Wed & Sat, 10.30am-3pm Thu, 10.30am-5pm Fri; ⊖Goldhawk Rd) Fenced in by the ethnic flavours of Shepherd's Bush, rock-solid A Cookes has been serving London pie and mash since the twilight years of Queen Vic's reign. The environment: moulded plastic furniture and Queens Park Rangers football banners. The food: honest, good-value and out-and-out London. Served in a jiffy and consumed with spoon and fork, a single pie and mash in a bowl with parsley liquor is £4; eels and mash will set you back £6.

ESARN KHEAW THAI £

Map p464 (www.esarnkheaw.com; 314 Uxbridge Rd, W12; mains £6.95-20.50; ⌚noon-3pm Mon-Fri, 6-11pm daily; ⊖Shepherd's Bush) Decor makeovers don't top the list at this superb long-standing restaurant serving food from the Esarn, the northeast of Thailand where people munch on chillies like chewing gum. The housemade Esarn Kheaw sausage and *som tom* (green papaya salad) are sublime.

PRINCESS VICTORIA GASTROPUB ££

Map p464 (www.princessvictoria.co.uk; 217 Uxbridge Rd, W12; weekday 2-course lunch £12.50; ⌚11.30am-midnight Mon-Sat, 11.30am-11.30pm Sun; 🚌207, 607, ⊖Shepherd's Bush Market) This imposing former Victorian gin palace is a quality boozer with ample elbow space. Grandly restored, the roomy interior soaks up pretty much any hubbub thrown at it, the menu is a gastronomic success while winelovers are rewarded with a strong selection.

GATE VEGETARIAN ££

Map p464 (☎020-8748 6932; http://thegaterestaurants.com/hammersmith.php; 51 Queen Caroline St, W6; mains £12.50-14.50; ⌚lunch Mon-Fri, dinner Mon-Sat; 🌱; ⊖Hammersmith) Widely considered one of London's very best vegetarian restaurants (with a newly opened branch in Islington), this newly refurbished eatery could do with better feng shui (behind the Hammersmith Apollo, off Hammersmith flyover), but the inventive menu (beetroot ravioli, aubergine schnitzel), friendly and welcoming staff, and relaxed atmosphere make the trek here worthwhile. Bookings crucial.

PATIO POLISH ££

Map p464 (www.patiolondon.com; 5 Goldhawk Rd, W12; mains £8.50-14.90, set meal with glass of vodka £16.50; noon-3pm Mon-Fri, 6-11pm daily; ; Shepherd's Bush, Goldhawk Rd) This cosy restaurant is cluttered with curios and antiques and serves fairly authentic home-style Polish food. It is presided over by a kindly matriarch who knows and sees all.

RIVER CAFÉ ITALIAN £££

(020-7386 4200; www.rivercafe.co.uk; Rainville Rd, Thames Wharf, W6; mains £12-35; 12.30-2.30pm & 7-9pm Mon-Sat, noon-3pm Sun; Hammersmith) The Thames-side restaurant that spawned the world-famous eponymous cookery books offers simple, precise cooking that showcases seasonal ingredients sourced with fanatical expertise; the menus change daily. Booking is essential, as it's a favourite of the Fulham set.

Paddington & Bayswater

COUSCOUS CAFÉ MOROCCAN ££

Map p462 (7 Porchester Gardens, W2; mains £9.95-15.95; Bayswater) This cosy and vividly decorated basement place excels in Moroccan-style couscous and *tagines* (spicy stews cooked in an earthenware dish), *pastillas* (filled savoury pastries) and slightly exaggerated service. Try the mixed meze plate (small/large £6.95/11.95). Alcohol is served or you can BYO (no corkage fee).

DRINKING & NIGHTLIFE

Notting Hill & Westbourne Grove

EARL OF LONSDALE PUB

Map p462 (277-281 Portobello Rd, W11; noon-11pm Mon-Sat, noon-10.30pm Sun; Notting Hill Gate, Ladbroke Grove) Named after the *bon vivant* founder of the AA (Automobile Association, *not* Alcoholics Anonymous), the Earl is peaceful during the day, with a mixture of old biddies and young hipsters inhabiting the reintroduced snugs. There are Samuel Smith's ales, a fantastic backroom, open fires and a magnificent beer garden.

Note the bricked-in windows in the wall onto the garden – the building was a victim of 'window tax' (see p330).

BEACH BLANKET BABYLON BAR

Map p462 (www.beachblanket.co.uk; 45 Ledbury Rd, W11; noon-midnight; ; Notting Hill Gate) This buzzing bar, decorated in baroque and rococo styles, is the place to come for a decadent night out. Famed for celebrity sightings, it's a favourite of Prince Harry and the moneyed set of the royal boroughs (so visit your manicurist and pop on your best togs).

PORTOBELLO STAR COCKTAIL BAR

Map p462 (www.portobellostarbar.co.uk; 171 Portobello Rd, W11; cocktails from £6; 11am-11.30pm Sun-Thu, 11am-12.30am Fri & Sat; ; Ladbroke Grove) See displays of cocktail chemistry with genuine flair at the hands of mixologist Jack Burger in this former pub given a refreshing makeover into a nifty, narrow cocktail bar. Frequently packed, the Portobello Star attracts a fair slice of Notting Hill's trendy drinkers, with eclectic sounds from weekend DJs.

NOTTING HILL ARTS CLUB CLUB

Map p462 (www.nottinghillartsclub.com; 21 Notting Hill Gate, W11; 6pm-late Mon-Fri, 4pm-late Sat & Sun; ; Notting Hill Gate) London simply wouldn't be what it is without places like NHAC. Cultivating the underground music scene, this small basement club attracts a musically curious and experimental crowd. The famous monthly Thursday Yo-Yo night is one of the best nights for R&B, '80s boogies, hip hop, ragga and diverse live sets; Wednesday's Death2Disco is indie night.

UNION TAVERN PUB

Map p462 (union-tavern.co.uk; 45 Woodfield Rd, W9; noon-11pm Mon-Thu, noon-midnight Fri & Sat, noon-10.30pm Sun; Westbourne Park) With just the right mix of shiny gastropub, rough-and-ready local appeal and a good location on the Grand Union Canal with a waterside terrace, this pub is a fabulous place to enjoy a couple of pints on your way to or from Portobello Road Market.

High Street Kensington

★KENSINGTON ROOF GARDENS CLUB

Map p464 (www.roofgardens.virgin.com; 99 Kensington High St, W8; ⏲10pm-3am Fri & Sat, May-Sep; ⊖High St Kensington) Atop the former Derry and Toms building high above Kensington High St is this enchanting venue – a nightclub with 0.6 hectares of gardens. There are three different gardens: the stunningly beautiful Spanish gardens inspired by the Alhambra in Granada; the Tudor gardens, all nooks, crannies and fragrant flowers; and the Woodlands gardens, home to ancient trees and four resident flamingos.

The gardens are only open from May to September; they have their own bars and often host live bands. The indoor part is the club proper (open year-round) where commercial dance music keeps the crowd of young socialites boogying until the early hours.

All of this wow-factor comes at a premium: entry is £20 to £25, you must register on the guest list before going and the drinks are £10 a pop. Still, it's a once-in-a-lifetime place. Entrance is on Derry St. Dress to impress.

WINDSOR CASTLE PUB

Map p464 (www.thewindsorcastlekensington.co.uk; 114 Campden Hill Rd, W11; ⏲noon-11pm Mon-Sat, noon-10.30pm Sun; 📶; ⊖Notting Hill Gate) A classic tavern on the brow of Campden Hill Rd, this place has history, nooks and charm on tap. It's worth the search for its historic compartmentalised interior, roaring fire (in winter), delightful beer garden (in summer) and affable regulars (most always). Legend attests the bones of Thomas Paine (author of *Rights of Man*) are in the cellar.

In the old days, Windsor Castle was visible from the pub, hence the name.

CHURCHILL ARMS PUB

Map p464 (www.churchillarmskensington.co.uk; 119 Kensington Church St; ⏲11am-11pm Mon-Wed, 11am-midnight Thu-Sat, noon-10.30pm Sun; 📶; ⊖Notting Hill Gate) With its cascade of geraniums and Union Jack flags swaying in the breeze, the Churchill Arms is quite a sight on Kensington Church St. Renowned for its Winston memorabilia and dozens of knick-knacks on the walls, the pub is a favourite of both locals and tourists. The attached conservatory has been serving excellent Thai food for two decades (mains £6 to £10).

Earl's Court & West Brompton

★TROUBADOUR BAR

Map p464 (www.troubadour.co.uk; 263-267 Old Brompton Rd, SW5; ⏲9am-midnight; ⊖Earl's Court) This eccentric, time-warped and convivial boho coffee-shop has been serenading drinkers since the 1950s. Bob Dylan, Adele, Joni Mitchell and Keith Moon have performed here and there's still live music (folk, blues) most nights and a large, pleasant garden open in summer. You'll be spoilt for choice with the wine list – Troubadour runs a wine club and has a wine shop (strong showing of Argentinean wines) next door and there's accommodation upstairs in the Garret (p348).

ATLAS PUB

Map p464 (www.theatlaspub.co.uk; 16 Seagrave Rd, SW6; ⏲noon-11pm Mon-Sat, noon-10.30pm Sun; ⊖West Brompton) A garrulous hubbub frequently pouring from its ivy-clad and port-coloured facade, this Victorian-era pub tempts locals and visitors alike with a delicious wood-panelled interior, winning Mediterranean menu, lovely side courtyard and fine range of beers and wines.

Maida Vale

WARRINGTON PUB

Map p462 (www.faucetinn.com/warrington; 93 Warrington Cres, W9; ⏲11am-11pm Mon-Thu, 11am-midnight Fri & Sat, 11am-10.30pm Sun; 📶; ⊖Warwick Ave, Maida Vale) Flung up in 1857, this former hotel and high-end brothel is an ornate, art nouveau pub with heaps of style. The huge saloon bar, dominated by a marble-topped hemispherical counter with a carved mahogany base and a huge stained-glass window by Tiffany, is a fabulous place to sample a range of four real ales.

Other alluring details include the imposing marble fireplace, eye-catching ceiling and magnificent porch; there's outside seating for al fresco drinking.

WATERWAY BAR

Map p462 (www.thewaterway.co.uk; 54 Formosa St, W9; ⏲noon-1am; ⊖Warwick Ave) Don't come here for the selection of beer or ales or the overly expensive nosh; this place, hard by the Grand Union Canal in Little Venice, is all about location, and it's hard to imagine a better place to while away a weekend afternoon.

Hammersmith

DOVE PUB

(www.dovehammersmith.co.uk; 19 Upper Mall, W6; ⊖Hammersmith, Ravenscourt Park) Severely inundated by the epic floodwaters of 1928, this gem of a 17th-century Fuller's pub revels in historic charm and superb Thames views. Scottish poet James Thompson was reputedly inspired to write the lyrics to 'Rule Britannia' here in the 18th century, it was Graham Greene's local, and Hemingway and Dylan Thomas drank here, too, while William Morris lived nearby.

To your right as you walk in is what was once listed as the smallest bar in London. If the sun comes out, fight for a spot on the lovely terrace (forget it on Boat Race day) and in winter, warm your toes by the open fire.

OLD SHIP W6 PUB

(www.oldshipw6.co.uk; 25 Upper Mall, W6; 9am-11pm Mon-Thu, 9am-midnight Fri-Sat, 9am-10.30pm Sun; ⊖Ravenscourt Park, Stamford Brook) With a ceiling decorated with sculls and oars, and walls hung with nautical prints, the Old Ship and its shiny, buttoned leather sofas would hardly merit a diversion but for its terrific waterside perch, which guarantees superb al fresco Thames views from the balcony upstairs or the ground floor terrace.

Dating to the 18th century, the pub is wall-to-wall with spectators for the annual Oxford and Cambridge Boat Race.

ENTERTAINMENT

O2 SHEPHERD'S BUSH EMPIRE CONCERT VENUE

Map p464 (www.o2shepherdsbushempire.co.uk; Shepherd's Bush Green, W12; ⊖Shepherd's Bush) Top acts (such as Mumford & Sons, Muse, PJ Harvey) get the crowds fired up in this famous midsized venue (capacity is 2000). The downer is the fact that the floor doesn't slope, so if you're not so tall you may not get much of a view from up the back in the stalls – it's worth paying for the balcony.

LYRIC HAMMERSMITH THEATRE

Map p464 (020-8741 6850; www.lyric.co.uk; King St, Lyric Sq, W6; ⊖Hammersmith) An excellent venue that turns classics on their head, the Lyric stages a stimulating choice of productions from the highbrow to more accessible theatre.

BUSH THEATRE THEATRE

Map p464 (www.bushtheatre.co.uk; 7 Uxbridge Rd, W12; ⊖Shepherd's Bush) This recently rehoused West London theatre is renowned for encouraging new talent. Its success over the past three decades is down to strong writing from the likes of Jonathan Harvey, Conor McPherson, Stephen Poliakoff and Mark Ravenhill.

INDIE CINEMAS

If you love cinema, you're in for a treat with West London's quirky picture houses. Q&A events with directors, sofas, alcoholic drinks allowed, and much more, this is how cinema should be. Tickets are slightly more expensive than run-of-the-mill cinemas.

Electric Cinema (Map p462; 020-7908 9696; www.electriccinema.co.uk; 191 Portobello Rd, W11; tickets £8-18; ⊖Ladbroke Grove) Having notched up its first centenary, the Electric is one of the UK's oldest cinemas, updated with luxurious leather armchairs, footstools and tables for food and drink in the auditorium.

Gate Picturehouse (Map p462; 0871 902 5731; www.picturehouses.co.uk; 87 Notting Hill Gate, W1; tickets £6.50-12.50; ⊖Notting Hill Gate) The Gate's single screen has one of London's most charming art deco cinema interiors, with director Q&As and live opera screenings from the famous Glyndebourne Festival. Cheapest tickets on Mondays.

Coronet (Map p462; www.coronet.org; 103 Notting Hill Gate, W8; tickets £7.50; ⊖Notting Hill Gate) The wonderful Edwardian interior, including a gorgeous balcony and even boxes, recalls the glory days of cinema, when filling a 400-seat house for every showing was easy. Cheap tickets on Tuesdays.

OPERA HOLLAND PARK OPERA

Map p464 (www.operahollandpark.com; Holland Park, W8; ⊖High St Kensington, Holland Park) Sit under the 800-seat canopy, temporarily erected every summer for a nine-week season in the middle of Holland Park for a mix of crowd pleasers and rare (even obscure) works.

RIVERSIDE STUDIOS PERFORMING ARTS

Map p464 (www.riversidestudios.co.uk; Crisp Rd, W6; ⊖Hammersmith) The Riverside hosts an eclectic mix of performing arts, from circus to theatre and comedy, and also doubles as an art-house cinema. There's a popular restaurant and bar to hand, with terrace views of the Thames and Hammersmith Bridge.

EARL'S COURT EXHIBITION CENTRE SPECTATOR SPORT

Map p464 (www.eco.co.uk; Warwick Rd, SW5; ⊖Earl's Court) This multipurpose venue hosts a range of events from sports fixtures to trade shows and concerts. There are current plans to demolish the iconic exhibition centre, which opened in 1937.

SHOPPING

CERAMICA BLUE HOMEWARES

Map p462 (www.ceramicablue.co.uk; 10 Blenheim Cres; ⊖Ladbroke Grove) A wonderful place for original and beautiful crockery, imported

LOCAL KNOWLEDGE

STAR HU'S LONDON

Originally from China, inspirational London fashion designer Star Hu (www.starhu.com) has a boutique in Portobello Green Arcade (p267). We caught up with her to get her lowdown on London.

How do you find London inspiring?

London's all about individuality. With its blend of cultures, traditions and subcultures, the most attractive thing about London is its diversity. There's a creative air, so if you're a naturally creative person, you're easily inspired. That's why I love London.

What parts of London really knock your socks off?

Where do I start? The London art scene, the V&A (p188), the Barbican (p161), the Tate Modern (p170), the Saatchi Gallery (p198), Royal Academy of Arts (p108), Hayward Gallery (p175) and Design Museum (p178). The markets, the pubs, Little Venice (p266) and Hampstead Heath (p246); Dalston Kingsland and Stokey (Stoke Newington); street fashion; London Fashion week; the South Bank, the music scene; **Lovebox** (www.mamacolive.com/lovebox; Victoria Park, E9); the Electric Cinema (p273). I could go on and on...

Any London shops you love to bits?

For designer fashion, there's **Browns Focus** (24 South Molton St, W1; ⌚10am-6.30pm Mon-Sat; ⊖Bond St) and **LN-CC** (18 Shacklewell Lane, E8; ⌚by appointment; Ⓡ Dalston Kingsland) in Dalston. For vintage fashion: Beyond Retro (p237), Absolute Vintage (p220) and **Blitz London** (55-59 Hanbury St, E1; 11am-7pm; ⊖Shoreditch High St). For high-street fashion the Topshop (p140) flagship store in Oxford Circus is a must.

For a drink at the end of the day? Your call.

I love going out in east and north London, but there's a great blues bar near Carnaby St called **Ain't Nothin But** (www.aintnothinbut.co.uk; 20 Kingly St) and that quirky little Spanish bar Bradley's (p131): they're my central London favourites. For somewhere more indie: the Old Blue Last (p219) and Catch (p218) are good live-music venues in east London. My gay friends love the George & Dragon (p216), the Joiners Arms (p235) on Hackney Rd and Dalston Superstore (p257).

And for Chinese nosh?

For authentic Chinese, **Ba Shan** (24 Romilly St, W1; ⌚noon-11pm; ⊖Leicester Sq) and Bar Shu (p123) in Soho. For something cheap and cheerful: Baozi Inn (p122) in Chinatown.

from more than a dozen countries. There are Japanese eggshell-glaze teacups, serving plates with tribal South African designs, gorgeous table cloths from Provence and much more.

NOTTING HILL BOOKSHOP BOOKS

Map p462 (www.thenottinghillbookshop.co.uk; 13 Blenheim Cres; ⌚9am-7pm Mon-Fri, 8.30am-7pm Sat, 10am-6pm Sun; ⊖Ladbroke Grove) Still milking every last drop as the inspiration behind the bookshop in Hugh Grant's and Julia Robert's monster rom-com, the former Travel Bookshop was recently repackaged as a more general bookshop. The new guise has done little to staunch the flow of visitors who pose outside for snaps. An understandable accent on travel books endures, but fiction provides equilibrium and there's a strong children's section at the rear.

BOOKS FOR COOKS BOOKS

Map p462 (www.booksforcooks.com; 4 Blenheim Cres, W11; ⌚10am-6pm Tue-Sat; ⊖Ladbroke Grove) All the recipe books from celeb and non-celeb chefs you can imagine are sold here – perfect for more adventurous cooks or for those looking for 'exotic' cookbooks. The cafe has a test kitchen where you can sample recipes at lunch and teatime.

VILLAGE BICYCLE CLOTHING

Map p462 (www.imavillagebicycle.com; 79-91 Ledbury Rd; ⌚10am-6pm Mon-Wed, Fri & Sat, 10am-7pm Thu, noon-5pm Sun; ⊖Notting Hill Gate, Westbourne Park) Opened by Jardine Matheson heir Willa Keswick and decorated with neon crosses and bling skulls, this hip two-floor boutique is a Notting Hillbilly hunting ground for edgy, fun and extrovert clothes and accessories, sequin-studded sneakers, hand-stitched bags, fluorescent, day-glo garb and other left-field, urban togs and trendy ephemera.

RELLIK VINTAGE

Map p462 (www.relliklondon.co.uk; 8 Golborne Rd; ⌚10am-6pm Tue-Sat; ⊖Westbourne Park) Incongruously located opposite one of London's most notorious tower blocks – the god-awful-yet-heritage-listed concrete Trellick Tower – Rellik is a fashionista favourite retro store. It stocks vintage numbers from the 1920s to the 1980s and, rummaging among the frippery, it's not unusual to find an Yves Saint-Laurent coat, a Chloe suit or an Ossie Clark dress.

WESTFIELD SHOPPING CENTRE

With a humungous cousin in Stratford (and one tipped for Croydon), this gigantic recession-busting shopping mecca was London's first mall. As well as the 380-odd shops that reside here (all franchises), **Westfield** (Map p464; http://uk.westfield.com/london; Ariel Way, W12; ⌚10am-10pm Mon-Sat, noon-6pm Sun; ⊖Wood Lane) has a raft of eateries (again, chains only), bars, a cinema, and regular events, from fashion shows to book signings.

PYLONES ACCESSORIES

Map p462 (www.pylones.com; 172 Portobello Rd; ⌚9.30am-6pm Sun-Fri, 9am-7pm Sat; ⊖Ladbroke Grove) Pop into Pylones and you're almost guaranteed to end up buying something entirely non-essential to flaunt to your nearest and dearest. Get your pointy elbows out and browse this vibrantly coloured and creative cosmos of knick-knacks before emerging with a nifty collapsible hairbrush, a psychedelic egg timer, a funky thermos flask, a day-glo wall clock, or whatever.

RETRO WOMAN VINTAGE

Map p462 (www.mgeshops.com; 20 Pembridge Rd, W11; ⌚10am-8pm; ⊖Notting Hill Gate) More secondhand than vintage, but very popular, Retro Woman has racks upon racks of hand-me-down fashion, including an astonishing selection of shoes (of Imelda Marcos proportions). There's another branch a bit further along Pembridge Rd, at No 32.

ORSINI VINTAGE

Map p464 (76 Earl's Court Rd, W8; ⌚10.30am-6pm Mon-Sat, noon-5pm Sun; ⊖Earl's Court) One of the best vintage designer collections in town, Orsini is small, beautiful and friendly. It's a little out of the way, but worth the effort if you're looking for a gem. Alterations are available in-store.

ROUGH TRADE WEST MUSIC

Map p462 (www.roughtrade.com; 130 Talbot Rd, W11; ⌚10am-6.30pm Mon-Sat, 11am-5pm Sun; ⊖Ladbroke Grove) With its underground, alternative and vintage rarities, this home of the eponymous punk-music label remains a haven for vinyl junkies.

BOOKS FOR AMNESTY BOOKS

Map p464 (139b King St; 10am-6pm Mon-Sat, 11.30am-4pm Sun; Hammersmith, Ravenscourt Park) Literary browsers can head to Amnesty International's secondhand bookshop for a well-considered and regularly refreshed collection of fiction, prose, poetry, biography, sci-fi, essays, art books and a solid crop of genre-spanning hardbacks, largely in good condition.

BOOK & COMIC EXCHANGE BOOKS

Map p462 (www.mgeshops.com; 14 Pembridge Rd; 10am-8pm; Notting Hill Gate) Full of surprises, this shop is inundated with early issues of *Superboy, Batman, Justice League, the Flash, the Hulk, Spiderman, the Silver Surfer* and a host of other comic superheroes, backed up by sizeable slabs of collectable music magazines and walls densely stuffed with secondhand books.

Stock is constantly reduced in price to make space for new items so there's always new literature turning up and bargains await.

HONEST JON'S MUSIC

Map p462 (020-8969 9822; www.honestjons.com; 278 Portobello Rd, W10; 10am-6pm Mon-Sat, 11am-5pm Sun; Ladbroke Grove) Selling old-school reggae, jazz, funk, soul, dance and blues vinyl to Notting Hill's musical purists since 1974, with a large volume of CDs.

SPORTS & ACTIVITIES

★**LONDON WATERBUS COMPANY** CRUISE

Map p462 (020-7482 2550; www.londonwaterbus.co.uk; 58 Camden Lock Pl, NW1; adult/child one-way £7.20/6, return £10.30/8.40; hourly 10am-5pm Apr-Sep; Warwick Ave, Camden Town) This enclosed barge runs enjoyable 50-minute trips on Regent's Canal between Little Venice and Camden Lock, passing by Regent's Park and stopping at London Zoo. There are fewer departures outside of high season – check the website for schedules.

QUEENS ICE & BOWL SKATING

Map p462 (www.queensiceandbowl.co.uk; 17 Queensway; 10am-6.45pm & 8-10.45pm daily, children's classes 4.45-5.30pm Tue & Thu; Queensway) London may have a generous crop of winter month outdoor ice rinks, but Queens Ice Rink in Queensway is open all year. A great hit with novices and ice-skaters of all ages, the rink has been sending generations of youngsters and adults, arms whirling, around its rink for decades. There's a fun bowling alley right alongside and disco skate nights on ice at weekends.

PORCHESTER SPA SPA

Map p462 (Porchester Centre, Queensway, W2; admission £26; 10am-10pm; Bayswater, Royal Oak) Housed in a gorgeous, art deco building, the Porchester is a no-frills spa run by Westminster Council. With a 30m swimming pool, a large Finnish-log sauna, two steam rooms, three Turkish hot rooms and a massive plunge pool, there are plenty of affordable treatments on offer including massages and male and female pampering/grooming sessions.

It's women only on Tuesdays, Thursdays and Fridays all day and between 10am and 4pm on Sundays; men only on Mondays, Wednesdays and Saturdays. Couples are welcome from 4pm to 10pm on Sundays.

RECIPEASE COOKING COURSE

Map p462 (www.jamieoliver.com; 92-94 Notting Hill Gate; children's classes from £15; Notting Hill Gate) Filling the spacious site left by WH Smiths, this Jamie Oliver food and kitchen emporium – with a restaurant above – has a kitchen at the busy heart of each floor. Here you can join a variety of adult and children's cookery classes: learn how to prepare sushi, Thai green curry or make pasta like a maestro, or have your kids learning the secret of perfect pancakes.

Greenwich & South London

GREENWICH | WOOLWICH | LAMBETH | KENNINGTON | ELEPHANT & CASTLE | BRIXTON | BATTERSEA | WANDSWORTH | DULWICH | FOREST HILL | CLAPHAM | CRYSTAL PALACE | CAMBERWELL | VAUXHALL

Neighbourhood Top Five

❶ Feasting on delicious views of London from beneath the statue of General Wolfe in **Greenwich Park** (p280).

❷ Hanging out at the fun and funky **Brixton Village** (p285).

❸ Exploring the **Cutty Sark's** (p282) history – and admiring its golden hull from beneath.

❹ Charting an eye-opening course through the oceanic exhibits of the **National Maritime Museum** (p283).

❺ Mooching about wild and wealthy **Wandsworth Common** (p286) and ogling the stunning Georgian mansions nearby.

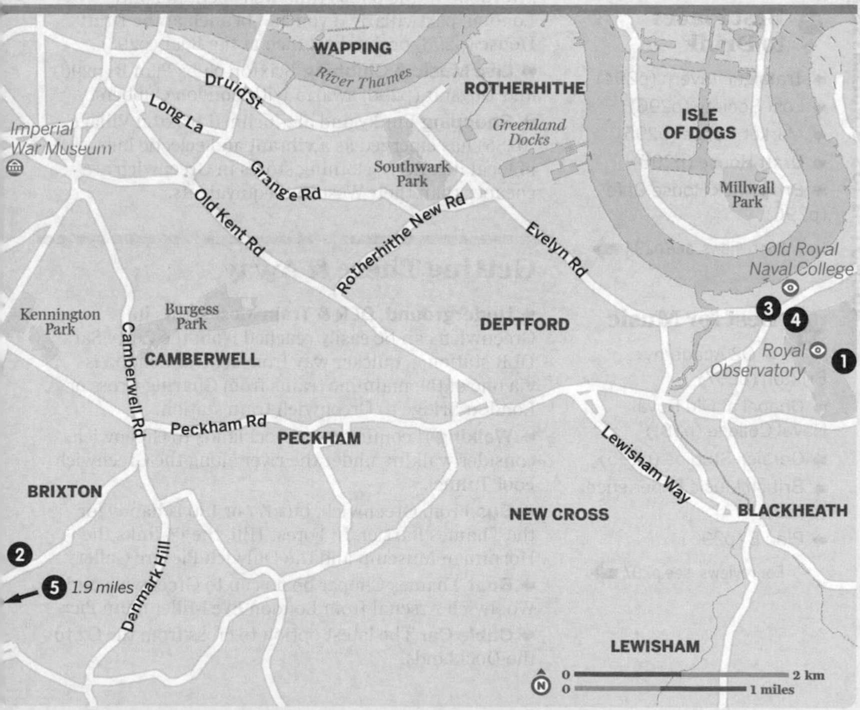

For more detail of this area see Maps p466, p468 and p469

Lonely Planet Top Tip

Join the harvesters in October scouring Greenwich Park for its huge bounty of windfall edible chestnuts (it's legal to pick them up off the ground, but illegal to swat them from the trees). A fun way to reach Docklands from Greenwich is via the foot tunnel under the Thames.

Best Places to Eat

- Buenos Aires Café (p292)
- Angels & Gypsies (p293)
- Abbeville Kitchen (p294)
- Franco Manca (p292)
- Chez Bruce (p293)

For reviews, see p291

Best Places to Drink

- Trafalgar Tavern (p294)
- Lost Society (p296)
- Market House (p295)
- Draft House (p296)
- Brunswick House Cafe (p296)

For reviews, see p294

Best for Music

- O2 Academy Brixton (p297)
- Chapel at Old Royal Naval College (p281)
- Corsica Studios (p295)
- British Music Experience (p282)
- Plan B (p296)

For reviews, see p297

Explore: Greenwich & South London

The existential divide between north and south London remains as stark as the Watford Gap, but growing numbers of North Londoners have warmed to South London's more affordable property prices and leafy charms. Quaint Greenwich (*gren*-itch) is packed with grand architecture, while some gorgeous parks and standout museums bring growing fleets of visitors. With the Royal Observatory and the fab newly re-opened Cutty Sark, Greenwich should be one of the highlights of any visit to London; allow a day, particularly if you want to head down the river to the Thames Barrier, passing the stunning O2 along the way.

Find time for an afternoon or a night out in edgy and artistic Brixton, or Clapham with its upmarket restaurants. Battersea and Wandsworth are home to lovely parks and a visit is ideally rounded off with a pint of beer in fantastic local pubs while Lambeth boasts both the episcopal seat of the Church of England and one of London's finest museums. Further afield, Dulwich and Forest Hill are home to excellent galleries and museums, while Bexleyheath will reward day trippers with unusual gems.

Local Life

- **Hang-outs** Spending a Saturday or Sunday afternoon in the pub is time well spent in South London, particularly if you add brunch at the Draft House (p296) or Sunday lunch at the Bear (p293).
- **Live Music & Clubbing** Brixton clubs Plan B (p296) and Dogstar (p296) swarm with London clubbers.
- **Shopping** Funky and art-inclined Brixton Village (p285) has emerged as a vibrant and eclectic hub of local life. Retro clothing stores in Greenwich are cheaper than their West End equivalents.

Getting There & Away

- **Underground, DLR & Train** Most sights in Greenwich can be easily reached from the Cutty Sark DLR station; a quicker way from central London is via one of the mainline trains from Charing Cross or London Bridge to Greenwich train station.
- **Walking** If coming from Docklands to Greenwich, consider walking under the river along the Greenwich Foot Tunnel.
- **Bus** From Greenwich, bus 177 or 180 is handy for the Thames Barrier. In Forest Hill, the P4 links the Horniman Museum and the Dulwich Picture Gallery.
- **Boat** Thames Clipper boats run to Greenwich and Woolwich Arsenal from London Eye Millennium Pier.
- **Cable Car** The latest option to cross from the O2 to the Docklands.

TOP SIGHT
ROYAL OBSERVATORY & GREENWICH PARK

One of London's most-visited attractions, the Royal Observatory is where the study of the sea and the stars converge within gorgeous Greenwich Park, London's oldest royal park. The Prime Meridian charts its line through the grounds of the observatory, chosen quite arbitrarily in 1884, cleaving the globe into the eastern and western hemispheres. The observatory sits on a hill within leafy and regal Greenwich Park, with its fabulous views, 73 hectares of trees and lush greenery.

Royal Observatory

The excellent Royal Observatory is divided into two sections. Note that access to the Astronomy Centre is free.

Flamsteed House & Meridian Courtyard

Charles II ordered construction of the Christopher Wren-designed Flamsteed House – the original observatory building – on the foundations of Greenwich Castle in 1675; it contains the magnificent **Octagon Room**, and the rather simple apartment where the Astronomer Royal and his family lived. Below is a series of brilliant galleries explaining how the longitude problem – how to accurately determine a ship's east-west location – was solved through astronomical means and the invention of the chronometer.

Outside Flamsteed House, the globe is decisively sliced into east and west, where delighted visitors can straddle both hemispheres in the Meridian Courtyard, with one foot either side of the meridian line. Every day at 1pm the red time-ball at the top of the Royal Observatory continues to drop as it has done since 1833.

DON'T MISS...

- Meridian Courtyard
- Flamsteed House
- Views from the statue of General Wolfe
- Astronomy Centre

PRACTICALITIES

- Map p469
- www.rmg.co.uk
- Greenwich Park, SE10
- Royal Observatory adult/child £6.35/1.80
- 10am-5pm
- DLR Cutty Sark

PRIME TARGET

On 15 February 1894, the Royal Observatory was the unexpected target of an anarchist bomb plot. The bomber – a 26-year-old French anarchist by the name of Martial Bourdin – managed to blow his left hand off in the bungled attack, and died from his wounds soon afterwards. The choice of the Royal Observatory as a target was never understood, but it was undamaged in the attack. The bombing later found literary recognition in Joseph Conrad's novel *The Secret Agent*.

The Greenwich meridian was selected as the global prime meridian at the International Meridian Conference in Washington DC in 1884. Greenwich therefore became the world's common zero for longitude and standard for time calculations, replacing the multiple meridians that had previously existed. Greenwich was assisted in its bid by the earlier US adoption of Greenwich Mean Time for its own national time zones. Furthermore, the majority of world trade already used sea charts that identified Greenwich as the prime meridian.

Astronomy Centre & Peter Harrison Planetarium

The southern half of the observatory contains the highly informative Astronomy Centre, where you can touch the oldest object you will ever encounter: part of the Gibeon meteorite, a mere 4.5 billion years old! Other engaging exhibits include an orrery (mechanical model of the solar system, minus Uranus and Neptune) from 1780, astronomical documentaries, a first edition of Newton's *Principia Mathematica* and the opportunity to view the Milky Way in multiple wavelengths. To take star-gazing further, pick up a Skyhawk telescope from the shop.

The state-of-the-art **Peter Harrison Planetarium** (Map p469; adult/child £6.50/4.50) – London's only one – can cast entire heavens onto the inside of its roof. It runs several informative shows a day.

Greenwich Park

Handsome venue of the 2012 Games equestrian events, this **park** (Map p469; www.royalparks.gov.uk; King George St, SE10; ⏲6am-6pm winter, 8pm spring & autumn, 9pm summer; 🚉Greenwich or Maze Hill, DLR Cutty Sark) is one of London's loveliest expanses of green, with a rose garden, picturesque walks and astonishing views from the crown of the hill near the Royal Observatory, towards Canary Wharf, the financial district across the Thames.

Covering a full 73 hectares, this is the oldest enclosed royal park and is partly the work of André Le Nôtre, the landscape architect who designed the palace gardens of Versailles for Louis XIV, the Sun King. The park is rich in historic sights, including a teahouse near the Royal Observatory, a cafe behind the National Maritime Museum, a deer park, tennis courts in the southwest and a boating lake at the Queen's House end. In October, look out for edible chestnuts on the ground.

Ranger's House (Wernher Collection)

This elegant Georgian **villa** (Map p469; www.english-heritage.org.uk; Greenwich Park, Chesterfield Walk, SE10; adult/child £6.70/4; ⏲tours only at 11am & 2pm Sun-Wed Apr-Sep; 🚉Greenwich or DLR Cutty Sark), built in 1723, once housed the park's ranger and now contains a collection of 700 works of art (medieval and Renaissance paintings, porcelain, silverware, tapestries) amassed by Julius Wernher (1850–1912), a German-born railway engineer's son who struck it rich in the diamond fields of South Africa in the 19th century. The Spanish Renaissance jewellery collection is the best in Europe, and the rose garden fronting the house defies description.

TOP SIGHT
OLD ROYAL NAVAL COLLEGE

When Christopher Wren was commissioned by King William III and Queen Mary II to construct a naval hospital here in 1692, he conceived it in two separate halves to protect the river views from the Queen's House, Inigo Jones' miniature masterpiece to the south. Built on the site of the Old Palace of Placentia, where Henry VIII was born in 1491, the hospital was initially intended for those wounded in the victory over the French at La Hogue. In 1869 the building was converted to a Naval College; today it is home to the University of Greenwich and Trinity College of Music, with two main rooms open to the public.

DON'T MISS...

- Painted Hall
- Concerts in the Chapel
- Artefacts from Henry VIII's old palace

PRACTICALITIES

- Map p469
- www.oldroyalnaval college.org
- 2 Cutty Sark Gardens, SE10
- ⏲10am-5pm
- DLR Cutty Sark

Painted Hall

Designed as a dining hall for sailors, the **Painted Hall** (Map p469; ⏲10am-5pm) in the King William Building is one of Europe's greatest banquet rooms, dressed in decorative 'allegorical baroque' murals by artist James Thornhill. The magnificent ceiling mural above the Lower Hall is a feast, showing William and Mary enthroned amid symbols of the Virtues. Beneath William's feet grovels the defeated French king Louis XIV, furled flag in hand. Head up to the Upper Hall where, on the western wall, George I is depicted with his family.

Off the Upper Hall is the **Nelson Room**, originally designed by Nicholas Hawksmoor. In January 1806 the brandy-soaked (for embalming purposes, of course) body of the great naval hero lay in state here before his funeral at St Paul's. Today the room contains a plaster replica of the statue atop Nelson's Column in Trafalgar Square, plus other memorabilia, including lots of hospital silver. Look to the courtyard through the window; the cobbles form an outline of the Union Flag (Union Jack).

Chapel

With its mix of ancient Greek and naval motifs, the beautiful **chapel** (Map p469; ⏲10am-5pm Mon-Sat, from 12.30pm Sun) in the Queen Mary Building is decorated in an elaborate rococo style. The eastern end of the chapel is dominated by a painting by the 18th-century American artist Benjamin West showing *The Preservation of St Paul after Shipwreck at Malta*. The chapel is famed for its excellent acoustics and regularly hosts concerts, many of them free; check the Old Royal Naval College's website for details.

Discover Greenwich

The new and mildly diverting **Discover Greenwich** (Map p469; www.ornc.org; The Pepys Building, King William Walk; ⏲10am-5pm) FREE exhibition delves into the history of Greenwich with models and hands-on exhibits, many aimed at children. It also contains artefacts from King Henry VIII's old palace, unearthed during a dig in 2005.

The Greenwich Tourist Office (p413) is also here. If you need a drink or a bite to eat, pop into the Old Brewery (p295) next door.

Guided Tours

Daily **guided tours** (adult/child £5/free) of the college run at noon and 2pm and take you behind the scenes as well as to the main sights. Tours must be booked at the Greenwich Tourist Office.

SIGHTS

Greenwich

ROYAL OBSERVATORY HISTORIC BUILDING
See p279.

GREENWICH PARK PARK
See p279.

OLD ROYAL NAVAL COLLEGE HISTORIC BUILDING
See p281.

QUEEN'S HOUSE HISTORIC BUILDING
Map p469 (www.rmg.co.uk/queens-house; Romney Rd, SE10; ⏲10am-5pm; DLR Cutty Sark) **FREE** The first Palladian building built by architect Inigo Jones after he returned from Italy is far more enticing than the art collection it contains, even though it includes some Turners, Holbeins, Hogarths and Gainsboroughs. The ceremonial Great Hall is the principal room – a gorgeous cube shape, with an elaborately tiled floor dating to 1637.

The house was begun in 1616 for Anne of Denmark, wife of James I, but was not completed until 1638, when it became the home of Charles I and his queen, Henrietta Maria. The beautiful helix-shaped Tulip Staircase (named for the flowers on the wrought-iron balustrade; sadly, no photos allowed) leads to a gallery on level 2 hung with paintings and portraits with a sea or seafaring theme from the National Maritime Museum's fine art collection. Look out for the strikingly modernist Sixty Degrees South by Herbert Barnard John Everett.

BRITISH MUSIC EXPERIENCE MUSEUM
(www.britishmusicexperience.com; O2, Millennium Way, SE10; adult/child £13/6.50; ⏲11am-7.30pm; North Greenwich) This musical attraction in the O2 'bubble' traces the history of British popular music from 1945 to the present day. There's star-studded memorabilia, from Spice Girls' Geri Halliwell's Union Jack dress to John Lennon's glasses. Film yourself playing guitar or pick up dance moves from a virtual instructor before standing next to holograms performing before a massive, cheering (filmed) audience.

TOP SIGHT CUTTY SARK

This Greenwich landmark, the last of the great clipper ships to sail between China and England in the 19th century, finally reopened in April 2012 after six years and £25 million of extensive renovations (and a disastrous fire in 2007). All we can say is that it was worth the wait: the Cutty Sark is a stunner and a brilliant attraction.

The exhibition in the ship's hold tells her story as a tea clipper at the end of the 19th century (and then wool and mixed cargo). Launched in 1869 in Scotland, she made eight voyages to China in the 1870s, sailing out with a mixed cargo and coming back with a bounty of tea. There are films, interactive maps and plenty of illustrations and props to give you an idea of what life on board was like.

On the top deck, you can visit the crew's cramped living quarters and the officer's plush cabins. Visits end in the basement gallery located underneath the ship: the hull, covered in golden Muntz metal plates, appears to be floating and is a breathtaking sight. There is also an intriguing collection of figureheads, one of the largest of its kind in the world.

DON'T MISS

- Views of the hull from the basement gallery
- Interactive displays on the Cutty Sark's voyages
- Top-deck living quarters

PRACTICALITIES

- Map p469
- www.cuttysark.org.uk
- King William Walk, SE10
- adult/child £12/6.50
- ⏲10am-5pm
- DLR Cutty Sark

TOP SIGHT
NATIONAL MARITIME MUSEUM

Narrating the long and eventful history of seafaring Britain, this museum is one of Greenwich's top attractions.

The exhibits are arranged thematically and highlights include **Miss Britain III** (the first boat to top 100mph on open water) from 1933, the 19m-long **golden state barge** built in 1732 for Frederick, Prince of Wales, and the huge **ship's propeller** installed on level 1. Families will love these, as well as the **ship simulator** and the **children's gallery** on the second floor where kids can let rip.

Adults are likely to prefer the fantastic (and slightly more serene) galleries. **Voyagers: Britons and the Sea** on the ground floor showcases some of the museum's incredible archives; **Traders: the East India Company and Asia** looks back on Britain's maritime trade with the East in the 19th century; while **Atlantic: Slavery, Trade, Empire** explores the triangular trade between Europe, Africa and America from the 1600s to the 1850s.

A new gallery, **Nelson, Navy, Nation 1688–1815**, focusing on the history of the Royal Navy during the conflict-ridden 18th century, was under preparation at the time of writing and was scheduled to open in October 2013. It'll likely feature the coat in which Nelson was fatally wounded.

DON'T MISS...

- Frederick's golden state barge
- Nelson's uniform coat
- *Miss Britain III*
- Ship simulator

PRACTICALITIES

- Map p469
- www.rmg.co.uk/national-maritime-museum
- Romney Rd, SE10
- 10am-5pm
- DLR Cutty Sark

O2 NOTABLE BUILDING
(www.theo2.co.uk; Peninsula Sq, SE10; North Greenwich) The 380m-wide circular O2 cost £750 million to build. Once the definitive white elephant, it has finally found its purpose as a multipurpose venue hosting big-ticket concerts, sporting events (it was the gymnastics and basketball venue for the London Olympics) and blockbuster exhibitions. There are dozens of bars and restaurants inside. The O2 is located on the Greenwich Peninsula, just 10 minutes by bus from Greenwich itself.

ST ALFEGE CHURCH CHURCH
Map p469 (www.st-alfege.org; Church St, SE10; 11am-4pm Mon-Wed, to 2pm Thu & Fri, 10am-4pm Sat, noon-4pm Sun; Greenwich or DLR Cutty Sark) Designed by Nicholas Hawksmoor in 1714 to replace a 12th-century building, this glorious parish church features a restored mural by James Thornhill (whose work includes the Painted Hall at the Royal Naval College and St Paul's Cathedral), a largely wood-panelled interior and an intriguing 'Tallis' keyboard with middle keyboard octaves from the Tudor period.

Free concerts take place on Thursdays at 1.10pm.

FAN MUSEUM MUSEUM
Map p469 (www.fan-museum.org; 12 Crooms Hill, SE10; adult/child £4/free; 11am-5pm Tue-Sat, noon-5pm Sun; ; Greenwich or DLR Cutty Sark) The world's only museum entirely devoted to fans has a wonderful collection of ivory, tortoiseshell, peacock-feather and

GREENWICH ARCHITECTURE

Greenwich is home to an extraordinary interrelated cluster of classical buildings. All the great architects of the Enlightenment made their mark here, largely due to royal patronage. In the early 17th century, Inigo Jones built one of England's first classical Renaissance homes, the Queen's House, which still stands today. Charles II was particularly fond of the area and had Sir Christopher Wren build both the Royal Observatory and part of the Royal Naval College, which John Vanbrugh then completed in the early 17th century.

THAMES BARRIER

This sci-fi looking barrier is designed to protect London from flooding and, with rising sea levels and surge tides, vulnerable London is likely to become increasingly dependent on the barricade. Completed three decades ago, the barrier consists of 10 movable gates anchored to nine concrete piers, each as tall as a five-storey building. The silver roofs on the piers house the operating machinery that rotates the gates against excess water. Tested monthly, they make a glitteringly surreal sight, straddling the river in the lee of a giant warehouse.

The Thames tide rises and falls quite harmlessly twice a day, and once a fortnight there's also a stronger 'spring' tide. The danger comes when the spring tide coincides with an unexpected surge, which pushes tons of extra water upriver. The barrier has been built to prevent that water pouring over the riverbanks and flooding nearby houses. Today environmentalists are already talking about a bigger, wider damming mechanism further towards the mouth of the river, before the current barrier comes to the expected end of its design life in 2030.

The barrier looks best when raised, and the only guaranteed time this happens is once a month, when the mechanisms are checked. For exact dates and times, check with the **Thames Barrier Information Centre** (☑020-8305 4188; 1 Unity Way, SE18; adult/child £3.75/2.25; ☺10.30am-5pm Thu-Sun; ⊜North Greenwich then ⌷472 or 161 or ⌷Charlton then ⌷472).

If you're coming from central London, take a train to Charlton from Charing Cross or London Bridge. Then walk along Woolwich Rd to Eastmoor St, which leads northward to the centre. If you're coming from Greenwich, you can pick up bus 177 or 180 along Romney Rd and get off at the Thames Barrier stop. The closest tube station is North Greenwich, from where you can pick up bus 472 or 161. Boats also travel to and from the barrier, although they don't land here.

folded-fabric examples alongside kitsch battery-powered versions and huge ornamental Welsh fans. The setting, an 18th-century Georgian town house, also has a Japanese-style garden plus the **Orangery** (half-/full tea £5/6; ☺3-5pm Tue & Sun), with lovely trompe l'œil murals and twice-weekly afternoon tea.

⊙ Woolwich

FIREPOWER (ROYAL ARTILLERY MUSEUM) MUSEUM

(www.firepower.org.uk; Royal Arsenal, Woolwich, SE18; adult/child £5.30/2.50; ☺10am-5pm Tue-Sat; ⌷DLR Woolwich Arsenal) Loud and reeking of adrenaline, Firepower is an explosive display of the evolution of artillery. The History Gallery traces artillery's development from catapults to nuclear warheads, while the multimedia, smoke-filled Field of Fire immerses you in the experience of artillery gunners from WWI to Bosnia in a 15-minute extravaganza. There's a Gunnery Hall packed with weapons and vehicles from the 20th century.

Kids will love the Camo Zone where they can try their hand on the firing range (£1.50).

GREENWICH HERITAGE CENTRE MUSEUM

(www.greenwichheritage.org; Royal Arsenal, Artillery Sq, SE18; ☺9am-5pm Tue-Sat; ⌷DLR Woolwich Arsenal) **FREE** This well-endowed centre examines the history of the Royal Arsenal, once Britain's main weapons manufacturing centre, and Woolwich Dockyards, with vivid testimonials by former employees and local residents, including tales of bombings during WWII.

⊙ Lambeth, Kennington and Elephant & Castle

FLORENCE NIGHTINGALE MUSEUM MUSEUM

Map p468 (☑020-7620 0374; www.florence-nightingale.co.uk; St Thomas's Hospital, 2 Lambeth Palace Rd, SE1; adult/child £5.80/4.80; ☺10am-5pm; ⊜Westminster or Waterloo) This small but excellent museum looks back at the life and legacy of Florence Nightingale (1820–1910), who led a team of nurses to Turkey in 1854 during the Crimean War. Nightingale worked to improve the care offered to soldiers. Back in London, she set up a training school for nurses at St Thomas's Hospital (where the museum is located) in 1859.

So popular did she become that baseball-card-style photos of the gentle 'Lady of the Lamp' were sold during her lifetime. There is no shortage of revisionist detractors who dismiss her as a 'canny administrator' and 'publicity hound'; Nightingale was, in fact, one of the world's first modern celebrities. But she is credited with being the mother of modern nursing. An audioguide is included in the admission price.

GARDEN MUSEUM MUSEUM

Map p468 (☎020-7401 8865; www.gardenmuseum.org.uk; St Mary-at-Lambeth, Lambeth Palace Rd, SE1; adult/concession £5/3; ⊙10.30am-5pm Sun-Fri, to 4pm Sat; ⊖Lambeth North) Housed in the church of St Mary-at-Lambeth, this peaceful, green-fingered museum's trump card is its charming **knot garden**, a replica of a 17th-century formal garden, with topiary hedges clipped into an intricate, twirling design. Keen gardeners will enjoy the displays on the 17th-century Tradescant *père* and *fils* – a father-and-son team who were gardeners to Charles I and Charles II.

Captain William Bligh (of mutinous Bounty fame) is buried here (he lived and died nearby at 100 Lambeth Rd). The excellent cafe serves vegetarian food. Temporary exhibitions are also staged and tours are reserved for the last Tuesday of the month at 2pm.

LAMBETH PALACE HISTORIC BUILDING

Map p468 (Palace Rd, SE1; ⊖Lambeth North) This gorgeous red-brick Tudor gatehouse located beside the church of St Mary-at-Lambeth leads to Lambeth Palace, the London residence of the Archbishop of Canterbury. Although the palace is not usually open to the public, the gardens occasionally are; check with a tourist office for more details.

Brixton

★BRIXTON VILLAGE MARKET

Map p466 (Atlantic Rd, SW9; ⊙8am-11.30pm Tue-Sun, to 6pm Mon; ⊖Brixton) This revitalised covered market has enjoyed an eye-catching renaissance since 2009, prompted by an initiative to offer a period of free rent to outfits setting up in the dilapidated 1930s Granville Arcade. Cafes and restaurants have

TOP SIGHT
IMPERIAL WAR MUSEUM

Fronted by a pair of intimidating 15in naval guns, this riveting museum is housed in what was once Bethlehem Royal Hospital, also known as Bedlam. Although the museum's focus is on military action involving British or Commonwealth troops during the 20th century, it rolls out the carpet to war in the wider sense.

In **Secret War** on the first floor, there's an intriguing rifle through the operations of the Secret Operations Executive (SOE), such as rubber soles resembling feet worn underneath boots to leave 'foot prints' on enemy beaches. One of the most challenging sections is the extensive **Holocaust Exhibition** (not recommended for under 14s) on the third floor.

The museum was partially closed at the time of writing for extensive refurbishment; complete reopening was scheduled for summer 2014, when the museum will unveil new state-of-the-art **First World War Galleries** to mark the 100th anniversary of the start of WWI.

A grand atrium will also be revealed in 2014; objects on display will include a Battle of Britain **Spitfire**, a towering German **V-2 rocket**, and as you work your way up the museum you will see everything from a Taliban motorbike to a lifelike replica of **Little Boy** (the atom bomb dropped on Hiroshima).

DON'T MISS...

- Holocaust Exhibition
- WWI Galleries
- Spitfire

PRACTICALITIES

- Map p468
- www.iwm.org.uk
- Lambeth Rd, SE1
- ⊙10am-6pm
- ⊖Lambeth North

BRIXTON WINDMILL

Built for one John Ashby in 1816, **Brixton Windmill** (Map p466; www.brixtonwindmill.org; Blenheim Gardens, SW2; ⊖Brixton then 🚌45 or 59) is the closest to central London still in existence. It was later powered by gas and milled as recently as 1934. It's been refitted with sails and machinery for a wind-driven mill and is not currently open to the public, but it can be admired from the outside.

swarmed in as well as a host of inventively inclined shops, which happily cohabit with butchers, greengrocers and bazaars.

The 'village' is lively day and night and has a lovely, eclectic atmosphere. Shops worth popping into include **Sweet Tooth** (Unit 66), selling sweets from around the world, and **Leftovers** (Unit 71), retailing antique French clothes and retro accessories. The village is full of restaurants: dine at Honest Burgers (p293) or get caffeinated at Federation Coffee (p295).

BRIXTON NEIGHBOURHOOD

The years that most shaped contemporary Brixton were the post-WWII 'Windrush' years, when immigrants arrived from the West Indies. (Windrush was the name of one of the leading ships that brought these immigrants to the UK.) Economic decline and hostility between the police and particularly the black community led to riots in 1981, 1985 and 1995.

Although violence returned to Brixton during the London riots of August 2011, the mood today is upbeat. Soaring property prices have sent in house-hunters, and pockets of gentrification sit alongside the more run-down streets. Apart from some great restaurants and clubs, the big sights are the fantastic Brixton Village – a current south London culinary and shopping hotspot – and Brixton Market.

⊙ Battersea & Wandsworth

BATTERSEA PARK PARK

Map p466 (www.batterseapark.org; ⏲8am-dusk; 🚉Battersea Park) With its Henry Moore and Barbara Hepworth sculptures, these 50 hectares of gorgeous greenery stretch between Albert and Chelsea Bridges. The park's tranquil appearance belies a bloody past: it was the site of an assassination attempt on King Charles II in 1671 and of a duel in 1829 between the Duke of Wellington and an opponent who accused him of treason.

The **Peace Pagoda** (Map p466), erected in 1985 by a group of Japanese Buddhists to commemorate Hiroshima Day, displays the Buddha in the four stages of his life. Refurbishment has seen the 19th-century landscaping reinstated and the grand riverside terraces spruced up. At the same time, the Festival of Britain pleasure gardens, including the spectacular Vista Fountains, have been restored. There are lakes, plenty of sporting facilities (including all-weather football pitches), an art space called the **Pump House Gallery** (Map p466; www.wandsworth.gov.uk/gallery; ⏲11am-5pm Wed-Sun) FREE and a small **Children's Zoo** (Map p466; www.batterseaparkzoo.co.uk; adult/child £8.75/6.50; ⏲10am-5.30pm Apr-Oct, to 4.30pm Nov-Mar).

BATTERSEA POWER STATION HISTORIC BUILDING

Map p466 (www.batterseapowerstation.co.uk; 🚉Battersea Park) Its four smokestacks famously celebrated on Pink Floyd's *Animals* album cover, Battersea Power Station is one of south London's best-known monuments. Built by Giles Gilbert Scott (who also designed the power station that is now the Tate Modern, and the iconic red telephone box) in 1933 with two chimneys (the other two were added in 1955), the power station was snuffed out in 1983 only to enter an existential limbo, slowly deteriorating as it passed from one optimistic developer to the next.

Luck finally turned for the mighty brick building in 2011 when a £5 billion masterplan to redevelop the site, right on the Thames, was approved. Plans include thousands of new homes, retail and corporate space and two new tube stations in Nine Elms and Battersea Park, an extension of the existing Northern Line. Work is scheduled to start in 2013, with the first new homes ready in 2016. The redevelopment won't be complete until 2024 however, so do make sure you schedule another trip to see the transformation in 10 years' time!

WANDSWORTH COMMON COMMON

(🚉Wandsworth Common or Clapham Junction) Wilder and more overgrown than the nearby common in Clapham, Wandsworth Common is full of couples pushing prams on a sunny day. On the western side is a pleasant collection of streets known as the **toast rack**, because of their alignment. Baskerville, Dorlcote, Henderson, Nicosia, Patten and Routh Rds are lined with Georgian houses. There's a blue plaque at 3 Routh Rd, home to the former British prime minister David Lloyd George.

◎ Dulwich & Forest Hill

DULWICH PICTURE GALLERY GALLERY
(www.dulwichpicturegallery.org.uk; Gallery Rd, SE21; adult/child £6/free; ⊙10am-5pm Tue-Fri, from 11am Sat & Sun; ⊠North Dulwich or West Dulwich) The UK's oldest public art gallery, the small Dulwich Picture Gallery was designed by the idiosyncratic architect Sir John Soane between 1811 and 1814 to house nearby Dulwich College's collection of paintings by Raphael, Rembrandt, Rubens, Reynolds, Gainsborough, Poussin, Lely, Van Dyck and others.

Unusually, the collectors Noel Desenfans and painter Sir Peter Francis Bourgeois chose to have their mausoleums, lit by a moody *lumière mystérieuse* (mysterious light) created with tinted glass, placed among the pictures.

The gorgeous, wood-panelled 17th-century **Christ's Chapel** (⊙1.30-3.30pm Tue) boasts an impressive copy of the *Transfiguration* by Raphael. It hosts regular concerts on Sunday evenings. The gallery also runs fantastic temporary exhibitions (additional £5 entry). Free guided tours of the museum depart at 3pm on Saturday and Sunday. The museum is a 10-minute walk northwards along Gallery Rd, which starts almost opposite West Dulwich train station. Bus P4 conveniently links the picture gallery with the Horniman Museum (p287).

DULWICH PARK PARK
(College Rd, SE21; ⊙8am-dusk; ⊠West Dulwich or North Dulwich) With its hectares of green space and much-loved bicycle hire putting fleets of novel, low-slung bikes under the feet of enthusiastic kids, Dulwich Park is one of London's most handsome and enjoyable parks. Bikes can be hired from **London Recumbents** (☑020-8299 6636; www.londonrecumbents.co.uk; Ranger's Yard, Dulwich Park; per hr £8-15; ⊙10am-5pm), near the Old

TOP SIGHT
HORNIMAN MUSEUM

Comprising the original collection of wealthy tea merchant Frederick John Horniman, this museum is a treasure-trove of discoveries, from a huge stuffed walrus to slowly undulating jellyfish, a fierce papier maché statue of Kali and a knock-out music exhibition.

On the ground and first floors is the **Natural History Gallery**, with animal skeletons and pickled specimens. When the magnificent 19th-century **apostle clock** strikes 4pm, the apostles troop out past Jesus and only Judas turns away from him. Children adore the **Hands On Base Gallery** where you can touch, wear and generally play around with objects.

On the lower ground floor you'll find the **African Worlds Gallery** and the **Music Gallery**. The latter displays instruments from 3500-year-old Egyptian clappers and early English keyboards, to Indonesian gamelan and Ghanaian drums. There are touch screens so you can hear what they sound like and a special **Hands On** room where you can try some of the instruments (which kids love).

The **aquarium** in the basement is small but state of the art and the 6.5 hectares of hillside **gardens** (complete with views of London) are magnificent.

DON'T MISS...

➡ Hands On Base Gallery
➡ Aquarium
➡ Music Gallery
➡ Gardens

PRACTICALITIES

➡ ☑020-8699 1872
➡ www.horniman.ac.uk
➡ 100 London Rd, Forest Hill, SE23
➡ free
➡ ⊙10.30am-5.30pm
➡ ⊠Forest Hill

DIVERSE IMAGES/UIG / GETTY IMAGES ©

1. Victoria Park (p227) 2. Hyde Park (p195) 3. Princess of Wales Conservatory, Kew Gardens (p306) 4. Richmond Park (p308)

DOUG MCKINLAY / GETTY IMAGES ©

Parks & Gardens

Glance at a colour map of town and be struck by how much is olive green. London has some of the world's most superb urban parkland: most of it well-tended, accessible and a delight in any season.

Victoria Park

Named after its eponymous royal benefactor, Victoria Park is one of East London's most pleasant and popular parks and has recently had an expensive regeneration. In summer it becomes a venue for live music and festivals.

Hyde Park

Perhaps London's most famous and easily accessed expanse of urban greenery, Hyde Park is astonishing for the variety of its landscapes and trees. The lovely Serpentine separates it from that other grand London park, Kensington Gardens.

Kew Gardens

To fall for Kew Gardens, all you need is an eye for fine architecture, a fondness for exploration and a sense of natural curiosity and aesthetics. Children will adore the treetop walkway and winter ice-skating.

Richmond Park

An epic expanse of greenery down southwest, royal Richmond Park is home to herds of deer, sublime views, a fantastic collection of trees, ponds, woodland and grass. Fling off the urban fumes and immerse yourself in its wild expanses.

Greenwich Park

Delightfully hilly, elegantly landscaped and bisected by the Meridian Line, Greenwich Park offers sweeping perspectives from its highest point. London's oldest enclosed royal park, it is home to herds of deer and some of Greenwich's top highlights.

College Gate in the west of the park. The park playground is great for toddlers.

Clapham

CLAPHAM NEIGHBOURHOOD

(Clapham Common) Famed for its huge **common** (Map p466), a verdant venue for many outdoor summer events (see http://claphamhighstreet.co.uk) and sports, Clapham is a popular neighbourhood in South London. The main thoroughfare, Clapham High St, starts at the common's northeastern edge and is lined with bars, restaurants and shops.

In the northwestern corner of the Common, the brick and stone **Holy Trinity Church** (Map p466; Clapham Common, SW4) (1776) was home to the Clapham Sect, a group of wealthy evangelical Christians that included William Wilberforce, a leading antislavery campaigner, active between 1790 and 1830. The sect also campaigned against child labour and for prison reform.

Beyond the church is **Clapham Old Town**, the historic heart of Clapham, with fine old buildings and a more sedate air than the high street.

Crystal Palace

CRYSTAL PALACE PARK PARK

(www.crystalpalacepark.org.uk; Crystal Palace, SE19; 7.30am-dusk Mon-Fri, from 9am Sat & Sun; Crystal Palace, Crystal Palace) Named after the prodigious glass and iron palace erected for the Great Exhibition in 1851 and moved here from Hyde Park in 1854, this huge park makes for intriguing exploration. Designed by Joseph Paxton, the palace burned down in 1936 with spectacular ferocity, the radiance of its conflagration visible across 10 counties.

In just a few hours, the palace was reduced to a smoking ruin, its goldfish, which swam in the ornamental ponds, 'missing – believed boiled', according to the *Times*. Nothing today remains of the Crystal Palace except the Victorian terrace and its crumbling statues. The park is great for kids though and you can find out more about the palace at the **Crystal Palace Museum** (www.crystalpalacemuseum.org.uk; Anerley Hill, SE19; 11am-4pm Sat & Sun) FREE down Anerley Hill.

TOP SIGHT
ELTHAM PALACE

This art deco house was built between 1933 and 1937 by the textile merchant Stephen Courtauld (of Courtauld Institute fame) and his wife Virginia. From the impressive entrance hall with its dome and huge circular carpet with geometric shapes, to the black-marble dining room with silver-foil ceiling and burlwood-veneer fireplace, it appears the couple had taste as well as money. They also, rather fashionably for the times, had a pet lemur; the heated cage, complete with tropical murals and a bamboo ladder leading to the ground floor for the spoilt (and vicious) 'Mah-jongg' is also on view.

A royal palace was built on this site in 1305 and was for a time the boyhood home of Henry VIII, before the Tudors decamped to Greenwich. Little of the palace remains, apart from the restored Great Medieval Hall. Its hammerbeam roof is generally rated the third best in the country, behind those at Westminster Hall and Hampton Court Palace. The eight hectares of gardens include a rockery and moat with working bridge.

The house was scheduled to close for renovations for the winter of 2013–14 at the time of writing. Check the website for details of the re-opening.

DON'T MISS

- Entrance hall
- Dining room

PRACTICALITIES

- www.english-heritage.org.uk
- Court Yard, Eltham, SE9
- adult/child £9.90/5.90
- 10am-5pm Sun-Wed Apr-Oct
- Eltham

WORTH A DETOUR

DANSON HOUSE & RED HOUSE

A couple of historic houses in Bexleyheath, once a village in Kent, now a typical suburb in southeast London, are well worth exploring.

From the outside, **Red House** (www.nationaltrust.org.uk/red-house; 13 Red House Lane, Bexleyheath, DA6; adult/child £7.20/3.60; 11am-5pm Wed-Sun; Bexleyheath then 15min walk south) conjures up a gingerbread house in stone. It was built in 1859 by Victorian designer William Morris – of Morris wallpaper fame. The nine rooms open to the public bear all the elements of the Arts and Crafts movement to which Morris adhered – a bit of Gothic art here, some religious symbolism there, an art nouveau–like sunburst over there. Furniture by Morris and the house's designer Philip Webb are in evidence, as are paintings and stained glass by Edward Burne-Jones. Entry prior to 1.30pm is by guided tour only. The surrounding gardens were designed by Morris 'to clothe' the house. Don't miss the well with a conical roof inspired by the oast houses of nearby Kent. The house is a 15-minute walk from Bexleyheath train station and is signposted.

Less than 10 minutes' walk from Red House is another gem: **Danson House** (www.dansonhouse.org.uk; Danson Park, Bexleyheath, DA6; adult/child/concession £7/free/5; noon-5pm Sun-Thu Apr-Oct; Bexleyheath then 20min walk southwest). It is a beautifully renovated Palladian villa dating to 1766 and was salvaged from demolition in 1995 and painstakingly renovated. Highlights include the dining room's reliefs and frescoes celebrating love and romance; the library and music room, with its functioning organ; the dizzying spiral staircase; and the (non renovated) Victorian kitchens. The English-style garden and surrounding park are a delight and the **tearoom** (Danson House, Danson Park, Bexleyheath, DA6; mains £5-8; noon-5pm daily Apr-Oct) deserves four stars for its wholesome, delicious food (everything from the scones to the pastries and soups is made fresh, daily, on the premises).

Trains to Bexleyheath run regularly from London Bridge (35 minutes). For those staying in Greenwich, shorten the journey by taking the train in Blackheath, where you could stop for dinner on your way back (see p292).

EATING

Eating in South London is a treat. The fine restaurants of Blackheath, Clapham, Camberwell or Wandsworth may be off the beaten track but take the opportunity to wander around these fine neighbourhoods and discover life as a local. The markets of Brixton and Greenwich are must-dos for lunch or an afternoon treat.

Greenwich

GREENWICH MARKET — MARKET £

Map p469 (www.shopgreenwich.co.uk/greenwich-market; College Approach, SE10; 10am-5.30pm Tue, Wed, Fri-Sun; ; DLR Cutty Sark) Perfect for snacking your way through a world atlas of food while browsing the other market stalls, come here for delicious food-to-go, from Spanish tapas to Thai curries, sushi, Polish doughnuts, French crêpes, Brazilian churros, smoked Louisiana sausages, *chivitos* and more; follow your nostrils and make your pick, and wash it all down with a glass of fresh farmhouse cider.

TAI WON MEIN — CHINESE £

Map p469 (39 Greenwich Church St, SE10; mains from £4.95; 11.30am-11.30pm; ; DLR Cutty Sark) The staff may be a bit jaded but this great snack spot – the Cantonese moniker just means 'Big Bowl of Noodles' – serves epic portions of carbohydrate-rich noodles to those overcoming Greenwich's titanic sights.

OLD BREWERY — MODERN BRITISH ££

Map p469 (www.oldbrewerygreenwich.com; Pepys Bldg, Old Royal Naval College, SE10; mains cafe £7-12, restaurant £10.50-18.50; cafe 10am-5pm, restaurant 6-11pm; ; DLR Cutty Sark) A working brewery with splendidly burnished 1000L copper vats at one end and a high ceiling lit with natural sunlight, the Old Brewery is a cafe serving lovely bistro fare by day and a restaurant by night, serving a choice selection of fine dishes carefully sourced from the best seasonal ingredients.

WORTH A DETOUR

GOURMET BLACKHEATH

Located south of Greenwich Park, across a grassy heath, the small neighbourhood of Blackheath feels like a quaint village from the home counties rather than a London suburb. For visitors, the main reason to come here – apart from a lovely stroll along the boutique-lined streets – is to eat: Blackheath has arguably better gourmet addresses than Greenwich and makes a fine culinary outing.

The **Buenos Aires Café** (www.buenosairesltd.com; 17 Royal Pde, SE3; mains £9-25; ⏲noon-2.30pm & 6-10.30pm Mon-Fri, noon-4pm & 6-10.30pm Sat & Sun; ✎; ⓡBlackheath) is without a doubt the pearl of the neighbourhood. As you would expect from an Argentinian eatery, the beef is superb but what seals it is the gorgeous decor (all wood furniture and over-sized posters), the excellent wine list, stellar service and wonderful homemade pasta and pizza (55% of today's population in Argentina is of Italian origin, hence this delightful culinary heritage). Booking essential.

Also warmly recommended is **Chapters All Day Dining** (www.chaptersrestaurants.com; 43-45 Montpelier Vale, SE3; mains £8.50-14.95; ⏲8am-11pm Mon-Sat, to 9pm Sun; ✎), a sophisticated brasserie offering, you guessed it, all day dining. Food and service are consistently high and you can come for anything from coffee and cake to dinner.

And if you'd rather have a picnic in the heath or Greenwich Park, stop at **Black Vanilla** (32 Tranquil Vale, SE3; cakes & ice creams £2-5; ⏲8am-6pm Mon-Sat, to 4pm Sun), a gelateria serving delightful (if pricey) ice cream and mountains of cupcakes.

You can easily walk to Blackheath from Greenwich through the park. Allow 40 minutes or so. Otherwise, bus 386 shuttles between Blackheath and Greenwich. Blackheath also has a train station (trains to London Bridge every 15 to 20 minutes).

INSIDE MODERN EUROPEAN £££

Map p469 (☎020-8265 5060; www.insiderestaurant.co.uk; 19 Greenwich South St, SE10; mains £13.95-21.95, 2-/3-course set menu £19.95/24.95; ⏲noon-2.30pm & 6.30-10.30pm Tue-Sat, noon-3.30pm Sun; ⓡDLR Greenwich) With white walls, modern art and linen tablecloths, Inside is a relaxed kind of place and one of Greenwich's best restaurant offerings. The fine food hits the mark, ranging tastily and affordably from pumpkin and red lentil soup to pan fried wild sea bass, and apple and rhubarb crumble.

SPREAD EAGLE FRENCH £££

Map p469 (www.spreadeaglerestaurant.co.uk; 1-2 Stockwell St, SE10; mains £12-24, lunch/dinner 2-course set-menu £13.50/22.50; ⏲noon-3pm & 6-10pm Tue-Sat, noon-5pm Sun; ⓡDLR Cutty Sark) Smart, French-inspired restaurant opposite the Greenwich Theatre in what was once the terminus for the coach service to/from London.

Lambeth, Kennington and Elephant & Castle

DRAGON CASTLE CHINESE ££

Map p468 (www.dragon-castle.com; 100 Walworth Rd, SE17; mains £9-20; ⏲noon-11pm Mon-Sat, 11.30am-10.30pm Sun; ✎; ⊖Elephant & Castle) Change may be afoot in Elephant & Castle (once one of the roughest areas of London but now the last bastion of real estate in Zone 1 not to be the preserve of millionaires) but Dragon Castle has been a constant. The duck, pork and seafood are renowned – but come for the dim sum (£1.90 to £3.80), especially at weekend lunch.

LOBSTER POT SEAFOOD £££

Map p468 (☎020-7582 5556; www.lobsterpotrestaurant.co.uk; 3 Kennington Lane, SE11; mains £17.50-28.50; ⏲noon-2.30pm & 7-10.30pm Tue-Sat; ⊖Kennington or Elephant & Castle) This charming French-owned restaurant hidden in the wastelands south of Elephant & Castle reels in diners hook, line and sinker with finely prepared fish and seafood dishes *à la française* (think lashings of butter and garlic). An eight-course tasting menu with/without lobster is £54.50/49.50.

Brixton & Camberwell

★**FRANCO MANCA** ITALIAN £

Map p466 (www.francomanca.co.uk; 4 Market Row, SW9; pizzas £5-7; ⏲noon-5pm Sun-Wed, to 10pm Thu-Sat; ✎; ⊖Brixton) Voted as the best pizza in London by practically everybody,

Franco Manca is a perennial favourite in Brixton. Beat those queues by arriving early, avoiding lunch hours and Saturday, and delight in some fine, fine pizza. The restaurant only uses its own sourdough (all made in the upstairs bakery with flour from a Neapolitan mill), fired up in a wood-burning brick oven.

MAMA LAN CHINESE £

Map p466 (www.mamalan.co.uk; Brixton Village, Unit 18, Coldharbour Lane, SW9; dishes £4.50-8.50; ⌚noon-4pm Sun-Wed, noon-4pm & 6-10pm Thu-Sat; ⊖Brixton) For authentic, handmade Beijing street food – dumplings, noodles, salads and snacks – Mama Lan is the business. This cute-as-a-button eatery in Brixton Village actually started life as a supper club – good thing they decided to spread the love with a restaurant because we can't get enough of their pork and Chinese leaf dumplings!

ROSIE'S DELI CAFÉ CAFE £

Map p466 (www.rosiesdelicafe.com; 14e Market Row, SW9; mains £4-6; ⌚9.30am-5.30pm Mon-Sat; ⊖Brixton) Park yourself on one of the mismatched wooden chairs at this much-loved Brixton cafe run by cook and author Rosie Lovell as it's a wholesome treat. She's certainly very charming and serves some fantastic cakes and biscuits (the fried banana bread is to die for). Quiches, wraps, ciabattas, sandwiches and pies also emerge from her kitchen.

ASMARA AFRICAN £

Map p466 (386 Coldharbour Lane, Brixton, SW9; mains £7.50-9; ⌚5.30pm-late; 🖉; ⊖Brixton) A rare Eritrean restaurant, unpretentious Asmara serves spicy chicken, lamb and beef stews and vegetable/vegan dishes that you scoop up with *injera,* the flat, slightly spongy sourdough bread that is a national dish. Staff add colour with traditional costumes, while the traditional *messob* meat dinner (£34 for two) with traditional coffee ceremony is pure enjoyment.

★ANGELS & GYPSIES SPANISH, MEXICAN ££

(www.angelsandgypsies.com; 29-33 Camberwell Church St, Camberwell, SE5; burritos £5, tapas £5-10; ⌚noon-3pm & 6-10.30pm; 🚉Denmark Hill, ⊖Oval then 🚌36, 185 or 436) This Spanish-Mexican restaurant is run by a half-English, half-Spanish brother duo who love all things Spanish and Mexican. Lunch is therefore an ode to Mexican street food, with burritos bursting at the seams, while dinner is all about tapas, with every product lovingly sourced from Spain (the ham from Salamanca, the chilli sauce is their Dad's recipe from Galicia etc).

The setting too is something to marvel at: customers sit on old church pews and wooden chairs, stunning stained-glass windows give the brick walls a warm glow and two magnificent *jamónes* stand guard on the horseshoe bar counter. Most amazing of all is the price: lunch for less than a tenner and dinner for under £20.

HONEST BURGERS BURGERS ££

Map p466 (www.honestburgers.co.uk; Unit 12, Brixton Village, SW9; mains £6.50-11.50; ⌚noon-4pm Mon, noon-5pm & 6-10pm Tue-Sun; ⊖Brixton) This burger outfit has deftly hopped onto the enterprising Brixton Village bandwagon. Plaudits for their juicy and tender burgers and gloriously rosemary seasoned triple-cooked chips have rained in from all corners and honest-to-God rightly so: they are well worth the wait for a table, which you could well have to do (it's titchy, seats around 30 and there are no bookings).

BEAR GASTROPUB ££

(www.thebear-freehouse.co.uk; 296a Camberwell New Road, Camberwell, SE5; mains £12-15; ⌚4-11pm Mon-Fri, noon-11pm Sat & Sun; 🚉Denmark Hill, ⊖Oval then 🚌36, 185 or 436) With its green leather banquettes, wooden floors, wood panelling and vintage furniture, the Bear is as cosy a gastropub as it gets and its cuisine, a mix of rustic English and French, hits the same comfort button: duck confit, old-school sausages, onglet, and some truly magnificent pies. Wash the lot down with the excellent selection of ales and wines.

Battersea & Wandsworth

★CHEZ BRUCE FRENCH £££

(☎020-8672 0114; www.chezbruce.co.uk; 2 Bellevue Rd, SW17; lunch/dinner 3-course menu £35/45; ⌚noon-2.30pm & 6.30-10pm; 🚉Wandsworth Common) Though Michelin-starred, Chez Bruce still insists on a winning local feel that accommodates all comers. The rustic facade, beside leafy Wandsworth Common, belies a crisp modern interior; the wine list is an all-star cast, the food sublime. Bookings essential.

SANTA MARIA DEL SUR ARGENTINE £££

Map p466 (020-7622 2088; www.santamariadelsur.co.uk; 129 Queenstown Rd, SW8; mains £14-28; noon-3pm & 6pm-midnight; Queenstown Rd or Battersea Park) Catering to carnivores with succulent grilled meats and sausages (and some token veggie dishes). Go for one of the *parrilladas* (mixed grill; £24 to £27.50 per person) to share and finish your meal with delicious pancakes and *dulce de leche* and a coffee with cream and cinnamon. Booking advised.

Dulwich & Forest Hill

DULWICH PICTURE GALLERY CAFE CAFE ££

(Dulwich Picture Gallery, Gallery Rd, SE21; mains £5-12; 9am-5pm Tue-Fri, 10am-5pm Sat & Sun; ; North Dulwich or West Dulwich) In a rarefied, modern extension of the Dulwich Picture Gallery, this cafe is a lifeline in the food desert that is Dulwich. Although the tea breaks are very English (coffee and walnut cake, scones etc), mains served for lunch are positively Mediterranean: Spanish tortilla, roasted sweet peppers with goat's cheese and paprika or spaghetti with chilli, garlic and pecorino cheese.

Clapham

MACARON BAKERY £

Map p466 (22 The Pavement, SW4; cakes £1.50-3; 8am-7pm Mon-Sat, from 9am Sun; Clapham Common) Among the spray of gift shops, cafes and delis along The Pavement, this gracious Parisian-style boulangerie welcomes with vast glass windows, an inviting sense of Gallic charm and mouthwatering pastries and macaroons.

★**ABBEVILLE KITCHEN** MODERN EUROPEAN ££

Map p466 (020-8772 1110; www.abbevillekitchen.com; 47 Abbeville Rd, SW4; mains £10-15; 6.30-11pm Mon-Thu, noon-3pm & 6.30-10.30pm Fri-Sun; Clapham Common or Clapham South) Nestled on a villagey street of Clapham, the Abbeville Kitchen has a local feel with its little terrace and cosy dining room yet its appeal is universal. The cuisine is a blend of modern British and European making great use of underrated products such as Jerusalem artichokes, dandelion or pigeon. The menu is succinct, listing the dishes' ingredients only, and very seasonal.

You'll always find a large piece of meat to share between two or three such as slow-cooked lamb or rib of Dexter beef.

TRINITY BRITISH £££

Map p466 (020-7622 1199; www.trinityrestaurant.co.uk; 4 The Polygon, SW4; 3-course lunch menu £27, mains £19-33; 12.30-2.30pm & 6.30-10pm Mon-Sat, noon-3pm Sun; Clapham Common) Named after the nearby church, Adam Byatt's good-looking Clapham Old Town restaurant is a light and delectable spot near the common. Service, attentive and unobtrusive, delivers a strong wine list and a mouth-watering menu displaying considerable culinary artistry. It's a formal, classic address that sees many returnees and also runs masterclasses in cookery. Reservations recommended.

DRINKING & NIGHTLIFE

The nightlife in South London is like a box of Quality Street chocolates: diverse; some of it an acquired taste! There is everything from historic boozers to flagship nightclubs, with everything in between. If you have an open mind, however, you'll have an absolutely brilliant time trying it all out.

Greenwich

The drinking in Greenwich is top-notch, a mix of superb, historic old pubs and trendy microbreweries. A must after a day's sightseeing, even if you're not staying in the area.

★**TRAFALGAR TAVERN** PUB

Map p469 (www.trafalgartavern.co.uk; 6 Park Row, SE10; noon-11pm Mon-Thu, to midnight Fri & Sat, to 10.30pm Sun; DLR Cutty Sark) Lapped by the brown waters of the Thames, this elegant tavern with big windows looking onto the river is steeped in history. Dickens apparently knocked back a few here – and used it as the setting for the wedding breakfast scene in *Our Mutual Friend* – and prime ministers Gladstone and Disraeli used to dine on the pub's celebrated whitebait.

CUTTY SARK TAVERN PUB

Map p469 (www.cuttysarktavern.co.uk; 4-6 Ballast Quay, SE10; ⏲11am-11pm Mon-Sat, noon-10.30 Sun; DLR Cutty Sark) Housed in a delightful bow-windowed, wood-beamed Georgian building directly on the Thames, the Cutty Sark is one of the few independent pubs left in Greenwich. Half a dozen cask-conditioned ales on tap line the bar, with an inviting riverside sitting-out area opposite. It's a 15-minute walk from the DLR station or hop on a bus along Trafalgar Rd and walk north.

GREENWICH UNION PUB

Map p469 (www.greenwichunion.com; 56 Royal Hill; ⏲noon-11pm Mon-Sat, 11.30am-10.30pm Sun; DLR Cutty Sark) The award-winning Union plies six or seven local microbrewery beers, including raspberry and wheat varieties, and a strong list of ales, plus bottled international brews. It's a handsome place, with duffed up leather armchairs and a welcoming long, narrow aspect that leads to the conservatory and beer garden at the rear.

OLD BREWERY BAR

Map p469 (www.oldbrewerygreenwich.com; Pepys Bldg, Old Royal Naval College, SE10; ⏲11am-11pm Mon-Sat, noon-10.30pm Sun; DLR Cutty Sark) Situated within the grounds of the old Royal Naval College, the Old Brewery is run by the Meantime Brewery, selling its own brew draught Imperial Pale Ale (brewed on site), along with a heady range of over 50 beers, from Belgian Trappist ales to fruity and smoked beers. We love the 'bottle chandelier' inside and the courtyard for sunny days.

Lambeth, Kennington and Elephant & Castle

★CORSICA STUDIOS DJ

Map p468 (www.corsicastudios.com; 4/5 Elephant Rd, SE17; admission £6-15; ⏲hours vary; Elephant & Castle) It is places like Corsica Studios that are starting to give the once-rough Elephant & Castle area an edge. This not-for-profit, underground club is a well-known venue for electronic music. It's a small, intimate space, with excellent sound and a mix of gigs and club nights.

MINISTRY OF SOUND CLUB

Map p468 (www.ministryofsound.com; 103 Gaunt St, SE1; admission £16-25; ⏲11pm-6.30am Fri & Sat; Elephant & Castle) This legendary club-cum-enormous-global-brand (four bars, four dance floors) lost some 'edge' in the early noughties but, after pumping in top DJs, the Ministry has firmly rejoined the top club ranks. Fridays is the Gallery trance night, while Saturday sessions offers the *crème de la crème* of house, electro and techno DJs.

Brixton

★MARKET HOUSE PUB

Map p466 (www.market-house.co.uk; 443 Coldharbour Lane, SW9; ⏲3-11pm Mon-Thu, 3pm-3am Fri, 1pm-4am Sat, 1-11pm Sun; Brixton) Brixton used to be well-known for its grotty pubs and rough music venues so the designer wall-papered, vintage-furnished, cocktail-serving Market House is something of a departure for the area – and a roaring success at that. The late (and free) opening hours at the weekend are especially popular with locals.

★PLAN B CLUB

Map p466 (www.planb-london.com; 418 Brixton Rd, SW9; admission £7-10; ⏲hours vary, check website; Brixton) This small venue, with its minimalist warehouse-like interior, has become a feature on the Brixton nightlife map with a shaken up roll call of hip hop, dubstep, R&B, house and electro acts. The Friday night Bump is a mix of pop and electronic.

FEDERATION COFFEE CAFE

Map p466 (www.federationcoffee.com; Unit 46, Brixton Village, SW9; ⏲8am-5pm Mon-Fri, from 9am Sat & Sun; Brixton) One of the fashionable new outlets in buzzing Brixton Village, funky Federation Coffee serves up fantastic coffee (the coffee is roasted locally in Brixton) and a large selection of teas in neat surroundings; it's an excellent spot to gauge the revitalised pulse of Brixton Village. Pastries (sweet and savoury) will soak up the caffeine.

EFFRA HALL TAVERN PUB

Map p466 (38A Kellet Rd, SW2; ⏲5-11pm Mon-Fri, 11am-11pm Sat, noon-10pm Sun; Brixton) This slightly run-down old boozer brings you closer to the heart of the Brixton Caribbean vibe than any other pub in the area, thanks to the spicy Jamaican menu and regular live jazz (or football on the big screens) in the evenings. The patio outback is fringed with palm trees, while the interior is all shabby Victorian splendour.

DOGSTAR DJ, BAR

Map p466 (www.antic-ltd.com/dogstar; 389 Coldharbour Lane, SW9; ⌚4-11pm Tue & Wed, 4pm-2am Thu & Fri, noon-4am Sat, noon-10.30pm Sun; ⊖Brixton) Downstairs, this long-running local institution has a cavernous DJ and live music bar, mobbed by a young South London crowd. The main bar is as casual as you'd expect from a converted pub – comfortable sofas, big wooden tables – so dressing to kill is not obligatory.

Battersea & Wandsworth

★LOST SOCIETY BAR

Map p466 (www.lostsociety.co.uk; 697 Wandsworth Rd, SW8; ⌚5pm-midnight Thu & Fri, 2pm-1am Sat, 2-7pm Sun; ⊞Wandsworth Rd, Battersea Park or Queenstown Rd) A fantastic bar-cum-restaurant whose six rooms are dedicated to delightful decadence, it's all 1920s glamour and aristocratic glitz at the Lost Society. There's a garden at the back where many a summer drinking session goes on; DJs and burlesque shows take over on weekends.

★DRAFT HOUSE PUB

(www.drafthouse.co.uk; 94 Northcote Rd, SW11; ⌚noon-11pm Mon-Fri, 10am-midnight Sat, noon-10.30pm Sun; ⊞Clapham Junction or Wandsworth Common) Its 18 ales, stouts and lagers on tap backed up by over 50 different bottled beers, Draft House is no slouch. A standout watering hole along urbane Northcote Rd, where middle-class cash and high expectations seamlessly dovetail, the seasonally-adjusted menu (served through the day) has also set local palates a-quiver with excellent brunches and standout burgers. Outside seating.

MASON'S ARMS PUB

Map p466 (www.masons-arms-battersea.co.uk; 169 Battersea Park Rd, SW8; ⌚noon-11pm; ☏; ⊞Battersea Park) This lovely boozer is a favourite of Battersea residents for its winning combination of relaxed atmosphere, beer garden on sunny days (and open fire for winter blues) and fantastic food.

Clapham

PRINCE OF WALES PUB

Map p466 (38 Old Town, SW4; ⌚5-11pm Mon-Thu, 5pm-1am Fri, 1pm-1am Sat, 1-11pm Sun; ⊖Clapham Common) While some pubs that festoon their ceilings with bric-a-brac and hang London Underground station signs on the walls can be tiresome, the Prince of Wales remains a very pleasant Clapham hangout, and its decor, unlike that of most pubs of the genre, is genuinely collected rather than supplied wholesale. Real ales appear regularly.

TWO BREWERS GAY

Map p466 (www.the2brewers.com; 114 Clapham High St, SW4; admission £3-6 after 10pm; ⌚4pm-2am Sun-Thu, to 4am Fri & Sat; ⊖Clapham Common) Clapham exudes an inner suburban feel, the High St in particular, but the long-standing Two Brewers endures as one of the best London gay bars outside the gay villages of Soho, Shoreditch and Vauxhall. Here there's a friendly, laid-back, local crowd who come for a quiet drink during the week and some madcap cabaret and dancing at weekends.

Vauxhall

The opening hours of Vauxhall's gay clubs can be something of a moving target because of club nights. Check the venues' websites or gay listings for up-to-date information.

★BRUNSWICK HOUSE CAFE CAFE

Map p468 (www.brunswickhousecafe.com; Brunswick House, 30 Wandsworth Rd, SW8; ⌚8.30am-11pm Mon-Fri, 10am-11pm Sat, 10am-5pm Sun; ☏) This boutique cafe, housed in a lone Georgian house marooned between high-rises and a roundabout, is an oasis of aesthetics in a world of urban ghastliness. Amidst oversized posters, assorted lanterns and vintage furniture come leaf teas, fresh fruit juices, elegant cocktails and wines by the carafe.

There is a restaurant out back, also warmly recommended: the food (mains £15 to £16) is modern British, simple and as elegantly executed as the surroundings.

FIRE GAY

Map p468 (www.firelondon.net; South Lambeth Rd, SW8; ⊖Vauxhall) Regularly hosting the

LOCAL KNOWLEDGE

VAUXHALL'S REGENERATION

Vauxhall has struggled to find its space on London's tourist map. A strange mix of derelict estates, transport hub, and MI6 headquarters (the UK's **Secret Intelligence Service** (Map p468) – the monstrous green glass buildings), it's not exactly appealing.

The area is changing, however; it's London's undisputed gay party village and boutique cafes and gastropubs are timidly opening. But what may clinch the deal of Vauxhall's renewal is the opening in 2014 of bad boy conceptual artist **Damien Hirst's new gallery**. It will host the artist's personal collection and will be located on Newport St in a series of converted industrial buildings.

best gay club nights in London, Fire is an expansive, smart space under Vauxhall's railway arches. Its most famous bill is the infamous Sunday all-nighter, Orange. Its (smoking) outdoor garden is a rare thing on the clubbing scene, good to watch the sunrise!

AREA GAY

Map p468 (67-68 Albert Embankment, SE1; ⊖Vauxhall) Home of classic club night Beyond, which runs from 3am to 7am on Sunday mornings, Area is a stalwart of Vauxhall's clubbing scene.

RVT GAY

Map p468 (www.rvt.org.uk; 372 Kennington Lane, SE11; ⏲7pm-midnight Mon, Wed & Thu, 6pm-midnight Tue, 9pm-2am Fri & Sat, 2pm-midnight Sun; ⊖Vauxhall) Rough around the edges to say the least, the Royal Vauxhall Tavern is the perfect antidote to the gleaming new wave of gay venues now crowding Vauxhall's gay village. Saturday's Duckie, tagged 'London's Authentic Honky Tonk' is the club's signature queer performance night.

Also check out S.L.A.G.S. on Sundays, and keep an eye out on the website for other upcoming events, including cabaret, bingo nights and open stage nights.

HOIST GAY

Map p468 (www.thehoist.co.uk; Arches 47C, South Lambeth Rd, SW8; ⏲9pm-2am Wed, 8pm-midnight Thu, 10pm-3am Fri, 10pm-4am Sat, 10pm-2am Sun; ⊖Vauxhall) One of Europe's most famous fetish clubs, the Hoist is a one-stop shop for guys into leather and uniforms. The dress code is very strict – everyone has to wear boots, and rubber, leather or uniform. Check out the array of fetish nights on the website.

☆ ENTERTAINMENT

Early September sees Greenwich play host to London's largest comedy festival, the Greenwich Comedy Festival (www.greenwichcomedyfestival.co.uk). Usually set in the grounds of the Old Royal Naval College, at the time of writing the festival was looking for a new venue and may be staged in a different month – check the website for updates.

★O2 ACADEMY BRIXTON LIVE MUSIC

Map p466 (www.o2academybrixton.co.uk; 211 Stockwell Rd, SW9; ⊖Brixton) It's hard to have a bad night at the Brixton Academy, even if you leave with your soles sticky with beer, as this cavernous former art deco theatre (holding 5000) always thrums with bonhomie. There's a properly raked floor for good views, as well as plenty of bars and an excellent mixed bill of established and emerging artists.

UP THE CREEK COMEDY

Map p469 (www.up-the-creek.com; 302 Creek Rd, SE10; admission £4-16; ⏲7.30-11pm Thu & Sun, to 2am Fri & Sat; 🚉Greenwich, DLR Cutty Sark) Bizarrely enough, the hecklers can be funnier than the acts at this great club. Mischief, rowdiness and excellent comedy are the norm with open mic nights on Thursdays (www.theopenmic.co.uk; £4) and Sunday specials (www.sundayspecial.co.uk; £6). There's an after-party disco on Fridays and Saturdays.

O2 ARENA LIVE MUSIC

(www.theo2.co.uk; Peninsula Sq, SE10; ⊖North Greenwich) One of the city's major concert venues, hosting all the biggies – the Rolling Stones, Britney Spears, Prince and many others – inside the 20,000-capacity stadium. It's also a popular venue for sporting events (tennis, horseriding etc). Ticket prices start at £20.

LOCAL KNOWLEDGE

FREE MUSIC IN GREENWICH

The **Trinity Laban Conservatoire of Music and Dance** (www.trinitylaban.ac.uk) offers regular free concerts in Greenwich: they're held in St Alfege Church (p283) at 1.10pm on Thursdays and at various times in the chapel (p281) of the Old Royal Naval College. Check the website for details.

LABAN THEATRE DANCE

Map p469 (www.trinitylaban.ac.uk; Creekside, SE8; admission £6-15; Deptford Bridge, DLR Greenwich) Home of the Trinity Laban Conservatoire of Music and Dance (p298), the Laban Theatre presents student dance performances, graduation shows and regular performances by the resident troupe, Transitions Dance Company. Its stunning £23 million home was designed by Herzog & de Meuron, designers of the Tate Modern.

BATTERSEA ARTS CENTRE THEATRE

Map p466 (www.bac.org.uk; Lavender Hill, SW11; 77 or 345, Clapham Junction) Closed at the time of writing because of extensive refurbishment, this arts centre planned to reopen over the course of 2013 with a brand new theatre, cafe and fully licensed bar, but the same busy schedule of innovative performances and activities.

SHOPPING

Greenwich is a paradise for lovers of retro clothes stores and handicrafts. Northcote Rd in Wandsworth has fine boutiques, from interior design to fashion.

GREENWICH MARKET HANDICRAFTS

Map p469 (www.shopgreenwich.co.uk/greenwich-market; Greenwich Market, SE10; 10am-5.30pm Tue-Sun) Greenwich may be one of the smallest of London's ubiquitous markets but it holds its own when it comes to quality: on Tuesdays, Wednesdays, Fridays and weekends, stallholders tend to be small, independent artists, offering original prints, wholesome beauty products, funky jewellery and accessories, cool fashion pieces and so on. On Tuesdays, Thursdays and Fridays, it's vintage, antiques and collectables.

BEEHIVE VINTAGE

Map p469 (320-322 Creek Rd, SE10; 10.30am-6pm Tue-Sun; DLR Cutty Sark) Funky meeting ground of old vinyl (Bowie, Rolling Stones, vintage soul) and retro togs (frocks, blouses, leather jackets and overcoats).

EMPORIUM VINTAGE, MUSIC

Map p469 (330-332 Creek Rd, SE10; 10.30am-6pm Wed-Sun; DLR Cutty Sark) Each piece is individual at this lovely vintage shop, where glass cabinets are crammed with costume jewellery, old perfume bottles and straw hats, while gorgeous jackets and blazers intermingle on the clothes racks. The men's offering is unusually good for a vintage shop.

20 STOREY GIFTS

Map p466 (2A Market Row, SW9; 10.30am-5pm Tue-Sun; Brixton) A shop with a sense of humour, 20 Storey is your essential stop for funky mugs, great cards, gadgets, posters and original books.

VILLAGE BOOKS BOOKS

(1D Calton Ave, Dulwich Village, SE21; 9am-5.30pm Mon-Sat, 11am-5pm Sun; North Dulwich) Village Books is so small you could swing the proverbial dead cat and dislodge books from all four walls. But tininess is this shop's forte, with a wealth of knowledge and experience from staff. There is an extensive and excellent children's book section.

BRIXTON MARKET MARKET

Map p466 (www.brixtonmarket.net; Electric Ave & Granville Arcade; 8am-6pm Mon-Sat, 8am-3pm Wed; Brixton) A heady, cosmopolitan blend of silks, wigs, knock-off fashion, Halal butchers and the occasional Christian preacher on Electric Ave. Tilapia fish, pig's trotters, yams, mangoes, okra, plantains and Jamaican *bullah* cakes (gingerbread) are just some of the exotic products on sale.

JOY FASHION

Map p466 (www.joythestore.com; 432 Coldharbour Lane, SW11; 10am-7.30pm Mon-Sat, 11am-7pm Sun; Brixton) This funky shop does a great line in retro floral frocks and blouses, hip T-shirts, polo shirts and an imaginative range of inventive gift ideas and quirky accessories.

ORIGINAL CROSSINGS

There are two ways to cross the Thames without using a boat.

Reached via glass-topped domes on either side of the river, the historic 370m-long **Greenwich Foot Tunnel** (Cutty Sark Gardens, SE10; 24 hr; DLR Cutty Sark) runs under the Thames from the Isle of Dogs to Greenwich. There are lifts – and about 100 stairs – on both sides.

Further downstream is London's latest river crossing option, the Emirates Air Line (p407) Cable Car. It runs between the O2 and the Excel exhibition centre in the Docklands and affords great views of Greenwich, Canary Wharf and the Docklands.

SPORTS & ACTIVITIES

UP AT THE O2 ADVENTURE SPORTS

(www.theo2.co.uk/upattheo2; O2, Greenwich Peninsula, SE10; tickets from £22; hours vary) London isn't exactly your thrill-seeking destination but this ascent of the O2 dome is definitely not for the faint-hearted. Equipped with climbing suit and a harness, you'll scale the famous white dome to arrive at a viewing platform perched 52m above the Thames with sweeping views of Canary Wharf, the river, Greenwich and beyond.

Not suitable for children under 10 (also check height and weight restrictions).

THE OVAL CRICKET GROUND

Map p468 (0844 375 1845; www.kiaoval.com; Kennington, SE11; international match £20-350, county £20-35; Oval) Home to the Surrey County Cricket Club, the Oval is London's second cricketing venue after Lord's. As well as Surrey matches, it also regularly hosts international test matches. Getting tickets for county games is relatively straightforward, but it's much harder for international fixtures. The season runs from April to September.

Richmond, Kew & Hampton Court

RICHMOND | KEW | PUTNEY | BARNES | CHISWICK | TWICKENHAM | WIMBLEDON

Neighbourhood Top Five

❶ Listening out for poltergeists along the galleries and vaults of majestic **Hampton Court Palace** (p302) before getting lost in the maze.

❷ Plunging into the luxuriant green expanses, wooded thickets and tropical foliage of **Kew Gardens** (p306).

❸ Turning your back on urban London to discover a pristine pocket of wilderness at the **London Wetland Centre** (p311).

❹ Sinking a pint of beer at the historic riverside **White Cross pub** (p314) while trying to avoid being cut off by the high tide.

❺ Exploring London's wild side, roaming at will around the verdant environs of **Richmond Park** (p308).

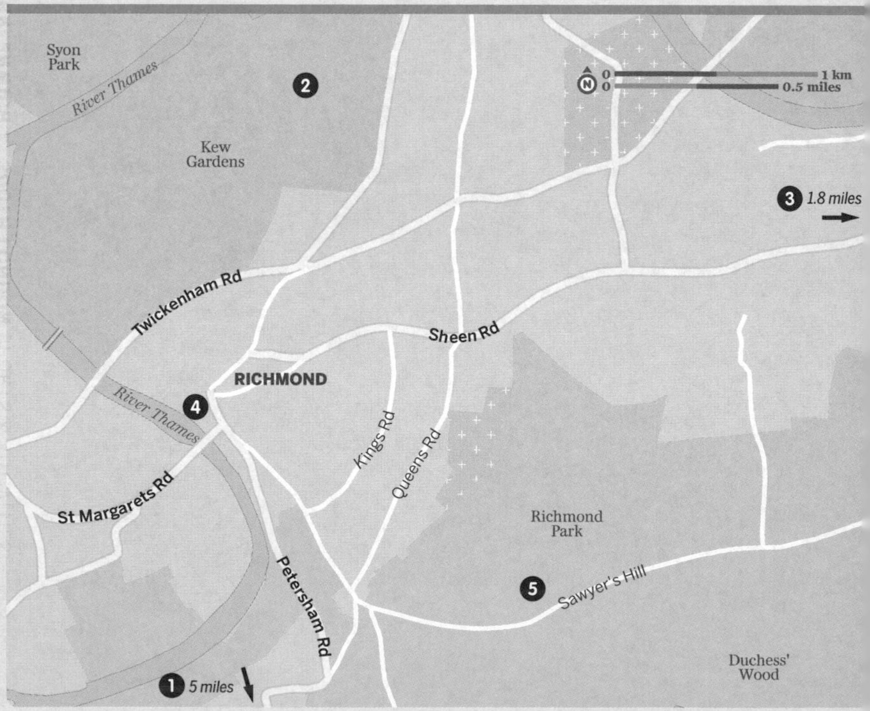

For more detail of this area see Map p470

Explore: Richmond, Kew & Hampton Court

If anywhere in London could be described as a village, Richmond – with its delightful green, riverside vistas and handsome architecture – is it. But the entire southwest from Putney to Twickenham is a refreshing alternative to central London's urban density. When the weather is fine, few London diversions can top time spent upriver by the Thames – whether exploring the major sights, walking along the riverbank or poking your head into a historic waterside pub. And if you really warm to the charms of London's green southwest, you'll also find a few lovely hotels to look after you.

You might not find yourself coming here to shop, but bring your wallet as there's no shortage of fine dining, and you'll find pubs aplenty. But it's exploration that should top your agenda, whether it be getting lost in the maze at splendid Hampton Court Palace, making endless botanic discoveries at Kew Gardens or walking the wilds of Richmond Park.

Local Life

➡ **Hang-outs** Get into the riverside pub lunch mood joining locals quaffing beer at the City Barge (p314) or White Cross (p314).

➡ **Greenery** Londoners from all over town bolt down to Richmond Park (p308) and Kew Gardens (p306) for weekend great escapes.

➡ **River Views** Join locals jogging by the river, walking their dogs or catching some sunshine north and south of Richmond Bridge (p308).

Getting There & Away

➡ **Train & Underground** Both Kew Gardens and Richmond are on the District Line and London Overground; Richmond train station can be reached from Clapham Junction. Trains run to Hampton Court station from Waterloo. East Putney, Putney Bridge, Fulham Broadway and Chiswick Park are on the District Line.

➡ **Boat** Boats run several times daily from Westminster Pier to Kew and on to Hampton Court Palace (boats sometimes stop at Richmond).

Lonely Planet's Top Tip

A manageable section of the fantastic Thames Path (p315) is the 4 miles between Putney Bridge and Barnes Footbridge. Taking around 90 minutes, most of the walk is very rural and at times you will only be accompanied by birdsong and the gentle swish of the river. From the footbridge, Chiswick train station is about 0.75 miles to the northwest. For more details, see the River Thames Alliance's Visit Thames site (www.visitthames.co.uk).

Best Places to Eat

➡ Al Boccon di'Vino (p313)
➡ Glasshouse (p313)
➡ Ma Goa (p313)
➡ Orange Pekoe (p314)

For reviews, see p312 ➡

Best Places to Drink

➡ White Cross (p314)
➡ Ye White Hart (p314)
➡ City Barge (p314)
➡ London Apprentice (p315)

For reviews, see p314 ➡

Best Guided Tours

➡ Kew Gardens (p306)
➡ Hampton Court Palace (p302)
➡ Richmond Park (p308)
➡ Strawberry Hill (p311)

For reviews, see p308 ➡

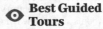

TOP SIGHT
HAMPTON COURT PALACE

London's most spectacular Tudor palace, this 16th-century icon concocts an imposing sense of history, from the huge kitchens and grand living quarters to the spectacular gardens, complete with 300-year-old maze.

History of the Palace

Hampton Court Palace was built by Cardinal Thomas Wolsey in 1515 but coaxed from him by Henry VIII just before Wolsey (as chancellor) fell from favour. It was already one of the most sophisticated palaces in Europe when, in the 17th century, Sir Christopher Wren was commissioned to build an extension. The result is a beautiful blend of Tudor and 'restrained baroque' architecture.

Entering the Palace

Passing through the magnificent main gate, you arrive first in the **Base Court** and beyond that **Clock Court**, named after its 16th-century astronomical clock. The panelled rooms and arched doorways in the **Young Henry VIII's Story** upstairs from Base Court provide a rewarding introduction: note the Tudor graffiti on the fireplace.

Henry VIII's Apartments

The stairs inside Anne Boleyn's Gateway lead up to Henry VIII's Apartments, including the stunning **Great Hall**. The **Horn Room**, hung with impressive antlers, leads to the **Great Watching Chamber** where guards controlled access to the king. Henry VIII's dazzling gemstone-encrusted **crown** has been recreated – the original was melted down by Oliver Cromwell – and sits in the **Royal Pew** (open 10am to 4pm Monday to Saturday

DON'T MISS...

- ➡ Great Hall
- ➡ Chapel Royal
- ➡ William III's Apartments
- ➡ Gardens and maze
- ➡ Mantegna's Triumphs of Caesar
- ➡ Henry VIII's Crown

PRACTICALITIES

- ➡ www.hrp.org.uk/HamptonCourtPalace
- ➡ adult/child £17.60/8.80
- ➡ ⌚10am-6pm Apr-Oct, to 4.30pm Nov-Mar
- ➡ Hampton Court Palace, Hampton Court

and 12.30pm to 1.30pm Sunday), which overlooks the beautiful **Chapel Royal** (still a place of worship after 450 years).

Tudor Kitchens & Great Wine Cellar

Also dating from Henry's day are the delightful Tudor kitchens, once used to rustling up meals for a royal household of some 1200 people. Don't miss the Great Wine Cellar, which handled the 300 barrels each of ale and wine consumed here annually in the mid-16th century.

William III's & Mary II's Apartments

A tour of William III's Apartments, completed by Wren in 1702, takes you up the grand **King's Staircase**. Highlights include the **King's Presence Chamber**, dominated by a throne backed with scarlet hangings. During the devastating fire of 1986, staff were ready to cut the huge portrait of William III from its frame with knives, if necessary. The sumptuous **King's Great Bedchamber**, with a bed topped with ostrich plumes, and the **King's Closet** (where His Majesty's toilet has a velvet seat) should not be missed.

William's wife Mary II had her own apartments, accessible via the fabulous **Queen's Staircase** (decorated by William Kent). When Mary died in 1694, work on her chambers was incomplete; they were finished during the reign of George II. At the time of writing, the apartments were being prepared for a new exhibition on the Royal bedchamber.

Georgian Private Apartments

The Georgian Rooms were used by George II and Queen Caroline on the court's last visit to the palace in 1737. Do not miss the fabulous Tudor **Wolsey Closet** with its early 16th-century ceiling and painted panels, commissioned by Henry VIII.

Cartoon Gallery

The Cartoon Gallery used to display the original Raphael Cartoons (now in the V&A Museum); nowadays it's just the late-17th-century copies.

Garden & Maze

Beyond the palace are the stunning gardens. Look out for the **Real Tennis Court**, dating from the 1620s. In the restored 24-hectare Riverside Gardens, you'll find the **Great Vine**. Planted in 1768, it's still producing just under 320kg of grapes per year.

No-one should leave Hampton Court without losing themselves in the 800m-long maze, included in entry; those not visiting the palace can enter for £4.40 (£2.75/13.20 for children/families).

VISIT BY BOAT

Between April and September, the palace can be reached by boat on the 22-mile route along the Thames from Westminster Pier in central London (via Kew and Richmond), but can take up to four hours (depending on the tide). Boats (one-way adult/child £15/7.50) are run by **Westminster Passenger Services Association** (www.wpsa.co.uk).

Hampton Court Palace presses up against 445-hectare Bushy Park (www.royalparks.gov.uk), a semiwild expanse with herds of red and fallow deer.

HAUNTED HAMPTON COURT

With a history this old and as eventful, a paranormal dimension is surely mandatory. Arrested for adultery and detained in the palace in 1542, Henry's fifth wife, Catherine Howard, was dragged screaming down a gallery at the palace by her guards after an escape bid. Her ghost is said to do a repeat performance, uttering 'unearthly shrieks' in the Haunted Gallery leading to the Royal Pew (she must be a tireless ghost as she also haunts the Tower of London).

A DAY AT THE PALACE

With so much to explore and seemingly infinite gardens, it can be tricky knowing where to begin. It helps to understand how the palace has grown over the centuries and how successive royal occupants embellished Hampton Court to suit their purposes and to reflect the style of the time.

As soon as he had his royal hands upon the palace from Cardinal Thomas Wolsey, Henry VIII began expanding the **Tudor architecture** 1, adding the **Great Hall** 2, the exquisite **Chapel Royal** 3, the opulent Great Watching Chamber and the gigantic **kitchens** 4. By 1540 it had become one of the grandest and most sophisticated palaces in Europe. James I kept things ticking over, while Charles I added a new tennis court and did some serious art-collecting – including acquiring **Mantegna's Triumphs of Caesar** 5.

Tudor Kitchens

These vast kitchens were the engine room of the palace. With a staff of 200 people, there were six spit-rack-equipped fireplaces, with roast meat always on the menu (to the tune of 8200 sheep and 1240 oxen per year).

7 The Maze

Around 150m north of the main bulding

Created from hornbeam and yew and planted in around 1700, the maze covers a third of an acre within the famous palace gardens. A must-see conclusion to Hampton Court, the maze takes the average visitor about 20 minutes to reach the centre.

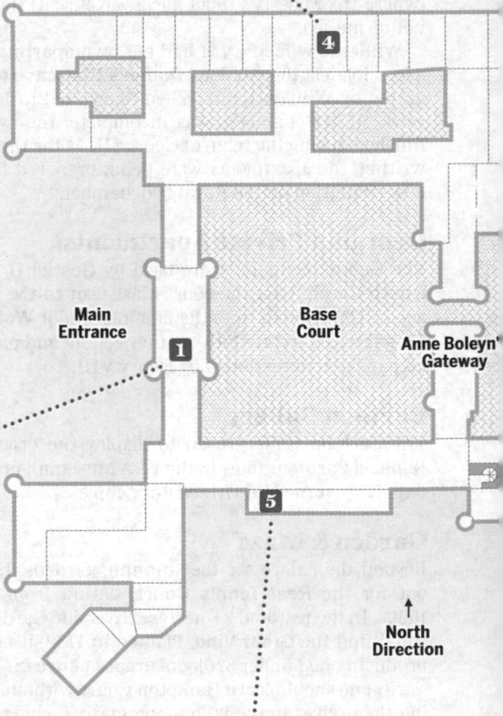

Tudor Architecture

Dating to 1515, the heart of the palace serves as one of the finest examples of Tudor architecture in the nation. Cardinal Thomas Wolsey was responsible for transforming what was originally a grand medieval manor house into a stunning Tudor palace.

The Triumphs of Caesar

Acquired by Charles I in 1629, Italian artist Andrea Mantegna's nine-painting series *The Triumphs of Caesar* portray Julius Caesar returning to Rome in a triumphant procession, accompanied by the spoils of war.

After the Civil War, puritanical Oliver Cromwell warmed to his own regal proclivities, spending weekends in the comfort of the former Queen's bedroom and selling off Charles I's art collection. In the late 17th century, William and Mary employed Sir Christopher Wren for baroque extensions, chiefly the William III Apartments, reached by the **King's Staircase** 6. William III also commissioned the world-famous **maze** 7.

TOP TIPS

- Ask one of the red-tunic-garbed warders for anecdotes and information.
- Tag along with a themed tour led by costumed historians or join a Salacious Gossip Tour for scandalous royal stories.
- Grab one of the audio tours from the Information Centre.

The Great Hall

This grand dining hall is the defining room of the palace, displaying what is considered England's finest hammer-beam roof, 16th-century Flemish tapestries telling the story of Abraham, and some exquisite stained-glass windows.

DAMIAN HARPER ©

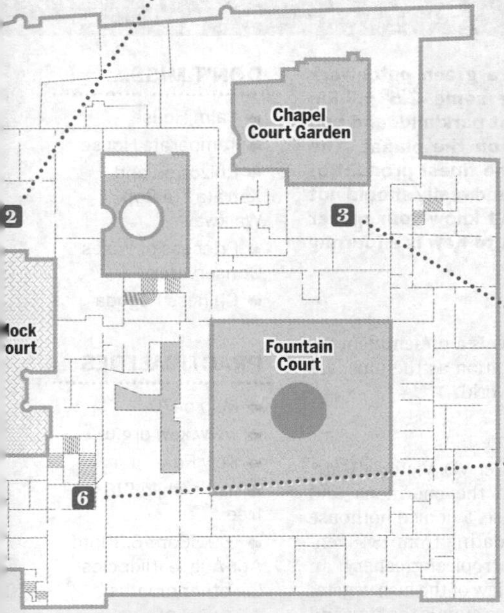

Chapel Royal

The blue-and-gold vaulted ceiling was originally intended for Christ Church, Oxford, but was installed here instead; the 18th-century oak reredos was carved by Grinling Gibbons. Books on display include a 1611 1st edition of the King James Bible, printed by Robert Barker.

The King's Staircase

One of five rooms at the palace painted by Antonio Verrio and a suitably bombastic prelude to the King's Apartments, the overblown King's Staircase adulates William III by elevating him above a cohort of Roman emperors.

DAMIAN HARPER ©

Open for Inspection

The palace was opened to the public by Queen Victoria in 1838.

JOHN LAMB / GETTY IMAGES ©

TOP SIGHT
KEW GARDENS

A staggering 24% of London is a green patchwork of domestic gardens, sprouting some 2.5 million trees. Throw in London's abundant parkland, and you have one of the greenest cities on the planet. The 121-hectare gardens at Kew are the finest product of the British botanical imagination and really should not be missed. No worries if you don't know your quiver tree from your ylang-ylang; a visit to Kew is a journey of discovery for everyone.

Botanical Collection

As well as being a public garden, Kew is a pre-eminent research centre, maintaining its reputation as the most exhaustive botanical collection in the world.

Palm House

Assuming you come by tube and enter via Victoria Gate, you'll come almost immediately to the enormous and elaborate 700-glass-paned Palm House, a domed hothouse of metal and curved sheets of glass dating from 1848, enveloping a splendid display of exotic tropical greenery; an aerial walkway offers a parrot's-eye view of the lush vegetation. Just northwest of the Palm House stands the tiny and irresistibly steamy **Waterlily House** (Map p470; Mar-Dec), sheltering the gigantic *Victoria cruziana* waterlily, whose vast pads can support the weight of a small adult.

DON'T MISS...

- Palm House
- Temperate House
- Rhizotron and Xstrata Treetop Walkway
- Princess of Wales Conservatory
- Chinese Pagoda

PRACTICALITIES

- Map p470
- www.kew.org.uk
- Kew Rd
- adult/child £16/free
- 9.30am-6.30pm Apr-Aug, earlier closing other months
- Kew Pier, Kew Bridge, Kew Gardens

Princess of Wales Conservatory

Further north, the angular Princess of Wales Conservatory houses plants in 10 different climatic zones – everything from a desert to a mangrove swamp. Look out for stone plants, which resemble pebbles (to deter grazing animals), carnivorous plants, gigantic waterlilies, cacti and a collection of tropical orchids.

Temperate House

The beautiful Temperate House in the southeast of Kew Gardens (north of the pagoda) is the world's largest surviving Victorian glasshouse, an astonishing feat of architecture housing an equally sublime collection of plants, including the towering Chilean wine palm. Nearby **Evolution House** traces plant evolution over 3500 million years.

Rhizotron & Treetop Walkway

In the **Arboretum** – a short walk from Temperate House – the fascinating Xstrata Treetop Walkway first takes you underground and then 18m up in the air into the tree canopy.

Kew Palace

Built in 1631 and the smallest of the royal palaces, adorable red-brick **Kew Palace** (www.hrp.org.uk/kew-palace; included in Kew Gardens ticket; ⌚9.30am-5.30pm Apr-Sep), in the northwest of the gardens, is a former royal residence once known as Dutch House. It was the favourite home of George III and his family; his wife, Queen Charlotte, died here in 1818 (you can see the very chair in which she expired). Don't miss the newly restored **Royal Kitchens** next door.

Other Highlights

Several long vistas (**Cedar Vista**, **Syon Vista** and **Pagoda Vista**) are channeled by trees from vantage points within Kew Gardens. The idyllic, thatched **Queen Charlotte's Cottage** (Map p470; ⌚11am-4pm Sat & Sun Apr-Sep) in the southwest of the gardens was popular with 'mad' George III and his wife; the carpets of bluebells around here are a drawcard in spring. The **Marianne North Gallery** displays the botanical paintings of Marianne North, an indomitable traveller who roamed the continents from 1871 to 1885, painting plants along the way. The **Orangery** near Kew Palace contains a restaurant, cafe and shop. Pieces of sculpture from British artist **David Nash** are positioned around Kew gardens, complementing and echoing the natural landscape. A traditional Japanese **Minka House** can be found among the bamboo fronds in the west of the gardens.

Getting Around

If you want a good overview of the gardens, jump aboard the **Kew Explorer** (adult/child £4/2), which allows you to hop on and off at stops along the way.

VISITING THE GARDENS

Spring is a spectacular season to visit, but any time of the year is fine. Most visitors arrive by tube or train, but from April to October, boats run by the **Westminster Passenger Services Association** (Map p440; ☎020-7930 2062; www.wpsa.co.uk; adult/child return to Kew Gardens £18/9) sail from Westminster Pier to Kew Pier. For eats, there's a restaurant in the 18th-century Orangery, the Pavilion restaurant, a cafe by Victoria Gate and the White Peaks Cafe. Kids can explore the fun-filled Treehouse Towers (an outdoor play area) and Climbers and Creepers (an interactive botanical zone). Popular summer concerts bring music to Kew (visit the website for more info).

Kew's 49.5m-tall eight-sided Chinese Pagoda (1762), designed by William Chambers (who designed Somerset House), is one of the gardens' architectural icons. During WWII, the pagoda withstood the blast from a stick of Luftwaffe bombs exploding nearby, and was also secretly employed by the Ministry of Defence to test bomb trajectories (which involved cutting holes in each floor!)

⊙ SIGHTS

⊙ Richmond & Kew

KEW GARDENS GARDENS
See p306.

RICHMOND PARK PARK
Map p470 (⊙7am-dusk Mar-Sep, from 7.30am Oct-Feb; ⊖Richmond) At almost 1000 hectares (the largest urban parkland in Europe), this park offers everything from formal gardens and ancient oaks to unsurpassed views of central London 12 miles away. It's easy to flee the several roads slicing up the rambling wilderness, making the park perfect for a quiet walk or a picnic with the kids, even in summer when Richmond's riverside heaves.

Herds of over 600 red and fallow deer basking under the trees are part of its magic, but they can be less than docile in rutting season (September and October) and when the does bear young (May to July), so keep your distance (over 50m) during these times. Birdwatchers will love the diverse habitats, from neat gardens to woodland and assorted ponds. Floral fans should visit **Isabella Plantation**, a stunning woodland garden created after WWII, in April and May when the rhododendrons and azaleas bloom.

Set in a beautiful 13-hectare garden and affording great views of the city from the back terrace, **Pembroke Lodge** (Map p470; www.pembroke-lodge.co.uk; ⊙9am-5.30pm summer, to just before dusk winter) was the childhood home of Bertrand Russell. The Georgian tea rooms can garnish your visit with warm scones and clotted cream after 3pm.

The pastoral vista from **Richmond Hill** has inspired painters and poets for centuries and still beguiles. It's the only view (which includes St Paul's Cathedral 10 miles away) in the country to be protected by an act of Parliament.

Coming from Richmond, it's easiest to enter via Richmond Gate or from Petersham Rd. Take a map with you and wander the grounds.

RICHMOND GREEN PARK
Map p470 (⊖Richmond, ⊖Richmond) A short walk west of the Quadrant, where you'll emerge from the tube, is Richmond Green with its mansions and delightful pubs. Cross the green diagonally for the attractive remains of **Richmond Palace** (Map p470), just the main entrance and red-brick gatehouse, built in 1501. Henry VII's arms are visible above the main gate: he built the Tudor additions to the edifice, although the palace had been in use as a royal residence since 1125. Elizabeth I died here in 1603.

HAM HOUSE HISTORIC BUILDING
Map p470 (☎020-8940 1950; www.nationaltrust.org.uk; Ham St, Ham, TW10; admission prices vary; ⊙house noon-4pm Sat-Thu late Mar–mid-Nov, gardens 11am-4pm Sat-Thu Jan–mid-Feb & Nov–mid-Dec, 11am-5pm Sat-Thu mid-Feb–Oct; ⊛; ☒371, ⊖Richmond, ⊖Richmond) Known as 'Hampton Court in miniature', Ham House was built in 1610 and became home to the first Earl of Dysart, unluckily employed as 'whipping boy' to Charles I. Inside it's grandly furnished; the Great Staircase is a magnificent example of Stuart woodworking. Look out for ceiling paintings by Antonio Verrio and for a miniature of Elizabeth I by Nicholas Hilliard.

THAMES AT RICHMOND

The stretch of the river from Twickenham Bridge to Petersham and Ham is one of the prettiest in London. The action is mostly around five-span **Richmond Bridge** (Map p470), built in 1777 and London's oldest surviving crossing, only widened for traffic in 1937. Just before it, along one of the loveliest parts of the Thames, is tiny Corporation Island, colonised by flocks of feral parakeets. The gorgeous walk to Petersham can be crowded in nice weather; best to cut across pastoral **Petersham Meadows** (Map p470) – where cows still graze – and continue to Richmond Park for peace and quiet. There are several companies near Richmond Bridge, including **Richmond Boat Hire** (☎8948 8270), that offer skiff hire (adult/child per hour £5/2.50, per day £15/7.50). Alternatively, walk north from Twickenham Bridge, alongside the Old Deer Park, past the two obelisks and climb onto **Richmond Lock** (Map p470) and footbridge, dating from 1894.

WORTH A DETOUR

SYON HOUSE

Just across the Thames from Kew Gardens, **Syon House** (Syon Park; Map p470; www.syonpark.co.uk; Brentford, TW7; adult/child £11/4.50, gardens only £6/3; ⌚house 11am-5pm Wed, Thu & Sun mid-Mar–Oct, gardens & conservatory 10.30am-5pm daily mid-Mar–Oct; ⊖Gunnersbury or 🚉Gunnersbury then 🚌237 or 267) was once a medieval abbey named after Mt Zion. In 1542 Henry VIII dissolved the order of Bridgettine nuns who peacefully lived here and rebuilt it into a residence. (They say God had the last laugh in 1547 when Henry's coffin was brought to Syon en route to Windsor for burial and burst open during the night, leaving his body to be set upon by the estate's dogs.)

The house from where Lady Jane Grey ascended the throne for her nine-day reign in 1553 was remodelled in the neoclassical style by Robert Adam in the 18th century and has plenty of Adam furniture and oak panelling. The interior was designed on gender-specific lines, with pastel pinks and purples for the ladies' gallery, and mock Roman sculptures for the men's dining room. Guests at the house have included the great Mohawk chieftain Thayendanegea (Joseph Brant) and Gunpowder plot–member Thomas Percy.

The estate's 16-hectare gardens, with a lake and a magnificent domed Great Conservatory (1826) – the latter inspiring Joseph Paxton to design the Crystal Palace – were landscaped by Lancelot 'Capability' Brown. Syon Park is filled with attractions for children, including an adventure playground and aquatic park.

Other notable paintings are by Constable and Reynolds. The grounds of Ham House slope down to the Thames, but there are also pleasant 17th-century formal gardens. Just opposite the Thames and accessible by small ferry is Marble Hill Park and its splendid mansion (p311). Special house tours run between December and March.

⊙ Putney & Barnes

PUTNEY & BARNES NEIGHBOURHOOD

Called *Putelei* in the Domesday Book of 1086, Putney is most famous as the starting point of the annual Oxford and Cambridge Boat Race (p30). Barnes is less well known and more 'villagey' in feel. The best way to approach Putney is to follow the signs from Putney Bridge tube station for the footbridge (which runs parallel to the rail track), admiring the gorgeous riverside houses, with their gardens fronting the Thames, and thereby avoiding the tatty High St until the last minute.

⊙ Chiswick

CHISWICK HOUSE HISTORIC BUILDING

(www.chgt.org.uk; Burlington Lane, Chiswick Park, W4; adult/child £5.90/3.50, gardens free; ⌚house 10am-5pm Sun-Wed Apr-Oct, gardens 7am-dusk daily; 📶; 🚉Chiswick, ⊖Turnham Green) Designed by the third Earl of Burlington (1694–1753) – fired up with passion for all things Roman after his grand tour of Italy – this stunner of a neo-Palladian pavilion with an octagonal dome and colonnaded portico is a delight. The almost overpoweringly grand interior includes the coffered dome of the Upper Tribunal – left ungilded, the walls below are decorated with eight enormous paintings.

Admire the stunningly painted ceiling (by William Kent) of the Blue Velvet Room and look out for carvings of the pagan vegetative deity, the Green Man, in the marble fireplaces of the Green Velvet Room.

Lord Burlington also planned the house's original gardens, now Chiswick Park, surrounding the house, but they have been much altered since his time. Children will love them – look out for the stone sphinxes near the Cedar of Lebanon trees (another sphinx made of lead can be found in the Lower Tribuna). Chiswick House also has an excellent cafe.

The house is about a mile southwest of the Turnham Green tube station and 750m northeast of Chiswick train station.

HOGARTH'S HOUSE HISTORIC BUILDING

(☎020-8994 6757; www.hounslow.info/arts/hogarthshouse; Hogarth Lane, W4; ⌚noon-5pm

LOCAL KNOWLEDGE

HAMPTON COURT PALACE

An enthusiastic communicator, Ian Franklin has been a State Apartment Warder at Hampton Court Palace for 16 years.

Are costumed tours the way to go?

Trained historians, our interpreters wear extremely accurate representations of period clothes, bringing historic scenarios to life. However, warders, such as myself, are found in most of the rooms and can answer questions face to face in a very personal way.

Any fascinating facts associated with the palace?

The Palace is home to the largest indigenous spider in England. *Tegenaria parietina*, nick-named the Cardinal Spider after Cardinal Wolsey, can measure up to 20cm from leg-tip to leg-tip. You probably won't encounter one, but their webs are often seen in places like the Tudor Kitchens and King's Stairs. If you don't like spiders – watch out!

Jane Seymour, Henry VIII's third wife, died at Hampton Court Palace. It is said that as there was no burial place ready, her body was laid out in the Chapel Royal. To prevent Jane's body decomposing too quickly, her internal organs were removed, and her heart placed in a casket and buried beneath the Chapel altar. There's no evidence the casket was ever dug up, so the heart could still be buried at the palace.

What's your favourite part of the Palace?

I love the Chapel Royal. As it's still used as a place of worship, and visitors are welcome to attend Sunday services, it gives a sense of life and community to the palace.

Any events you can recommend throughout the year?

The special cooking days in the Tudor Kitchens on the first full weekend in any month, and at Easter and Christmas. Where else in the UK can you regularly see cooks creating Tudor dishes, or meals from period recipes, in the greatest surviving Tudor Kitchens in the country?

Any spooky treats?

Our famous ghost tours, which run from Halloween to March, allow visitors to enter the palace after dark, and take in the most 'haunted' areas. You can visit the infamous 'Haunted Galley' in almost total darkness!

Tue-Sun; ⊖Turnham Green) FREE Home between 1749 and 1764 to artist and social commentator William Hogarth, this recently restored small house displays his caricatures and engravings, with such works as the haunting *Gin Lane* (and the less well-known, more affirmative *Beer Street*), *Marriage-à-la-mode* and copies of *A Rake's Progress* and *The Four Stages of Cruelty*.

The low ceiling of the narrow staircase is a head-bumping reminder that the Sergeant Painter to the King was under five foot at full stretch. The house was bombed by the Luftwaffe in 1940, but the artist's mulberry tree survived and still flourishes in the garden (which would be a quiet retreat were it not for the roaring dual carriageway beyond the wall), accompanied by daffodils in spring. Prints and postcards are available from the downstairs shop.

FULLER'S GRIFFIN BREWERY BREWERY

(☎020-8996 2063; www.fullers.co.uk; Chiswick Lane South, W4; admission incl tasting £10-12; ⏲tours hourly 11am-3pm Mon-Fri; 🚉Chiswick, ⊖Turnham Green) If you're a total beer fiend, hop (excuse the pun) on a tour to see it being brewed up and join in a good-old tasting session (over-18s only). Informative 90-minute guided tours of the brewery (minimum four people) depart regularly on weekdays, and must be booked in advance by phone.

Twickenham

MARBLE HILL HOUSE HISTORIC BUILDING

Map p470 (020-8892 5115; www.english-heritage.org.uk; Richmond Rd, TW1; adult/child/family £5.70/3.40/14.80; tours 10.30am & noon Sat, 10.30am, 12pm, 2.15pm & 3.30pm Sun Apr-Oct, park 7am-dusk; ; St Margaret's or Richmond, Richmond) An 18th-century Palladian peach conceived as an idyllic escape from the hurly burly of city life, this majestic love nest was originally built for George II's mistress Henrietta Howard and later occupied by Mrs Fitzherbert, the secret wife of George IV. The Georgian interior contains some astonishing flourishes, including the hand-painted Chinese wallpaper in the dining parlour and some delectable furniture.

The poet Alexander Pope had a hand in designing the park, which stretches leisurely down to the Thames. To get there from St Margaret's station, turn right along St Margaret's Rd, then take the right fork along Crown Rd and turn left along Richmond Rd. Turn right along Beaufort Rd and walk across Marble Hill Park to the house. It is also easily accessible by pedestrian ferry from Ham House. It's a 25-minute walk from Richmond station.

STRAWBERRY HILL HISTORIC BUILDING

(www.strawberryhillhouse.org.uk; 268 Waldegrave Rd, TW1; adult/child £8.40/5.25; house 2-5.30pm Mon-Wed, noon-5.30pm Sat & Sun Mar-Oct, garden 10am-6pm daily; Richmond then R68) With its snow-white walls and Gothic turrets, this fantastical and totally restored 18th-century creation in Twickenham is the work of art historian, author and politician Horace Walpole. Studded with elaborate stained glass, the building reaches its astonishing apogee in the gallery, with its magnificent papier-mâché ceiling. For the full magic, join a twilight tour (£20).

Wimbledon

WIMBLEDON COMMON COMMON

(www.wpcc.org.uk; Wimbledon or Wimbledon then 93) Surging on into Putney Heath, Wimbledon Common blankets a staggering 460 hectares of southwest London. An astonishing expanse of open, wild and

TOP SIGHT
LONDON WETLAND CENTRE

One of Europe's largest inland wetland projects, this 42-hectare centre run by the Wildfowl & Wetlands Trust (WWT) was successfully transformed from four Victorian reservoirs and attracts some 180 species of bird, as well as 300 types of moth and butterfly.

From the visitor centre and glassed-in observatory overlooking the ponds, meandering paths and boardwalks lead visitors around the grounds, penetrating the reedbed, marsh, fen and watery habitats of its many residents and transients, including black swans, ducks, Bewick's swans, geese, red-crested pochards, sand martins, coots and the rarer bitterns, herons and kingfishers. Don't miss the **Peacock Tower**, a three-storey hide on the main lake's eastern edge; other hides sprinkled around the reserve include the fantastic **Headley Discovery Hide** in the west. The wetland is also well-populated with eight different species of bats that feed on the abundant moths. A short walk north of the entrance, the wetland's family of sleek-coated otters are fed daily at 11am and 2pm (Monday to Friday). Free **tours** depart daily at 11.30am and 2.30pm; bird feed walks set out at 3pm. Binoculars can be hired from the shop.

DON'T MISS...

- Peacock Tower
- Headley Discovery Hide
- Otter Feeding
- Daily Tours

PRACTICALITIES

- 020-8409 4400
- www.wwt.org.uk
- Queen Elizabeth's Walk, SW13
- adult/child/family £10.60/5.90/29.55
- 9.30am-6pm Apr-Oct, 9.30am-5pm Nov-Mar
- Hammersmith then 283 (Duck Bus)

wooded space for walking, nature trailing and picnicking – the best mode of exploration – the common has its own **Wimbledon Windmill** (www.wimbledonwindmill.org.uk; Windmill Rd, SW19; adult/child £2/1; ⌚2-5pm Sat, 11am-5pm Sun late Mar-Oct; ⊖Wimbledon), a fine smock mill (ie octagonal-shaped with sloping weatherboarded sides) dating from 1817.

The windmill, which ceased operating in 1864, contains a museum with working models on the history of windmills and milling. The adjacent Windmill Tearooms can supply tea, caffeine and sustenance. On the southern side of the common, the misnamed **Caesar's Camp** is what's left of a roughly circular earthen fort built in the 5th century BC.

WIMBLEDON LAWN TENNIS MUSEUM MUSEUM

(☎020-8946 6131; www.wimbledon.org; Gate 3, Church Rd, SW19; adult/child £12/7, museum & tour £22/13; ⌚10am-5pm; ⊖Wimbledon or 🚆Wimbledon then 🚌93) This well-presented museum details the history of tennis – from its French precursor *jeu de paume* (which employed the open hand) to the supersonic serves of today's champions. It's a state-of-the-art presentation, with plenty of video clips and a projection of John McEnroe in the dressing room at Wimbledon, but the highlight is the chance to see Centre Court from the **360-degree viewing box**.

WIMBLEDON TICKETS

For a few weeks each June and July, the sporting world's attention is fixed on the quiet southern suburb of Wimbledon, as it has been since 1877. Most show-court tickets for the **Wimbledon** (☎020-8944 1066; www.wimbledon.com) Championships are allocated through public ballot, applications for which usually begin in early August of the preceding year and close at the end of December. Entry into the ballot does not mean entrants will get a ticket. A quantity of show court, outer court, ground tickets and late-entry tickets are also available if you queue on the day of play, but if you want a show-court ticket it is recommended you camp the night before in the queue. See www.wimbledon.com/championships/tickets for details.

Riveting facts and figures abound: tennis clothes worn by female tennis players in 1881 weighed up to a grueling 4.9kg! Compare this with Maria Sharapova's skimpy 2004 Ladies Singles outfit, also on display. The museum is only open to ticket holders during the championships; it houses a cafe and a shop selling all manner of tennis memorabilia. Audio guides are available. Regular tours of Wimbledon that take in Centre Court, No 1 Court and other areas of the All England Club also include access to the museum.

BUDDHAPADIPA TEMPLE TEMPLE

(☎020-8946 1357; www.buddhapadipa.org; 14 Calonne Rd, SW19; admission free; ⌚temple 9am-6pm Sat & Sun, grounds 9am-5pm daily; ⊖Wimbledon then 🚌93) Immersed within 4 acres of tranquil Wimbledon land, this delightful Thai Buddhist temple actively welcomes all and sundry. Along with its reflective Buddhist repose, a community feel permeates the temple grounds, with visitors invited in for coffee and a chat. The *wat* (temple) boasts a *bot* (consecrated chapel) decorated with traditional scenes by two leading Thai artists (take your shoes off before entering).

Sundays are generally the most eventful times to visit, when Dhamma talks and discussions are given in the main temple between 1pm and 2pm. The temple also holds regular meditation classes and retreats (see the website). To reach the temple, take the tube or train to Wimbledon and then bus 93 up to Wimbledon Parkside. Calonne Rd leads off it on the right.

EATING

Richmond

STEIN'S GERMAN £

Map p470 (Richmond Towpath, TW10; mains from £3.90; ⌚noon-dusk, longer hours in summer; 🚆Richmond, ⊖Richmond) On sunny Richmond days, this popular riverside *biergarten* not far from Richmond Bridge is a natural choice for sampling the lazy Thames-side vibe as well as affordable *würstchen*, other Bavarian specialities and a stein or two of chilled *weissbier*.

Shaded by two tall yew trees and parasols, the setting is choice, and overloaded parents can rejoice at the small playground for under-fours at the back.

GELATERIA DANIELI GELATERIA £

Map p470 (www.gelateriadanieli.com; 16 Brewers Lane; ice cream from £2.25; ⏲10am-8pm Mon-Wed, 10am-10pm Thu-Sat, 11am-10pm Sun; Richmond, Richmond) Stuffed away down delightful narrow, pinched and flagstone-paved Brewer's Lane off Richmond Green, this titchy gelateria is a joy, and often busy. The handmade ice cream arrives in some lip-smacking flavours, from Christmas pudding through pistachio, walnut and nougat to peanut and chocolate, scooped into small tubs or chocolate and hazelnut cones.

PIER 1 FISH & CHIPS ££

Map p470 (www.pier1fishandchipshop.co.uk; 11-13 Petersham Rd, TW10; mains from £10.95; ⏲11.30am-11pm Mon-Sat, to 10.30pm Sun; Richmond, Richmond) There's little by way of charm in the white, bright and voluminous interior of Pier 1, but the fish here is what it's all about, ferried to tables by helpful waiting staff in black trilbies. The fish – served with chips and a small dish of mushy peas – is prodigiously sized and succulently cooked, either fried in batter or grilled.

CHEZ LINDSAY FRENCH ££

Map p470 (020-8948 7473; www.chez-lindsay.co.uk; 11 Hill Rise, TW10; mains £10-20.50; ⏲noon-11pm Mon-Sat, to 10pm Sun; Richmond, Richmond) An appetising slice of Brittany at the bottom of Richmond Hill, enduringly popular Chez Lindsay's simply furnished dining room has won consistent praise for its wholesome Breton cuisine, comfortable ambience and river views. There's an accent on seafood and house specialities include adorable galettes (buckwheat pancakes) with countless tasty fillings (or plain), washed down with a variety of hearty (and very dry) Breton ciders.

★AL BOCCON DI'VINO ITALIAN £££

Map p470 (020-8940 9060; www.nonsolovinoltd.co.uk; 14 Red Lion St, TW9; set meal £40; ⏲dinner from 7pm Tue & Wed, lunch from 1pm & dinner from 7pm Thu-Sun; Richmond, Richmond) This stellar Venetian restaurant is generally rammed with eager gourmands. Rather audaciously, there's neither menu nor wine list, but this adds adventurousness to the culinary occasion, as overseen by owner Riccardo. You may get *pasta fresca ripiena* or *agnello al forno*, depending on the availability of the freshest ingredients (and fresh they are).

Meals consist of a sequence of ten or more courses, at a flat fee of £40 (wine is also a take-it or leave-it £25), so take along an empty tummy. Book well ahead, especially for weekends.

PETERSHAM NURSERIES CAFE MODERN EUROPEAN £££

Map p470 (020-8940 5230; www.petershamnurseries.com; Church Lane, off Petersham Rd, TW10; mains £19-27, 2-/3-course menu Wed-Fri £23/28; ⏲cafe noon-2.45pm Tue-Sun, teahouse 10am-4.30pm Tue-Sat, from 11am Sun) In a greenhouse at the back of the fabulously located Petersham Nurseries is this award-winning cafe straight out of the pages of *The Secret Garden*. The confidently executed cuisine includes organic ingredients harvested from the nursery gardens as well as seasonal plates, ranging from pan-fried wild sea bass to osso buco with polenta. Booking in advance is essential. There's also a **teahouse** for coffee, tea and cakes through the day and an Italian lunch menu.

Because of local residents' and council concerns about traffic increasing with the cafe's popularity, patrons are asked to walk here via the picturesque river towpath, or to use public transport.

Kew

GLASSHOUSE MODERN EUROPEAN ££

Map p470 (020-8940 6777; www.glasshouse-restaurant.co.uk; 14 Station Pde, TW9; 3-course lunch £27.50-32.50, 3-course dinner £42.50; ⏲noon-2.30pm & 6.30-10.30pm Mon-Sat, 12.30-3pm & 7-10pm Sun; ; Kew Gardens, Kew Gardens) A day at Kew Gardens finds a perfect conclusion at this gastronomic highlight. The glass-fronted exterior envelops a delicately lit, low-key interior, where the focus remains on divinely cooked food. Diners are rewarded with a consistently accomplished menu from chef Daniel Mertl that combines English mainstays with modern European innovation. There's a great children's lunch menu on weekends.

Putney & Barnes

MA GOA INDIAN ££

(www.ma-goa.com; 242-244 Upper Richmond Rd, SW15; mains £8.75-15.50, daily 2-course set meal

£10; noon-2.30pm Tue-Fri & 12.45-3pm Sun, 6.30-11pm Mon-Sat & 6-10pm Sun; ; Putney, Putney Bridge) The speciality at this much-loved restaurant is the subtle cuisine of Portugal's former colony on India's west coast. Winning dishes include the lovely *chini raan achari* (pot roasted lamb shank with spices), Ma's *fish caldin* (swordfish with coconut, mustard & fenugreek sauce) and the stir-fried *Goa chorizo*. Vegetarian options are available plus there's a good value Sunday buffet lunch (£11).

ORANGE PEKOE TEAHOUSE ££

(www.orangepekoeteas.com; 3 White Hart Lane, SW13; cream tea £8; 7.30am-5pm Mon-Fri, 9am-5pm Sat & Sun; Barnes Bridge) This delightful Barnes tea shop is a consummate haven for lovers of the tea leaf. Surround yourself with all types of tea and present all your tricky leaf-related questions to the on-site tea sommelier; there's fine coffee, too, plus tasty breakfasts and cakes, ravishing cream teas (scones with clotted cream, strawberry jam and a pot of tea) throughout the day and the guilty pleasure of full-on traditional afternoon teas, presented in thoroughly English fashion. Reservations recommended.

ENOTECA TURI ITALIAN ££

(www.enotecaturi.com; 28 Putney High St, SW15; mains £9.50-22.50, 2-course set lunch/dinner £17.50/27.50; noon-2.30pm & 7-10.30pm Mon-Sat; Putney, Putney Bridge) The atmosphere at this stylish place is serene, the service charming, the menu enticing. Enoteca Turi devotes equal attention to the grape as to the food, which means that each dish, be it *fedelini* with clams or braised rabbit with white wine, comes recommended with a particular glass of wine (or you can pick from the huge wine selection if you have ideas of your own).

Chiswick

FRANCO MANCA PIZZA £

(020-8747 4822; www.francomanca.co.uk; 144 Chiswick High Rd, W4; pizzas £4.50-6.95; noon-11pm; Turnham Green) Branching out from its original Brixton pizzeria, Franco Manca has brought its deliciously aromatic thin crust, sourdough pizzas (and culinary pizzazz) to Chiswick, with longer hours and more elbow room. Never be put off by its stark choice of six pizzas; this place is entirely about quality, not quantity. Even fussy and hard-to-please Italian diners applaud and the highly affordable price tag is a further fillip.

DRINKING & NIGHTLIFE

Richmond & Kew

WHITE CROSS PUB

Map p470 (www.thewhitecrossrichmond.com; Water Lane, TW9; 10am-11pm Mon-Sat, to 10.30pm Sun; Richmond) The riverside location and fine food and ales make this bay-windowed pub on the site of a former friary a winner. There are entrances for low and high tides, but when the river is at its highest, Cholmondeley Walk running along the Thames floods and the pub is out of bounds to those not willing to wade. Wellies are provided.

Very occasionally boats have to pick up stranded boozers: a chalkboard lists high-tide times and depths (you can also check the website). Quirky detail: there's a tiny working fireplace under the window on your right as you enter.

Putney & Barnes

YE WHITE HART PUB

(www.whitehartbarnes.co.uk; The Terrace, SW13; 11am-11pm Mon-Thu, 11am-midnight Fri, 10am-midnight Sat, 10am-11pm Sun; ; Barnes Bridge) This riverside Young's pub in Barnes was formerly a Masonic lodge; it's huge, traditional and welcoming downstairs, but the temptation in warmer months is to head to the balcony upstairs for Thames views, or plonk yourself down at one of the riverside tables. When **Boat Race** (p30) day arrives, the pub is deluged with beer-toting spectators.

Chiswick

CITY BARGE PUB

(27 Strand on the Green, W4; 11am-11pm; ; Gunnersbury) In a line of small riverside cottages facing wooded Oliver's Island (where Cromwell is alleged to have taken refuge), this gem of a pub, with a purple-painted interior, looks straight onto the muddy

Thames. There has been a pub here since the Middle Ages (1484, to be exact), although the Luftwaffe gave it a dramatic facelift.

Once known as the Navigators Arms, it is split into two bars (go for the cosy old downstairs one) and drinkers spill outside in clement weather. A scene from the Beatles' film *Help!* was shot here, celebrated in framed photo stills next to the bar. The hefty steel door clangs shut during high tides, which inundate the towpath.

Twickenham

LONDON APPRENTICE PUB

Map p470 (www.thelondonapprentice.co.uk; 62 Church St, TW7; 11am-11pm Sun-Thu, to midnight Fri & Sat; Isleworth) This riverside pub (apparently unconnected with the Cornish village of the same name) trumpets a lineage dating back to Tudor days, although the building you drink in today is 18th century. Henry VIII is said to have dallied with wife-to-be number five, Catherine Howard, at the tavern's older incarnation; other regulars included smugglers and highwaymen, including Dick Turpin.

WHITE SWAN PUB

Map p470 (www.whiteswantwickenham.com; Riverside, TW1; Twickenham) This traditional pub in Twickenham overlooks a quiet stretch of the Thames from what must be one of the most English-looking streets in London. It boasts a fantastic riverside location, a great selection of beer and a loyal crowd of locals. Even if you are not in Twickenham, the White Swan is worth a detour.

Wimbledon

CROOKED BILLET PUB

(www.thecrookedbilletwimbledon.com; 14-15 Crooked Billet, SW19; Wimbledon) This historic Young's boozer south of Cannizaro Park just off Wimbledon Common is brimful of character, with flagstone floors, open fires and a cosy village-pub personality. Drinkers collapse on the green opposite in summer, while home-cooked food, award-winning ale and seasonal drinks welcome weary ramblers and Wimbledon wayfarers. The Hand in Hand pub next door is another snug option, packed at weekends.

THAMES PATH

The entire Thames Path National Trail is a 184-mile walk stretching from the river's source at Thames Head, near Kemble in the Cotswolds, to the Thames Barrier. It's truly magnificent, particularly in its upper reaches, but tackling the entire course is for the truly ambitious and will need a couple of weeks. Most visitors walk sections of it, such as the 16-mile chunk from Battersea to the barrier, which takes about 6½ hours. There is also a short but lovely riverside walk from Putney to Barnes, or the gorgeous stretch of river from Twickenham Bridge to Petersham and Ham.

SPORTS & ACTIVITIES

TWICKENHAM RUGBY STADIUM STADIUM

(020-8892 2000; www.rfu.com; Rugby Rd, Twickenham, TW1; Hounslow East then 281 or Twickenham) The home of English rugby union. A **museum** (0870 405 2001; adult/child £7/5; 10am-5pm Tue-Sat, 11am-5pm Sun) showcases old matches in the video theatre and boasts a collection of 10,000 items of rugby memorabilia. Guided tours of the stadium (adult/child/family £15/9/45) take place at various times every day (except Mondays and match days) and include entry to the museum; see the website for details on times. Tickets for international matches are hard to obtain.

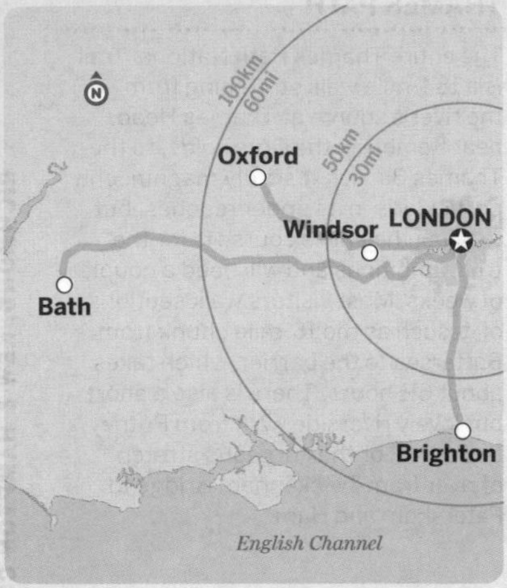

Day Trips from London

Windsor Castle p317

That bastion of British royalty, Windsor Castle, overlooks the affluent town of Windsor, picturesquely located by the Thames.

Oxford p320

The world's oldest university town, Oxford's allure doesn't stop with its prestigious colleges; there's delightful architecture and world-class museums, too.

Brighton p324

With its heady mix of seaside, seediness and sophistication, Brighton is London's favourite coastal resort – with a mock-Mogul summer palace thrown in to boot.

Bath p327

A cultural trendsetter and fashionable haunt for three centuries, Bath has so many architectural gems that the entire city has been named a World Heritage site.

TOP SIGHT
WINDSOR CASTLE

The world's largest and oldest occupied fortress, this redoubtable mass of battlements and towers dominates the Berkshire town of Windsor, 25 miles west of London. British monarchs have holed up in Windsor Castle for over 900 years, and it is well known as the Queen's residence of choice and the place she calls home after returning from her work 'week' (now just Tuesday to Thursday) at the 'office' (Buckingham Palace). One of the world's greatest surviving medieval castles, Windsor Castle's longevity and popularity are assured by its easy accessibility from the Big Smoke (London).

Some History

A wooden castle was erected around 1080 by William the Conqueror; it was rebuilt in stone by Henry II in 1165; Charles II gave the state apartments a baroque makeover; George IV swept in with his preference for Gothic style; and Queen Victoria refurbished a beautiful chapel in memory of her beloved Albert. Consequently, the castle displays a lively range of architectural styles from half-timbered red brick to Gothic stonework. A disastrous fire in 1992 nearly wiped out this incredible piece of English cultural heritage; luckily damage, though severe, was limited and a £37 million restoration returned the state apartments to their former glory.

State Apartments

The castle area, covering more than five hectares, is divided into three wards. In the Upper Ward, the State Apartments,

DON'T MISS

- The Grand Vestibule
- St George's Hall
- St George's Chapel
- Queen Mary's Dolls' House
- Changing of the Guard

PRACTICALITIES

- www.royalcollection.org.uk
- adult/child £17.75/10.60, when State Apartments closed £9.70/6.45
- 9.45am-5.15pm Mar-Oct, 9.45am-4.15pm Nov-Feb
- Bus 701 or 702 from Victoria coach station, Windsor Central or Windsor Riverside

LOCAL EATS

There are some great local dining and drinking options. Small but perfectly formed **Gilbey's** (01753-854921; www.gilbeygroup.com; 82-83 High St, Eton; mains from £16.50, 2-/3-course menu £19.50/25.50; noon-2.30pm & 6-9.30pm;) is a British restaurant in Eton and one of the area's finest. The homely but modern restaurant and bar **Bel & the Dragon** (01753-866056; www.belandthedragon.co.uk; 1 Datchet Rd, by Thames St, Windsor; mains £9-28; lunch & dinner;) is in an old 11th-century Windsor house. **Two Brewers** (34 Park St, Windsor; 11.30am-11pm Mon-Thu, 11.30am-11.30pm Fri-Sat, noon-10.30pm Sun) is a cosy 17th-century inn perched by Cambridge Gate on the edge of Windsor Great Park.

Join a free guided tour (every half-hour) or take a multilingual audio tour of the lavish state rooms and beautiful chapels. At times, the State Apartments and St George's Chapel are closed. If the Queen is in residence, you'll see the Royal Standard flying from the Round Tower.

which are closed at certain times (check the website) reverberate with history. The cannons, suits of armour, banners and pageantry of the **Grand Staircase** sets the tone for the rooms.

The **Grand Vestibule** displays gifts to Queen Victoria from her global dominion and spoils from the empire, including a life-size tiger's head of gold from the throne of Tipu, Sultan of Mysore, an Ethiopian crown and a dagger from Negeri Sembilan in Malaysia, presided over by a statue of Queen Victoria. You can also weigh up the bullet than killed Nelson. The **Waterloo Chamber** commemorates the Battle of Waterloo, filled with portraits of the great and the good by Sir Thomas Lawrence (1769–1830).

The voluptuous **King's Dressing Room** has some of the most important Renaissance paintings in the royal collection: alongside Sir Anthony van Dyck's magnificent Triple Portrait of Charles I, you will see works by Hans Holbein, Rembrandt, Peter Paul Rubens and Brueghel. A magnificent portrait of Henry VIII hangs over the fireplace in the **Queen's Drawing Room**; more splendour is encapsulated in the Adam fireplace, paintings and tapestries of the **Queen's Presence Chamber**.

The **Queen's Guard Chamber** positively bristles with pistols and swords. Named after the patron saint of the Order of the Garter, fabulous **St George's Hall** is the venue of state banquets: on the ceiling, the shields of the Knights of the Garter (originally from George IV's time here) were recreated after the devastating fire of 1992. The blank shields record 'degraded' knights, who fell from favour. The fire of 1992 commenced in the **Lantern Lobby**, a former chapel; a plaque records the tragedy. The tour ends in the **Garter Throne Room**.

Queen Mary's Dolls' House

This astonishing creation located in the Upper Ward is not a toy but a work of artful miniaturisation, designed by Sir Edwin Lutyens for Queen Mary. Completed in 1924 on a 1:12 scale, an exquisite attention to detail holds sway – with running water, electricity and lighting, tiny Crown Jewels, a silver service, vintage wine in the cellar and even a vacuum cleaner!

St George's Chapel

Moving westward through the Middle Ward and past the distinctive **Round Tower**, rebuilt in stone from the original Norman keep in 1180, you enter the Lower Ward. One of Britain's finest examples of early English architecture, this chapel (begun by Edward IV in 1475, but not completed until 1528) has a superb nave fashioned in Perpendicular Gothic style, with gorgeous fan vaulting. Serving as a **royal mausoleum**, the chapel contains the royal tombs of 10 monarchs including Edward IV, Henry VIII, Charles I, George VI and the late Queen Mother. Note the magnificent **Quire**, hung with Garter Knights' banners above the beautifully carved 15th-century wooden stalls. St George's Chapel closes on Sunday, but time your visit well and you can attend choral evensong at 5.15pm daily except Wednesday.

Albert Memorial Chapel

Originally built in 1240 and dedicated to Edward the Confessor, this small and highly decorated chapel was the place of worship for the Order of the Garter until St George's Chapel snatched that honour. After the death of Prince Albert at Windsor Castle in 1861, Queen Victoria ordered its elaborate redecoration as a tribute to her husband. A major feature of the restoration is the magnificent vaulted roof, whose gold mosaic pieces were crafted in Venice. The chapel stands alongside St George's Chapel.

The Drawings Gallery & China Museum

Among the Royal Collection are a large volume of **drawings by Leonardo da Vinci**, some of which are often displayed in the Drawings Gallery in the Upper Ward, along with other masterpieces. The gallery is also used for temporary exhibitions of pieces from the collection. Among displays in the China Museum is the fabulous and highly elaborate Rockingham Service (1830–37).

Windsor Great Park

South of the castle is this beautiful **park** (☎01753-860222; ⏲8am-dusk) ranging over a staggering area of some 10,500 hectares. The **Long Walk** is a 3-mile jaunt along a tree-lined path from King George IV Gate to the Copper Horse statue (of George III) on Snow Hill, the park's highest point. The **Savill Garden** (www.theroyallandscape.co.uk; adult/child £9/4; ⏲10am-6pm) is particularly lovely and located about 4 miles south of Windsor Castle. Take the A308 out of town and follow the brown signs.

Changing of the Guard

A must for any visitor is the changing of the guard, a fabulous spectacle of pomp and ceremony that draws large crowds to the castle gates. You'll get a better view if you stay to the right of the crowd, and if you're just interested in watching the marching bands, find a spot along High or Sheet Sts; the guards leave from Victoria Barracks on the latter at 10.45am and return an hour later.

ETON

A 15-minute walk over the River Thames from Windsor Castle, **Eton** (www.etoncollege.com; adult/child £7.50/6.50, extended tour £11; ⏲guided tours 2pm & 3.15pm daily school holidays, Wed, Fri, Sat & Sun term time) is arguably the world's most famous public (ie private) school, one that has educated 19 prime ministers and a host of explorers, authors and economists. Several buildings, including the Lower School, date from its founding in 1440 during the reign of Henry VI. All boys are boarders and must wear formal tailcoats, waistcoats and white collars to lessons (though the top hats went out in 1948).

Tour tickets must be purchased in advance at the visitor centre, a cream building with blue railings on Eton High St near the college. Stops on the tour include School Yard, Cloisters Court, Lower School, College Chapel and the Museum of Eton Life.

Oxford

Explore

The Victorian poet Matthew Arnold described Oxford as 'that sweet city with her dreaming spires'. These days the spires coexist with a flourishing commercial city that has some typical urban social problems. But for visitors, the superb architecture and the unique atmosphere of the more than three-dozen colleges – synonymous with academic excellence – and their courtyards and gardens, remain major attractions.

The town dates back to the early 12th century (having developed from an earlier Saxon village) and has been responsible for educating some 26 British prime ministers, including Margaret Thatcher, Tony Blair and the current PM, David Cameron.

The Best...

- **Sight** Ashmolean Museum (p322)
- **Place to Eat** Edamame (p323)
- **Place to Drink** Turf Tavern (p324)

Top Tip

For fine views of the Radcliffe Camera, the Oxford skyline and surrounding countryside, clamber up the 127 steps of the 14th-century tower of the beautiful **University Church of St Mary the Virgin** (www.university-church.ox.ac.uk; High St; tower adult/child £3/2.50; church 9am-5pm, tower 9.30am-4.30pm Mon-Sat & 11.45am-4.30pm Sun). On Sunday the tower opens just before noon, after the morning service.

Getting There & Away

- **Bus Oxford Tube** (01865-772250; www.oxfordtube.com) and **Oxford Express** (01865-785400; www.oxfordbus.co.uk) buses depart every 10 to 30 minutes round the clock from London's Victoria coach station (return from £16) and can be boarded at various other points in London too, including Marble Arch, Notting Hill Gate and Shepherd's Bush. Journey time is an hour and 40 minutes.
- **Train** There are two **trains** (0845 7484950; www.nationalrail.co.uk) per hour from London's Paddington station (return from £23, one hour).

Need to Know

- **Area code** 01865
- **Location** 59 miles northwest of London
- **Tourist Office** (252200; www.visitoxfordandoxfordshire.com; 15-16 Broad St; 9.30am-5pm Mon-Sat, 10am-3.30pm Sun, closes 30 mins later in winter)

SIGHTS

CHRIST CHURCH COLLEGE NOTABLE BUILDING

(www.chch.ox.ac.uk; St Aldate's; adult/child £8/6.50; 9am-5pm Mon-Sat, 2-5pm Sun) Founded in 1525 and massively popular with Harry Potter fans, having appeared in several of the films, Christ Church is the grandest of all Oxford's colleges. The main entrance is below the imposing **Tom Tower** (1681), designed by Christopher Wren and containing a 7-tonne bell called Great Tom.

The bell chimes 101 times each evening at 9.05pm to sound the curfew imposed on the original 101 students.

Visitors enter farther down St Aldate's via the wrought-iron gates of the War Memorial Gardens and Broad Walk. Immediately on entering is the 15th-century **cloister**, a relic of the ancient Priory of St Frideswide, whose shrine was once a focus of pilgrimage. From here, you go up to the **Great Hall**, the college's magnificent dining room that served as the model for the Great Hall at Hogwarts, with its hammer-beam roof and imposing portraits of past scholars.

The college chapel is **Christ Church Cathedral**, the smallest in the country. To the south of the college is **Christ Church Meadow**, a leafy expanse bordered by the Cherwell and Isis Rivers and ideal for leisurely walking. Christ Church is a working college, and the hall often closes between 11.40am and 2.30pm and the cathedral in late afternoon.

OTHER COLLEGES NOTABLE BUILDINGS

(www.ox.ac.uk/colleges) If time and opening hours permit (check the website for details), consider visiting any of the following important colleges: **Magdalen College** (www.magd.ox.ac.uk; High St; adult/child £5/4; noon-7pm), pronounced *maud-lin*, with huge grounds bordering the River Cherwell; **Merton College** (www.merton.ox.ac.uk; Merton St; admission £2, guided tour £2; 2-5pm

Oxford

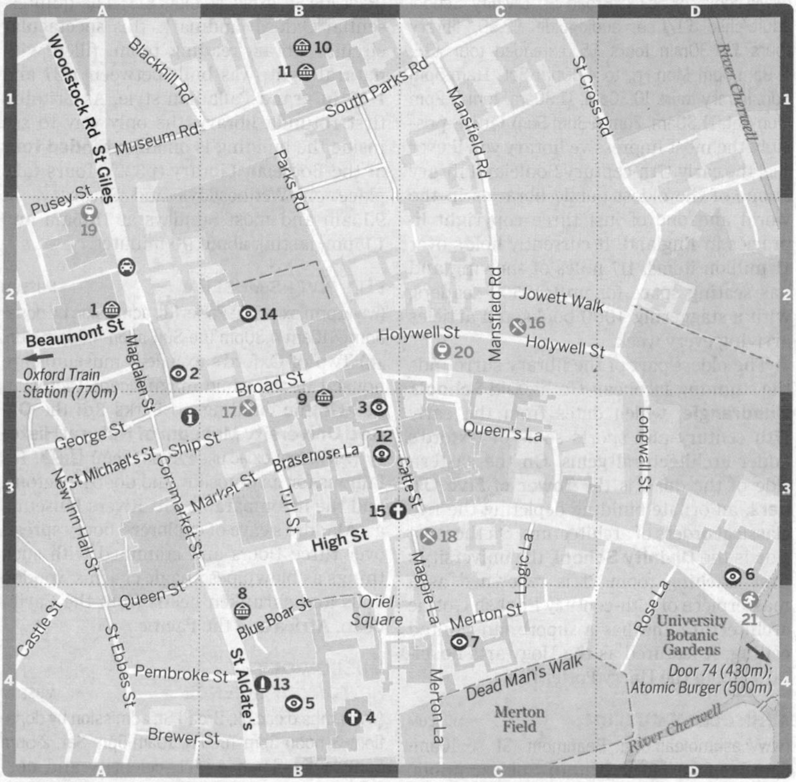

Oxford

Sights (p320)

1 Ashmolean Museum A2
2 Balliol College A2
3 Bodleian Library B3
4 Christ Church Cathedral B4
5 Christ Church College B4
6 Magdalen College D3
7 Merton College C4
8 Museum of Oxford B4
9 Museum of the History of Science B3
10 Oxford University Museum of Natural History B1
11 Pitt Rivers Museum B1
12 Radcliffe Camera B3
13 Tom Tower B4
14 Trinity College B2
15 University Church of St Mary the Virgin B3

Eating (p323)

16 Edamame C2
17 Missing Bean B3
18 Quod C3

Drinking & Nightlife (p323)

19 Eagle & Child A2
20 Turf Tavern C2

Sports & Activities (p322)

21 Magdalen Bridge Boathouse D4

Mon-Fri, 10am-5pm Sat & Sun, guided tour 45min), with a 14th-century library where JRR Tolkien wrote much of the *Lord of the Rings;* **Trinity College** (www.trinity.ox.ac.uk; Broad St; adult/child £1.75/1; ⌚10am-noon & 2-4pm Sun-Fri, 2-4pm Sat), with an exquisitely carved chapel; and **Balliol College** (www.balliol.ox.ac.uk; Broad St; adult/child £2/1; ⌚10am-5pm, dusk in winter), founded in 1263 and thought to be the oldest college in Oxford.

BODLEIAN LIBRARY LIBRARY

(www.bodley.ox.ac.uk; Broad St; Divinity School adult/child £1/free, audioguide £2.50, library tours £7, 30min tours £5, extended tour £13; ⏲9am-5pm Mon-Fri, to 4.30pm Sat, 11am-5pm Sun, library tours 10.30am, 11.30am, 1pm & 2pm Mon-Sat, 11.30am, 2pm & 3pm Sun) Quite possibly the most impressive library you'll ever see, the early 17th-century Bodleian Library is one of the oldest public libraries in the world and one of just three copyright libraries in England. It currently holds over 11 million items, 117 miles of shelving and has seating space for up to 2500 readers, with a staggering 4000 books and articles arriving every week.

The oldest part of the library surrounds the stunning Jacobean-Gothic **Old Schools Quadrangle**, which dates from the early 17th century and sports some of Oxford's odder architectural gems. On the eastern side of the quad is the **Tower of Five Orders**, an ornate building depicting the five classical orders of architecture. On the west side is the **Divinity School**, the university's first teaching room. It is renowned as a masterpiece of 15th-century English Gothic architecture and has a superb fan-vaulted ceiling; it featured as the Hogwarts hospital wing in the Harry Potter films.

ASHMOLEAN MUSEUM MUSEUM

(www.ashmolean.org; Beaumont St; ⏲10am-6pm Tue-Sun) FREE Britain's oldest public museum (1683) is now among its finest after a recent £60 million makeover. Its five floors of bright, spacious galleries contain everything from Egyptian artefacts and Chinese art to European and British paintings by the likes of Rembrandt, Michelangelo, Turner and Picasso. There's a wonderful rooftop terrace restaurant with stunning views of the city.

RADCLIFFE CAMERA LIBRARY

(Radcliffe Sq; extended tours £13) The quintessential Oxford landmark, this spectacular circular library/reading room, filled with natural light, was built between 1737 and 1749 in grand Palladian style. As Britain's first rotunda library, the only way to see inside the building is on an **extended tour** of the Bodleian Library (p322). Tours take place on Wednesdays and Saturdays at 9.15am and most Sundays at 11.15am and 1.15pm, lasting about 90 minutes.

PITT RIVERS MUSEUM MUSEUM

(www.prm.ox.ac.uk; Parks Rd; admission by donation; ⏲10am-4.30pm Tue-Sun, noon-4.30pm Mon; 👪) Two of Oxford's excellent museums are housed in the same magnificent Victorian neo-Gothic building on Parks Rd: the **Oxford University Museum of Natural History** (www.oum.ox.ac.uk; ⏲10am-5pm) FREE. It's famous for its dinosaur and dodo skeletons, and the incomparable Pitt Rivers Museum, an Aladdin's cave of explorers' booty spread over three floors and crammed with such things as blowpipes, magic charms, voodoo dolls and shrunken heads from the Caribbean, Africa and the Pacific.

MUSEUM OF THE HISTORY OF SCIENCE MUSEUM

(www.mhs.ox.ac.uk; Broad St; admission by donation; ⏲noon-5pm Tue-Fri, 10am-5pm Sat, 2-5pm Sun) FREE Science, art, celebrity and nostalgia come together at this fascinating museum where the exhibits include everything from a blackboard used by Einstein to the world's finest collection of historic scientific instruments, all housed in a beautiful 17th-century building.

MUSEUM OF OXFORD MUSEUM

(www.museumofoxford.org.uk; St Aldate's; ⏲10am-5pm Tue-Sat) FREE Though it often

IN FOR A PUNT

Punting is the pastime of choice on the River Cherwell in Oxford and along the Backs in Cambridge (p323). It looks fairly straightforward, but we've landed in the drink enough times to assure you that it ain't. Still, that shouldn't deter anyone who isn't afraid of getting a bit wet.

The secret to propelling the flat-bottomed boats is to push gently on the pole to get the punt moving and then to use the pole as a rudder to keep on course.

Punts are available daily from 9.30am to dusk, March to October. If you'd like to give it a go, head for **Magdalen Bridge Boathouse** (www.oxfordpunting.co.uk; High St; punting max 5 people per hour weekday/weekend £18/20, chauffeured boat max 4 people per 30 mins £25) just below the northeast end of Magdalen Bridge.

CAMBRIDGE: CLASSIC UNIVERSITY TOWN

If you liked Oxford, you'll love Cambridge. Awash in exquisite architecture, steeped in history and tradition and renowned for its quirky rituals, Cambridge is the quintessential English university town and has produced more Nobel prize winners than any other educational institution in the world.

Must-see sites include 16th-century **King's College Chapel** (www.kings.cam.ac.uk/chapel; King's Pde; adult/child £7.50/free, Evensong free; ⏲9.45am-4.30pm Mon, from 9.30am Tue-Sun, Evensong 5.30pm Mon-Sat, 10.30am & 3.30pm Sun, term time only), one of the most sublime buildings in Europe, and **Trinity College** (www.trin.cam.ac.uk; Trinity St; adult/child £1.50/1; ⏲10.30am-4.30pm), the largest and wealthiest of Cambridge's 31 colleges established by Henry VIII in 1546. But don't miss the rich **Fitzwilliam Museum** (www.fitzmuseum.cam.ac.uk; Trumpington St; admission by donation, guided tour £5; ⏲10am-5pm Tue-Sat, noon-5pm Sun), one of the first art museums in the UK, and a spot of punting, which is even more of a tradition here than at Oxford (see p322). Punt hire costs from £18 per hour and a 45-minute chauffeured trip is £16.50. Two recommended firms are **Granta Punt Hire Company** (www.puntingincambridge.com; Newnham Rd; per hr/day £18/80) and **Scudamore's** (www.scudamores.com; Granta Pl; per hr £22).

Some 60 miles north of London, Cambridge is accessible by bus from London's Victoria coach station (return from £18, two hours, every 10 minutes) and by train from both Liverpool St station (return from £15) and King's Cross station (return from £23). The journey by rail takes between 45 minutes and 1¼ hours.

gets overlooked in favour of Oxford's other museums, the Museum of Oxford is an absorbing romp through the city's history – from the Roman and Saxon eras to the Victorian era and 20th-century industries, such as marmalade-making and car manufacture. The reconstructions of period interiors, such as a 19th-century Jericho kitchen, are particularly good.

EATING & DRINKING

EDAMAME
JAPANESE £

(www.edamame.co.uk; 15 Holywell St; mains £6-9; ⏲11.30am-2.30pm Wed-Sat, 5-8.30pm Thu-Sat, noon-3.30pm Sun) The queue out the door speaks volumes about the quality of the food at this tiny joint. All light wood and friendly bustle, Edamame is the best place in town for genuine Japanese and the sushi (Thursday night 5pm to 8.30pm only, £2.50 to £8) is divine. Arrive early; be prepared to wait.

ATOMIC BURGER
AMERICAN £

(www.atomicburger.co.uk; 96 Cowley Rd; mains £5.25-11; ⏲10am-10.30pm) Frequently pumping, retro-styled Atomic Burger does a brisk business with its reams of inventively named platters – Woody Allen, Dead Elvis, Sergio Leoni – and a good line of gob-smacking shakes. Hardcore diners can have a shot at the Wall of Flame with the fiery triple burger stack with ghost chilli sauce Fallout Challenge. Vegetarians don't get the cold shoulder, there's loads of non-meat choices.

MISSING BEAN
CAFE £

(www.themissingbean.co.uk, 14 Turl St; mains £3-6; ⏲8am-6.30pm Mon-Fri, 9am-6.30pm Sat, 10.30am-5.30pm Sun;) Worshippers of the coffee bean single out this independent specialist coffee shop, if they can grab a seat. Loose-leaf teas, fruit juices, shakes and smoothies have less-caffeine-dependent fans approving, while the fresh muffins, doughnuts, cakes and ciabatta sandwiches are great for snackers. The *affogato* (espresso on bourbon vanilla ice cream) is a rich, decadent delight.

DOOR 74
MODERN BRITISH ££

(☎01865-203374; www.door74.co.uk; 74 Cowley Rd; mains £10-14; ⏲noon-11pm Tue-Sat, 11am-4pm Sun) This cosy and relaxed bistro keeps things successfully straightforward with its simple formula of friendly service and a consistently fine menu. The weekend brunches (full English breakfast, pancakes) are supremely filling. Space is intimate – tight is another word – so book ahead.

QUOD
MODERN BRITISH ££

(☎01865-202505; www.quod.co.uk; 92-94 High St; mains £11.50-22; ⏲7am-11pm Mon-Sat, to 10.30pm Sun) Perennially popular for its smart surroundings and buzzing atmosphere (not to mention its fine grills, fish dishes and pasta), this restaurant dishes up modern brasserie-style food to the Oxford masses. The two-course Monday to Friday set lunch (£12.95) is great value and if you're caught between meals, opt for afternoon tea (£6.95 to £22.95) from 3pm to 5.30pm. The live jazz on Sundays (5pm to 7pm) is a treat.

TURF TAVERN PUB

(4-5 Bath Pl; ⏲11am-11pm) Hidden away down a narrow alleyway, this tiny medieval pub is one of the town's best loved and bills itself as 'an education in intoxication' (this is also where president Bill Clinton 'did not inhale'). Home to 11 real ales, it's always packed with a mix of students, professionals and the lucky tourists who manage to find it. One of the few pubs in town with plenty of outdoor seating.

EAGLE & CHILD PUB

(49 St Giles; ⏲11am-11pm Mon-Thu, to midnight Fri & Sat, noon-10.30pm Sun) Affectionately known as the 'Bird & Baby', this atmospheric place, dating from 1650, was once the favourite haunt of Tolkien and CS Lewis. Its wood-panelled rooms and good selection of real ales still attract a mellow crowd.

Brighton

Explore

With its large student population, the country's biggest gay scene outside London, and working-class families down for a jolly, this city by the sea caters to everyone. It offers in one outstretched hand atmospheric cafes, excellent restaurants, old-style beach seafood huts and a good-for-a-laugh amusement pier.

The town's character essentially dates from the 1780s when the dissolute, music-loving prince regent (the future King George IV) built his outrageous summer palace, the Royal Pavilion, here as a venue for lavish parties by the sea. And that charmingly seedy 'great-place-for-a-dirty-weekend' vibe lasted throughout the gang-ridden 1930s of Graham Greene's novel *Brighton Rock* and the mods-versus-rockers deckchair-smashing rivalry of the '60s.

The Best...

➡ **Sight** Royal Pavilion (p324)

➡ **Place to Eat** The Gingerman (p327)

➡ **Place to Drink** Basketmakers Arms (p327)

Top Tip

Brighton offers the best entertainment line-up on the south coast, with clubs to rival London's for cool. Keep tabs on what's hot by searching out publications such as *Brighton Source* (www.brightonsource.co.uk) and *Brighton What's On* (http://whatson.brighton.co.uk).

Getting There & Away

➡ **Bus** Hourly **National Express** (☎0871 781 8181; www.nationalexpress.com) buses run from Victoria coach station (return from £13, 2¼ hours).

➡ **Train** There are about 40 fast trains (p320) each day from London's Victoria station (return from £25, 50 minutes), and slower ones from Blackfriars, London Bridge and King's Cross (return from £16, 70 minutes).

Need to Know

➡ **Area code** ☎01273

➡ **Location** 53 miles south of London

➡ **Tourist Office** (☎01273-290337; www.visitbrighton.com; 4-5 Pavilion Buildings; ⏲9am-5.15pm Apr-Oct, 10am-5pm Nov-Mar) Next to the Royal Pavilion.

SIGHTS

ROYAL PAVILION PALACE

(www.royalpavilion.org.uk; Royal Pavilion Gardens; adult/child £10.50/5.90; ⏲9.30am-5.45pm Apr-Sep, 10am-5.15pm Oct-Mar) The interior of Brighton's top attraction, the Royal Pavilion, is one of the most opulent in England. An outstanding folly – Indian palace on the outside and over-the-top Chinoiserie within – it's an apt symbol of Brighton's reputation for decadence and high living. The entire confection, which Queen Victoria sold to the town in 1850 for £53,000 (apparently she found Brighton 'far too crowded'), is an eye-popping spectacle, but some interiors stand out even amid the riot of decoration.

The self-paced audioguide tour takes you through a dozen or so rooms, including the magnificent ground floor **Long Gallery**, with its metal bamboo staircases. A blaze of red and gold infested with coiling dragons, a glorious dome and a 1 tonne chandelier, the **Banqueting Room** must be the most incredible in all of England. More dragons and snakes writhe within the overblown **Music Room** with its ceiling of 26,000 gold scales, and the then-state-of-the-art **Great Kitchen** must have wowed Georgians with its automatic spits and hot tables. Not to be missed on the 1st floor are **Queen Victoria's Apartments** (including her water closet).

BRIGHTON MUSEUM & ART GALLERY MUSEUM

(www.brighton-hove-museums.org.uk; Royal Pavilion Gardens; ⊙10am-5pm Tue-Sun) FREE This fantastic museum and art gallery in the Royal Pavilion's renovated stable block has a glittering collection of 20th-century art-deco, nouveau and postwar art and design, including a crimson Salvador Dalí sofa modelled on Mae West's lips and elegant pieces by Charles Rennie Mackintosh. There's also an enthralling gallery of world art, an impressive collection of Egyptian artefacts, an 'images of Brighton' multimedia exhibit, a costume gallery (garbs include a mod suit and a rocker leather jacket) and temporary exhibitions. A lovely upstairs cafe with tables overlooking the main hall rounds it all off.

BRIGHTON WHEEL VIEWPOINT

(www.brightonwheel.com; Madeira Dr; adult/child £8/6.50; ⊙10am-9pm Sun-Thu, to 11pm Fri & Sat) Just slightly smaller than the London Eye, Brighton's seafront wheel is best ridden at sunset for gobsmacking views of the Channel, the pier and the town below. Book tickets online during busy times.

BRIGHTON PIER AMUSEMENT PARK

(www.brightonpier.co.uk; Madeira Dr) This grand old centenarian pier is the place to experience Brighton's tackier side. There are plenty of stomach-churning fairground rides and dingy amusement arcades to keep you amused, plus candy floss and Brighton rock to chomp on while you're doing so.

There's still no sign of the long-awaited 183m-tall i360 observation tower, planned to loom above the Brighton seafront by the sad remains of West Pier come 2015.

BRIGHTON SEA LIFE CENTRE AQUARIUM

(www.visitsealife.com/brighton; Marine Pde; adult £17.40; ⊙10am-6pm Apr-Sep, to 5pm Oct-Mar) Dating from Victorian times, the world's oldest operational sea-life centre underwent a major revamp in 2012. Old favourites such as stingrays and giant turtles have been joined by new creatures of the deep, and the general visitor experience has been brought into the 21st century. Buy in advance online for a cheaper rate.

EATING & DRINKING

SCOOP & CRUMB ICE CREAM £

(www.scoopandcrumb.com; 5-6 East St; snacks £3-5, sundaes £2.50-6; ⊙10am-6pm Sun-Fri, to 7pm Sat) Great for a pick-me-up, the sundaes (over 50 types) stacked at this pastel-shaded, light and bright ice-cream parlour, belonging to the city's artisan ice-cream producer, are second to none. Outsize hot waffles and monster toasties are further reasons to stop by.

TEA COSY TEAHOUSE £

(www.theteacosy.co.uk; 3 George St; teas £3.50-12; ⊙noon-5pm Wed-Fri & Sun, to 5.30pm Sat) Fans of the British monarchy can go weak-kneed in this kitsch shrine to the Royal Family, where every square inch is devoted to monarchical memorabilia, including ample Kate and Wills paraphernalia. The simple menu runs to toast, scones, cake and finger sandwiches.

SAM'S OF BRIGHTON MODERN BRITISH ££

(☎01273-676222; www.samsofbrighton.co.uk; 1 Paston Pl; mains £12.50-20, 2-/3-course set lunch £12.50/15; ⊙noon-3pm & 6-10pm Tue-Fri, 10am-3pm & 6-10pm Sat, 10am-4pm Sun) Not exactly in the thick of things, this family-owned restaurant (those are pictures of the kids on the wall) in easternmost Kemp Town is well worth the journey for its innovative takes on dishes like roast breast of guinea fowl and steamed black bream. Brunch is served from 10am on Saturday and Sunday.

TERRE À TERRE VEGETARIAN ££

(☎01273-729051; www.terreaterre.co.uk; 71 East St; mains £14; ⊙noon-10.30pm Mon-Fri, 11am-11pm Sat, 11am-10pm Sun; ✍) A gourmet vegetarian experience is not an oxymoron. This

Brighton

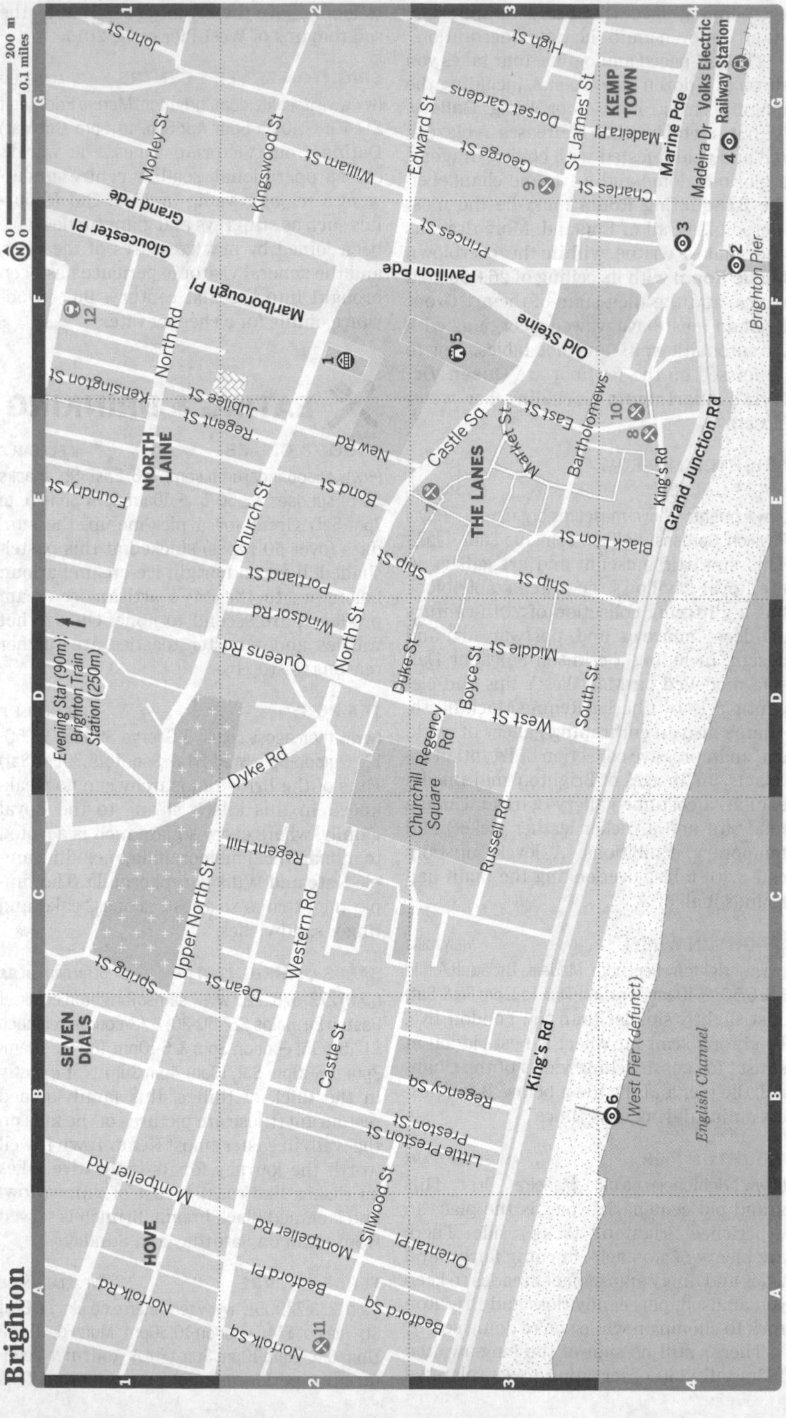
200 m
0.1 miles
Evening Star (90m); Brighton Train Station (250m)
SEVEN DIALS
HOVE
NORTH LAINE
THE LANES
KEMP TOWN
John St
Morley St
Grand Pde
Gloucester Pl
Marlborough Pl
North Rd
Kensington St
Jubilee St
Regent St
Foundry St
Church St
Portland St
Windsor Rd
Queens Rd
Dyke Rd
Spring St
Upper North St
Dean St
Regent Hill
Western Rd
Castle St
Montpelier Rd
Norfolk Rd
Norfolk Sq
Bedford Pl
Bedford Sq
Sillwood St
Oriental Pl
Little Preston St
Preston St
Regency Sq
King's Rd
West Pier (defunct)
English Channel
Russell Rd
Churchill Square
Regency Rd
West St
Boyce St
Duke St
North St
Middle St
South St
Ship St
Black Lion St
New Rd
Bond St
Castle Sq
Market St
East St
Bartholomews
King's Rd
Grand Junction Rd
Old Steine
Pavilion Pde
Princes St
Edward St
William St
Kingswood St
George St
Charles St
St James' St
Dorset Gardens
High St
Madeira Pl
Marine Pde
Madeira Dr
Volks Electric Railway Station
Brighton Pier

Brighton

Sights (p324)

1 Brighton Museum & Art Gallery F2
2 Brighton Pier F4
3 Brighton Sea Life Centre F4
4 Brighton Wheel G4
5 Royal Pavilion F3
6 West Pier B4

Eating (p325)

7 Riddle & Finns E3
8 Scoop & Crumb E4
9 Tea Cosy G3
10 Terre à Terre E4
11 The Gingerman A2

Drinking & Nightlife (p325)

12 Basketmakers Arms F1

fantastic restaurant is a sublime dining experience, from the vibrant, modern space and the entertaining menus, to the delicious, inventive dishes full of rich, robust flavours.

RIDDLE & FINNS SEAFOOD ££
(www.riddleandfinns.co.uk; 12b Meeting House Lane; mains £12-19; ⊙noon-10pm Sun-Thu, noon-11pm Fri & Sat, also 9.30-11.30am Sat & Sun) We're told that Gordon Ramsay called the fare served in this elegant candelabra-lit oyster bar 'seafood as it should be'. We don't care about that, but we'll come back for our favourite bivalves (from £12 a half-dozen) and more bubbly. With an open kitchen busy with chefs looking onto the street, it's hidden down The Lanes

THE GINGERMAN MODERN EUROPEAN £££
(☎01273-326688; www.gingermanrestaurant.com; 21a Norfolk Sq; 2/3-course menu £15/18; ⊙12.30-2pm & 7-10pm Tue-Sun) Seafood from Hastings, Sussex beef, Romney Marsh lamb, local sparkling wines and countless other seasonal, local and British treats go into the adroitly flash-fried and slow-cooked dishes at this snug, 32-cover eatery. Reservations advised.

BASKETMAKERS ARMS PUB
(www.basket-makers-brighton.co.uk; 12 Gloucester Rd; ⊙11am-11pm Mon-Thu, 11am-midnight Fri & Sat, noon-11pm Sun) Probably the best traditional pub in Brighton, mellow and cheerful Basketmakers in the North Laine district, is a boozy delight. Southeast of the train station, eight ales on tap and around 100 types of whisky wet whistles all round. Food is way above average and served daily from noon to 8.30pm (7pm on Saturday, 8pm on Sunday).

EVENING STAR PUB
(www.eveningstarbrighton.co.uk; 55-56 Surrey St; ⊙noon-11pm Sun-Thu, 11.30am-midnight Fri & Sat) With an outstanding selection of award-winning real ales, Belgian beers, organic lagers and seasonal brews on the chalkboard, the Evening Star is a diamond in the Brighton rough. Within staggering distance of Brighton train station.

Bath

Explore

England has some handsome towns, but few can hold a candle to this delightful city of honey-coloured stone and elegant streets. Always renowned for its Roman baths and architecture – especially its fine Georgian terraces – Bath is celebrated in equal measure for its association with the novelist Jane Austen – not so much for her actual works but for the films based on them. Sometimes it seems the crowds just can't get enough.

The Romans established the town of Aquae Sulis in AD 44 and built an extensive baths complex and a temple to the goddess Sulis-Minerva. Throughout the Middle Ages, Bath was an ecclesiastical centre and a wool-trading town, but it was not until the early 18th century that Bath and its spas became the centre of fashionable society. Certain districts in Bath still vie with some in London as the nation's top 'des res' (desirable residences).

The Best...

- **Sight** Roman Baths (p329)
- **Place to Eat** Menu Gordon Jones (p330)
- **Place to Drink** Star Inn (p331)

Top Tip

The Roman Baths have been off-limits to bathers since 1976 for health reasons. But should you want to take the plunge in

Bath

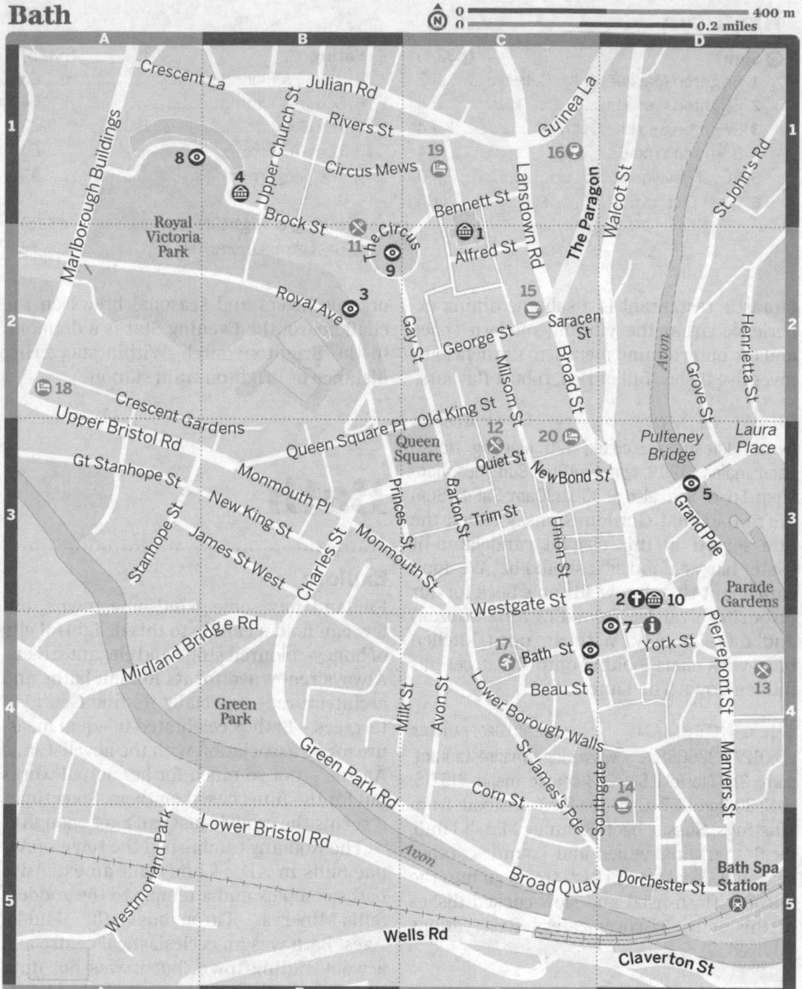

Bath's thermal waters there is finally a way: **Thermae Bath Spa** (☎0844-888 0844; www.thermaebathspa.com; Bath St; ⏱9am-9.30pm, last entry 7pm), an ultramodern shell of stone and glass sitting comfortably beside a Georgian spa building, that has steam rooms, waterfall showers and a choice of bathing venues, including an open-air rooftop pool with jaw-dropping views of Bath.

Getting There & Away

➡ **Bus** Bath is linked to London's Victoria coach station (one-way from £20, 3½ hours) by **National Express** (☎0871 781 8181; www.nationalexpress.com) up to 10 times a day.

➡ **Train** There are direct trains (p320) from London Paddington and Waterloo stations (return from £39, 1½ hours) at least hourly.

Need to Know

➡ **Area code** ☎01225

➡ **Location** 115 miles west of London

➡ **Tourist Office** (www.visitbath.co.uk; Abbey Churchyard; ⏱9.30am-5pm Mon-Sat, 10am-4pm Sun)

Bath

SIGHTS

ROMAN BATHS — HISTORIC SITE

(www.romanbaths.co.uk; Abbey Churchyard; adult/child/family £12.75/8.50/36; ⏲9am-10pm July & Aug, 9am-6pm Mar-Jun, Sep & Oct, 9.30am-5.30pm Nov-Feb) Ever since the Romans arrived in Bath, life in the city has revolved around the three geothermal springs that bubble up near Bath Abbey. Situated alongside an important temple dedicated to the healing goddess Sulis-Minerva, the 2000-year-old baths form one of the best-preserved ancient Roman spas in the world.

The audioguide walk-through route takes in the entire complex, at the heart of which is the **Great Bath**, a large lead-lined pool filled with steaming, geothermally heated water. Bathers would hop from the warm bath to the circular **frigidarium** (cool pool), to close the pores. Note the gemstones found in the surviving Roman drain – possibly loosened from bathers' rings by the steaming waters.

Other highlights are the 12th-century **King's Bath**, built around the original sacred spring, and the remains of the **Temple of Sulis-Minerva**. The pediment from the temple is an imposing relic – the tangle-haired deity at its centre is believed to be a Gorgon, yet is male, so Neptune is also suggested, as are Oceanus and Mithras. Don't miss the astonishing gilt bronze **Head of Minerva**, an exquisite work of art and the sole surviving remnant from a life-size statue that once stood in the temple. Gilded six times over the centuries, it was rescued from the ground in 1727 after lying undisturbed for over a millennium.

Admission includes an audioguide in a choice of eight languages, featuring a special commentary by bestselling author Bill Bryson. You can also serve yourself a cup of warm mineral water, said to cure everything under the sun.

ROYAL CRESCENT — STREET

Bath is the proud owner of some glorious Georgian architecture, and it doesn't get any grander than on Royal Crescent, a semicircular terrace of majestic townhouses overlooking the green sweep of Royal Victoria Park. Designed by John Wood the Younger (1728–82) and built between 1767 and 1775, the houses were designed to appear perfectly symmetrical from the outside, but the original owners were allowed to design the interiors to their own specifications; consequently no two houses on the crescent are quite the same. They would originally have been rented for the summer season by wealthy socialites, who descended on Bath to indulge in a whirlwind program of masquerades, dances, concerts and tea parties.

For a glimpse into the splendour and razzle-dazzle of Georgian life, head for the newly restored house at **No 1 Royal Crescent** (http://no1royalcrescent.org.uk; 1 Royal Cres; adult/child/family £8.50/3.50/17; ⏲noon-5.30pm Mon, 10.30am-5.30pm Tue-Sun), given to the city by the shipping magnate Major Bernard Cayzer, and since restored using only 18th-century materials. Among the

WINDOW TAX

When wandering the streets of Bath, you may note bricked-in windows, often high up on the walls of historic properties. Introduced in England and Wales during the reign of William III in 1696, a tax became payable on houses depending on its number of windows. The more windows a house had, the greater the tax; consequently some house-owners filled in surplus windows to avoid the tax. As the levy was interpreted as a tax on light, it may have given rise to the phrase 'daylight robbery'. The tax was finally repealed in 1851.

rooms on display are the drawing room, several bedrooms and the huge kitchen, complete with massive hearth, roasting spit and mousetraps.

BATH ABBEY CHURCH

(www.bathabbey.org; requested donation £2.50; ⏲9.30am-6pm Mon, 9am-6pm Tue-Sat, 1-2.30pm & 4.30-5.30pm Sun) Looming above the centre of the city, Bath's huge abbey church was built between 1499 and 1616 (upon the site of the former Norman cathedral), making it the last great medieval church raised in England. Its most striking feature is the west facade, where angels climb up and down stone ladders, commemorating a dream of the founder, Bishop Oliver King. Among those buried here are Sir Isaac Pitman (who devised the Pitman method of shorthand) and the celebrated *bon viveur* Beau Nash. In **St Alphege's Chapel**, look under the floor for the original pillar bases of the Norman cathedral. Hunt for the face reflected in the surface of the brass plaque of the Rectors of Bath, between the dates 1634 and 1859. Frequent tours (adult/child £6/3, Monday to Saturday) of the **tower** head up the 212 steps to the roof for fine views.

On the abbey's southern side, the small **Vaults Heritage Museum** (⏲10am-4pm Mon-Sat) explores the abbey's history and its links with the nearby baths.

ASSEMBLY ROOMS HISTORIC BUILDING

(www.nationaltrust.org.uk/bath-assembly-rooms; 19 Bennett St; adult/child £2/free; ⏲10.30am-6pm) Opened in 1771, the city's glorious Assembly Rooms were where fashionable Bath socialites once gathered to waltz, play cards and listen to the latest chamber music. You're free to wander around the rooms, as long as they haven't been reserved for a special function; rooms open to the public include the card room, tearoom and the truly splendid ballroom, all of which are lit by their original 18th-century chandeliers. The Assembly Rooms were all but gutted by incendiary bombs during WWII but have since been carefully restored. A rewarding **fashion museum** (www.fashionmuseum.co.uk; adult/child £7.75/5.75; ⏲10.30am-5pm) is in the basement.

PULTENEY BRIDGE BRIDGE

Built in 1773 and suspended gracefully above the rushing waters of Pulteney Weir, this elegant bridge is one of only a handful in the world to be lined with shops (the most famous other example is the Ponte Vecchio in Florence).

THE CIRCUS HISTORIC AREA

(The Circus) Inspired by the Roman Colosseum, the Circus is a Georgian masterpiece of John Wood the Elder's design. Arranged over three equal terraces, the 33 mansions overlook a garden populated by plane trees; a German bomb fell into the square in 1942 and demolished several houses, although they've since been rebuilt in seamless style. Look out for plaques to Thomas Gainsborough, Clive of India and David Livingstone, all former Circus residents.

To the south along Gravel Walk is the **Georgian Garden**, restored to resemble a typical 18th-century townhouse garden.

EATING & DRINKING

★MENU GORDON JONES MODERN BRITISH ££

(☎01225-480871; www.menugordonjones.co.uk; 2 Wellsway; 5-course lunch £35, 6-course dinner £45; ⏲12.30-2pm & 7-9pm Tue-Sat) You'll have to book aeons ahead to dine at this pocket-sized restaurant, besieged as it is with diners and accolades. The multicourse 'surprise menus' are dreamt up by Gordon Jones on the day, and showcase his taste for experimentation, both in terms of ingredients and presentation, displaying artistry and flair. The dining space is tiny and ambience very much plays second fiddle to the menu, but as a culinary experience, the food is second to none.

SOTTO SOTTO
ITALIAN ££

(☑01225-330236; www.sottosotto.co.uk; 10a North Pde; pasta £9, mains £13-17; ⊙noon-2.30pm & 5-10.30pm) This centrally located diner exudes romantic charm in a cellar setting complete with barrel-brick roof, overseen by busy and efficient staff. Everything's just like mama made, from the *osso bucco* (veal shank) to the *orecchiette mare e monti* (top-hat pasta with seafood, beans and pancetta). Book ahead.

CIRCUS
MODERN BRITISH ££

(☑01225-466020; www.thecircuscafeandrestaurant.co.uk; 34 Brock St; mains lunch £5.50-10, dinner £11-14; ⊙10am-midnight Mon-Sat) Just off the namesake Circus (p330), this bistro is still one of Bath's best. The food, prepared by chef Alison Golden, is excellent, ample and beautifully presented and the warm welcome serves as a splendid entrée. Choose between the ground floor overlooking a small courtyard or the intimate (but cramped when full) cellar. Reserve ahead.

SALAMANDER
BRITISH ££

(☑01225-428889; www.bathales.com/pubs/salamander.html; 3 John St; mains £10-14; ⊙restaurant noon-9.30pm Mon-Sat, to 8pm Sun) Owned by the city's bespoke brewery, Bath Ales, the Sally's ground-floor bar is the place to sample amber-coloured Gem and Golden Hare and the stronger (5.2%) and darker Rare Hare. The supper room upstairs has moved on from 'steak and chops' to some far more adventurous dishes made with locally sourced meat and produce.

JIKA JIKA
CAFE

(www.jikajika.co.uk; 4a Princes Buildings, George St; ⊙8am-5pm Mon-Tue, 8am-11pm Wed-Fri, 8.30am-11pm Sat, 9am-5pm Sun) If you know your coffee beans, this award-winning cafe is a fine place to settle down if you simply can't function without espresso, roasted by hand and sourced from rare estates. There's a second branch in Brunel Square.

STAR INN
PUB

(www.star-inn-bath.co.uk; 23 The Vineyards, off The Paragon; ⊙noon-2.30pm & 5.30pm-midnight Mon-Thu, to 1am Fri, noon-1am Sat, noon-midnight Sun; ⊛) Not many pubs are registered relics, but the Star is – it still has many of its 19th-century bar fittings. It's the brewery tap for Bath-based Abbey Ales; some ales are served in traditional jugs, and you can even ask for a pinch of snuff in the 'smaller bar'. It's along the raised pavement of The Paragon – a delightful curve of Georgian terraced buildings (bombed during the Blitz).

🛏 SLEEPING

Bath is just 90 minutes from London, but spending the night is an attractive option. The tourist office (p328) has a free accommodation-booking service.

ST CHRISTOPHER BATH
HOSTEL £

(☑01225-481444; www.st-christophers.co.uk/bath-hostels; 6 Green St; dm £16-19, d £55; @⊛) A branch of a chain of successful UK-based hostels with the signature Belushi's pub on the ground floor, centrally located St Christopher Bath is housed in a former street corner bakers, with five dormitory rooms with six to 12 beds, a twin and two doubles (one with bathroom) and 24-hour reception.

MARLBOROUGH HOUSE
B&B ££

(☑01225-318175; www.marlborough-house.net; 1 Marlborough Lane; s £80-95, d £95-130, tr £95 125; ⊛) This charming B&B offers six tastefully themed, clean rooms and a welcoming host, Peter, who is a font of information. The Victorian (No 2) and Georgian (No 3) rooms have four-post beds, the complimentary sherry goes down well and the breakfasts are heavenly.

★QUEENSBERRY HOTEL
HOTEL £££

(☑01225-447928; www.thequeensberry.co.uk; 4 Russell St; d £150-270, ste £460; ⊛) With a lovely drawing room where the floorboards creak and a gorgeous garden, this fine and individual boutique hotel on sloping Russell St rolls four Georgian townhouses into one, offering a modish choice of rooms, each uniquely presented. The hotel's Olive Tree restaurant is a rewarding choice for some of the best dishes in Bath.

Sleeping

Landing the right accommodation is integral to your London experience, and there's no shortage of choice. But just because London is a city that never sleeps doesn't mean it doesn't go to bed: rooms in sought-after hotels can be booked solid. There are some fantastic hotels about, whatever the price tag, but plan ahead.

Hotels

London has a grand roll-call of stately hotels and many are experiences in their own right. The lead up to the 2012 Olympics saw big-profile openings and a host of less well-known new operations flinging open their doors. Standards across the top end and much of the boutique bracket are high, but so are prices. Quirkiness and individuality can be found in abundance (this is London), alongside dyed-in-the-wool traditionalism. A wealth of budget boutique hotels has exploited a lucrative niche, while a rung or two down in overall quality and charm, midrange chain hotels generally offer good locations and dependable comfort. Demand can often outstrip supply – especially on the bottom step of the market – so book ahead, particularly during holiday periods and in summer.

B&Bs

Housed in good-looking old properties, bed and breakfasts come in a tier below hotels, often promising boutique-style charm and a more personal level of service. Handy B&B clusters appear in South Kensington, Victoria, Fulham and Bloomsbury.

Hostels

After B&Bs the cheapest form of accommodation is hostels, both the official Youth Hostel Association (YHA) ones and the (usually) hipper, more party-orientated independent ones. Hostels vary in quality so select carefully; most offer twins as well as dorms.

Rates & Booking

Deluxe hotel rooms will cost from around £350 per double but there's good variety at the top end, so you should find a room from about £180 offering superior comfort without the prestige. Some boutique hotels also occupy this bracket. There's a noticeable dip in quality below around £180 for a double, but we have listed the best in this range. Under £100 and you're at the more serviceable, budget end of the market. Look out for weekend deals that can put a better class of hotel within reach. Rates often slide in winter. Book through the hotels' websites for the best online deals or promotional rates. Unless otherwise indicated, accommodation prices quoted include breakfast. International Youth Hostel Federation (IYHF) members net discounts on YHA accommodation.

Apartments

If you're in London for a week or more, a short-term or serviced apartment such as 196 Bishopsgate (p339), Number 5 Maddox Street (p337) or Beaufort House (p342) may make sense; rates at the bottom end are comparable to a B&B.

Websites

Londontown (☎020-7437 4370; www.londontown.com)

Lonely Planet (www.lonelyplanet.com/hotels) Bookings.

YHA Central Reservations System (www.lonelyplanet.com/london) Hostels.

Lonely Planet's Top Choices

York & Albany (p345) North London Georgian elegance meets luxurious comfort.

Dorset Square Hotel (p336) Regency architecture and restful views.

Hoxton Hotel (p343) Cool location, nifty looks, £1 room offers for the lucky few.

Clink78 (p344) Heritage hostel and former magistrates court.

Threadneedles (p339) Fresh new look but same old impeccable service.

Best by Budget

£

Clink261 (p344) Best facilities in London, and still one of the best value.

Church Street Hotel (p349) Boutique Mexican decor at diminutive prices.

££

No 10 Manchester Street (p336) Quintessential boutique hotel in quiet neighbourhood.

Citizen M (p339) High-tech, innovative and intimate.

£££

Dean Street Townhouse (p335) Georgian Soho gem.

Brown's Hotel (p337) London's oldest hotel remains top of the heap.

Best Romantic Hotels

Ritz (p338) So grand it lent its name to the English language.

Goring (p341) Delectable slice of classy, classic England.

Best Boutique Hotels

Zetter Hotel & Townhouse (p343) Sustainable two-part hotel with a mix of luxurious sleek and period interiors.

Charlotte Street Hotel (p338) London's first boutique hotel and arguably its best.

Hotel Indigo Tower Hill (p339) Welcome new stylish addition to the City accommodation scene.

Best B&Bs

Aster House (p341) Charming, comfortable and expertly run South Kensington B&B.

Barclay House (p346) Ticks every box and a few more.

Best for Contemporary Cool

Soho Hotel (p338) Very hip, very central, with original artwork throughout.

Citizen M (p339) Tablet-controlled rooms and square beds; this is hotel 2.0.

W (p337) More film set than hotel – for those with a sense of humour.

Best for Heritage

Claridge's (p337) Art-deco palace with designs by Viscount Linley.

Ritz (p338) There's only one Ritz and it reigns supreme.

Best for Views

W (p337) Quirky hotel shrouded in glass looking in all directions.

One Aldwych (p337) Costly but priceless river views from the uppermost rooms.

NEED TO KNOW

Price Ranges

In our listings we've used the following codes to represent the price of an en-suite double room in high season:

£	under £90
££	£90 to £180
£££	over £180

Reservations

➡ Book rooms as far in advance as possible, especially for weekends and peak periods.

➡ **British Hotel Reservation Centre** (☎020-7592 3055; www.bhrconline.com) has desks at airports and major train stations.

➡ **Visit London** (☎0871-222 3118, per minute 10p; www.visitlondonoffers.com) offers a free booking service with a wide range of properties and has a list of gay-friendly options.

Tax

➡ Value-added tax (VAT, now a staggering 20%) is added to hotel rooms. Some hotels include this in their advertised rates, some don't. Prices listed here include VAT.

Checking In & Out

➡ Check in is usually 2pm, though most places will let you check in earlier, or at least leave your luggage. Check out is usually between 10am and noon.

Breakfast

➡ Breakfast may be included in the room rate. Sometimes this is a continental breakfast; full English breakfast could cost extra.

Where to Stay

NEIGHBOURHOOD	FOR	AGAINST
The West End	Close to main sights; ubercentral; great transport links; wide accommodation range in all budgets; great restaurants	Busy tourist areas; expensive
The City	St Paul's and Tower of London; good transport links; handy central location; quality hotels; some cheaper weekend rates	Very quiet at weekends; a business district so high prices during week
The South Bank	Near Tate Modern, London Eye and Southbank Centre; cheaper than West End; excellent pubs and views	Many chain hotels; choice and transport limited
Kensington & Hyde Park	Excellent for South Kensington museums and shopping; great accommodation range; stylish area; good transport	Quite expensive; drinking and nightlife options limited
Clerkenwell, Shoreditch & Spitalfields	Trendy area with great bars and nightlife; excellent for boutique hotels	Few top sights; transport options limited
The East End & Docklands	Markets, multicultural feel; great restaurants and traditional pubs	More limited sleeping options; some areas less safe at night
Hampstead & North London	Leafy textures; vibrant and energetic nightlife; pockets of village charm; excellent boutique hotels and hostels; great gastropubs; quiet during week	Non-central and away from main sights
Notting Hill & West London	Cool cachet; great shopping, markets and pubs; fab boutique hotels; good transport	Pricey; light on sights
Greenwich & South London	Ace boutique options; leafy escapes; near top Greenwich sights	Sights spread out beyond Greenwich; transport limited
Richmond, Kew & Hampton Court	Smart riverside hotels; semi-rural pockets; close to Kew Gardens, Hampton Court Palace and Richmond; quiet; fantastic riverside pubs	Sights spread out; long way from central London

The West End

GENERATOR HOSTEL £

Map p436 (020-7388 7666; www.generatorhostels.com/london; 37 Tavistock Pl, WC1; dm/r from £12/50; @; Russell Sq) With its industrial decor, blue neon lights and throbbing techno, the huge Generator (more than 850 beds) is one of the grooviest budget places in central London. The bar, complete with pool tables, stays open until 2am and there are frequent themed parties. Dorm rooms have between four and 12 beds.

There is no kitchen but breakfast is provided and the large canteen serves bargain dinners from £4.50.

OXFORD ST YHA HOSTEL £

Map p432 (020-7734 1618; www.yha.org.uk; 14 Noel St, W1; dm/tw from £18/46; @; Oxford Circus) The most central of London's eight YHA hostels is also one of the most intimate, with just 104 beds and excellent shared facilities: we love the fuchsia kitchen and the bright, funky lounge. Dormitories have three and four beds and there are doubles and twins. Internet costs £1 per 20 minutes on their computers; wi-fi is £5/9 per day/week.

The in-house shop sells coffee and beer.

RIDGEMOUNT HOTEL B&B £

Map p436 (020-7636 1141; www.ridgemounthotel.co.uk; 65-67 Gower St, WC1; s/d/tr/q £67/98/123/136, without bathroom £52/78/102/124; @; Goodge St) This old-fashioned hotel offers its guests a warmth and consideration that you don't come across very often in the city these days. About half of its 30 utilitarian rooms have bathrooms; there are a number of triples and quadruples that will be useful for groups of friends and families. It also has a laundry service and free internet use.

GEORGE HOTEL B&B £

Map p436 (020-7387 8777; www.georgehotel.com; 58-60 Cartwright Gardens, WC1; s/d/tr from £85/110/115, without bathroom £65/85/97; WC1; @; Russell Sq) A friendly chap, this George, if a little old-fashioned. Cheaper rooms share bathrooms. Don't expect much but with this location, who's complaining? It's housed in a building built around 1810. Hotel guests get access to the gardens in front.

★**HOTEL LA PLACE** HOTEL ££

Map p438 (020-7486 2323; www.hotellaplace.com; 17 Nottingham Pl, W1; s/d from £105/152; @; Baker St) The 18 rooms here are very much in the traditional mode, but impeccably cared for, with updated bathrooms. All double rooms have king-size beds with orthopaedic mattresses, and the friendly family management has installed a 24-hour wine bar downstairs, an ice machine on the 2nd floor and a little computer room. The two-level suite and connecting rooms are good for families.

FIELDING HOTEL BOUTIQUE HOTEL ££

Map p430 (020-7836 8305; www.the-fielding-hotel.co.uk; 4 Broad Ct, Bow St, WC2; s/d from £90/140; ; Covent Garden) Hidden away in a pedestrianised court in the heart of Covent Garden, this pretty, 25-room hotel named after the novelist Henry Fielding, who lived nearby, has been furnished to a very high standard: the bathrooms have lovely walk-in showers and the rooms are beautifully done up and are fully air-conditioned. The hotel doesn't provide breakfast but the area is full of cafes.

ACADEMY BOUTIQUE HOTEL ££

Map p436 (020-7631 4115; www.theetoncollection.com; 21 Gower St, WC1; weekend/weekday d from £138/200; ; Goodge St) This beautiful, terribly English hotel is set across five Georgian town houses in Bloomsbury. The 49 lovely rooms are kitted out with fluffy feather duvets, elegant furnishings and the latest in creature comforts. There's a conservatory overlooking a leafy back garden with a fish pond, and a cosy breakfast room but no lift.

DEAN STREET TOWNHOUSE BOUTIQUE HOTEL ££

Map p432 (020-7434 1775; www.deanstreettownhouse.com; 69-71 Dean St, W1; r £180-440; ; Tottenham Court Rd) This 39-room gem in the heart of Soho has a wonderful boudoir atmosphere with its Georgian furniture, retro black-and-white tiled bathroom floors, beautiful lighting and girly touches (Cowshed bathroom products, hairdryer *and* straighteners in every room!). 'Medium' and 'bigger' rooms have four-poster beds and antique-style bathtubs right in the room.

HARLINGFORD HOTEL HOTEL ££

Map p436 (020-7387 1551; www.harlingfordhotel.com; 61-63 Cartwright Gardens, WC1; s/d/tr £88/120/140; ; Russell Sq) With its 'H' logo proudly sewn on the bedroom cushion, a modern interior with lots of lavender and mauve, and green-tiled bathrooms, this stylish Georgian hotel with 43 rooms is arguably the best on a street where competition is fierce. The welcome is always warm and the price is unbeatable but there's no lift and lots of stairs.

MORGAN HOTEL
B&B ££

Map p436 (☑020-7636 3735; www.morgan-hotel.co.uk; 24 Bloomsbury St, WC1; s/d/tr £110/135/185; ✳@☎; ⊖Tottenham Court Rd) In a row of 18th-century Georgian houses just west of the British Museum, the family-owned Morgan is distinguished by its friendliness, great service (free computer downstairs, breakfast fit for a king) and good value. The decor in the rooms is somewhat dated, but impeccably clean. The larger suites (doubles/triples £195/235 but no air-con) are worth the extra money.

NO 10 MANCHESTER STREET
BOUTIQUE HOTEL ££

Map p438 (☑020-7317 5900; www.tenman-chesterstreethotel.com; 10 Manchester St, W1; r £175-245; ☎; ⊖Baker St) In a wonderful Edwardian town house, this 45-room stunner epitomises 'boutique hotel': print wallpaper, designer beiges and browns, splashes of colour (note the bright 'star' carpet in the lobby), high-tech must-haves (iPods, free wi-fi, DVD player – DVD collection in reception – Nespresso machines etc) and impeccable service. Go for one of the four courtyard rooms with private terrace.

No 10 Manchester also prides itself on its humidor and outdoor heated lounge, where you can try one of the 60 different kinds of cigars and cigarillos.

SEVEN DIALS HOTEL
HOTEL ££

Map p430 (☑020-7240 0823; www.seven dialshotellondon.com; 7 Monmouth St, WC2; s/d/tr/q £95/105/130/150; ☎; ⊖Covent Garden or Tottenham Court Rd) The Seven Dials is a clean and comfortable almost-budget option in a very central location. Half of the 18 rooms face onto charming Monmouth St; the ones at the back don't get much of a view but are quieter.

AROSFA HOTEL
B&B ££

Map p436 (☑020-7636 2115; www.arosfalondon. com; 83 Gower St, WC1; s/d/tr/q £72/107/130/160; ⊖Goodge St) The old Arosfa has come a long way, with Philippe Starck furniture in the

lounge and a new modern look. The 17 rooms are less lavish, with cabin-like bathrooms in many of them. About half have been refurbished; they are small but remain good value. There are a couple of family rooms; room 4 looks onto a small garden.

JESMOND HOTEL
B&B ££

Map p436 (☑020-7636 3199; www.jesmond hotel.org.uk; 63 Gower St, WC1; s/d/tr/q £60/110/145/160, without bathroom £50/85/115/150; @☎; ⊖Goodge St) We've received more than a few letters from readers singing the praises of this family-run B&B in Bloomsbury. The 15 guest rooms – a dozen with bathroom – are basic but clean and cheerful, and it has a small, pretty garden. There's laundry service and internet on their computer is free.

ARRAN HOUSE HOTEL
B&B ££

Map p436 (☑020-7636 2186; www.arranho-tel-london.com; 77-79 Gower St, WC1; s/d/tr/q £105/125/155/175, without bathroom £70/95/105/125; @☎; ⊖Goodge St) This welcoming Bloomsbury B&B provides excellent value for the location. The 30 rooms range from basic singles with shared facilities to bright, well-furnished doubles with bathrooms. There is a cosy lounge at the front and gorgeous gardens at the back, perfect for a few drinks or a quiet read. Guests can use the microwave, fridge and dining room.

★DORSET SQUARE HOTEL
HOTEL £££

Map p438 (☑020-7723 7874; www.firmdale hotels.com; 39 Dorset Sq, NW1; d from £260, ste from £350; ✳☎; ⊖Baker St) Two combined Regency town houses contain this enchanting new 38-room hotel overlooking leafy Dorset Sq, where the very first cricket ground was laid in 1814 (which explains the cricket memorabilia in glass cases in the lobby and cricket balls as doorknobs). Guestrooms are smallish but almost dreamily decorated with a blend of antiques, sumptuous fabrics and crown-canopied or four-poster beds.

The in-house restaurant, the Potting Shed (mains £12.50 to £20.50), is a cut above.

HAZLITT'S
HISTORIC HOTEL £££

Map p432 (☑020-7434 1771; www.hazlittshotel. com; 6 Frith St, W1; s £222, d/ste from £288/660; ✳☎; ⊖Tottenham Court Rd) Built in 1718 and comprising four original Georgian houses, this is the one-time home of essayist William Hazlitt (1778–1830). The 30 guestrooms have been furnished with original antiques from the Georgian era and boast a wealth of seductive details, including panelled walls, mahogany four-poster beds, antique desks, Victorian claw-foot tubs and sumptuous fabrics.

A nod to modern times includes such creature comforts as iPod docking stations and flat-screen TVs.

CLARIDGE'S
LUXURY HOTEL £££

Map p438 (☑020-7629 8860; www.claridges. co.uk; 55 Brook St, W1; r/ste from £299/555; ✳@⚭; ⊖Bond St) Claridge's, with 203 rooms, is one of the greatest of London's five-star hotels. Well known for its sumptuous art-deco features (including 1930s vintage furniture that once graced the staterooms of the decommissioned SS *Normandie*), it recently added a more modern touch with a series of rooms and suites designed by David Linley, the Queen's grandson.

The result is muted colours and elegant, classic furniture designs. Check out his magnificent Map Room and its wall-size inlaid map of the world.

HAYMARKET HOTEL
HOTEL £££

Map p432 (☑020-7470 4000; www.haymarket hotel.com; 1 Suffolk Pl, off Haymarket, SW1; r £325-425, ste from £505; ✳⚭✳; ⊖Piccadilly Circus) The progeny of hoteliers and designers Tim and Kit Kemp, the Haymarket is opulently beautiful, with hand-painted Gournay wallpaper, signature fuchsia and green designs in the 50 guestrooms, a sensational 18m pool with mood lighting, an exquisite library lounge with honesty bar, and original artwork throughout. Just love the dog silhouettes on the chairs and bar stools.

ONE ALDWYCH
HOTEL £££

Map p430 (☑020-7300 1000; www.onealdwych. co.uk; 1 Aldwych, WC2; d/ste from £250/450; ✳⚭✳; ⊖Covent Garden) Housed in former art-nouveau newspaper offices (1907), One Aldwych is an upbeat hotel with 105 rooms and modern art throughout. The spacious and stylish rooms are replete with raw silk curtains, natural tones, daily fresh flowers and huge bathtubs. The circular suites have fabulous views of The Strand and Waterloo Bridge and the chlorine-free swimming pool is a plus.

BROWN'S HOTEL
HOTEL £££

Map p432 (☑020-7493 6020; www.brownshotel. com; 30 Albemarle St, W1; r/ste from £335/1100; ✳⚭; ⊖Green Park) This landmark hotel was created in 1837 from 11 town houses and is London's oldest hostelry. Each of the 117 rooms has been individually decorated by designer Olga Polizzi and many feature antiques and original artworks. The rest of the hotel is similarly attractive: the traditional English Tea Room has Edwardian oak panelling and working fireplaces and the Donovan Bar a stunning stained-glass window.

The in-house restaurant Hix Mayfair by celebrity chef Mark Hix is decorated with original art by Tracy Emin, Michael Landy, Bridget Riley and other contemporary names.

NUMBER 5 MADDOX STREET
APARTMENT £££

Map p432 (☑020-7647 0200; www.5maddox street.com; 5 Maddox St, W1; ste £290-800; ✳⚭; ⊖Oxford Circus) Right off Regent St, this luxury establishment, with 12 suites/apartments, will feel like your own London pad. Along with all the facilities the contemporary traveller could require, including iPod docking stations, each apartment has a fully equipped kitchen, and some even get their own little balcony or patio. Rooms are on five floors but there is no lift.

No 8 is the largest apartment. Wi-fi costs £10/50 a day/week.

COVENT GARDEN HOTEL
BOUTIQUE HOTEL £££

Map p430 (☑020-7806 1000; www.coventgarden hotel.co.uk; 10 Monmouth St, WC2; d/ste from £310/490; ✳⚭; ⊖Covent Garden) This 58-room boutique hotel housed in a former French hospital features antiques like the beautiful marquetry desk in the drawing room, gorgeous, bright fabrics and quirky bric-a-brac to mark its individuality. There's an excellent bar-restaurant called Brasserie Max just off the lobby, and two stunning guest lounges with fireplaces on the 1st floor that come into their own in the winter.

W
LUXURY HOTEL £££

Map p432 (☑020-7758 1000; www.whotels. com; 10 Wardour St, W1; r weekend/weekday from £289/539; ✳⚭; ⊖Leicester Sq) Everything has been designed for fun at the W: from the disco-ball-adorned reception to the curved walls and furniture, the cartoon cushions and the room entrances via the bathroom. The bold retro decor, with padded walls and red and gold themes, is slightly reminiscent of an Austin Powers film, but the 192-room W is definitely more sophisticated than that.

Being right at the heart of the West End, room prices increase as you go up the building. Great in-house spa oddly called Away.

SOHO HOTEL
HOTEL £££

Map p432 (☑020-7559 3000; www.sohohotel. com; 4 Richmond Mews, off Dean St W1; r/ste from £350/515; ❋❦; ⊖Oxford Circus) One of London's hippest hotels, the Soho has all the hallmarks of the eclectically chic duo Tim and Kit Kemp writ large over 91 individually designed guestrooms; the colours lean towards the limes and raspberries, and there's original artwork throughout the hotel, including a stunning black cat sculpture by Fernando Botero at the entrance.

CHARLOTTE STREET HOTEL
BOUTIQUE HOTEL £££

Map p436 (☑020-7806 2000; www.charlotte streethotel.com; 15-17 Charlotte St, W1; d/ste from £300/490; ❋❦; ⊖Goodge Street) London's first boutique hotel and arguably its best, this 52-room property, where Laura Ashley goes postmodern and comes up smelling of roses, is a favourite of visiting media types. The Drawing Room, with its working fireplace and oversized sofas, is a delightful place to wind down. The Charlotte also has its own cinema and shows on Sunday night (£35, with three-course meal).

RITZ
LUXURY HOTEL £££

Map p440 (☑020-7493 8181; www.theritzlondon. com; 150 Piccadilly, W1; r/ste from £380/700; ❋❦; ⊖Green Park) What can you say about a hotel that has lent its name to the English lexicon? This 136-room caravanserai has a spectacular position overlooking Green Park and is supposedly the Royal Family's home away from home (it does have a royal warrant from the Prince of Wales and is very close to the palace). All rooms have period interiors and antique furniture.

The Long Gallery and Palm Court restaurants, done in Louis XVI themes, have a strict formal-dress code (shirt and tie).

WALDORF HILTON
HISTORIC HOTEL £££

Map p430 (☑020-7836 2400; www.hilton.co.uk/ waldorf; Aldwych, WC2; r from £350; ❋❦❦; ⊖Temple or Covent Garden) The glorious Edwardian splendour of this renovated old pile still lives on in the heritage-listed Palm Court. The rooms feature some very contemporary designs but the hotel is working hard to make the best of its heritage and anecdote-filled history, with afternoon teas, historic tours, a pianist in the reception area, and a Louis XVI–style restaurant. Great swimming pool too.

CHESTERFIELD MAYFAIR
HOTEL £££

Map p438 (☑020-7491 2622; www.chesterfield-mayfair.com; 35 Charles St, W1; s/d/ste from £220/290/570; ❋❦; ⊖Green Park) Just a block west of Berkeley Sq, the 108-room Chesterfield comprises five floors of refinement and lustre hidden behind a fairly plain Georgian facade. It has ceilings with mouldings, marble floors, upholstered walls and period-style furnishings, as you'd expect from one of the grande dames of London digs. Room 102 has a lovely bay window.

BLOOMS TOWNHOUSE
HOTEL £££

Map p436 (☑020-7323 1717; www.grangehotels. com; 7 Montague St, off Russell Sq WC1; r from £229; ❋❦; ⊖Tottenham Court Rd or Holborn) This elegant 18th-century town house has the feel of a country home, which belies its position in what were the grounds of the British Museum. The decor in the 26 guestrooms is all carpets and print fabrics and there's a delightful terrace garden at the back where breakfast can be served. Unusually they still charge £10 per day for wi-fi.

CUMBERLAND HOTEL
HOTEL £££

Map p438 (☑0871-376 9014; www.thecumber-land.co.uk; Great Cumberland Pl, W1; s £180, d from £200; ❋❦; ⊖Marble Arch) You'll be forgiven for thinking you've accidentally stumbled into a contemporary art gallery in the hangar-sized lobby with larger-than-life sculptures and backlit floor. The 1000-plus guestrooms at this colossus all have cheerful, modern decor, many with views of nearby Hyde Park. It might be worth paying the £50 supplement for an executive room, which comes with extra amenities and access to the executive lounge.

🛏 The City

LONDON ST PAUL'S YHA
HOSTEL £

Map p442 (☑020-7236 4965; www.yha.org.uk; 36 Carter Lane , EC4; dm £17-25, d £40-50; @❦; ⊖St Paul 's) This 213-bed hostel, housed in a heritage-listed building, stands in the very shadow of St Paul's. Dorms have between three and 11 beds, and twins and doubles are available. There's a licensed cafeteria (breakfast £5, dinner from £6 to £8) but no kitchen, plus a lot of stairs and no lift. There's a seven-night maximum stay.

★THREADNEEDLES HOTEL ££

Map p442 (☎020-7657 8080; www.hotelthreadneedles.co.uk; 5 Threadneedle St, EC2; r weekend/weekday from £150/250; ❄📶; ⊖Bank) You have to know this place is here. It's wonderfully anonymous, though once through the doorway the grand circular lobby, furnished in a vaguely art-deco style and covered with a hand-painted glass dome, comes into view. The 74 refurbished rooms over five floors are smallish but pleasantly kitted out, all with high ceilings and dark, sleek furnishings.

HOTEL INDIGO TOWER HILL BOUTIQUE HOTEL ££

Map p442 (☎020-7423 6310; www.hotelindigo.com/lontowerhill; 142 Minories, EC3; r weekend/weekday from £100/200; ❄📶; ⊖Aldgate) A welcome addition to the City's accommodation scene is this new branch of the US InterContinental group's boutique-hotel chain. The 46 differently styled rooms all feature four-poster beds, iPod docking stations and a 'unique scent' system that allows you to choose your own fragrance. Larger-than-life drawings and photos of the neighbourhood won't let you forget where you are.

GRANGE ST PAUL'S HOTEL ££

Map p442 (☎020-7074 1000; www.grangehotels.com; 10 Godliman St , EC4; r weekend/weekday from £100/250; ❄📶🏊; ⊖St Paul's) The sheer size of the lobby atrium will have you gasping on entering this contemporary hostelry just south of St Paul's. The 133 well-proportioned rooms are fully loaded with high-tech gadgetry, and there's a 'female friendly' wing designed specifically with women in mind. Add to that a fully equipped health and fitness club and spa with a 20m swimming pool.

ANDAZ LIVERPOOL STREET HOTEL ££

Map p442 (☎020-7961 1234; www.london.liverpoolstreet.andaz.com; 40 Liverpool St, EC2; r weekend/weekday from £145/290; ❄📶; ⊖Liverpool St) This is the London flagship for Hyatt's sophisticated Andaz chain. There's no reception, just black-clad staff who check you in on mini laptops. The 267 rooms are cool and spacious, with interesting furnishings and lighting scheme. On top of this there are four restaurants, two bars and a subterranean Masonic temple discovered during the hotel's refit in the '90s.

196 BISHOPSGATE APARTMENT £££

Map p442 (☎020-7621 8788; www.196bishopsgate.com; 196 Bishopsgate , EC2; studio/1-bed apt £242/270; ❄📶; ⊖Liverpool St) These 48 luxury serviced apartments are well equipped and in a very handy location opposite Liverpool St station. Two-bedroom and executive studios (with balcony) are also available. Prices drop after six nights, making apartments a good option for a longer stay.

The South Bank

WALRUS HOSTEL £

Map p444 (☎07545 589214; www.walrussocial.com; 172 Westminster Bridge Rd, SE1; dm £18.50-25.50; 📶; ⊖Waterloo) This little hostel gets top marks for trying so hard (and succeeding!) at making a welcoming, individual, friendly and cosy hostel in the big smoke. The corridors and stairs are on the shabby side but the dorms (sleeping four to 18) and bathrooms are well kept and homely. The downside is the noise from the street and railway but at this price...

The vintage kitchen is fun, as is the tip-top shabby-chic pub downstairs, which is just as popular with the locals as it is with hostel residents. Breakfast, linen and towels are all included in the price.

ST CHRISTOPHER'S VILLAGE HOSTEL £

Map p444 (☎020-7939 9710; www.st-christophers.co.uk; 163 Borough High St, SE1; dm/r from £14/62; @📶; ⊖London Bridge) This 185-bed place is the flagship of a hostel chain with basic but cheap and clean accommodation (the bathrooms are looking a little tired however). There's a roof garden with bar, barbecue and excellent views of the Shard skyscraper, as well as a cinema and Belushi's bar below for serious partying. Dorms have four to 14 beds.

The hotel has two nearby branches (same contact details): **St Christopher's Inn** (Map p444; 121 Borough High St, SE1), with 50 beds, brand new bathrooms, another pub and a small veranda; and the **Oasis** (Map p444; 59 Borough High St), a woman-only 40-bed hostel.

★CITIZEN M BOUTIQUE HOTEL ££

Map p444 (☎020-3519 1680; www.citizenm.com/london-bankside; 20 Lavington Street, SE1; r £109-189; ❄@📶; ⊖Southwark) If Citizen M had a motto, it would be 'less fuss, more comfort'. The hotel has done away with

FEW-FRILLS CHAINS

London has several discount hotel chains that offer clean and modern – if somewhat institutional – accommodation for reasonable rates.

Express by Holiday Inn (Map p450; ☎0800-434 040; www.hiexpress.co.uk; weekday d £229, weekend £100-150) The most upmarket of the chains listed here, and notable for its clever locations.

Premier Inn (☎0870-242 8000; www.premierinn.com; r from £119) London's original cheap chain; in large numbers.

Tune Hotel (www.tunehotels.com; r from £55) Clean, neat and pared down; pay for extras as required. Four branches in town.

Travelodge (☎0871-984 8484; www.travelodge.co.uk; r from £70) Pleasant rooms, few public facilities.

Days Hotel (Map p454; ☎0800-028 0400; www.daysinn.co.uk; r £69-125) Just three branches in central London.

easyHotel (www.easyhotel.com; r from £45) Functional, with orange-moulded-plastic rooms, some without windows; five branches in town.

things it considers superfluous (room service, reception, bags of space) and instead gone all out on mattress and bedding (heavenly super king-size beds), state-of-the-art technology (everything in the room from mood-lighting to TV is controlled through a tablet computer) and superb decor.

Downstairs, the canteen-restaurant works on a self-service basis so that you can grab a meal whenever you feel like it (breakfast at 1pm and midnight chef encouraged) and the bar-lounge is an uncanny blend of designer and homely.

BERMONDSEY SQUARE HOTEL — BOUTIQUE HOTEL ££

Map p444 (☎020-7378 2450; www.bermondseysquarehotel.co.uk; Bermondsey Sq, Tower Bridge Rd, SE1; r £99-250, ste £300-500; ❄@📶; ⊖Borough) Just the ticket for Bermondsey is this hip, purpose-built, 80-room boutique hotel. Lobby photos of Brigitte Bardot and a young Anthony Hopkins set the '60s mood. The smallish but stylish standard rooms are fine but the best are the far-pricier suites at the top, named after iconic '60s songs.

Kensington & Hyde Park

CHERRY COURT HOTEL — B&B £

Map p448 (☎020-7828 2840; www.cherrycourthotel.co.uk; 23 Hugh St, SW1; s/d/tr £60/68/105; ❄📶; ⊖Victoria) Rooms (12 in all) may be a tad small but are very clean and tidy at this space-challenged, five-floor Victorian house hotel adorned with a Union Jack flag (the US and EU flags also go up occasionally) not far from Victoria train station. Rates are very attractive for this part of town, but there's no lift. A 5% credit-card surcharge applies.

Breakfast is a fruit basket in the morning but what really swings it for guests is the affable service from the owners.

MEININGER — HOSTEL £

Map p448 (☎020-3318 1407; www.meininger-hostels.com; Baden Powell House, 65-67 Queen's Gate, SW7; dm £16-22, s/tw from £75/90; ❄@📶; ⊖Gloucester Rd or South Kensington) In late-1950s Baden Powell House, opposite the Natural History Museum, this 48-room German-run 'city hostel and hotel' has spic-and-span rooms, most of which are dorms of between four and 12 beds, with pod-like showers. The 11 private rooms all have bathrooms and a good-size working area. Service is efficient and correct, there's good security and a bar in-house plus a great roof terrace hosting barbecues in warm weather.

ASTOR HYDE PARK — HOSTEL £

Map p448 (☎020-7581 0103; www.astorhostels.co.uk; 191 Queen's Gate, SW7; dm/tw Sun-Thu £22/28, Fri & Sat £35/40; @; ⊖Gloucester Rd or High St Kensington) With its wood-panelled walls, bay windows with leaded lights, 19th-century vibe and posh address just over from the Royal Albert Hall, this hostel has 150 beds in rooms over five floors (no lift), including dorms with three to 12 beds, and a good kitchen complete with incongruous pool tables.

ASTOR VICTORIA
HOSTEL £

Map p448 (☑020-7834 3077; www.astorhostels.co.uk; 71 Belgrave Rd, SW1; dm £18-20, d £45-90; ☞; ⊖Pimlico) Mothership of the Astor group of five hostels, this sedate place has 194 beds, including four- and eight-bed dorms and a handful of twins and doubles with shared shower and toilet. The hostel is helpfully staffed by travellers in between trips who are loaded with useful information.

ASTER HOUSE
B&B ££

Map p448 (☑020-7581 5888; www.asterhouse.com; 3 Sumner Pl, SW7; s £150, d £228-324; ✳@☞; ⊖South Kensington) This award-winning Singaporean-run property is truly excellent. From the lovely house and quintessential English aura, the welcoming staff, the comfortable rooms with quality furnishings and sparkling bathrooms to the delightful plant-filled Orangerie and Jemima the duck in the charming garden, it's all enchanting.

LIME TREE HOTEL
B&B ££

Map p448 (☑020-7730 8191; www.limetreehotel.co.uk; 135-137 Ebury St, SW1; s £99, d £150-175; @☞; ⊖Victoria) Family run for over 40 years, this smartly renovated Georgian town-house hotel has a pleasant back garden to catch the late afternoon rays while contemporary renovations and polite staff make it an appealing choice. No lift.

B+B BELGRAVIA
B&B ££

Map p448 (☑020-7259 8570; www.bb-belgravia.com; 64-66 Ebury St, SW1; d/apt from £84/225, studio £89-140; @☞; ⊖Victoria) This spiffing six-floor Georgian B&B, remodelled with contemporary flair, boasts crisp common areas and a chic lounge echoing the black-and-white tiled floor. The 18 rooms (some with shower, others with bath) aren't enormous but there's a further batch of studio rooms with compact kitchens at No 82 Ebury St. A pleasant courtyard garden is out back. No lift.

NUMBER SIXTEEN
HOTEL ££

Map p448 (☑020-7589 5232; www.numbersixteenhotel.co.uk; 16 Sumner Pl, SW7; s from £168, d £222-360; ✳@☞; ⊖South Kensington) With uplifting splashes of colour, choice art and a sophisticated-but-fun design ethos, ravishing Number Sixteen is four properties in one and a lovely (and rather labyrinthine) place to stay, with 42 individually designed rooms, a cosy drawing room and a fully stocked library. And wait till you see the idyllic, long back garden set around a fish pond, or have breakfast in the light-filled conservatory.

WINDERMERE HOTEL
B&B ££

Map p448 (☑020-7834 5163; www.windermere-hotel.co.uk; 142-144 Warwick Way, SW1; s £145-175, d £185-215, tw £195-215, f £235; @☞; ⊖Victoria) The attractive, award-winning and recently refurbished and expanded Windermere has 19 small but bright and individually designed rooms in a sparkling-white, mid-Victorian townhouse (with lift and brasserie). A 10% discount is offered if rooms are booked in advance.

LUNA SIMONE HOTEL
B&B ££

Map p448 (☑020-7834 5897; www.lunasimonehotel.com; 47-49 Belgrave Rd, SW1; s £70-75, d £95-120; @; ⊖Pimlico) This central and welcoming 35-room hotel is a popular choice among the hotels along Belgrave Rd. Compact rooms come with clean showers, double-glazed windows and innocuous blonde-wood furniture. Luggage storage is free; no lift. English breakfast included.

★GORING
HOTEL £££

Map p440 (☑020-7396 9000; www.thegoring.com; Beeston Place; r £540-1090; ⊖Victoria) Kate Middleton spent her last night as a commoner in the Royal Suite here before joining the ranks of the Royal Family, propelling the Goring into an international media glare. Glistening with chandeliers, dotted with trademark fluffy sheep and overseen by highly professional staff, this family-owned hotel is a supremely grand, albeit highly relaxed slice of England and Englishness (and the garden is sumptuous).

LEVIN HOTEL
HOTEL £££

Map p448 (☑020-7589 6286; www.thelevinhotel.co.uk; 28 Basil St, SW3; r from £350; ✳☞; ⊖Knightsbridge) As close as you can get to sleeping in Harrods, the luxury 12-room Levin is a bijou boutique gem. Attention to detail and highly hospitable service creates a delightful stay, while elegance and sophistication permeate this tiny hotel from top to toe, fashioning a highly personable choice in the heart of Knightsbridge.

HALKIN BY COMO
HOTEL £££

Map p448 (☑020-7333 1000; www.halkin.como. bz; Halkin St, SW1; r/ste from £470/670, breakfast £28.50; ✳@☎; ⊖Hyde Park Corner) With muted Asian influences, the chichi Halkin is for business travellers of a minimalist bent. Bedroom doors are hidden within curved wooden hallways, and the 41 swish rooms are filled with natural light, cream walls, burlwood panelling and large all-marble bathrooms. The staff, togged up in Armani-designed uniforms, are all obliging. There's no rear garden, though guests can use the key for nearby Belgrave Square. A fantastic new in-hotel Basque restaurant provides the culinary flair.

BLAKES
HOTEL £££

Map p448 (☑020-7370 6701; www.blakeshotels. com; 33 Roland Gardens, SW7; s £195, d £295-395, ste from £695, breakfast £12.50-19.50; ✳@☎; ⊖Gloucester Rd) Recently refurbished Blakes oozes panache: five Victorian houses cobbled into one hotel and incomparably designed by Anouska Hempel. Each of its 48 guest rooms is elegantly decked out in a distinctive, flamboyant style: expect four-poster beds (with and without canopies), rich fabrics and antiques set on bleached hardwood floors.

AMPERSAND HOTEL
BOUTIQUE HOTEL £££

Map p448 (☑020-7589 5895; www.ampersandhotel.com; 10 Harrington Road; s & d £372; ✳@☎; ⊖South Kensington) Housed in the old Norfolk Hotel building, a light, fresh and bubbly feel fills the new Ampersand, its (narrow) corridors and (stylish but smallish) rooms decorated with wallpaper designs celebrating the nearby arts and sciences of South Kensington's museums, a short stroll away. The wrapping recently off, there's a spring in its step, zest in the service and an eagerness to please.

Apero, the cellar Mediterranean restaurant, is excellent.

GORE
HOTEL £££

Map p448 (☑020-7584 6601; www.gorehotel. com; 190 Queen's Gate, SW7; r from £205; @☎; ⊖Gloucester Rd) With obliging staff in tails, twinkling chandeliers, walls crowded with framed portraits and prints and enough wood-paneling to put paid to a sizeable chunk of woodland, this fantastic 50-room hotel wallows in old England charm. Rolling Stones fans can celebrate the Beggars Banquet launch in the bar; Judy Garland aficionados can sleep on her bed (shipped over from the US) in her namesake suite.

The attached Bistrot One Ninety Queen's Gate is a fine place for brunch or a pre- or post-concert drink for the nearby Royal Albert Hall.

BEAUFORT HOUSE
APARTMENT £££

Map p448 (☑020-7584 2600; www.beauforthouse.co.uk; 45 Beaufort Gardens SW3; 1-4 bed apt £306-1176; ☎; ⊖Knightsbridge) Run by very helpful, friendly and welcoming staff, these stylish, comfortable and fully-equipped serviced apartments in a grand building on a quiet cul-de-sac off Brompton Rd are ideally located for Harrods and the breathless shopping vortex of Knightsbridge. Free access to a nearby health club; no minimum stay requirement outside of high season. Check out 10am.

KNIGHTSBRIDGE HOTEL
HOTEL £££

Map p448 (☑020-7584 6300; www.knightsbridgehotel.com; 10 Beaufort Gardens, SW3; s/d/ste from £235/290/475; ✳@☎; ⊖Knightsbridge) The lovely six-floor, 44-room Knightsbridge occupies a 200-year-old house just around the corner from Harrods on a particularly quiet, no-through-traffic, tree-lined street. Each room is different, with elegant and beautiful interiors done in a sumptuous, subtle and modern English style. Some of the singles, although beautifully furnished, are very small for the price. Check out is 11am (Sundays noon).

LANESBOROUGH
HOTEL £££

Map p448 (☑020-7259 5599; www.lanesborough. com; Hyde Park Corner, SW1; r from £495; ✳@☎; ⊖Hyde Park Corner) Where visiting divas doze and foreign royalty hang their crowns, this former hospital's (St George's) lavishly appointed guest rooms exude a regal opulence. All guests receive personal round-the-clock butlers, and staff are impeccably turned out in bowler hats and morning suits.

Push the boat out and check into the Lanesborough Suite: ranging over 380 sq m, you'll secure four bedrooms, five and a half bathrooms, a kitchen, two living rooms, a dining room (and an £18,000 a night price tag).

Clerkenwell, Shoreditch & Spitalfields

★HOXTON HOTEL — HOTEL ££

Map p450 (020-7550 1000; www.hoxtonhotels.com; 81 Great Eastern St, EC2; d & tw £59-199; @; Old St) This is hands down the best hotel deal in London. In the heart of Shoreditch, this sleek 208-room hotel aims to make its money by being full each night. You get an hour of free phone calls, free computer terminal access in the lobby, free printing and breakfast from Prêt à Manger. Rooms are small but stylish.

There are flat-screen TVs, a desk and fridge with complimentary bottled water and milk. Best of all is the price – while you have to be very lucky to get one of the £1 rooms (which sell out in minutes every three months), depending on the date you can find a room for £49 to £69 – still excellent deals for this level of comfort.

★ROOKERY — LUXURY HOTEL £££

Map p450 (020-7336 0931; www.rookeryhotel.com; 12 Peter's Lane, Cowcross St, EC1; s £235, d £238-625; ; Farringdon) This absolute charmer is a warren of 33 rooms built within a row of 18th-century Georgian houses and fitted out with antique furniture (including a museum-piece collection of Victorian baths, showers and toilets), original wood panelling, statues in the bathrooms and artworks selected personally by the owner. There's a small courtyard garden and a wonderfully private and whimsical feel to the whole place.

ZETTER HOTEL & TOWNHOUSE — BOUTIQUE HOTEL £££

Map p450 (020-7324 4444; www.thezetter.com; 86-88 Clerkenwell Rd, EC1M; d from £235, studio £300-450; ; Farringdon) The Zetter comprises two quite different properties, both exemplary in their execution. The original Zetter is a temple of cool with an overlay of kitsch on Clerkenwell's titular street. Built using sustainable materials on the site of a derelict office, its 59 rooms are small but perfectly formed. The **Zetter Townhouse** (Map p450; 49-50 St John's Sq; r £222-294, ste £438-480), on a pretty square behind the Zetter, has just 13 rooms in a characterful Georgian pile.

There are Penguin Classics on the bookshelves and hi-tech flat-screens and air-conditioning (using water from the hotel's very own bore hole). The rooftop studios are the real treat though, with terraces commanding superb views across the city. Top-quality fare is available in the ground-floor restaurant.

The rooms in Zetter Townhouse are uniquely decorated in period style but with witty touches such as headboards made from reclaimed fairground carousels. Further treats include the Roberts radios, beautiful roll-top baths and the hand-painted lifts. The fantastic hotel bar is a destination in itself.

13 PRINCELET ST — APARTMENT £££

Map p450 (01628 825925; www.landmarktrust.org.uk; 13 Princelet St, E1; r around £310; Liverpool St) Built in 1719 this fantastic old town house was lovingly restored in 1987 before being bequeathed to the Landmark Trust, offering a rare opportunity to stay in a period property in this area. It's beautifully decorated, with tiled fireplaces and three large bedrooms (two twins, one double) set over four sloping floors. There's also a patio garden and fully equipped kitchen.

Prices vary depending on dates and there's a minimum stay of three nights.

FOX & ANCHOR — BOUTIQUE HOTEL £££

Map p450 (0121 6163614; www.foxandanchor.com; 115 Charterhouse St, EC1; r £222-246, ste £324, weekends r £138-162, ste £234; @; Farringdon or Barbican) Characterful option in a handy location above a glorious pub, this place offers just six small but sumptuous rooms, each individually decorated and with all mod cons.

SHOREDITCH ROOMS — BOUTIQUE HOTEL £££

Map p450 (020-7739 5040; www.shoreditchhouse.com; Shoreditch House, Ebor St, E2; r around £225, breakfast £10; ; Shoreditch High St) Part of private members' club Shoreditch House, but with rooms available to all, they're quite upfront here about the size of the rooms, categorising them tiny, small and small plus. Each room is freshly decorated in a beach-house style, with light wood panelling and sparkly white linen. Small-plus rooms have a balcony.

Areas available to guests include the gorgeous rooftop pool, secret garden and lazy lawn. Prices vary considerably depending on the date and can go as low as £85 on selected nights.

BOUNDARY BOUTIQUE HOTEL £££

Map p450 (020-7729 1051; www.theboundary.co.uk; 2-4 Boundary St, E2; d £260-300, ste £450-570; ; Shoreditch High St) Terence Conran's impressive design hotel in a converted factory towers over the shops on achingly hip Redchurch St. Each room or suite takes its theme from a particular designer or design style, such as Eames, Bauhaus or Scandinavian. Mod cons are as flash as you'd expect. Rates are reduced for all rooms on Sunday nights.

MALMAISON HOTEL £££

Map p450 (020-7012 3716; www.malmaison-london.com; 18-21 Charterhouse Sq, EC1; r £300-325, breakfast £16-19; ; Farringdon) Facing a picture-postcard leafy square in Clerkenwell, this conservatively chic 97-room hotel feels more like a dangerously expensive cocktail bar when you enter its lobby. Public areas are moodily low-lit, with the exception of the luminous subterranean restaurant. Rooms are simple and elegant. Prices vary considerably and can be much cheaper at the weekends.

The East End & Docklands

★40 WINKS BOUTIQUE HOTEL ££

Map p454 (020-7790 0259; www.40winks.org; 109 Mile End Rd, E1; s/d £105/175; ; Stepney Green) Short on space but not on style, this two-room boutique guesthouse in less-than-desirable Stepney Green oozes charm. It is housed in an early-18th-century town house owned by a successful designer and has been used as a location for a number of fashion shoots. The rooms (the single is quite compact) are uniquely decorated with an expert's eye. Book early.

OLD SHIP HOTEL ££

Map p454 (020-8986 1641; www.urbaninns.co.uk; 2 Sylvester Path, E8; ; 38 or 55, Hackney Central) This bright, 10-room place has surprisingly cheerful rooms and public areas, and represents good value for money, putting you close to the action of lively Broadway Market and surrounds. The pub of the same name below serves, among other things, excellent British 'tapas' and pies.

TOWN HALL HOTEL & APARTMENTS LUXURY HOTEL APARTMENT £££

Map p454 (020-7871 0460; www.townhallhotel.com; Patriot Square, E2; d £355-389, apt £410-554, breakfast £17; ; Bethnal Green) Set in an erstwhile Edwardian town hall (1910), updated with art-deco features in the 1930s, it was the council's headquarters until 1965. The design aesthetic of the hotel combines these eras beautifully, with the addition of cutting-edge contemporary art by London-based artists. No rooms are the same, and the apartments are extremely well equipped.

The marble lobby and central staircase are an impressive welcome and a world away from the scruffy neighbourhood outside. Each room has quirks from the original structure, along with carefully designed contemporary features throughout.

Hampstead & North London

★CLINK78 HOSTEL £

Map p456 (020-7183 9400; www.clinkhostels.com; 78 King's Cross Rd, WC1; dm/r from £9/40; @; King's Cross St Pancras) This fantastic 500-bed hostel is housed in a 19th-century magistrates courthouse where Dickens once worked as a scribe and members of the Clash made an appearance in 1978. Rooms feature pod beds (including storage space) in four- to 16-bed dormitories (there is a female aisle). There's a top kitchen with a huge dining area and a busy bar in the basement.

Parts of the hostel, including seven spooky (and vaguely claustrophobic) cells converted to bedrooms and a pair of wood-panelled court rooms used as a TV lounge and an internet room, are heritage-listed.

CLINK261 HOSTEL £

Map p456 (020-7833 9400; www.clinkhostels.com; 261-265 Grays Inn Rd, WC1X; dm/r from £9/50; @; King's Cross St Pancras) A top-notch hostel with bright, funky dorms, good bathrooms, bunk beds fitted with a privacy panel and individual lockers for valuables, a brilliant self-catering kitchen that looks straight out of a design magazine, and a fab TV lounge and computer room.

LONDON ST PANCRAS YHA HOSTEL £

Map p456 (020-7388 9998; www.yha.org.uk; 79 Euston Rd, NW1; dm/r from £20/61; @; King's Cross St Pancras) This 185-bed hostel has modern, clean dorms sleeping four to six (nearly all with private facilities) and some private rooms. There's a good bar and cafe, although there are no self-catering facilities.

★**YORK & ALBANY** BOUTIQUE HOTEL £££

Map p460 (020-7388 3344; www.gordonramsay.com/yorkandalbany; 127-129 Parkway, NW1; r from £205; ; Camden Town) Luxurious yet cosy, the York & Albany oozes Georgian charm: there are feature fireplaces in many of the rooms, antique furniture, beautiful floor-to-ceiling windows and lush bathrooms (with underfloor heating, ideal on cold winter days). All rooms have flatscreen TV, DVD player (and DVDs at reception) and free wi-fi. The hotel is right by Regent's Park, and just five minutes' walk from happening Camden.

★**GREAT NORTHERN HOTEL** BOUTIQUE HOTEL £££

Map p456 (020-3388 0800; www.gnhlondon.com; King's Cross Rd, N1; r from £300; ; King's Cross St Pancras) Rising like a phoenix from the ashes of the 'old' King's Cross – once the city's red-light district – the Great Northern Hotel, with its curving brick facade, would make its 1854 incarnation proud. The world's first railway hotel is back in business with a boutique, classic style reminiscent of luxury sleeper trains.

Exquisite craftsmanship is in evidence everywhere – with noble materials and custom designs – without losing sight of practical details: there are European as well as English sockets; there's a 'pantry' on every floor from which you can help yourself to hot or cold drinks, cakes, books and newspapers; and there's great in-room entertainment with films, music playlists and audio books. There is also a lively bar and an excellent restaurant.

MEGARO BOUTIQUE HOTEL £££

Map p456 (020-7843 2222; www.hotelmegaro.co.uk; Belgrove St, WC1H; d £160-240, f £260; ; King's Cross St Pancras) There are many things that commend Megaro to this guidebook: the indulgently large rooms, lovely decor, the creature comforts in the rooms (espresso machine, fresh milk, hairdryer, rainforest showerhead), attentive service, and Karpo (p249), its excellent bar-restaurant. There is some noise from the street so if you're a light sleeper, go high or go at the back.

ROUGH LUXE BOUTIQUE HOTEL £££

Map p456 (020-7837 5338; www.roughluxe.co.uk; 1 Birkenhead St, WC1H; r £229-289; ; King' s Cross St Pancras) Half rough, half luxury is the strapline of this unique hotel, and the interior is true to its words: scraps of old newspaper adorn the walls along with original works of art; the bathrooms are utterly gorgeous but the vintage 1970s TV doesn't work. Rooms are tiny but service and location more than make up for it.

The little patio at the back is a lovely surprise – guests are welcome to bring food and enjoy a glass of wine on balmy nights.

ST PANCRAS RENAISSANCE LONDON HOTEL LUXURY HOTEL £££

Map p456 (020-7841 3540; www.marriott.co.uk; Euston Rd, NW1; d from £230; ; King's Cross St Pancras) It took the best part of a decade and £150 million to revive the former Midland Grand Hotel but, boy, was it worth it. The Gothic, red-brick building is a Victorian marvel. Disappointingly, only 38 of the 245 rooms are in the original building; the rest are in an extension at the back and rather bland.

The hotel's spa is anything but bland, however, with Victorian tiling in the pool. Victoriana can also be found in abundance in the hotel bar (p255) and restaurant.

Notting Hill & West London

TUNE HOTEL HOTEL £

Map p462 (020-7258 3140; www.tunehotels.com; 41 Praed St W2; r £35-80; ; Paddington) This new 137-room Malaysian-owned budget hotel offers super-duper rates for early birds who book a long way in advance. The ethos is you get the bare bones – a twin or double room, the cheapest without window – and pay for add-ons (towel, wi-fi, TV) as you see fit, giving you the chance to just put a roof over your head, if that's all you need.

You don't even get a wardrobe, just hangers. Things are super hygienic, everything's clean as a whistle and staff are welcoming.

STYLOTEL HOTEL £

Map p462 (020-7723 1026; www.stylotel.com; 160-162 Sussex Gardens, W2; s/d/tr/q £60/85/105/120, studio/1-bedroom ste £142/185; ; Paddington) The crisp industrial design – scored aluminium treads, opaque green glass, plentiful riveted stainless steel, metal bed frames – of this 40-room niche hotel is contemporary and well-priced. Elbow room is at a minimum: 'stylorooms' are small, but the largely carpet-free floor surfaces help keep things dapper. The eight more spacious 'stylosuites' above the Sussex Arms around the corner are newer and more swish.

YHA EARL'S COURT
HOSTEL £

Map p464 (☑020-7373 7083; www.yha.org.uk; 38 Bolton Gardens, SW5; dm from £20, tw/d from £48.50/50.50; @🕏; ⊖Earl's Court) There's some lovely original tiling on the floor as you enter this fine old property on a quiet, leafy street in Earl's Court, although most other period detailing has been overlaid. Most accommodation (186 beds) is in clean, airy dormitories of between four and 10 bunk beds. There's a sense of space in the common areas; showers and toilets are clean and staff helpful.

There's a huge gravel garden out back strewn with tables plus a good-sized kitchen, two lounges and a bright, modern cafe.

YHA HOLLAND HOUSE
HOSTEL £

Map p464 (☑020-7937 0748; www.yha.org.uk; Holland Walk, W8; dm from £15; @; ⊖High St Kensington) Built into the Jacobean wing of Holland House (1607) and an ugly 1959 attachment in the middle of delightful Holland Park, this functional hostel has 201 beds in large rooms with between six and 20 beds. It's all about location here, as it's always busy and rather institutional.

ST CHRISTOPHER'S SHEPHERD'S BUSH
HOSTEL £

Map p464 (☑020-8600 7500; www.st-christophers.co.uk; 13-15 Shepherd's Bush Green; dm £19-25; 🕏; ⊖Shepherd's Bush) St Christopher's Shepherd's Bush may be unscenically located slap bang by the massive Shepherd's Bush roundabout, but you're right by the tube station for the Central line into town via nearby Notting Hill Gate, the hostel has a lively pub and staff are friendly. Accommodation is rather cramped, but there are nifty lockable drawers under the beds and special off-peak, weekday offers booked online can fall to just over £10 per night.

★LA SUITE WEST
BOUTIQUE HOTEL ££

Map p462 (☑020-7313 8484; www.lasuitewest.com; 41-51 Inverness Tce; r £130-354; ❋@🕏; ⊖Bayswater) The black-and-white foyer of the Anouska Hempel–designed La Suite West – bare walls, a minimalist slit of a fireplace, an iPad for guests' use on an otherwise void white marble reception desk – presages the OCD neatness of rooms hidden away down dark corridors. The straight lines, spotless surfaces and sharp angles are accentuated by impeccable bathrooms and softened by comfortable beds and warm service.

Downstairs suites have gardens and individual gated entrances.

BARCLAY HOUSE
B&B ££

Map p464 (☑020-7384 3390; www.barclayhouselondon.com; 21 Barclay Rd, SW6; r £110-125; @🕏; ⊖Fulham Broadway) The two dapper, thoroughly modern and comfy bedrooms in this charmingly ship-shape Victorian house are a dream, from the Phillipe Starck shower rooms, walnut furniture, new double-glazed sash windows and underfloor heating to the small, thoughtful details (fumble-free coat hangers, drawers packed with sewing kits and maps). The cordial, music-loving owners – bursting with tips and London knowledge – concoct an inclusive, homely atmosphere. Usually there is a four-night minimum stay.

ROCKWELL
BOUTIQUE HOTEL ££

Map p464 (☑020-7244 2000; www.therockwell.com; 181-183 Cromwell Rd, SW5; s from £90, d £100-115, ste from £160; ❋🕏; ⊖Earl's Court) With an understated-cool design ethos, things are muted, dapper and more than

STUDENT DIGS

During university holidays (generally mid-March to late April, late June to September and mid-December to mid-January), student dorms and halls of residence are open to paying visitors. Choices include **LSE Vacations** (☑020-7955 7676; www.lsevacations.co.uk; s/tw/tr from £45/60/83), whose eight halls include the 800-bed **Bankside House** (Map p444; 24 Sumner St, SE1; ⊖Southwark) and **High Holborn Residence** (Map p430; 178 High Holborn, WC1; ⊖Holborn). **King's College Conference & Vacation Bureau** (☑020-7848 1700; www.kingsvenues.com; s £45-55, tw £65) handles the centrally-located **Great Dover St Apartments** (Map p444; 165 Great Dover St, SE1; ⊖Borough), the **Stamford St Apartments** (Map p444; 127 Stamford St, SE1; ⊖Waterloo) with a further residence in **Hampstead** (Kidderpore Ave).

a tad minimalist at 'budget boutique' 40-room Rockwell. Spruce and stylish, all rooms have shower, the mezzanine suite is an absolute peach and the three rooms (LG1, 2 and 3) giving on to the garden are particularly fine.

Diagonally across from the Cromwell Hospital (where George Best saw out his last day), rooms on Cromwell Rd are triple-glazed to stifle the roar.

HOTEL INDIGO BOUTIQUE HOTEL ££

Map p462 (020-7706 4444; www.indigopaddington.com; 16 London St, W2; r from £152; ; Paddington) This 64-room gem, part of the boutique division of the huge US InterContinental group of hotels, is a top choice in Paddington. The decoration takes its inspiration from the 13th-century Fibonacci sequence of numbers that finds miraculous expression in nature. Each of the four floors has its own colour scheme in the rooms and bathrooms are stunning, with fabulous fittings.

17 HOMESTEAD RD B&B ££

Map p464 (020-7385 6773; www.fulhambedandbreakfastlondon.co.uk; 17 Homestead Rd; d & tw from £90; Fulham Broadway or Parsons Green) With its pristine buff-coloured carpets, this charming and entirely spotless two-room B&B is housed in a Victorian terraced property. The ambience is lovingly maintained with lashings of elbow grease (and a no-shoes policy) from the friendly and welcoming owner, Fiona. Phoning ahead to book is important. Breakfasts are simple (muesli, toast, orange juice, tea or coffee); single occupancy prices are £20 cheaper than the double occupancy price and check-in time is usually after 5pm.

VANCOUVER STUDIOS APARTMENT ££

Map p462 (020-7243 1270; www.vancouverstudios.co.uk; 30 Prince's Sq, W2; apt £97-350; ; Bayswater) Everyone will feel at home in this appealing terrace of stylish and affordable studios, with a restful and charming walled garden. Very well maintained rooms all contain kitchenettes but otherwise differ wildly – ranging from a tiny but well-equipped single to a spacious three-bedroom garden apartment (minimum stay three nights) that sleeps up to six.

SPACE APART HOTEL HOTEL ££

Map p462 (020-7908 1340; www.aparthotellondon.co.uk; 36-37 Kensington Gardens Sq W2; apt £139-194; ; Bayswater or Royal Oak) Light, bright and spic-and-span studio apartments with kitchenette at eye-catching rates in this converted 30-room Georgian building is the name of the game at neatly designed Space Apart, which provides a handy and affordable stay not far from the Notting Hill action. The studios are not big, but for around £20 you can upgrade to a roomier double studio. There's usually a two-night minimum stay.

BASE2STAY HOTEL ££

Map p464 (020-7244 2255; www.base2stay.com; 25 Courtfield Gardens, SW5; s/d from £93/99; ; Earl's Court) Breezy, fresh and cost-efficient Base2stay has endeavoured to filter out all the 'unnecessary' extras most hotels offer and concentrate on the 'important' things like good wi-fi, music systems, kitchenettes and discounts at local restaurants. The result is a pared-down, stylistically functional and extremely comfortable 67-room hotel (sans bar or restaurant) committed to sustainability (recycling, energy-saving light bulbs, water savings, fair-trade tea and coffee etc) that encourages guests to embrace the same principles.

TWENTY NEVERN SQUARE HOTEL ££

Map p464 (020-7565 9555; www.20nevernsquare.com; 20 Nevern Sq, SW5; r from £115; ; Earl's Court) Each room is different at this elegant and stylish four-floor brick hotel overlooking a lovely London square. Cosy, but not especially large, rooms are decorated with Asian-style woodwork, imposing carved-wood beds (some of them four-poster), venetian blinds and heavy fabrics. Some rooms have bath, others shower. There is a gorgeous conservatory where breakfast is served, and a tiny patio. Wi-fi is complimentary and there's a lift.

NEW LINDEN HOTEL BOUTIQUE HOTEL ££

Map p462 (020-7221 4321; www.newlinden.co.uk; Hereford Rd, 59 Leinster Sq, W2; s/d from £79/105; ; Bayswater) Light, airy and beautifully designed, the New Linden is a very classy option located between Westbourne Grove and Notting Hill. Some of the rooms are on the small side due to the Georgian buildings' quirky layout, but they feel cosy rather than cramped. Staff are charming, too.

VICARAGE HOTEL B&B ££
Map p464 (020-7229 4030; www.londonvicaragehotel.com; 10 Vicarage Gate, W8; s/d £110/138, without bathroom £65/110; ; High St Kensington or Notting Hill Gate) Gilt mirrors, sconces, chandeliers and striped red-and-gold wallpaper – this affordable mid-terrace house hotel almost on Palace Gardens Tce (where the phenomenal cherry trees in spring have to be seen to be believed) is exquisitely located. The 17 rooms are less lavish, but atmospherically old-world-English and slightly larger than usual. The 3rd- and 4th-floor rooms have shared bathrooms.

GARRET APARTMENT ££
Map p464 (020-7370 1434; www.troubadour.co.uk; 263-267 Old Brompton Rd, SW5; 1-/2-person apt £160/175; ; West Brompton) Slung out above the Troubadour, this roomy suite/apartment is a fab boho choice in Earl's Court. There's loads of space, lovely window arches onto Old Brompton Road, pull chains on the loos, overhead skylights, roses on arrival and you're suspended way above the traffic din below. You've your own access, so you feel like you're kipping in your best mate's flat. There's no lift, so pack light.

GARDEN COURT HOTEL HOTEL ££
Map p462 (020-7229 2553; www.gardencourthotel.co.uk; 30-31 Kensington Gardens Sq, W2; s/d/tr/f £76/125/150/175, s/d with shared bathroom £50/79; ; Bayswater) Run by the same family since 1954, the spotless Garden Court is a reliable choice in its price range. The decor is simple, with decorative wallpaper and basic furniture, and a great bonus for guests is access to both the hotel garden and the leafy square across the street. Wi-fi is £5 per stay.

PORTOBELLO GOLD INN ££
Map p462 (020-7460 4910; www.portobellogold.com; 95-97 Portobello Rd, W11; r/apt from £75/150; ; Notting Hill Gate) This friendly guesthouse above a pleasant restaurant and pub has seven rooms of varying sizes and quality of furnishings. There are several small doubles (with minuscule shower room). The four-poster suite has antique furnishings, a foldaway four-poster bed and (decorative) open-hearth fireplace. The Roof Terrace studio has a microwave and fridge and exclusive access to the roof (with a putting green).

RUSHMORE HOTEL ££
Map p464 (020-7370 3839; www.rushmore-hotel.co.uk; 11 Trebovir Rd, SW5; s/d £69/89; ; Earl's Court) The gentle pastel shades, Mediterranean murals, terracotta and faux marbling of this modest hotel create a different and rather charming atmosphere. All 22 guest rooms are of a decent size and are impeccably clean. It's prudent to compare rooms: four rooms on the 1st floor have balconies: Nos 11 and 12 face the street and Nos 14 and 15, the courtyard. There's no lift.

PARKWOOD HOTEL HOTEL ££
Map p462 (020-7402 2241; www.parkwoodhotel.com; 4 Stanhope Pl, W2; s/d/tr/f £89/119/135/155, s/d/tr with shared bathroom £69/89/109; ; Marble Arch) You certainly get value for money at this small hotel where rooms are simple but pretty spacious on the whole. Bathrooms are basic but the whole place is run with pride and the staff are very friendly. You're a hop and a skip from Oxford St and Hyde Park, and wi-fi is free.

GATE HOTEL B&B ££
Map p462 (020-7221 0707; www.gatehotel.co.uk; 6 Portobello Rd, W11; s/d/tr from £60/85/115; ; Notting Hill Gate) The half-dozen guest rooms in this old town house with classic frilly English decor and flowery facade all have private facilities. You're as close as you're going to get to the buying and selling of Portobello Road. Breakfast is continental only and served in the rooms since there is no dining room; prices rise at weekends.

PORTOBELLO HOTEL BOUTIQUE HOTEL £££
Map p462 (020-7727 2777; www.portobellohotel.co.uk; 22 Stanley Gardens, W11; s/d/feature r from £174/234/276; ; Notting Hill Gate) This splendidly located, 21-room property has been a firm favourite with rock and rollers and movie stars down the decades. Feature rooms are presented with stylish colonial decor, four-poster beds and inviting roll-top baths; room 16 has an ample round bed, a Victorian bathing machine and a roll-call of past celebrity lodgers.

Things are simpler and rooms much smaller lower down the tariff registry, while the overall decor could do with some attention. Rooms at the back have views of the neighbouring properties' beautiful gardens, but the hotel itself has no garden.

K + K HOTEL GEORGE
BOUTIQUE HOTEL £££

Map p464 (☎020-7598 8700; www.kkhotels.com; 1-15 Templeton Place; s/d/tr £300/336/360; ❄📶; ⊖Earl's Court) From the niftily designed, wide-open foyer to the joyfully huge garden with its glorious lawn, this tidy 154-room boutique hotel just round the corner from Earl's Court tube station has smallish rooms, but they are attractively presented, comfy and come with neat shower. There's a snazzy bar, helpful service throughout, soft colours and the location is great for zipping into the centre of town.

Greenwich & South London

SAFESTAY
HOSTEL £

(☎020-7703 8000; www.safestay.co.uk; 144-152 Walworth Rd, SE17; dm/tw/d from £18/58/66; @📶; ⊖Elephant & Castle) Who would have thought that the Labour Party's former headquarters would make such a bling hostel? The 18th-century Georgian building has been stunningly renovated: inside it's all pink, stripes and bright lights, though the rooms are more sober. Most dorms (four to eight beds) are en suite. Our only criticism is that it lacks soul – perhaps it'll come with time.

ST CHRISTOPHER'S INN GREENWICH
HOSTEL £

Map p469 (☎020-8858 3591; www.st-christophers.co.uk; 189 Greenwich High Rd, SE10; dm £10-25, tw £40-55; 📶; 🚆Greenwich, ⊖Greenwich) The Greenwich branch of this successful chain of hostels has 55 beds and is quieter than some of its more centrally located sister properties (though it stands cheek by jowl to Greenwich train station). The hostel has a lively pub but the dorms (six to eight beds) are pretty cramped and the bathrooms, though clean, are in need of a revamp.

★CHURCH STREET HOTEL
BOUTIQUE HOTEL ££

(☎020-7703 5984; www.churchstreethotel.com; 29-33 Camberwell Church St, SE5; s £60-90, d £90-170, f £190; ❄📶; 🚆Denmark Hill) 🍃 One of London's most individual boutique hotels, this vibrant establishment is a much needed shot of tequila into the hotel landscape of London. Run by a half-Spanish, half-English brother duo in love with Mexico, the hotel brims with colour, vibrant details and Mexicana (the tiled bathrooms will perk up anyone's day). The smallest rooms share bathrooms. Prices include a sensational breakfast.

NUMBER 16 ST ALFEGE'S
B&B ££

Map p469 (☎020-8853 4337; www.st-alfeges.co.uk; 16 St Alfege Passage, SE10; s/d £75/125; 📶; 🚆DLR Greenwich) One-time sweet shop, this gay-owned B&B has two well-appointed doubles and a single, individually decorated in shades of blue, green or yellow and all with bathroom. The owners do their best to make everyone, gay or straight, feel at home, with chats and cups of tea in the charming basement kitchen. The main entrance is on Roan St.

CAPTAIN BLIGH GUESTHOUSE
B&B ££

Map p468 (☎020-7928 2735; www.captainblighhouse.co.uk; 100 Lambeth Rd, SE1; s/d £78/108; 📶; ⊖Lambeth North) This late-18th-century property and former home of Bligh is a leafy corner of South London. Pros: the fully equipped suites (complete with kitchen) are gorgeous (we love the Royal Suite), quiet and kept immaculate. Cons: no credit cards, a four-night minimum stay and one night's nonrefundable deposit required. A welcome pack, which basically covers breakfast for four days, is included.

KENNINGTON B&B
B&B ££

Map p468 (☎020-7735 7669; www.kenningtonbandb.com; 103 Kennington Park Rd, SE11; d £120-150; 📶; ⊖Kennington) With gorgeous bed linen, well-preserved Georgian features and just a small number of bedrooms, this lovely B&B in an 18th-century house is tasteful in every regard, from the shining, tiled shower rooms and Georgian shutters to the fireplaces and cast-iron radiators. Bathrooms are private but off-suite (located on the landing).

PARK PLAZA WESTMINSTER BRIDGE
HOTEL £££

Map p444 (☎0844-415 6780; www.parkplaza.com; 200 Westminster Bridge Rd, SE1; d £159-289, studio £289-349; ❄@📶🏊; ⊖Waterloo) The 1019 (yes) rooms of the Park Plaza are contemporary, stylish and very comfortable but the cheapest merely face unspectacularly into the atrium; upgrade to the studios (equipped with kitchenette and sofa-bed, perfect for families) or penthouse rooms for great views of the Thames, Big Ben and the London Eye.

Richmond, Kew & Hampton Court

FOX AND GRAPES PUB ££

(☎020-8619 1300; www.foxandgrapeswimbledon.co.uk; 9 Camp Rd; r £125 ; 📶; ⊖Wimbledon) This popular gastropub sees the rambling barbour-clad Wimbledon set decamping with mud-flecked canines in tow. The location is lovely and the three modern rooms-with-shower upstairs – each one named after a Womble – can cast a (pricey) roof over your head if you take to Wimbledon's semi-rural charms. Room includes continental breakfast.

★BINGHAM BOUTIQUE HOTEL £££

Map p470 (☎020-8940 0902; www.thebingham.co.uk; 63 Petersham Rd, TW10; s £175, d £195-290; ❄📶; ⊖Richmond or 🚉Richmond then 🚌65) Just upriver from Richmond Bridge, this lovely riverside Georgian town house is an enticing boutique escape from central London, with 15 very stylish and well-presented, art-deco-inspired rooms. Each room takes its name from a poem (the house holds a literary history). Riverside rooms are naturally pricier, but worth it, as roadside rooms – although deliciously devised and double-glazed – look out over busy Petersham Rd. Further treasures are the excellent restaurant and the lounge bar where some irresistible cocktail mixing takes place.

PETERSHAM HOTEL £££

Map p470 (☎020-8940 0061; www.petershamhotel.co.uk; Nightingale Lane, TW10; s £135-175, d £185-250, ste £320, weekend s £95-135, d £165; 📶; ⊖Richmond or 🚉Richmond then 🚌65) Neatly perched on the slope down Richmond Hill leading across Petersham Meadows towards the Thames, the impressive Petersham offers stunning, Arcadian views at every turn. And its restaurant, with its large windows gazing down to the river, has some choice panoramas. The 60 rooms are classically styled but those with good river views are dearer.

SLEEPING

Understand London

London Today

By hosting the 2012 Olympic Games, London attracted a staggering amount of attention and scrutiny from talking heads, the media and the chattering classes. The city was appraised, reappraised, examined and compared against a raft of expectations that would capsize a lesser city, especially one in the grip of a nationwide recession. Yet London has reaffirmed itself as a capital of transformative ideas, cultural dynamism and change.

Best on Film

Withnail & I (1986) Cult black comedy about two unemployed actors in 1969 Camden.

Love Actually (2003) Syrupy romantic comedy with great shots of the city.

Skyfall (2012) Sam Mendes' masterful contribution to the James Bond franchise.

Notting Hill (1999) Soppy rom-com with Hugh Grant and Julia Roberts in an atypically all-white Notting Hill.

Shaun of the Dead (2004) The zombie hordes come to...Crouch End.

Best in Print

London Fields (Martin Amis; 1989) Gripping, dark postmodern study of London lowlife.

Journal of the Plague Year (Daniel Defoe; 1722) Defoe's classic reconstruction of the Great Plague of 1665.

London Under (Peter Ackroyd; 2012) Mesmerising exploration of the city's subterranean world.

Oliver Twist (Charles Dickens; 1837) Unforgettable characters and a vivid depiction of Victorian London seen through the eyes of a hapless orphan.

Sour Sweet (Timothy Mo; 1982) Moving portrayal of a Hong Kong Chinese family moving to London in the 1960s.

London (Edward Rutherfurd; 1997) Sweeping drama that brings London's epic history vividly to life.

London vs the Rest?

As the economic downturn double-dips its way into the record books, the UK is increasingly a nation of two halves: London (plus the Southeast), and the rest. Between 2007 and 2011, the London economy grew by a huge 12.4% against a backdrop of negative growth in many other parts of the British Isles. London is the world's sixth largest city economy: in most parts of the city, property prices have continued to gallop ahead, with many areas registering double-digit increases. In 2013, the cost of an average London home surged past £500,000, double the national mean. Other parts of the UK seem catatonic in comparison. London employment has been rosier than the rest of the nation since 2007 while average incomes are 30% higher than elsewhere in the country. And London is increasingly attractive to foreigners: in 2012 London was amusingly declared France's sixth biggest city in terms of French population, according to the number of French nationals living in the UK capital (as many as 400,000).

The Olympic Effect

The UK's most painful recession since records began was briefly forgotten during the ebullience of the 2012 Olympic Games in London, when Team GB seized their best gold medal haul since the 1908 event. After seven years of planning, it was the city's big moment in the global spotlight: the £8.92 billion price-tagged sporting event in London won almost universal media acclaim, with many hailing it as one of the best Olympic Games ever. International Olympic Committee (IOC) President Jacques Rogge even declared that the games had 'refreshed the Olympic movement'. The games left an area of East London with world-class sports facilities and gave added gloss (and brand new transport infrastructure) to one of the most visited cities in the world. A signature challenge since the athletes took their last bows in August 2012 has been to ensure the Olympics legacy – investing in sport in school and society to produce the UK champions of tomorrow – outlasts the short-lived glow of the games themselves.

Ethnicity & Multiculturalism

London is undergoing its most thorough ethnic transformation in its history. The 2011 census revealed that white Britons in London now constitute a minority (45%) for the first time in its 2000-year history. The figures coincided with a period of growing skepticism over the EU, exacerbated by the ongoing Eurozone crisis. Many Londoners have called for greater efforts to promote integration of ethnic communities into British culture, but the subject remains a political minefield, especially since the terrorist bombings on the London Transport network in 2005. The 2013 murder of off-duty soldier Lee Rigby in Woolwich by two Islamist extremists underscored fears. Some Londoners insist immigrants should somehow conform to a national credo, while others point the finger at UK foreign policy, insisting it is divisive.

Austerity & Change

After the 2010 general election, the Conservative Party and Liberal Democrats were forced to forge the first coalition cabinet since WWII, with David Cameron as prime minister. Rarely has a UK government taken charge in more economically blighted circumstances: with an economy crippled by debt and overspend, a new Age of Austerity dawned. Some pundits linked the devastating London riots of 2011 with cutbacks and economic hardship; others blamed the erosion of social and personal responsibility in modern Britain. Despite the disorder and buoyed by popular support, tousle-haired and bouncy Conservative Boris Johnson defied his critics, securing a narrowly won re-election for a second term as Mayor of London in 2012.

Moving Forwards

An ambitious redesign of London's transport options is either in the pipeline or already on the streets. Launched in 2010, the popular Barclays Cycle Hire Scheme has transformed the way a large number of people – including visitors – get about town. The London Overground was expanded and a cable car over the River Thames now lashes together North Greenwich and the Royal Docks. Crossrail will bring high-frequency underground trains linking east and west London along two brand new lines costing £15.9 billion, due to commence operation in 2018. The already iconic Shard in London Bridge was completed in 2012 and the 37-storey Walkie-Talkie (20 Fenchurch St) and 225m-tall Cheesegrater (the Leadenhall Building) in the City should be finished by 2014.

if London were 100 people

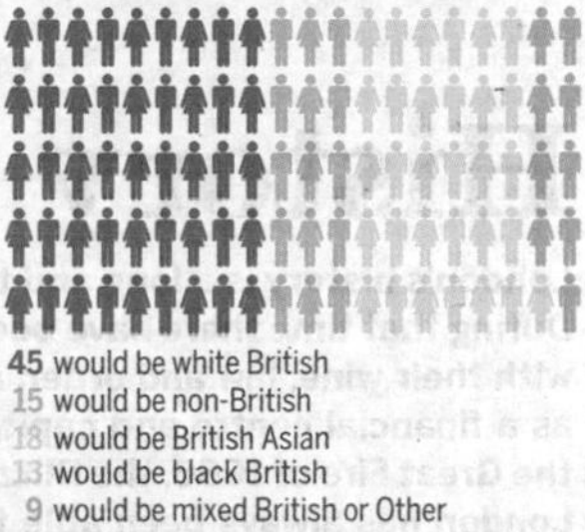

belief systems

(% of population)

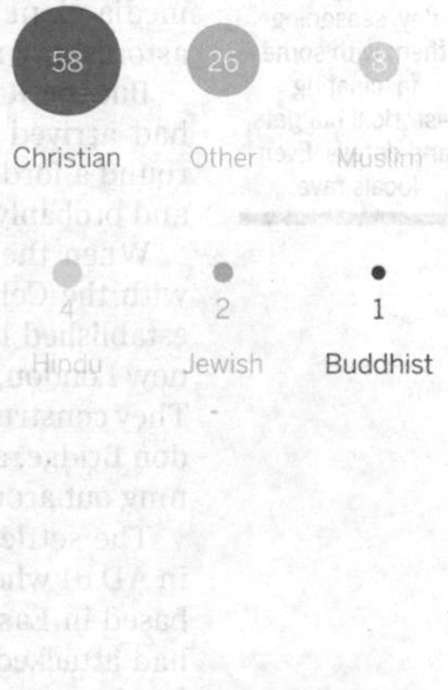

population per sq km

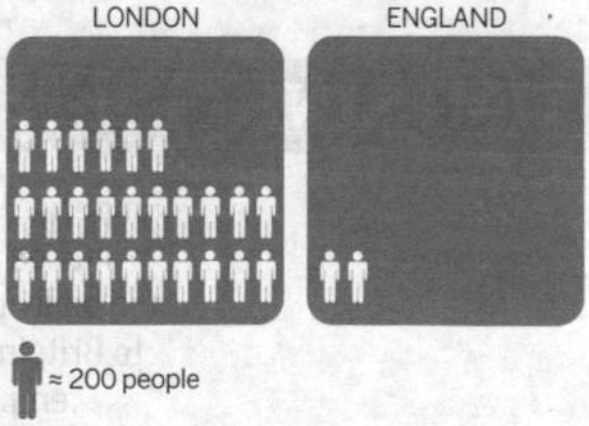

History

London's history is a long and turbulent narrative spanning more than two millennia. During that time there have been good times (the arrival of the Romans, for example, with their wine, law and order, and road-building skills, and the expansion of London as a financial centre and capital of an empire) and bad times (apocalyptic plagues, the Great Fire of 1666, the Blitz carpet bombing of WWII). But even when on its knees London has always been able to get up, dust itself off and move on, constantly re-inventing itself along the way.

Hidden London (www.hidden-london.com) exposes London's 'minor districts and localities' to the light of day, seasoning them with some fascinating historical nuggets and details. Even locals rave.

Londinium

London was settled by the Romans, and the area, particularly the City of London, has been inhabited continuously ever since. As a result, archaeologists have had to dig deep to discover the city's past, relying more often than not on redevelopment to allow excavations. The Walbrook Sq building site, for example, future headquarters of the financial media giant Bloomberg in the heart of the City, continues to yield an astonishing number of Roman finds.

But the Romans were not the first on the block. The Iron Age Celts had arrived in Britain sometime in the 4th century BC and settled round a ford in the Thames. The river was twice as wide as it is today, and probably served as a barrier separating tribal groups.

When the Romans first visited in the 1st century BC, they traded with the Celts. In 43 AD, an invasion force led by Emperor Claudius established the port of Londinium, the first real settlement at what is now London, and used it as a springboard to capture Celtic strongholds. They constructed a wooden bridge across the Thames near today's London Bridge, and this became the focal point for a network of roads fanning out around the region.

The settlement's development as a trading centre was interrupted in AD 61 when an army led by Boudicca, queen of the Celtic Iceni tribe based in East Anglia, exacted violent retribution on the Romans, who had attacked her kingdom, flogged her and raped her daughters. The Iceni overran Camulodunum (now Colchester), which had become the

TIMELINE

55–54 BC

Emperor Julius Caesar makes a fast-paced and badly planned visit to Britain and returns empty-handed – though the Senate declares a celebration lasting 20 days.

AD 43

The Romans invade Britain, led by Emperor Claudius, and stay for many years.

47–50

A defensive fort at Londinium is built. The name Londinium is probably taken from a Celtic place name (a common Roman practice) but there is no evidence as to what it actually means.

capital of Roman Britannia, and then turned on Londinium, massacring its inhabitants and razing the settlement before the Romans defeated them. They say that if you dig deep enough in the City you'll find a layer of rubble and soft red ash dating from that great conflagration.

The Romans rebuilt Londinium around Cornhill, the highest elevation north of the bridge, between 80 and 90 AD. About a century later they wrapped a defensive wall some 2.7m thick and 6m high around it. Towers were added to strengthen it, and the original gates – Aldgate, Ludgate, Newgate and Bishopsgate – are remembered as place names in today's London. By then Londinium, a centre for business and trade but not a fully fledged *colonia* (settlement), was an imposing city with a massive basilica, an amphitheatre, a forum and the governor's palace.

By the middle of the 3rd century Londinium was home to some 30,000 people of various ethnic groups, with temples dedicated to a large number of cults. When Emperor Constantine converted to Christianity in 312, the fledgling religion became the empire's – and London's – official cult, seeing off its rival, Mithraism.

In the 4th century, the Roman Empire in Britain began to decline, with increasing attacks by the Picts and Scotti in the north and the Saxons, Germanic tribes originating from north of the Rhine, in the southeast. In 410, when the embattled Emperor Honorius refused them military aid, the Romans abandoned Britain, and Londinium was reduced to a sparsely populated backwater.

Lundenwic

What happened to Londinium after the Roman withdrawal is still the subject of much historical debate. While there is no written record whatsoever of the town from 457 to 604, most historians now think that Romano-Britons continued to live here even as Saxon settlers established farmsteads and small villages in the area.

Lundenwic (or 'London settlement') was established outside the city walls due west of Londinium and around present-day Aldwych and Charing Cross as a Saxon trade settlement. By the early 7th century the Saxons had been converted to Christianity by the Pope's emissary Augustine. Lundenwic was an episcopate and the first St Paul's Cathedral was established at the top of Ludgate Hill.

This infant trading community grew in importance and attracted the attention of the Vikings in Denmark. They attacked in 842 and again nine years later, burning Lundenwic to the ground. Under the leadership of King Alfred the Great of Wessex, the Saxon population fought back, driving the Danes out in 886. Alfred resettled the old Roman city, now known as Lundunburg or Lunduntown, farther east

Historical Reads

- *London: The Biography (Peter Ackroyd)*
- *London: A History in Maps (Peter Barber)*
- *Unearthing London: The Ancient World beneath the Metropolis (Simon Webb)*
- *A Traveller's History of London (Richard Tames)*
- *London: The Illustrated History (John Clark & Cathy Ross)*
- *London at War (Philip Ziegler)*

c 120–125

A vast conflagration, known as the 'Hadrianic Fire' after Emperor Hadrian, sweeps through Londinium, devastating the settlement.

122

Emperor Hadrian pays a visit to Londinium and many impressive municipal buildings are constructed. Roman London reaches its peak, with temples, bathhouses, a fortress and a port.

190–225

London Wall is constructed around Londinium after outsiders breach Hadrian's Wall to the north. The wall encloses an area of just 132 hectares and is 5m high.

410

The Emperor Honorius decrees that the colony of Britannia should take care of its own defences, thus effectively ending the Roman presence in Londinium.

towards the River Lea, with a trading wharf at Billingsgate, and south of the Thames to Sudwerke (south work), today's Southwark.

Saxon London grew into a prosperous and well-organised town divided into 20 wards, each with its own alderman, and resident colonies of German merchants and French vintners. But attacks by the Danes continued apace, and the Saxon leadership was weakening; in 1016 Londoners were forced to accept the Danish leader Knut (Canute) as king of England.

With the death of Knut's brutal son Harthacanute in 1042, the throne passed to the Saxon Edward the Confessor, who went on to found an abbey and palace at Westminster on what was then an island at the mouth of the (now underground) River Tyburn. When Edward moved his court to Westminster, the port, now the City, became the trading and mercantile centre, while Westminster became the seat of politics, administration and justice – an arrangement that continues today.

EAST LONDON

For trivia, little-known facts and endless specialist information on the history of the East End and its personalities, click on East London History (www.eastlondonhistory.com).

The Normans

The most famous date in English history, 1066, marks the real birth of England as a unified nation state. After the death of Edward the Confessor in 1066, a dispute over who would take the English throne spelled disaster for the Saxon kings. Harold Godwinson, the Earl of Wessex, was anointed successor by Edward on his deathbed, but this enraged William, the Duke of Normandy, who claimed that Edward had promised him the throne. William mounted a massive invasion of England from France and on 14 October defeated Harold at the Battle of Hastings, before marching on London to claim his prize. William, now dubbed 'the Conqueror', was crowned king of England in the new Westminster Abbey on 25 December 1066, ensuring the Norman conquest was complete. He subsequently found himself in control of what was by then the richest and largest city in the kingdom.

William distrusted the 'vast and fierce populace' of London, and to intimidate his new subjects as well as protect himself from them, he built 10 castles within a day's march of London, including the White Tower, the core of the Tower of London. Cleverly, he kept the prosperous merchants on side by confirming the city's independence in exchange for taxes. London soon became the principal town of England.

Medieval London

The last of the Norman kings, Stephen, died in 1154, and the throne passed to Henry II of the powerful House of Plantagenet, which would rule England for the next two and a half centuries. Always short of a penny, Henry's successors were happy to to let the City of London

597

Ethelbert, the first English monarch to convert to Christianity, welcomes St Augustine and his missionaries to Canterbury, ensuring that city's religious supremacy.

c 600

The Saxon trade settlement of Lundenwic – literally 'London settlement' – is formed to the west of the Roman site of Londinium.

604

The first Christian cathedral dedicated to St Paul is built on the site of the current cathedral; fashioned from wood, it burns down in 675 and is later rebuilt.

852

Vikings settle in London, having attacked the city 10 years before; a period of great struggle between Wessex and Denmark begins for control of the Thames.

A BOY, A PUSS & CITY HALL

Boris Johnson may be London's most popular mayor in recent memory, but he has a long way to go before he can compete with his 15th-century predecessor, Dick Whittington.

Legend tells us that Dick was a country lad who came to the city to seek his fortune with his faithful feline in tow. Soon disillusioned with the Big Smoke, he was about to turn back when he heard the bells of the Church of St Mary-le-Bow ringing out the message, 'Turn again, Whittington, thrice mayor of London'. Dick did just that and went on to find fame and fortune. A 19th-century stone on Highgate Hill, at the point where he is said to have heard the bells, features a bronze cat and makes reference to the 'thrice' mayor 'Sir' Richard Whittington.

It's a nice story but almost entirely inaccurate. Dick Whittington was the third son of an affluent Gloucestershire family who arrived in London in a 'cat', as coastal boats were then called. He may indeed have heard those bells but they told lies too: he was mayor four times between 1397 and 1419. Oh, and Dick was never knighted.

keep its independence as long as its merchants continued to finance their wars and building projects. When Richard I (known as 'the Lionheart'), a king who spent a mere six months of his life in England, needed funds for his crusade to the Holy Land, he recognised the city as a self-governing commune in return for cash.

A city built on trade and commerce, London would always guard its independence fiercely, as Richard's successor, King John, learnt the hard way. In 1215 John was forced to cede to the powerful barons, and to curb his arbitrary demands for pay-offs from the city. Among those pressing him to put his seal to the landmark Magna Carta, which effectively diluted royal power, was the by-then powerful lord mayor of the City of London; the first holder of this office, Henry Fitz Aylwin, had taken office just a quarter-century before.

Commerce and trade with Europe in wine, furs, cloth and other goods boomed, and the nobles, barons and bishops built lavish houses for themselves along what is now The Strand, which connected the City with the Palace of Westminster, the new seat of royal power. The first stone London Bridge was completed in 1209, although it was frequently too crowded to cross, and most people traversed the river on a small boat called a wherry. The watermen's touting shouts of 'Oars? Oars?' are said to have confused many a country visitor tempted by more carnal services.

Fire was a constant hazard in the cramped and narrow houses and lanes of 14th-century London, but disease caused by unsanitary living

Work on the first stone London Bridge was completed in 1209 after the earlier Norman wooden bridge was destroyed twice, once by a gale in 1091 and again by fire in 1136. The current bridge dates from 1972.

886

King Alfred the Great, first king of England, reclaims London for the Saxons and founds a new settlement within the walls of the old Roman town.

1016

The Danes return to London and Knut is crowned king of England. Most famous in English folklore for failing to command the waves, Knut ushers in two decades of peace.

1065

Westminster Abbey is first consecrated, even though the building is not completed for another quarter-century.

Westminster Abbey (p86)

conditions and impure drinking water from the Thames was the greatest threat to the burgeoning city. In 1348 rats on ships from Europe brought the Black Death, a bubonic plague that wiped out almost half the population of about 80,000 over the next year and a half.

With their numbers down, there was growing unrest among labourers, for whom violence became a way of life, and rioting was commonplace. In 1381, miscalculating – or just disregarding – the mood of the nation, the young Richard II tried to impose a poll tax on everyone in the realm. Tens of thousands of peasants, led by the soldier Wat Tyler and the prelates Jack Straw and John Ball, marched in protest on London. The Archbishop of Canterbury was dragged from the Tower and beheaded, several ministers were murdered and many buildings were razed before the Peasants' Revolt ran its course and its leaders executed.

Sanitation in London could have taken an evolutionary leap forwards in 1596 when Sir John Harrington invented a flushing loo with a cistern, but the novel concept failed to find a market.

London gained wealth and stature under the Houses of Lancaster and York in the 15th century, but the two houses' struggle for ascendancy led to the catastrophic Wars of the Roses. The century's greatest episode of political intrigue occurred during this time: in 1483 the 12-year-old Edward V of the House of York reigned for only two months before vanishing with his younger brother into the Tower of London, never to be seen again. Whether or not their uncle, Richard III – who became the next king – murdered the boys has been the subject of much conjecture over the centuries (Shakespeare would have us believe he did the evil deed). In 1674 workers found a chest containing the skeletons of two children near the White Tower, which were assumed to be the princes' remains and reburied in Westminster Abbey.

Richard III didn't have long to enjoy the hot seat: he was killed in 1485 at the Battle of Bosworth by Henry Tudor, who as Henry VII became the first monarch of the eponymous dynasty. In September 2012 Richard's remains, confirmed by rigorous DNA tests, were excavated beneath a car park in central Leicester.

The House of Tudor

Though the House of Tudor lasted but 120 years and three generations it is the best-known English dynasty. London became one of the largest and most important cities in Europe during its reign, which coincided with the discovery of the Americas and thriving world trade.

Henry's son and successor, Henry VIII, was the most extravagant of the clan, instructing new palaces to be built at Whitehall and St James's, and bullying his lord chancellor, Cardinal Thomas Wolsey, into giving him Hampton Court.

Henry's life was dominated by the need to produce a male heir, which indirectly led to his split with the Catholic Church. This occurred in

1066

After his great victory over King Harold at the Battle of Hastings, William, Duke of Normandy, aka William the Conqueror, is crowned in Westminster Abbey.

1078

William builds 10 castles within a day's march of London, first in earth and timber and then in stone, including the White Tower.

1091

The Great London Tornado sweeps through town, destroying much of the original church of St Mary-le-Bow, the wooden London Bridge and countless houses.

1097

William Rufus, son of William the Conqueror, commences the construction of Westminster Hall. The hall, possibly the largest in Europe at the time, is completed two years later.

1534 after the Pope refused to annul his marriage to Catherine of Aragon, who had borne him only a daughter after 24 years of marriage. Turning his back on Rome, he made himself the supreme head of the church in England and married Anne Boleyn, the second of his six wives. He 'dissolved' (abolished) London's monasteries, seized the church's vast wealth and property and smashed ecclesiastical culture. The face of the medieval city was transformed: much of the land requisitioned for hunting later became Hyde, Regent's and Richmond Parks, while many of the religious houses disappeared, leaving only their names in particular areas, such as Whitefriars and Blackfriars (after the colour of the habits worn by Carmelite and Dominican monks).

Despite his penchant for settling differences with the axe (two of his six wives and Wolsey's replacement as lord chancellor, Thomas More, were beheaded, along with 32 other leaders) and his persecution of both Catholics and fellow Protestants who didn't toe the line, Henry VIII remained a popular monarch until his death in 1547. The reign of Mary I, his daughter by Catherine of Aragon, saw a brief return to Catholicism, during which the queen sanctioned the burning to death of 200 Protestants at Smithfield and earned herself the nickname 'Bloody Mary'. By the time Elizabeth I, Henry VIII's daughter by Anne Boleyn, took the throne, Catholicism was a waning force, and hundreds of people who dared to suggest otherwise were carted off to the gallows at Tyburn near today's Marble Arch.

BEGGARS

Begging was treated very harshly in 16th-century London. Henry VIII instructed that able-bodied beggars and vagabonds be whipped, beaten or even imprisoned, but such policies failed to stem the tide of vagrants.

Elizabethan London

The 45-year reign (1558–1603) of Elizabeth I is still looked upon as a 'golden age' of English history, and it was just as significant for London. During these four decades English literature reached new and still unbeaten heights, and religious tolerance gradually became accepted doctrine, although Catholics and some Protestants still faced persecution. England became a naval superpower, having defeated the Spanish Armada in 1588, and the city established itself as the premier world trade market with the opening of the Royal Exchange by Elizabeth in 1570.

London was blooming economically and physically: in the second half of the 16th century the population doubled to 200,000. The first recorded map of London was published in 1558, and John Stow produced *A Survey of London,* the first history of the city, in 1598.

This was also the golden era of English drama, and the works of William Shakespeare, Christopher Marlowe and Ben Jonson packed new playhouses, such as the Rose (built in 1587) and the Globe (1599). Both were in Southwark, a notoriously 'naughty' place at the time, teeming with stews (brothels) and bawdy taverns. Most importantly, they

1170

Archbishop of Canterbury Thomas Becket, born in Ironmongers Lane and known as Thomas of London in his lifetime, is murdered by four of Henry II's knights.

1176

London Bridge is built in stone for the first time, though it is frequently too crowded to cross, and most people traverse the river by boat.

1189

The coronation of Richard I sees a pogrom in which Jews of both sexes and all ages are killed in London.

1215

King John signs the Magna Carta (literally 'Great Charter'), an agreement with England's barons forming the basis of constitutional law in England.

WHAT'S IN THE NAME?

Many of London's street names, especially in the City, recall the goods that were traded there: Poultry, Cornhill, Sea Coal Lane, Milk and Bread Sts and the more cryptic Friday St, where you bought fish for that fasting day. Other meanings are not so obvious. The '-wich' or '-wych' in names like Greenwich, Aldwych and Dulwich come from the Saxon word *wic*, meaning 'settlement'. *Ea* or *ey* is an old word for 'island' or 'marsh'; thus Chelsea (Island of Shale), Bermondsey (Bermond's Island), Battersea (Peter's Island) and Hackney (Haca's Marsh). In Old English *ceap* meant 'market'; hence Eastcheap is where the plebs shopped in medieval times, while Cheapside (originally Westcheap) was reserved for the royal household. 'Borough' comes from *burg*, Old English for 'fort' or 'town'. And the odd names East Ham and West Ham come from the Old English *hamm* or 'hem'; they were just bigger enclosed (or 'hemmed-in') settlements than the more standard hamlets.

were outside the jurisdiction of the city, which frowned upon and even banned theatre.

When Elizabeth died without an heir in 1603, she was succeeded by her second cousin, who was crowned James I. Although the son of the Catholic Mary, Queen of Scots (not to be confused with Elizabeth's half-sister Mary), James was slow to improve conditions for England's Catholics and drew their wrath. He narrowly escaped death when the plot by Guy Fawkes and his co-conspirators to blow up the Houses of Parliament on 5 November 1605 was uncovered. The discovery of the audacious plan is commemorated on this date each year with bonfires and fireworks.

The Civil Wars & Restoration

When James I's son, Charles I, came to the throne in 1625, his intransigent personality and total belief in the 'divine right of kings' set the monarchy on a collision course with an increasingly confident parliament at Westminster and a City of London tiring of extortionate taxes. The crunch came when Charles tried to arrest five antagonistic members of parliament, who fled to the city, and in 1642 the country slid into civil war.

The Puritans (extremist Protestants) and the city's expanding merchant class threw their support behind Oliver Cromwell, leader of the Parliamentarians (the so-called Roundheads), who battled the Royalist troops (the Cavaliers). London firmly backed the Roundheads, and Charles I was defeated in 1646, although a Second Civil War (1648–49)

1241

Cock Lane in Smithfields effectively becomes London's first red-light district.

1340

The population of London reaches to between 50,000 and 80,000, similar to other large cities in Europe at the same time.

1348

Rats on ships from Europe bring the so-called Black Death, a bubonic plague that wipes out almost two-thirds of the city's residents over the following decades.

1455

The Wars of the Roses, a series of rebellions and battles between two houses of the Plantagenet Dynasty – Lancaster (red rose) and York (white rose) – erupts and rages for three decades.

and a Third Civil War (1649–51) continued to wreak havoc on what had been a stable and prosperous nation.

Charles I was beheaded for treason outside Banqueting House in Whitehall on 30 January 1649, famously wearing two shirts on the cold morning of his execution so as not to shiver and appear cowardly. Cromwell ruled the country as a republic for the next 11 years, during which time Charles' son, Charles II, continued fighting for the restoration of the monarchy. During this period Cromwell banned theatre, dancing, Christmas and just about anything remotely fun.

After Cromwell's death, parliament decided that the royals weren't so bad after all, refused to recognise the authority of Cromwell's successor, his son Richard, and restored the exiled Charles II to the throne in 1660. Death was deemed too good for Cromwell, who was exhumed, hung, drawn and quartered at Tyburn. His rotting head was displayed on a spike at Westminster Hall for two decades. Richard went into exile.

Plague & Fire

In mid-17th-century London, the shout 'garde loo' alerted all passers-by that a chamberpot was about to be emptied into the street from an upstairs window. Crowded, filthy London had suffered from recurrent outbreaks of bubonic plague since the 14th century, but nothing had prepared it for the Great Plague of 1665, which dwarfed all previous outbreaks.

As the plague spread, families affected were forced to stay inside for 40 days until the victim recovered or died. Previously crowded streets were deserted, the churches and markets were closed, and an eerie silence descended. To make matters worse, the mayor believed that dogs and cats were the spreaders of the plague and ordered them all killed, thus ridding the disease-carrying rats of their natural predators. By the time the winter cold arrested the epidemic, an estimated 100,000 people had perished, their corpses collected and thrown into vast 'plague pits'.

Previously crowded streets were deserted, and an eerie silence descended

The plague finally began to wane in November 1665, leaving the population devastated and superstitious that the deaths had been punishment from God for London's moral squalor. Londoners scarcely had a year to recover when another disaster struck. The city had for centuries been prone to fire, as nearly all buildings were constructed from wood and thatch, but the mother of all blazes broke out on 2 September 1666 in a bakery in Pudding Lane.

It didn't seem like much to begin with – the mayor himself dismissed it as 'something a woman might pisse out' before going back to bed –

1476

William Caxton, a prominent merchant from Kent, establishes his press at Westminster, printing nearly 100 volumes of works by the likes of Geoffrey Chaucer and the poet John Gower.

LEEMAGE / GETTY IMAGES ©

William Caxton

1558

The first detailed map of London is commissioned by a group of German merchants; a golden age of peace, art and literature begins when Queen Elizabeth I takes the throne.

1569

In order to raise money, Elizabeth I holds the world's first national lottery, with a top prize of $5000; tickets cost 10 shillings and the draw takes place next to old St Paul's Cathedral.

LONDON'S UNDERGROUND RIVERS

The Thames is not London's only river: many now course underground. Some survive only in place names: the Hole Bourne, Wells, Tyburn, Walbrook and Westbourne, which was dammed in 1730 to form the Serpentine in Hyde Park. The most famous of all, the Fleet, rises in Hampstead and Kenwood ponds and flows south through Camden Town, King's Cross, Farringdon Rd and New Bridge St, where it empties into the Thames at Blackfriars Bridge. It had been used as an open sewer and dumping area for entrails by butchers for centuries; the Elizabethan playwright Ben Jonson describes a voyage on the Fleet on a hot summer's night in which every stroke of the oars 'belch'd forth an ayre as hot as the muster of all your night-tubs discharging their merd-urinous load'. After the Great Fire, Christopher Wren oversaw the deepening and widening of the Fleet into a canal, but this was covered over in 1733 and the rest of the river three decades later.

but the unusual autumn heat combined with rising winds meant the fire raged out of control for days, reducing some 80% of London to carbon. Only eight people died (officially at least), but most of London's medieval, Tudor and Jacobean architecture was obliterated. The fire was finally stopped at Pye Corner in Smithfield, on the very edge of London, by blowing up all the buildings in the inferno's path. It is hard to overstate the scale of the destruction: 88 churches, including St Paul's Cathedral, and more than 13,000 houses were razed, leaving tens of thousands of people homeless. Many Londoners left for the countryside, or sought their fortunes in the New World.

For a real-time experience of a 17th-century blogger, click on The Diary of Samuel Pepys (www.pepysdiary.com), where a new entry written by the celebrated diarist is published daily.

Wren's London

One positive outcome of the inferno was that it created a blank canvas upon which master architect Christopher Wren could build his 51 magnificent new churches and cathedral. Wren's plan for rebuilding the entire city was deemed too expensive and many landlords opposed it; the familiar pattern of streets that had grown up over the centuries since the time of the Romans quickly reappeared. However, new laws stipulated that brick and stone designs replace the old timber-framed, overhanging Tudor houses and that many roads be widened. The fire accelerated the movement of the wealthy away from the City and into what is now the West End.

By way of memorialising the blaze – and symbolising the restoration and resurgence of the subsequent years – the Monument, designed by Wren, was erected in 1677 near the site of the fire's outbreak. At the time the 61m-tall column was by far the highest structure in the city, visible from everywhere in the capital.

1599

The Globe opens in Southwark alongside other London theatres such as the Rose and the Swan; most of Shakespeare's plays written after 1599 are staged here, including *Macbeth* and *Hamlet*.

1605

A Catholic plot to blow up James I by hiding gunpowder under the House of Commons is foiled; Guy Fawkes, one of the alleged plotters, is executed the following year.

1613

The Globe Theatre catches fire and burns to the ground; it is rebuilt the following year but closed by the Puritans and demolished in 1642.

1649

King Charles I is executed at the height of the English Civil Wars, a series of armed conflicts and political machinations between Royalists and Parliamentarians.

In 1685 some 1500 Huguenot refugees arrived in London, fleeing persecution in Catholic France; another 3500 would follow. Many of them turned their hands to the manufacture of luxury goods such as silks and silverware in and around Spitalfields and Clerkenwell, which were already populated with Irish, Jewish and Italian immigrants and artisans. London was fast becoming one of the world's most cosmopolitan places.

The Glorious – ie bloodless – Revolution in 1688 brought the Dutch King William of Orange to the English throne. He relocated from Whitehall Palace to a new palace in Kensington Gardens, and the surrounding area smartened itself up accordingly. In order to raise finances for his war with France – and as a result of the City's transformation into a centre of finance rather than manufacturing – William III established the Bank of England in 1694.

London's growth continued unabated, and by 1700 it was Europe's largest city, with some 600,000 people. The influx of foreign workers brought expansion to the east and south, while those who could afford it headed to the more salubrious environs of the north and west. London remains today, more or less, divided along these lines.

The crowning glory of the 'Great Rebuilding', Wren's St Paul's Cathedral, was completed in 1710. A masterpiece of English baroque architecture, it remains one of the city's most prominent landmarks.

ST PAUL'S

For superb city views from London's most iconic piece of ecclesiastical architecture, climb the 528 stairs (no lift) to the Golden Gallery in the dome of Sir Christopher Wren's magnum opus: 300-year-old St Paul's Cathedral.

Georgian London

The last of the Stuart monarchs, Queen Anne, died without an heir in 1714. Although there were some 50 Catholic relatives with stronger claims, a search was immediately launched to find a Protestant relative since the 1701 Act of Settlement forbade Roman Catholics from taking the throne. Eventually George of Hanover, a great-grandson of James I, arrived from Germany and was crowned king of England, though he never learned to speak English. Meanwhile, the increasingly literate population got their first newspapers, which began to cluster around Fleet St.

Robert Walpole's Whig Party controlled parliament during much of George I's reign and, as 'First Lord of the Treasury', effectively became Britain's first prime minister. He was presented with 10 Downing St, which has been the official residence of nearly every prime minister since.

London grew at a phenomenal pace during this time, and measures were taken to make the city more accessible. The Roman wall surrounding the City of London was torn down, and Westminster Bridge opened in 1750, only the second span over the Thames after London Bridge.

Georgian London saw a great creative surge in music, art and architecture. Court composer George Frederick Handel wrote *Water Music* (1717) and *Messiah* (1741) while living here, and in 1755 Dr Johnson published the first English dictionary. William Hogarth, Thomas Gainsborough

1661

Oliver Cromwell's body is dug up from Westminster Abbey and given a posthumous 'execution'; his head is then stuck on a spike and displayed above Westminster Hall.

1665

The Great Plague ravages London, wiping out a fifth of the population. Less catastrophic than the 14th-century Black Death, it is remembered as one of Europe's last outbreaks.

1666

The Great Fire of London burns for five days, destroying the city Shakespeare had known, leaving four-fifths of the metropolis in smoking ruins.

1702

The *Daily Courant*, London's first daily newspaper, is published in Fleet St, consisting of a single page of news.

and Joshua Reynolds produced some of their finest paintings and engravings, and many of London's most elegant buildings, streets and squares were erected or laid out by the likes of architects John Soane, his pupil, Robert Smirke, and the prolific John Nash.

All the while, though, London was becoming ever more segregated and lawless. Indeed, contemporary newspapers suggest it was the most crime-ridden city in Europe, and even George II was relieved of 'purse, watch and buckles' during a stroll through Kensington Gardens. This was Hogarth's London, in which the wealthy built fine mansions in attractive squares and gathered in fashionable new coffee houses while the poor huddled together in appalling slums and drowned their sorrows with cheap gin. To curb rising crime, two magistrates, including the writer Henry Fielding, established the Bow Street Runners in 1749. This voluntary group – effectively a forerunner to the Metropolitan Police Force (set up in 1829) – challenged the official marshals, or thief-takers, who were suspected (often correctly) of colluding with the criminals.

The stench on the streets of medieval London would have been unbearable, an overpowering and grotesque blend of urine, excrement, rotting meat, muck, offal, blood and the hideous aromas that emanated from the tanneries.

In 1780 parliament proposed to lift the law preventing Catholics buying or inheriting property. One MP, Lord George Gordon, led a 'No Popery' demonstration that turned into the so-called Gordon Riots. A mob of 30,000 went on a rampage, attacking Irish labourers, and burning prisons, 'Papishe dens' (chapels) and several law courts. As many as 850 people died during the riots, including some who drank themselves to death after breaking into a Holborn distillery. The army managed to restore order only after five days of rioting.

As George III, forever remembered as the king who lost the American colonies, slid into dementia towards the end of the 18th century, his son, the Prince Regent, set up an alternative and considerably more fashionable court at Carlton House in Pall Mall. By this time London's population had mushroomed to just under a million.

Victorian London

In 1837 George III's 18-year-old granddaughter, Victoria, ascended the throne. During her long reign London would become the nerve centre of the largest and richest empire the world had ever known, covering a quarter of the globe's surface and ruling more than 500 million people.

New docks were built to facilitate the booming trade with the colonies, and railways began to fan out from the capital. The world's first underground railway opened between Paddington and Farringdon Rd in 1863 and was such a success that other lines quickly followed. Many of London's most famous buildings and landmarks were built at this time:

1707

The first-ever sitting of the parliament of the Kingdom of Great Britain occurs in London as the 1707 Act of Union brings England and Scotland together under one parliament.

1711

Sir Christopher Wren's St Paul's Cathedral is officially completed, 35 years after old St Paul's Cathedral is gutted in the Great Fire.

1759

The British Museum opens to the public for the first time, housed in Montagu House in Bloomsbury and levying no admission fee to all 'studious and curious persons'.

1812

Charles Dickens, Victorian England's greatest novelist, is born in Portsmouth; many of his novels paint London in all its Victorian squalor.

ALBERT & THE GREAT EXHIBITION

In 1851 Queen Victoria's consort, the German-born Prince Albert, organised a huge celebration of new technology from around the world in Hyde Park. The so-called Great Exhibition was held in a 7.5-hectare iron and glass hothouse, a 'Crystal Palace' designed by gardener and architect Joseph Paxton using the newfangled plate glass. Some two million people flocked from elsewhere in Britain and abroad to marvel at the more than 100,000 exhibits. So successful was this first world's fair that Albert arranged for the profits to be ploughed into building two permanent exhibitions, which eventually became the Science and the Victoria & Albert Museums. The original (and revolutionary) structure itself was moved to Sydenham, where it burned down in 1936, but the area in southeast London – and its popular football club – retain the name. Exactly ten years after the exhibition the prince died of typhoid, and Victoria was so prostrate with grief that she wore mourning clothes until her death in 1901.

the recently renamed Elizabeth Tower (popularly known as 'Big Ben'; 1859), Royal Albert Hall (1871) and the magnificent Tower Bridge (1894).

The city, however, heaved under the burden of its vast size, and in 1858 London was in the grip of the 'Great Stink', when the population explosion so overtook the city's sanitation facilities that raw sewage seeped in through the floorboards of wealthy merchants' houses and the Houses of Parliament were draped with sheets soaked in lime chloride to allay the stench. Leading engineer Joseph Bazalgette tackled the problem by creating an underground network of sewers in the late 1850s. London had truly become the first modern metropolis.

Though the Victorian age is chiefly seen as one of great imperial power founded on industry, trade and commerce, intellectual achievement in the arts and sciences was enormous. The greatest chronicler of the times was Charles Dickens, whose *Oliver Twist* (1837) and other works explored the themes of poverty, hopelessness and squalor among the working classes. In 1859 Charles Darwin published his seminal and immensely controversial *On the Origin of Species* here, in which he outlined the theory of evolution.

Some of Britain's most capable prime ministers served during Victoria's 64-year reign, most notably William Gladstone (four terms between 1868 and 1894) and Benjamin Disraeli (who served in 1868 and again from 1874 to 1880). And with the creation of the London County Council (LCC) in 1889, the capital had its first-ever directly elected government.

Waves of immigrants, from Irish and Jews to Chinese and Indian sepoys, arrived in London during the 19th century, when the population exploded from one million to six million people. This breakneck

DEA, FRESMAN / GETTY IMAGES ©

Charles Dickens by Daniel Maclise

1814

The Great Beer Flood of London sees a flash-flood of almost 1.5 million litres of beer, causing death and destruction in the streets around a brewery in St Giles when vats rupture.

1829

London's first regular bus service – the 'omnibus' – begins, running from Paddington to Bank. The fare is 1 shilling.

1838

The coronation of Queen Victoria at Westminster Abbey ushers in a new era for London; the British capital becomes the economic and political centre of the world.

expansion was not beneficial to all – inner-city slums housed the poor in atrocious conditions of disease and overcrowding, while the affluent expanded to leafy suburbs, where new and comfortable housing was built. The inner suburbs of London are still predominantly made up of Victorian terraced housing.

Queen Victoria (she of 'We are not amused' fame) is often seen as a dour, humourless old curmudgeon but was an intelligent, progressive and passionate woman. Like the present monarch, Elizabeth II, she lived to celebrate her Diamond Jubilee in 1897, but died four years later at the age of 81 and was buried in Windsor. Her reign can be seen as the climax of British world supremacy.

From Empire to World War

Victoria's self-indulgent son Edward, the Prince of Wales, was already 60 by the time he was crowned Edward VII in 1901. London's *belle époque* was marked with the introduction of the first motorised double-decker buses in 1904, which replaced the horse-drawn versions that had plodded their trade since 1829; and a touch of glamour came in the form of luxury hotels, such as the Ritz in 1906, and department stores, such as Selfridges, in 1909. The first London Olympics were held at White City Stadium in 1908.

What became known as the Great War (or WWI) broke out in August 1914, and the first German bombs fell from zeppelins near the Guildhall a year later, killing 39 people. In all, some 670 Londoners were killed by bombs (half the national total of civilian casualties) and another 2000 wounded.

You may worry about today's vehicle emissions, but at the end of the 19th century, 1000 tonnes of horse dung would fall on the streets of London daily. Crossing sweepers, often young boys, made meagre earnings clearing a path for pedestrians to cross.

The Interwar Years

After the war ended in 1918, London's population continued to rise, reaching nearly 7.5 million in 1921. The LCC busied itself clearing slums and building new housing estates, while the suburbs spread ever deeper into the countryside.

Unemployment rose steadily, and in May 1926 a wage dispute in the coal industry escalated into a nine-day general strike, in which so many workers downed tools that London virtually ground to a halt. The army was called in to maintain order and to keep the buses and the Underground running, but the stage was set for more than half a century of industrial strife.

Despite the economic woes, the era brought a wealth of intellectual success. The 1920s were the heyday of the Bloomsbury Group, which counted writers Virginia Woolf and EM Forster and the economist John Maynard Keynes in its ranks. The spotlight shifted westwards

1843
Connecting Rotherhithe and Wapping, the Thames Tunnel, the first tunnel to be constructed under a navigable river, opens.

1851
The Great Exhibition, the brainchild of Victoria's consort, Albert, who would die a decade later, opens to great fanfare in the purpose-built Crystal Palace in Hyde Park.

1878
London's first electric lights are installed in Billingsgate Fish Market, using Jablochkoff candles; Holborn Viaduct and Victoria Embankment are illuminated at the same time.

1884
Greenwich Mean Time is established, making Greenwich Observatory the centre of world time, against which all clocks around the globe are set.

RICHARD TAMES: HISTORIAN

Prolific historian Richard Tames has published hundreds of books, including a score on London. Among them are the seminal *A Traveller's History of London* and the best-selling *Shakespeare's London on Five Groats a Day*.

Where in London is the past most palpable for you?
Well, there is big history and little history, isn't there? For big history it would be Westminster Abbey stuffed with all those statues. For little history it would be the East End, specifically the Brick Lane area. To think the likes of Jack London and Israel Zangwill walked up and down those streets.

Which period of history most closely reflects our own?
It would have to be the late Victorian and early Edwardian periods. If you consider the time from the 1890s into the early 20th century till 1910, along came the telephone, motorcar, powered flight and radio. They all fundamentally changed the dimensions of human experience in a way that was very difficult to work out or foresee at the time. With the information revolution we're doing exactly the same thing.

Which London street is the most diverse architecturally?
Probably the stretch of Woburn Place, Southampton Row and King's Way from Euston to Aldwych: Arts and Crafts LCC fire station, St Pancras New Church, Hotel Russell and so on.

Help settle the ultimate London argument. Which is the oldest...
Not the oldest pub in London question again? Ugh. Ye Olde Mitre (p215) probably deserves the title; Hoop and Grapes (p167) might claim it but it has not continuously functioned as a pub over the years. If you want to know how old a building is go backwards and downwards – no one fills in cellars. Ye Olde Cheshire Cheese (p167) has a wonderful array of cellars.

London in a word or two...
Semre eadem – it's always the same – yet always different. People still come for St Paul's and the Tower, but also now for the Shard and the Tate Modern.

to Fitzrovia in the following decade, when George Orwell and Dylan Thomas raised glasses with contemporaries at the Fitzroy Tavern on Charlotte St. Cinema, TV and radio arrived: the BBC aired its first radio broadcast from the roof of Marconi House on The Strand in 1922, and the first TV program from Alexandra Palace 14 years later.

The royal family took a knock when Edward VIII abdicated in 1936 to marry a woman who was not only twice divorced but – egad! – an American. The same year Oswald Mosley attempted to lead the black-

1893
The world's first outdoor aluminium statue, the Shaftesbury Memorial Fountain, topped with a statue of the Angel of Christian Charity (better known as Eros), is unveiled in Piccadilly Circus.

1901
Queen Victoria dies after reigning more than 63 years – the longest reign in British history. Elizabeth II could break the record in 2015.

1908
London hosts its first Olympic Games in the now-demolished White City Stadium; a total of 22 teams take part and the entire budget is £15,000.

1928
Parts of central London are deluged as the River Thames floods, killing 14 people and inundating streets and properties.

shirted British Union of Fascists on an anti-Jewish march through the East End but was repelled by a mob of around half a million at the famous Battle of Cable St.

WWII & the Blitz

Prime Minister Neville Chamberlain's policy of appeasing Adolf Hitler during the 1930s eventually proved misguided as the Führer's lust for expansion appeared insatiable. When Germany invaded Poland on 1 September 1939, Britain declared war, having signed a mutual-assistance pact with the Poles a few days beforehand. WWII (1939–45), Europe's darkest hour, had begun.

The first year was one of anxious waiting for London. Some 600,000 women and children had been evacuated to the countryside and the Battle of Britain raged elsewhere, primarily around Royal Air Force bases in England, but no bombs fell to disturb the blackout in the capital. On 7 September 1940 that all came to a swift and brutal end when the German Air Force, the Luftwaffe, dropped hundreds of bombs on the East End, killing 430 people.

The Blitz (from the German '*blitzkrieg*' or 'lightning war') lasted for 57 nights, and then continued intermittently until mid-May 1941. Some Underground stations were turned into giant bomb shelters, although one bomb rolled down the escalator at Bank station and exploded on the platform, killing more than 100 people. Londoners responded with

THE WORLD IN ONE CITY

London is historically made up of immigrants. Whether Roman, Viking, Anglo-Saxon, Norman, Huguenot, Irish or Jamaican, large numbers of ethnically diverse people have always been assimilated into the city. Africans are well documented to have served in the Roman army, but they first came to England in significant numbers as slaves in Elizabethan times and settled around St Giles. The first truly large influx of foreigners was in the late 17th century, when Huguenots, French Protestant refugees fleeing religious persecution at home, settled in Spitalfields and Soho. Jews have arrived over the past four centuries; their traditional areas have been the East End (particularly Spitalfields and Whitechapel) and northwest London. WWII brought Poles, Ukrainians and other Eastern Europeans to London, and today the Poles are a long-established community in Hammersmith and Shepherd's Bush.

The single biggest wave of immigration came in the 1950s, when, facing a labour shortage, the government allowed anyone born in a UK colony to have British citizenship. This brought a huge black population from the Caribbean and a large Asian diaspora from India, Bangladesh and Pakistan. The black population settled in West London and South London, while those from the subcontinent were concentrated in the East End. A third of all Londoners are now foreign-born, representing 270 different nationalities and 300 languages.

1936

The 'Year of Three Kings': George VI ascends the throne following the death of his father and abdication of his brother, who gave up his throne for an American divorcée.

1940–41

London is devastated by the Blitz, although miraculously St Paul's Cathedral and the Tower of London escape the bombing unscathed.

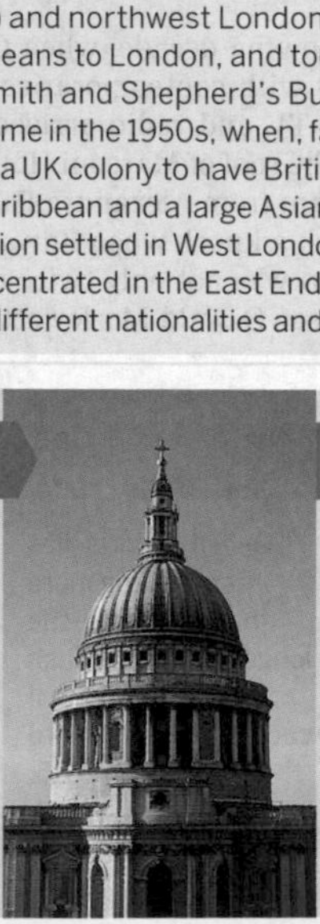

BARBARA VAN ZANTEN / GETTY IMAGES ©

St Paul's Cathedral (c 1943; p154)

1944

The Blackout is downgraded to a dim-out over London in autumn; Big Ben is again illuminated in April of the following year, along with full street lighting.

legendary resilience and stoicism. To the great admiration and respect of the people, the royal family refused to leave London during the bombing. When begged to allow her children to leave, Queen Elizabeth (the present monarch's late mother) apparently replied, 'the children could not possibly go without me, I wouldn't leave without the King, and the King won't leave'. Buckingham Palace took a direct hit during a bombing raid early in the campaign, famously prompting the Queen to announce that 'now we can look the East End in the face'. Winston Churchill, prime minister from 1940, orchestrated much of Britain's war strategy from the Cabinet War Rooms deep below Whitehall, and it was from here that he made his stirring wartime speeches.

London's spirit was tested again in June 1944, when Germany launched pilotless V-1 bombers (known as doodlebugs) over East London. By the time Nazi Germany capitulated in May 1945, up to a third of the East End and the City of London had been flattened, almost 30,000 Londoners killed and a further 50,000 seriously wounded. The scale of the destruction can be felt by taking a walk around East London and the City – where postwar buildings have been erected, this is generally where German bombs hit.

The night of 29th December 1940 has been called the 'Second Great Fire of London', when German bombers dropped more than 100,000 bombs on London in a few hours, starting 1500 fires raging across the City – which became a furnace – and up to Islington. St Paul's was hit 28 times but escaped, largely due to the bravery of 100 Fire Watch volunteers. There's a memorial plaque in their honour in St Paul's Cathedral.

Postwar London & the '60s

Once the Victory in Europe (VE) celebrations had died down, the nation began to confront the war's appalling toll and to rebuild. The years of austerity had begun, with rationing of essential items and the building of high-rise residences on bomb sites in areas like Pimlico and the East End to solve the chronic housing problem. To help boost morale London hosted the 1948 Olympics (dubbed 'the austerity Games') and the Festival of Britain in 1951, a century after the Great Exhibition in Hyde Park.

The gloom returned, quite literally, on 6 December 1952 in the form of the Great Smog. A lethal blend of fog, smoke and pollution descended, and some 4000 people died of respiratory disorders. This prompted the Clean Air Act of 1956, which introduced zones to central London where only smokeless fuels could be burned.

Rationing of most goods ended in 1953, the year the current queen, Elizabeth II, was crowned following the death of her much-loved father King George VI.

Immigrants from around the world – particularly the former colonies – flocked to London, where a dwindling population had led to labour shortages. However, as the Notting Hill race riots of 1958 attest, despite being officially encouraged to come, new immigrants weren't always welcomed on the streets.

Some economic prosperity returned in the late 1950s, and Prime Minister Harold Macmillan told Britons they'd 'never had it so good'.

1951

The Festival of Britain is opened by King George VI; the festival celebrates the centenary of the Great Exhibition and aims to lift the national mood after the destruction of WWII.

1952

London is brought to a virtual standstill for four days in December by a thick pea-souper smog that smothers and chokes the city.

1953

Queen Elizabeth II's coronation is held at Westminster Abbey, the first major event to be broadcast live around the world on TV; many English families buy their first television.

1956

Red Routemaster double-decker buses make their first appearance in London and instantly become an iconic symbol of the city.

London became the place to be during the 1960s, when the bottled-up creative energy of the postwar era was spectacularly uncorked. London found itself the epicentre of cool in fashion and music: the streets were awash with colour and vitality, the iconic Mini car (1959) became a British icon and the Jaguar E-type (1961) was launched to adoring crowds.

Social norms underwent a revolution: the introduction of the contraceptive pill, the legalisation of homosexuality, and the popularisation of drugs such as marijuana and LSD through the hippy movement created an unprecedented permissive and liberal climate. Popular music in mid-to-late 1960s 'Swinging London' became increasingly alloyed with drug use, political activism and a counter-cultural mindset. The Beatles recording at Abbey Rd and the Rolling Stones performing free in front of half a million people in Hyde Park were seminal moments. Carnaby St and the King's Rd were the most fashionable places on earth, and pop-culture figures from Twiggy and David Bailey to Marianne Faithfull and Christine Keeler became the icons of the new era.

The Punk Era

The party didn't last long, and London returned to the doldrums in the harsh economic climate of the 1970s. The city's once-important docks never recovered from the loss of empire, the changing needs of modern container ships and poor labour relations, disappearing altogether between 1968 and 1981. Shipping moved 42km east to Tilbury, and the Docklands declined to a point of decay, until they were rediscovered by property developers a decade later. In 1973 a bomb went off at the Old Bailey (the Central Criminal Court), signalling the arrival on English soil of the Irish Republican Army (IRA) and its campaign for a united Ireland.

Post-1960s music became more formulaic as glam rock ruled, despite the blossoming of London legends Marc Bolan and David Bowie. Economic stagnation, cynicism and the superficial limits of disco and glam rock spawned a novel London aesthetic: punk. Largely white, energetic, abrasive and fast, punk transformed popular music and fashion at one stroke as teenagers traded in denim bell-bottoms for black drainpipes, and long hair for spiked Mohicans. The late 1970s were exhilarating times for London youth as punk opened the door for new wave, a punchy mod revival and the indulgent new romantics.

While the music and fashion scene was popping, torpor had set into Britain's body politic. Seen as weak and in thrall to the all-powerful trade unions, the brief and unremarkable Labour premiership of James Callaghan (1976–79) was marked by crippling strikes in the late 1970s, most significantly the 'Winter of Discontent' of 1978–79.

For a fascinatingly informative blog reviewing the social, musical and popular-cultural history of 20th-century London, take a look at Another Nickel in the Machine (www.nickelinthemachine.com), covering everything from suffragettes to vintage Bowie.

1959

The Notting Hill Carnival is launched by Claudia Jones to promote good race relations following the riots of 1958 when white and Afro-Caribbean communities clashed.

1966

England beats Germany to win the World Cup at Wembley – possibly the greatest day in the history of British sport and one seared into the consciousness of every schoolboy.

1979

Margaret Thatcher is elected prime minister. Her policies will transform Britain beyond recognition – part vital modernisation, part radical right-wing social policy.

1981

Brixton sees the worst race riots in London's history; Lord Scarman, delivering his report on the events, puts the blame squarely on 'racial disadvantage that is a fact of British life'.

The Thatcher Years

In 1979 the Conservative (or Tory) leader Margaret Thatcher became the UK's first female prime minister. In power for all of the 1980s and embarking on an unprecedented program of privatisation, Margaret Thatcher – aka the 'Iron Lady' – is arguably the most significant of Britain's postwar leaders. While her critics decry her approach to social justice and the large gulf that developed between the haves and have nots during her time in power, her defenders point to the massive modernisation of Britain's trade-union-dominated infrastructure and the vast wealth creation her policies generated.

In the beginning her monetarist policy sent unemployment skyrocketing; an inquiry following the Brixton riots of 1981 found that an astonishing 55% of men aged under 19 in that part of London were jobless. Meanwhile the Greater London Council (GLC), under the leadership of 'Red' Ken Livingstone, proved to be a thorn in Thatcher's side. County Hall, which faces the Houses of Parliament across the Thames, was hung with a giant banner recording the number of unemployed in the capital and goading the prime minister to do something about it. Thatcher responded in 1986 by abolishing the GLC, leaving London the only European capital without a unified local government.

While poorer Londoners suffered under Thatcher's significant trimming back of the welfare state, things had rarely looked better for the business community. Riding a wave of confidence partly engendered by the deregulation of the stock exchange in 1986 (the so-called Big Bang), London underwent explosive economic growth. Property developers proved to be only marginally more discriminating than the Luftwaffe, though some outstanding modern structures, including the Lloyd's of London building, went up.

Like previous booms, the one of the late 1980s proved unsustainable. As unemployment started to rise again and people found themselves living in houses worth much less than they had paid for them, Thatcher introduced a flat-rate poll tax. Protests around the country culminated in a 1990 march on Trafalgar Sq that ended in a fully fledged riot. Thatcher's subsequent resignation after losing a confidence vote in Parliament brought to an end this divisive era in modern British history. Her successor, the former Chancellor of the Exchequer, John Major, employed a far more collective form of government.

In 1992, to the amazement of most Londoners, the Conservatives were elected for a fourth successive term in government, without the inspiring leadership of Thatcher. The economy went into a tailspin shortly after, and the IRA detonated two huge bombs, one in the City

IRON LADY

The Iron Lady (2011) is a very watchable biopic of the late Margaret Thatcher starring Meryl Streep. It seamlessly traces the former prime minister's life and career from politically astute grocer's daughter to grieving widow suffering from dementia.

1984

The Thames Barrier, designed to protect London from flooding as a consequence of high tides and storm surges, is officially opened by the Queen.

1987

A fire, probably started by a dropped match or cigarette, at King's Cross Underground station causes the deaths of 31 people.

1990

Britain erupts in civil unrest, culminating in the poll tax riots in Trafalgar Sq; the deeply unpopular tax is ultimately Thatcher's undoing and she resigns in November.

1997

Labour sweeps to victory after almost two decades of Tory power. Tony Blair's radical relaunch of the Labour Party as centrist 'New Labour' gives him a majority of 179 in the House of Commons.

in 1992 and another in the Docklands four years later. The writing was on the wall for the Conservatives, as the Labour Party, apparently unelectable for a decade, came back with a new face.

Blair's Britain

Invigorated by its sheer desperation to return to power, the Labour Party selected the thoroughly telegenic Tony Blair to lead it. The May 1997 general election returned a Labour government to power for the first time in 18 years, but it was a much changed 'New Labour' party, one that had shed most of its socialist credo and supported a market economy, privatisation and integration with Europe. The Conservatives were thrashed, and the Blair era had begun.

Most importantly for London, Labour recognised the legitimate demand the City had for local government, and created the London Assembly and the post of mayor. Former leader of the GLC Ken Livingstone stood as an independent candidate and stormed the contest. For London, this meant big change. Livingstone introduced a successful congestion charge to limit private vehicles in central London and sought to bring London's backward public transport network into the 21st century.

O2

The shock of the new has traditionally knocked London sideways and the Millennium Dome on the Greenwich Peninsula failed to impress when it opened in 2000. Designed by Richard Rogers and sometimes mockingly referred to as the Millennium Tent, the dome eventually triumphed when rebranded as the O2 in 2007.

London's resurgence as a great world city seemed to be going from strength to strength, culminating in its selection to host the Olympic Games in 2012. London's buoyant mood was, however, shattered the very next morning when extremist Muslim terrorists detonated a series of bombs on the city's public transport network, killing 52 people. Triumph turned to terror, followed quickly by anger and then defiance. Just two weeks later the attempted detonation of several more bombs on London's public transport system sent the city into a state of severe unease, which culminated in the tragic and shocking shooting by the Metropolitan Police of an innocent Brazilian electrician Jean Charles de Menezes, mistaken for Hussain Osman, one of the failed bombers. Summer 2005 marked London's lowest ebb for some time.

Enter Boris

Ken Livingstone's campaign to get a third term as London mayor in 2008 was fatally undermined when the Conservative Party fielded maverick MP and popular TV personality Boris Johnson as its candidate. Even more of a populist than Livingstone, Eton-educated Johnson, portrayed by the media as a gaffe-prone toff, actually proved to be a deft political operator and surprised everyone by sailing past Livingstone to become the first Conservative mayor of London.

2000

Ken Livingstone is elected mayor of London as an independent, despite the government's attempts to shoehorn its own candidate into the job.

2003

London's congestion charge is introduced by Livingstone, creating an outcry that grows more muted as traffic flow improves.

2005

A day after London is awarded the 2012 Olympics, 52 people are killed by extremist Muslim suicide bombers attacking the London transport network on 7 July.

2008

Boris Johnson, a Conservative MP and journalist famed for his gaffes and rather eccentric appearance, beats Ken Livingstone to become London's new mayor.

With his wild mop of blond hair, shapeless suits and in-your-face eagerness, Johnson cut an almost eccentric and oddball figure, a persona Londoners – even dyed-in-the-wool Labour supporters – warmed to. He disagreed with Livingstone on many issues, but continued to support several of his predecessor's policies, including the congestion charge and the expansion of bicycle lanes. A keen cyclist himself, Boris is forever associated with the Barclays Cycle Hire Scheme, now called 'Boris bikes' (though Livingstone proposed it first). Johnson pledged to replace Livingstone's unloved 'bendy buses' with remodelled Routemasters, which were introduced on some routes in 2012; the new mayor also oversaw the banning of alcohol consumption on London Transport.

Johnson's first mayoral term coincided with London's transformation for the 2012 Olympic Games. Neglected areas of the recession-hit city were showered with investment and a vast building program in East London took shape. The era also saw a transferral of government power from the lacklustre Labour Party under Gordon Brown's leadership to a Conservative-Liberal Democrat coalition government with fellow Etonian David Cameron as prime minister and Nick Clegg deputy prime minister.

London's Year

2012 promised to be London's year, and few people – at home or abroad – were disappointed.

A wet early summer was predicted for the capital, but that did little to dampen spirits in June during the four-day holiday that marked the Queen's Diamond Jubilee – the 60th anniversary of her ascension to the throne. London was bedecked in red, white and blue bunting, and lavish street parties knitted together neighbourhoods across the city. As celebratory and joyous as the Jubilee was, it was but a prelude to *the* London event of the year: the all-singin', all-dancin' Olympics and Paralympics that welcomed some 15,000 athletes competing in almost 50 sports for 800 medals. Over the course of 29 days there were many expected highs (Britain took 65 Olympic and 120 Paralympic medals, to rank third in each games) and some surprising ones (London's transport system did not just cope but excelled). But nothing quite came close to Danny Boyle's Olympics Opening Ceremony, in which the world was treated to an extravagant potted history of London and the UK, and James Bond (in the form of Daniel Craig) jumped out of a helicopter into the Olympic Stadium accompanied by none other than Her Majesty, 'the Queen'.

Relive the excitement, thrills and spills (including Her Maj's famous bailout from that helicopter) of the 2012 Olympic Games by logging onto the official London 2012 site (www.london2012.com).

2010

Labour is defeated in the general elections, which results in a hung Parliament and a Conservative-Liberal Democrat coalition government with David Cameron as prime minister.

2011

A demonstration in Tottenham on 6 August turns into a riot and episodes of mass looting which then spreads to numerous London boroughs and towns across the UK.

2012

Boris Johnson narrowly beats Ken Livingstone to win his second election as mayor; the Queen celebrates 60 years on the throne; London hosts the 2012 Olympics and Paralympics.

2013

The Shard, at 310m/1016ft the tallest building in the European Union, opens to the public; MPs vote in favour of the Marriage (Same Sex Couples) Bill, legalising gay marriage.

Architecture

Unlike other world-class cities, London has never been methodically planned. Rather, it has developed in an organic (read haphazard) fashion. London retains architectural reminders from every period of its long history, but they are often hidden: part of a Roman wall enclosed in the lobby of a modern building near St Paul's Cathedral, say, or a galleried Restoration coaching inn tucked away in a courtyard off Borough High St. This is a city for explorers. Bear that in mind and you'll make discoveries at virtually every turn.

FESTIVAL

The London Festival of Architecture (www.lfa2010.org) is an annual month-long event in June celebrating the capital's buildings with a range of events, walks, talks, tours and debates.

Laying the Foundations

London's architectural roots lie within the walled Roman settlement of Londinium, established in AD 43 on the northern banks of the River Thames, pretty much on the site of today's City. Few Roman traces survive outside museums, though a Temple of Mithras, built in AD 240, will be relocated to the eastern end of Queen Victoria St in the City when the Bloomberg headquarters are completed at Walbrook Sq. Stretches of the Roman wall remain as foundations to a medieval wall outside Tower Hill tube station and in a few sections below Bastion Highwalk, next to the Museum of London.

The Saxons, who moved into the area after the decline of the Roman Empire, found Londinium too small, ignored what the Romans had left behind and built their communities further up the Thames. Excavations carried out by archaeologists from the Museum of London during renovations at the Royal Opera House in the late 1990s uncovered extensive traces of the Saxon settlement of Lundenwic, including some wattle-and-daub housing. But the best place to see what the Saxons left behind, in situ, is the church of All Hallows-by-the-Tower, northwest of the Tower of London, which boasts an important archway, the walls of a 7th-century Saxon church and a Roman pavement. St Bride's, Fleet St, has a similar pavement.

With the arrival of William the Conqueror in 1066, the country received its first example of Norman architecture with the White Tower, the sturdy keep at the heart of the Tower of London. The church of St Bartholomew-the-Great at Smithfield also has Norman arches and columns marching down its nave. The west door and elaborately moulded porch at the Temple Church in Inner Temple, the undercroft at Westminster Abbey and the crypt at St-Mary-le-Bow are other outstanding details of Norman architecture.

Medieval London

Enlarged and refurbished in the 13th and 14th centuries by the 'builder king' Henry III and his son, Edward I, Westminster Abbey is a splendid reminder of the work of master masons in the Middle Ages. Perhaps the finest surviving medieval church in the city is the 13th-century church of St Ethelburga-the-Virgin near Liverpool St station, heavily restored after Irish Republican Army (IRA) bombings in 1993. The 15th-century Church of St Olave, northwest of Tower Hill, is one of the City's few re-

OPEN SESAME

If you want to see the inside of buildings you wouldn't normally be allowed to, the third weekend in September is the time to visit London. That's when the charity **Open House London** (☎020-3006 7008; www.londonopenhouse.org) arranges for owners of some 750 private buildings to throw open their front doors and let in the public free of charge. Major buildings (eg the Gherkin, City Hall, Lloyd's of London, Royal Courts of Justice, BT Tower) have participated in the past; the full program becomes available in August. An architectural London Night Hike winds its way through the city during the same period, and its tours branch Open City (p408) offers architect-led tours year-round.

maining Gothic parish churches, while the crypt at the largely restored Church of St Etheldreda, north of Holborn Circus, dates from about 1250. Southwark Cathedral includes some remnants from the 12th and 13th centuries.

Secular medieval buildings are even scarcer, although the ragstone Jewel Tower, opposite the Houses of Parliament, dates from 1365, and most of the Tower of London goes back to the Middle Ages. Staple Inn in Holborn dates from 1378, but the half-timbered shopfront facade (1589) is mostly Elizabethan, and heavily restored in the mid 20th century. Westminster Hall was originally built in 1199; the hammer-beam roof came 300 years later. The great Medieval Hall (1479) at Eltham Palace also has a splendid hammer-beam roof.

A Trinity of Architects

The finest London architect of the first half of the 17th century was Inigo Jones (1573–1652), who spent a year and a half in Italy and became a convert to the Renaissance architecture of Andrea Palladio. His *chefs-d'œuvre* include Banqueting House (1622) in Whitehall and Queen's House (1635) in Greenwich. Often overlooked is the much plainer church of St Paul's in Covent Garden, which Jones designed in the 1630s and described as 'the handsomest barn in England'.

The greatest architect to leave his mark on London was Christopher Wren (1632–1723), responsible not just for his masterpiece and monument St Paul's Cathedral (1710) but also for many of central London's finest churches. He oversaw the building (or rebuilding) of more than 50 of them, many replacing medieval churches lost in the Great Fire, as well as the Royal Hospital Chelsea (1692) and the Old Royal Naval College, begun in 1694 at Greenwich. His English baroque buildings and churches are taller and lighter than their medieval predecessors. Perhaps the most striking features of Wren's newly designed churches were the graceful steeples that were to take the place of the solid square towers of the medieval ones.

The lovely row of houses at 52-55 Newington Green, N16, are London's oldest surviving brick terrace houses. Predating the Great Fire of London, they were built in 1658.

Nicholas Hawksmoor (1661–1736) was a pupil of Wren and worked with him on several churches before going on to design his own masterpieces. The restored Christ Church (1729) in Spitalfields, St George's Bloomsbury (1731), St Anne's, Limehouse (1725) and St George-in-the-East (1726) at Wapping are among the finest of his half-dozen London churches.

Georgian Manners

The Georgian period saw the return of classicism (or neo-Palladianism). Among the greatest exponents of this revived style was Robert Adam (1728–92), much of whose work in London was demolished by the Victorians.

Excellent examples that managed to survive are remodelled Kenwood House (1779) on Hampstead Heath and some of the interiors of Apsley House (1778) in Hyde Park Corner.

Adam's fame has been eclipsed by that of John Nash (1752–1835), whose contribution to London's architecture compares to that of Wren. Nash was responsible for the layout of Regent's Park and its surrounding elegant crescents. To give London a 'spine', he created Regent St as a straight axis from St James's Park in the south to the new Regent's Park in the north. This grand scheme also involved the formation of Trafalgar Sq, and the development of the Mall and the western end of The Strand. Nash refashioned the old Buckingham House into Buckingham Palace (1830) for George IV.

Nash's contemporary John Soane (1753–1837) was the architect of the Bank of England, completed in 1833 (though much of his work was lost during the bank's rebuilding by Herbert Baker in 1925–39), as well as the Dulwich Picture Gallery (1814). Robert Smirke (1780–1867) designed the British Museum in 1823; it's one of the finest expressions of the so-called Greek Revivalist style.

London's smallest house – 3ft wide at its narrowest point – is 10 Hyde Park Pl, now part of Tyburn Convent (p197). Despite being such a small target, it was damaged by a German bomb during WWII.

A 'Gothick' Rethink

In the 19th century a reaction emerged in the form of the highly decorative neo-Gothic style, also known as Victorian High Gothic or 'Gothick'. Champions were the architects George Gilbert Scott (1811–78), Alfred Waterhouse (1830–1905) and Augustus Pugin (1812–52). Scott was responsible for the elaborate Albert Memorial (1872) in Kensington Gardens and the 1872 Midland Grand Hotel (later St Pancras Chambers and now once again a hotel). Waterhouse designed the flamboyant Natural History Museum (1881), while Pugin worked from 1840 with the designer Charles Barry (1795–1860) on the Houses of Parliament after the Palace of Westminster burned down in 1834. The last great neo-Gothic public building to go up in London was the Royal Courts of Justice (1882), designed by George Edmund Street.

The emphasis on the artisanship and materials necessary to create these elaborate neo-Gothic buildings led to the so-called Arts and Crafts movement – 'British art nouveau' for lack of a better term – of which William Morris (1834–96) was the leading exponent. Morris' work can be enjoyed in the Green Dining Room of the Victoria & Albert Museum. The 1902 Euston Fire Station, opposite St Pancras New Church, is a wonderful example of Arts and Crafts architecture.

Flirting with Modernism

Relatively few notable public buildings emerged from the first 15 years of the 20th century, apart from Admiralty Arch (1910) in the Edwardian baroque style of Aston Webb (1849–1930), who also designed the 1911 Queen Victoria Memorial, opposite Buckingham Palace, and worked on the front facade of the palace itself. County Hall, designed by Ralph Knott in 1909, was not completed until 1922. More modern imagination is evident in commercial design, for example the superb art-nouveau design of Michelin House on Fulham Rd, dating from 1911.

In the period between the two world wars, English architecture was barely more creative, though Edwin Lutyens (1869–1944) designed the Cenotaph (1920) in Whitehall as well as the impressive 1927 Britannic House, now Triton Court, in Moorgate. Displaying the same amount of Edwardian optimism is the former Port of London Authority (1922) designed by Edwin Cooper and now being redeveloped as an apartment block and hotel.

Designed by US architect Harvey Wiley Corbett (1873–1954), Bush House, at the southern end of Kingsway and until recently the home of the BBC World Service, was built between 1923 and 1935. The delicious curves of the Daily Express Building (1932, Ellis Clarke with Owen Williams) on Fleet St are a splendid example of art deco grace. Designed by HS Goodhart-Rendel in 1928, iconic St Olaf House, an office block fronting the Thames, is another art-deco classic.

Russian architect Berthold Lubetkin (1901–90) is perhaps best remembered for his Penguin Pool at the London Zoo, with its concrete spiral ramp. Built in 1934, it is considered to be London's earliest modernist structure.

The famous art-nouveau stained glass of the Michelin Building was removed for storage at the start of WWII, but subsequently vanished. The current stained glass is a reproduction, based on photographs. The hunt for the original continues. See www.michelinonline.co.uk/centenary/amnesty.htm.

Postwar Reconstruction

Hitler's bombs during WWII wrought the worst destruction on London since the Great Fire of 1666 and the immediate postwar problem was a chronic housing shortage. Low-cost developments and ugly high-rise housing were thrown up on bomb sites and many of these blocks still scar the horizon today.

The Royal Festival Hall, designed by Robert Matthew (1906–75) and J Leslie Martin (1908–99) for the 1951 Festival of Britain and overhauled more than half a century later, attracted as many accolades as brickbats when it opened as London's first major public building in the modernist style. Equally controversial is the proposal to link the RFH with other disparate units of the Southbank Centre (ie Queen Elizabeth Hall and Hayward Gallery) with a glassed-in Festival Wing. Even now hardly anyone seems to have a good word to say about the neighbouring National Theatre, a brutalist structure by Denys Lasdun (1914–2001) begun in 1966 and finished a decade later.

The 1960s saw the ascendancy of the workaday glass-and-concrete high-rises exemplified by the mostly unloved 1967 Centre Point by Richard Seifert (1910–2001). But the once-vilified modernist tower has

SCOTT E BARBOUR / GETTY IMAGES ©

Financial district skyline, including 30 St Mary Axe (Gherkin; p157), designed by Foster and Partners

now been listed by English Heritage, meaning that it represents a particular style, is of great value to the patrimony and largely cannot be altered. The 1964 BT Tower, formerly known as the Post Office Tower and designed by Eric Bedford (1909–2001), has also received Heritage-listed status.

Little building was undertaken in the 1970s apart from roads, and the recession of the late 1980s and early 1990s brought much development and speculation to a standstill. Helping to polarise traditionalists and modernists still further was Prince Charles, who described a proposed extension to the National Gallery as being like 'a monstrous carbuncle on the face of an elegant and much loved friend'. For these and other reasons, the London skyline had little to compare with that of New York or Hong Kong.

Postmodernism Lands

London's contemporary architecture was born in the City and the revitalised Docklands in the mid-1980s. The City's centrepiece was the 1986 Lloyd's of London, Richard Rogers' 'inside-out' masterpiece of ducts, pipes, glass and stainless steel. Taking pride of place in the Docklands was Cesar Pelli's 244m-high 1 Canada Sq (1991), commonly known as Canary Wharf and easily visible from central London. But London's very first postmodern building (designed in the late 1980s by James Stirling but not completed till 1998) is considered to be Number One Poultry, a playful shiplike City landmark faced with yellow and pink limestone. The graceful British Library (Colin St John Wilson, 1998), with its warm red-brick exterior, Asian-like touches and wonderfully bright interior, met a very hostile reception but has now become a popular and much-loved London landmark.

With a youthful New Labour in power at the end of the 1990s, Britain's economy on the up and the new millennium looming, attention turned to public buildings, including several landmarks that would define London in the early 21st century.

From the disused Bankside Power Station (Giles Gilbert Scott, 1947–1963), the Tate Modern (Herzog & de Meuron, 1999) was refashioned as an art gallery that scooped international architecture's most prestigious prize, the Pritzker. The stunning Millennium Bridge (Norman Foster and Anthony Caro, 2000), the first new bridge to cross the Thames in central London since Tower Bridge went up in 1894, is much loved and much used. Even the white-elephant Millennium Dome (Richard Rogers), the class dunce of 2000, won a new lease of life as the 02 concert and sports hall, the world's most successful entertainment venue.

SCALE MODEL

For a good look at how London's built environment looks and will look in future visit New London Architecture (p106) – don't miss the ever-updated scale model.

Today & Tomorrow

Early in the millennium such structures as the 2002 glass 'egg' of City Hall and the ever-popular, ever-present 2003 30 St Mary Axe – or 'the Gherkin' – gave the city the confidence to continue planning more heady buildings.

By the middle of the decade London's biggest urban development project ever was under way, the 200-hectare Olympic Park in the Lea River Valley near Stratford, where most of the events of the 2012 Summer Olympics and Paralympics would take place. The park would offer few architectural surprises – except for Zaha Hadid's stunning Aquatics Centre, a breathtaking structure suitably inspired by the fluid geometry of water; and the ArcelorMittal Orbit, a zany public work of art with viewing platforms designed by the sculptor Anish Kapoor.

BROKEN GLASS & RAZOR SHARP

Londoners have a predilection for nicknaming new towers – whether built or planned – and many of them go on to replace the original name. Here are some of the popular ones, inspired, of course, by the building's outline:

Hubble-Bubble (p228) A shisha, or water pipe, is what Mayor Boris Johnson imagined the 115m-tall tangle-of-metal called the ArcelorMittal Orbit, the centrepiece of the Olympic Park, to be when he first saw it.

Cheese Grater (Leadenhall Building; Map p442; 122 Leadenhall St, EC3) Piling work finally commenced in 2011 for this recession-delayed 48-storey, 225m-tall tower in the form of a stepped wedge that faces architect Richard Rogers' other icon, the Lloyd's of London building. It will open in 2014.

Gherkin (p157) The 180m-tall bullet-shaped tower that seems to pop up at every turn has also been known as the Swiss Re Tower (after its first major tenants), Cockfosters (after its architect, Norman Foster), the exotic (or erotic) pickle etc.

Shard (p177) This needle-like 87-storey tower by Italian architect Renzo Piano (who originally dismissed tall buildings as 'statements of arrogance') is one mother of a splinter you wouldn't want to tussle with. At 310m, it is the EU's tallest building.

Stealth Bomber (One New Change; Map p442; www.onenewchange.com) French architect Jean Nouvel's office block and shopping mall next to St Paul's was built to bring new life to the City, especially at the weekend. Its nickname, only occasionally used, comes from its distinctive low-slung design.

Walkie Talkie (20 Fenchurch Street; Map p442; 20 Fenchurch St, EC3) This 37-storey, 177m-tall tower, expected in 2014, bulges in and bulges out, vaguely resembling an old-fashioned walkie talkie. It's probably the least popular new building as it dominates the skyline.

Razor (Strata; Map p468; 8 Walworth Rd SE1, SE1) One of our favourite towers in South London is this 43-storey, turbine-topped tower (officially the Strata building) rising over Elephant & Castle, resembling an electric razor and completed in 2010. It's London's tallest residential building.

Although the 2008 recession undermined for several years what was the most ambitious building program in London since WWII, an improved economic climate at the start of this decade saw those buildings under construction completed and 'holes in the ground' filled in with the start of new structures.

Topped out in 2010 were the 230m-tall Heron Tower in the City, then London's third-tallest building, and the very distinctive Strata (150m) south of the river with three wind turbines embedded in its roof. But nothing could compare with the so-called Shard, at 310m the EU's tallest building, completed in 2012. The glass-clad upturned icicle, dramatically poking into Borough skies and visible from across London, houses offices, residences, a five-star hotel, restaurants and, on the 72nd floor, London's highest public viewing gallery.

Other innovative designs in recent years include include top-heavy (and ultra-green) Palestra House, at 197 Blackfriars Rd; and Kings Place (90 York Way, N1), a music and arts venue and office development in the King's Cross area which is home to the *Guardian* newspaper. With its 133m-high arch and 1km stadium circumference, redesigned Wembley Stadium (Norman Foster) has re-emerged as a dramatic sporting icon. The new Tate Modern Project extension will add a dramatically modern and inspirational add-on to the southern side of the Tate Modern when it opens in 2016. The striking multifaceted Siemens Crystal (Wilkins Eyre, 2012) next to the Emirates Air Line cable car at Royal Docks houses an incubator and exhibition centre on how to make cities sustainable.

Literary London

For nigh on seven centuries, London has been the setting for works of prose. Indeed, the capital has been the inspiration for the masterful imaginations of such eminent wordsmiths as Shakespeare, Defoe, Dickens, Thackeray, Wells, Orwell, Conrad, Eliot, Greene and Woolf (even though not all were native to the city, or even British).

Built in 1567, the Old Curiosity Shop (13–14 Portsmouth St, WC2) made famous by Charles Dickens' eponymous novel, can still be seen today (although it's now a shoe shop and some say the name was added after publication).

The Middle Ages & Renaissance

It's hard to reconcile the bawdy portrayal of London in Geoffrey Chaucer's *Canterbury Tales* with Charles Dickens' bleak hellhole in *Oliver Twist,* let alone Daniel Defoe's plague-ravaged metropolis in *Journal of the Plague Year* with Zadie Smith's multiethnic romp *White Teeth.* Ever-changing, yet somehow eerily consistent, London has left its mark on some of the most influential writing in the English language.

Chaucerian London

The first literary reference to London appears in Chaucer's *Canterbury Tales,* written between 1387 and 1400: the 30-odd pilgrims of the tale gather for their trip to Canterbury at the Tabard Inn in Southwark and agree to share stories on the way there and back. Sadly, the inn burned down in 1676; a blue plaque to the poet marks the site of the building today.

Shakespearian London

Born in Warwickshire, William Shakespeare spent most of his life as an actor and playwright in London around the turn of the 17th century. He trod the boards of several theatres in Shoreditch and Southwark and wrote his greatest tragedies, among them *Hamlet, Othello, Macbeth* and *King Lear,* for the original Globe theatre on the South Bank. Although London was his home for most of his life, Shakespeare was an ardent fantasist and set nearly all his plays in foreign or imaginary lands. Even his English historical plays are hardly ever set in the capital; only *Henry IV: Part II* includes a London setting – a tavern called the Boar's Head in Eastcheap.

18th-Century London

Daniel Defoe was perhaps the first true London writer, both living in and writing about the city during the early 18th century. He is most famous for his novels *Robinson Crusoe* (1719–20) and *Moll Flanders* (1722), which he wrote while living at two addresses in Church St in Stoke Newington. Defoe's *Journal of the Plague Year* is his most absorbing account of London life, documenting the horrors of the Great Plague during the summer and autumn of 1665, when the author was a young child.

Dickensian & 19th-Century London

Two early 19th-century Romantic poets drew inspiration from London. John Keats, born above a Moorgate public house in 1795, wrote 'Ode to a Nightingale' while living near Hampstead Heath in 1819 and 'Ode on a Grecian Urn' reportedly after viewing the Parthenon frieze in the British

Museum the same year. William Wordsworth discovered inspiration for the poem 'Upon Westminster Bridge' while visiting London in 1802.

Charles Dickens (1812–70) was the definitive London author. When his father and family were interned at Marshalsea Prison in Southwark for not paying their debts, the 12-year-old Charles was forced to fend for himself on the streets. His family was released three months later, but that grim period was seared into the boy's memory and provided a font of experiences on which to draw. His novels most closely associated with London are *Oliver Twist,* with its gang of thieves led by Fagin in Clerkenwell, and *Little Dorrit,* whose hero was born in the Marshalsea. *Our Mutual Friend* is a scathing criticism of modern values, both monetary and social, and a spirited attack on the corruption, complacency and superficiality of 'respectable' London. The house in Bloomsbury where he wrote *Oliver Twist* and two other novels has now reopened as the Charles Dickens Museum.

Sir Arthur Conan Doyle (1858–1930) portrayed a very different London, his pipe-smoking, cocaine-snorting sleuth, Sherlock Holmes, coming to exemplify a cool and unflappable Englishness. Letters to the mythical hero and his admiring friend, Dr Watson, still arrive at 221b Baker St, where there's a museum to everyone's favourite Victorian detective.

London at the end of the 19th century appears in many books. HG Wells' early science-fiction story *The War of the Worlds* captures the sense and mood of the times. W Somerset Maugham's first novel, *Liza of Lambeth,* was based on his experiences as an intern in the slums of South London, while *Of Human Bondage,* so English, provides a portrait of late-Victorian London.

Top Literary Sites

Shakespeare's Globe (p172)

Charles Dickens Museum (p106)

Keats House (p246)

Carlyle's House (p199)

Sherlock Holmes Museum (p117)

Bloomsbury (p105)

20th-Century Writing

American Writers & London

Of Americans who wrote about London at the turn of the century, Henry James, who settled and died here, stands supreme with his *Daisy Miller* and *The Europeans. The People of the Abyss,* by socialist writer Jack London, is a sensitive portrait of poverty and despair in the East End. And we couldn't forget Mark Twain's *The Innocents Abroad,* in which the inimitable humorist skewers both the Old and New Worlds. St Louis-born TS Eliot settled in London in 1915, where he published his poem 'The Love Song of J Alfred Prufrock' almost immediately and moved on to his ground-breaking epic 'The Waste Land', where London is portrayed as an 'unreal city'.

THE BLUE PLAQUES SCHEME

You won't be in London long before you'll start noticing round, very blue plaques placed outside various buildings, which identify them as the homes of the great and the good. The very first plaque was put up in 1867, identifying the birthplace of the poet Lord Byron at 24 Holles St, W1, off Cavendish Sq. Since then a large percentage – some 25% of the 850 in place – have honoured writers and poets. These include everything from the offices of publisher Faber & Faber at 24 Russell Sq, where TS Eliot worked, to the Primrose Hill residence of Irish poet and playwright WB Yeats at 23 Fitzroy Rd, NW1 (where, incidentally, the US poet Sylvia Plath committed suicide in 1963). Candidates for a blue plaque go through a rigorous selection process. The minimum requirements are they must have been dead for at least two decades or have been born 100 years before, and be known to the 'well-informed passer-by'.

LITERARY READINGS, TALKS & EVENTS

A host of literary events are regularly held across London, ranging from book and poetry readings to talks, open-mic performances, writing workshops and other occasions celebrating the written word.

To catch established and budding authors, attend the monthly **Book Slam** (www.bookslam.com) usually held from 6.30pm on the last Thursday of the month at various clubs around London. Guests have included Nick Hornby, Hanif Kureishi and Will Self, and the event features readings, slam poetry, live music, DJs and comedians. Check the website for dates and venues.

Covent Garden's **Poetry Café** (Map p430; ☎020-7420 9888; www.poetrysociety.org.uk; 22 Betterton St, WC2; ⏲11am-11pm Mon-Fri, from 6.30pm Sat; ⊖Covent Garden) is a favourite for lovers of verse, with almost daily readings and performances by established poets, open-mic evenings and writing workshops.

The Institute of Contemporary Arts (p110) has excellent talks every month, with well-known writers from all spectrums, from the hip to the seriously academic.

Bookshops, particularly **Waterstone's** (www.waterstones.com), Foyle's (p140) and the London Review Bookshop (p140), often stage readings. Some major authors also now appear at the Southbank Centre (p184). Many such events are organised on an ad-hoc basis, so keep an eye on the listings in the freebie *Time Out* or any of the weekend newspaper supplements, including the *Guardian Guide* distributed with Saturday's paper.

Held over two weeks in late May/early June, the **London Literature Festival** (www.londonlitfest.com) at the Southbank Centre holds talks and events featuring writers and the literati.

Interwar Developments

Between the world wars, PG Wodehouse (1881–1975), the quintessential 20th-century British writer, depicted London high life with his hilarious lampooning of the English upper classes in the Jeeves stories. Quentin Crisp, the self-proclaimed 'stately homo of England', provided the flipside, recounting in his ribald and witty memoir *The Naked Civil Servant* what it was like to be openly gay in sexually repressed pre-war London. George Orwell's experience of living as a beggar in London's East End coloured his book *Down and Out in Paris and London* (1933).

The sternly modernist Senate House (1937) on Malet St in Bloomsbury contained offices of the Ministry of Information, where George Orwell worked during WWII. It is thought to have been the inspiration for the Ministry of Truth in his classic dystopian 1949 novel *Nineteen Eighty-Four*.

The Modern Age

The End of the Affair, Graham Greene's novel chronicling a passionate and doomed romance, takes place in and around Clapham Common just after WWII, while *The Heat of the Day* is Elizabeth Bowen's sensitive, if melodramatic, account of living through the Blitz.

Colin MacInnes described the bohemian, multicultural world of 1950s Notting Hill in *Absolute Beginners,* while Doris Lessing captured the political mood of 1960s London in *The Four-Gated City,* the last of her five-book *Children of Violence* series. She also provided some of the funniest and most vicious portrayals of 1990s London in *London Observed.* Nick Hornby, nostalgic about his days as a young football fan in *Fever Pitch* and obsessive about vinyl in *High Fidelity,* found himself the voice of a generation.

Before it became fashionable, Hanif Kureishi explored London from the perspective of ethnic minorities, specifically young Pakistanis, in his best-known novels *The Black Album* and *The Buddha of Suburbia.* He also wrote the screenplay for the groundbreaking film *My Beautiful Laundrette.* Author and playwright Caryl Phillips won plaudits for his description of the Caribbean immigrant's experience in *The Final Passage,* while Timothy Mo's *Sour Sweet* is a poignant and funny account of a Chinese family in the 1960s trying to adjust to English life.

The decades leading up to the turn of the millennium were great ones for British literature, bringing a dazzling new generation of writers to the fore. Martin Amis *(Money, London Fields)*, Julian Barnes *(Metroland, Talking it Over)*, Ian McEwan *(Enduring Love, Atonement)*, Salman Rushdie *(Midnight's Children, The Satanic Verses)*, AS Byatt *(Possession, Angels & Insects)* and Alan Hollinghurst *(The Swimming Pool Library, The Line of Beauty)* all need little introduction to keen readers.

A larger-than-life statue of John Betjeman (1906–84) gazing up in wonder above the departures hall at St Pancras International Station recalls the former poet laureate's campaign in the 1960s to save the Victorian High Gothic structure.

Millenium London

Helen Fielding's *Bridget Jones's Diary* and its sequel, *Bridget Jones: The Edge of Reason*, launched the 'chick lit' genre, one that transcended the travails of a young single Londoner to become a worldwide phenomenon. *Enfant terrible* and incisive social commentator Will Self's *Grey Area* is a superb collection of short stories focusing on skewed and surreal aspects of the city. *The Book of Dave* is his hilarious, surreal story of a bitter, present-day London cabbie burying a book of his observations, which are later discovered and regarded as scripture by the people on the island of Ham (future Britain is an archipelago due to rising sea levels).

Peter Ackroyd names the city as the love of his life. *London: the Biography* is his inexhaustible paean to the capital, while *The Clerkenwell Tales* brings to life the 14th-century London of Chaucer, and his more recent *The Canterbury Tales: A Retelling* renders Chaucer's timeless tales in lucid, compelling modern English. *Thames: Sacred River* is Ackroyd's fine monument to the muck, magic and mystery of the river through history.

Iain Sinclair is the bard of Hackney, who, like Ackroyd, has spent his life obsessed with and fascinated by the capital. His acclaimed and ambitious *London Orbital*, a journey on foot around the M25, London's mammoth motorway bypass, is required London reading, while *Hackney, That Rose-Red Empire* is an exploration of one of London's most notorious (though rapidly becoming trendy) boroughs.

Current Scene

Home to most of the UK's major publishers and its best bookshops, London remains a vibrant place for writers and readers alike. But the frustrating predominance of several powerful corporations within publishing can occasionally limit pioneering writing.

This state of affairs has, however, stimulated an exciting literary fringe, which, although tiny, is very active and passionate about good writing. London still has many small presses where quality and innovation are prized over public relations skills, and events kick off in bookshops and in the back rooms of pubs throughout the week.

Back in the mainstream, the big guns of the 1980s, such as Martin Amis, Ian McEwan, Salman Rushdie and Julian Barnes, are still going strong, although new voices have broken through in the last decade – indeed, there have been some outstanding new London writers in recent years, from Monica Ali, who brought the East End to life in *Brick Lane,* and Zadie Smith, whose *NW* was shortlisted for the Women's Prize for Fiction in 2013, to Jake Arnott's intelligent Soho-based gangster yarn *The Long Firm* and Gautam Malkani's much-hyped *Londonstani*.

At the same time, other writers have been 'rediscovered'. Howard Jacobson, variously called the 'Jewish Jane Austen' and the 'English Philip Roth' won the Man Booker Prize in 2010 for *The Finkler Question,* the first time the prestigious award had gone to a comic novel in a quarter-century.

Browse any London bookshop and you should find a London section, where you will find many of these titles and lots more.

Literary Pubs

Newman Arms (West End; p130)

George Inn (South Bank; p182)

Museum Tavern (West End; p130)

French House (West End; p131)

Dove (Hammersmith; p273)

Theatre & Dance

London has more theatrical history than almost anywhere else in the world, and it's still being made nightly on the stages of the West End, the South Bank and the vast London fringe. No visit to the city is complete without taking in a show, and a mere evening walk through 'theatreland' in the West End is an electrifying experience as thousands of people make their way to one of London's many playhouses. If dance tops your list, you can visit any of numerous London venues to applaud classical and contemporary repertoires.

Consult London's *Time Out* for weekly theatrical listings.

Theatre

Dramatic History

Elizabethan Period

Very little is known about London theatre before the Elizabethan period, when a series of 'playhouses', including the Globe, were built on the south bank of the Thames and in Shoreditch. Although the playwrights of the time – Shakespeare, Christopher Marlowe *(Doctor Faustus, Edward II)* and Shakespeare's great rival, Ben Jonson *(Volpone, The Alchemist)* – are now considered timeless geniuses, theatre then was more about raucous popular entertainment, where the crowd drank and heckled the actors. The Puritans responded by shutting the playhouses down after the Civil War in 1642.

Restoration

Three years after the return of the monarchy in 1660, the first famous Drury Lane theatre was built and the period of 'restoration theatre' began, under the patronage of the rakish Charles II. Borrowing influences from Italian and French theatre, Restoration theatre incorporated drama (such as John Dryden's *All For Love,* 1677) and comedy. The first female actors appeared (in Elizabethan times men played female roles), and Charles II is recorded as having had an affair with at least one, Nell Gwyn.

Victorian Period

Despite the success of John Gay's *The Beggar's Opera* (1728), Oliver Goldsmith's farce *She Stoops to Conquer* (1773) and Richard Sheridan's *The Rivals* and *The School for Scandal* (also in the 1770s) at Drury Lane, popular music halls replaced serious theatre during the Victorian era. Light comic operetta, as defined by Gilbert and Sullivan *(HMS Pinafore, The Pirates of Penzance, The Mikado)*, was all the rage. A sea change only arose with the emergence at the end of the 19th century of such compelling playwrights as Oscar Wilde *(An Ideal Husband, The Importance of Being Earnest)* and George Bernard Shaw *(Pygmalion)*.

The 20th Century

Comic wits, including Noël Coward *(Private Lives, Brief Encounter)*, and earnest dramatists, such as Terence Rattigan *(The Winslow Boy, The Browning Version)* and JB Priestley *(An Inspector Calls)*, followed. However, it wasn't until the 1950s and 1960s that English drama yet again experienced such a fertile period as the Elizabethan era.

Perfectly encapsulating the social upheaval of the period, John Osborne's *Look Back in Anger* at the Royal Court Theatre in 1956 heralded a rash of new writing, including Harold Pinter's *The Homecoming,* Joe Orton's *Loot,* Tom Stoppard's *Rosencrantz and Guildenstern are Dead* and Alan Ayckbourn's *How the Other Half Loves*. During the same period many of today's leading theatre companies were formed, including the National Theatre.

Though somewhat eclipsed by the National Theatre, today's Royal Court Theatre retains a fine tradition of new writing. In the past decade it has nurtured such talented playwrights as Jez Butterworth *(Mojo, The Night Heron),* Ayub Khan-Din *(East Is East),* Conor McPherson *(The Weir, Shining City)* and Joe Penhall *(Dumb Show).*

If innovation and change are too much for you, drop by St Martin's Theatre where the same production of *The Mousetrap* has been running since 1952!

Current Scene

London remains a thrilling place for theatre-lovers. Nowhere else, with the possible exception of New York, offers such a diversity of high-quality drama, first-rate musical theatre and such a sizzling fringe. Whether it's Hollywood A-listers gracing tiny stages and earning Equity minimum for their efforts, or lavish West End musicals, London remains an undisputed theatrical world leader and innovator.

West End & Off West End

In recent years the mainstream West End has re-established its credentials, with extraordinary hits, while the smarter end of the fringe continues to shine with risky, controversial and newsworthy productions. The hottest tickets are still for the National Theatre, which has gone from strength to strength under its current director, Nicholas Hytner, who is sadly standing down in 2015. His productions have enjoyed both huge box-office success and critical acclaim. Other innovative venues are off–West End theatres such as the Arcola, the Almeida, the Royal Court Theatre, the Soho Theatre and the Donmar Warehouse.

Big names can often be seen treading London's hallowed boards – think Jude Law playing Hamlet at the Donmar, Dame Judi Dench in Mishima's *Madame de Sade* at the Wyndham's Theatre or Daniel Radcliffe in *The Cripple of Inishmaan.*

There's something for all dramatic tastes in London's Theatreland, from contemporary political satire to creative reworking of old classics and all shades in between. Recent productions that have won critical acclaim include *Globe to Globe,* in which 37 theatre companies from around the world presented Shakespeare's works in 37 different languages, the highly praised musical *Singing in the Rain,* the children's musical *Matilda* and the 2012 West End production of *Sweeney Todd.* In 2013, Britain's theatre pioneers, Punchdrunk, staged *The Drowned Man* and director Sam Mendes' version of *Charlie and the Chocolate Factory* became an autumn hit.

London's Best Theatres

- *National Theatre (South Bank)*
- *Shakespeare's Globe (South Bank)*
- *Old Vic (South Bank)*
- *Donmar Warehouse (West End)*
- *Royal Court Theatre (Kensington & Hyde Park)*
- *Arcola Theatre (Hampstead & North London)*
- *Young Vic (South Bank)*
- *Hampstead Theatre (Hampstead & North London)*
- *Barbican (City)*
- *Menier Chocolate Factory (South Bank)*

Shakespearean Offerings

Shakespeare's legacy is generously honoured on the city's stages, most notably by the Royal Shakespeare Company (RSC) and at the Globe theatre. The RSC stages one or two of the bard's plays in London annually, although it currently has no London home (its productions are based in Stratford-upon-Avon and usually transfer to the capital later in their run), while the open-air Shakespeare's Globe on the South Bank attempts to re-create the Elizabethan theatre experience. The Globe's new Sam Wanamaker Playhouse, looking to open in early 2014, will be a unique place to savour Shakespeare's words, with an intimate candle-lit atmosphere. Artistic director Dominic Dromgoole, having taken over the reins at the Globe in 2006, has ensured that Shakespeare's plays remain at the core of the theatre's program, but at the same time has produced a wider range of European and British classics, as well as new material.

Dance

Whether contemporary, classical or crossover, London will have the right dance moves for you. As one of the world's great dance capitals, London's artistic habitat has long created and attracted talented choreographers with both the inspiration and aspiration to fashion innovative dance.

London's most celebrated choreographer is award-winning Matthew Bourne *(Swan Lake, Play Without Words, Edward Scissorhands, Dorian Gray, Oliver!, Cinderella)*, who has been repeatedly showered with praise for his reworking of classics. Other leading London-based talents who have helped take London's dance message to the wider world include Rafael Bonachela, who scripted Kylie Minogue's Showgirl tour, and Wayne McGregor, who worked as movement director on *Harry Potter and the Goblet of Fire*.

However, Bonachela and McGregor are not alone in the vanguard. The Place in Euston was the original birthplace of modern British dance, and the training school Laban has emerged with strong cutting-edge performances. Meanwhile, the revamped Sadler's Wells – the birthplace of English classical ballet in the 19th century – continues to stage an exciting program of various styles featuring dance performances choreographed by Carlos Acosta, Twyla Tharp and Alvin Ailey and international troupes such as the Dance Theatre of Harlem.

Covent Garden's redeveloped Royal Opera House is the stunning home of London's leading classical-dance troupe, the world-famous Royal Ballet. The company largely sticks to the traditional, but more contemporary influences occasionally seep into productions. Recent highlights include the 2012 production of *Gloriana* by Richard Jones, a new production of *Nabucco* from Daniele Abbado, and the perennially popular *Swan Lake*, which opened the 2012–13 Royal Ballet season. Contemporary fairytale *Raven Girl* was a 2013 collaboration between Wayne McGregor and Audrey Niffenegger, author of the award-winning novel *The Time Traveler's Wife*.

For more cutting-edge work, the innovative **Rambert Dance Company** (☎020-8630 0640; www.rambert.org.uk) is the UK's foremost contemporary dance troupe. It is possibly the most creative force in UK dance and its autumn 2013 move from Chiswick to purpose-built premises in Doon St (behind the National Theatre) in the far more creative milieu of the South Bank has made its dance concepts that much more accessible.

One of the world's best companies, the **English National Ballet** (www.ballet.org.uk), is a touring ballet company. You may be fortunate enough to catch it at one of its various venues in London – principally at the London Coliseum.

Another important venue for experimental dance is the Barbican; for the latest, check www.londondance.com.

DANCE UMBRELLA

Running for six weeks from early October, Dance Umbrella (www.danceumbrella.co.uk) is one of the world's leading dance festivals of its kind.

Art & Fashion

London today is the art capital of Europe, with a vibrant gallery scene and some of the world's leading modern-art collections. Many of the world's greatest artists have spent time in London, including Monet and Van Gogh. Although Britain's artists have historically been eclipsed by their European confreres, some distinctly innovative artists have emerged from London, a city also considered to be a major citadel of contemporary fashion.

Art

Holbein to Turner

It wasn't until the rule of the Tudors that art began to take off in London. The German Hans Holbein the Younger (1497–1543) was court painter to Henry VIII, and one of his finest works, *The Ambassadors* (1533), hangs in the National Gallery. A batch of great portrait artists worked at court during the 17th century, the best being Anthony Van Dyck (1599–1641), who painted *Charles I on Horseback* (1638), also in the National Gallery. Charles I was a keen collector and it was during his reign that the Raphael Cartoons, now in the Victoria & Albert Museum, came to London.

Local artists began to emerge in the 18th century, including landscapist Thomas Gainsborough (1727–88), William Hogarth (1697–1764), and poet, engraver and watercolourist William Blake (1757–1827). A superior visual artist to Blake, John Constable (1776–1837) studied the clouds and skies above Hampstead Heath, sketching hundreds of scenes that he'd later match with subjects in his landscapes.

JMW Turner (1775–1851), equally at home with oils and watercolours, represented the pinnacle of 19th-century British art. Through innovative use of colour and gradations of light he created a new atmosphere that seemed to capture the wonder, sublimity and terror of nature. His later works, including *Snow Storm – Steam-boat off a Harbour's Mouth* (1842), *Peace – Burial at Sea* (1842) and *Rain, Steam and Speed – the Great Western Railway* (1844), now in the Tate Britain and the National Gallery, were increasingly abstract, and although widely vilified at the time, later inspired the Impressionist works of Claude Monet.

The Palace Art Fair (www.palaceartfair.co.uk), held in stunning surroundings at Fulham Palace every October, showcases more than 100 contemporary artists working across a variety of media.

The Pre-Raphaelites to Hockney

The brief but splendid flowering of the Pre-Raphaelite Brotherhood (1848–54) took its inspiration from the Romantic poets, abandoning the pastel-coloured rusticity of the day in favour of big, bright and intense depictions of medieval legends and female beauty. The movement's main proponents were William Holman Hunt, John Everett Millais and Dante Gabriel Rossetti; artists Edward Burne-Jones and Ford Madox Brown were also strongly associated with the movement.

In the early 20th century, cubism and futurism helped generate the short-lived Vorticists, a modernist group of London artists and poets, centred on the dapper Wyndham Lewis (1882–1957), that sought to capture dynamism in artistic form.

Sculptors Henry Moore and Barbara Hepworth both typified the modernist movement in British sculpture, but by the post-WWII years, art had transformed yet again. In 1945, the tortured, Irish-born painter Francis Bacon (1909–92) caused a stir when he exhibited his *Three Studies for Figures at the Base of a Crucifixion* – now on display at the Tate Britain – and afterwards continued to spook the art world with his repulsive yet mesmerising visions.

Australian art critic Robert Hughes has eulogised Bacon's contemporary, Lucian Freud (1922–2011), as 'the greatest living realist painter'. Freud's early work was often surrealist, but from the 1950s the bohemian Freud exclusively focused on pale, muted portraits – often nudes, and frequently of friends and family (although he has also painted the Queen).

Popular art classes are held at the Dulwich Picture Gallery and other museums and galleries around London.

London in the swinging 1960s was perfectly encapsulated by pop art, its vocabulary best articulated by the brilliant David Hockney (b 1937). Hockney gained a reputation as one of the leading pop artists through his early use of magazine-style images (although he rejected the label), but after a move to California, his work became increasingly naturalistic. Two of his most famous works, *Mr and Mrs Clark and Percy* (1971) and *A Bigger Splash* (1974), are displayed at the Tate Britain.

Gilbert & George were quintessential English conceptual artists of the 1960s. The Spitalfields odd couple are still at the heart of the British art world, having now become a part of the establishment by representing Britain at the 2005 Venice Biennale, and holding a very successful retrospective at the Tate Modern in 2007.

Brit Art

Despite its incredibly rich collections, Britain had never led, dominated or even really participated in a particular artistic epoch or style. That all changed in the twilight of the 20th century, when 1990s London became the beating heart of the art world.

Brit Art sprang from a show called *Freeze*, which was staged in a Docklands warehouse in 1988, organised by artist and showman Damien Hirst and largely featuring his fellow graduates from Goldsmiths' College. Influenced by pop culture and punk, this loose movement was soon catapulted to notoriety by the advertising guru Charles Saatchi, who bought an extraordinary number of works and came to dominate the scene.

Brit Art was brash, decadent, ironic, easy to grasp and eminently marketable. Hirst chipped in with a cow sliced into sections and preserved in formaldehyde; flies buzzed around another cow's head and were zapped in his early work *A Thousand Years*. Chris Ofili provoked with *The Holy Virgin Mary*, a painting of the black Madonna made partly with elephant poo; brothers Jake and Dinos Chapman produced mannequins of children with genitalia on their heads; and Marcus Harvey created a portrait of notorious child-killer Myra Hindley made entirely with children's hand-prints, whose value skyrocketed when it was repeatedly vandalised with ink and eggs by the public.

Since 1999, the Fourth Plinth Project in Trafalgar Sq has offered a platform for novel, and frequently controversial, works by contemporary artists.

The areas of Shoreditch, Hoxton and Whitechapel – where many artists lived, worked and hung out – became the epicentre of the movement, and a rash of galleries moved in. Among these was White Cube, owned by one of the most important patrons of early Brit Art, Jay Jopling.

For the 10 years or so that it rode a wave of publicity, the defining characteristics of Brit Art were notoriety and shock value. Damien Hirst and Tracey Emin inevitably became celebrities.

LONDON ARTISTS TODAY

London continues to generate talent across a range of artistic media, keeping critics on their toes. These are some of the biggest-name artists working in contemporary London:

Banksy The anonymous street artist whose work is a worldwide phenomenon.

Antony Gormley This sculptor is best known for the 22m-high *Angel of the North*, beside the A1 trunk road near Gateshead in northern England.

Anish Kapoor An Indian sculptor working in London since the 1970s, whose fantastic installations and sculpture are extremely popular with Londoners – his ArcelorMittal Orbit in the Queen Elizabeth Olympic Park was a hit during the Olympics.

Marc Quinn *Self* is a sculpture of the artist's head made from his own frozen blood, which Quinn recasts every five years. *Self* can be seen – in all its refrigerated glory – at the National Portrait Gallery.

Chantal Joffe This London-based artist is well known for her naive, expressionist portraits of women and children.

One critic argued the hugely hyped movement was the product of a 'cultural vacuum', an example of the emperor's new clothes, with people afraid to criticise the works for fear they'd look stupid.

Beyond Brit Art

On the fringes of Brit Art are a lot of less-stellar but equally inspiring artists exploring other directions. A highlight is Richard Wilson's iconic installation *20:50* (1987; now a permanent installation at the Saatchi Gallery) – a room filled waist-high with recycled oil. Entering down the walkway, you feel as if you've just been shot out into space. In Douglas Gordon's most famous work, *24 Hour Psycho* (1993), the Scottish video artist slowed Alfred Hitchcock's masterpiece so much it was stripped of its narrative and viewed more like a moving sculpture. Gary Hume first came to prominence with his *Doors* series: full-size paintings of hospital doors, which can be seen as powerful allegorical descriptions of despair – or just perfect reproductions of doors.

The biggest date on the art calendar is the controversial Turner Prize at the Tate Britain. Any British artist under the age of 50 is eligible to enter, although there is a strong preference for conceptual art. The 2012 award went to Elizabeth Price, for her powerful and political video piece, *The Woolworths Choir of 1979*.

London's Greatest Artworks

Sunflowers, by Vincent Van Gogh (National Gallery)

Fighting Temeraire, by JMW Turner (National Gallery)

Whaam!, by Roy Lichtenstein (Tate Modern)

Ophelia, by Sir John Everett Millais (Tate Britain)

Three Studies for Figures at the Base of a Crucifixion, by Sir Francis Bacon (Tate Britain)

Fashion

The British fashion industry has always been about younger, directional and more left-field designs. London fashion focuses on streetwear and the wow factor, with a few old reliables keeping the frame in place and mingling with hot new designers, who are often unpolished through inexperience, but bursting with talent and creativity. As a result, London is definitely exciting in a global sense and nobody with an interest in street fashion will be disappointed.

London weathered a tough few years that saw its status as an international fashion centre drop, but the city has returned to the heart of the fashion universe, boasting a bright new firmament of young stars.

London's Who's Who

With his witty designs and eclectic references, St Martin's graduate Giles Deacon took London by storm with his own label, Giles. Other

Brit stars making a buzz are Henry Holland, Jonathan Saunders, Christopher Kane and Greek-Austrian import Marios Schwab. Nu-rave darling Gareth Pugh is also someone to look out for, another St Martin's alumnus who took the underground club fashions of Shoreditch and transposed them for the shop floor. Stella McCartney can't be missed, with her ethical fashion and world-wide profile. Born and living in London, McCartney was Team GB's Olympic creative director and was also voted one of the UK's 100 most powerful women by the BBC in February 2013.

London Fashion Abroad

The influence of London's designers continues to spread well beyond the capital. The 'British Fashion Pack' still work at, or run, many of the major Continental fashion houses such as Chanel, Givenchy and Chloé. Fashion houses such as Alexander McQueen retain design studios in London, and erstwhile defectors to foreign catwalks, such as Luella Bartley and Matthew Williamson, have returned to London to show their collections.

FASHION WEEK

The high point on the London fashion calendar is London Fashion Week (www.londonfashionweek.co.uk), held in February and September each year. The main venue is Somerset House.

Fame & Celebrity

With its eccentricity when compared to the classic feel of the major Parisian and Milanese houses or the cool street-cred of New York designers, the London fashion spirit was best exemplified by Isabella Blow. This legendary stylist discovered Alexander McQueen, Stella Tennant and Sophie Dahl (among many others) during her career at *Vogue* and *Tatler*. Blow sadly committed suicide in 2007. A further shock for the industry was the tragic suicide of Alexander McQueen in 2010 at the age of 40.

British fashion's 'bad girl' Kate Moss has been in and out of the news since the start of her career – for both her sense of style and Top Shop clothes line and her off-runway antics. The fashion world thrives on notoriety and John Galliano's much-publicised arrest in 2011 for an anti-Semitic diatribe against a couple in a Paris cafe was a nadir for Dior's chief designer, who was consequently dropped by the fashion house. Despite these tragic losses and moments of scandal, London retains all the innovative ingredients for exhilarating developments in fashion, today and tomorrow.

The Music Scene

Drawing upon a deep and often gritty reservoir of talent, London's modern music scene is one of the city's greatest sources of artistic power, and a magnet for bands and hopefuls from all musical hemispheres. Periodically a world leader in musical fashion and innovative soundscapes, London blends its homegrown talent with a continuous influx of styles and cultures, keeping currents flowing and inspiration percolating.

The Swinging '60s

London's prolific output began with the Kinks and their North London songwriter Ray Davies, whose lyrics read like a guide to the city. 'You Really Got Me', 'All Day and All of the Night' and 'Dedicated Follower of Fashion' brilliantly capture the anti-establishment mood of the '60s, while 'Waterloo Sunset' is the ultimate feel-good London song.

Another London band, the Rolling Stones, first stepped up to a paying audience at the old Bull & Bush in Richmond in 1963. An R&B band with frequent trajectories into American blues and rock and roll, the Stones quickly set up as a more rough-edged counterpoint to the cleaner boy-next-door image of The Beatles (famously from Liverpool but who recorded most of their best-known songs in London).

Struggling to be heard above the din was inspirational mod band the Small Faces, formed in 1965. The Who, from West London, innovated by smashing guitars on stage ('instrument destruction'), propelling TVs from hotel windows and driving cars into swimming pools. Jimi Hendrix came to London and took guitar playing to unseen heights before tragically dying in a flat in the Samarkand Hotel in West London in 1970. In some ways, the swinging '60s ended in July 1969 when the Stones famously staged their free concert in Hyde Park in front of more than 250,000 liberated fans.

The '70s

A local band called Tyrannosaurus Rex had enjoyed moderate success throughout the '60s. In 1970 they changed their name to T.Rex, frontman Marc Bolan donned a bit of glitter and the world's first 'glam' band had arrived. Glam encouraged the youth of uptight

LONDON IN MUSIC THROUGH THE YEARS

1967

Waterloo Sunset (The Kinks) Unimpeachable classic from the '60s.

1978

(I Don't Want to Go to) Chelsea (Elvis Costello) Punchy Costello from the early years.

1978

Hong Kong Garden (Siouxsie and the Banshees) Stirring goth-punk ode to a Chinese takeaway in Chislehurst High St.

1978

Baker Street (Gerry Rafferty) With an iconic and roof-raising saxophone riff.

1979

London Calling (The Clash) Raw and potent punk anthem.

1984

West End Girls (Pet Shop Boys) Smooth and glossy first chart success from the British pop duo.

1989

Twenty-Four Minutes from Tulse Hill (Carter the Unstoppable Sex Machine) SW2 finds fame in this throbbing indie track.

1993

Buddha of Suburbia (David Bowie) One of the Thin White Duke's most sublime songs.

Britain to come out of the closet and be whatever they wanted to be. Baritone-voiced Brixton boy David Jones (aka David Bowie) then altered the rock landscape with his astonishing *The Rise and Fall of Ziggy Stardust and the Spiders from Mars* in 1972, one of the decade's seminal albums. Genre-spanning Roxy Music, blending art rock and synth pop, generated a more sophisticated glam sound.

Back at the rock face, a little band called Led Zeppelin (who formed in 1968) was busy cultivating the roots of heavy metal. And 17-year-old Farok Bulsara changed his name to Freddie Mercury and led Queen to become one of the greatest rock-and-roll stars of all time. British-American band Fleetwood Mac left blues for pop rock and stormed the charts in the US as well as in Britain; their landmark *Rumours* became the fifth-highest-selling album in history.

Punk's unexpected arrival kicked in the complacent mid-'70s commercial edifice of disco, rock and glam. Few saw it coming but none could miss it. The Sex Pistols were the most notorious of a wave of bands that began pogoing around London in 1976.

Fellow Londoners The Clash harnessed the raw anger of the time into a collar-grabbing brand of political protest that would see them outlast their peers, treading the fine line between angry punks and great songwriters. The disillusioned generation finally had a plan and a leader in frontman Joe Strummer; *London Calling* is a spirited call to arms.

Punk cleared the air and into the oxygen-rich atmosphere swarmed a gaggle of late '70s acts. London band The Damned sought out an innovative niche as Goth punk pioneers. The Jam deftly vaulted the abyss between punk and mod revivalism (lead singer and 'Modfather' Paul Weller followed up with a hugely successful solo career after middle-of-the-road sophisti-pop hits with The Style Council) and Madness put the nutty sound on the London map. New Wave and the New Romantics quickly shimmied into the fast-changing music scene... And before London knew it, the '80s had arrived.

The '80s

Guitars disappeared, swiftly replaced by keyboard synthesisers and drum machines. Fashion and image became indivisible from music. Thin ties, winklepickers, velcro-fastening white sneakers, spandex, densely-pleated trousers and make-up dazzled at every turn. Big hair was big. Overpriced, oversexed and way overdone, '80s London was a roll-call of hair-gelled pop: Spandau Ballet, Culture Club, Bananarama, Wham! and Howard Jones. Wham!'s Georgios Panayiotou changed his name to George Michael and gained massive success as a solo artist.

Overpriced, oversexed and way overdone, '80s London was a roll-call of hair-gelled pop

Depeche Mode broke new ground in dark neo-synth pop, while northern-lads-turned-Londoners the Pet Shop Boys found success and an impressive longevity, Neneh Cherry started rapping and south-east London samplers Colourbox strongly hinted at things to come.

While the late '80s brought blond boy-band Bros and the anodyne starlets and one-hit wonders of the Hit Factory: Stock Aitken & Waterman, relief had already been assured from up north with the arrival of The Smiths and their alternative rock innovations. In the closing years of the decade, the Stone Roses and the Happy Mondays devised a new sound that had grown out of the recent acid-house raves. Dance exploded in 1988's summer of love, with dilated pupils and a stage set for rave anthems such as the KLF's mighty 'What Time is Love?' A generation was gripped by dance music and a new lexicon ruled: techno, electronica, hip hop, garage, house and trance.

The '90s

The early 1990s saw the explosion of yet another scene: Britpop, a genre broadly defined as back to (Beatles) basics. A high-profile battle between two of the biggest bands, Blur from London and Oasis from Manchester, drew a line in the musical sand.

Weighing in on the London side were the brilliant and erratic Suede and Elastica (the latter fronted by the punky, poppy Justine Frischmann), not to mention Sheffield defectors to the capital, Pulp (with their irrepressible lead man, Jarvis Cocker). Skirting around the edges, doing their own thing, were Radiohead (from Oxford, close enough to London).

Arguably the most world-wide fame in this period was taken by the London-based boy and girl bands Take That, All Saints, East 17 and the then-ubiquitous Spice Girls. Their enduring popularity is reflected in the reunions of some of these bands two decades later and the Spice Girls' appearance in the London Olympics closing ceremony in 2012, which cemented them as an inherent part of British music culture.

As Britpop ebbed in the late '90s, other currents were flowing into town, and drum 'n' bass and electronica found an anthem-packed sound with DJs such as Goldie and London band Faithless stylishly seeing out the millennium.

The Noughties (or the '00s)

London band Coldplay – melodic rockers led by falsetto front man Chris Martin – first made a big splash in the UK at the dawn of the new century, before finding international fame. After four best-selling albums, their position as one of London's leading rock bands appears unshakeable.

But other musical styles were cooking. London's Asian community made a big splash in the early 21st century, with Talvin Singh and Nitin Sawhney fusing dance with traditional Indian music to stunning effect, and Asian Dub Foundation bringing their unique brand of a mix of rapcore, dub, dancehall and ragga, and political comment to an ever-widening audience.

Pete Doherty and Carl Barât single-handedly renewed interest in guitar music despite its post-Britpop malaise. Their band, The Libertines, created a huge splash with their 2002 debut single 'What a Waster', and their first album went platinum. Kicked out, Doherty went on to form Babyshambles and a controversial public persona.

Fronted by eponymous Alison, Goldfrapp brought a seductive and sensual electronica to the fore on the albums *Black Cherry* and *Supernature,* before abruptly departing in a mystical pastoral-folk direction on the band's much-applauded *Seventh Tree* (2008). The band then backpedaled with 2010's *Head First* as Goldfrapp rediscovered 1980s synthpop.

Other London noughties talents include the bellowing Florence and the Machine, quirky West London singer-songwriter Lily Allen and

2004

Round Here (George Michael) Moving song drawing on the singer's recollections of his first day at school.

2006

LDN (Lily Allen) Catchy ska-beat hit from the London popster.

2007

Hometown Glory (Adele) Exquisite celebration of West Norwood from the Tottenham-born songster.

2007

London Town (Kano) London rapper on his hometown.

2008

Warwick Avenue (Duffy) The beautiful voice of this Welsh starlet puts Warwick Ave tube station on the musical map.

2011

The City (Ed Sheeran) Dubstep-folkie Sheeran has a cynic's eye for the joys and trials of the Big Smoke.

2013

Goin' Crazy (Dizzee Rascal ft Robbie Williams) Rascal and Williams meet up in Dalston on souped-up mobility scooters.

A MUSICAL JOURNEY THROUGH LONDON

Zebra crossing on Abbey Rd, St John's Wood The Beatles' most famous album cover.

Heddon St, Soho Where the cover for *Ziggy Stardust* was photographed.

23 Brook St, Mayfair Former home to composers Handel and Hendrix.

St Martin's College, Mayfair First Sex Pistols gig.

Tree on Queen's Ride, Barnes Where Marc Bolan died as a passenger in a Mini in 1977.

3 Savile Row, Mayfair Site of the last Beatles performance on the roof of the Apple building in 1969.

extraordinary but tragic (she passed away in July 2011, aged just 27) Southgate chanteuse Amy Winehouse.

London Music Today

The London scene has fought its way back from being an overhyped late-'90s destination for those seeking cool by association and is again one of the major creative musical hubs on earth.

With her second album, Tottenham-born soulster-songwriter Adele won not just the nation's hearts but spent 10 weeks at number one in the US album charts with *21* (2011).

Grime and its successor genre, dubstep (two real indigenous London musical forms born in the East End out of a fusion of hip-hop, drum 'n' bass and UK garage), are at the cutting edge of London music. Dizzee Rascal, Lady Sovereign, Lethal Bizzle, Roll Deep, GoldieLocks and Kano are perhaps the best-known singers and groups working in the genre.

The ethereal singer James Blake won critical acclaim for his eponymous and soulful first post-dubstep album and released his second offering, *Overgrown*, in 2013. Popular London folk-rock ensemble Mumford & Sons have also assailed the American charts, and Londoner Tinie Tempah is the first British rapper to make it big in the US. Brixton-based Jessie Ware has won the hearts of soul and electro-loving audiences with her first album *Devotion* (2012), gathering fans worldwide.

Film & Media

The UK punches well above its weight for its standing on the international film scene, but London is far from the glittering hub of the film industry that it might be, despite notable celluloid triumphs. Nonetheless, London forms the backdrop to a riveting array of films, while the city's media sphere is a vibrant and influential force.

London & Film

The Local Cinematic Industry

Londoners are proud of their hometown, but few see London at the forefront of the film industry. Despite frequent originality and creative novelty, British films can be hit and miss (certainly at the box office); commercial triumphs include recent Oscar-winners *The King's Speech* (2010) and *The Queen* (2006), and further back the classics *Four Weddings and a Funeral* (1994) and *Shakespeare in Love* (1998), but a frustrating inconsistency persists (despite the disproportionate influence of Brits in Hollywood).

A system of public funding through the British Film Institute exists alongside private investment, taking over from the defunct UK Film Council (set up in 2000 to nurture a self-sustaining film industry). Channelling lottery money into British film, the system has been only partially successful in fostering quality, world-beating cinema. Critics accused the UK Film Council of extravagance, wasting money backing film projects that would have difficulty finding buoyancy in a colder sink-or-swim commercial environment, spawning cinematic flops and effectively managing a welfare system for local film.

Film fans nostalgically dwell on the golden – but honestly rather brief – era of Ealing comedies, when the London-based Ealing Studios turned out a steady stream of hits. Between 1947 and 1955, after which the studios were sold to the BBC, it produced enduring classics such as *Passport to Pimlico, Kind Hearts and Coronets, Whisky Galore, The Man in the White Suit, The Lavender Hill Mob* and *The Ladykillers*. This was also the time of legendary film-makers Michael Powell and Emeric Pressburger, the men behind *The Life and Death of Colonel Blimp* and *The Red Shoes*.

Today the industry finds itself habitually stuck in a deep groove of romantic comedies, costume dramas and gangster pics, while setting periodic benchmarks for horror. Producers, directors and actors complain about a lack of adventurousness in those holding the purse strings, while film investors claim there are not enough scripts worth backing.

Recent notable British films include the unsettling horror *The Woman in Black* (2012), musical drama *Les Misérables* (2012) and *Great Expectations* (2012). Educated in London, Essex-born British director Ben Wheatley has won plaudits for *Down Terrace* (2009), set in Brighton and shot on a budget of £6000, the award-winning horror *Kill List* (2011) and black comedy *Sightseers* (2012).

Well-known British actors such as Ewan McGregor, Daniel Craig, Ralph Fiennes, Jude Law, Christian Bale, Liam Neeson, Hugh Laurie, Kate Winslet, Keira Knightley and Emily Watson spend time working abroad, as

OUTDOOR CINEMA

Outdoor cinema is rolled out in London in the warmer months at Somerset House Film4 Summer Screen (www.somersethouse.org.uk/film; tickets £14.50), where films can be enjoyed in a sublime setting.

BEST CINEMATIC FESTIVALS

A host of London festivals celebrating cinema and ranging across the film spectrum entertains film enthusiasts from the popcorn crowd to art-house intelligentsia and shades in between.

London Film Festival (www.bfi.org.uk/lff) Held in October; the highlight of London's many festivals celebrating cinema.

Raindance Festival (www.raindance.co.uk) Europe's leading independent film-making festival. It's a terrific celebration of independent, non-mainstream cinema from across the globe, screening just before the London Film Festival.

Portobello Film Festival (www.portobellofilmfestival.com) Held in September; features largely independent works by London film-makers and international directors. The UK's largest independent film competition, it's free to attend.

London Lesbian & Gay Film Festival (www.bfi.org.uk/llgff) One of the best of its kind with hundreds of independent films from around the world shown over a fun, party-intensive fortnight at BFI Southbank.

do many British directors, including Ridley Scott (*Blade Runner*, *Alien*, *Thelma & Louise*, *Black Hawk Down*), Michael Winterbottom (*The Claim*, *The Killer Inside Me*), Christopher Nolan (*Memento*, *Insomnia*, *The Prestige*, *Inception*, *The Dark Knight Rises*) and Sam Mendes (*American Beauty*, *Revolutionary Road*, *Skyfall*).

London on the Screen

From the impressions of an interwar Harley St in *The King's Speech* (2010) to the seedy South Kensington and Earl's Court of Roman Polanski's *Repulsion* (1965), London remains a hugely popular location to make films. That most die-hard of New Yorkers, Woody Allen, has made *Match Point*, *Scoop*, *Cassandra's Dream* and *You Will Meet a Tall Dark Stranger* in the capital over the past decade. The city's blend of historic and modern architecture works massively to its advantage: Ang Lee's *Sense and Sensibility* (1995) retreated to historic Greenwich for its wonderful parkland and neoclassical architecture. Merchant Ivory's costume drama *Howard's End* (1992) and the biopic *Chaplin* (1992) feature the neo-Gothic St Pancras Chambers, while David Lynch's *The Elephant Man* (1980) took advantage of the moody atmosphere around the then-undeveloped Shad Thames (the site of today's Butler's Wharf). *Withnail & I* (1987) remains a quintessential classic of offbeat British comedy, partly set in Camden.

Get the low-down on British films, as well as films made in London and the UK, at the London Film Museum (p175).

London also serves as an effective backdrop to the horror genre and dystopian cinema. Danny Boyle's shocking *28 Days Later* (2002) haunted viewers with images of an entirely deserted central London in its opening sequences, scenes rekindled in the gore-splattered sequel *28 Weeks Later* (2006). Much of Stanley Kubrick's controversial and bleak *A Clockwork Orange* (1971) was filmed in London, while Alfonso Cuarón's *Children of Men* (2006) forged a menacing and desperate vision of a London to come. Further dystopian visions of a totalitarian London-to-come coalesce in James McTeigue's *V for Vendetta* (2005).

Other parts of town to look out for include the eponymous West London neighbourhood in *Notting Hill* (1999) and the Dickensian backstreets of Borough that feature in such polar opposites as chick-flick *Bridget Jones's Diary* (2001) and Guy Ritchie's gangster-romp *Lock, Stock and Two Smoking Barrels* (1998), while Smithfield conveys a certain bleak glamour in *Closer* (2004) and Brick Lane finds celluloid fame in its namesake drama (2007). Farringdon and other parts of town north of the Thames provide the backdrop to David Cronenberg's ultra-violent *Eastern Promises* (2007) while Crouch End and New Cross Gate is overrun by zombies in the hilarious *Shaun of the Dead* (2004). Mike Newell's moving drama *Soursweet* (1988) follows the travails of a newly married Hong Kong couple moving to London in the 1960s. Sam Mendes' well-received *Skyfall* puts London into action-packed context in James Bond's spectacular 2012 outing, while awkward British monster movie *Attack the Block* (2011) sees a south London council-estate gang fighting off an alien invasion. British director Terence Davies' critically acclaimed dramatic adaption of Terence Rattigan's *The Deep Blue Sea* (2011) conjures up a tragic portrait of post-WWII London.

The urban environment's capacity to isolate people in one of the world's most densely populated cities forms the background of Carol Morley's poignant *Dreams of a Life* (2011), a moving examination of the life of Joyce Vincent, a sociable 38-year-old woman whose dead body lay undiscovered for three years in her North London flat.

For an overview of cinemas in London see the Entertainment chapter (p65), and check the Entertainment sections within each neighbourhood chapter for local cinema details.

Television

Most countries would give their eye teeth to have TV this good, from the extraordinary films of the BBC natural history unit to the cutting-edge comedy and drama across the channels.

When it comes to televisual output, London plays with a stronger hand than it does in film: a huge amount of global TV content originates in Britain, from the *Teletubbies* to *Planet Earth* and *Who Wants to be a Millionaire*. British TV shows adapted to localised versions garnering huge followings include *The X Factor*, *MasterChef* and *Top Gear*. There are five free-to-air national TV stations: BBC1, BBC2, ITV1, Channel 4 and Five.

First airing on BBC1 in 2007 and tipped for a 5th series, award-winning *Outnumbered*, a charmingly comic portrayal of life in a South London middle-class family, is much-loved for its uncontrived yet painfully amusing insights into parenthood.

Radio

BBC London (94.9 FM) is largely a talk station with great sports coverage, broadcasting across the capital. BBC Radio 4 (93.5 FM) is an excellent spoken word station with first-rate news coverage. If you're stuck in traffic, tune into Capital FM (95.8 FM), the most popular pop station in the city and the commercial equivalent of the BBC's national Radio 1 (98.8 FM). For indie music, there's Xfm (104.9 FM), for dance tune into Kiss (100 FM) and for soul, R&B and hip hop there's Choice FM (96.9 FM). Classical listeners can swivel the dial to Classic FM (100.9 FM).

Media

Newspapers & Magazines

National newspapers in England and London are almost always financially independent of any political party, although their political leanings are quite obvious. There are two broad categories of newspapers, most commonly distinguished as broadsheets (or 'qualities') and tabloids (the distinction is more about content than physical size).

Daily Papers

The main London newspaper is the centre-right *Evening Standard*, a free tabloid published between Monday and Friday and handed out around mainline train stations, tube stations, retailers and stands. *Metro* (published Monday to Friday) is another skimpy morning paper designed to be read in 20 minutes, littering tube stations and seats, giving you an extra excuse to ignore your fellow passengers.

Broadsheet readers are extremely loyal to their paper and rarely switch from one to another. Liberal and middle-class, the *Guardian* has excellent reporting, an award-winning website and a progressive agenda. A handy small-format entertainment supplement, the *Guide,* comes with Saturday's paper. Dubbed the 'Torygraph', the right-wing *Daily Telegraph* is the unofficial Conservative party paper, and fogeyish perhaps, but with first-rate foreign news coverage. The *Times* is a stalwart of the British press and part of the Murdoch stable; it's a decent read with a wide range of articles and strong foreign reporting. Not aligned with any political party, the *Independent* is a left-leaning serious-minded tabloid with a focus on lead stories that other papers ignore. The *Financial Times* is a heavyweight business paper with a fantastic travel section in its weekend edition.

For sex and scandal over your bacon and eggs, turn to the *Mirror,* a working class and Old Labour paper; the *Sun* – the UK's bestseller – a gossip-hungry Tory-leaning tabloid legendary for its sassy headlines; or the lowbrow *Daily Star.* Other tabloid reads include the midlevel *Daily Express* and the centre-right *Daily Mail.*

Sunday Papers

Most dailies have Sunday stablemates, and (predictably) the tabloids have bumper editions of trashy gossip, star-struck adulation, fashion extras and mean-spirited diatribes. The *Observer,* established in 1791, is the oldest Sunday paper and sister of the *Guardian,* with a great Sunday arts supplement *(New Review).* The *Sunday Telegraph* is as serious and politically blue as its weekly sister paper, while the *Sunday Times* is brimful of fashion and scandal and probably puts paid to a rainforest per issue (but most of it can be arguably tossed in the recycling bin upon purchase).

Magazines

An astonishing range of magazines is published and consumed in London, from celebrity gossip to ideological heavyweights.

Political magazines are particularly strong. The satirical *Private Eye* has no political bias and lampoons everyone equally, although anyone in a position of power is preferred. The excellent weekly *Economist* cannot be surpassed for international political and business analysis. Claiming to be Britain's oldest-running magazine, the right-wing weekly *Spectator* is worshipped by Tory voters, but its witty articles are often loved by left-wingers, too. The *New Statesman* is a stalwart left-wing intellectual news magazine.

A freebie available from tube stations, big museums and galleries, *Time Out* is the listings guide par excellence and great for taking the city's pulse, with strong arts coverage, while the *Big Issue,* sold on the streets by the homeless, is not just an honourable project, but a damned fine read.

London loves celebrities with *Heat, Closer* and *OK!* the most popular purveyors of the genre. US import *Glamour* is the queen of the women's glossies; *Marie Claire, Elle* and *Vogue* are regarded as the thinking-woman's glossies. The smarter men's magazines include *GQ* and *Esquire,* while less edifying reads are the so-called 'lads' mags': *FHM, Loaded, Maxim* and *Nuts.* A slew of style magazines are published here, including *i-D,* an übercool London fashion and music gospel, and rival *Dazed & Confused.*

New Media Websites

Londonist (www.londonist.com) City-centric blog.

Urban 75 (www.urban75.com) Outstanding community website, with a counter-cultural edge.

Survival Guide

Transport

ARRIVING IN LONDON

Most people arrive in London by air, but an increasing number of visitors coming from Europe let the train take the strain, while buses from across the Continent are a further option.

The city has five airports: Heathrow, which is the largest, to the west; Gatwick to the south; Stansted to the northeast; Luton to the northwest; and London City in the Docklands.

Most transatlantic flights land at Heathrow (average flight time from the US East Coast is between 6½ and 7½ hours, 10 to 11 hours from the West Coast; slightly more on the return).

Visitors from Europe are more likely to arrive at Gatwick, Stansted or Luton (the latter two are used exclusively by low-cost airlines such as easyJet and Ryanair). Most flights to continental Europe last from one to three hours.

An increasingly popular form of transport is the Eurostar – the Channel Tunnel train – between London and Paris or Brussels. The journey lasts 2¼ hours to Paris and less than two hours to Brussels. Travellers depart from and arrive in the centre of each city.

Flights and tours can be booked online at lonelyplanet.com/bookings.

Heathrow Airport

Some 15 miles west of central London, **Heathrow** (LHR; www.heathrowairport.com) is the world's busiest international airport and counts five terminals, including the totally revamped Terminal 2.

Each terminal has currency-exchange facilities, information counters and accommodation desks.

Left-luggage Facilities are in each terminal and open 5.30am to 11pm. The charge per item is £5 for up to four hours, £8.50 for 24 hours (or part thereof), up to a maximum of 90 days.

Hotels There are three international-style hotels that can be reached on foot from the terminals, and another 20 or so nearby. The **Hotel Hoppa** (www.hotelbybusheathrow.com; adult/child £4/free) bus links nearby hotels with the airport's terminals, running every 15 to 30 minutes from 4am to midnight.

Train

Underground (www.tfl.gov.uk) Three stations on the Piccadilly line serve Heathrow: one for Terminals 1, 2 and 3, another for Terminal 4, and the terminus for Terminal 5. The Underground, commonly referred to as 'the tube' (one way £5, from central London one hour, every three to nine minutes) is the cheapest way of getting to Heathrow. It runs from just after 5/5.45am from/to the airport (just after 5.45/7am Sunday) to 11.45pm/12.30am (about 11.30pm Sunday in both directions). Buy tickets at the station.

Heathrow Express (www.heathrowexpress.com; one way/return £20/34) This high-speed train whisks passengers from Heathrow Central station (serving Terminals 1, 2 and 3) and Terminal 5 to Paddington. Terminal 4 passengers should take the free inter-terminal shuttle train available to Heathrow Central and board there. Trains run every 15 minutes from just after 5am in both directions to between 11.25pm (from Paddington) and just before midnight (from the airport). The journey takes 15 minutes.

Heathrow Connect (www.heathrowconnect.com; one way £9.50) Travelling between Heathrow and Paddington station, this modern passenger train service departs every 25 minutes and makes five stops en route at places like Southall and Ealing Broadway. The first trains leave Heathrow at just after 5.20am (6am Sunday) and the last service is just after 11pm. From Paddington, services leave between approximately 5am (6am Sunday) and just after 11pm. The journey takes 30 minutes.

Bus

National Express (www.nationalexpress.com) Coaches (one way from £5.50, 45 minutes to 90 minutes, every 30 minutes to one hour) link the Heathrow Central Bus Station with **Victoria coach station** (Map p448; 164 Buckingham Palace Rd, SW1; ⊖Victoria) about 45 times per day. The first bus leaves the Heathrow Central Bus station (at Terminals 1, 2 and 3) at 5.35am, with the last departure at 9.40pm. The first bus leaves Victoria at 7.45am, the last at 11.30pm.

At night the **N9 bus** (£1.40, 1¼ hours, every 20 minutes) connects Heathrow with central London, terminating at Aldwych.

Taxi

A metered black cab trip to/from central London will cost between £45 and £65 (£60 from Oxford St) and take 45 minutes to an hour, depending on traffic and your departure point.

Gatwick Airport

Located some 30 miles south of central London, **Gatwick** (LGW; www.gatwickairport.com) is smaller than Heathrow. The North and South Terminals are linked by a 24-hour shuttle train, with the journey time about three minutes. There are left-luggage facilities in both terminals, open 5am to 9pm. The charge is £8 per item for 24 hours (or part thereof), up to a maximum of 90 days' storage.

Train

National Rail (☎0845-7484950; www.nationalrail.co.uk) There are regular train services to/from London Bridge (30 minutes, every 15 to 30 minutes), King's Cross (55 minutes, every 15 to 30 minutes) and London Victoria (30 minutes, every 10 to 15 minutes). Fares vary depending on the time of travel and the train company, but allow £8 to £10 for a single.

Gatwick Express (www.gatwickexpress.com; one way/return £19.90/34.90) This dedicated train service links the station near the South Terminal with Victoria station in central London every 15 minutes. From the airport, there are services between 4.30am and 1.35am. From Victoria, they leave between 3.30am and just after 12.30am. The journey takes a half-hour.

Bus

National Express (www.nationalexpress.com) coaches (one way from £7, 65 minutes to 90 minutes) run throughout the day from Gatwick to Victoria coach station. Services leave the airport at least once an hour usually on the hour round the clock and operate at least hourly on the half-hour from Victoria.

easyBus (www.easybus.co.uk; one way £10, return from £12) This budget outfit runs 19-seater minibuses every 10 to 20 minutes from Earl's Court/West Brompton to Gatwick from 3am to 12.30am daily. Departures from Gatwick are between 4.20am and 1.30am. Tickets can be purchased from the driver and there are ticket outlets at the airport in both the North and South Terminals. Journey time averages 75 minutes.

Taxi

A metered black cab trip to/from central London costs about £100 and takes just over an hour.

Stansted Airport

Stansted (STN; www.stanstedairport.com) is 35 miles north-east of central London in the direction of Cambridge.

Train

The **Stansted Express** (☎0845 8500150; www.stanstedexpress.com) rail service (one way/return £23.40/32.80, 45 minutes, every 15 to 30 minutes) links the airport and Liverpool St station. From the airport the first train leaves at 5.30am, the last at 1.30am (12.30am on Saturday). Trains depart Liverpool St station from 4.10am to just before 11.30pm.

Bus

National Express (www.nationalexpress.com) Coaches run around the clock, offering well over 100 services per day. The A6 runs to Victoria coach station (one way from £10, 85

GETTING HERE FOR LESS

Check any of the websites below for good deals on airline tickets:

- www.cheapflights.co.uk
- www.ebookers.com
- www.expedia.com
- www.lastminute.com
- www.opodo.co.uk
- www.skyscanner.net

Or try either of the following for rail bookings:

- www.eurostar.com
- www.raileurope.co.uk

to 110 minutes, every 10 to 20 minutes) via North London. The A9 runs to Liverpool St Station (one way from £8, 70 minutes, every 30 minutes).

easyBus (www.easybus.co.uk) Minibuses (one way £10, from £12 return, 75 minutes, every 15 to 30 minutes) from Baker St to Stansted run 24 hours a day.

Terravision (www.terravision.eu) Coaches link Stansted to both Liverpool St train station (bus A51, one way/return from £9/15, 55 minutes) and Victoria coach station (bus A50, one way/return from £8/14, 75 minutes) every 20 to 40 minutes between 6am and 1am.

Taxi

A metered black cab trip to/from central London costs around £125.

Luton Airport

A smallish airport 32 miles northwest of London, **Luton** (LTN; www.london-luton.co.uk) generally caters for cheap charter flights and discount airlines.

Train

National Rail (☎0845 7484950; www.nationalrail.co.uk) services (one way from £15, 30 to 40 minutes, every six to 15 minutes, from 7am to 10pm) run from London Bridge and King's Cross St Pancras stations to Luton Airport Parkway station, from where an airport shuttle bus will take you to the airport in eight minutes.

Bus

easyBus (www.easybus.co.uk) Minibuses (one way £10, from £12 return, one hour, every 30 minutes) run from Victoria coach station to Luton via Marble Arch, Baker St and Finchley Rd tube stations every half-hour round the clock, with the same frequencies coming from the airport.

Green Line Bus 757 (www.greenline.co.uk) Buses from/to Luton (one way/return £17/25, tickets valid three months, 75 to 90 minutes) run to/from Buckingham Palace Rd just south of Victoria station, leaving approximately every half-hour round the clock.

Taxi

A metered black cab trip to/from central London costs about £110.

London City Airport

Its proximity to central London, which is just 6 miles to the west, as well as to the commercial district of the Docklands, means **London City Airport** (LCY; www.londoncityairport.com) is predominantly a gateway airport for business travellers, although it does also serve holidaymakers with its 40-odd continental European and half-dozen national destinations. You can also now fly to New York from here.

Train

The **Docklands Light Railway** (DLR; www.tfl.gov.uk/dlr) stops at the London City Airport station (one way £4.50, with an Oyster card £2.10 to £3.90). The journey to Bank takes just over 20 minutes, and trains go every eight to 10 minutes from just after 5.30am to 12.15am Monday to Saturday, and 7am to 11.15pm Sunday.

Taxi

A metered black cab trip to or from the City/Oxford St/Earl's Court costs about £25/35/50.

Train

Main national rail routes are served by InterCity trains, which are neither cheap nor particularly punctual. Check **National Rail Enquiries** (☎0845 748 4950; www.nationalrail.co.uk) for timetables and fares.

Eurostar (www.eurostar.com) The high-speed passenger rail service links St Pancras International Station with Gare du Nord in Paris (or Bruxelles Midi in Brussels), with between 14 and 16 daily departures. Fares vary enormously, from £69 for the cheapest return to

CLIMATE CHANGE & TRAVEL

Every form of transport that relies on carbon-based fuel generates CO_2, the main cause of human-induced climate change. Modern travel is dependent on aeroplanes, which might use less fuel per kilometre per person than most cars but travel much greater distances. The altitude at which aircraft emit gases (including CO_2) and particles also contributes to their climate change impact. Many websites offer 'carbon calculators' that allow people to estimate the carbon emissions generated by their journey and, for those who wish to do so, to offset the impact of the greenhouse gases emitted with contributions to portfolios of climate-friendly initiatives throughout the world. Lonely Planet offsets the carbon footprint of all staff and author travel.

almost £310 for a fully flexible return at busy periods.

Eurotunnel (www.eurotunnel.com) High-speed shuttle trains transport motor vehicles and bicycles between Folkestone in England and Coquelles (5km southwest of Calais) in France. Services run round the clock – up to four times an hour during the day but hourly from 1am to 6am. Booking online is cheapest, where day-overnight return fares start at £46 and two- to five-day excursion fares from £94. All prices include a car and passengers.

Bus

Eurolines (Map p448; www.eurolines.com; SW1) Has buses operated by National Express to continental Europe leaving from **Victoria coach station** (Map p448; 164 Buckingham Palace Rd, SW1; ⊖Victoria).

National Express (www.nationalexpress.com) The main coach operator in the UK, with generally comfortable and reliable services.

Green Line (www.greenline.co.uk) Another national coach operator on main UK routes.

Megabus (www.megabus.com) Operates no-frills, airline-style seat pricing.

GETTING AROUND LONDON

Public transport in London is extensive, often excellent and always pricey. It is managed by **Transport for London** (www.tfl.gov.uk), which has a user-friendly, multilingual website with a journey planner, maps, detailed information on every mode of transport in the capital and live updates on traffic.

The cheapest way to get around London is with an Oyster card, a smart card. Paper tickets still exist and, although day travel cards cost the same on paper as on Oyster, using paper singles or returns is substantially more expensive than using an Oyster.

The tube, DLR and Overground network are ideal for zooming across different parts of the city; buses and the new Barclays bikes are great for shorter journeys.

Left-luggage facility

Excess Baggage (☎0800 7831085; www.left-baggage.co.uk) operates at London's main train stations: St Pancras, Paddington, Euston, Victoria, Waterloo, King's Cross, Liverpool St and Charing Cross. The service costs £8.50 per bag for the first 24 hours and £5 for each additional day.

OYSTER CARD

The Oyster card is a smart card on which you can store credit towards 'prepay' fares, as well as Travelcards valid for periods from a day to a year. Oyster cards are valid across the entire public transport network in London. All you need to do when entering a station is touch your card on a reader (which has a yellow circle with the image of an Oyster card on them) and then touch again on your way out. The system will then deduct the appropriate amount of credit from your card, as necessary. For bus journeys, you only need to touch once upon boarding.

The benefit lies in the fact that fares for Oyster card users are lower than standard ones. If you are making many journeys during the day, you will never pay more than the appropriate Travelcard (peak or off peak) once the daily 'price cap' has been reached.

Oyster cards can be bought (£5 refundable deposit required) and topped up at any Underground station, travel information centre or shop displaying the Oyster logo.

To get your deposit back along with any remaining credit, simply return your Oyster card at a ticket booth.

London Underground

The London Underground ('the tube'; 11 colour-coded lines) is part of an integrated transport system that also includes the Docklands Light Railway (DLR; a driverless overhead train operating in the eastern part of the city) and Overground network (mostly outside of Zone 1 and sometimes underground). Despite the never-ending upgrades and 'engineering works' requiring weekend closures, it is overall the quickest and easiest way of getting around the city, if not the cheapest.

The first trains operate from around 5.30am Monday to Saturday and 6.45am Sunday. The last trains leave around 12.30am Monday to Saturday and 11.30pm Sunday.

During weekend closures, schedules, maps and alternative route suggestions are posted in every station, and staff are at hand to help redirect you.

Some stations, most famously Leicester Square and Covent Garden, are much closer in reality than they appear on the map.

Fares

- London is divided into nine concentric fare zones.
- It will always be cheaper to travel with an Oyster card than a paper ticket.
- Children under the age of 11 travel free.
- If you're in London for a longer period and plan to travel every day, consider a weekly or even a monthly Travelcard.
- If you're caught without a valid ticket, you're liable for an on-the-spot fine of £80. If paid within 21 days, the fine is reduced to £40. Inspectors accept no excuses.

Bus

London's iconic double-decker 'jump-on-jump-off' Routemaster was phased out in 2005 except for two 'heritage routes' (9 and 15). The move caused such an uproar, however, that a sleek, newly designed version was introduced on certain routes (eg 38) in early 2012. Still, less-sexy double-deckers on other routes offer just as good a view of the city as the Routemasters but be aware that the going can be slow, thanks to traffic jams and dozens of commuters getting on and off at all the stops.

There are excellent bus maps at every stop detailing all routes and destinations served from that particular area (generally a few bus stops within two to three minutes' walk, shown on a local map).

Bus services normally operate from 5am to 11.30pm.

Night bus

More than 50 night bus routes (prefixed with the letter 'N') run from around 11.30pm to 5am.

There are also another 60 bus routes operating 24 hours; the frequency decreases between 11pm and 5am.

Oxford Circus, Tottenham Court Rd and Trafalgar Sq are the main hubs for night routes.

Night buses can be infrequent and stop only on request, so remember to ring for your stop.

Fares

Oyster cards are valid on all bus services, including night buses, and are cheaper than cash fares. Bus journeys cost a flat fare (non-Oyster/Oyster £2.40/1.40) regardless of how far you go. The daily price cap on buses is £4.40.

At bus stops with a yellow background, if you don't have an Oyster card, you must buy your ticket *before* boarding the bus at the stop's ticket machine (you will need the exact amount in coins).

Children under 11 travel free.

Bicycle

Tens of thousands of Londoners cycle to work every day, and it is generally a good way to get around the city, although traffic can be intimidating for less confident cyclists. The city has tried hard to improve the cycling infrastructure, however, opening new 'cycle superhighways' for commuters and launching the Barclays Cycle Hire Scheme, which is particularly useful for visitors. In a few short years bicycle cafes have sprouted up around London like mushrooms after rain.

Transport for London (www.tfl.gov.uk) publishes 14 free maps of London's cycle routes. You can order them via the website or by ringing ☎0843-222 1234.

Hire

London Bicycle Tour Company (Map p444; ☎020-3318 3088; www.londonbicycle.com; 1a Gabriel's Wharf, 56 Upper Ground, SE1; ⏲10am-6pm Jun-Sep, to 4pm Oct-May; ⊖Waterloo or Blackfriars) Rentals cost £3.50 per hour or £20 for the first day, £10 for days two and three, £5 for days four and five, £50 for the first week, £25 for the second and £20 for subsequent weeks. You will need to provide credit-card details as a deposit and must show ID.

TUBE, DLR & OVERGROUND FARES

ZONE	NON-OYSTER SINGLE	OYSTER PEAK SINGLE	OYSTER OFF-PEAK SINGLE	PEAK CAP (OYSTER DAY TRAVEL CARD)	OFF-PEAK CAP (OYSTER DAY TRAVEL CARD)
Zone 1 only	£4.50	£2.10	£2.10	£8.40	£7
Zone 1& 2	£4.50	£2.80	£2.10	£8.40	£7
Zone 1-3	£4.50	£3.20	£2.70	£10.60	£7.70
Zone 1-4	£5.50	£3.80	£2.70	£10.60	£7.70
Zone 1-5	£5.50	£4.60	£3	£15.80	£8.50
Zone 1-6	£5.50	£5	£3	£15.80	£8.50
Children 11-15 (Zone 1 & 2)	£2.20	£0.80	£0.75	£4.20	£1.50

BARCLAYS CYCLE HIRE SCHEME

Like Paris and other European cities, London has its own cycling-hire scheme called **Barclays bikes** (☎0845-026 3630; www.tfl.gov.uk.), but universally known as 'Boris bikes' after the city's unstoppable mayor, Boris Johnson, who launched the initiative. The bikes have proved as popular with visitors as with Londoners.

The idea is simple: pick up a bike from one of the 570 docking stations dotted around the capital. Cycle. Drop it off at another docking station.

Access Fee & Hire rates

➡ The access fee is £2 for 24 hours, £10 for a week. All you need is a credit or debit card. Up to 30min is free.

➡ Up to one hour costs £1, up to 1½ hours costs £4, up to two hours costs £6, up to three hours costs £15 and up to 24 hours (maximum) costs £50.

➡ You can take as many bikes as you like during your access period (24 hours or one week), leaving five minutes between each trip.

➡ The pricing structure is designed to encourage short journeys rather than longer rentals; for those, go to a hire company. You'll also find that although easy to ride, the bikes only have three gears and are quite heavy. You must be 18 to buy access and at least 14 to ride a bike.

Hiring a Bike

➡ Insert your debit or credit card in the docking station to pay your access fee (only once for the access period).

➡ Request a cycle release code slip at the docking station every time you want to take a bike during your access period.

➡ Enter the release code at your chosen bike dock; wait for the green light to release the bike.

➡ If you find it difficult to pull the bike free from its dock, bounce the back wheel up and down first.

➡ Ride!

➡ Return the bike at any free dock; wait for the green light to make sure the bike is locked.

➡ If the docking station is full, consult the terminal to find available docking points nearby. iPhone users may also want to download the free cyclehire app, which locates nearby docking stations and shows you how full they are.

It also offers daily bike tours (routes on website) of central London for £18.95 (East London and Royal London tours at £21.95 are also available weekends).

On Your Bike (Map p444; ☎020-7378 6669; www.onyourbike.com; The Vaults, Montague Close, SE1; ⏲7.30am-7.30pm Mon-Fri, 10am-6pm Sat, 11am-5pm Sun; ⊖London Bridge) Rentals cost £18 for the first day, £10 for subsequent days and £45 per week. Prices include hire of a helmet but not a lock. A deposit of £150 (via credit card) is required and you will need to show ID.

Bicycles on Public Transport

Bicycles can be taken only on the Circle, District, Hammersmith & City and Metropolitan tube lines, though not during peak times (7.30am to 9.30am and 4pm to 7pm Monday to Friday). Folding bikes can be taken on any line at any time, however. Bicycles can also travel on the Overground (with the same time restrictions as on the tube) and the Emirates Air Line cable car but not on the DLR.

Restrictions on taking a bike on suburban and mainline trains vary from company to company, but many now have carriages with very generous handicapped sections that cyclists can take advantage of when not in use. For details call **National Rail Enquiries** (☎0845-748 4950; www.nationalrail.co.uk).

Taxi

Black Cabs

The **black cab** (www.londonblackcabs.co.uk) is as much a feature of the London cityscape as the red double-decker bus. Licensed black-cab drivers have 'The Knowledge', acquired after rigorous training and a series of exams. They are supposed to know 25,000 streets within a six-mile radius of Charing Cross/Trafalgar Sq and the 100 most visited spots of the moment, including clubs and restaurants.

➡ Cabs are available for hire when the yellow sign above the windscreen is lit; just stick your arm out to signal one.

➡ Fares are metered, with the flagfall charge of £2.40 (covering the first 310m during a weekday), rising by increments of 20p for each subsequent 168m.

➡ Fares are more expensive in the evenings and overnight.

➡ You can tip taxi drivers up to 10% but most Londoners simply round up to the nearest pound.

➡ To order a cab by phone, try **Computer Cabs** (☎cash 020-7908 0207, credit card 020-7432 1432; www.comcablondon.com); it charges a £2 booking fee.

➡ **Hailo** (hailocab.com) uses uses GPS to connect your mobile phone to that of the nearest free black-cab driver; download the free app from its website. You pay only the metered fare.

Minicabs

➡ Minicabs, which are licensed, are cheaper (usually) competitors of black cabs.

➡ Unlike black cabs, minicabs cannot legally be hailed on the street; they must be hired by phone or directly from one of the minicab offices (every high street has at least one and most clubs work with a minicab firm to send revellers home safely).

➡ Don't accept unsolicited offers from individuals claiming to be minicab drivers – they are just guys with cars.

➡ Minicabs don't have meters; there's usually a fare set by the dispatcher. Make sure you ask before setting off.

➡ Your hotel or host will be able to recommend a reputable minicab company in the neighbourhood; every Londoner has the number of at least one company. Or phone a large 24-hour operator such as **Addison Lee** (☎0844-800 6677; www.addisonlee.com).

➡ Women travelling alone at night can choose **Lady Mini Cabs** (☎020-7272 3300; www.ladyminicabs.co.uk), which has women drivers.

Boat

There are a number of companies operating along the River Thames. Only **Thames Clippers** (www.thamesclippers.com; adult/child £6.50/3.25) really offers commuter services, however. It's fast, pleasant and you're almost always guaranteed a seat and a view.

Boats run every 20 to 30 minutes from 6am to between 10pm and midnight, depending on the day of the week and whether there is an event at the O2. The route goes from London Eye Millennium Pier to Woolwich Arsenal Piers, serving London Eye, Tate Modern, Shakespeare's Globe, Borough Market, Tower Bridge, Canary Wharf, Greenwich and the O2.

Discounts apply for pay-as-you-go Oyster card holders (£5.85) and travel-card holders (paper ticket or on an Oyster card; £4.30).

Car & Motorcycle

As a visitor, it's very unlikely you'll need to drive in London. Mayors Ken Livingstone (2000–08) and Boris Johnson (elected in 2008 and voted in for another four years in 2012) have done everything in their power to encourage Londoners to get out of their car and into public transport (or on their bikes!) and the same disincentives should keep you firmly off the road: the congestion charge, extortionate parking fees, traffic jams, high price of petrol, fiendishly efficient traffic wardens and wheel clampers and so on.

If you get a parking ticket or your car gets clamped, call the number on the ticket. If the car has been removed, ring the free 24-hour service called **TRACE** (Tow-Away Removal & Clamping Enquiries; ☎0845-206 8602) to find out where your car has been taken to. It will cost you a minimum of £200 to get your vehicle back on the road.

Driving

ROAD RULES

➡ Get a copy of the *The Highway Code* (www.gov.uk/highway-code), available at Automobile Association (AA) and Royal Automobile Club (RAC) outlets, as well as some bookshops and tourist offices.

➡ A foreign driving licence is valid in Britain for up to 12 months from the time of your last entry into the country.

➡ If you bring a car from continental Europe, make sure you're adequately insured.

➡ All drivers and passengers must wear seatbelts, and motorcyclists must wear a helmet.

CONGESTION CHARGE

London followed Singapore's lead in 2003 and introduced a congestion charge to reduce the flow of traffic into its centre. For full details log on to www.tfl.gov.uk/roadusers/congestioncharging.

The congestion charge zone encompasses Euston Rd and Pentonville Rd to the north, Park Lane to the west, Tower Bridge to the east and Elephant & Castle and Vauxhall Bridge Rd to the south. As you enter the zone, you will see a large white 'C' in a red circle.

If you enter the zone between 7am and 6pm Monday to Friday (excluding public holidays), you must pay the £10 charge (payable in advance or on the day) or £12 on the first charging day after travel to avoid receiving a fine (£120 or £60 if paid within 14 days).

You can pay online, at newsagents, petrol stations or any shop displaying the 'C' sign, by telephone on ☎0845-900 1234 (or ☎44 20-7649 9122 from abroad) and even by text message/SMS once you've registered online.

Hire

There is no shortage of car rental agencies in London. Book in advance for the best fares, especially at weekends.

A godsend for those who need a car for just a couple of hours or half a day is the self-service pay-as-you-go scheme, **Zipcar** (☎0333-2409000; www.zipcar.co.uk). After registering and paying the £59.50 annual membership, you locate the closest available Zipcar vehicle to where you are staying, unlock the car with your membership card, release the key with a PIN and drive on. Prices start at £5 (£6.50 Friday to Sunday) per hour and £49 (£55) per day. You get 40 miles of free petrol per day for bookings of less than 24 hours, and about 500 miles per week for longer bookings.

The following rental agencies have several branches across the capital:

Avis (www.avis.com)

easyCar (www.easycar.com)

Hertz (www.hertz.com)

Cable Car

The **Emirates Air Line** (www.emiratesairline.co.uk; adult/child single £4.30/2.20, return £8.60/4.40, with Oyster or Travelcard single £3.20/1.60, return £6.40/3.20; ⌚7am-9pm Mon-Fri, from 8am Sat, from 9am Sun Apr-Sep, closes 1hr earlier Oct-Mar; DLR Royal Victoria, ⊖North Greenwich), a cable car linking the Royal Docks in East London with North Greenwich some 90m above the Thames, opened to great fanfare on the eve of the Olympics in 2012 and proved immensely popular throughout the summer. Numbers have dropped off significantly since then as the cable car is really only useful as a form of transport if you are travelling between the ExCel Convention Centre and the O2. Still, though the journey is brief (a mere five minutes) the views of Canary Wharf, the Olympic Park, Greenwich, the Thames Barrier and the distant City skyscape are stunning.

TOURS

From erudite to eccentric, tours on offer to see the sights are legion in London. The organised bus and cab tours, although not particularly cool, are good for those who are short on time. Those with special interests – Jewish London, bird-watching, pop music – might consider hiring their own guide.

Air Tours

Adventure Balloons (☎01252 844222; www.adventureballoons.co.uk; Winchfield Park, London Rd, Hartley Wintney, Hampshire RG27) Weather permitting, there are weekday morning London flights (£199 per person) shortly after dawn from late April to mid-August. The flight lasts one hour, but allow four to six hours, including take-off, landing and recovery. See website for meeting points.

London Helicopter (☎020-7887 2626; www.thelondonhelicopter.com; POD Building, Bridges Ct, Battersea, SW11) Panoramic flights over London lasting 20 minutes for £199 depart daily throughout the day. Call or book online.

Boat Tours

Travel-card holders get one-third off all boating fares listed here (RIB London Voyages excluded). Boat services cruise along the Thames in central London but also go as far as the Thames Barrier and Hampton Court. If you're not bothered about commentary see Boat, p406.

Circular Cruise (☎020-7936 2033; www.crownriver.com; adult/child/family one way £9.50/4.75/28.50, return £12.30/6.15/36.90; ⌚11am-6.30pm late May-early Sep, to 5pm early Apr-late May & early Sep-Oct) Vessels travel east from Westminster Pier to St Katharine's Pier near the Tower of London and back, calling at Embankment, Festival and Bankside Piers. You can travel just one way, make the return trip or use the boat as a hop-on/hop-off service to visit sights on the way. Tours depart half-hourly late May to early September, every 40 minutes the rest of the year.

RIB London Voyages (Map p444; ☎020-7928 8933; www.londonribvoyages.com; Westminster Bridge Rd, Boarding Gate 1, London Eye, Waterloo Millennium Pier, SE1; adult/child £34.95/20.95; ⌚hourly 10am-6pm) Feel like James Bond – or David Beckham en route to the 2012 Olympic Games – on this high-speed inflatable boat that flies down the Thames at 30 to 35 knots. RIB also does a Captain Kidd–themed trip between the London Eye and Canary Wharf for the same price.

Thames River Services (Map p469; www.thamesriverservices.co.uk; adult/child single £12/6, return £15.50/7.75) These cruise boats leave Westminster Pier for Greenwich, stopping at the Tower of London. Every second service continues on from Greenwich to the Thames Barrier (one way adult/child £14/7, return £17/8.50, hourly 11.30am to 3.30pm) but does not land there, passing the O2 along the way.

From Westminster it's a two-hour round trip to Greenwich, three hours to the Thames Barrier; from Greenwich the round trip to the Thames Barrier takes one hour. From November to late March there's a reduced service from Westminster to Greenwich, with eight daily departures between 10.40am and 3.20pm.

Thames River Boats (Map p440; ☎020-7930 2062; www.wpsa.co.uk; Westminster Pier, Victoria Embankment, SW1; Kew adult/child/family one way £12/6/30, return £18/9/45, Hampton Court one way £15/7.50/37.50, return £22.50/11.25/56.25; ⏰11am & 2pm Apr-Oct) These boats go upriver from Westminster Pier to the Royal Botanic Gardens at Kew (1½ hours) and on to Hampton Court Palace (another 1½ hours, first sailing only), a distance of 22 miles. It's possible to get off the boats at Richmond, but it depends on the tides; check before you sail.

Bus Tours

The following companies offer commentary and the chance to get off at each sight and rejoin the tour on a later bus. Tickets are valid for 24 hours.

Big Bus Tours (www.bigbustours.com; adult/child/family £29/12/70; ⏰every 20min 8.30am-6pm Apr-Sep, to 5pm Oct & Mar, to 4.30pm Nov-Feb) Informative commentaries in eight languages. The ticket includes a free river cruise with City Cruises and three thematic walking tours (Royal London, Harry Potter film locations and Ghosts by Gaslight). Online booking discounts available.

Original Tour (www.theoriginaltour.com; adult/child/family £26/13/91; ⏰every 20min 8.30am-5.30pm) Another hop-on-hop-off option with a river cruise thrown in as well as three themed walks: Changing of the Guard, Rock 'n' Roll and Jack the Ripper.

Specialist Tours

Guide London (Association of Professional Tourist Guides; ☎020-7611 2545; www.guidelondon.org.uk; half-/full day £140/225) Hire a prestigious Blue Badge Tourist Guide, know-it-all guides who have studied for two years and passed a dozen written and practical exams to do their job. They can tell you stories behind the sights that you'd only hear from them or take you on a themed tour – from royalty and the Beatles to parks and shopping. Go by car, public transport, bike or on foot.

London Duck Tours (Map p444; ☎020-7928 3132; www.londonducktours.co.uk; County Hall, SE1; adult/child/family £21/14/62; ⊖Waterloo) Amphibious craft based on D-Day landing vehicles depart from behind the London Eye near the County Hall and cruise the streets of central London before making a dramatic descent into the Thames at Vauxhall. Tours last 75 minutes.

Open City (☎020-7383 2131; www.open-city.org.uk; tours £14.50-35.50) This not-for-profit organisation focusing on the built environment organises architectural tours to various parts of London, including the Square Mile, Bankside and King's Cross on foot, by bus or by boat. Some are photography tours. The tours (2½ to three hours) include lively, well-informed commentary.

Walking Tours

London Walks (☎020-7624 3978; www.walks.com; adult £9) A huge choice of walks, including Jack the Ripper tours at 7.30pm daily and 3pm Saturday, Beatles tours at 11.20am Tuesday and Saturday, a Sherlock Holmes tour at 2pm Friday and a tour of Harry Potter film locations at 2pm Saturday and Sunday.

London Mystery Walks (☎07957-388280; www.tourguides.org.uk; adult/child £10/9) Tour Jack the Ripper's old haunts at 7pm on Monday, Wednesday and Friday. You must book in advance.

Directory A–Z

Customs Regulations

The UK distinguishes between goods bought duty-free outside the EU and those bought in another EU country, where taxes and duties will have already been paid.

If you exceed your duty-free allowance, you will have to pay tax on the items. For European goods, there is officially no limit to how much you can bring but customs use certain guidelines to distinguish between personal and commercial use.

Discount Cards

Of interest to visitors who want to take in lots of paid sights in a short time is the **London Pass** (www.londonpass.com; per 1/2/3/6 days £47/64/77/102). The pass offers free entry and queue-jumping to all major attractions and can be altered to include use of the Underground and buses. Check the website for details.

Electricity

Emergency

Dial ☎999 to call the police, fire brigade or ambulance in the event of an emergency.

Internet Access

Almost all hotels in London now provide wi-fi, although a few, particularly top-end places, continue to charge for the service.

A number of hotels (and especially hostels) also provide computer terminals for guests who may not be travelling with a laptop or hand-held device.

A huge number of cafes offer free wi-fi to customers, including chains such as Starbucks, Cafe Nero, Costa and Pret a Manger as well as McDonalds.

Open-air and street wi-fi access is available in areas across London, including Oxford St, Trafalgar Sq, Piccadilly Circus, the City of London and Islington's Upper St. Users have to register but there is no charge.

Most major train stations, airport terminals and even certain Underground stations also have wi-fi access, but it can be quite pricey depending on your provider.

Legal Matters

Should you face any legal difficulties while in London, visit a branch of the **Citizens Advice Bureau** (www.citizensadvice.org.uk).

Driving Offences

The laws against drink-driving are very strict in the UK and treated seriously. Currently the limit is 80mg of alcohol in 100mL of blood. The safest approach is not to drink anything at all if you're planning to drive.

Drugs

Illegal drugs of every type are widely available in London, especially in clubs. Nonetheless, all the usual drug warnings apply. Cannabis was down-

IMPORT RESTRICTIONS

ITEM	DUTY-FREE	TAX & DUTY PAID
Tobacco	200 cigarettes, 100 cigarillos, 50 cigars or 250g tobacco	800 cigarettes, 400 cigarillos, 200 cigars, 1kg tobacco
Spirits & liqueurs	1L spirit or 2L of fortified wine (eg sherry or port)	10L spirit, 20L fortified wine
Beer & wine	16L beer and 4L still wine	110L beer, 90L still wine
Other goods	Up to a value of £390	n/a

graded to a Class C drug in 2004 but reclassified as a Class B drug in 2009 following new studies that prompted a government rethink. If you're caught with pot today, you're likely to be arrested. Possession of harder drugs, including heroin and cocaine, is always treated seriously. Searches on entering clubs are common.

Fines

In general you rarely have to pay on the spot for an offence. The exceptions are trains, the tube and buses, where people who can't produce a valid ticket for the journey when asked to by an inspector can be fined there and then. No excuses are accepted, though if you can't pay, you'll be able to register your details (if you have some sort of ID with you) and be sent a fine in the post.

Medical Services

EU nationals can obtain free emergency treatment (and, in some cases, reduced-cost healthcare) on presentation of a **European Health Insurance Card** (www.ehic.org.uk).

Reciprocal arrangements with the UK allow Australians, New Zealanders and residents and nationals of several other countries to receive free emergency medical treatment and subsidised dental care through the **National Health Service** (NHS; ☎0845 4647; www.nhs.uk). They can use hospital emergency departments, GPs and dentists. For a full list, click on 'Services near you' on the NHS website.

Visitors staying 12 months or longer, with the proper documentation, will receive care under the NHS by registering with a specific practice near their residence.

Travel insurance is advisable for non-EU residents as it offers greater flexibility over where and how you're treated and covers expenses for an ambulance and repatriation that will not be picked up by the NHS.

Dental Services

For emergency dental care, visit the NHS website or call into **University College London Hospital** (☎020-3447 0083; www.uclh.org; 235 Euston Rd, NW1; ⊖Euston Sq or Warren St).

Note that many travel insurance schemes do not cover emergency dental care.

Hospitals

The following hospitals have 24-hour accident and emergency departments. However, in an emergency just call 999 and an ambulance will normally be dispatched from the hospital nearest to you.

Charing Cross Hospital (☎020-3311 1234; www.imperial.nhs.uk/charingcross; Fulham Palace Rd, W6; ⊖Hammersmith)

Chelsea & Westminster Hospital (☎020-8746 8000; www.chelwest.nhs.uk; 369 Fulham Rd, SW10; ⊖South Kensington or Fulham Broadway then 🚌14 or 414)

Guy's Hospital (☎020-7188 7188; www.guysandstthomas.nhs.uk; Great Maze Pond, SE1; ⊖London Bridge)

Homerton Hospital (☎020-8510 5555; www.homerton.nhs.uk; Homerton Row, E9; 🚆Homerton)

Royal Free Hospital (☎020-7794 0500; www.royalfree.nhs.uk; Pond St, NW3; 🚆Hampstead heath, ⊖Belsize Park)

Royal London Hospital (☎020-3416 5000; www.bartshealth.nhs.uk; Whitechapel Rd, E1; ⊖Whitechapel)

University College London Hospital (☎020-3447 0083; www.uclh.org; 235 Euston Rd, NW1; ⊖Euston Sq or Warren St)

Pharmacies

The main pharmacy chains in London are Boots and Superdrug; a branch of either – or both – can be found on virtually every high street.

The **Boots** (☎020-7734 6126; www.boots.com; 44-46 Regent St, W1B; ⏲8am-midnight Mon-Fri, 9am-midnight Sat, noon-6pm Sun; ⊖Piccadilly Circus) in Piccadilly Circus is one of the biggest and most centrally located and has extended opening times.

Money

Although it is a member of the EU, the UK has not adopted the euro and has retained the pound sterling (£) as its unit of currency.

One pound sterling is made up of 100 pence (called 'pee', colloquially).

Notes come in denominations of £5, £10, £20 and £50, while coins are 1p ('penny'), 2p, 5p, 10p, 20p, 50p, £1 and £2.

Unless otherwise noted, all prices are in pounds sterling.

ATMs

ATMs are everywhere and will generally accept Visa, MasterCard, Cirrus or Maestro cards, as well as more obscure ones. There is almost always a transaction surcharge for cash withdrawals with foreign cards. There are nonbank-run ATMs that charge £1.50 to £2 per transaction. These are normally found inside shops and are particularly expensive for foreign bank card holders. The ATM generally warns you before you take money out that it will charge you but be vigilant.

Also, always beware of suspicious-looking devices attached to ATMs. Many London ATMs have now been made tamperproof, but certain fraudsters' devices are capable of sucking your card into the machine, allowing the fraudsters to release it when you have given up and left.

Changing Money

The best place to change money is in any local post office branch, where no commission is charged.

You can also change money in most high-street banks and some travel agencies, as well as at the numerous bureaux de change throughout the city.

Compare rates and watch for the commission that is not always mentioned very prominently. The trick is to ask how many pounds you'll receive in total before committing – you'll lose nothing by shopping around.

Credit & Debit Cards

Londoners live off their debit cards, which can also be used to get 'cash back' from supermarkets.

➡ Credit and debit cards are accepted almost universally in London, from restaurants and bars to shops and even by some taxis.

➡ American Express and Diners Club are far less widely used than Visa and MasterCard.

Tipping

Many restaurants add a 'discretionary' service charge to your bill. It's legal for them to do so but this should be clearly advertised.

In places that don't include a service charge, you are expected to leave 10% extra unless the service was unsatisfactory. A tip of 15% is for extraordinary service.

You never tip to have your pint pulled or wine poured in a pub.

Some guides and/or drivers on Thames boat trips will solicit you – sometimes rather forcefully – for their commentary. Whether you pay is up to you but it is not required.

You can tip taxi drivers up to 10% but most people just round up to the nearest pound.

Opening Hours

The following table summarises standard opening hours. Reviews will list exact times for each venue.

Sights	10am-6pm
Banks	9am-5pm Mon-Fri
Shops	9am-7pm Mon-Sat, noon-6pm Sun
Restaurants	noon-2.30pm & 6-11pm
Pubs & bars	11am-11pm

Post

The **Royal Mail** (www.royalmail.co.uk) is no longer the humdinger it once was but is generally very reliable.

Postcodes

The unusual London postcode system dates back to WWI. The whole city is divided up into districts denoted by a letter (or letters) and a number. For example, W1, the postcode for Mayfair and Soho, stands for 'West London, district 1'. EC1, on the other hand, stands for 'East Central London, district 1'. The number a district is assigned has nothing to do with its geographic location, but rather its alphabetical listing in that area. For example, in North London N1 and N16 are right next to each other as are E1 and E14 in East London.

Public Holidays

Most attractions and businesses close for a couple of days over Christmas and sometimes Easter. Places that normally shut on Sunday will probably close on bank holiday Mondays.

New Year's Day 1 January

Good Friday Late March/April

Easter Monday Late March/April

May Day Holiday First Monday in May

Spring Bank Holiday Last Monday in May

Summer Bank Holiday Last Monday in August

PRACTICALITIES

Weights & Measures The UK uses a confusing mix of metric and imperial systems.

Smoking Forbidden in all enclosed public places nationwide. Most pubs have some sort of smoking area outside.

Christmas Day 25 December

Boxing Day 26 December

School Holidays

These change from year to year and often from school to school. As a general rule, however, they are as follows:

Spring half term One week in mid-February

Easter holidays One week either side of Easter Sunday

Summer half term One week in late May/early June

Summer holiday Late July to early September

Autumn half term One week in late October/early November

Christmas holidays Roughly 20 December to 6 January

Safe Travel

London is a fairly safe city for its size, so exercising common sense should keep you secure.

If you're getting a cab after a night's clubbing, make sure you go for a black taxi or a licensed minicab firm. Many of the touts operating outside clubs and bars are unlicensed and can therefore be unsafe. The areas where you should avoid wandering alone at night are King's Cross, Brixton, parts of Dalston and Peckham, though sticking to the main roads offers a certain degree of safety.

Pickpocketing does happen in London, so keep an eye on your handbag and wallet, especially in bars and nightclubs, and in crowded areas such as the Underground.

Taxes & Refunds

Value-added tax (VAT) is a sales tax of up to 20% levied on most goods and services except food, books and children's clothing. Restaurants must, by law, include VAT in their menu prices, although VAT is not always included in hotel room prices so always ask when booking to avoid unpleasant surprises at bill time.

It's sometimes possible for visitors to claim a refund of VAT paid on goods. You're eligible if you have spent fewer than 365 days out of the two years prior to making the purchase living in the UK, and if you're leaving the EU within three months of making the purchase.

Not all shops participate in what is called either the VAT Retail Export Scheme or Tax Free Shopping, and different shops will have different minimum purchase conditions (normally around £75 in any one shop). On request, participating shops will give you a special form (VAT 407). This must be presented with the goods and receipts to customs when you depart the country. (VAT-free goods can't be posted or shipped home.) After customs has certified the form, it should be returned to the shop for a refund (minus an administration or handling fee), which usually takes about eight to 10 weeks to come through.

Telephone

British Telecom's famous red phone boxes survive in conservation areas only (notably Westminster). Some people use them as shelter while using their mobile phones.

Some BT phones still accept coins, but most take phonecards (available from retailers, including most post offices and some newsagents) or credit cards.

Useful phone numbers (charged calls):

International dialing code (☎00)

Local call rate applies (☎08457)

National call rate applies (☎0870 & ☎0871)

Premium rate applies (☎09) From 65p per minute

Toll-free (☎0800)

Directory Enquiries (International) (☎118 505, 118 102; www.bt118500.com)

Directory Enquiries (Local & National) (☎118 500, 118 118; www.bt118500.com)

Operator (International) (☎155)

Operator (Local & National) (☎100)

Reverse Charge/Collect Calls (☎155)

Calling London

London's area code is ☎020, followed by an eight-digit number beginning with 7 (central London), 8 (Greater London) or 3 (non-geographic).

You only need to dial the ☎020 when you are calling London from elsewhere in the UK or if you're dialling from a mobile.

To call London from abroad, dial your country's international access code (usually ☎00 but ☎011 in Canada and the USA), then 44 (the UK's country code), then 20 (dropping the initial 0), followed by the eight-digit phone number.

International Calls & Rates

International direct dialling (IDD) calls to almost anywhere can be made from nearly all public telephones. Direct dialling is cheaper than making a reverse-charge (collect) call through the international operator (☎155).

Many private firms offer cheaper international calls than BT. In such places you phone from a metered booth and then pay the bill. Some cybercafes and internet shops also offer cheap rates for international calls.

International calling cards with stored value (usually £5,

£10 or £20) and a PIN, which you can use from any phone by dialling a special access number, are usually the cheapest way to call abroad. These cards are available at most corner shops.

Note that the use of Skype may be restricted in hostels and internet cafes because of noise and/or band-width issues.

Local & National Call Rates

Local calls are charged by time alone; regional and national calls are charged by both time and distance.

Daytime rates apply from 7am to 7pm Monday to Friday.

The cheap rate applies from 7pm to 7am Monday to Friday and again over the weekend from 7pm Friday to 7am Monday.

Mobile Phones

The UK uses the GSM 900 network, which covers Europe, Australia and New Zealand, but is not compatible with the North American GSM 1900 or Japanese mobile technology.

If you have a GSM phone, check with your service provider about using it in the UK and enquire about roaming charges.

It's usually better to buy a local SIM card from any mobile-phone shop, though in order to do that you must ensure your handset from home is unlocked.

Time

Wherever you are in the world, the time on your watch is measured in relation to the time at Greenwich in London – Greenwich Mean Time (GMT). British Summer Time, the UK's form of daylight-savings time, muddies the water so that even London is ahead of GMT from late March to late October.

Paris	GMT +1
New York	GMT -5
San Francisco	GMT -8
Sydney	GMT +10

Toilets

It's now an offence to urinate in the streets. Train stations, bus terminals and attractions generally have good facilities, providing also for people with disabilities and those with young children. You'll also find public toilets across the city, some operated by local councils, others automated and self-cleaning. Most now charge 50p.

Tourist Information

Visit London (☎0870 156 6366; www.visitlondon.com) Visit London can fill you in on everything from tourist attractions and events (such as the Changing of the Guard and Chinese New Year parade) to river trips and tours, accommodation, eating, theatre, shopping, children's London, and gay and lesbian venues.

Heathrow Airport (Terminal 1, 2 & 3 Underground station; ⏲7.15am-8pm Mon-Sat, 8.15am-8pm Sun)

King's Cross St Pancras Station (⏲7.15am-9.15pm Mon-Sat, 8.15am-8.15pm Sun)

Liverpool Street Station (⏲7.15am-7pm Mon-Sat, 8.15am-7pm Sun)

Piccadilly Circus Underground Station (⏲9.15am-7pm)

Victoria Station (⏲7.15am-9.15pm Mon-Sat, 8.15am-7pm Sun)

Local tourist offices include the following:

City of London Information Centre (Map p442; www.visitthecity.co.uk; St Paul's Churchyard, EC4; ⏲9.30am-5.30pm Mon-Sat, 10am-4pm Sun; ⊖St Paul's) Tourist information, fast-track tickets to City attractions and guided walks (adult/child £6/4).

Greenwich Tourist Office (www.visitgreenwich.org.uk/tourist-information-centre; Pepys House, 2 Cutty Sark Gardens, SE10; ⏲10am-5pm; DLR Cutty Sark)

Travellers with Disabilities

For travellers with disabilities, London is an odd mix of user-friendliness and downright disinterest. New hotels and modern tourist attractions are legally required to be accessible to people in wheelchairs, but many historic buildings, B&Bs and guesthouses are in older buildings, which are hard to adapt.

Transport is equally hit and miss, but slowly improving:

- Only 66 of London's 270 tube stations have step-free access; the rest have escalators or stairs.
- The above-ground DLR is entirely accessible for wheelchairs.
- All buses can be lowered to street level when they stop; wheelchair users travel free.
- Guide dogs are universally welcome on public transport and in hotels, restaurants, attractions etc.

Transport for London (www.tfl.gov.uk) publishes the *Getting Around London* guide, which contains the latest information on accessibility for passengers with disabilities. Download it from the website.

The following organisations can provide helpful information before you travel:

Royal Association for Disability & Rehabilitation (Radar; 020-7250 3222; www.radar.org.uk; 12 City Forum, 250 City Rd, EC1; Old St) This is an umbrella organisation for voluntary groups for people with disabilities. Many wheelchair-accessible toilets across London can be opened only with a special key, which can be obtained from tourist offices or for £4 (plus a brief statement of your disability) via the Radar website.

Royal National Institute for the Blind (020-7388 1266; www.rnib.org.uk; 105 Judd St, WC1H) This is the best point of initial contact for sight-impaired visitors to London. It can also be contacted via its confidential **helpline** (0303 123 9999; 8.45am-5.30pm Mon-Fri).

Royal National Institute for Deaf People (0808 808 0123, textphone 0808 808 9000; www.rnid.org.uk; 19-23 Featherstone St, EC1) This is the main organisation working with deaf and hard of hearing people in the UK. Many ticket offices and banks are fitted with hearing loops to help the hearing-impaired; look for the ear symbol.

VISA REQUIREMENTS

COUNTRY	TOURISM	WORK	STUDY
European Economic Area	X	X	X
Australia, Canada, New Zealand, South Africa, USA	X (for stay of up to 6 months)	√	√
Other nationalities	√	√	√

Visas

Immigration to the UK is becoming tougher, particularly for those seeking to work or study. The above table indicates who will need a visa for what, but make sure you check the website of the UK Border Agency or with your local British embassy or consulate for the most up-to-date information.

Visa Extensions

Tourist visas can only be extended in clear emergencies (eg an accident, death of a relative). Otherwise you'll have to leave the UK (perhaps going to Ireland or France) and apply for a fresh one. To extend (or attempt to extend) your stay in the UK, ring the **Visa & Passport Information Line** (0870 606 7766; 40 Wellesley Rd, Home Office's Immigration & Nationality Directorate, Lunar House, Croydon, CR9 2BY; 8am-4pm Mon-Fri; East Croydon) before your current visa expires. The process takes a few days in France and Ireland and longer in the UK.

Women Travellers

Female visitors to London are unlikely to have many problems provided they take the usual big-city precautions. Don't get into an Underground carriage with no one else in it or with just one or two men. And if you feel unsafe, you should take a taxi or licensed minicab.

Lady Mini Cabs (020-7272 3300; www.ladyminicabs.co.uk) based in Archway in North London has women drivers.

Apart from the occasional wolf whistle and unwelcome body contact on the tube, women will find male Londoners reasonably enlightened. Going into pubs alone may not always be a comfortable experience, though it is in no way out of the ordinary.

Marie Stopes International (0845 300 8090; www.mariestopes.org.uk; 108 Whitfield St, W1; 8.30am-5pm Mon, Wed & Fri, 9.30am-6pm Tue & Thu; Warren St) provides contraception, sexual-health checks and abortions.

Behind the Scenes

SEND US YOUR FEEDBACK

We love to hear from travellers – your comments keep us on our toes and help make our books better. Our well-travelled team reads every word on what you loved or loathed about this book. Although we cannot reply individually to postal submissions, we always guarantee that your feedback goes straight to the appropriate authors, in time for the next edition. Each person who sends us information is thanked in the next edition – and the most useful submissions are rewarded with a selection of digital PDF chapters.

Visit **lonelyplanet.com/contact** to submit your updates and suggestions or to ask for help. Our award-winning website also features inspirational travel stories, news and discussions.

Note: We may edit, reproduce and incorporate your comments in Lonely Planet products such as guidebooks, websites and digital products, so let us know if you don't want your comments reproduced or your name acknowledged. For a copy of our privacy policy visit lonelyplanet.com/privacy.

OUR READERS

Many thanks to the travellers who used the last edition and wrote to us with helpful hints, useful advice and interesting anecdotes: Aarti Abhyankar, Euijoo Yeo, James Rea, Jill Abney, Joe Radmore, John Rodda, Josefina Boston, Kareen MacDonald, Marcelo J S Cano, Nicolas Combremont, Rosemary Dunne-Smith, Rosina Licciardello, Watson Aphiwatanakoon, Yasar Ozkul

AUTHOR THANKS

Emilie Filou

Big thanks to my fellow authors Steve Fallon, Damian Harper and Vesna Maric – this book was a truly collaborative effort. Thanks also to the many friends (hello Nikki, Chris, Van, Sid, Alex, Nic, Phil, Cake, Zanthy and Cos) who chipped in with recommendations and came along for the ride: your dedication to finding a good time knows no bounds! And finally, thanks to chief critic and husband extraordinaire Adolfo for his patience and company.

Steve Fallon

I can't remember working with such a wonderful group of authors as the *London 9* Dream Team: Emilie Filou, Damian Harper and Vesna Maric. A million thanks for all their help, advice and suggestions. Fellow Blue Badge Tourist Guide Lia Lalli was a goldmine for eating ideas; Stephen Unwin went beyond the call of duty with help on the gay and lesbian sections. As always, I'd like to state my admiration, gratitude and great love for my partner Michael Rothschild.

Damian Harper

Thanks to everyone who helped along the way: my co-authors, Emma Gough, Laura Hutchinson, Amaya Wang, Laura Teale, Star Hu, Ian Franklin, Bill Moran and anyone else I may have overlooked. Thanks also to my wife Dai Min and my two children, as ever.

Vesna Maric

Thanks to Jo Potts and James Smart for commissioning and guiding the title, and big thanks to my co-authors Emilie Filou, Steve Fallon and Damian Harper – a wonderful bunch to work with.

ACKNOWLEDGMENTS

Cover photograph: Houses of Parliament, Big Ben and London Eye/Alan Copson. London Eye designed by David Marks and Julia Barfield.

THIS BOOK

This 9th edition of Lonely Planet's *London* guidebook was researched and written by Emilie Filou, Steve Fallon, Damian Harper and Vesna Maric. This guidebook was commissioned in Lonely Planet's London office, and produced by the following:

Commissioning Editors James Smart, Jo Cooke
Coordinating Editor Saralinda Turner
Senior Cartographer Jennifer Johnston
Coordinating Layout Designer Adrian Blackburn
Managing Editors Bruce Evans, Martine Power
Managing Layout Designer Jane Hart
Assisting Editors Laura Gibb, Rosie Nicholson, Monique Perrin, Kirsten Rawlings, Helen Yeates
Assisting Cartographers Rachel Imeson, Valentina Kremenchutskaya, Anthony Phelan
Assisting Layout Designers Frank Deim, Wibowo Rusli
Cover Research Naomi Parker
Internal Image Research Kylie McLaughlin
Illustrators Javier Zarracina, Michael Weldon
Thanks to Anita Banh, Ryan Evans, Larissa Frost, Genesys India, Jouve India, Wayne Murphy, Trent Paton, Kerrianne Southway, Gerard Walker

See also separate subindexes for:
- EATING P421
- DRINKING & NIGHTLIFE P423
- ENTERTAINMENT P424
- SHOPPING P425
- SPORTS & ACTIVITIES P426
- SLEEPING P426

Index

Sights 000
Map Pages **000**
Photo Pages **000**

Sights 000
Map Pages **000**
Photo Pages **000**

Sights 000
Map Pages **000**
Photo Pages **000**

EATING

Sights 000
Map Pages **000**
Photo Pages **000**

DRINKING & NIGHTLIFE

Sights 000
Map Pages **000**
Photo Pages **000**

SHOPPING

SPORTS & ACTIVITIES

SLEEPING

London Maps

Sights

- Beach
- Bird Sanctuary
- Buddhist
- Castle/Palace
- Christian
- Confucian
- Hindu
- Islamic
- Jain
- Jewish
- Monument
- Museum/Gallery/Historic Building
- Ruin
- Sento Hot Baths/Onsen
- Shinto
- Sikh
- Taoist
- Winery/Vineyard
- Zoo/Wildlife Sanctuary
- Other Sight

Activities, Courses & Tours

- Bodysurfing
- Diving
- Canoeing/Kayaking
- Course/Tour
- Skiing
- Snorkelling
- Surfing
- Swimming/Pool
- Walking
- Windsurfing
- Other Activity

Sleeping

- Sleeping
- Camping

Eating

- Eating

Drinking & Nightlife

- Drinking & Nightlife
- Cafe

Entertainment

- Entertainment

Shopping

- Shopping

Information

- Bank
- Embassy/Consulate
- Hospital/Medical
- Internet
- Police
- Post Office
- Telephone
- Toilet
- Tourist Information
- Other Information

Geographic

- Beach
- Hut/Shelter
- Lighthouse
- Lookout
- Mountain/Volcano
- Oasis
- Park
- Pass
- Picnic Area
- Waterfall

Population

- Capital (National)
- Capital (State/Province)
- City/Large Town
- Town/Village

Transport

- Airport
- Border crossing
- Bus
- Cable car/Funicular
- Cycling
- Ferry
- Metro station
- Monorail
- Parking
- Petrol station
- S-Bahn/Subway station
- Taxi
- T-bane/Tunnelbana station
- Train station/Railway
- Tram
- Tube station
- U-Bahn/Underground station
- Other Transport

Note: Not all symbols displayed above appear on the maps in this book

Routes

- Tollway
- Freeway
- Primary
- Secondary
- Tertiary
- Lane
- Unsealed road
- Road under construction
- Plaza/Mall
- Steps
- Tunnel
- Pedestrian overpass
- Walking Tour
- Walking Tour detour
- Path/Walking Trail

Boundaries

- International
- State/Province
- Disputed
- Regional/Suburb
- Marine Park
- Cliff
- Wall

Hydrography

- River, Creek
- Intermittent River
- Canal
- Water
- Dry/Salt/Intermittent Lake
- Reef

Areas

- Airport/Runway
- Beach/Desert
- Cemetery (Christian)
- Cemetery (Other)
- Glacier
- Mudflat
- Park/Forest
- Sight (Building)
- Sportsground
- Swamp/Mangrove

MAP INDEX

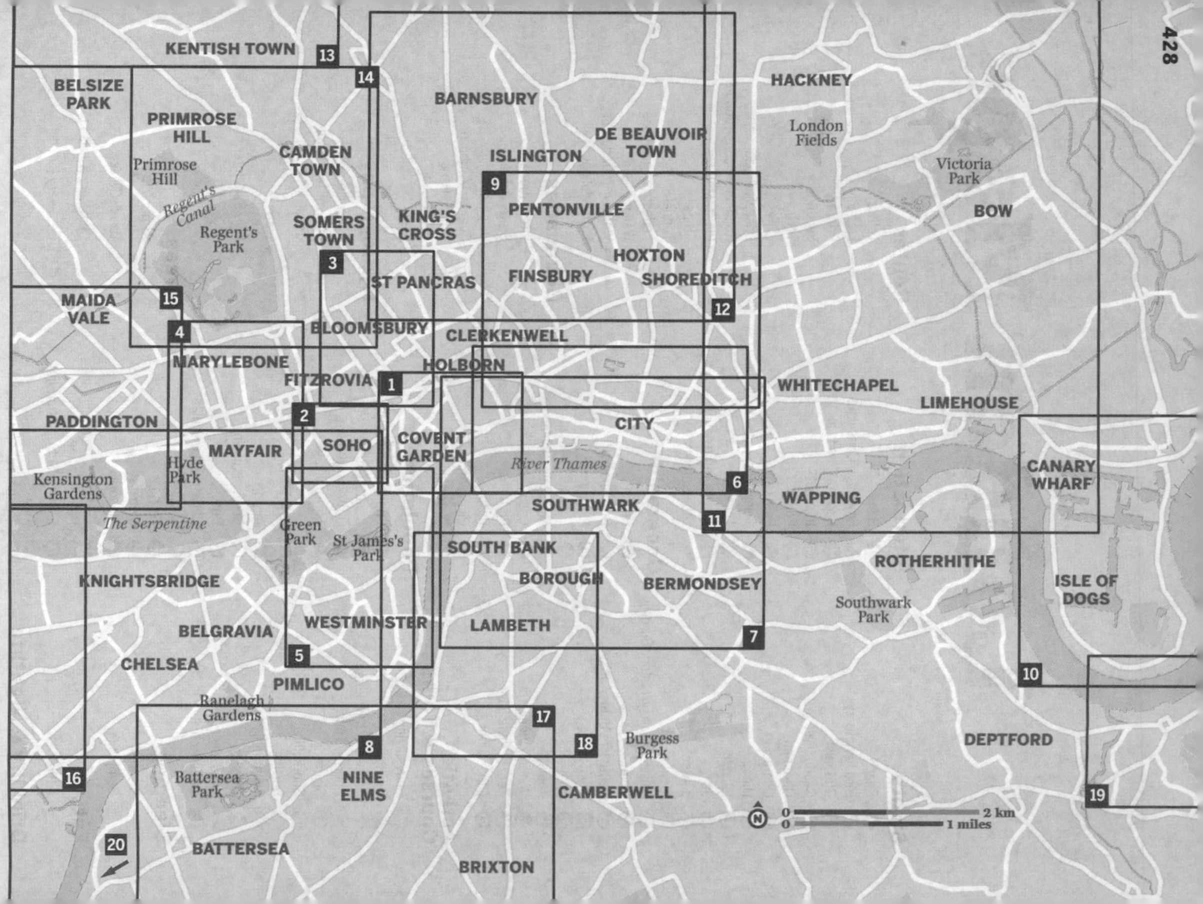

KENTISH TOWN
BELSIZE PARK
PRIMROSE HILL
Primrose Hill
Regent's Canal
Regent's Park
CAMDEN TOWN
SOMERS TOWN
KING'S CROSS
BARNSBURY
ISLINGTON
DE BEAUVOIR TOWN
HACKNEY
London Fields
Victoria Park
BOW
PENTONVILLE
HOXTON
FINSBURY
SHOREDITCH
ST PANCRAS
MAIDA VALE
BLOOMSBURY
CLERKENWELL
MARYLEBONE
HOLBORN
FITZROVIA
WHITECHAPEL
LIMEHOUSE
PADDINGTON
SOHO
CITY
MAYFAIR
COVENT GARDEN
River Thames
CANARY WHARF
Hyde Park
Kensington Gardens
WAPPING
SOUTHWARK
The Serpentine
Green Park
St James's Park
SOUTH BANK
ROTHERHITHE
KNIGHTSBRIDGE
BOROUGH
BERMONDSEY
ISLE OF DOGS
Southwark Park
WESTMINSTER
LAMBETH
BELGRAVIA
CHELSEA
PIMLICO
Ranelagh Gardens
Burgess Park
DEPTFORD
Battersea Park
NINE ELMS
CAMBERWELL
BATTERSEA
BRIXTON
0 2 km
0 1 miles
1
2
3
4
5
6
7
8
9
10
11
12
13
14
15
16
17
18
19
20

WEST END: COVENT GARDEN *Map on p430*

Key on p429

A
B
C
D
1
2
3
4
5
6
7
See map p436
See map p432
See map p440
Bloomsbury St
Great Russell St
Little Russell St
Bloomsbury Square
Bloomsbury Way
Southampton Pl
Southampton Row
Catton St
Procter St
Barter St
New Oxford St
Holborn
High Holborn
Newton St
Museum St
Shaftesbury Ave
Grape St
Bucknall St
St Giles High St
Stukely St
Macklin St
Parker St
Great Queen St
Wild Ct
Wild St
Drury La
Shorts Gdns
Endell St
New Compton St
Charing Cross Rd
Neal St
Shelton St
COVENT GARDEN
Kemble St
Flower Market
Earlham St
Long Acre
Bow St
Crown Ct
Russell St
West St
Langley St
Mercer St
Covent Garden
Catherine St
SOHO
CHINATOWN
James St
Floral St
Covent Garden Market
Wellington St
Rose St
King St
Tavistock St
Exeter St
Lisle St
Cranbourn St
Garrick St
Henrietta St
Southampton St
Leicester Sq
New Row
Bear St
Bedfordbury
Bedford St
The Strand
Leicester Square
St Martin's La
Chandos Pl
Agan St
Carting La
Irving St
William IV St
Adam St
Orange St
St Martin's St
National Portrait Gallery
John Adam St
Savoy Pl
Whitcomb St
National Gallery
Duncannon St
Victoria Embankment
Victoria Embankment Gardens
Villiers St
Pall Mall
Trafalgar Square
Charing Cross
Craven St
Cockspur St
Trafalgar Sq
Embankment
ST JAMES'S
1
2
4
5
8
9
12
14
17
20
21
22
23
25
29
30
31
32
33
35
37
38
39
40
41
42
44
45
46
47
48
49
50
51
52
53
54
56
57
58
59
60
61
62
63
64
65
66
67
69
70
71
72
73
74
75
76
77
78
79
80
81
82
83
84
85
86
87
88
89
90
91
92
93
94
95
96
98

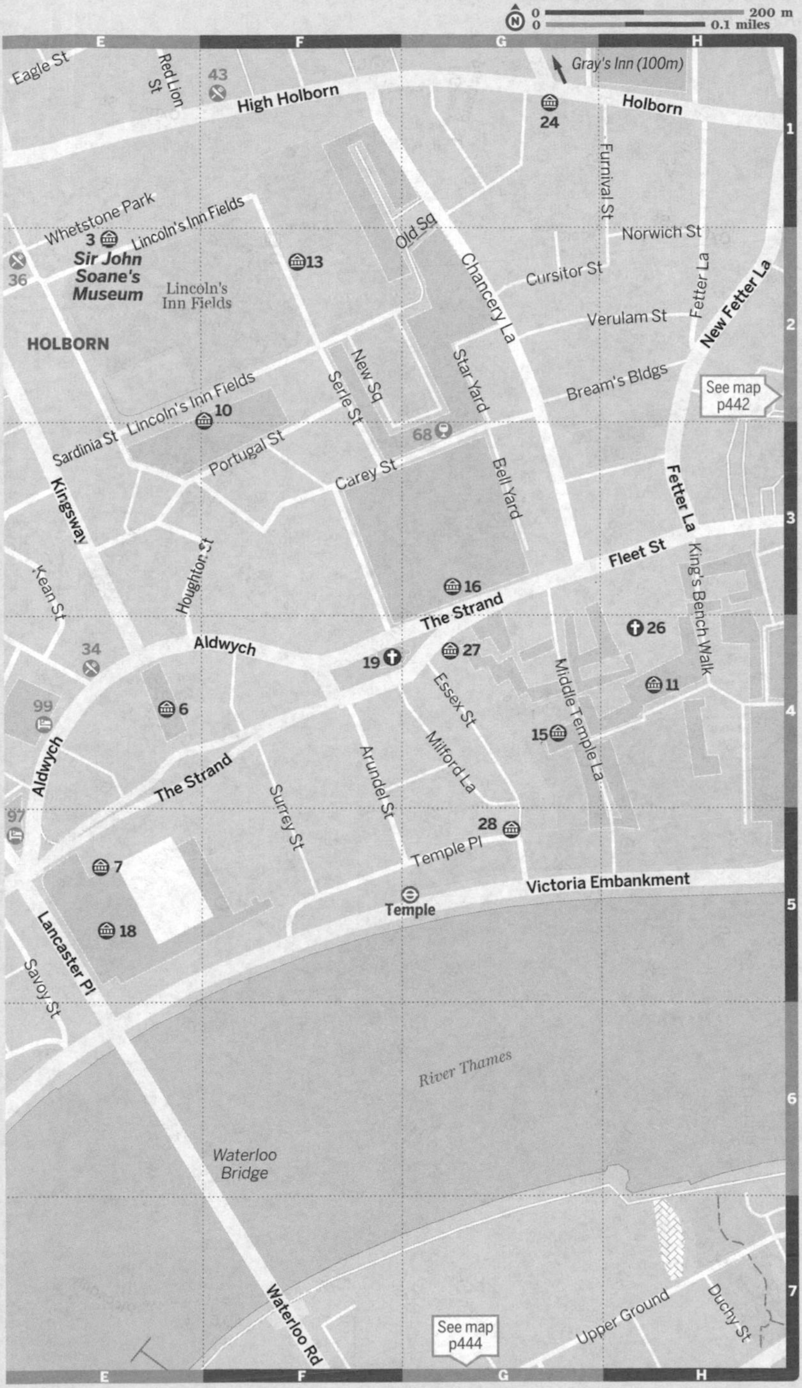
0 200 m
0 0.1 miles
E
F
G
H
1
2
3
4
5
6
7
Gray's Inn (100m)
Eagle St
Red Lion St
43
High Holborn
24
Holborn
Furnival St
Whetstone Park
Lincoln's Inn Fields
3
Sir John Soane's Museum
36
Lincoln's Inn Fields
13
Old Sq
Chancery La
Norwich St
Cursitor St
Fetter La
New Fetter La
Verulam St
HOLBORN
New Sq
Serle St
Star Yard
Bream's Bldgs
See map p442
Lincoln's Inn Fields
10
Sardinia St
Portugal St
68
Carey St
Bell Yard
Kingsway
Fetter La
Houghton St
Fleet St
Kean St
16
King's Bench Walk
The Strand
26
Aldwych
34
19
27
Middle Temple La
11
99
6
Essex St
Aldwych
15
Milford La
The Strand
Arundel St
Surrey St
97
28
Temple Pl
7
Victoria Embankment
Temple
18
Lancaster Pl
Savoy St
River Thames
Waterloo Bridge
Waterloo Rd
See map p444
Upper Ground
Duchy St

Key on p434

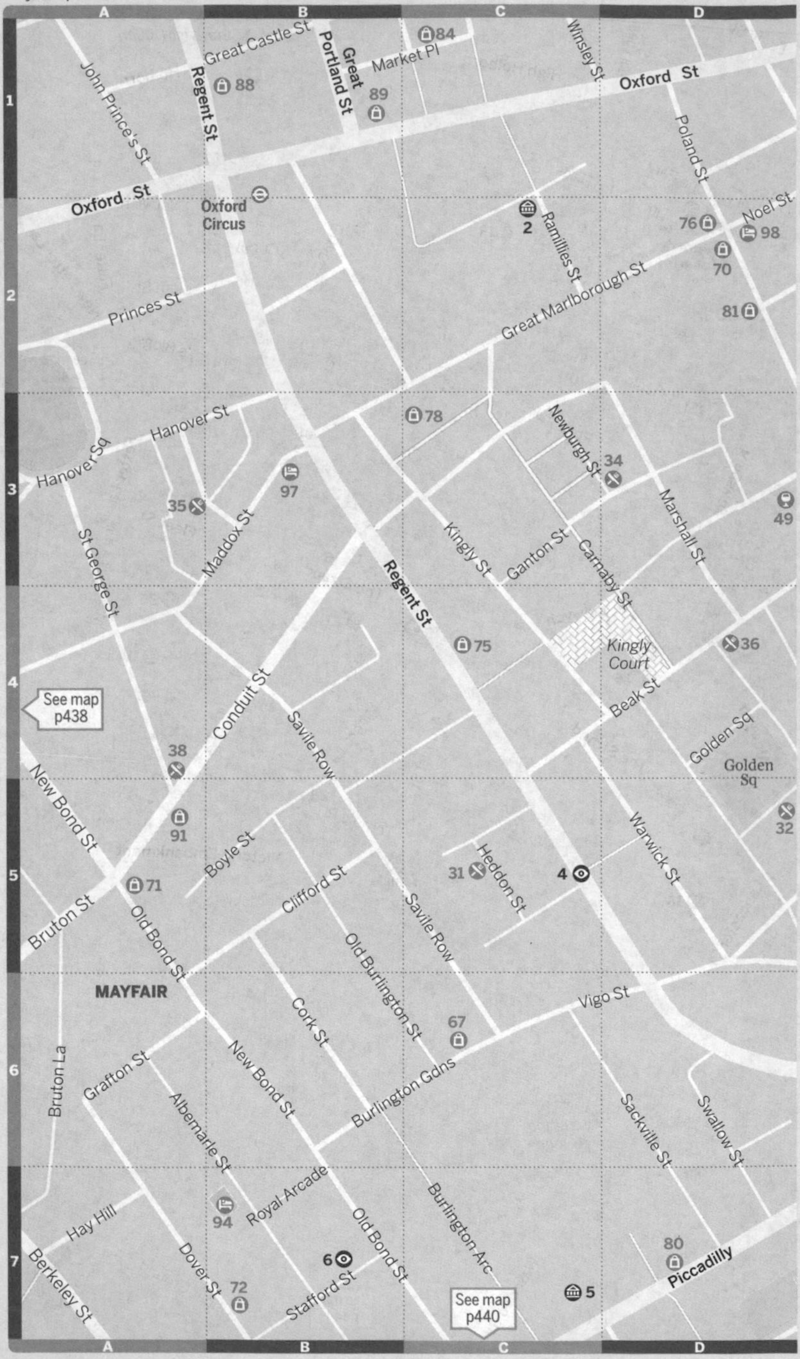

A
B
C
D
1
2
3
4
5
6
7
Great Castle St
Market Pl
Great Portland St
Regent St
John Prince's St
Winsley St
Oxford St
Poland St
Oxford Circus
Ramillies St
Noel St
Great Marlborough St
Princes St
Hanover St
Hanover Sq
Newburgh St
Marshall St
Maddox St
St George St
Kingly St
Ganton St
Carnaby St
Regent St
Kingly Court
Beak St
Golden Sq
Golden Sq
Conduit St
Savile Row
See map p438
New Bond St
Boyle St
Heddon St
Warwick St
Clifford St
Bruton St
Old Bond St
Savile Row
Old Burlington St
MAYFAIR
Vigo St
Cork St
Bruton La
Grafton St
New Bond St
Burlington Gdns
Albemarle St
Sackville St
Swallow St
Royal Arcade
Hay Hill
Burlington Arc
Old Bond St
Berkeley St
Dover St
Stafford St
Piccadilly
See map p440
84
88
89
2
76
98
70
81
78
34
97
35
49
75
36
38
91
32
31
4
71
67
94
6
80
72
5

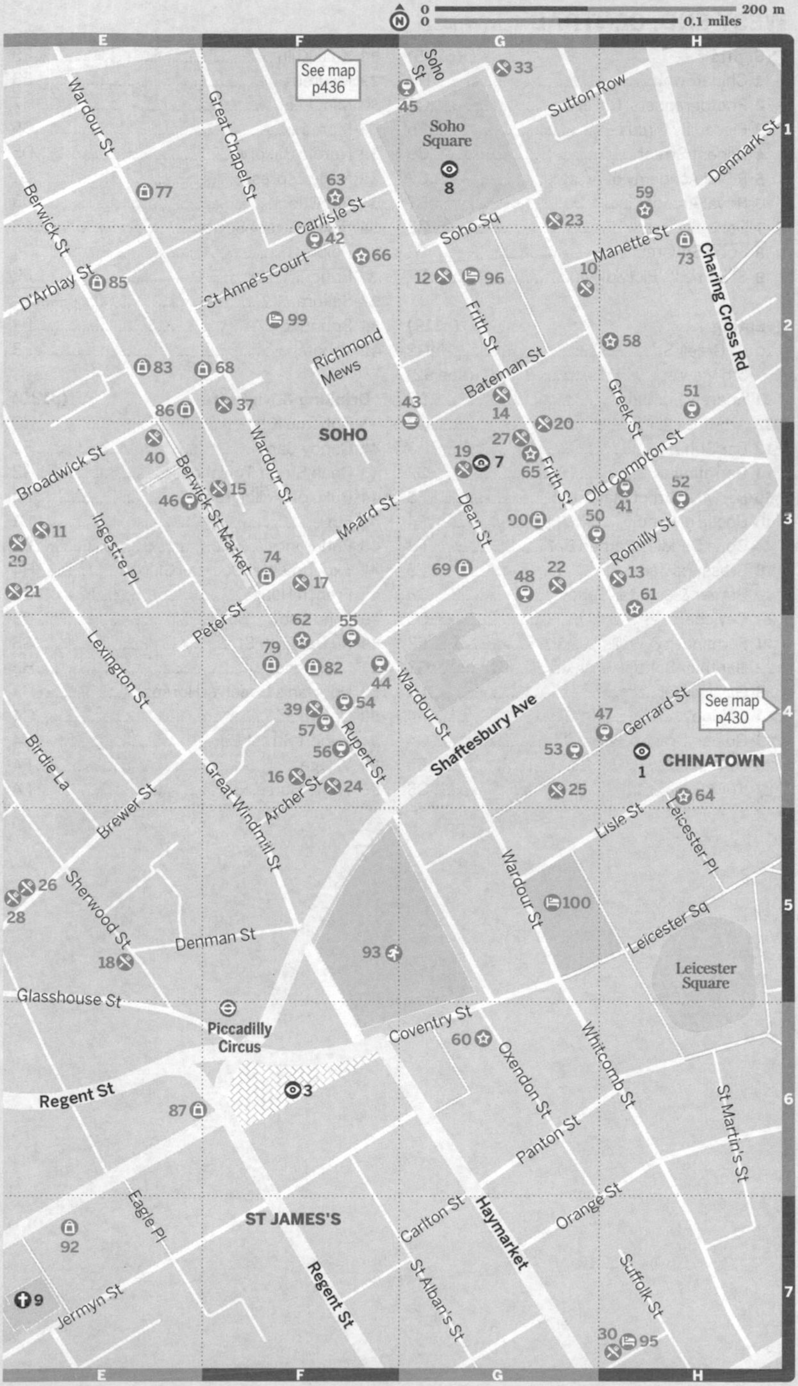
0 200 m
0 0.1 miles
E
F
G
H
1
2
3
4
5
6
7
See map p436
See map p430
Soho St
Soho Square
Sutton Row
Denmark St
Wardour St
Great Chapel St
Berwick St
Carlisle St
Soho Sq
Manette St
Charing Cross Rd
D'Arblay St
St Anne's Court
Richmond Mews
Frith St
Bateman St
Greek St
SOHO
Broadwick St
Old Compton St
Meard St
Dean St
Ingestre Pl
Berwick St Market
Romilly St
Peter St
Lexington St
Shaftesbury Ave
Gerrard St
CHINATOWN
Birdie La
Rupert St
Great Windmill St
Archer St
Brewer St
Lisle St
Leicester Pl
Sherwood St
Denman St
Leicester Sq
Leicester Square
Glasshouse St
Piccadilly Circus
Coventry St
Oxendon St
Whitcomb St
Regent St
Panton St
St Martin's St
Eagle Pl
ST JAMES'S
Carlton St
Haymarket
Orange St
St Alban's St
Suffolk St
Jermyn St
Regent St

WEST END: CENTRAL *Map on p432*

Sights **(p105)**

1 Chinatown H4
2 Photographers' Gallery C2
3 Piccadilly Circus F6
4 Regent Street C5
5 Royal Academy of Arts C7
6 Royal Arcade B7
7 Soho G3
8 Soho Square G1
9 St James's Piccadilly E7

Eating **(p119)**

10 10 Greek St G2
5th View (see 92)
11 Andrew Edmunds E3
12 Arbutus G2
13 Bar Shu H3
14 Barrafina G2
15 Berwick Street Market F3
16 Bocca di Lupo F4
17 Bone Daddies Ramen Bar F3
18 Brasserie Zédel E5
19 Burger & Lobster Soho G3
20 Ceviche G3
21 Fernandez & Wells E3
22 Gauthier Soho G3
23 Gay Hussar G1
24 Gelupo F4
25 Golden Dragon G4
26 HIX E5
27 Koya G3
28 Kulu Kulu E5
29 Mildreds E3
30 Mint Leaf H7
31 Momo C5
32 Nordic Bakery D5
33 Nude Espresso G1
34 Pitt Cue D3
35 Pollen Street Social A3
36 Polpo D4
37 Princi F2
38 Sakura A4
39 Spuntino F4
40 Yauatcha E3

Drinking & Nightlife **(p130)**

41 Boheme Kitchen & Bar H3
42 Candy Bar F2
43 Dean Street Townhouse G2
44 Duke of Wellington F4
45 Edge G1
46 Endurance E3
47 Experimental Cocktail Club H4
48 French House G3
49 John Snow D3
50 Ku Bar Frith St G3
51 LAB Soho H2
52 Norman's Coach & Horses H3
53 Opium G4
54 Rupert Street Bar F4
55 Village F4
56 White Horse F4

57 Yard F4

Entertainment (p135)

58 Amused Moose Soho H2
59 Borderline H1
60 Comedy Store G6
61 Curzon Soho H3
62 Madame Jo Jo's F4
63 Pizza Express Jazz Club F1
64 Prince Charles H4
65 Ronnie Scott's G3
66 Soho Theatre F2

Shopping (p138)

67 Abercrombie & Fitch C6
68 Agent Provocateur F2
69 Algerian Coffee Stores G3
70 Beyond Retro D2
71 Burberry A5
72 Dover Street Market B7
73 Foyle's H2
74 Gosh! F3
Grant & Cutler .... (see 73)
75 Hamleys C4
76 Harold Moore's Records D2
77 Joy E1
78 Liberty C3
79 Lina Stores F4
80 Minamoto Kitchoan D7
81 Phonica D2
82 Prowler F4
Ray's Jazz .... (see 73)
83 Reckless Records E2
84 Reiss C1
85 Sister Ray E2
86 Sounds of the Universe E2
87 Sting E6
88 Topshop B1
89 Urban Outfitters B1
90 Vintage House G3
91 Vivienne Westwood A5
92 Waterstone's E7

Sports & Activities (p110)

93 London Trocadero F5

Sleeping (p335)

94 Brown's Hotel B7
Dean Street Townhouse .... (see 43)
95 Haymarket Hotel H7
96 Hazlitt's G2
97 Number 5 Maddox Street B3
98 Oxford St YHA D2
99 Soho Hotel F2
100 W G5

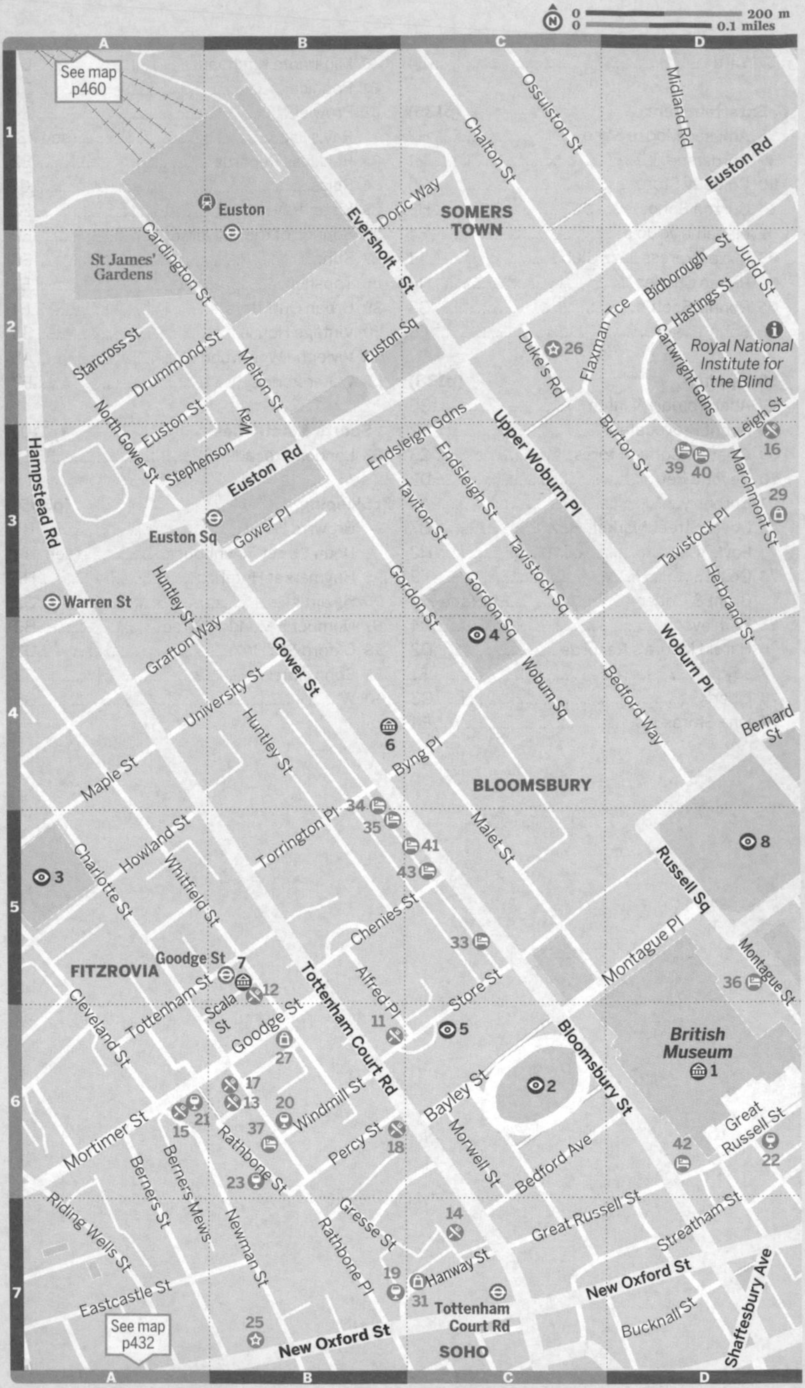
0
200 m
0
0.1 miles
A
B
C
D
1
2
3
4
5
6
7
See map p460
See map p432
Euston
St James' Gardens
SOMERS TOWN
Ossulston St
Chalton St
Midland Rd
Euston Rd
Doric Way
Eversholt St
Cardington St
Starcross St
Drummond St
Melton St
Euston Sq
North Gower St
Euston St
Stephenson Way
Hampstead Rd
Bidborough St
Judd St
Hastings St
Flaxman Tce
Duke's Rd
Cartwright Gdns
Royal National Institute for the Blind
Leigh St
Marchmont St
Burton St
Upper Woburn Pl
Endsleigh Gdns
Endsleigh St
Taviton St
Gower Pl
Tavistock Sq
Tavistock Pl
Herbrand St
Gordon St
Gordon Sq
Warren St
Huntley St
Grafton Way
Gower St
University St
Woburn Sq
Bedford Way
Woburn Pl
Bernard St
Byng Pl
Maple St
BLOOMSBURY
Torrington Pl
Howland St
Charlotte St
Whitfield St
Malet St
Russell Sq
Chenies St
Montague Pl
Montague St
FITZROVIA
Goodge St
Tottenham St
Scala St
Alfred Pl
Store St
Tottenham Court Rd
Cleveland St
Goodge St
Bloomsbury St
British Museum
Windmill St
Bayley St
Mortimer St
Rathbone St
Percy St
Morwell St
Bedford Ave
Great Russell St
Berners St
Berners Mews
Riding Wells St
Newman St
Gresse St
Rathbone Pl
Hanway St
Great Russell St
Streatham St
Eastcastle St
New Oxford St
Tottenham Court Rd
SOHO
Bucknall St
Shaftesbury Ave
1
2
3
4
5
6
7
8
11
12
13
14
15
16
17
18
19
20
21
22
23
25
26
27
29
31
33
34
35
36
37
39
40
41
42
43

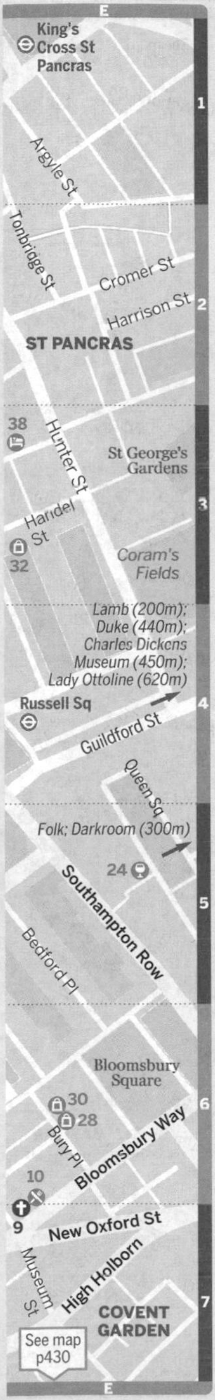

Top Sights (p89)
1 British Museum D6

Sights (p105)
2 Bedford Square C6
3 BT Tower A5
4 Gordon Square C4
5 New London Architecture .. C6
6 Petrie Museum of Egyptian Archaeology B4
7 Pollock's Toy Museum B5
8 Russell Square D5
9 St George's, Bloomsbury E7

Eating (p119)
10 Abeno E6
11 Busaba Eathai B6
12 Dabbous B5
13 Fino B6
14 Hakkasan C7
15 Newman Street Tavern A6
16 North Sea Fish Restaurant . D3
17 Roka B6
18 Sagar B6

Drinking & Nightlife (p130)
19 Bradley's Spanish Bar B7
20 Fitzroy Tavern B6
21 London Cocktail Club A6
22 Museum Tavern D6
23 Newman Arms B6
24 Queen's Larder E5

Entertainment (p135)
25 100 Club B7
26 Place C2

Shopping (p138)
27 Bang Bang Clothing Exchange B6
28 Blade Rubber Stamps E6
29 Gay's the Word D3
30 London Review Bookshop ... E6
31 On the Beat C7
32 Skoob Books E3

Sleeping (p335)
33 Academy C5
34 Arosfa Hotel B4
35 Arran House Hotel B5
36 Blooms Townhouse D5
37 Charlotte Street Hotel B6
38 Generator E3
39 George Hotel D3
40 Harlingford Hotel D3
41 Jesmond Hotel C5
42 Morgan Hotel D6
43 Ridgemount Hotel C5

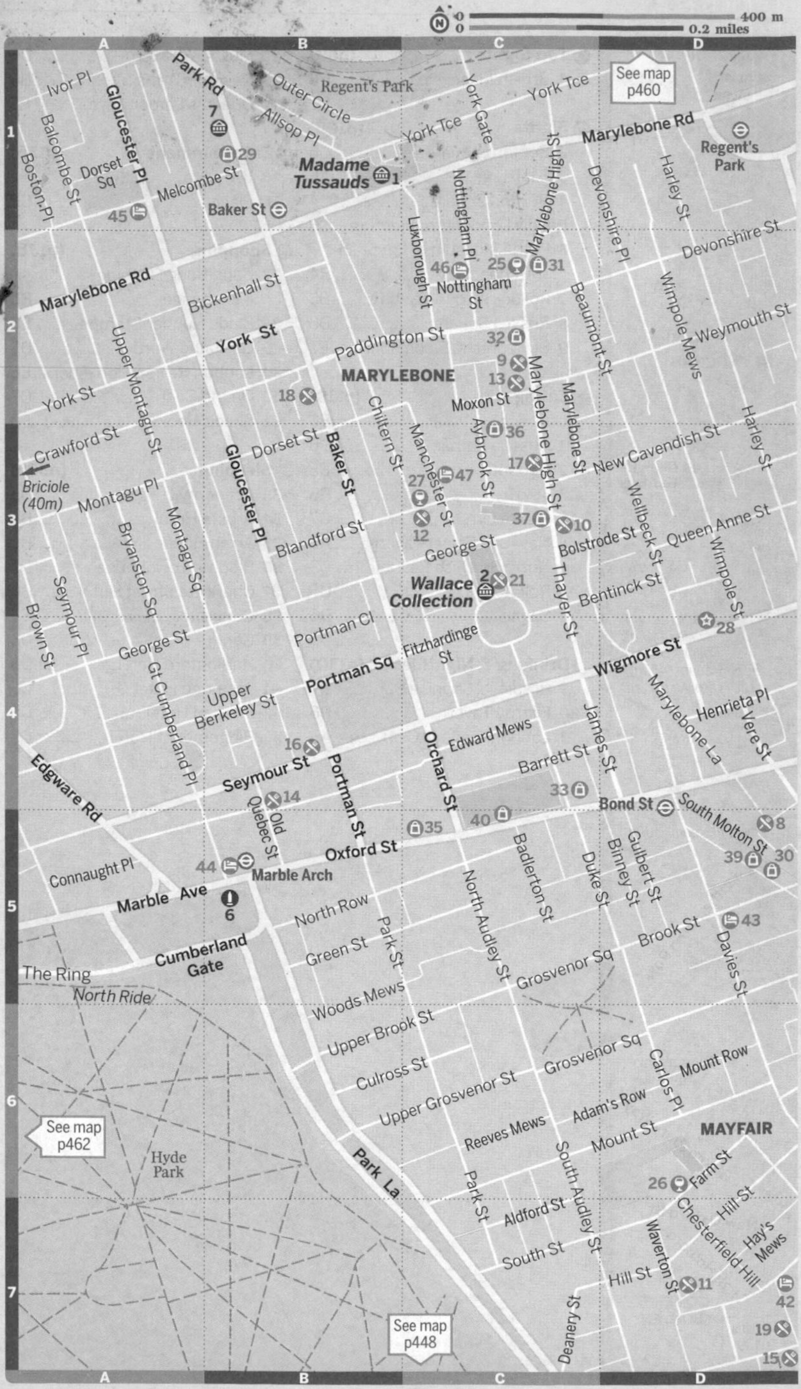
400 m
0.2 miles
A
B
C
D
1
2
3
4
5
6
7
See map p460
See map p462
See map p448
Regent's Park
Outer Circle
Park Rd
Allsop Pl
York Gate
York Tce
Marylebone Rd
Regent's Park
Ivor Pl
Gloucester Pl
Balcombe St
Boston Pl
Dorset Sq
Melcombe St
Madame Tussauds
Baker St
Nottingham Pl
Luxborough St
Marylebone High St
Devonshire Pl
Harley St
Devonshire St
Bickenhall St
Nottingham St
Beaumont St
Wimpole Mews
Weymouth St
York St
Paddington St
Upper Montagu St
MARYLEBONE
Chiltern St
Manchester St
Moxon St
Aybrook St
Marylebone St
New Cavendish St
Crawford St
Briciole (40m)
Dorset St
Baker St
Montagu Pl
Montagu Sq
Bryanston Sq
Blandford St
George St
Wellbeck St
Queen Anne St
Bolstrode St
Thayer St
Wallace Collection
Bentinck St
Wimpole St
Seymour Pl
Brown St
George St
Portman Cl
Fitzhardinge St
Gt Cumberland Pl
Upper Berkeley St
Portman Sq
Wigmore St
Marylebone La
Henrieta Pl
Vere St
Edward Mews
James St
Barrett St
Edgware Rd
Seymour St
Portman St
Orchard St
Old Quebec St
Bond St
South Molton St
Oxford St
Connaught Pl
Marble Arch
Badlerton St
Duke St
Binney St
Gulbert St
Marble Ave
North Row
North Audley St
Park St
Green St
Brook St
Davies St
Cumberland Gate
The Ring
North Ride
Grosvenor Sq
Woods Mews
Upper Brook St
Grosvenor Sq
Carlos Pl
Mount Row
Culross St
Upper Grosvenor St
Adam's Row
Reeves Mews
MAYFAIR
Hyde Park
Park La
Mount St
South Audley St
Farm St
Park St
Alldford St
Hill St
Chesterfield Hill
Hay's Mews
South St
Hill St
Waverton St
Deanery St
1
2
6
7
8
9
10
11
12
13
14
15
16
17
18
19
21
25
26
27
28
29
30
31
32
33
35
36
37
39
40
42
43
44
45
46
47

Top Sights (p116)
1 Madame Tussauds B1
2 Wallace Collection C3

Sights (p105)
3 All Souls Church.................... E3
4 Broadcasting House............. E3
5 Handel House Museum........ E5
6 Marble Arch B5
7 Sherlock Holmes Museum .. B1

Eating (p128)
8 Bar Trattoria Semplice D5
9 Fishworks C2
10 Golden Hind C3
11 Greenhouse D7
12 Il Baretto C3
13 La Fromagerie C2
14 La Porte des Indes B4
15 Le Boudin Blanc D7
16 Locanda Locatelli B4
17 Providores & Tapa Room C3
18 Reubens B2
19 Tamarind D7
20 Villandry E2
21 Wallace C3
22 Wild Honey E5

Drinking & Nightlife (p130)
23 Guinea E6
24 Loop Bar E4
25 Prince Regent C2
26 Punch Bowl D6
27 Purl C3

Entertainment (p135)
28 Wigmore Hall D4

Shopping (p138)
29 Beatles Store B1
30 Butler & Wilson D5
31 Cath Kidston C2
32 Daunt Books C2
33 French Connection UK C4
34 John Lewis E4
35 Marks & Spencer C5
36 Marylebone Farmers Market C3
37 Monocle Shop C3
38 Mulberry E5
39 Poste D5
40 Selfridges C5
41 Stella McCartney E6

Sleeping (p335)
42 Chesterfield Mayfair D7
43 Claridge's D5
44 Cumberland Hotel B5
45 Dorset Square Hotel A1
46 Hotel La Place C2
47 No 10 Manchester Street C3

WEST END: ST JAMES'S

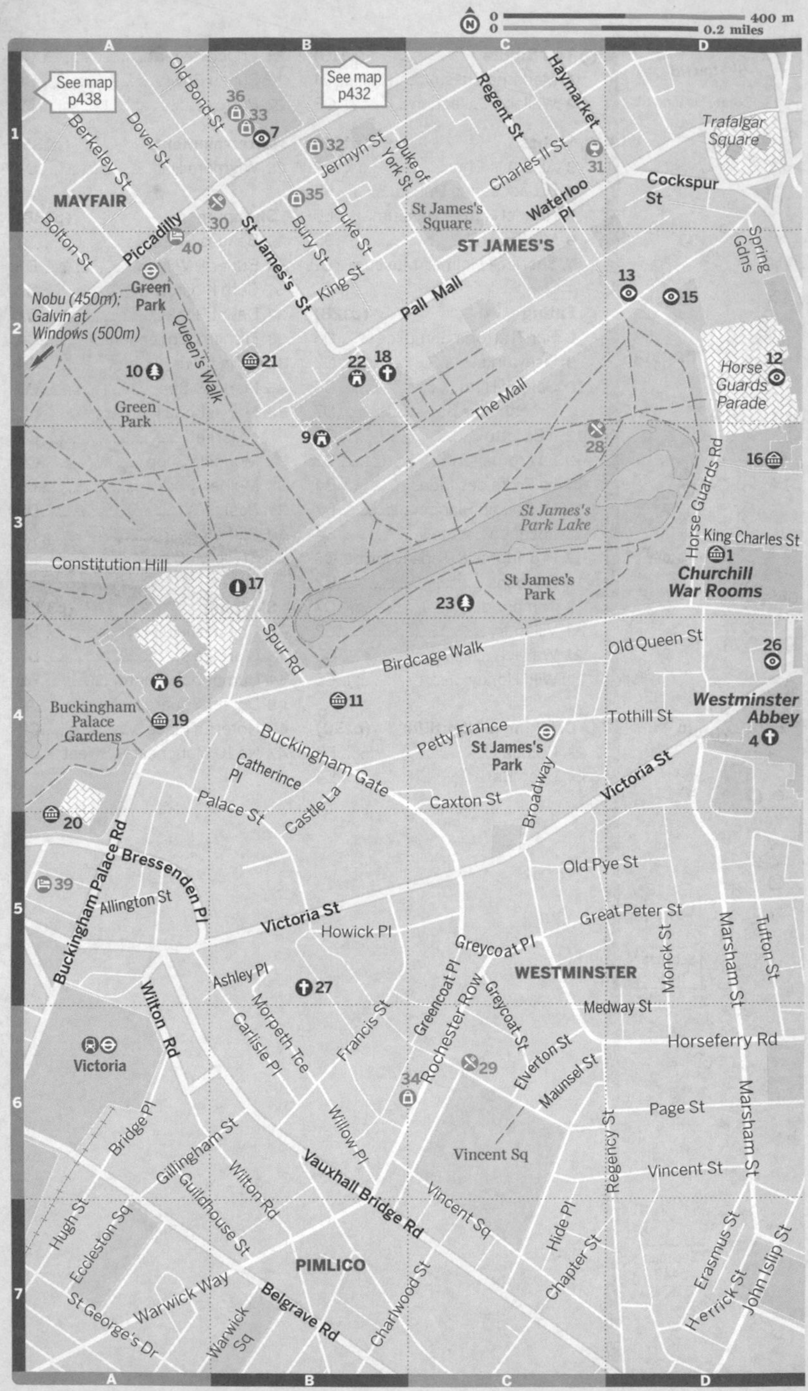

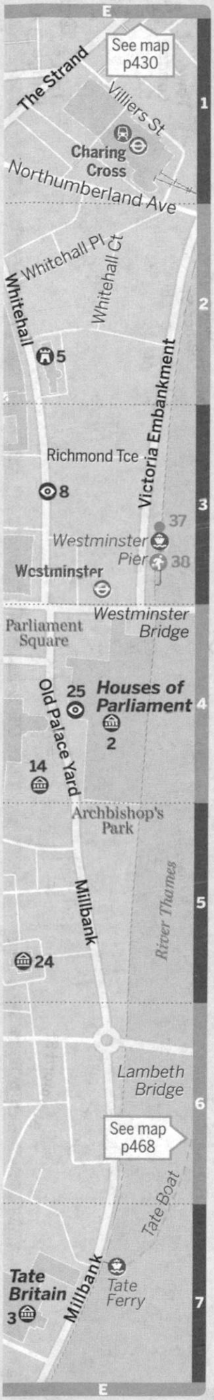

Top Sights (p86)

1 Churchill War Rooms D3
2 Houses of Parliament........... E4
3 Tate Britain E7
4 Westminster Abbey............ D4

Sights (p105)

5 Banqueting House................ E2
6 Buckingham Palace.............A4
7 Burlington Arcade................ B1
8 Cenotaph E3
9 Clarence House....................B3
10 Green Park...........................A2
11 Guards Museum B4
12 Horse Guards Parade......... D2
13 Institute of Contemporary Arts D2
14 Jewel Tower......................... E4
15 National Police Memorial.... D2
16 No 10 Downing Street D3
17 Queen Victoria Memorial B3
18 Queen's Chapel B2
19 Queen's Gallery A4
20 Royal Mews..........................A5
21 Spencer House.....................B2
22 St James's Palace................B2
23 St James's Park C3
24 St John's, Smith Square E5
25 St Stephen's Entrance E4
26 Supreme Court D4
27 Westminster Cathedral B5

Eating (p119)

28 Inn the Park C3
29 Vincent Rooms C6
30 Wolseley................................ B1

Drinking & Nightlife (p133)

31 Sports Cafe C1
Wolseley......................(see 30)

Entertainment (p135)

ICA Cinema..................(see 13)

Shopping (p138)

32 Fortnum & Mason................ B1
33 Penhaligon's......................... B1
34 Shepherds C6
35 Taylor of Old Bond Street.... B1
36 Wright & Teague.................. B1

Sports & Activities (p408)

37 Thames River Boats............ E3
38 Westminster Passenger Services Association......... E3

Sleeping (p335)

39 Goring.................................A5
40 Ritz......................................A2

THE CITY

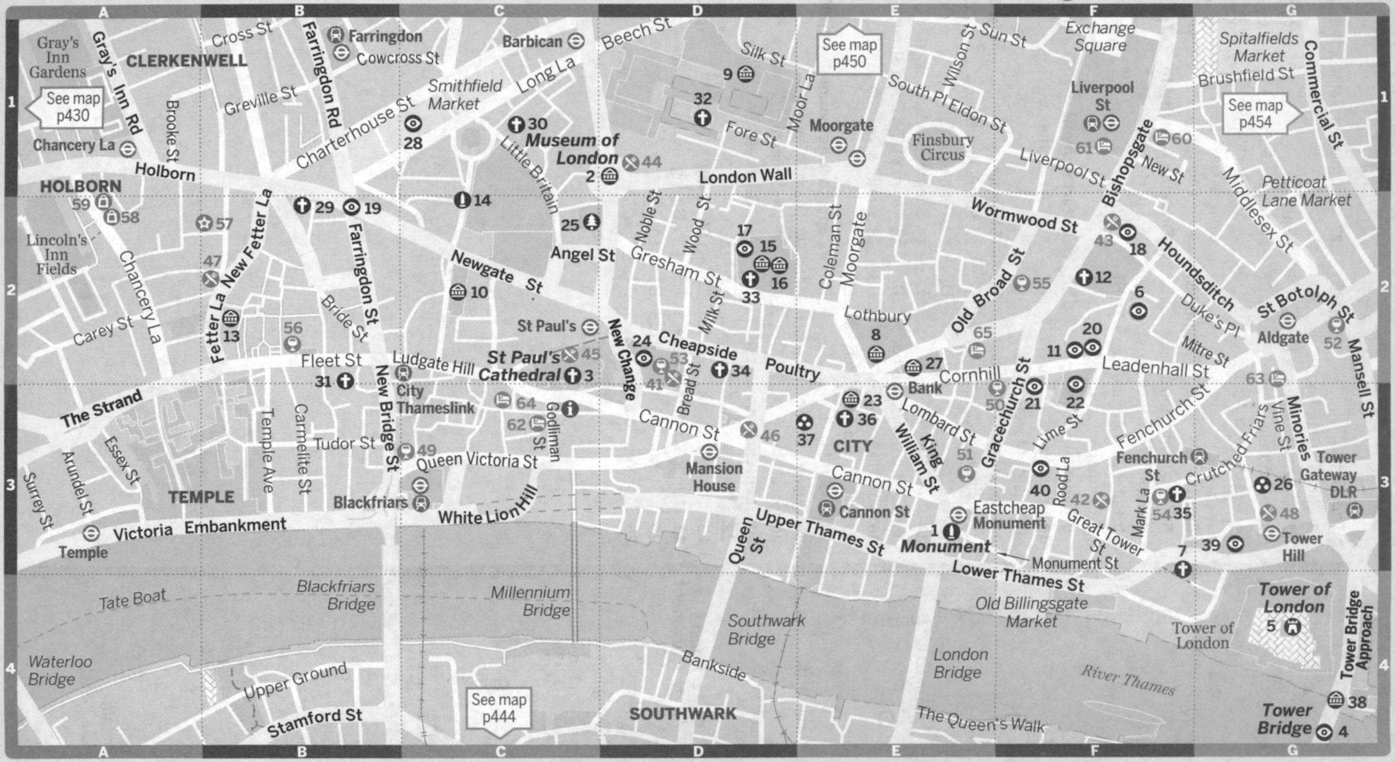

0 500 m
0 0.25 miles
N
Gray's Inn Gardens
Gray's Inn Rd
CLERKENWELL
Cross St
Farringdon
Cowcross St
Barbican
Beech St
Silk St
See map p450
Wilson St
Sun St
Exchange Square
Spitalfields Market
Brushfield St
Commercial St
See map p430
Brooke St
Greville St
Farringdon Rd
Charterhouse St
Smithfield Market
Long La
Museum of London
Moor La
Moorgate
South Pl
Eldon St
Finsbury Circus
Liverpool St
Liverpool St
Bishopsgate
New St
See map p454
Petticoat Lane Market
Middlesex St
Chancery La
Holborn
HOLBORN
Little Britain
Fore St
London Wall
Wormwood St
Houndsditch
Lincoln's Inn Fields
New Fetter La
Farringdon St
Newgate St
Angel St
Noble St
Wood St
Gresham St
Coleman St
Moorgate
Old Broad St
Chancery La
Fetter La
Bride St
Milk St
Lothbury
Duke's Pl
St Botolph St
Aldgate
Mansell St
Carey St
Fleet St
Ludgate Hill
St Paul's
St Paul's Cathedral
New Change
Cheapside
Poultry
Cornhill
Mitre St
Leadenhall St
City Thameslink
Bread St
Bank
Gracechurch St
The Strand
Temple Ave
Carmelite St
New Bridge St
Godliman St
Cannon St
Lombard St
Lime St
Fenchurch St
Crutched Friars
Vine St
Minories
Tudor St
Queen Victoria St
Mansion House
CITY
King William St
Fenchurch St
Tower Gateway DLR
Essex St
Arundel St
Surrey St
TEMPLE
Blackfriars
White Lion Hill
Cannon St
Cannon St
Eastcheap
Monument
Rood La
Great Tower St
Mark La
Temple
Victoria Embankment
Queen St
Upper Thames St
Monument
Monument St
Tower Hill
Lower Thames St
Tate Boat
Blackfriars Bridge
Millennium Bridge
Southwark Bridge
Old Billingsgate Market
Tower of London
Tower of London
Tower Bridge Approach
Waterloo Bridge
Bankside
London Bridge
River Thames
Upper Ground
See map p444
Stamford St
SOUTHWARK
The Queen's Walk
Tower Bridge

THE CITY

Top Sights (p148)

1 Monument E3
2 Museum of London D1
3 St Paul's Cathedral C2
4 Tower Bridge G4
5 Tower of London G4

Sights (p157)

6 30 St Mary Axe F2
7 All Hallows-by-the-Tower F3
8 Bank of England Museum E2
9 Barbican D1
10 Central Criminal Court (Old Bailey) C2
11 Cheese Grater F2
12 Church of St Ethelburga-the-Virgin F2
Clockmakers' Museum (see 17)
13 Dr Johnson's House B2
14 Golden Boy of Pye Corner C2
15 Guildhall D2
16 Guildhall Art Gallery & Roman Amphitheatre D2
17 Guildhall Library D2
18 Heron Tower F2
19 Holborn Viaduct B2
20 Leadenhall Building F2
21 Leadenhall Market F3
22 Lloyd's of London F3
23 Mansion House E3
24 One New Change D2
25 Postman's Park C2
26 Roman Wall G3
27 Royal Exchange E2
28 Smithfield Market C1
29 St Andrew Holborn B2
30 St Bartholomew-the-Great C1
31 St Bride's, Fleet Street B2
32 St Giles' Cripplegate D1
33 St Lawrence Jewry D2
34 St Mary-le-Bow D2
35 St Olave's F3
36 St Stephen Walbrook E3
37 Temple of Mithras E3
38 Tower Bridge Exhibition G4
39 Trinity Square Gardens G3
40 Walkie Talkie F3

Eating (p165)

41 Bread Street Kitchen D2
Café Below (see 34)
42 Camino Monumento F3
43 Duck & Waffle F2
44 London Wall Bar & Kitchen D1
45 Restaurant at St Paul's C2
Royal Exchange Grand Café & Bar (see 27)
46 Sweeting's D3
47 White Swan Pub & Dining Room E2
48 Wine Library G3

Drinking & Nightlife (p166)

49 Blackfriar C3
50 Counting House F3
51 Folly E3
52 Hoop and Grapes G2
53 Madison D2
54 Ship F3
55 Vertigo 42 F2
56 Ye Olde Cheshire Cheese B2

Entertainment (p167)

Barbican (see 9)
57 Volupté B2

Shopping (p167)

58 London Silver Vaults A2
59 Silver Vaults A2

Sleeping (p338)

60 196 Bishopsgate F1
61 Andaz Liverpool Street F1
62 Grange St Paul's C3
63 Hotel Indigo Tower Hill G2
64 London St Paul's YHA C3
65 Threadneedles E2

Key on p446

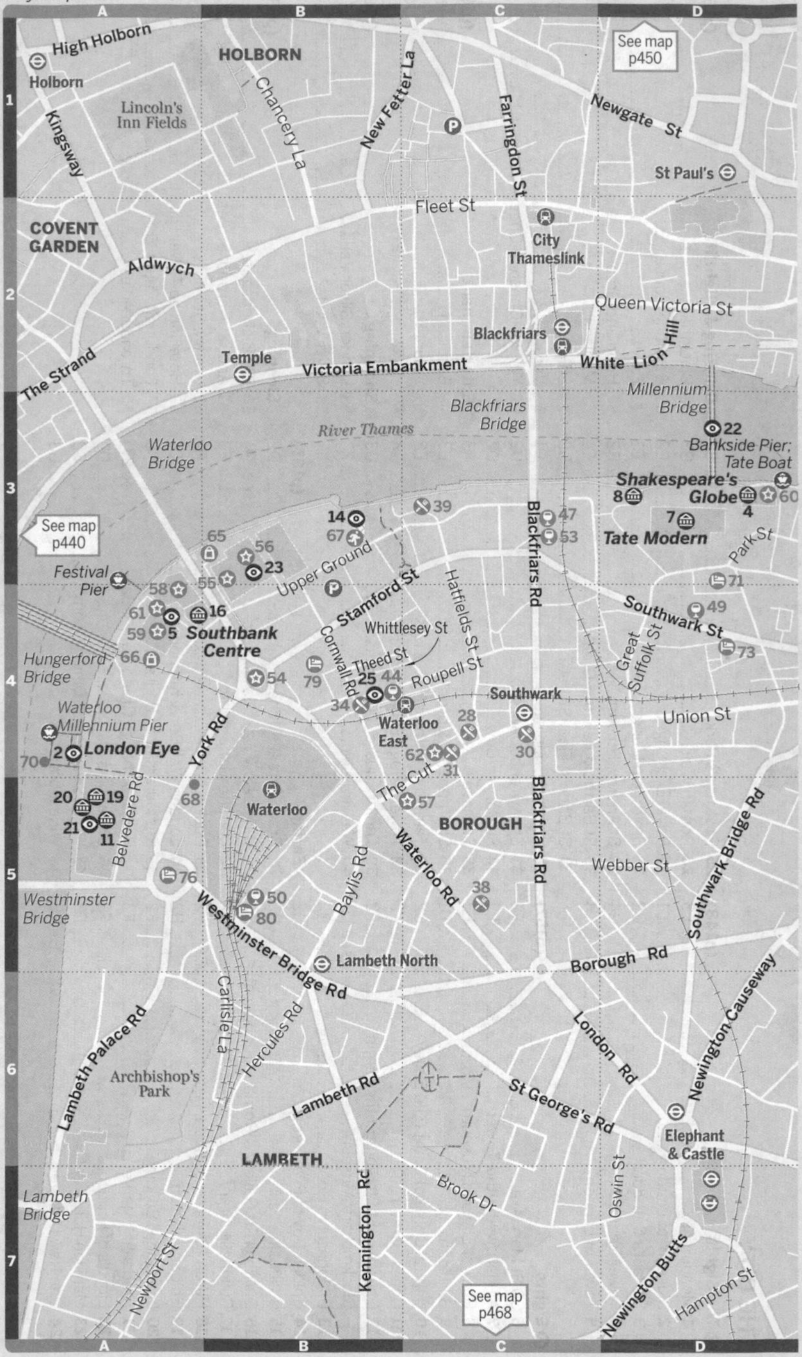
A
B
C
D
1
2
3
4
5
6
7
High Holborn
Holborn
HOLBORN
Lincoln's Inn Fields
Kingsway
Chancery La
New Fetter La
Farringdon St
See map p450
Newgate St
St Paul's
COVENT GARDEN
Aldwych
Fleet St
City Thameslink
Queen Victoria St
Blackfriars
White Lion Hill
The Strand
Temple
Victoria Embankment
Millennium Bridge
Blackfriars Bridge
River Thames
Waterloo Bridge
22
Bankside Pier; Tate Boat
Shakespeare's Globe
8
4
60
39
14
47
7
Tate Modern
See map p440
65
67
56
53
Park St
23
Upper Ground
Festival Pier
58
55
Stamford St
Hatfields St
71
Blackfriars Rd
61
16
49
Southwark St
5
Southbank Centre
Whittlesey St
59
Cornwall Rd
Great Suffolk St
73
Hungerford Bridge
66
Theed St
Roupell St
54
79
25
44
Southwark
34
Union St
Waterloo Millennium Pier
Waterloo East
28
York Rd
2
London Eye
62
30
70
31
The Cut
20
19
68
Waterloo
57
21
11
Belvedere Rd
BOROUGH
Blackfriars Rd
Webber St
Waterloo Rd
Southwark Bridge Rd
76
Baylis Rd
Westminster Bridge
50
80
38
Westminster Bridge Rd
Lambeth North
Borough Rd
Carlisle La
Hercules Rd
London Rd
Newington Causeway
Lambeth Palace Rd
Archbishop's Park
St George's Rd
Lambeth Rd
Elephant & Castle
LAMBETH
Kennington Rd
Brook Dr
Osvin St
Lambeth Bridge
Newport St
See map p468
Newington Butts
Hampton St

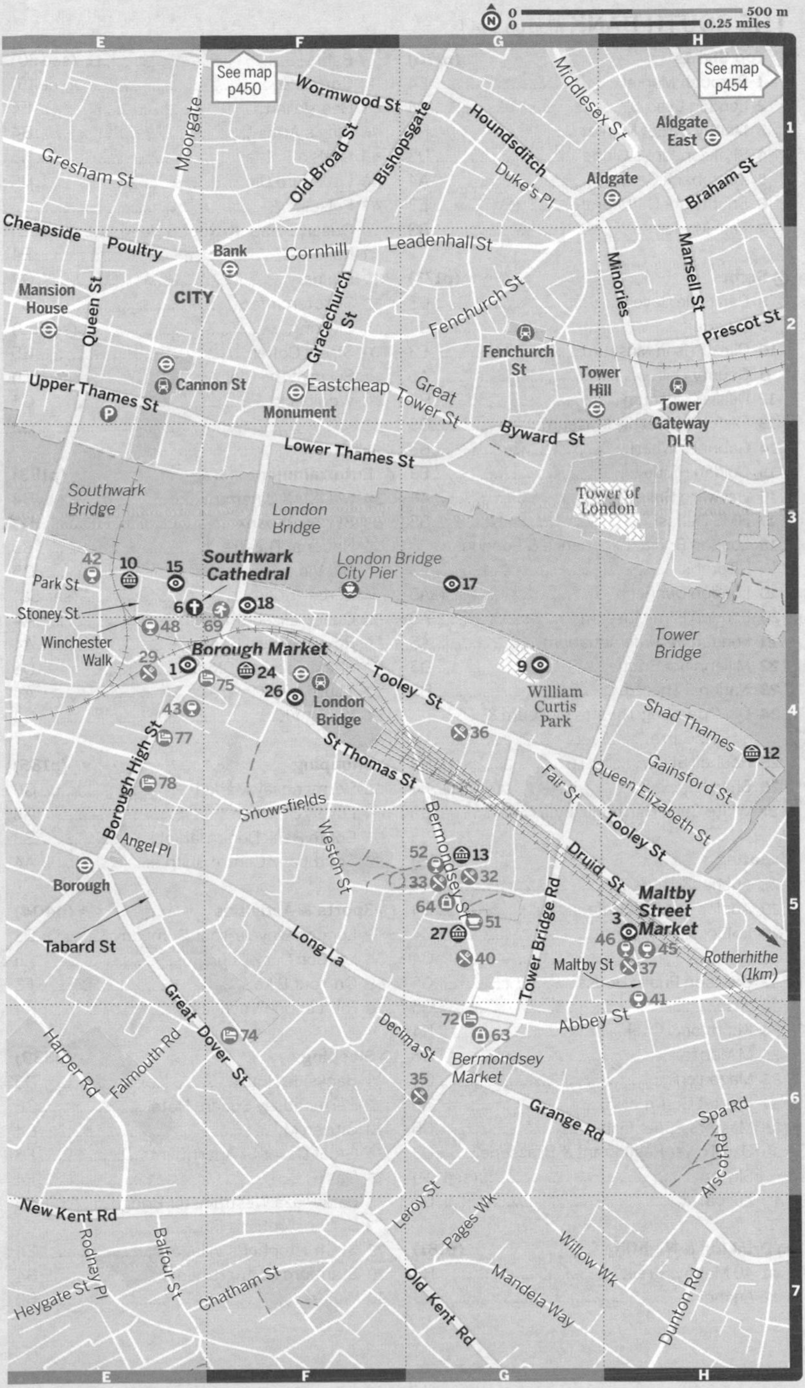
0 500 m
0 0.25 miles
E
F
G
H
1
2
3
4
5
6
7
See map p450
See map p454
Wormwood St
Middlesex St
Houndsditch
Moorgate
Old Broad St
Bishopsgate
Duke's Pl
Aldgate East
Aldgate
Braham St
Gresham St
Cheapside
Poultry
Bank
Cornhill
Leadenhall St
Minories
Mansell St
Mansion House
Queen St
CITY
Gracechurch St
Fenchurch St
Prescot St
Fenchurch St
Cannon St
Eastcheap
Great Tower St
Tower Hill
Tower Gateway DLR
Upper Thames St
Monument
Byward St
Lower Thames St
Southwark Bridge
London Bridge
Tower of London
Southwark Cathedral
London Bridge City Pier
Park St
Stoney St
Winchester Walk
Borough Market
Tooley St
London Bridge
William Curtis Park
Tower Bridge
Shad Thames
Gainsford St
St Thomas St
Fair St
Queen Elizabeth St
Tooley St
Borough High St
Snowsfields
Weston St
Bermondsey St
Druid St
Maltby Street Market
Angel Pl
Borough
Tabard St
Long La
Tower Bridge Rd
Maltby St
Rotherhithe (1km)
Abbey St
Great Dover St
Decima St
Bermondsey Market
Harper Rd
Falmouth Rd
Grange Rd
Spa Rd
Alscot Rd
New Kent Rd
Rodney Pl
Balfour St
Leroy St
Pages Wk
Willow Wk
Heygate St
Chatham St
Old Kent Rd
Mandela Way
Dunton Rd
1
3
6
9
10
12
13
15
17
18
24
26
27
29
32
33
35
36
37
40
41
42
43
45
46
48
51
52
63
64
69
72
74
75
77
78

THE SOUTH BANK *Map on p444*

KENSINGTON & HYDE PARK *Map on p448*

Key on p447

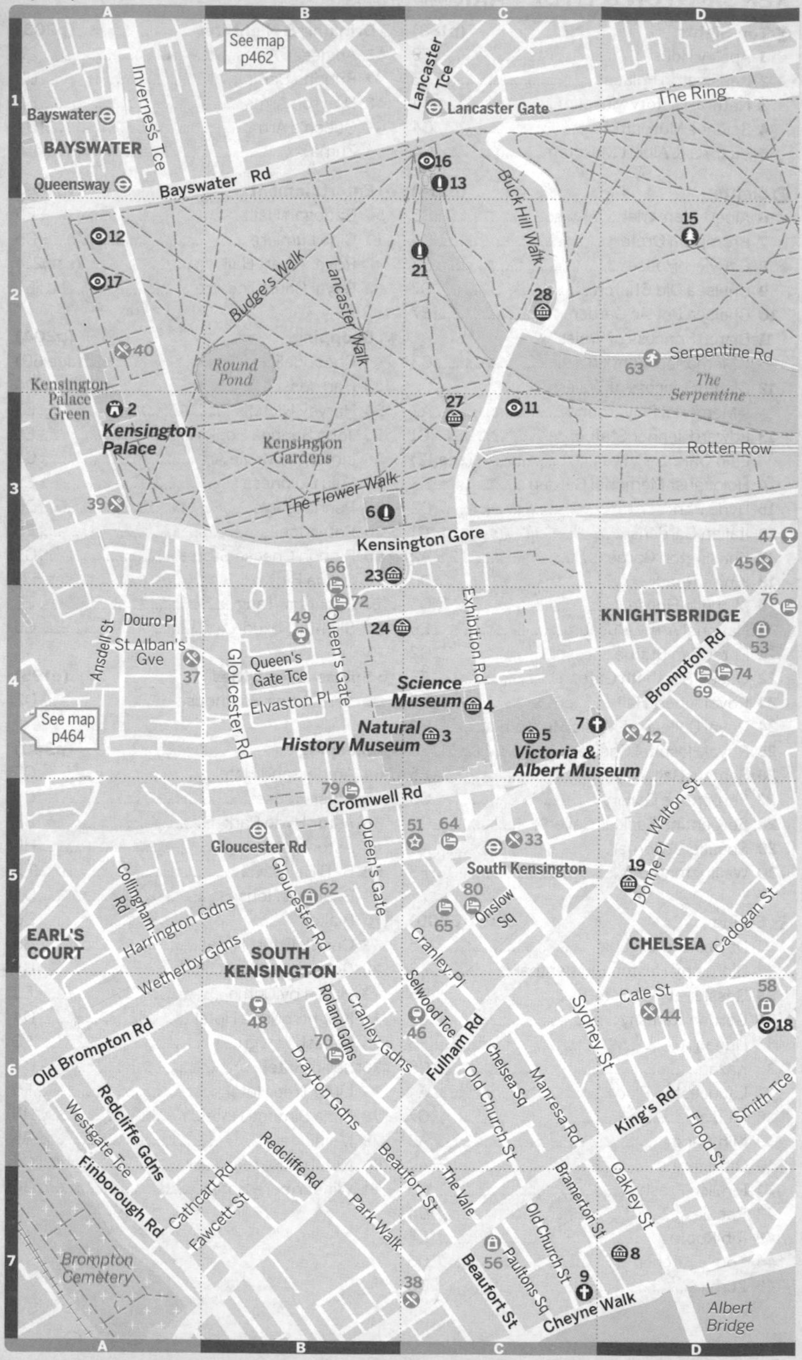
A
B
C
D
1
2
3
4
5
6
7
See map p462
Lancaster Tce
Lancaster Gate
The Ring
Bayswater
BAYSWATER
Inverness Tce
Queensway
Bayswater Rd
16
13
Buck Hill Walk
15
12
17
Budge's Walk
Lancaster Walk
21
28
40
Round Pond
Serpentine Rd
63
The Serpentine
Kensington Palace Green
2
Kensington Palace
27
11
Kensington Gardens
Rotten Row
The Flower Walk
39
6
Kensington Gore
47
45
66
23
72
Exhibition Rd
76
KNIGHTSBRIDGE
Douro Pl
49
24
53
Ansdell St
St Alban's Gve
Queen's Gate Tce
Queen's Gate
Gloucester Rd
Brompton Rd
37
69
74
Science Museum
4
Elvaston Pl
See map p464
Natural History Museum
3
5
7
Victoria & Albert Museum
42
79
Cromwell Rd
Walton St
51
64
33
Gloucester Rd
South Kensington
Collingham Rd
19
Donne Pl
62
80
Onslow Sq
65
Cadogan St
Harrington Gdns
EARL'S COURT
Cranley Pl
CHELSEA
Wetherby Gdns
SOUTH KENSINGTON
Cale St
58
48
Roland Gdns
Selwood Tce
Cranley Gdns
Sydney St
44
18
46
Fulham Rd
Old Brompton Rd
70
Chelsea Sq
Manresa Rd
Drayton Gdns
Old Church St
Smith Tce
King's Rd
Redcliffe Gdns
Westgate Tce
Flood St
Redcliffe Rd
Beaufort St
Finborough Rd
Cathcart Rd
The Vale
Bramerton St
Oakley St
Fawcett St
Park Walk
Old Church St
8
56
Paultons Sq
Brompton Cemetery
38
Beaufort St
9
Cheyne Walk
Albert Bridge

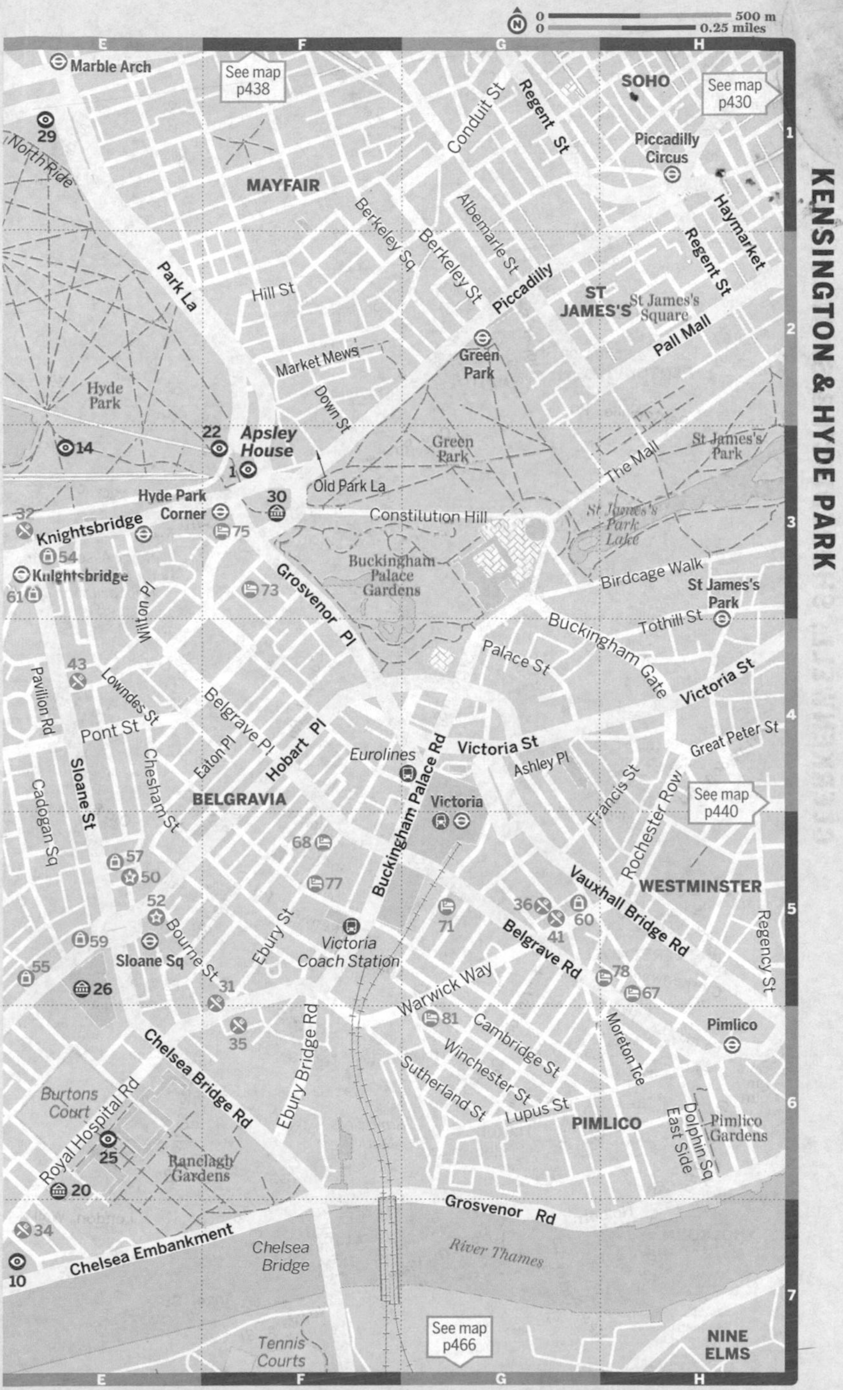
KENSINGTON & HYDE PARK
0 500 m
0 0.25 miles
Marble Arch
See map p438
SOHO
See map p430
Conduit St
Regent St
Piccadilly Circus
North Ride
MAYFAIR
Berkeley Sq
Albemarle St
Haymarket
Berkeley St
Regent St
Park La
Hill St
Piccadilly
ST JAMES'S
St James's Square
Pall Mall
Market Mews
Green Park
Hyde Park
Down St
Green Park
Apsley House
The Mall
St James's Park
Old Park La
Hyde Park Corner
Constitution Hill
Knightsbridge
St James's Park Lake
Buckingham Palace Gardens
Knightsbridge
Grosvenor Pl
Birdcage Walk
St James's Park
Wilton Pl
Tothill St
Buckingham Gate
Palace St
Pavilion Rd
Lowndes St
Belgrave Pl
Victoria St
Pont St
Hobart Pl
Eurolines
Victoria St
Great Peter St
Eaton Pl
Chesham St
Ashley Pl
Sloane St
Cadogan Sq
BELGRAVIA
Buckingham Palace Rd
Victoria
Francis St
Rochester Row
See map p440
WESTMINSTER
Vauxhall Bridge Rd
Bourne St
Ebury St
Victoria Coach Station
Belgrave Rd
Regency St
Sloane Sq
Warwick Way
Cambridge St
Pimlico
Moreton Tce
Chelsea Bridge Rd
Ebury Bridge Rd
Winchester St
Sutherland St
Lupus St
Burtons Court
Royal Hospital Rd
PIMLICO
Dolphin Sq East Side
Pimlico Gardens
Ranelagh Gardens
Grosvenor Rd
Chelsea Embankment
Chelsea Bridge
River Thames
Tennis Courts
See map p466
NINE ELMS

Key on p452

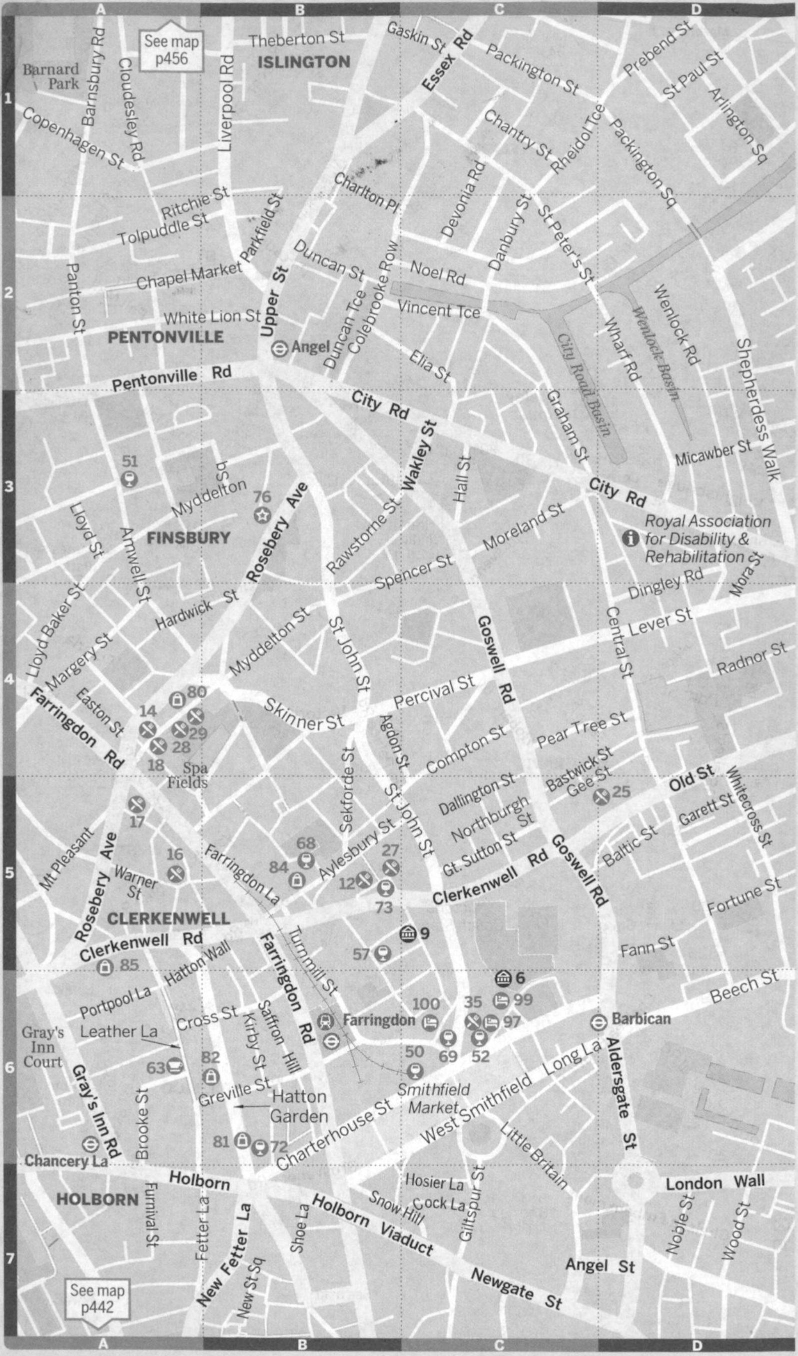
A
B
C
D
1
2
3
4
5
6
7
See map p456
See map p442
ISLINGTON
PENTONVILLE
FINSBURY
CLERKENWELL
HOLBORN
Barnard Park
Barnsbury Rd
Cloudesley Rd
Liverpool Rd
Theberton St
Gaskin St
Essex Rd
Packington St
Prebend St
St Paul St
Arlington Sq
Copenhagen St
Chantry St
Rheidol Tce
Packington Sq
Charlton Pl
Devonia Rd
Danbury St
St Peter's St
Ritchie St
Tolpuddle St
Parkfield St
Chapel Market
Duncan St
Noel Rd
Panton St
Upper St
Duncan Tce
Colebrooke Row
Vincent Tce
White Lion St
Angel
Elia St
City Road Basin
Wharf Rd
Wenlock Basin
Wenlock Rd
Shepherdess Walk
Pentonville Rd
City Rd
Wakley St
Graham St
Micawber St
51
Myddelton Sq
76
Rosebery Ave
Hall St
Lloyd St
Amwell St
Rawstorne St
Moreland St
Royal Association for Disability & Rehabilitation
Mora St
Spencer St
Dingley Rd
Lloyd Baker St
Hardwick St
Goswell Rd
Central St
Lever St
Margery St
Myddelton St
St John St
Radnor St
Farringdon Rd
80
Percival St
Easton St
14
29
28
18
Skinner St
Agdon St
Compton St
Pear Tree St
Spa Fields
Sekforde St
Bastwick St
Gee St
25
Old St
Whitecross St
17
Dallington St
Northburgh St
Garett St
Baltic St
Mt Pleasant
68
Aylesbury St
27
Gt. Sutton St
Clerkenwell Rd
16
Warner St
84
12
73
Fortune St
Farringdon La
9
Fann St
Clerkenwell Rd
Hatton Wall
Turnmill St
57
85
6
Beech St
Portpool La
100
35
99
Cross St
Farringdon
97
Barbican
Gray's Inn Court
Leather La
Saffron Hill
Kirby St
69
52
50
63
82
Long La
Aldersgate St
Greville St
Hatton Garden
Smithfield Market
Brooke St
Gray's Inn Rd
Charterhouse St
West Smithfield
Little Britain
81
72
Chancery La
Holborn
Hosier La
London Wall
Furnival St
Fetter La
New Fetter La
Shoe La
Snow Hill
Cock La
Giltspur St
Holborn Viaduct
Noble St
Wood St
Angel St
New St Sq
Newgate St

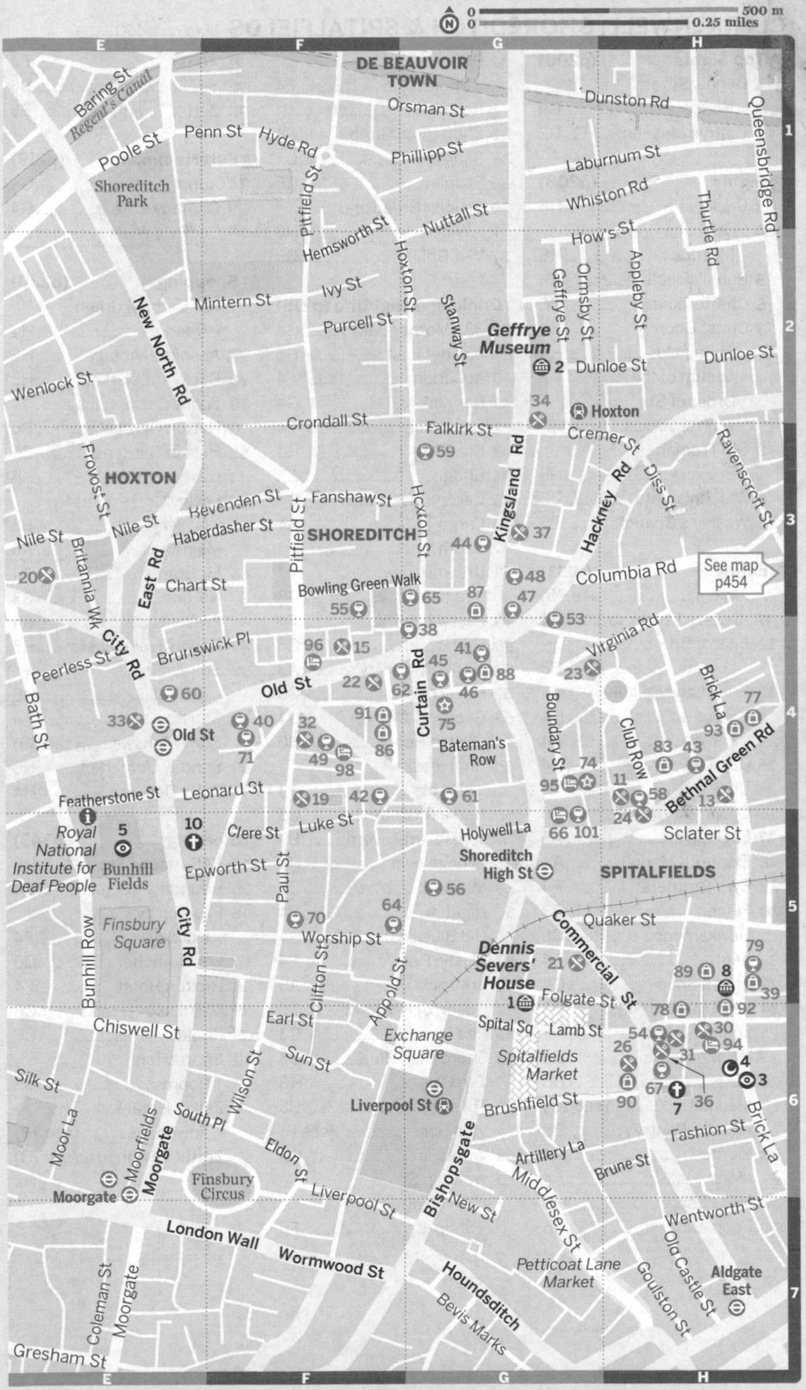
0 500 m
0 0.25 miles
E
F
G
H
1
2
3
4
5
6
7
DE BEAUVOIR TOWN
Baring St
Regent's Canal
Orsman St
Dunston Rd
Queensbridge Rd
Poole St
Penn St
Hyde Rd
Phillipp St
Laburnum St
Shoreditch Park
Pitfield St
Whiston Rd
Thurtle Rd
Nuttall St
How's St
Hemsworth St
Hoxton St
Geffrye St
Ormsby St
Appleby St
Mintern St
Ivy St
Stanway St
Purcell St
Geffrye Museum
New North Rd
2
Dunloe St
Dunloe St
Wenlock St
34
Hoxton
Crondall St
Falkirk St
Cremer St
Kingsland Rd
59
Ravenscroft St
Frovost St
HOXTON
Hackney Rd
Diss St
Fanshaw St
Bevenden St
Haberdasher St
SHOREDITCH
Nile St
Nile St
Britannia Wk
East Rd
44
37
20
Chart St
Bowling Green Walk
48
Columbia Rd
See map p454
55
65
87
47
53
City Rd
38
Brunswick Pl
96
15
41
Virginia Rd
Peerless St
45
Curtain Rd
88
23
Bath St
60
22
62
46
Old St
Boundary St
Brick La
77
33
Old St
40
32
91
75
Club Row
93
71
86
Bateman's Row
83
43
49
98
74
Bethnal Green Rd
Featherstone St
Leonard St
95
11
58
19
42
61
13
24
Royal National Institute for Deaf People
5
10
Clere St
Luke St
Holywell La
66
101
Sclater St
Bunhill Fields
Epworth St
Shoreditch High St
SPITALFIELDS
Paul St
56
64
Quaker St
Finsbury Square
70
Commercial St
79
Worship St
Dennis Severs' House
21
89
8
39
Bunhill Row
City Rd
Clifton St
Appold St
1
Folgate St
78
92
Chiswell St
Earl St
Exchange Square
Spital Sq
Lamb St
54
30
26
94
31
Sun St
Spitalfields Market
4
3
Silk St
Wilson St
67
36
Liverpool St
90
7
Brushfield St
South Pl
Brick La
Moor La
Moorfields
Moorgate
Eldon St
Bishopsgate
Fashion St
Artillery La
Finsbury Circus
Brune St
Moorgate
Liverpool St
Middlesex St
New St
Wentworth St
London Wall
Old Castle St
Wormwood St
Houndsditch
Petticoat Lane Market
Goulston St
Aldgate East
Coleman St
Moorgate
Bevis Marks
Gresham St

CLERKENWELL, SHOREDITCH & SPITALFIELDS *Map on p450*

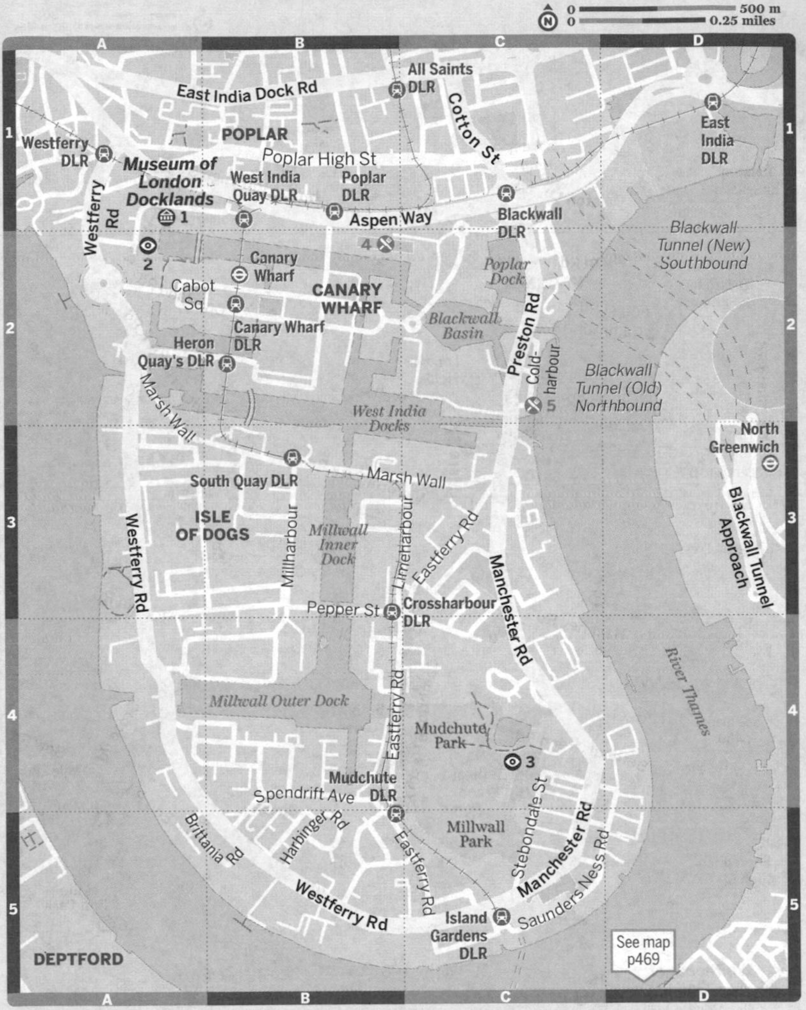

Top Sights (p229)

1 Museum of London Docklands A1

Sights (p229)

2 Isle of Dogs A2

3 Mudchute Park & Farm C4

Eating (p234)

4 Billingsgate Fish Market B2

5 Gun C2

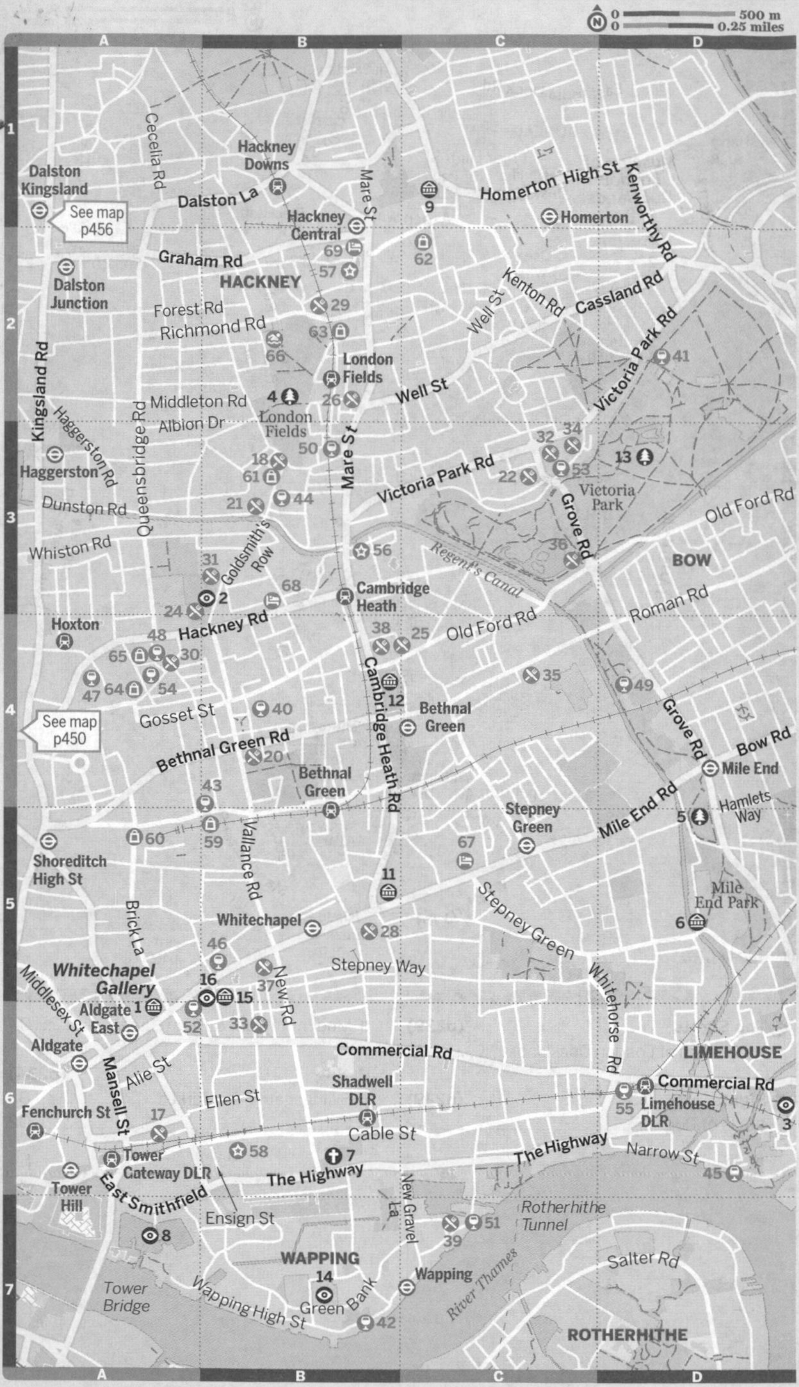
0 500 m
0 0.25 miles
A
B
C
D
1
2
3
4
5
6
7
Dalston Kingsland
See map p456
Cecelia Rd
Hackney Downs
Dalston La
Hackney Central
Mare St
9
Homerton High St
Homerton
Kenworthy Rd
Graham Rd
69
57
62
HACKNEY
Dalston Junction
Forest Rd
Richmond Rd
29
63
Kenton Rd
Cassland Rd
Well St
Victoria Park Rd
41
66
London Fields
Kingsland Rd
Middleton Rd
4
London Fields
26
Well St
Albion Dr
Haggerston Rd
Queensbridge Rd
50
32
34
Haggerston
18
61
Mare St
Victoria Park Rd
22
53
13
Victoria Park
21
44
Grove Rd
Dunston Rd
Old Ford Rd
Whiston Rd
Goldsmith's Row
56
Regent's Canal
36
BOW
31
68
2
Cambridge Heath
24
Hackney Rd
Roman Rd
Hoxton
48
38
25
Old Ford Rd
65
30
47
64
54
35
49
12
40
Gosset St
Bethnal Green
See map p450
Bethnal Green Rd
20
Cambridge Heath Rd
Grove Rd
Bow Rd
Mile End
Bethnal Green
43
Stepney Green
Mile End Rd
5
Hamlets Way
60
59
Vallance Rd
67
Shoreditch High St
11
Brick La
Mile End Park
Stepney Green
Whitechapel
28
6
46
Stepney Way
Whitehorse Rd
Middlesex St
Whitechapel Gallery
16
37
New Rd
Aldgate
1
15
East
52
33
Aldgate
Commercial Rd
LIMEHOUSE
Mansell St
Alie St
Shadwell DLR
Commercial Rd
Ellen St
55
Limehouse DLR
3
Fenchurch St
17
Cable St
58
7
The Highway
Narrow St
Tower Gateway DLR
The Highway
45
Tower Hill
East Smithfield
Ensign St
New Gravel La
Rotherhithe Tunnel
39
51
8
WAPPING
Salter Rd
14
Wapping
Tower Bridge
Wapping High St
Green Bank
River Thames
42
ROTHERHITHE

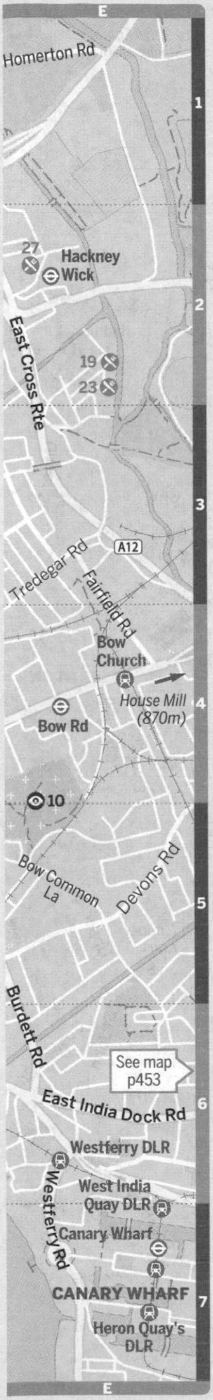

Top Sights (p224)

1 Whitechapel Gallery A6

Sights (p224)

2 Hackney City Farm B3
3 Limehouse D6
4 London Fields B2
5 Mile End Park.........................D5
6 Ragged School Museum......D5
7 St George-in-the-East B6
8 St Katharine Docks..............A7
9 Sutton House C1
10 Tower Hamlets Cemetery Park.................................E4
11 Trinity Green Almshouses...B5
12 V&A Museum of Childhood.................................B4
13 Victoria Park......................... D3
14 Wapping B7
15 Whitechapel Bell Foundry....B5
16 Whitechapel Road................B5
William Booth Statue ..(see 11)

Eating (p230)

17 Café Spice Namasté............A6
18 Climpson & Sons B3
19 Counter Cafe E2
20 E Pellici B4
21 F. Cooke B3
22 Fish House C3
23 Formans E2
24 Frizzante@City Farm............A3
25 Gallery Cafe C4
26 Green Papaya........................B2
27 Hackney Pearl E2
28 Kolapata B5
29 Lardo B2
30 Laxeiro....................................A4
31 Little Georgia B3
32 Loafing.................................... C3
33 Mirch Masala B6
34 Namô C3
35 Palmers C4
36 Pavilion................................... C3
37 Tayyabs...................................B5
38 Viajante B4
39 Wapping Food C7
Whitechapel Gallery Dining Room.........................(see 1)

Drinking & Nightlife (p234)

40 Bethnal Green Working Men's Club..........................B4
41 Britannia D2
42 Captain Kidd.......................... B7
43 Carpenter's Arms B4
44 Dove Freehouse....................B3
45 Grapes.....................................D6
46 Indo..B5
47 Joiners Arms A4
48 Nelsons Head A4
49 Palm Tree D4
50 Platform Café, Bar & Terrace.............................B3
51 Prospect of Whitby C7
52 Rhythm Factory A6
53 Royal Inn on the Park...........C3
54 Royal Oak...............................A4
55 White Swan............................D6

Entertainment (p236)

56 Bistrotheque B3
57 Hackney Empire B2
58 Wilton's B6

Shopping (p237)

59 Beyond Retro B5
60 Brick Lane Market A5
61 Broadway Market B3
62 Burberry Outlet Shop...........C2
63 Carhartt Outlet Store B2
64 Columbia Road Flower Market A4
65 Jones Dairy............................A4

Sports & Activities (p225)

66 London Fields Lido B2

Sleeping (p344)

67 40 Winks C5
68 Days Hotel B3
69 Old Ship..................................B2
Town Hall Hotel & Apartments ....(see 38)

NORTH LONDON: ISLINGTON & KING'S CROSS

Key on p458

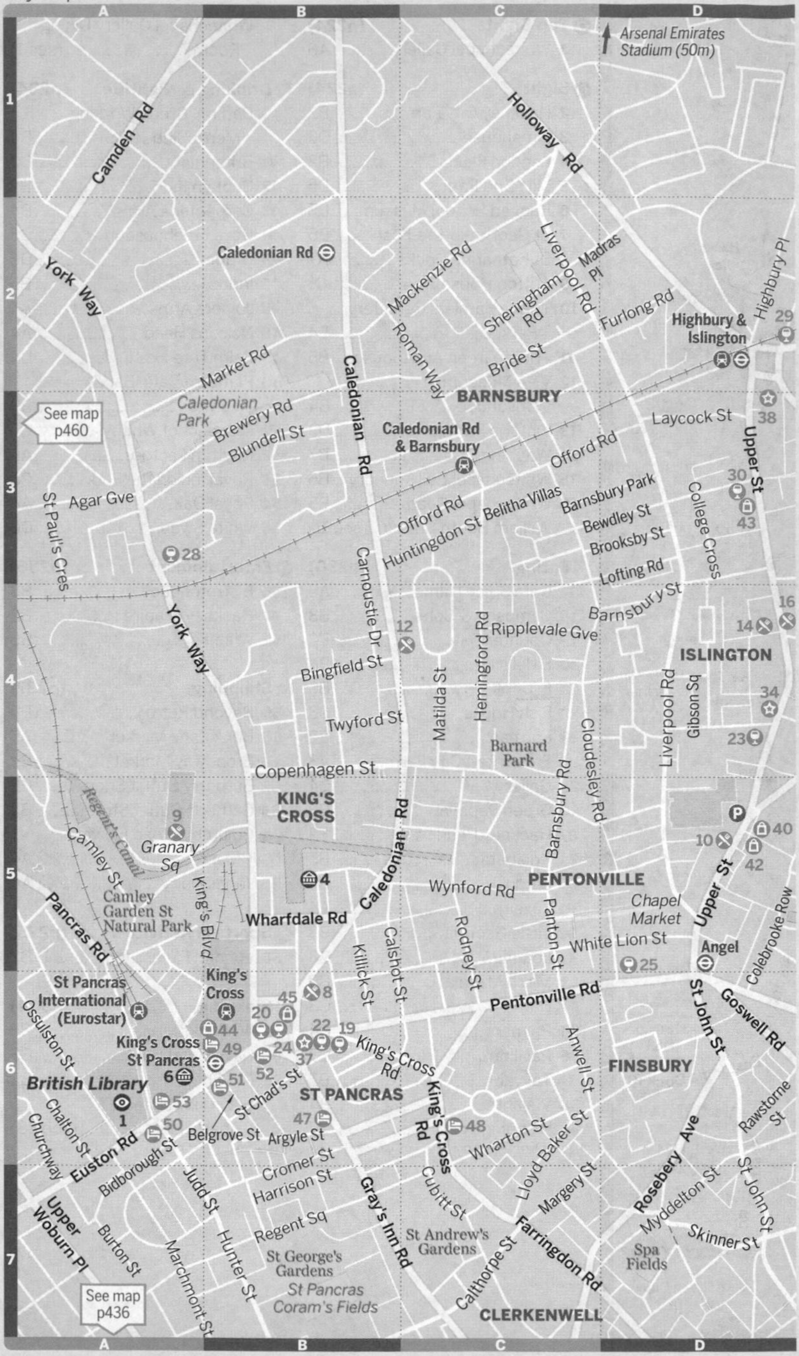

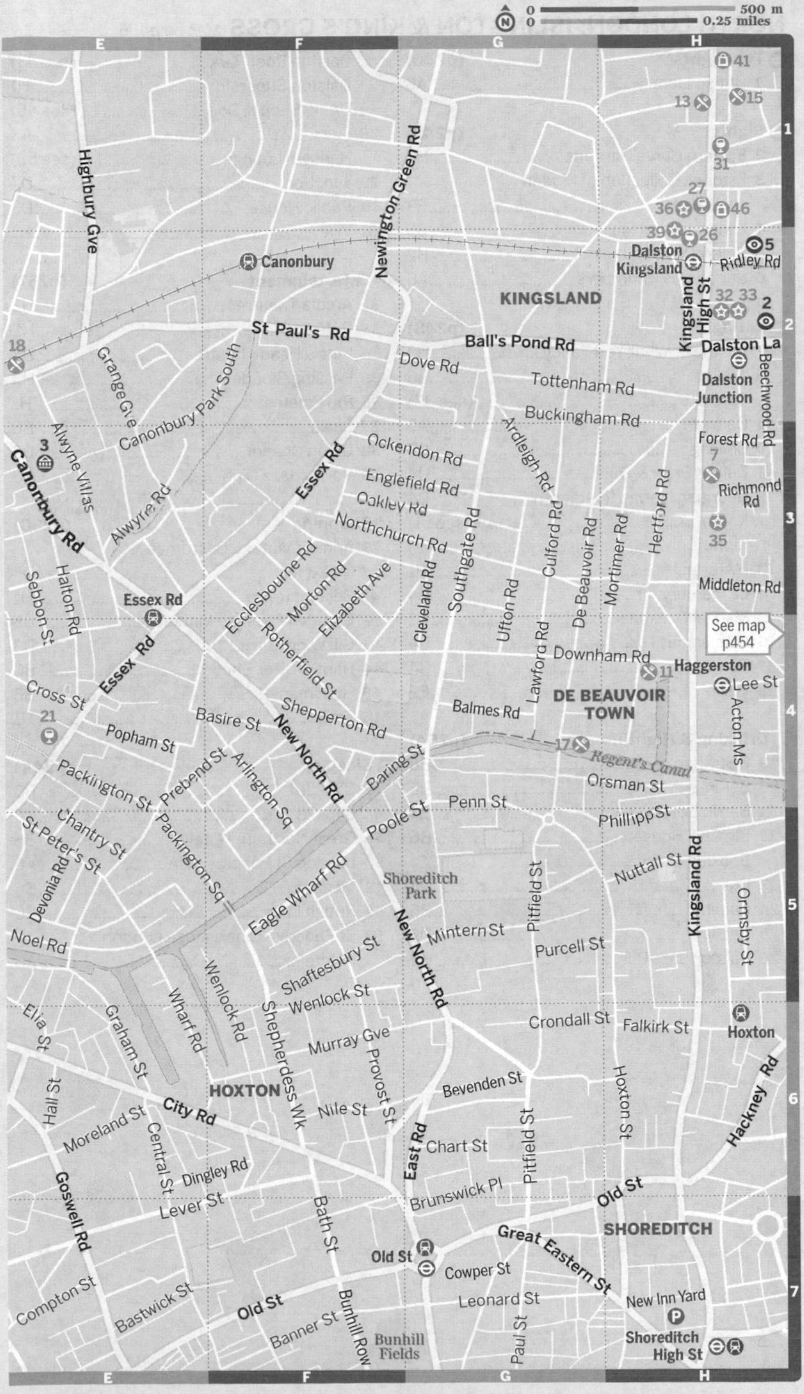
0 500 m
0 0.25 miles
E
F
G
H
1
2
3
4
5
6
7
41
13
15
31
27
36
46
39
26
5
Dalston Kingsland
Ridley Rd
KINGSLAND
Kingsland High St
32
33
2
Dalston La
Dalston Junction
Beechwood Rd
Highbury Gve
Canonbury
Newington Green Rd
St Paul's Rd
Ball's Pond Rd
18
Dove Rd
Tottenham Rd
Buckingham Rd
Grange Gve
Canonbury Park South
Canonbury Rd
Alwyne Villas
3
Alwyne Rd
Essex Rd
Ockendon Rd
Englefield Rd
Oakley Rd
Northchurch Rd
Ardleigh Rd
Forest Rd
7
Richmond Rd
35
Hertford Rd
Mortimer Rd
De Beauvoir Rd
Culford Rd
Southgate Rd
Cleveland Rd
Ufton Rd
Elizabeth Ave
Morton Rd
Ecclesbourne Rd
Middleton Rd
See map p454
Sebbon St
Halton Rd
Rotherfield St
Downham Rd
Lawford Rd
Haggerston
11
Lee St
Acton Ms
DE BEAUVOIR TOWN
Balmes Rd
Cross St
21
Popham St
Basire St
Shepperton Rd
New North Rd
17
Regent's Canal
Orsman St
Packington St
Prebend St
Arlington Sq
Baring St
Penn St
Phillipp St
Chantry St
St Peter's St
Devonia Rd
Packington Sq
Poole St
Eagle Wharf Rd
Shoreditch Park
Pitfield St
Nuttall St
Kingsland Rd
Ormsby St
Noel Rd
Mintern St
Purcell St
Shaftesbury St
Wenlock St
Wenlock Rd
Wharf Rd
Graham St
Elia St
Shepherdess Wk
Murray Gve
Provost St
Crondall St
Falkirk St
Hoxton
Hoxton St
Hackney Rd
HOXTON
City Rd
Hall St
Bevenden St
Nile St
Moreland St
Central St
Chart St
East Rd
Dingley Rd
Goswell Rd
Lever St
Bath St
Brunswick Pl
Old St
SHOREDITCH
Great Eastern St
Cowper St
Compton St
Bastwick St
Leonard St
New Inn Yard
Banner St
Bunhill Row
Bunhill Fields
Paul St
Shoreditch High St

NORTH LONDON: ISLINGTON & KING'S CROSS *Map on p456*

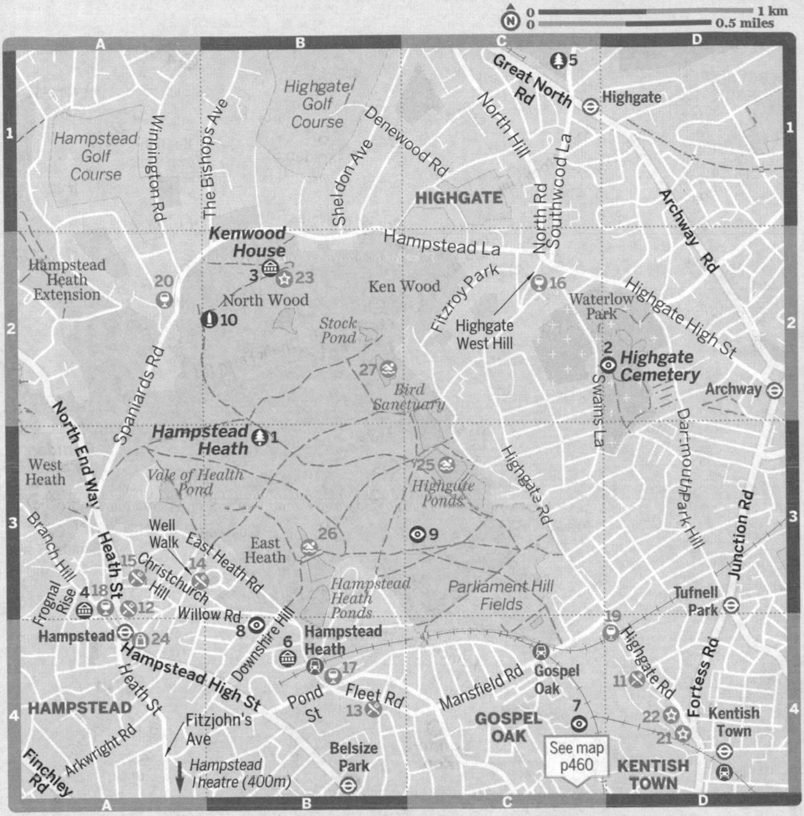

Top Sights (p246)
1 Hampstead Heath ... B3
2 Highgate Cemetery ... D2
3 Kenwood House ... B2

Sights (p245)
4 Fenton House ... A3
5 Highgate Wood ... C1
6 Keats House ... B4
7 Kentish Town City Farm ... C4
8 No 2 Willow Road ... B4
9 Parliament Hill ... C3
10 Sculptures by Henry Moore & Barbara Hepworth ... B2

Eating (p248)
11 Dirty Burger ... D4
12 Gaucho Grill ... A3
13 Stag ... B4
14 Wells Tavern ... A3
15 Woodlands ... A3

Drinking & Nightlife (p256)
16 Flask Tavern ... C2
17 Garden Gate ... B4
18 Holly Bush ... A3
19 Southampton Arms ... D4
20 Spaniard's Inn ... A2

Entertainment (p257)
21 Bull & Gate ... D4
22 Forum ... D4
23 Live by the Lake ... B2

Shopping (p260)
24 Exclusivo ... A4

Sports & Activities (p261)
25 Hampstead Heath Men's Pond ... C3
26 Hampstead Heath Ponds ... B3
27 Hampstead Heath Women's Pond ... B2

NORTH LONDON: CAMDEN

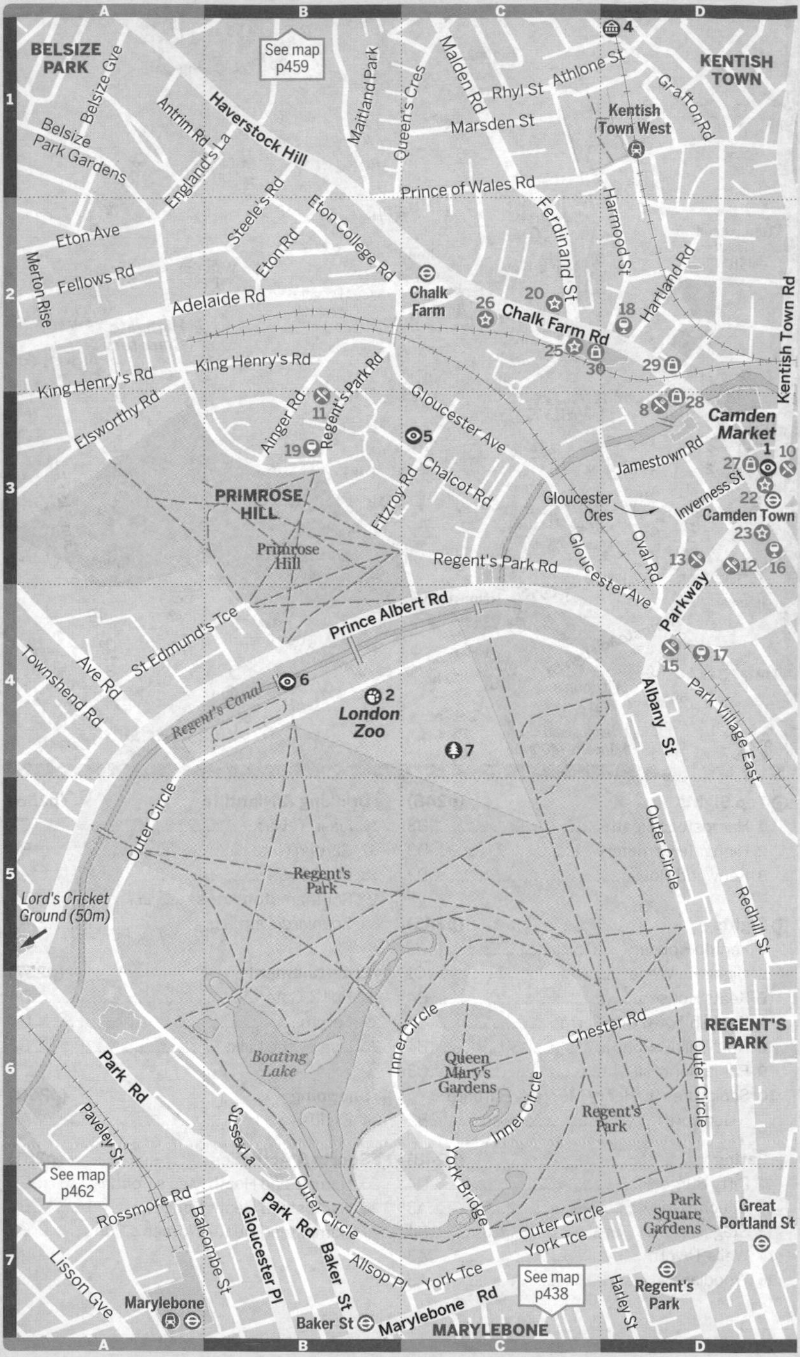
A
B
C
D
1
2
3
4
5
6
7
See map p459
See map p462
See map p438
BELSIZE PARK
KENTISH TOWN
PRIMROSE HILL
Primrose Hill
REGENT'S PARK
MARYLEBONE
Belsize Gve
Belsize Park Gardens
Antrim Rd
England's La
Haverstock Hill
Maitland Park
Queen's Cres
Malden Rd
Rhyl St
Athlone St
Marsden St
Kentish Town West
Grafton Rd
Prince of Wales Rd
Ferdinand St
Harmood St
Hartland Rd
Kentish Town Rd
Steele's Rd
Eton College Rd
Eton Rd
Eton Ave
Fellows Rd
Merton Rise
Adelaide Rd
Chalk Farm
Chalk Farm Rd
King Henry's Rd
Elsworthy Rd
Ainger Rd
Regent's Park Rd
Gloucester Ave
Chalcot Rd
Fitzroy Rd
Camden Market
Jamestown Rd
Inverness St
Gloucester Cres
Camden Town
Oval Rd
Parkway
Prince Albert Rd
St Edmund's Tce
Ave Rd
Townshend Rd
Regent's Canal
London Zoo
Albany St
Park Village East
Outer Circle
Regent's Park
Redhill St
Lord's Cricket Ground (50m)
Boating Lake
Inner Circle
Queen Mary's Gardens
Chester Rd
Park Rd
Paveley St
Sussex La
York Bridge
Rossmore Rd
Balcombe St
Gloucester Pl
Baker St
Allsop Pl
York Tce
Harley St
Park Square Gardens
Great Portland St
Lisson Gve
Marylebone
Marylebone Rd
1
2
4
5
6
7
8
10
11
12
13
15
16
17
18
19
20
22
23
25
26
27
28
29
30

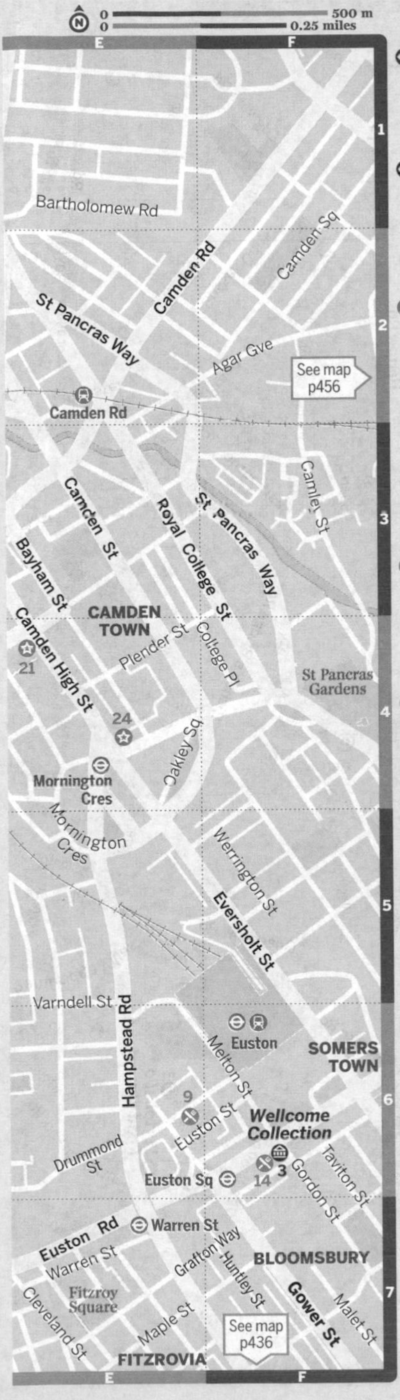

Top Sights (p242)

1 Camden Market D3
2 London Zoo B4
3 Wellcome Collection F6

Sights (p244)

4 Annroy D1
5 Primrose Hill C3
6 Regent's Canal B4
7 Regent's Park C4

Eating (p248)

8 Chin Chin Labs D3
9 Diwana Bhel Poori House E6
10 Mango Room D3
11 Manna B3
12 Market D3
13 Namaaste Kitchen D3
14 Peyton & Byrne at the Wellcome Collection F6
15 York & Albany D4

Drinking & Nightlife (p255)

16 Black Cap D3
17 Edinboro Castle D4
18 Lock Tavern D2
19 Queen's B3

Entertainment (p257)

20 Barfly C2
21 Blues Kitchen E4
22 Electric Ballroom D3
23 Jazz Café D3
24 KOKO E4
25 Proud Camden C2
26 Roundhouse C2

Shopping (p260)

27 Buck Street Market D3
28 Camden Lock Market D3
29 Canal Market D2
30 Stables Market C2

Sleeping (p344)

York & Albany .... (see 15)

NOTTING HILL & WEST LONDON

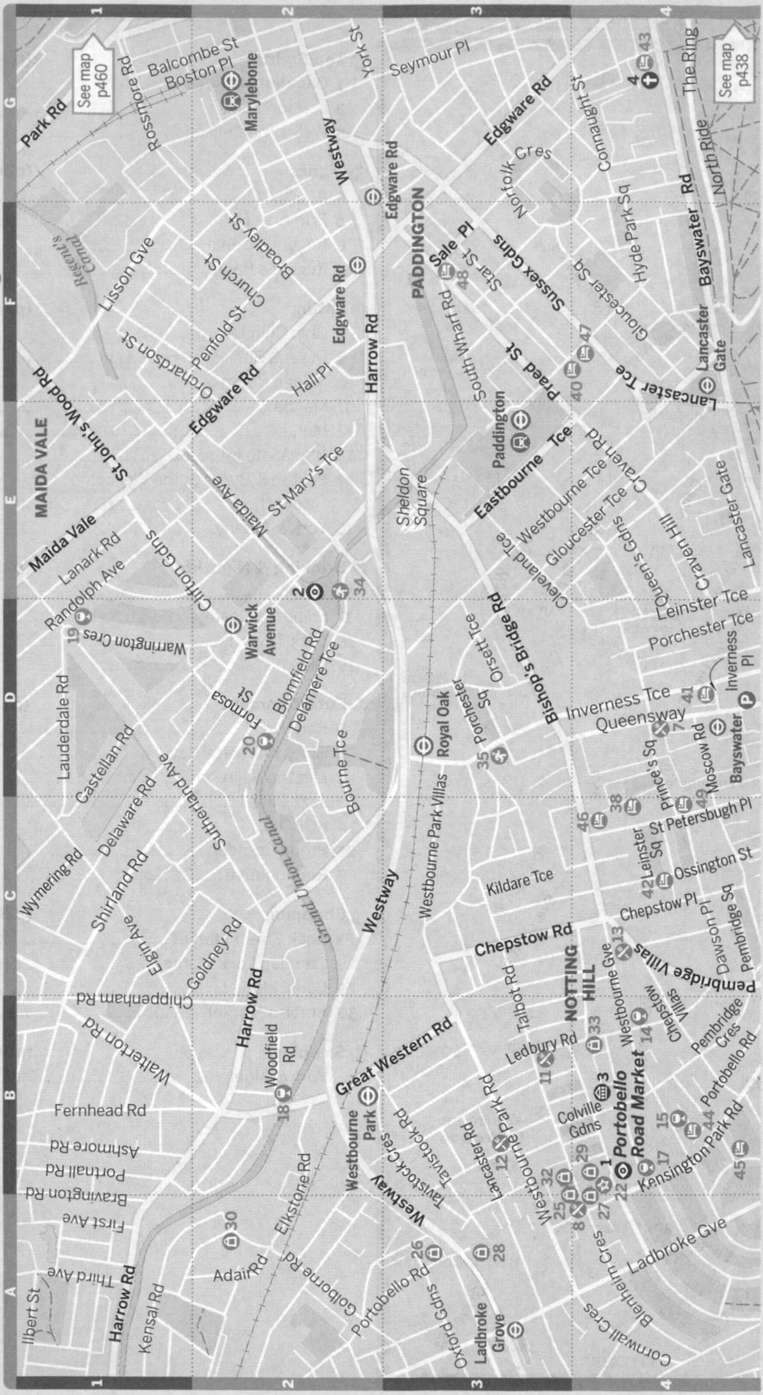

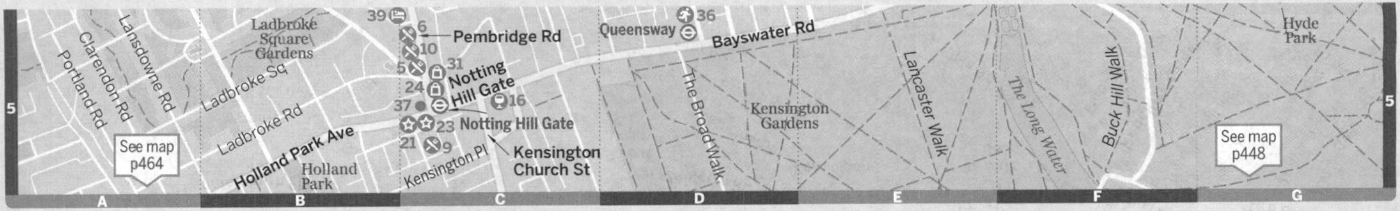

Top Sights (p267)
1 Portobello Road Market ... B4

Sights (p265)
2 Little Venice ... E2
3 Museum of Brands, Packaging and Advertising ... B4
4 Tyburn Convent ... G4

Eating (p267)
5 Arancina ... C5
6 Bubbleology ... C5
7 Couscous Café ... D4
8 E&O ... A4
Electric Diner ... (see 22)
9 Geales ... C5
10 Gelato Mio ... C5
11 Ledbury ... B3
12 Rum Kitchen ... B3
13 Taquería ... C4

Drinking & Nightlife (p271)
14 Beach Blanket Babylon ... B4
15 Earl of Lonsdale ... B4
16 Notting Hill Arts Club ... C5
17 Portobello Star ... B4
18 Union Tavern ... B2
19 Warrington ... D1
20 Waterway ... D2

Entertainment (p273)
21 Coronet ... C5
22 Electric Cinema ... B4
23 Gate Picturehouse ... C5

Shopping (p274)
24 Book & Comic Exchange ... C5
Books for Cooks ... (see 25)
25 Ceramica Blue ... A3
26 Honest Jon's ... A3
27 Notting Hill Bookshop ... A4
28 Portobello Green Arcade ... A3
29 Pylones ... B4
30 Rellik ... A2
31 Retro Woman ... C5
32 Rough Trade West ... B3
33 Village Bicycle ... B4

Sports & Activities (p276)
34 London Waterbus Company ... E2
35 Porchester Spa ... D3
36 Queens Ice & Bowl ... D5
37 Recipease ... C5

Sleeping (p345)
38 Garden Court Hotel ... C4
39 Gate Hotel ... B5
40 Hotel Indigo ... F4
41 La Suite West ... D4
42 New Linden Hotel ... C4
43 Parkwood Hotel ... G4
44 Portobello Gold ... B4
45 Portobello Hotel ... B4
46 Space Apart Hotel ... C4
47 Stylotel ... F4
48 Tune Hotel ... F3
49 Vancouver Studios ... C4

WEST LONDON: SHEPHERD'S BUSH & EARL'S COURT

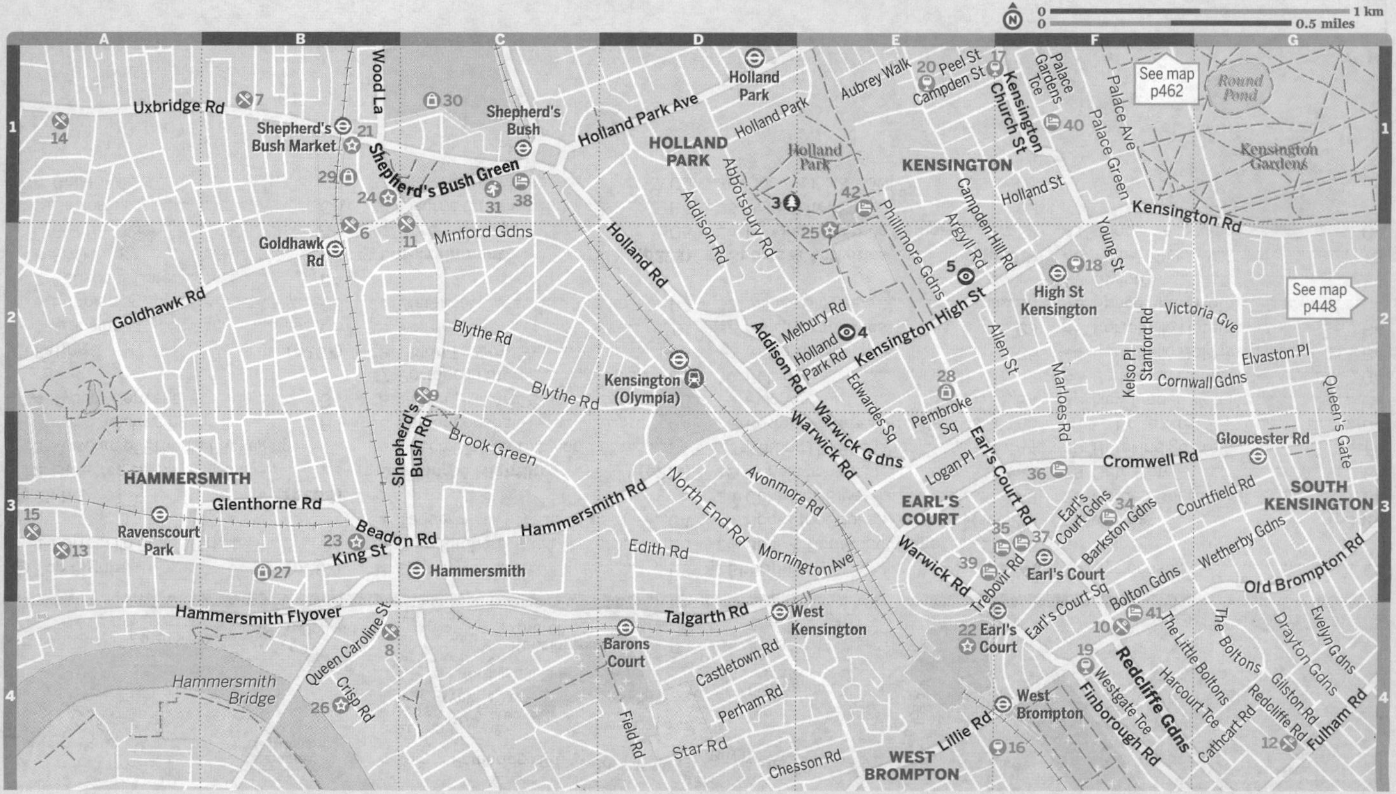

WEST LONDON: SHEPHERD'S BUSH & EARL'S COURT

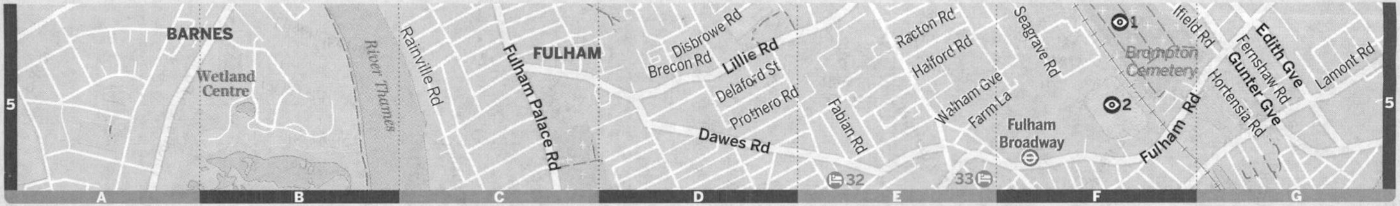

Sights (p265)

1 Brompton Cemetery ... F5
2 Chelsea Football Club ... F5
3 Holland Park ... D1
4 Leighton House ... E2
5 Linley Sambourne House ... E2

Eating (p269)

6 A Cookes ... B2
Bush Theatre Cafe & Bar ... (see 21)
7 Esarn Kheaw ... B1
8 Gate ... B4
9 Kerbisher & Malt ... C2
10 Mr Wing ... F4
11 Patio ... C2
12 Penny Black ... G4
13 Potli ... A3
14 Princess Victoria ... A1
15 Tosa ... A3

Drinking & Nightlife (p272)

16 Atlas ... F4
17 Churchill Arms ... F1
18 Kensington Roof Gardens ... F2
19 Troubadour ... F4
20 Windsor Castle ... E1

Entertainment (p273)

21 Bush Theatre ... B1
22 Earl's Court Exhibition Centre ... E4
23 Lyric Hammersmith ... B3
24 O2 Shepherd's Bush Empire ... B1
25 Opera Holland Park ... E2
26 Riverside Studios ... B4

Shopping (p274)

27 Books for Amnesty ... B3
28 Orsini ... E2
29 Shepherd's Bush Market ... B1
30 Westfield ... C1

Sports & Activities (p76)

31 Fitness First ... C1

Sleeping (p345)

32 17 Homestead Rd ... E5
33 Barclay House ... E5
34 Base2stay ... F3
Garret ... (see 19)
35 K + K Hotel George ... F3
36 Rockwell ... F3
37 Rushmore ... F3
38 St Christopher's Shepherd's Bush ... C1
39 Twenty Nevern Square ... E3
40 Vicarage Hotel ... F1
41 YHA Earl's Court ... F4
42 YHA Holland House ... E1

SOUTH LONDON: BRIXTON, CLAPHAM & BATTERSEA

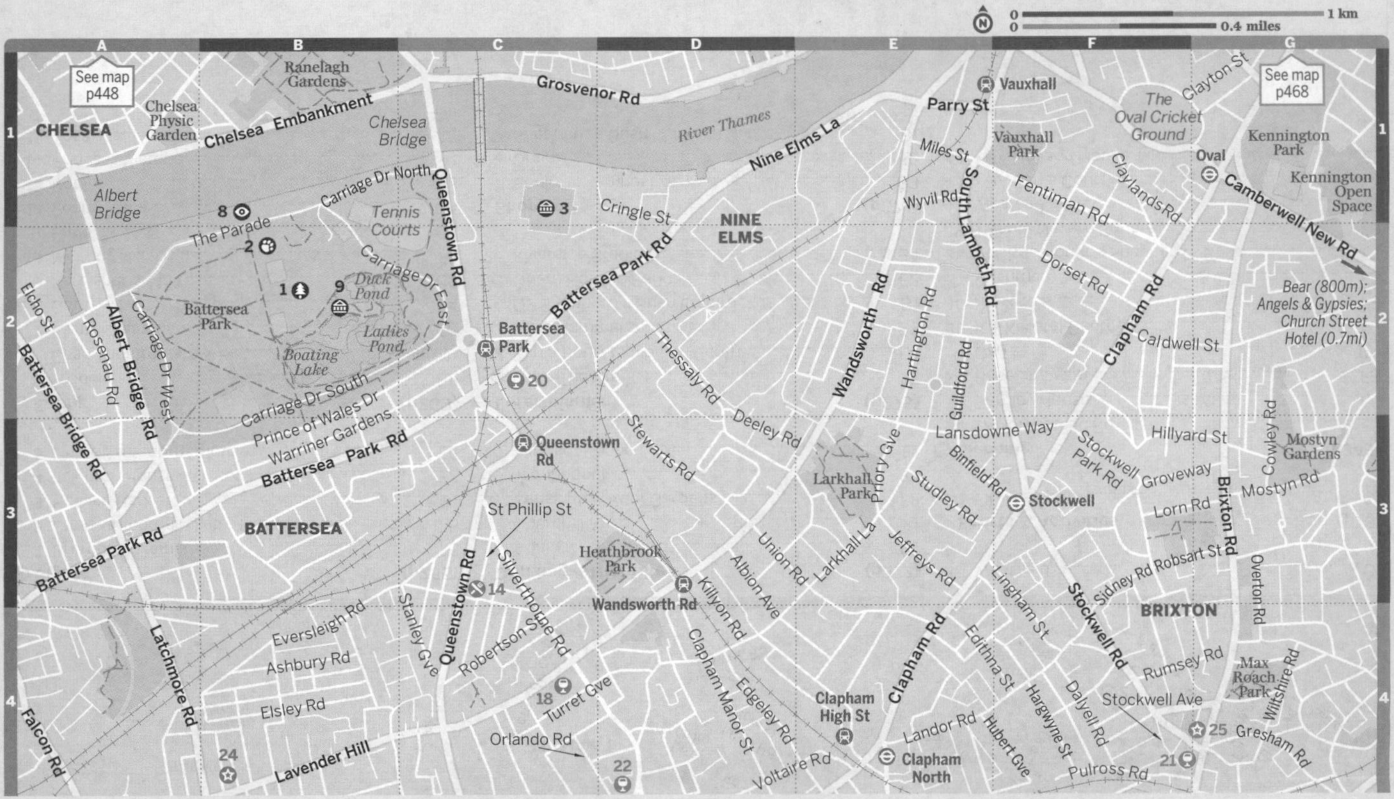

SOUTH LONDON: BRIXTON, CLAPHAM & BATTERSEA

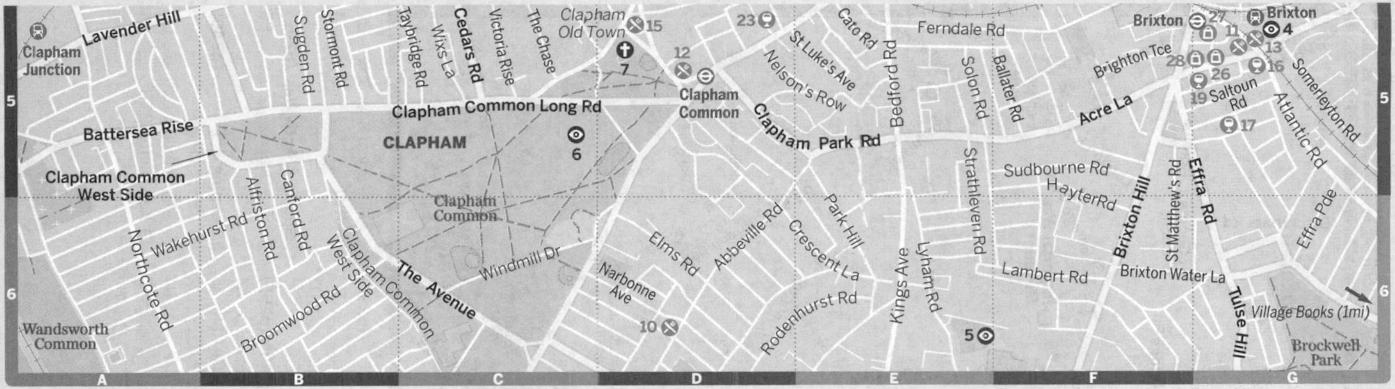

Sights (p285)

1 Battersea Park ... B2
2 Battersea Park Children's Zoo ... B2
3 Battersea Power Station ... C1
4 Brixton Village ... G5
5 Brixton Windmill ... E6
6 Clapham Common ... C5
7 Holy Trinity Church ... D5
8 Peace Pagoda ... B1
9 Pump House Gallery ... B2

Eating (p292)

10 Abbeville Kitchen ... D6
11 Asmara ... G5
Franco Manca ... (see 27)
Honest Burgers ... (see 4)
12 Macaron ... D5
13 Mama Lan ... G5
Rosie's Deli Café ... (see 27)
14 Santa Maria del sur ... C3
15 Trinity ... D5

Drinking & Nightlife (p295)

16 Dogstar ... G5
17 Effra Hall Tavern ... G5
Federation Coffee ... (see 4)
18 Lost Society ... C4
19 Market House ... G5
20 Mason's Arms ... C2
21 Plan B ... F4
22 Prince of Wales ... D4
23 Two Brewers ... D5

Entertainment (p297)

24 Battersea Arts Centre ... B4
25 O2 Academy Brixton ... G4

Shopping (p349)

26 20 Storey ... G5
27 Brixton Market ... G5
28 Joy ... G5

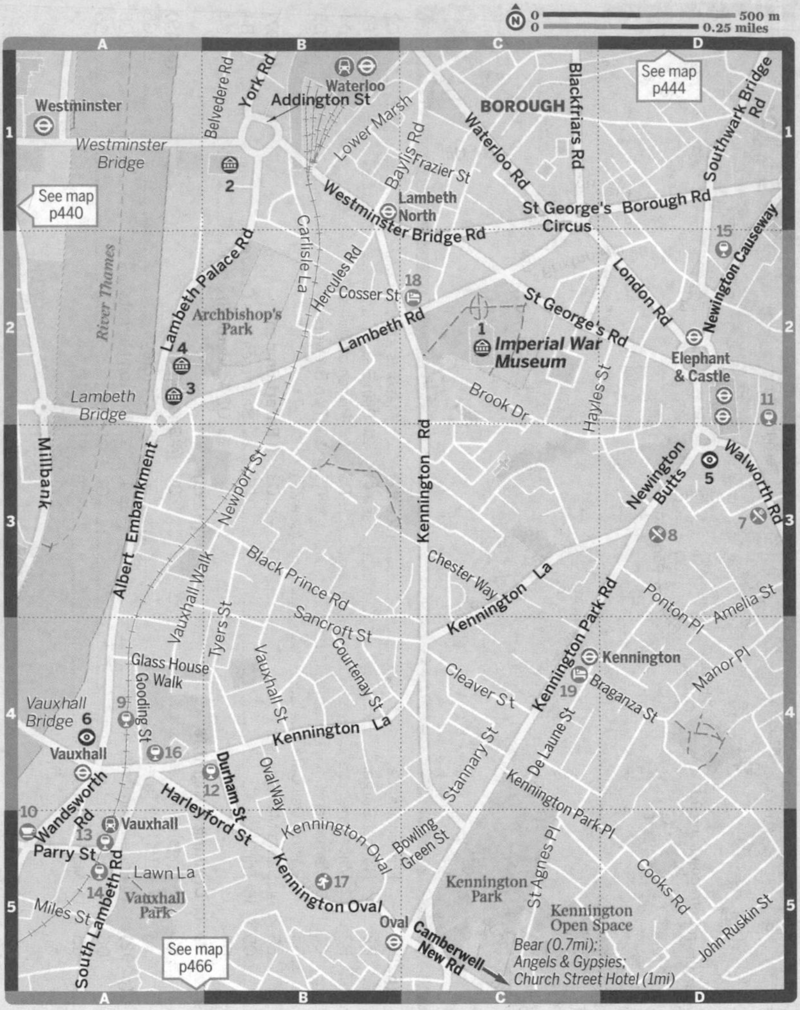

Top Sights (p285)

1 Imperial War Museum .. C2

Sights (p284)

2 Florence Nightingale Museum B1
3 Garden Museum A2
4 Lambeth Palace A2
5 Razor D3
6 Secret Intelligence Services (MI6) A4

Eating (p292)

7 Dragon Castle D3
8 Lobster Pot D3

Drinking & Nightlife (p295)

9 Area A4
10 Brunswick House Cafe . A5
11 Corsica Studios D2
12 Eagle B4
13 Fire A5
14 Hoist A5
15 Ministry of Sound D2
16 RVT A4

Sports & Activities (p299)

17 The Oval B5

Sleeping (p349)

18 Captain Bligh Guesthouse C2
19 Kennington B&B C4

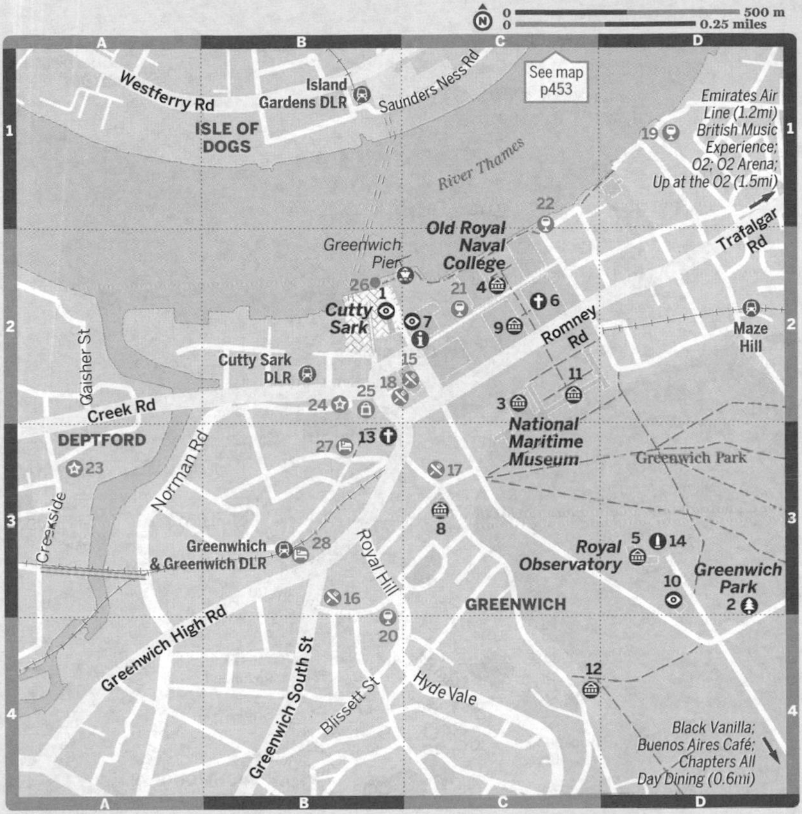

Top Sights (p279)
1 Cutty Sark B2
2 Greenwich Park D3
3 National Maritime Museum C2
4 Old Royal Naval College C2
5 Royal Observatory D3

Sights (p282)
6 Chapel C2
7 Discover Greenwich C2
8 Fan Museum C3
9 Painted Hall C2
10 Peter Harrison Planetarium D3
11 Queen's House C2
12 Ranger's House (Wernher Collection) C4
13 St Alfege Church B3
14 Statue of General Wolfe D3

Eating (p291)
15 Greenwich Market C2
16 Inside B3
Old Brewery .... (see 21)
17 Spread Eagle C3
18 Tai Won Mein B2

Drinking & Nightlife (p294)
19 Cutty Sark Tavern D1
20 Greenwich Union B4
21 Old Brewery C2
22 Trafalgar Tavern C1

Entertainment (p297)
23 Laban Theatre A3
24 Up the Creek B2

Shopping (p298)
Beehive .... (see 25)
25 Emporium B2
Greenwich Market (see 15)

Sports & Activities (p408)
26 Thames River Services B2

Sleeping (p349)
27 Number 16 St Alfege's B3
28 St Christopher's Inn Greenwich B3

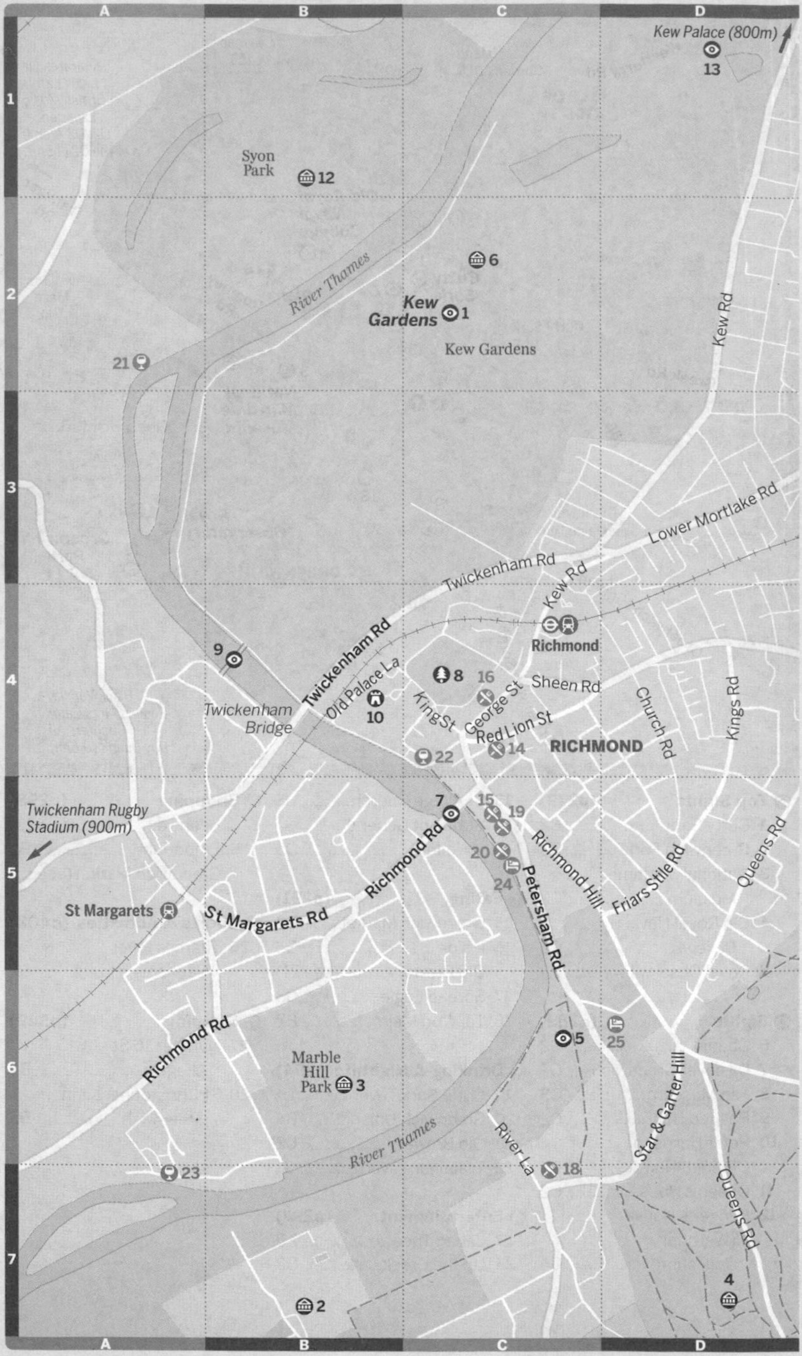
A
B
C
D
1
2
3
4
5
6
7
Kew Palace (800m)
13
Syon Park
12
6
River Thames
Kew Gardens
1
Kew Gardens
Kew Rd
21
Lower Mortlake Rd
Twickenham Rd
Kew Rd
Richmond
9
Twickenham Rd
Old Palace La
8
16
Sheen Rd
George St
King St
10
Twickenham Bridge
Red Lion St
14
RICHMOND
Church Rd
Kings Rd
22
7
15
19
Twickenham Rugby Stadium (900m)
Richmond Rd
Richmond Hill
Friars Stile Rd
Queens Rd
20
24
Petersham Rd
St Margarets
St Margarets Rd
5
25
Richmond Rd
Marble Hill Park
3
Star & Garter Hill
River Thames
River La
23
18
Queens Rd
4
2

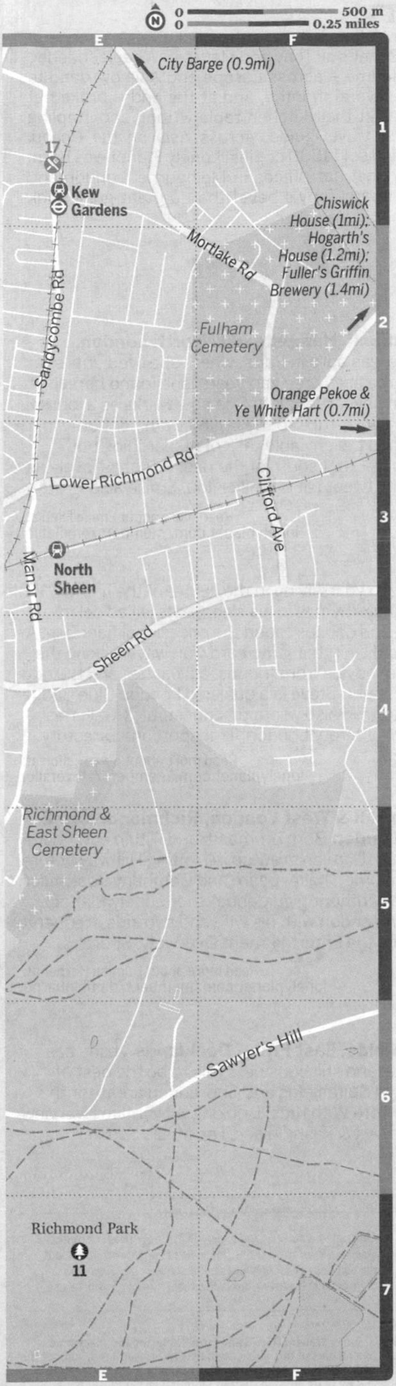

Top Sights (p306)

1 Kew Gardens C2

Sights (p308)

2 Ham House B7
3 Marble Hill House B6
4 Pembroke Lodge D7
5 Petersham Meadows C6
6 Queen Charlotte's Cottage C2
7 Richmond Bridge C5
8 Richmond Green C4
9 Richmond Lock B4
10 Richmond Palace Remains B4
11 Richmond Park E7
12 Syon House B1
13 Waterlily House D1

Eating (p312)

14 Al Boccon di'Vino C4
15 Chez Lindsay C5
16 Gelateria Danieli C4
17 Glasshouse F1
18 Petersham Nurseries Cafe C7
19 Pier 1 .... C5
20 Stein's C5

Drinking & Nightlife (p314)

21 London Apprentice A2
22 White Cross C4
23 White Swan A7

Sleeping (p350)

24 Bingham C5
25 Petersham D6

Our Story

A beat-up old car, a few dollars in the pocket and a sense of adventure. In 1972 that's all Tony and Maureen Wheeler needed for the trip of a lifetime – across Europe and Asia overland to Australia. It took several months, and at the end – broke but inspired – they sat at their kitchen table writing and stapling together their first travel guide, *Across Asia on the Cheap*. Within a week they'd sold 1500 copies. Lonely Planet was born.

Today, Lonely Planet has offices in Melbourne, London and Oakland, with more than 600 staff and writers. We share Tony's belief that 'a great guidebook should do three things: inform, educate and amuse'.

Our Writers

Emilie Filou

Coordinating Author, The South Bank, Hampstead & North London, Greenwich & South London Emilie was born in Paris, where she lived until she was 18. Following her three-year degree and three gap years, she found herself in London, fell in love with the place and never really left. She now works as a journalist, specialising in Africa and makes regular trips to the region from her home in North London. For this book, Emilie had the enviable task of researching both North and South London and concluded – controversially – that south of the river is just as lovely as north! You can see her work on www.emiliefilou.com; she tweets at @EmilieFilou. Emilie also wrote the Plan Your Trip section and Eating Overview.

Read more about Emilie Filou at:
lonelyplanet.com/members/emiliefilou

Steve Fallon

The West End, The City After a dozen years living in the centre of the known universe – East London – Steve cockney-rhymes in his sleep, eats jellied eel for brekkie, drinks lager by the bucketful and dances round the occasional handbag. As always, for this edition of London he did everything the hard/fun way: walking the walks, seeing the sights, taking (some) advice from friends, colleagues and the odd taxi driver and digesting everything in sight. Steve is a qualified London Blue Badge Tourist Guide; find out more at www.steveslondon.com. Steve also wrote the Museums & Galleries Overview, Gay & Lesbian Overview, History, Architecture, Literary London, Transport and Directory.

Read more about Steve Fallon at:
lonelyplanet.com/members/stevefallon

Damian Harper

Kensington & Hyde Park, Notting Hill & West London, Richmond, Kew & Hampton Court, Day Trips from London Born off the Strand within earshot of Bow Bells (favourable wind permitting), Damian grew up in Notting Hill way before it was discovered by Hollywood. A onetime Shakespeare and Company bookseller and radio presenter, Damian has been authoring guidebooks for Lonely Planet since the late 1990s. He lives in South London with his wife and two kids, frequently returning to China (his second home). Damian also wrote the Entertainment Overview, Sports & Activities Overview, London Today and Film & Media.

Read more about Damian Harper at:
lonelyplanet.com/members/damianharper

Vesna Maric

Clerkenwell, Shoreditch & Spitalfields, East End & Docklands Vesna has lived in London for nearly two decades and still considers this to be the best of all cities. Researching the East End and Spitalfields and Shoreditch areas for this edition has been a treat. Vesna also wrote With Kids, Drinking & Nightlife Overview, Shopping Overview, Theatre & Dance, Art & Fashion and The Music Scene.

Published by Lonely Planet Publications Pty Ltd
ABN 36 005 607 983
9th edition – Feb 2014
ISBN 978 1 74220 873 2

10 9 8 7 6 5 4 3 2
Printed in China